Small Claims Court: Procedure and Practice

THIRD EDITION

S. Patricia Knight

2014
Emond Montgomery Publications
Toronto, Canada

Emond Montgomery Publications Limited
60 Shaftesbury Avenue
Toronto ON M4T 1A3
http://www.emp.ca/highered

Printed in Canada.
Reprinted November 2014.

We acknowledge the financial support of the Government of Canada through the Canada Book Fund for our publishing activities.

Emond Montgomery Publications has no responsibility for the persistence or accuracy of URLs for external or third-party Internet websites referred to in this publication, and does not guarantee that any content on such websites is, or will remain, accurate or appropriate.

Publisher: Mike Thompson
Acquisitions editor: Lindsay Sutherland
Senior developmental editor: Sarah Gleadow
Director, editorial and production: Jim Lyons
Production editor: Andrew Gordon
Copy editor and indexer: Paula Pike
Proofreader: Cindy Fujimoto
Cover and text designer: Tara Wells
Typesetter: Shani Sohn
Cover image: iStockphoto.com / KaleviTamm

Library and Archives Canada Cataloguing in Publication

Knight, S. Patricia, author
    Small claims court : procedure and practice / S. Patricia Knight. — Third edition.

Includes index.
ISBN 978-1-55239-558-5 (pbk.)

    1. Small claims courts—Ontario.   2. Civil procedure—Ontario.   3. Actions and defenses—Canada.   I. Title.

KEO1090.K55 2013   347.713'04   C2013-902618-5
KF8769.K55 2013

This book is dedicated to Jean Higgins,
Dr. Sheila Cheeseman, and Dr. Michael Cheeseman.

Contents

APPENDIXES

List of Figures and Tables

Acknowledgments

I would like to thank the following: Sarah Gleadow and Anthony Rezek for their encouragement and helpful advice as we went forward with the third edition; Cindy Fujimoto and Paula Pike for their painstaking editing; my family for their understanding and support; and my students in the Sheridan Paralegal program—my partners in teaching and learning.

S. Patricia Knight, 2013

Introduction to Small Claims Court

1

LEARNING OUTCOMES

After reading this chapter, you will understand:

- What type of action is heard in Small Claims Court

- What the *Courts of Justice Act* is and what it does

- Small Claims Court monetary jurisdiction

- Who may hear and decide Small Claims Court matters

- The purpose of Small Claims Court

- Who may represent a party in Small Claims Court

- Orders for payment of money and costs in Small Claims Court

- Appeals of Small Claims Court trial decisions

- How to read the *Small Claims Court Rules*

What Is Small Claims Court?

Small Claims Court is a civil trial court. In Ontario, Small Claims Court is a division of the Superior Court of Justice.

Unlike the Ontario Court of Justice and the Trial Division of the Superior Court of Justice, Small Claims Court has no criminal or quasi-criminal jurisdiction. **Jurisdiction** is a court's area of legal authority. Small Claims Court hears civil actions only—that is, actions in which one party sues another party for some form of private relief. In Small Claims Court, the relief sought is usually money. Small Claims Court also has jurisdiction to make orders for the return of property.

For legal purposes, an **action** is a proceeding brought in a court. The persons involved in the action or proceeding are called the **parties** to the action. Parties to a civil action are also known as **litigants** because they are engaged in civil litigation.

BOX 1.1 Who May Litigate?

When we think of the word "person," most of us think of an individual human being. However, for legal purposes, a corporation is a person, and may be named as a party to an action along with individuals.

Other business entities, such as sole proprietorships, partnerships, and unincorporated organizations, may also be named as parties in an action.

In civil actions, the parties to the proceeding usually take the stand as witnesses at the trial of the matter (if it goes all the way to trial). A sole proprietorship, partnership, or corporation cannot take the stand, so the owners, senior officers, or directors will give evidence on its behalf.

The party who commences the action is called the **plaintiff**. The party who defends the action is called the **defendant**. There may be multiple plaintiffs, or co-plaintiffs, in an action, so long as the relief they are seeking from the defendant is based on a common set of facts or issues. There may be multiple defendants or co-defendants in an action if the plaintiff has reason to believe that one or more persons may be liable for the relief sought.

BOX 1.2 Naming Multiple Plaintiffs or Defendants

On the plaintiff's claim (Form 7A) there is space on the first page for the name, address, and telephone number of one plaintiff and his legal representative, and one defendant and his legal representative. What do you do if there are two plaintiffs, or more than one defendant? This may happen in a debt collection proceeding—for example, where a credit card company is suing a husband and wife who both use the same credit card and are both liable for the unpaid balance on the account.

When this happens, tick off the box marked "Additional plaintiff(s) listed on attached Form 1A" or "Additional defendant(s) listed on attached Form 1A." Then fill in the information about the additional parties on Form 1A—Additional Parties, or a Form 1A.1—Additional Debtors, and insert it in Form 7A after page 1. See figures 1.1, 1.2, and 1.3 below. See also Small Claims Court Rule 1.06(3)—Additional Parties.

A Small Claims Court plaintiff may also be called a **claimant**. A claimant is a person who commences a claim. In Small Claims Court, claimants are charged filing fees according to the frequency of their court use.

An **infrequent claimant** is anyone who files fewer than 10 Small Claims Court claims in a Small Claims Court office on or after January 1 in any calendar year. Infrequent claimants are charged $75.00 to file a claim.

A **frequent claimant** is anyone who files 10 or more claims in a Small Claims Court office on or after January 1 in any calendar year. A frequent claimant is charged $145.00 per claim.

Access to Justice

Litigation can be an expensive and time-consuming method of resolving a dispute. In the civil courts, the parties themselves bear the costs of litigating. They must pay for legal representation and all other expenses connected with advancing the matter through the court. A civil proceeding in the Superior Court of Justice is governed by complex procedural rules and requirements. This makes it very difficult to advance or defend an action in the Superior Court of Justice without a lawyer's assistance. In other words, your access to justice depends on whether or not you can afford a lawyer. At the same time, the complicated rules and procedures drive the cost of legal representation up. A plaintiff who is suing for $100,000.00 does not want to have to pay a lawyer $75,000.00 to recover that amount, but that can happen in a lengthy proceeding that is fiercely contested.

Small Claims Court is intended to improve the public's access to justice by providing a forum for proceedings where the parties are likely to be self-represented and the amount being claimed is comparatively modest—that is, proceedings where it is not cost-effective for the parties to hire a lawyer to represent them. Small Claims rules and procedures have been simplified with a view to resolving these matters expeditiously. The court's simplified procedures are also intended to be easily understood by self-represented parties.

Keep in mind that "simple" is a relative term. Something that is simple for a person with some legal background and experience can be very confusing and intimidating for a person without that knowledge. Completing a plaintiff's claim can be extremely difficult for someone who has no experience with legal drafting or whose first language is not English. Issuing the claim and complying with the rules for proper service are almost impossible for such a plaintiff.

Another thing to consider is the time commitment required by any legal proceeding. Often a self-represented party who is working full time at a day job cannot take three hours off to attend on a motion for set aside or a pretrial—let alone take a whole day off to attend at trial.

It is arguable that, in spite of the best intentions of legislators and the Civil Rules Committee, many people who appear in Small Claims Court would prefer to have legal representation if they had the resources to pay for it and if it were cost-effective to do so. Section 26 of the *Courts of Justice Act* states that a party may be represented in a proceeding in Small Claims Court by a person authorized by the *Law Society Act* to represent the party—that is, a licensee who is a lawyer or a paralegal, or a student-

FIGURE 1.1 **Plaintiff's Claim (Form 7A)**

ONTARIO
Superior Court of Justice
Cour supérieure de justice

Plaintiff's Claim
Demande du demandeur
Form / *Formule* 7A Ont. Reg. No. / *Règl. de l'Ont.* : 258/98

Small Claims Court / *Cour des petites créances de*

Claim No. / *N° de la demande*

Seal / *Sceau*

Address / *Adresse*

Phone number / *Numéro de téléphone*

☐ Additional plaintiff(s) listed on attached Form 1A.
Le ou les demandeurs additionnels sont mentionnés sur la formule 1A ci-jointe.

☐ Under 18 years of age.
Moins de 18 ans.

Plaintiff No. 1 / *Demandeur n° 1*

Last name, or name of company / *Nom de famille ou nom de la compagnie*		
First name / *Premier prénom*	Second name / *Deuxième prénom*	Also known as / *Également connu(e) sous le nom de*
Address (street number, apt., unit) / *Adresse (numéro et rue, app., unité)*		
City/Town / *Cité/ville*	Province	Phone no. / *N° de téléphone*
Postal code / *Code postal*		Fax no. / *N° de télécopieur*
Representative / *Représentant(e)*		LSUC # / *N° du BHC*
Address (street number, apt., unit) / *Adresse (numéro et rue, app., unité)*		
City/Town / *Cité/ville*	Province	Phone no. / *N° de téléphone*
Postal code / *Code postal*		Fax no. / *N° de télécopieur*

Defendant No. 1 / *Défendeur n° 1*

☐ Additional defendant(s) listed on attached Form 1A.
Le ou les défendeurs additionnels sont mentionnés sur la formule 1A ci-jointe.

☐ Under 18 years of age.
Moins de 18 ans.

Last name, or name of company / *Nom de famille ou nom de la compagnie*		
First name / *Premier prénom*	Second name / *Deuxième prénom*	Also known as / *Également connu(e) sous le nom de*
Address (street number, apt., unit) / *Adresse (numéro et rue, app., unité)*		
City/Town / *Cité/ville*	Province	Phone no. / *N° de téléphone*
Postal code / *Code postal*		Fax no. / *N° de télécopieur*
Representative / *Représentant(e)*		LSUC # / *N° du BHC*
Address (street number, apt., unit) / *Adresse (numéro et rue, app., unité)*		

FIGURE 1.2   Additional Parties (Form 1A)

ONTARIO
Superior Court of Justice
Cour supérieure de justice

PAGE 1A

Additional Parties
Parties additionnelles
Form / *Formule* 1A Ont. Reg. No. / *Régl. de l'Ont.* : 258/98

Claim No. / *N° de la demande*

☐ **Plaintiff No. /** *Demandeur n°*   ☐ **Defendant No. /** *Défendeur n°*

Last name, or name of company / *Nom de famille ou nom de la compagnie*		
First name / *Premier prénom*	Second name / *Deuxième prénom*	Also known as / *Également connu(e) sous le nom de*
Address (street number, apt., unit) / *Adresse (numéro et rue, app., unité)*		
City/Town / *Cité/ville* Province		Phone no. / *N° de téléphone*
Postal code / *Code postal*		Fax no. / *N° de télécopieur*
Representative / *Représentant(e)*		LSUC # / *N° du BHC*
Address (street number, apt., unit) / *Adresse (numéro et rue, app., unité)*		
City/Town / *Cité/ville* Province		Phone no. / *N° de téléphone*
Postal code / *Code postal*		Fax no. / *N° de télécopieur*

☐ **Plaintiff No. /** *Demandeur n°*   ☐ **Defendant No. /** *Défendeur n°*

Last name, or name of company / *Nom de famille ou nom de la compagnie*		
First name / *Premier prénom*	Second name / *Deuxième prénom*	Also known as / *Également connu(e) sous le nom de*

Address (street number, apt., unit) / *Adresse (numéro et rue, app., unité)*

FIGURE 1.3   Additional Debtors (Form 1A.1)

ONTARIO
Superior Court of Justice
Cour supérieure de justice

Additional Debtors
Débiteurs additionnels
Form / *Formule* 1A.1 Ont. Reg. No. / *Régl. de l'Ont.* : 258/98

Claim No. / *N° de la demande*

If a debtor has "also known as names", list each also known as name in a separate set of boxes below. / *Si un débiteur a d'autres noms sous lesquels il est également connu, indiquez chacun de ces noms ci-dessous dans un ensemble séparé de cases.*

Last name of debtor, or name of company / *Nom de famille du débiteur/de la débitrice ou nom de la compagnie*		
First name / *Premier prénom*	Second name / *Deuxième prénom*	Third name / *Troisième prénom*

Last name of debtor, or name of company / *Nom de famille du débiteur/de la débitrice ou nom de la compagnie*		
First name / *Premier prénom*	Second name / *Deuxième prénom*	Third name / *Troisième prénom*

Last name of debtor, or name of company / *Nom de famille du débiteur/de la débitrice ou nom de la compagnie*		
First name / *Premier prénom*	Second name / *Deuxième prénom*	Third name / *Troisième prénom*

at-law working under the supervision of a lawyer. Small Claims Court presents excellent opportunities for paralegals, who can provide legal services at rates that are often more affordable than those of a lawyer. For litigants who are self-represented, either because they cannot afford legal representation or for other reasons, Small Claims Court provides a comparatively inexpensive and user-friendly forum.

Fee Waiver

Parties who cannot afford to pay court fees may apply for a fee waiver. The fee waiver forms can be found at the Attorney General's website, or can be obtained from the Small Claims Court office. To find the forms at the Attorney General's website, select the "Court Services" link. In the "Court Fees" section, select "A Guide to Fee Waiver Requests." See figure 1.4 below.

FIGURE 1.4 Requesting a Fee Waiver

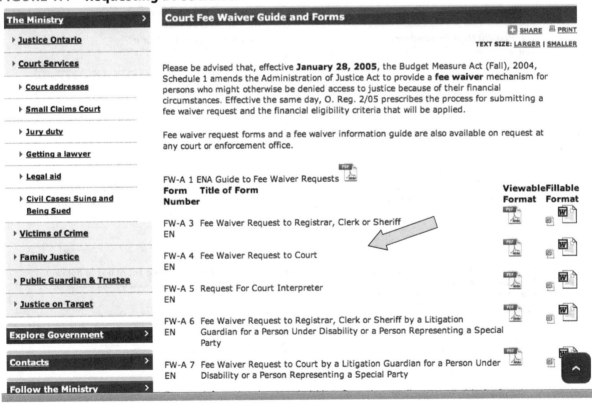

The Courts of Justice Act

The *Courts of Justice Act* is the statute that sets out the court system in Ontario. It governs all courts from the Ontario Court of Justice to the Court of Appeal for Ontario. The procedural rules for Ontario courts, as well as other matters such as the salaries of provincial court judges and the monetary jurisdiction of Small Claims Court, are contained in the regulations to the *Courts of Justice Act*.

The general principles governing Small Claims Court are set out at ss. 22 to 33.1 of the *Courts of Justice Act*. Anyone who practises in Small Claims Court should be thoroughly familiar with these principles.

BOX 1.3 What Is the Courts of Justice Act?

The *Courts of Justice Act* is a statute. Statutes are laws that are put in place by the federal Parliament in Ottawa, or by the legislatures of the provinces and territories.

Federal statutes apply to all of Canada. Provincial or territorial statutes apply only to the province or territory in which they were passed. The *Courts of Justice Act* is a provincial statute that applies only to the court system in Ontario. Other provinces have similar legislation. Because the court system in each province is set up by that province's legislature, the courts in each province often have different names and different (though similar) procedural rules. For example, in British Columbia, the superior trial court is called the British Columbia Supreme Court. In Alberta, the superior trial court is called the Alberta Court of Queen's Bench.

In Ontario, the superior trial court is called the Ontario Superior Court of Justice. The Small Claims Court is a branch of the Ontario Superior Court of Justice.

When reading statutes, you will often come across the Latin word "Idem." See, for example, the heading for s. 22(2) of the *Courts of Justice Act*. "Idem" means "the same as previous." In other words, the content of subsection 22(2) deals with the same subject matter as subsection 22(1).

Monetary Jurisdiction of Small Claims Court

General

Monetary jurisdiction is the amount of money that the court may order one party to pay another, not including pre- and post-judgment interest and costs. Pre- and post-judgment interest, and how it is calculated, will be discussed in later chapters.

Costs are amounts that the court orders one party to pay to the other party. Costs are awarded in addition to any other relief, monetary or otherwise, that may be ordered. The general rule is that costs are awarded to the successful party, to reimburse the successful party for legal fees and disbursements incurred in the course of litigation.

Legal fees are what you are charged by a lawyer or paralegal for legal representation and advice.

Disbursements are the out-of-pocket expenses of a legal proceeding. Disbursements include court filing fees, charges for service of documents, photocopying charges, postage, courier charges, and so on.

In Small Claims Court, court filing fees tend to be modest, in comparison to other civil trial courts. For example, it costs $75.00 for an infrequent claimant (someone who files fewer than 10 claims per calendar year in a Small Claims Court office) to file a plaintiff's claim in Small Claims Court. By contrast, it costs $181.00 to file a statement of claim or notice of action in the Superior Court of Justice. It costs $157.00 to file an application for divorce in Family Court, and $280.00 to place the application for divorce on the list for hearing (trial).

Small Claims Court fees and allowances can be found in the regulations to the *Administration of Justice Act*. Links to these regulations can also be found at the Attorney General's website under "Court Fees" on the Court Services page (see figure 1.4 above), and at the e-Laws website (see figure 1.5 below). You will find a schedule of Small Claims Court fees in Appendix D at page 559.

FIGURE 1.5   Finding Court Fees and Allowances on e-Laws

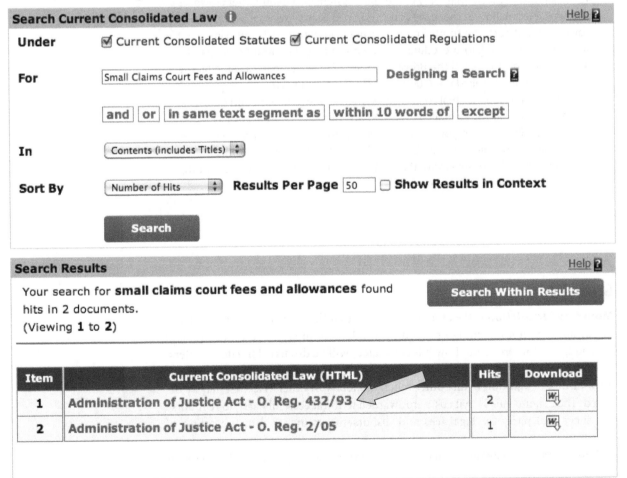

Maximum Recoverable Amount

The monetary jurisdiction of Small Claims Court in Ontario is the maximum amount of money a party may recover in a Small Claims action in Ontario, exclusive of interest and costs. It is established by s. 23(1) of the *Courts of Justice Act*, and by regulations published pursuant to ss. 23 and 53. Effective January 1, 2010, the monetary jurisdiction of Small Claims Court throughout Ontario, as set out in O. Reg. 626/00, is $25,000.00, exclusive of interest and costs. "Exclusive of interest and costs" means that interest on the money recovered, plus the successful party's costs, will be awarded in addition to the amount of money ordered to be paid. If the action is for the recovery of possession of personal property, the value of that personal property cannot exceed $25,000.00.

The Small Claims Court monetary jurisdiction changes from time to time. In 1970, it was $1,000.00. In 1979, this amount was increased to $3,000.00 for Small Claims Court (then known as the Ontario Court (Civil Division)) in Metropolitan Toronto only. In 1993, the Small Claims Court monetary jurisdiction was increased to $6,000.00 throughout Ontario. In 2001, that amount was increased to $10,000.00, and effective January 1, 2010 the amount recoverable was increased to $25,000.00.

Every time the monetary jurisdiction of Small Claims Court increases, there will be actions pending in the Superior Court of Justice (the higher court) that will then fall within the Small Claims Court jurisdiction. Section 23(2) of the *Courts of Justice Act* provides that an action that is commenced in the Superior Court of Justice for a money payment or return of property with a value that falls within Small Claims Court jurisdiction may be transferred to Small Claims Court at any time before trial if all the parties consent. If all parties do not consent, the party seeking the transfer must make a motion to a Superior Court judge for an order authorizing the transfer.

Note that, at present, paralegals are not allowed to appear in the Superior Court of Justice.

Transfer to Small Claims—Consent

If all parties to an action in the Superior Court of Justice consent to a transfer to Small Claims Court at any time before trial, the party requesting the transfer must obtain written, signed consents from all other parties. The party requesting the transfer then fills out a requisition (Form 4E of the *Rules of Civil Procedure*) and files it, along with the written consent of all other parties, at the court office of the Superior Court of Justice. The party requesting the transfer must pay a court fee of $75.00 to transfer the file. The Registrar will then arrange the transfer.

You will find a sample Form 4E at figure 1.6.

Transfer to Small Claims—No Consent

If all parties to an action do not consent, at any time before trial a party wishing to transfer an action from the Superior Court of Justice to Small Claims Court may bring a motion in the Superior Court of Justice for permission to do so. The party requesting the transfer must contact the court office of the Superior Court of Justice where the action was commenced, and obtain a hearing date after January 1, 2010 that is convenient for all parties or their representatives. If the action was brought under the Rule 76 Simplified Procedure, the motion will be made using the simplified procedure motion form (Form 76B). If the action was brought in the ordinary procedure, the motion will be made under Rule 37 using a notice of motion (Form 37A) supported by affidavit evidence. The motion may be made in writing. See Rule 37.12.1(4) of the *Rules of Civil Procedure*, which permits opposed motions to be made in writing where the issues of fact and law are not complex.

FIGURE 1.6   Form 4E Requisition—Rules of Civil Procedure

FORM 4E

Courts of Justice Act

REQUISITION

(General heading)

REQUISITION

TO THE LOCAL REGISTRAR at *(place)*

    I REQUIRE *(Set out a concise statement of what is sought and include all particulars necessary for the registrar to act. Where what is sought is authorized by an order, refer to the order in the requisition and attach a copy of the entered order. Where an affidavit or other document must be filed with the requisition, refer to it in the requisition and attach it.)*

(Date)   *(Name, address and telephone number of lawyer or other person filing requisition)*

(The following are examples of different kinds of requisition.)

(Simple requisition)

    I REQUIRE a certified copy of the *(identify document by nature and date).*

(Order attached)

    I REQUIRE, in accordance with the order dated *(date)*, a copy of which is attached, a commission authorizing the taking of evidence before the commissioner named in the order and a letter of request.

    I REQUIRE, in accordance with the order dated *(date)*, a copy of which is attached, a certificate of pending litigation in respect of the land described in the statement of claim.

(Affidavit attached)

    I REQUIRE an order to continue this action with *(name)* as plaintiff and *(name)* as defendants. An affidavit stating that the defendant *(name)* has reached the age of majority is attached.

RCP-E 4E (July 1, 2007)

Who May Hear and Determine a Small Claims Court Proceeding?

Section 22(1) of the *Courts of Justice Act* establishes Small Claims Court as a branch of the Superior Court of Justice. Pursuant to ss. 22(2) and (3), justices of the Superior Court of Justice may also preside as judges in Small Claims Court matters. A **justice** is the same thing as a judge.

Section 24(2) provides that, in addition to judges of the Superior Court of Justice, provincial judges and deputy judges may hear and determine Small Claims Court matters.

Superior Court judges are appointed federally, by the governor general. Provincial judges are appointed provincially, by the lieutenant governor. An appointment to the bench is a lifetime appointment, which ends only when a judge retires, is dismissed for serious wrongdoing, becomes incapacitated, or dies.

Deputy judges are found only in Small Claims Court. Unlike other judges in the Superior Court of Justice and the Ontario Court of Justice, deputy judges are not granted lifetime appointments. They are lawyers who are appointed for a term of three years by a regional senior judge of the Superior Court of Justice, with the approval of the attorney general. A deputy judge's appointment is renewable for one or more terms.

Sections 24(2) and (3) of the *Courts of Justice Act* give deputy judges unrestricted authorization to hear and determine any Small Claims Court matter.

General Mandate of Small Claims Court

The general mandate of Small Claims Court, as set out in s. 25 of the *Courts of Justice Act*, is "to hear and determine in a summary way all questions of law and fact and … make such order as is considered just and agreeable to good conscience." In other words, the parties to a Small Claims Court action are entitled to have the matter resolved and enforce their judgment, if any, without being hindered or prejudiced by complex, expensive, and time-consuming procedures.

Like all procedural rules for Ontario courts, the *Rules of the Small Claims Court* (also known as the *Small Claims Court Rules*) are published as a regulation to the *Courts of Justice Act*. The Rules implement the mandate set out in s. 25 by establishing a simplified (or summary) procedure that is designed to be user-friendly for self-represented or unsophisticated users, while preserving and protecting the rights of the parties. The basic steps in a Small Claims Court proceeding are the same as those in the Superior Court of Justice (Civil Division), but at every stage, the Small Claims Court forms and procedures have been simplified and streamlined.

To understand how streamlined the Small Claims Court procedure is, compare the "Summary of Contents" for the *Rules of Civil Procedure*, which govern proceedings in the Superior Court of Justice, with the "Summary of Contents" for the *Rules of the Small Claims Court*. In the Superior Court of Justice, 58 rules are required to cover procedure from commencement of a claim through discoveries, pretrial, and trial, to assessment of costs. Additional rules govern enforcement of orders and particular proceedings such as mortgage actions, administration of estates, applications for judicial review, and the simplified procedure.

By contrast, the *Rules of the Small Claims Court* consist of 22 rules. Rules 1 to 20 govern all aspects of procedure from commencement of an action to enforcement of orders. Rule 21 sets out the role of referees in Small Claims Court matters.

Rule 22 sets out procedures for money paid into or out of court pursuant to a court order or a statutory provision or rule, or where the payment is made pursuant to a court order under Rule 4.08.

For an overview of Small Claims Court procedure, along with timelines for each step, see Appendix 1.1 to this chapter. For the basic steps in an undefended Small Claims Court proceeding, see Figures 5.2 and 5.4 in Chapter 5. For the basic steps in a defended proceeding, see Figures 6.2 and 6.3 in Chapter 6.

BOX 1.4 What Are Questions of Law and Questions of Fact?

A **question of law** is an issue that requires the application or interpretation of a law or legal principle. In both jury and non-jury trials, questions of law are determined by judges.

A **question of fact** is a factual dispute. All actions involve factual disputes. The plaintiff makes a series of assertions, or **allegations**, that tell his version of the story. The defendant then makes a series of allegations that tell her version of the story. Both parties and their witnesses give evidence at trial, and, based on that evidence, the finder of fact decides which allegations to accept as facts, on a balance of probabilities, and which allegations to reject as untrue.

In jury trials, the finder of fact is the jury. Being a court of summary procedure, Small Claims Court does not have jury trials. The judge determines all questions of fact and law.

Who May Represent a Party in Small Claims Court?

Section 26 of the *Courts of Justice Act* provides that a party may be represented in a proceeding by a person authorized under the *Law Society Act* to represent the party. If a representative is not licensed under the *Law Society Act*, the court may exclude that representative from appearing on behalf of a party if the court finds that the representative is not competent to properly represent the party, or does not understand and comply with the duties and responsibilities of an advocate.

Examples of licensed persons are **lawyers** and **paralegals**. Lawyers are persons who have been called to the Bar of Ontario and are licensed to practise law in Ontario. Paralegals are non-lawyer legal representatives who are licensed to provide legal services to clients for a fee in Ontario.

Non-licensees may provide legal services to the public if they fall within any of the exemptions set out in By-law 4, s. 30 to the *Law Society Act*. The exemptions are reviewed and amended from time to time. Some examples of non-licensees who might appear in Small Claims Court as of this writing are:

1. An individual who is employed by a single employer that is not a licensee or a licensee firm, who provides legal services only for and on behalf of the employer, and who does not provide any legal services to any person other than the employer.

2. A law student who volunteers in or is completing a clinical education course at a student legal aid services society, provides legal services through the clinic to that clinic's designated community only, and acts under the direct supervision of a lawyer.

3. Any individual whose profession or occupation does not include the provision of legal services or the practice of law; who provides legal services only occasionally for or on behalf of a related person, a friend, or a neighbour; and who does not ask for and does not receive any form of compensation or benefit for providing those legal services.

Evidence

With respect to evidence that is admissible by the Small Claims Court at a hearing, s. 27 of the *Courts of Justice Act* states:

Evidence

s. 27(1) Subject to subsections (3) and (4), the Small Claims Court may admit as evidence at a hearing and act upon any oral testimony and any document or other thing so long as the evidence is relevant to the subject-matter of the proceeding, but the court may exclude anything unduly repetitious.

Idem

(2) Subsection (1) applies whether or not the evidence is given or proven under oath or affirmation or admissible as evidence in any other court.

Idem

(3) Nothing is admissible in evidence at a hearing,

(a) that would be inadmissible by reason of any privilege under the law of evidence; or

(b) that is inadmissible by any Act.

Conflicts

(4) Nothing in subsection (1) overrides the provisions of any Act expressly limiting the extent to or purposes for which any oral testimony, documents or things may be admitted or used in evidence in any proceeding.

Copies

(5) A copy of a document or any other thing may be admitted as evidence at a hearing if the presiding judge is satisfied as to its authenticity.

Section 27 permits the court to consider any evidence, so long as it is relevant and not unduly repetitious, regardless of whether that evidence would be admissible in any other court. The court may also accept as evidence a copy of a document instead of an original, so long as the judge is satisfied that the copy is an authentic copy of the original document.

The general rule with respect to **hearsay** evidence is that a witness is not allowed to repeat in court what they were told by a third party, if the reason for presenting the evidence is to prove the truth of the contents of the third-party statement. The effect of s. 27 is to allow hearsay evidence at Small Claims Court hearings, so long as it is relevant and not unduly repetitious, unless the evidence is subject to exclusion because of privilege or any statutory rules with respect to evidence (as set out in the Ontario *Evidence Act*, for example). The judge hearing the matter must decide how much weight, or credibility, to give the hearsay evidence.

This relaxed approach to evidence is in keeping with the general mandate of Small Claims Court to provide a forum where parties may have their proceedings resolved in a just, speedy, inexpensive, and simple manner. Where comparatively modest sums of money are involved, unsophisticated or self-represented parties should be able to present their case without being obliged to master complex rules of evidence.

Other Procedural Matters

Payment Terms

Section 28 of the *Courts of Justice Act* permits a judge to impose terms when making an order with respect to payment of money. A Small Claims Court order may provide for a **lump-sum payment**—that is, the entire amount owing is to be paid in a single payment. Or the court may order **installment (or partial) payments**, stating the amount of each partial payment and the date on which it is to be paid.

Costs (Rule 19)

General

The general rule is that costs are awarded to the successful party in order to reimburse the successful party for legal fees and expenses incurred in the course of litigation. In a Small Claims Court proceeding, a successful party is entitled, at a minimum, to an order that his reasonable disbursements, including any costs of effecting service, preparing a plaintiff's or defendant's claim or a defence, and expenses for travel, accommodation, photocopying and experts' reports, shall be paid by the unsuccessful party (Rule 19.01(1)).

BOX 1.5 Reminder: Costs and Disbursements

Costs are money amounts that the court orders one party to pay to another party. Costs are awarded in addition to any other relief, for money or return of property, that may be ordered.

> Legal fees are what you are charged by a lawyer or paralegal for legal representation and advice.
>
> Disbursements are the out-of-pocket expenses of a legal proceeding. These include court filing fees, charges for service of documents, photocopying charges, postage, courier charges, and witness fees.
>
> Ordinarily, a costs award does not reimburse the successful party for all of her legal fees and expenses connected with the litigation. In Small Claims Court, the costs that may be awarded by the court to a successful party are subject to the *Courts of Justice Act* and the *Rules of the Small Claims Court*. See the discussion below.

The clerk shall assess (that is, determine the amount of) the successful party's disbursements in accordance with Rules 19.01(3) and (4), and O. Reg. 432/93 to the *Administration of Justice Act*, which sets out Small Claims Court fees and allowances (Rule 19.01(2)). The amount assessed for effecting service shall not exceed $60.00 (Rule 19.01(3)). The amount assessed for preparing a plaintiff's or defendant's claim or a defence shall not exceed $100.00 (Rule 19.01(4)). The clerk's assessment of disbursements is subject to review by the court.

If the successful party is represented by a lawyer, student-at-law, or paralegal, the court may award a reasonable representation fee at trial or an assessment hearing (Rule 19.04).

If the successful party is self-represented, the court may order that the unsuccessful party pay the self-represented successful party an amount not exceeding $500.00 as compensation for inconvenience or expense (Rule 19.05).

If the court is satisfied that any party, successful or unsuccessful, has unduly complicated or prolonged an action or has engaged in other unreasonable behaviour, the court may order that party to pay compensation to another party (Rule 19.06).

Any order for costs made pursuant to Rule 19 is subject to s. 29 of the *Courts of Justice Act*. Section 29 states that an award of costs in a Small Claims Court proceeding cannot exceed 15% of the amount claimed or the value of the property to be recovered, excluding disbursements unless the court considers it necessary in the interests of justice to penalize a party or a party's representative for unreasonable behaviour in the proceeding. Fifteen percent of the current Small Claims Court maximum monetary jurisdiction of $25,000.00 is $3,750.00.

Appeals

Section 31 provides that, in an action for payment of money in excess of $2,500.00 or recovery of property with a value in excess of $2,500.00, excluding interest and costs, a final order may be appealed to a single judge of the Divisional Court. Note that whether or not a party may appeal depends on how much they claimed originally, not how much they were awarded at trial (*Action Auto Leasing & Gallery Inc. v. Robillard*).

The Divisional Court is the appellate branch of the Superior Court of Justice. Appeals to the Divisional Court are governed by Rule 61 of the *Rules of Civil Procedure*.

Paralegals are not allowed to appear in the Superior Court of Justice at present. The parties to an appeal may be self-represented or represented by a lawyer.

The Rules of the Small Claims Court

What Are They?

As was discussed above, in Ontario, the *Courts of Justice Act* sets up the court structure for all courts in the province. The rules of the various courts are published as regulations to the *Courts of Justice Act*. See figure 1.7 for the e-Laws link to the *Rules of the Small Claims Court*.

The rules of any court establish its procedural requirements. You must be thoroughly familiar with the processes of the courts and tribunals you appear before, because failure to comply with procedural requirements may result in prejudice to your client.

How to Use the Rules

No matter how familiar you may think you are with a court's process, it is difficult to remember everything. If you are not sure about a procedure, do not guess. Check the applicable Rules. Read them carefully.

Whenever you are appearing for a client in Small Claims Court, you should have a copy of the Rules with you, so that you can refer to them if the need arises. You should never appear before any court or tribunal without having a copy of the rules of that court or tribunal handy.

Rule 1—General

Rule 1 deals with general matters that are not specifically covered by other rules.

FIGURE 1.7   Finding the Rules of the Small Claims Court on e-Laws

Item	Current Consolidated Law (HTML)	Hits	Download
1	Administration of Justice Act - O. Reg. 2/05	2	
2	Courts of Justice Act - O. Reg. 258/98	2	
3	Courts of Justice Act - R.R.O. 1990, Reg. 194	1	

Definitions (Rule 1.02)

Rule 1.02 contains a list of definitions to be used when interpreting and applying other rules. For example, in order to understand Rule 4—Parties Under Disability—you must know what "disability" means in the Small Claims Court context. You will find the definition of "disability" in Rule 1.02.

Whenever you take a procedural step in a Small Claims Court matter, you are required to give the other parties **notice**—serving documents on other parties to make them aware that a procedural step is about to take place. The **notice period** is the minimum amount of time you have to serve the documents, as prescribed by the Rules. Rule 3.01 of the *Small Claims Court Rules* provides that when calculating a notice period, you exclude the first day and include the last day of the period. If the last day of the notice period falls on a holiday, the periods ends on the next day that is not a holiday. If you are not sure whether a day is a holiday for purposes of calculating a notice period, you should consult the definition of "holiday" in Rule 1.02.

Although Rule 3.01 of the *Small Claims Court Rules* is silent on this point, it is prudent, when calculating notice periods, to apply the formula set out in Rule 3.01 of the *Rules of Civil Procedure*. When a notice period is seven days or less, you do not count holidays when calculating the end date of the notice period. When a notice period is more than seven days, holidays are included when you calculate the end date of the notice period. If a notice period ends on a holiday, you move the end date over to the next business day.

In Small Claims Court, "order" means an order or a judgment. A self-represented person is someone who is representing herself—that is, she does not have a lawyer, paralegal, or student-at-law assisting her.

BOX 1.6 Failing to Meet Procedural Deadlines

You are acting for the defendant in a Small Claims Court action for recovery of an unpaid debt of $3,500.00, plus interest and costs. Your client was served with the plaintiff's claim on September 1, 20—. Your client came to see you to discuss the claim on September 6.

September is a busy month for you. You put the copy of the plaintiff's claim into your inbox, where it slowly gets buried under a stack of paper.

Early in October, your client phones you to say that he just received a default judgment against him in the mail. He wants to know what is going on. At this point, you dig the plaintiff's claim out of your inbox, and pick up your copy of the *Small Claims Court Rules*. This is what you discover.

According to Small Claims Court Rule 9.01(1), a defendant must file a defence with the court within 20 days of being served with the plaintiff's claim. When you missed the 20-day deadline, the plaintiff filed proof of service of the claim with the court, and had your client noted in default (Rule 11.01). Because this was an action for a debt, the plaintiff was also entitled to have default judgment signed by the clerk against your client (Rule 11.02(1)). The default judgment can be enforced against your client under Rule 20.

Being noted in default means that your client is not permitted to take any further steps in the proceeding, except to bring a motion for an order setting aside the noting in default and the default judgment (Rule 11.05). Rule 11.05 permits you to correct your error, but in order to do so, you must draft additional documents, pay a $40.00 filing fee on the motion, serve the other side, and make an additional court appearance. Even if you are successful on the motion, the court may award costs against your client.

This error could have been prevented by having a proper tickler system in place for notifying you of approaching procedural deadlines on your files. As it is, your mistake may result in additional procedural delay and possible prejudice to your client by way of a costs award.

A tickler system is a list of tasks with deadlines for their completion. The deadline for a task may be a statutory limitation period or a procedural deadline set by the rules of a tribunal. A tickler system also contains tickler or bring-forward dates notifying you that a deadline is approaching, and that you should start working on a task in order to get it completed before the deadline.

Interpretation of the Rules (Rule 1.03)

Rule 1.03(1) provides that the rules shall be **liberally construed** with a view to obtaining a just (fair), expeditious (speedy), and inexpensive resolution of every proceeding on its merits. Rule 1.03(1) makes specific reference to s. 25 of the *Courts of Justice Act*, which was discussed above.

"Liberally construed" means that the Rules will be interpreted in such a way as to bring about a just and fair conclusion, without undue emphasis on strict compliance with all procedural requirements and technicalities, so long as the rights of all parties are protected. In other words, the court may apply the Rules in a way that is not strictly provided for in the language on the page, but which is in keeping with the court's mandate under s. 25 to hear and decide matters without needless procedural delay, with a view to bringing about a fair and just resolution within a reasonable time.

Rule 1.03(2) provides further direction with respect to interpreting the Rules in a situation that the Rules do not cover adequately. In this kind of situation, the court may look at the Rules themselves, and may also look outside the Rules, at the *Courts of Justice Act*, the statute governing the action (if there is one), and, if appropriate, the *Rules of Civil Procedure*, for guidance in arriving at a decision. This is called "deciding by analogy."

BOX 1.7 How to Read the Rules

When taking any procedural step, you must be careful to look at all the relevant rules. This may seem a bit confusing at first, but it gets easier as you become more familiar with Small Claims Court procedures. Continuing with the example from

Box 1.6, let's look at some rules and subrules that would be relevant when making arrangements for the set aside motion.

As you already know, Rule 11.05 permits you to bring the motion. Since you missed the deadline for filing a defence, one of the things you will have to ask the court for on the motion is an order extending the time for filing a defence. Rule 3.02(1) authorizes the court to make this kind of order.

If you are not sure what forms to use on the motion, you will need to consult Rule 15, which governs motions. You will find the name and number of the form to use at Rule 15.01(1).

Rule 15.01(2) tells you that you must obtain a hearing date for the motion before serving the notice of motion on the other party. Rule 15.01(3) tells you the minimum number of days before the hearing date that the motion must be served on the other party. If you are not sure how to calculate the notice period, you must read Rule 15.01(3) together with Rule 3.01 (Time—Computation) of the *Small Claims Court Rules*. You should also consider Rule 3.01 (Time—Computation) of the *Rules of Civil Procedure*. You may also wish to clarify the definition of "holiday" in the list of definitions at Rule 1.02 of the *Small Claims Court Rules*. Finally, you must check Rule 8 (Service) to find out how a motion may be served on another party, and what document you use to prove service.

Rule 15.02 tells you about methods of hearing a motion (in person, by telephone or video conference, and so on). If you want the motion to be heard by telephone or video conference, you must make a request to the court under Rules 1.07 and 15.02(1)(b).

How many rules and subrules did you count?

Orders on Terms (Rule 1.04)

Rule 1.04 authorizes the court to impose terms and give directions when making an order, so long as the terms and directions are just.

Telephone and Video Conferences (Rule 1.07)

If a court has facilities for telephone or video conferencing, a settlement conference, a motion, or all or part of an examination of a debtor or other person under Rule 20.10 may be heard or conducted by telephone or video conference (Rules 1.07(1) and 1.07(1.1)).

To schedule a telephone or video conference, a party must file a request in Form 1B with the court, giving reasons for the request (Rule 1.07(2)). Before granting the request, the judge must consider whether the **balance of convenience** favours the party requesting the telephone or video conference, or that of any party opposing it; plus any other relevant matter (Rule 1.07(3)). A court applying the balance of convenience test will balance the prejudice to one party of denying the relief asked for, against the prejudice to an opposing party if the relief is granted.

If the balance of convenience favours the party requesting a telephone or video conference, the request will be granted, and the court will make the necessary arrangements and notify the parties (Rule 1.07(4)).

On motion by a party opposing a telephone or video conference, an order granting a telephone or video conference may be set aside or varied by a judge presiding over the proceeding or over a step in the proceeding (Rule 1.07(5)).

BOX 1.8 What Does "Liberally Construe" Really Mean?

No matter how carefully procedural rules are drafted, they cannot cover every possible situation that arises. Sometimes there is a "gap" in the rules—that is, there is no language that deals directly with a particular issue. Sometimes the existing language is ambiguous—that is, it can be read as having more than one meaning.

To **construe** the language of a rule (or, for that matter, a statute or a legal document such as a will or contract) means to interpret it—to read it and decide what it means. Construe is the verb. Construction is the noun.

Strict construction (also known as narrow construction) means that the language of the rule is read and applied using its exact, technical meaning. An example of strict construction would be the definition of "holiday" in Rule 1.02. If the rule says that, in a Small Claims Court proceeding, certain days are holidays, then they are holidays. It does not matter whether you, as a defendant, have to work on Saturdays and Sundays, New Year's Day, Good Friday, and Easter Monday—they are still holidays as far as the *Small Claims Court Rules* are concerned.

Liberal construction (also known as equitable construction) means that, when applying the Rules, the court goes beyond the exact meaning of the language in order to implement the principles behind the Rules, as stated in s. 25 of the *Courts of Justice Act* and Rules 1.03(1) and 1.03(2).

Let's consider service of a plaintiff's claim, which is governed by Rules 8.01(1), 8.02, 8.03, and 8.04. The rules of service are complex, and can be very confusing for the self-represented. When interpreting these rules, the court may not insist on strict technical compliance, so long as it is clear that the plaintiff has made good-faith efforts to deliver the claim to the defendant, and the defendant has received the claim.

What if the way the plaintiff serves the claim is in strict technical compliance with the Rules, but the defendant never receives it? Let's say that the plaintiff uses an alternative to personal service, Rule 8.03(2)—Service at Place of Residence. The plaintiff leaves the claim in a sealed envelope addressed to the defendant with an apparent adult member of the household, and mails a copy to the defendant on the same day. This is proper service under the Rules. However, for one reason or another, the defendant does not receive the claim. After the 20-day period for filing a defence set out in Rule 9.01(1) has passed, the plaintiff notes the defendant in default. When served with the default judgment, the defendant brings a motion to set aside the noting of default.

At the hearing of the motion, can the plaintiff rely on technical compliance with the letter of the law as set out in Rules 8.03(2) and 9.01(1) to argue that the defendant's motion should be dismissed?

The plaintiff may make the argument, but the court is unlikely to deny the defendant her right to be heard, based on a narrow, technical argument of this nature.

Instead, the court will look at what is fair in all of the circumstances when coming to its decision. If appropriate, the court may compensate the plaintiff for any inconvenience, delay, and expense caused by the defendant's conduct with an order that the defendant pay the plaintiff some costs.

Procedure in the civil courts tends to be forgiving, in that it makes allowances for errors by parties or their legal representatives. Legal representatives should not use this as an excuse for carelessness. Know your rules and stay on top of your deadlines. If you are too busy to give a client's case the attention it needs, refer the matter to another paralegal with expertise in the area, or to a lawyer.

Rule 2—Non-Compliance with the Rules

Rule 2 complements Rule 1.03 (liberal construction of the Rules). Rule 2.01 states that a failure to comply with the rules is an irregularity—a mistake that can be corrected. If you make a mistake, it does not mean that a particular procedural step, document, or order has no legal force and effect. Instead, the court has discretion to grant amendments or other relief, with a view to obtaining a just resolution of the real issues that are in dispute. The court must exercise this discretion on such terms as are just to both or all parties. In other words, the party that made the mistake requiring correction may have to pay some costs to other parties; or the order may contain other terms intended to minimize potential prejudice to other parties.

Rule 2.02 provides that the court may dispense with compliance with any rule at any time, if it is just to do so.

Rule 3—Time

When calculating a period of time for taking a certain procedural step, you exclude the first day and include the last day of the period. If the last day of the period falls on a holiday as defined in Rule 1.02, then it ends on the next business day (Rule 3.01).

The court has discretion to lengthen or shorten the time prescribed by the Rules for doing anything, on such terms as are just (Rule 3.02(1)).

The time prescribed by the Rules for serving or filing a document may be lengthened or shortened by filing the consent of the parties (Rule 3.02(2)).

Closing Comment

You need to know the *Rules of the Small Claims Court* well, if you propose to practise in this area, or if you are working under the supervision of someone who practises in this area (for example, in debt collection). But the most important thing to remember is—when in doubt, do not guess. Read your Rules.

CHAPTER SUMMARY

Small Claims Court is a division of the Ontario Superior Court of Justice. It is a civil trial court that hears actions for money in amounts up to $25,000.00, excluding interest and costs, or for recovery of property with a value of $25,000.00 or less.

Small Claims Court is intended to improve the public's access to justice by providing a forum with simplified rules and procedures where claimants may have their matters resolved in a just, speedy, inexpensive, and simple manner.

The *Courts of Justice Act* sets up the court system in Ontario. Sections 22 to 31 of the *Courts of Justice Act* set out the general principles governing Small Claims Court, including who may be a judge of Small Claims Court (s. 24); monetary jurisdiction (s. 23 and O. Reg. 626/00); the general mandate or purpose of Small Claims Court (s. 25); legal representation (s. 26); evidence (s. 27); installment orders for payment of money (s. 28); costs (s. 29); and appeals (s. 31).

The *Rules of the Small Claims Court* are published as a regulation to the *Courts of Justice Act*. The Rules implement the mandate set out in s. 25 of the *Courts of Justice Act* by establishing a summary procedure that is designed to be user-friendly for self-represented or unsophisticated parties, while preserving and protecting the rights of all parties.

Anyone practising in Small Claims Court should be familiar with its procedural rules. This does not mean that you must have them memorized; but you should know them well enough so that, when you are not sure about a procedural point, you know where to look in the Rules to find the answer.

KEY TERMS

action: a proceeding brought in a court *(p. 2)*

allegation: an assertion made in a pleading by a party to an action, setting out what she hopes to prove *(p. 12)*

balance of convenience: a common-law test; a court applying this test will balance the prejudice to one party of denying the relief asked for, against the prejudice to the opposing party if the relief is granted *(p. 19)*

claimant: another word for plaintiff; a claimant is anyone who commences a claim *(p. 3)*

construe: to interpret *(p. 20)*

costs: the expenses connected with a legal proceeding; costs include a party's legal fees, plus disbursements, or out-of-pocket expenses, including court filing fees *(p. 7)*

defendant: the party who defends a civil action *(p. 2)*

disbursements: the out-of-pocket expenses of a legal proceeding; these include court filing fees, charges for service of documents, photocopying charges, postage, etc. *(p. 8)*

frequent claimant: anyone who files 10 or more claims in a Small Claims Court office on or after January 1 in any calendar year *(p. 3)*

hearsay rule: a witness is not allowed to repeat in court what they were told by a third party, if the reason for putting the evidence in is to prove the truth of the contents of the third-party statement *(p. 14)*

infrequent claimant: anyone who files fewer than 10 Small Claims Court claims in a Small Claims Court office on or after January 1 in any calendar year *(p. 3)*

installment (or partial) payments: a partial payment of a sum of money owing at regular intervals over a period of time until the amount owing is paid in full *(p. 14)*

jurisdiction: a court's area of legal authority; in Ontario, jurisdiction is established by the *Courts of Justice Act* and by the common law *(p. 2)*

justice: a justice is the same thing as a judge; "justice," "judge," and "court" are often used interchangeably in reported decisions *(p. 11)*

lawyer: a person who has been called to the Bar of Ontario and who is licensed to practise law in Ontario *(p. 12)*

legal fees: fees charged by a lawyer or paralegal for legal representation and advice *(p. 7)*

liberal construction: means that, when applying the Rules, the court goes beyond the exact meaning of the language in order to implement the principles behind the Rules *(p. 20)*

liberally construed: interpreting the Rules without undue emphasis on strict compliance with all procedural requirements and technicalities, with a view to bringing about a resolution that is just and fair to all parties within a reasonable time *(p. 18)*

litigant: a party to a civil action; someone engaged in civil litigation *(p. 2)*

lump-sum payment: a one-time payment of the full amount owing or a portion thereof *(p. 14)*

monetary jurisdiction: the amount of money that the court may order one party to pay another, not including interest and costs *(p. 7)*

notice: service of documents on other parties to make them aware of an intended procedural step or other matter *(p. 17)*

notice period: the minimum period of time for serving documents on other parties before a procedural step takes place *(p. 17)*

paralegal: a non-lawyer who is not an articling student and who is licensed to provide legal services in permitted areas of practice to clients for a fee in the province of Ontario *(p. 12)*

party: a person who commences or defends an action or proceeding *(p. 2)*

plaintiff: the party who commences a civil action *(p. 2)*

question of fact: a factual dispute; in jury trials, questions of fact are determined by the jury; in non-jury trials, questions of fact are determined by the trial judge *(p. 12)*

question of law: an issue that requires the application or interpretation of a law or legal principle; in both jury and non-jury trials, questions of law are determined by judges *(p. 12)*

strict construction: means that the language of a rule is read and applied using its exact, technical meaning; also known as "narrow construction" *(p. 20)*

REFERENCES

Action Auto Leasing & Gallery Inc. v. Robillard, [2011] OJ No. 2453 (OSCJ Div. Ct.).
Administration of Justice Act, RSO 1990, c. A.6.
Courts of Justice Act, RRO 1990, Reg. 194, as amended.
Courts of Justice Act, RSO 1990, c. C.43.
Evidence Act, RSO 1990, c. E.23, as amended.
Law Society Act, RSO 1990, c. L.8.
Law Society of Upper Canada (LSUC), By-laws (Toronto: LSUC, 2005, as amended); available online at http://www.lsuc.on.ca.

Libel and Slander Act, RSO 1990, c. L.12.
Proceedings Against the Crown Act, RSO 1990, c. P.27.
Rules of Civil Procedure, RRO 1990, Reg. 194.
Rules of the Small Claims Court, O. Reg. 258/98.
Small Claims Court—Fees and Allowances, O. Reg. 432/93.

REVIEW QUESTIONS

1. What is jurisdiction?
2. What is an action? What types of actions does Small Claims Court hear?
3. What is a frequent claimant? What is an infrequent claimant? Why is the distinction important?
4. What is the *Courts of Justice Act*? What is its purpose?
5. What is the monetary jurisdiction of Small Claims Court? Does the maximum amount that can be claimed include interest and costs?
6. What is the difference between costs, legal fees, and disbursements?
7. What is a deputy judge? What is the difference between deputy judges and other judges in Small Claims Court?
8. What is the general mandate of Small Claims Court? Please provide the statutory authority.
9. Who may appear as a legal representative in Small Claims Court? Please provide the statutory authority.
10. a. What is hearsay evidence?
    b. What is the general rule with respect to hearsay evidence?
    c. What is the general rule with respect to hearsay evidence in Small Claims Court? Please provide the statutory authority.
11. What are the *Small Claims Court Rules* and what is their purpose?
12. What is the general principle governing interpretation of the *Small Claims Court Rules*? Please provide the number of any rule(s) you are relying upon in support of your answer.
13. What is the general rule with respect to orders for payment of costs in Small Claims Court? Please provide the statutory authority.
14. If a party wants to appeal a final order of the Small Claims Court, what court do they appeal to? What procedural rule or rules govern the appeal?

APPENDIX 1.1 Overview of Small Claims Court Procedure and Timelines

PROCEDURAL STEP	TIME PERIOD	START DATE	AUTHORITY
Issue plaintiff's claim	2 years *Note: There are statutory notice periods for some defendants. See, for example:* • *Libel and Slander Act, s. 5(1)* • *Proceedings Against the Crown Act, ss. 7(1), (3)*	The day the claim is discovered *Note: "Claim" is defined as "a claim to remedy an injury, loss or damage that occurred as a result of an act or omission."*	*Limitations Act, 2002,* ss. 4, 5 *Limitations Act, 2002,* s. 1
Serve plaintiff's claim	6 months *Note: Court may extend time for service before or after 6-month period ends*	The day the claim is issued	*Rules of the Small Claims Court* (RSCC), O. Reg. 258/98, Rule 8.01(2)
File defence to plaintiff's claim or defendant's claim	Personal service: 20 days	The day personal service takes place	RSCC, Rule 9.01(1)
	Alternative to personal service: Depends on method of service	The day service is effective	
	Substituted service: By court order	By court order	RSCC, Rule 8.04
Issue defendant's claim	20 days	The day the defence is filed	RSCC, Rule 10.01(2)(a)
	After the 20-day period has expired but before trial or default judgment, with leave of the court	By court order	RSCC, Rule 10.01(2)(b)
File defence to defendant's claim	20 days	The day service of defendant's claim becomes effective	RSCC, Rule 10.03
File defence to plaintiff's claim—third party added by defendant's claim	20 days	The day service of defendant's claim becomes effective	RSCC, Rule 10.03
Default proceedings	Noting in default: Immediately after the time for filing a defence has expired, if no defence to a plaintiff's claim or a defendant's claim has been filed.		RSCC, Rule 11.01(1)
	Default judgment: In a plaintiff's claim for a debt or liquidated amount, if a defendant has been noted in default, the clerk may sign default judgment for all or part of the amount claimed, plus interest if claimed.		RSCC, Rule 11.02(1)

PROCEDURAL STEP	TIME PERIOD	START DATE	AUTHORITY
Settlement conference *Note: This date is set by the clerk*	90 days	The day the first defence is filed	RSCC, Rule 13.01(3)
Offer to settle	May be made any time up until the court makes a final disposition of the matter. May be accepted any time up until the offer is withdrawn or expires, or there is a final disposition of the matter.		RSCC, Rule 14.03
Request a trial date	ASAP by plaintiff upon receipt of notice from the clerk stating that a party must request a trial date if the matter does not settle within 30 days after the settlement conference.		RSCC, Rule 13.07
Motion for new trial	30 days	The day the final order is made	RSCC, Rule 17.04
Appeal to Divisional Court *Note: The Divisional Court is the appeal branch of the Superior Court of Justice*	30 days	The day the order appealed from is made, unless a statute or the *Rules of Civil Procedure* provides otherwise	*Courts of Justice Act*, RSO 1990, c. C.43, s. 31 *Rules of Civil Procedure*, RRO 1990, Reg. 194, Rule 61.04(1)
	At present, paralegals are not allowed to appear on appeals to the Divisional Court. However, if your client indicates that she wishes to appeal an order, you should advise her of the 30-day window and tell her to seek the services of a lawyer. You may wish to direct her to the Lawyer Referral Service (1-800-268-8326 or 416-947-3330 (within the GTA)).		

You and Your Client

2

LEARNING OUTCOMES

After reading this chapter, you will understand:

- The duty of competence

- The duty of honesty and candour

- The purpose and scope of the duty of confidentiality

- Permitted disclosure

- The duty to avoid conflicts of interest

- Compliance with client identification and verification (By-law 7.1, Part III)

- The basic concepts of effective communication

- The purpose of the engagement letter or retainer agreement

- How to handle the money retainer

- The purpose of the reporting letter

- Management of client files

Introduction

Many of a paralegal's duties and obligations to a client arise out of the fiduciary relationship between the paralegal and the client. A **fiduciary relationship** is a relationship of absolute trust and confidence between two persons, in which one person (the **fiduciary**) is required to act with scrupulous good faith, honesty, and candour for the benefit of the other person (the beneficiary). In the paralegal–client relationship, the paralegal is the fiduciary and the client is the beneficiary. The paralegal must put the client's interests ahead of her own in all dealings with the client. The client is entitled to place absolute confidence, reliance, and trust in the paralegal.

In this chapter, we will discuss the following duties owed by the paralegal to the client:

- the duty to be competent (Rule 3.01);
- the duty to be honest and candid with the client (Rule 3.02);
- the duty to hold client information in strict confidence (Rule 3.03); and
- the duty to avoid conflicts of interest (Rule 3.04).

The importance of effective communication with the client will also be considered.

In the following discussion, the *Paralegal Rules of Conduct* are referred to as the Paralegal Rules, and the *Paralegal Professional Conduct Guidelines* are referred to as the Guidelines.

Competence (Paralegal Rule 3.01; Guideline 6)

Like all professionals, paralegals are required to be knowledgeable about the areas in which they provide services to the public. A client hires a paralegal because the paralegal has knowledge and skills the client does not have. A paralegal who holds herself out as having certain kinds of expertise must ensure that she does in fact possess that expertise and can apply it for the benefit of her clients.

Paralegals who fail to meet standards of professional competence when providing legal services to the public may cause harm to their clients, and to their business partners and associates. They may also bring the paralegal profession and the justice system into disrepute.

The Competent Paralegal (Paralegal Rules 3.01(1), (2), and (3))

Paralegal Rule 3.01(1) imposes a general obligation to perform any legal services undertaken on a client's behalf to the standard of a competent paralegal. A **competent paralegal** is a paralegal who has and applies the relevant skills, attributes, and values appropriate to each matter undertaken on behalf of a client, including but not limited to (1) knowledge; (2) client service and communication; and (3) skills and judgment.

You shall not undertake to represent a client in a matter unless you are familiar with the legal principles and procedures governing the applicable area of law, or are confident that you can become familiar with those legal principles and procedures in a timely and cost-effective manner (Paralegal Rule 3.01(2)).

If at any stage of the matter you discover that you are not competent to complete the tasks for which you were retained, you shall (Paralegal Rule 3.01(3)):

1. decline to act; or
2. obtain the client's consent to retain, consult, or collaborate with another licensee who is competent to perform the task and is licensed to do so.

When you are first approached by a client about a particular matter, you shall carefully consider whether you are competent to provide the legal services required. When assessing your own competence, keep in mind that a lack of competence on your part may do the client a disservice, bring discredit to the paralegal profession, and bring the administration of justice into disrepute. The best time to turn your mind to this is before accepting the retainer, at which time you may decline to act if you are not satisfied that you possess the required knowledge and skills. If you decline to act, you should consider referring the client to another paralegal or a lawyer with the required expertise. You should also consider sending a **non-engagement letter** to the client confirming that you have not accepted the retainer and stating your reasons. A non-engagement letter is a letter confirming that the paralegal has declined to accept the retainer, or that the client has declined to retain the paralegal.

BOX 2.1 What Is a Retainer?

In a legal services context, the word "retainer" may be used to mean several different things.

The **paralegal–client retainer** is the contractual relationship between the client and the paralegal. The terms of the paralegal–client retainer should be discussed with the client at the initial consultation.

The **retainer agreement** is the written contract between the paralegal and the client. It sets out the important terms of the paralegal–client retainer, including the scope of the legal services to be provided, the likely cost of those services, expected outcomes, billing practices, and events of termination of the retainer, among other things. It is called an agreement because it is signed back to the paralegal by the client. An **engagement letter** may be used for the same purpose. An engagement letter confirms the terms of the paralegal–client retainer, but is not signed back by the client.

A **money retainer** is money paid by the client to the paralegal for future legal services. A money retainer for future legal services belongs to the client, and must be held in trust for the client until legal services have been provided and billed to the client.

Sometimes a matter takes a direction that could not be anticipated when you accepted the retainer. If you are no longer competent to act for a client because of unforeseen developments in an ongoing matter, you must advise the client that you are not competent to perform a particular task, and obtain the client's consent to retain, consult, or collaborate with another licensee who is competent to perform the task and is licensed to do so. If the client will not consent to such an arrangement, you must withdraw from representation. Lack of competence is a ground for mandatory withdrawal of legal representation (Paralegal Rule 3.08(5)(e)).

Regardless of expertise, no paralegal licensee should provide legal services to a client in an unauthorized area of law (Paralegal Rule 3.02(2)). Clients with such matters should be advised to seek the services of a lawyer and be referred to a lawyer with expertise in that area of law or directed to the Law Society Referral Service (1-800-268-8326 or 416-947-3330 (within the GTA)). There is no charge for the Law Society Referral Service. You should also consider sending a non-engagement letter to the client confirming that you have terminated the retainer and stating your reasons.

Honesty and Candour (Paralegal Rule 3.02(1); Guideline 7)

A paralegal must be honest and candid when advising a client. This is true whether the client is seeking to retain you in a matter or is a casual client seeking quick advice.

In this context, being **candid** means being forthright and sincere, and looking at both sides of each issue without bias. You must advise the client honestly and candidly of the applicable law, the client's options, possible outcomes, and possible risks. Your advice should enable the client to make informed decisions and give appropriate instructions in the matter.

You should always ensure that clients, including prospective clients, understand that you are a paralegal, not a lawyer.

You must never undertake or provide advice regarding a matter that is outside the scope of permissible practice for paralegals.

When advising a client, you must never knowingly assist in or encourage any dishonesty, fraud, crime, or illegal conduct. You must not instruct a client on how to violate the law and avoid punishment.

Bad News

Clients like to hear good news. If they intend to sue someone in Small Claims Court for an unpaid debt, they want to hear that they have a good case and will get their money back. If they are trying to evict a tenant from rental housing, they want to hear that they will get an eviction order. If they are fighting a speeding ticket, they want to hear that the case will be thrown out due to a deficiency on the face of the charging document.

Your duty to be honest and candid applies when the news is good and when it is bad. The downside of being honest and candid about bad news is that, if the client is not happy with what he hears, he may seek legal assistance elsewhere. In a competitive market, it can be difficult to let any client walk out the door, however unreasonable his expectations. Nonetheless, your professional duty requires you to give honest, candid advice as to the merits of the matter and whether the client's objectives are achievable.

In situations where you decline to accept a retainer or a client declines to retain you after the initial consultation, you should send the client a non-engagement letter, confirming that you will not be acting in the matter. The non-engagement letter should advise the client of any limitation periods, and recommend that the client seek other legal representation.

The Duty of Confidentiality (Paralegal Rule 3.03; Guideline 8)

General

You have a professional and ethical duty to hold in strict confidence anything you learn at any stage of your professional relationship with the client about any aspect of the client's affairs. In other words, you must not share client information (including client information that other people may already know) with anyone, unless authorized by your client or required by law to do so (Paralegal Rule 3.03).

The duty of confidentiality is grounded in the principle that effective legal representation requires full and unreserved communication between the legal representative and the client. The client must be confident that anything discussed with or disclosed to you will not be disclosed to others, unless she authorizes that disclosure or the nature of the matter requires it. The duty applies whether your client is an individual or a business entity such as a corporation.

Scope of the Duty of Confidentiality

The duty of confidentiality applies to all information of any kind that you acquire from a client or on behalf of a client during the professional relationship. This includes:

1. The identity of the client and the fact that the client has consulted or retained you;

2. Information about the client that is not relevant to the specific matter on which you have been retained; and

3. Information that others may have knowledge of. For example, others may know your client's home address and telephone number. That does not release you from your obligation not to disclose that information, except with your client's consent or as required by law.

The duty to keep information confidential applies to you, your associates, and anyone in your employ or acting under your supervision, including students.

In the office, client information should not be left in places where it is visible to others. If you are meeting a client in your office, your desk should be clear of other client files and any other documents that might serve as client identifiers. Computer monitors should be situated so that their screens are not visible to the public. If screens are visible to the public, they should be filtered.

When Does the Duty of Confidentiality Arise, and When Does It End?

The duty of confidentiality arises when you enter into a professional relationship with a client. It applies to **casual** or **prospective clients** as well as to regular **clients**.

BOX 2.2 Gossip: What Not to Do

You are representing Rosemary Lawson, the plaintiff in a personal injury action. Over time, you have come to distrust your client. You think she is lying about the circumstances in which the injury (a sprained wrist) took place, and that she has unreasonable expectations about how much money she can expect to get. The defendant has made what you think is a reasonable settlement offer. You have been urging Ms. Lawson to accept it, but she refuses.

One evening after work you meet your husband for dinner at a restaurant near your office. The restaurant is crowded and noisy. You have told your husband about several incidents when Rosemary Lawson was particularly difficult. She has become a kind of joke between you. When you have ordered, your husband says, "So, how'd it go today? How's Rosemary?" While the waiter serves your drinks, you tell your husband the latest "Rosemary anecdote." It is an entertaining story, and makes your husband laugh. You and your husband have a pleasant dinner.

Comment: You should not discuss a client with your spouse or any other member of your family. You should not discuss a client in a public place like a restaurant, where wait staff and other diners can overhear what you are saying.

You should never discuss a client or anything connected with a client file with anyone who is not entitled to hear the information. Nor should you talk about these things in circumstances where third parties may overhear what you are saying. Your friends and relatives have no obligation to keep the information confidential, nor do third parties who may overhear your conversation. If they repeat the information to others, your client could be prejudiced. Even if no prejudice to your client results, you have breached the duty to hold all client information in strict confidence.

Even if you do not mention the client's name and remove other identifiers, you breach the duty of confidentiality when you share client information with someone who has no right to hear it and owes the client no duty to hold it in confidence.

A casual client is a client who consults with you about a legal issue, but then decides not to proceed, or not to hire you to act as his legal representative. A prospective client is a person who consults you about a legal issue but has not yet retained you. A client is a person who consults with you and hires you to represent her in a matter or a number of matters. The professional relationship with casual clients, prospective clients, and clients who retain you as their legal representative begins when they first approach you for legal advice. The duty of confidentiality arises at that point.

The duty of confidentiality continues indefinitely. It continues after the professional relationship has ended. It continues regardless of how the professional relationship ended. A client may fire you. You still owe that client the duty to hold his information in strict confidence. A client may die. You must continue to hold his information in strict confidence. Your associates, employees, and students must do the same.

Your duty to hold client information in strict confidence does not end when your association with a particular paralegal practice or law firm ends. It continues indefinitely. You may never use confidential information for your own benefit, whether personal or financial, even if doing so would not harm your client. You may never use confidential information for the personal or financial benefit of a third party. You may never use confidential information to the disadvantage of a client, including a former client.

When May You Disclose Confidential Information?

You may disclose confidential information to others if you have the client's **express consent** or **implied consent** to do so.

Express (or explicit) consent means that the client has given you written authorization to disclose particular information to specified third parties. For example, you must obtain a written authorization from your client before releasing medical records or reports from the client's treating physician to other parties.

Written authorizations should clearly state any restrictions on disclosure, and should specify to whom you may disclose the information, and for what period of time, if that is appropriate. You will find a sample authorization at Appendix 2.10 to this chapter.

Implied consent is not written down—it is implied by the professional relationship. Unless the client directs otherwise, you have implied consent to disclose confidential information to colleagues, employees, and students who are working on the client file. However, anyone to whom confidential information is disclosed must be aware of and comply with their duty to hold the information in strict confidence.

You also have implied consent to reveal a certain amount of client information because the matter requires it. For example, in court proceedings, client information that would otherwise be confidential may be disclosed in pleadings and other documents filed with the court. The contents of court files are open to the public unless legislation prohibits public access or the court imposes a publication ban.

The Duty to Avoid Conflicts of Interest

(Paralegal Rule 3.04; Guideline 9)

General

A **conflict of interest** is any circumstance that may negatively affect a paralegal's ability to act in the client's best interests. Conflicts of interest may arise at any time in a client matter, as the matter evolves, new parties are added, and new circumstances or information comes to light.

Paralegal Rule 3.04(1) defines "conflict of interest" or "conflicting interest" as an interest, financial or otherwise,

(a)   that would be likely to have an adverse effect on a paralegal's judgment on behalf of, or loyalty to, a client or prospective client; or

(b)   that a paralegal might be prompted to give preference to over the interests of a client or a prospective client.

A paralegal shall not advise or represent more than one side in a dispute (Paralegal Rule 3.04(2)). A **dispute** is an argument or disagreement between two or more sides in which the interest of one side is in direct opposition to the interest of another side. A paralegal cannot act for persons with adverse interests in a dispute, because to do so would influence the paralegal's judgment and loyalty to the adverse persons.

Because conflicts of interest may result in harm to the client, paralegals have an obligation to prospective clients, current clients, and former clients to avoid conflicts of interest and potential conflicts of interest.

Conflict-Checking System

How do you find out whether or not there may be a conflict of interest in a particular client matter? To assist in complying with the duty of avoidance of conflicts of interest, paralegals should maintain a searchable database of information about prospective, current, and former clients, as well as information about related persons and conflicting or adverse parties. The database should include fields for the following information (the list is not exhaustive):

- client's name, and aliases and former names, if applicable;
- client contact information;
- date the file was opened;
- client file name and active client matter number;
- subject matter of the file;
- date the file was closed, and closed client matter number; and
- names and contact information of related persons, and of conflicting or adverse parties (if available), cross-referenced to the client file.

The database may be maintained in a paper or electronic format. Some legal software applications automatically enter client and other data into a conflicts databank as new electronic files are opened.

As part of your conflict-checking system, you should have standard office procedures in place for conducting conflict searches at critical points in the paralegal–client relationship. Your first search should take place after the initial contact with a prospective client. You should search for conflicts again when you have more information about the client, and related or adverse parties. If a retainer is entered into, you should conduct a conflict search any time a new party is added in a proceeding. If a conflict arises after you are retained, you may be required to withdraw from representing the client.

BOX 2.3 Conflicts of Interest—Who Is the Client?

Any person who is a client of the paralegal firm of which you are a partner or an employee is a client, regardless of whether you actually handle that person's work (Paralegal Rule 1.02). In a busy firm with many clients and/or a high client turnover, you may have no knowledge of a client's existence or that your firm ever represented him. Nevertheless, a paralegal–client relationship exists between you and that client and entails various duties, including the duty of confidentiality and the duty to avoid conflicts of interest.

Since every client of a paralegal firm is also the client of every other paralegal in the firm, if one paralegal has a conflict of interest in a matter, then all paralegals in the firm have a conflict of interest in that matter (Guideline 9).

This means that when you check for conflicts, you must review the names of all current and former clients of the firm, not just the clients you personally represented.

Client Consent

The existence of a conflict or potential conflict does not always mean that you cannot represent the client. Paralegal Rule 3.04(3) permits you to act or continue to act if the client consents to your doing so.

CONSENT—PROSPECTIVE CLIENT

If practicable, whenever a prospective client contacts your firm, certain information (such as the client's name, including any aliases, and contact information) should be obtained from the client and entered immediately into your conflict-checking system. A conflict search should be carried out before there is any further contact with the prospective client. The results of the search should be reviewed by the paralegal.

If the search reveals a conflict or potential conflict, you must consider whether you should accept the retainer or decline to represent the prospective client. Paralegal Rule 3.04(3) permits you to accept the retainer if the prospective client consents. To comply, you must first disclose the conflict or potential conflict to the client. You must provide sufficient detail about the conflict to enable the client to make an informed decision about whether retaining you is in her best interests in the circumstances. This is called **informed consent**. Guideline 9 recommends that you give the prospective client some time to consider the disclosure and ask for further clarification.

If there are other persons who are involved in or connected with the client matter, you may have a duty to avoid conflicts of interest with respect to those persons as well. Examples of such individuals are members of the client's family, the client's spouse, and the client's business associates or employees. You must obtain informed consent from those persons as well (Paralegal Rule 3.04(4)).

If, having reviewed the information provided, the prospective client consents to your representation, you may accept the client retainer. The prospective client's consent, and the consents of any client associates, should be in writing.

Conflict of Interest—Prospective Client Declines Retainer. If, having reviewed the information provided, the prospective client declines to retain you, you should confirm the client's decision in a non-engagement letter. The non-engagement letter must advise the client of any limitation periods and recommend that the client obtain independent legal representation from a competent paralegal or lawyer with no personal interest in the matter.

Conflict of Interest—Paralegal Declines Retainer. There may be situations where you cannot provide full disclosure about the conflict of interest without revealing confidential information about another client or clients. When that happens, you must advise the prospective client that there is a conflict of interest and that you cannot accept the retainer (Guideline 9). You should confirm your decision in writing in a non-engagement letter. The non-engagement letter must advise the client of any limitation periods and recommend that the client obtain independent legal representation from a competent paralegal or lawyer with no personal interest in the matter.

Guideline 9 recommends that you consider whether to accept or decline a prospective client's retainer any time you become aware of a conflict or potential conflict. You should do this even if you have the client's consent and if, in your opinion, the retainer would not breach the Paralegal Rules. When considering whether to accept the client matter, you should take into account the delay, expense, and inconvenience that will arise for the client and/or for you, should you be required to withdraw at a later stage in the proceeding.

Guideline 9 also notes that, in some cases, even though the client has indicated that he wants to retain you, the only way to deal with the conflict is to decline the retainer.

In both of the above cases, if you decide to decline the retainer, you should confirm your decision in writing in a non-engagement letter. The non-engagement letter should advise the client of any limitation periods and recommend that the client obtain independent legal representation from a competent paralegal or lawyer with no personal interest in the matter.

You will find examples of non-engagement letters at Appendixes 2.1 and 2.2.

CONSENT—EXISTING CLIENT

Existing client matters should be checked for conflicts at critical points throughout the paralegal–client retainer. You should conduct a conflict search any time a new party is added in a proceeding or new information about the client matter comes to light. If a conflict arises after you are retained, you may be required to withdraw from representing the client.

If a conflict search reveals a conflict or potential conflict in an existing client matter, you must consider whether or not to continue to act in the matter. Paralegal Rule 3.04(3) permits you to continue to act if the client gives you informed consent based on disclosure of all information regarding the conflict that the client requires to make a decision. The client should be given some time to consider the disclosure and ask for further clarification.

If there are other persons who are involved in or connected with the client matter, you may have a duty to avoid conflicts of interest with respect to those persons as well. You must obtain informed consent from those persons as well.

If, having reviewed the information provided, the client and any client associates consent to your continuing representation, you may continue to act in the client matter. The client's consent, and the consents of any client associates, should be in writing.

Conflict of Interest—Existing Client Terminates Retainer. If an existing client decides to terminate the retainer after having been advised that a conflict has arisen in an ongoing matter and having reviewed the information provided, you should confirm the termination of the retainer in writing. If the client requests that the matter be transferred to another paralegal or a lawyer, you should obtain a direction, in writing and signed by the client, for release of the client's file to the successor licensee. If the client collects the file herself, you should obtain an acknowledgment in writing and signed by the client confirming that she has received the file.

Conflict of Interest—Paralegal Withdraws from Representation. There may be situations where you cannot provide full disclosure about a conflict of interest without revealing confidential information about another client or clients. When that happens, you must advise the client that there is a conflict of interest and that you must refuse the retainer or, in the case of an ongoing matter, withdraw from representation. You should confirm your decision in writing to the client.

Any time you become aware of a conflict or potential conflict, you should consider whether or not to continue to act in the client matter. You should do this even if you have the client's consent to continue to act and are satisfied that your continued involvement would not put you in breach of the Paralegal Rules. When coming to a decision about whether to continue to act in the matter, you should take into account the delay, expense, and inconvenience that will arise for the client and/or for you, should you be required to withdraw at a later stage in the proceeding.

Sometimes the only way to deal with the conflict in an ongoing client matter is to withdraw from representation, even though the client may want you to continue to act in the matter. When withdrawing your services, you must comply with Paralegal Rule 3.08. You shall not withdraw from representation unless you are satisfied that there is good cause. You must give the client notice that is appropriate in the circumstances; try to minimize expense and avoid prejudice to the client; and do all that reasonably can be done to facilitate the orderly transfer of the client matter to a successor licensee.

Client Identification and Verification (By-law 7.1)

Amendments to By-law 7.1 with respect to client identification and verification came into effect in Ontario on December 31, 2008. They are part of a Canada-wide initiative by provincial law societies to fight fraud and money laundering.

By-law 7.1, Part III applies to retainers in matters for new or existing clients entered into on or after December 31, 2008 (s. 21).

Unless otherwise noted, all references to section numbers in the following discussion refer to By-law 7.1, Part III.

Compliance with the By-law 7.1 Client Identification and Verification Requirements

Section 22(1) requires a licensee to comply with the client identification and verification requirements set out in s. 23 whenever he is retained to provide legal services to a new or existing client on or after December 31, 2008.

You do not have to identify or verify clients on matters that were in existence prior to December 31, 2008. However, if you are retained in a new or related matter for any of those clients on or after December 31, 2008, you must comply with the client identification and verification requirements in Part III.

Licensees Who Are Exempt from the Section 23 Client Identification and Verification Requirements

You are not required to comply with the s. 23 client identification and verification requirements if you provide legal services and/or engage in or give instructions for the receiving, paying, or transferring of funds (s. 22(2)):

(a)   while acting on behalf of your employer;

(b)   while acting as an agent for another licensee or paralegal who has already identified the client;

(c)   while acting for a client who was referred to you by another paralegal or a lawyer who has already identified the client; or

(d)   while acting as duty counsel or providing summary legal services under the *Legal Aid Services Act* or providing legal services through a duty counsel program of a non-profit organization, unless a financial transaction is involved.

With respect to (b) and (c) above, you should require the paralegal or lawyer for whom you are acting as an agent, or the paralegal or lawyer who made the referral, to confirm that they have already identified the client in compliance with the requirements of the by-law.

What Is the Difference Between Client Identification and Client Verification?

Client identification refers to information you obtain from the client regarding who the client is and what the client does. **Client verification** refers to information you must obtain in order to confirm that the client is who he says he is.

Licensees must obtain and record client identification information in accordance with the criteria set out in s. 23(1) for the client in every new client matter opened on or after December 31, 2008. This includes existing clients who retain you in new or related matters on or after December 31, 2008.

If you engage in or give instructions for the receiving, paying, or transferring of funds, then you must obtain the additional client identification information set out in s. 23(2) and you must comply with the client verification requirements set out in s. 23(4) (s. 22(1)(b)).

Funds include cash, currency, securities, negotiable instruments, or other financial instruments that indicate a person's title or interest in them (s. 20). A **negotiable instrument** is an unconditional order or promise to pay an amount of money, which can be transferred—for example, cheques or banknotes (paper money).

Exemptions for Certain Types of Funds (s. 22(3))

You do not have to comply with the s. 23(2) client identification requirements and the s. 23(4) client verification requirements if the funds you are handling fall within one of the following exemptions (the list is not exhaustive) (s. 22(3)):

(a) funds paid to or received from a financial institution such as a bank, credit union, trust company, and so on; a public body such as a government ministry or a municipality; or a reporting issuer (public company) or subsidiary of a reporting issuer;

(b) funds received from the trust account of another paralegal or a lawyer;

(c) funds received from a peace officer, law enforcement agency, or other public official acting in an official capacity;

(d) funds paid or received pursuant to a court order;

(e) funds paid for a fine or penalty;

(f) funds paid or received in settlement of legal or administrative proceedings;

(g) funds paid or received for professional fees, disbursements, expenses, or bail;

(h) funds paid, received, or transferred by electronic funds transfer.

Clients Who Are Exempt from Client Identification and Verification

You are not required to comply with the Part III client identification and verification requirements if your client is (s. 22(4)):

1. a financial institution as defined at By-law 7.1, s. 20,

2. a public body as defined at By-law 7.1, s. 20, or

3. a reporting issuer as defined at By-law 7.1, s. 20.

BOX 2.4 Reminder

A **public company** (referred to as a "reporting issuer" in By-law 7.1, Part III) is a corporation whose shares are for sale to the general public. Public companies are subject to rigorous disclosure requirements under securities legislation.

A **private corporation** (also called a closely held corporation) is a corporation whose shares are not publicly traded. Its incorporating documents (1) restrict the right to sell shares, (2) limit the number of its shareholders (excluding employees) to 50, and (3) prohibit public trading of its shares or securities.

The Criteria for Client Identification and Verification

The criteria for identifying and verifying clients are set out in Table 2.1. Verification of identity forms for individuals, organizations, third-party beneficiaries, and principals are available at the Law Society of Upper Canada website. You will find samples, adapted for use in paralegal firms, at Appendixes 2.3 and 2.4.

Client Verification, Not Face to Face (s. 23(8))

You may use this form of client verification if you engage in or give instructions for the receiving, paying, or transferring of non-exempt funds on behalf of an individual client who is elsewhere in Canada, so that you are unable to receive instructions from the client face to face (s. 23(8)). To comply with the s. 23(4) verification requirements, you must obtain an attestation from a commissioner of oaths or a guarantor certifying that he has verified the client's identity by looking at the appropriate independent source documents (s. 23(8)). Section 23(9) provides a list of professionals who may be used as guarantors, including dentists, lawyers, physicians, and accountants. You must exercise due diligence in confirming that the attestor is a member of one of these professions. **Due diligence** means exercising the prudence and vigilance that a reasonable and prudent paralegal would exercise in similar circumstances.

The attestation must be printed on a legible photocopy of the document. It must include the name, occupation, address, and signature of the attestor, and the type and number of the document seen by the attestor (s. 23(10)). A sample attestation form for use by paralegal firms is available at the Law Society website. You will find the text of a sample attestation at Appendix 2.5.

TABLE 2.1   Criteria for Client Identification and Verification

		CLIENT	
		Individual	*Organization**
IDENTIFICATION CRITERIA	*Exempt funds: ss. 22(1)(a), 22(3), 23(1)*	• Full name • Business address and phone number, if applicable • Home address and phone number • Occupation(s)—does not have to be employment *If the client refuses to provide this information, you must inform the client that you will be in breach of By-law 7.1 if you do not obtain this information, and will be obliged to decline the retainer.*	• Full name • Business address and phone number • Incorporation or business identification number (and its place of issue), if applicable • General nature of the business or activity engaged in by the client (not applicable to a financial institution, a public body, or a public company) • Name, position, and contact information for the person(s) authorized to provide instructions in the matter
	Non-exempt funds: ss. 22(1)(b)(i), 23(2)	• None	• Name and occupation(s) of each director of the organization (unless the organization is a securities dealer) • Name, address, and occupation(s) of each person who owns 25% or more of the organization or shares of thereof *You must make reasonable efforts to obtain the above information. Asking your client may be sufficient; or you may consult the corporate minute books if they are available, or an online corporate registry service.*
	Note	• If the client (whether an individual or an organization) is acting for or representing another person, you must obtain the same identification information for that person as for your client.	

		CLIENT	
		Individual	*Organization**
VERIFICATION CRITERIA	***Non-exempt funds: ss. 22(1)(b)(ii), 23(4)***	• Verification must take place immediately after you first engage in or give instructions for the receiving, paying, or transferring of funds (s. 23(5)).	• Verification must take place by not later than 60 days after you first engage in or give instructions for the receiving, paying, or transferring of funds (s. 23(6)).
	Note	<ul><li>You shall take reasonable steps to verify the identity of the client using what the licensee reasonably considers to be reliable, independent source documents (see examples below), data, or information.</li><li>You shall take reasonable steps to comply with the verification requirement as early as possible in the retainer.</li><li>If the client (whether an individual or an organization) is acting for or representing another person, you shall take the same steps to verify the identity of that person that you take to verify the identity of your client.</li><li>You shall complete and sign a verification of identity form for each individual, organization, third-party beneficiary, or principal, with photocopies of the documentation relied on attached.</li></ul>	
		Examples of independent source documents (s. 23(7)):	
		If the client is an individual: An original government-issued identification that is valid and has not expired, and that you reasonably believe to be independent and reliable: – driver's licence – birth certificate – passport – provincial or territorial health card (if such use is not prohibited by law)	**If the client is a private company or society created under legislative authority:** – a certificate of corporate status, if the client is a private company or society created under legislative authority – an annual filing – a similar record confirming the organization's existence **If the client is a trust:** – a trust agreement – other documents establishing or amending the trust – documents identifying the trustees **If the client is a partnership:** – the partnership agreement

* Private company, partnership, fund, trust, co-operative, or unincorporated association.

Client Verification, Use of Agent (s. 23(11))

You may use this form of client verification if you engage in or give instructions for the receiving, paying, or transferring of non-exempt funds on behalf of a client who is outside Canada, or as an alternative to the s. 23(8) procedure for verifying the identity of an individual client who is elsewhere in Canada. Section 23(11) permits you to enter into a written agreement with an agent specifying the steps that the agent will be taking on your behalf to comply with the verification requirements and to provide you with the information. If the agent acting on your behalf is not an employee of your firm or a paralegal who provides legal services through your firm, you shall enter into a written agreement with the agent specifying the steps that the agent will be taking on your behalf to comply with the verification requirements (s. 23(11)). The agent may provide the information to you in the form of an attestation. See Appendix 2.5 for a sample attestation.

Previous Client Verification (s. 23(12))

For an individual client, a licensee complies with the s. 23(4) verification requirement if she has already verified the individual client's identity and recognizes the individual (s. 23(12)(a)).

For a client that is an organization, a licensee complies with the s. 23(2) identification requirements and the s. 23(4) verification requirements if she has already complied with those requirements with respect to the organization (s. 23(12)(b)).

Documentation (ss. 23(13), (14))

You must obtain copies of every document used to verify the identity of a client, a third-party beneficiary, or a principal, including copies of documents used by agents for client verification under s. 23(11) (s. 23(13)).

You must keep records of all information obtained for purposes of client identification and verification, including copies of supporting documents, attestations, and so on, for the longer of (s. 23(14)):

(a) the duration of the paralegal–client relationship, and for as long as is necessary to provide service to the client; and

(b) at least six years following completion of the work for which you were retained.

Criminal Activity (s. 24)

In the course of complying with the s. 23 client identification and verification requirements, you may begin to reasonably suspect that you are or will be assisting the client in dishonesty, fraud, crime, or illegal conduct. If that happens, you shall immediately cease to engage in any activities that would assist the client in dishonesty, fraud, crime, or illegal conduct (s. 24(a)), and, if necessary, withdraw from providing legal services to the client (s. 24(b)).

Communicating with the Client

General

Competent paralegals communicate effectively with their clients. This does not mean spending hours chatting on the phone with them. It means providing clients with the information they need as efficiently as possible.

Effective communication means advising the client during your initial contact with him that you are a paralegal, and explaining what that means; interviewing the client to find out what he wants; providing the client with honest advice as to the merits of his case and likely outcomes; keeping the client posted on next steps; obtaining and confirming client instructions when necessary; and generally keeping the client informed on the progress of the matter as things occur.

Advising Clients That You Are a Paralegal

Paralegals shall not hold themselves out as lawyers (Paralegal Rules 3.02(1) and 8.02(2)(a)) or undertake or provide advice with respect to a matter outside the permissible scope of paralegal practice (Paralegal Rule 3.02(2)).

When meeting a client for the first time, you should advise the client that you are a paralegal, not a lawyer, and you should explain the difference. You should inform the client that the legal services you provide are restricted to permissible areas of paralegal practice; and that if the client's problem falls outside these areas, the client should seek the services of a lawyer.

Small Claims Court is a permissible area of practice for paralegals (*Courts of Justice Act*, s. 26; By-law 4, s. 6).

The Initial Client Consultation

Although it does not have to take place in person, the initial client consultation is often the first time you meet a new client face to face. This is when the client gathers the information about you and your firm that he needs to decide whether he wants to hire you. This is also when you find out what the client's problem is and what the client's goals are; gather the information about the client's case that you need to decide whether he has a valid claim or defence; and determine what additional information or documents, if any, you need to go forward in the matter.

Prior to the consultation, you or your staff should perform a conflict check, and you should review the results. If there is a conflict or a potential conflict, you should comply with Paralegal Rule 3.04 and Guideline 9, discussed above.

You should take careful notes of what is said at the consultation. If the client gives you instructions to proceed, you should go over the notes with him before he leaves, to make sure that you have all the relevant details, correct any errors, and fill in any gaps. You should make a list of any relevant documents. If he has not brought all of them with him to the interview, you should give the client a copy of the list and advise him to provide the missing documents as soon as possible. You should discuss the terms of the paralegal–client retainer with the client to ensure that he understands them. You should discuss next steps with the client and answer any questions he may have.

Your notes of the initial consultation should be dated and filed in the client file. You will need them to draft the retainer agreement or engagement letter, as well as the claim or defence. You should have a consistent practice with respect to where they are filed, so that you can always find them when you need them. For instance, you may wish to have a subfile in every client file that is dedicated to notes of interviews and telephone conversations, plus copies of emails.

If the client retains you, you must comply with the client identification and verification requirements set out in By-law 7.1, Part III.

Interviewing Strategies

Your interviewing strategy at the initial consultation will depend on whether you are talking to a plaintiff or a defendant. With a plaintiff, it is best to begin with open-ended questions, which let the plaintiff tell her story. When you have a sense of what she is there for, and what the likely legal issues are, you can start asking for details (such as dates, amounts owed or paid, and documentation), plus any other information you need to shape the plaintiff's story into a persuasive legal narrative.

When you are meeting with a defendant, one of the first questions you should ask her is when she was served with the claim, so that you know whether you are likely to be dealing with a noting of default. You will then want to review the claim itself. Your interview questions will be structured by the allegations in the claim. It is a good idea to go through the allegations one by one, and find out whether the defendant admits them, denies them, or has an alternative version of what happened. This will help you to develop a theory of what the defence should be. You can then ask additional questions to find out whether there is any evidence to support that theory.

If the defendant wishes to make a defendant's claim, your questions should be open-ended until you have a sense of what the story is; then, as in a plaintiff interview, you can start asking more specific questions with a view to "shaping" the narrative.

When you are interviewing clients, you will find that they tell you a lot of things that may or may not be relevant to their matter. During the interview, and afterward, when you are going over your notes, keep the following questions in mind: What does the client want? What do I need to say to support the client's case? Which client statements support the client's case? Which client statements do not support the client's case? Which client statements are completely irrelevant to any issue that I am aware of in the client's case at this stage of the action?

When you have decided what the relevant facts are, you have to turn them into a persuasive narrative—one that is carefully organized for maximum clarity. Sometimes, as in the case of a simple debt collection, this will be easy to do. In other cases, the narrative will be more complex, and will require careful thought, editing, and rewriting.

You cannot decide which facts are relevant unless you are familiar with the law applicable to a client matter. If you need a refresher in the applicable law, do some legal research at no cost to the client. If you are completely unfamiliar with the applicable legal principles, remember that Paralegal Rule 3.01(2) requires that you shall not undertake to represent a client in a matter unless you are familiar with the legal principles and procedures governing the applicable area of law, or are confident that you can become familiar with those legal principles and procedures in a timely and cost-effective manner.

Confirming the Retainer

Paralegal–Client Retainer

At the outset of the paralegal–client relationship, you should establish the scope of the paralegal–client retainer—that is, the terms of the contractual relationship between you and your client. You should discuss some or all of the following terms with the client at the initial consultation:

- specific client goals;
- if the client is an organization, identify the individual(s) in the organization who are authorized to give you instructions in the matter;
- the scope of the retainer (that is, the nature and extent of the legal services to be provided to achieve the client's goals);
- an estimate of the time it will take to complete key steps, if appropriate;
- an estimate of the likely cost of those services, along with any assumptions upon which your estimate is based;
- the fee structure (hourly rate, flat or fixed rate, fees by stages, or contingency fee);
- if an hourly rate is charged, your hourly rates and those of any associates who may be working on the file;
- standard disbursements and expenses for this type of matter;
- when and how often money retainers will be required, with confirmation that the money will be held in trust until the client is invoiced;
- your billing policies, and the consequences of late payment, including the interest charged on accounts that have been outstanding for more than 30 days;
- how settlement funds are to be handled;
- events of termination of the retainer; and
- a stipulation that any changes to the agreement are to be made in writing.

The agreed-upon terms should be confirmed in writing in a retainer agreement or engagement letter.

Whether you use an engagement letter or a retainer agreement to confirm the retainer, the document should advise the client that you are a licensed paralegal; that there are restrictions on the legal services you may provide; and that the client's matter falls within areas of practice authorized for paralegals.

You will find examples of an engagement letter and a retainer agreement at Appendixes 2.6 and 2.7.

Money Retainer

A money retainer is money paid to you by the client on account of future legal services and/or disbursements to be incurred. It is a deposit that secures your legal services. The money retainer belongs to the client until legal services have been provided and the client has been invoiced for those legal services.

Your paralegal practice should have, at the minimum, two bank accounts: a general account and a mixed trust account.

The **general account** is your operating account. You use the general account to pay ongoing business expenses, such as salaries, rent, insurance premiums, professional fees, client disbursements and expenses, and so on.

The **mixed trust account** is used for client money. It is called a mixed trust account because it holds money for many different clients.

You should never deposit a money retainer to your general account. You should never transfer money out of the mixed trust account to your general account to pay yourself for legal services without first providing the client with an invoice for those services.

It is permissible to reimburse yourself from the mixed trust account for proper disbursements and expenses that were paid from your general account for items like court filing fees, courier expenses, and so on in a client matter without first invoicing the client, so long as proper books and records of the transaction are kept (By-law 9, s. 9(1)2; Guideline 14). However, it is recommended that you pay disbursements and expenses from your general (operating) account and recover them from a money retainer held in trust to the credit of the client matter after you have invoiced the client.

Paying Yourself Out of Settlement Funds Payable to the Client

Settlement funds that are payable to the client or payable by the client to another person belong to the client. There should be a term in the retainer agreement or engagement letter stating that any settlement funds payable to the client or payable by the client to another person are to be paid to you in trust. There should also be a term that, after full and final releases have been signed by all parties and the client has been invoiced, any outstanding fees and disbursements may be paid in full from settlement funds payable to the client, with any balance remaining to be paid out to the client or otherwise in accordance with the client's written direction.

If the client matter settles (that is, it is resolved without a trial) on terms that another party is to pay your client money, the settlement agreement should state that the funds are to be paid to your firm in trust. If the other party is self-represented, the funds should be paid by certified cheque. The settlement funds will be deposited to your mixed trust account because it is the client's money. When full and final releases have been signed by all parties, you may send the client your final report, along with your final invoice, which will be paid from the settlement funds held in trust. Any balance remaining in trust will be paid by trust cheque to your client or otherwise in accordance with the client's written direction.

When Should I Ask My Client for Instructions?

Clients hire you because you have professional knowledge and competence that they do not, and they pay you for that knowledge and competence.

For example, if you are representing a plaintiff in a Small Claims Court proceeding, you are expected to apply your knowledge and skills to advance the matter through the various procedural stages without seeking the client's instructions at every stage. However, you should keep the client informed of the progress of the matter. Often, this can be done by means of an **interim reporting letter**, which is delivered to the client, along with an **interim invoice**, before the client matter is concluded. An interim reporting letter reports the steps taken in the client matter to that point, the results obtained, and the likely next steps. An interim invoice is a bill delivered to the client before the client matter is concluded, in accordance with your billing policy.

If anything unusual occurs in a client matter, or if a procedure or required expense (such as hiring an expert witness) will result in significant additional cost to the client, you should advise the client and seek instructions. You should also seek client instructions before agreeing to an adjournment, or accepting or rejecting an offer of settlement.

If the other party makes an offer to settle, you should inform your client of the terms of the offer. Keeping in mind your duty to promote compromise and settlement (Paralegal Rule 3.02(5)), you should advise him whether you think the offer is reasonable or unreasonable, and why. Depending on the circumstances, you may wish to advise your client to make a counter-offer.

The final decision about accepting the offer, rejecting the offer, or making a counter-offer must be the client's, unless you have a written agreement or written instructions to the contrary. You cannot accept or reject the offer, or make a counter-offer, without first obtaining the client's instructions to do so.

Any time you talk to a client about his file, whether it is a casual telephone conversation or a scheduled meeting, you should keep a written record. This rule applies whether you are using paper files or file management software. Your notes should be identified by client name and dated. They should specify the nature of the contact, and describe what was discussed in a reasonable amount of detail. Any client instructions should be carefully and thoroughly noted. Your notes should be filed in a subfile in the client file. Depending on the circumstances, it may be advisable to confirm client instructions in writing to the client.

A **final reporting letter**, along with your final invoice for fees and disbursements incurred since the last interim invoice, should be sent to the client at the conclusion of the client matter. A final reporting letter provides a summary of the client's problem, steps taken, and results achieved in the client matter. If you are returning unused trust funds to the client, your trust cheque for the funds will be enclosed with the final reporting letter. You will find a sample of a final reporting letter at Appendix 2.11.

Client File Management

General

You do not need file management software to run an efficient practice. Whether you use file management software or set up your client files manually, the same principles of effective file management apply. File management software, if used properly, makes file management fast and easy by doing most of the organizing for you; but if you have proper procedures in place, you can provide timely, effective client service whatever your level of technology.

If you have office staff, they should understand the importance of setting up client files properly and maintaining orderly office systems. New staff should be trained in proper file management procedures. You should consider setting up and maintaining an office procedures manual for staff use.

You should also consider developing a database of precedent documents for use by paralegal employees and staff. The database should include routine correspondence, forms, standard retainer agreements and retainer letters, simple pleadings, etc. The contents of the database should be reviewed and updated on a regular basis.

The office procedures manual and database of precedents are intended to assist staff and paralegal employees to perform their duties efficiently. However, keep in mind that you shall assume complete professional responsibility for all business entrusted to you; and you shall directly supervise staff and assistants to whom particular tasks and functions are delegated. See Paralegal Rule 8.01 and By-law 7.1.

Setting Up a File System

The Client File

The client file is a file that is created either manually (that is, using paper) or electronically (using file management software) to contain all information pertaining to a particular client matter. Even if you do not use file management software, keep in mind that many of the documents in your client files will be assembled electronically. Electronic documents should be filed in an orderly fashion in folders cross-referenced to their client matters by **client matter number**. You should consider establishing a firm protocol for filing electronic documents and paper documents.

A separate client file with a unique matter number should be opened for each client matter. File management software will do this for you automatically. If you are handling several different matters for the same client, you should open a separate file with a unique matter number for each matter. The client matter number is used to track all transactions in a particular client matter, including time spent on the client matter, money held in trust to the credit of the client matter, billings, payments, and so on.

All correspondence, notes, pleadings and other documents connected with a particular client matter should be kept in appropriate subfiles in the client file folder. All subfiles should be cross-referenced to the client matter using the client matter number.

The client matter number is not the same as the claim number. The client matter number is a unique number assigned by the paralegal firm (or the file management software) to a particular client matter in order to identify that matter for filing, accounting, docketing, and billing purposes. The claim number is a unique number assigned to a particular proceeding by the Small Claims Court clerk for purposes of filing pleadings and other documents, identifying the matter on court dockets, monitoring the progress of the matter, and so on.

The client matter name that appears on file labels, correspondence, and so on should state, at a minimum, the client name and the client matter number.

Client Information

The client file should contain complete client contact information, including the client's name, address, telephone and cell phone numbers, and email address. If the client is an institution or business entity of some kind, the name and other essential information of the person providing you with instructions should also be recorded in the client file.

There should be a record of the name (and address, if known) of the other party, and the name and other contact information for the other party's legal representative, if any. This information should be readily accessible, so that anyone opening the client file has it at their fingertips.

For a paper file, it should be standard procedure when opening a new file to complete a file information sheet containing a record of the above information. The file information sheet should be stapled to the inside front cover of the client file or kept in some other readily accessible place in the client file. See the sample file information sheet at Appendix 2.8.

Checking for Conflicts

If practicable, whenever a prospective client contacts your firm, certain information (such as the client's name, including any aliases, and contact information) should be obtained from the client and entered into your conflict-checking system. A conflict search should be carried out before there is any further contact with the prospective client. The search results should be reviewed by the paralegal. The paralegal's decision should be noted on the file, and the search should be filed in the client file.

See the discussion of conflicts of interest above at pages 33–37.

The Checklist and Tickler System

For each client file you open, you should have a file-specific tickler and checklist that set out tasks to be performed along with bring-forward dates and deadlines for their completion.

You should also have a general tickler system. For a small firm, this could be a calendar or desk diary. In the general tickler, all important dates and deadlines for all active client matters should be recorded, along with bring-forward reminders.

A tickler or bring-forward reminder (also called "diarizing") is a reminder to yourself that a particular matter will require attention in the near future. This gives you advance notice of work to be completed, along with the deadline for doing so. For example, if you have a Small Claims Court trial coming up, you should give yourself bring-forward reminders on a weekly basis starting at least two months before the scheduled court date, so that you can obtain and serve on all parties any documents, written statements, or audio or visual records that you intend to use as evidence (Rule 18.02(1)); summon witnesses; review the file and any relevant case law, etc.; and prepare your witnesses.

How much advance notice you give yourself for preparation depends on the applicable procedural rules, the complexity of the task to be completed, how much reliable support you have, and how busy your practice is.

You should also diarize for deadlines to be met by the other party, if the next steps on your file will depend on what action the other party takes. For example, if you are acting for the plaintiff in a Small Claims Court proceeding, you should always note the deadline for the defendant to deliver a defence (this will vary, depending on how service of the claim was effected). If the defendant fails to deliver a defence within that time, you must take steps to have the defendant noted in default, and, if appropriate, default judgment signed.

As tasks on the checklist are completed, they are initialled by the person who completed them and the date of completion is noted. This procedure allows you to pick up the file, look at the checklist, and know exactly where the file is at procedurally.

A sample checklist/tickler can be found at Appendix 2.9.

LIMITATION PERIODS

A limitation period is a deadline prescribed by statute for commencing a court proceeding or otherwise protecting your legal rights. In Ontario, the *Limitations Act, 2002*, establishes a general limitation period for commencement of claims of no later than two years from the day on which the basis for the claim was discovered by the plaintiff. Limitation periods should be noted on your checklist/tickler in the client file. Serious prejudice to your client will result if you miss a limitation period. Limitation periods are dealt with in more detail in Chapter 3.

OTHER DEADLINES

The rules governing courts and tribunals provide deadlines for procedural steps in matters before the court or tribunal to which they apply. These procedural deadlines should also be noted on your checklist/tickler and diarized for follow-up.

It is extremely important to check for and note down any procedural deadlines when opening a new client file. Usually, missing a procedural deadline in a court proceeding does not result in permanent prejudice to your client, because courts have discretion to extend procedural deadlines. However, you must apply to the court for an order extending the deadline. This means an extra expense for your client. If the other party has been inconvenienced or prejudiced in any way, the court will likely order that your client pay them some costs.

If the missed deadline was your error, you should not bill the client for whatever action you must take to correct the error. If costs are awarded against your client because of your error, the amount of those costs should be deducted from your fee.

Organization of File Contents

The contents of the client file should be organized into subfiles. Subfiles are separate, labelled folders that are kept in the client file. In an electronic file, they would be subfolders.

As with client documents, each subfile should be clearly labelled. The label on each subfile should state its contents, the client name, and the client matter number. This system of cross-referencing to the client file ensures that any subfiles that are pulled from the client file can be easily put back into the correct client file.

The number and type of subfiles you open for a particular client file will vary, depending on the nature of the proceeding. Client files may contain the following subfiles:

- Correspondence: All correspondence related to the file should be filed in this subfile. Notes of telephone conversations may also be kept in this file, along with hard copies of email correspondence. Every document should have a date on it. The contents of this subfile should be arranged in reverse chronological order, with the most recent communication on top.

- Pleadings: All court documents (plaintiff's claim, defence, other pleadings if any, affidavits or certificates of service, motions, etc.) are kept in this subfile.
- Documents: The originals of any documentary evidence upon which you intend to rely at the hearing of the matter should be kept in this subfile.
- Retainer agreement and billing information.
- Documentation confirming client identification and verification.
- Relevant case law and legal research.

You may not need all of the above subfiles in every case. Decide what is efficient for your practice. However, at a minimum, client files should have subfiles for correspondence, client identification and verification documents, pleadings, and documentary evidence.

Storage of Files

When in use, active client files, such as file boxes, files, diskettes, CDs, etc., should not be left out in any area to which the public has access. This includes your office, if that is where you meet clients.

Staff who work in public areas should not be assigned to work on client files unless their work area is set up in such a way as to protect client confidentiality.

If your client files are electronic, computer monitors should be turned so that they are not visible to the public. Monitors that are visible to the public should be filtered. All electronic data of a personal nature should be password-protected or encrypted.

When not in use, all documentation connected with an active client file should be properly stored in the correct client file. The client file should be properly filed in the correct place in your filing system. That filing system should be in a secure place. For example, if you use filing cabinets, the filing cabinets should be in a separate area to which access is restricted.

Active client files should not be stored with closed files. Closed files should be pulled from the active client file system and stored separately, also in a secure place.

Closing Out Client Files

Client files may be closed when all services connected to the file have been completed, and the client has received a final account and reporting letter. The client is also entitled to receive her original documents back (after the appeal period of 30 days from the date of trial has elapsed), as well as any other documents that were not provided to her in the course of the retainer. You should have the client sign and return an acknowledgment of receipt of these documents.

When closing out client files, staff should check to ensure that appropriate data about the file have been entered into the conflict-checking database.

Closed files should be coded as closed. They should be stored in a secure place, separate from active client files. Closed electronic files should be stored in a format that will be retrievable by future technology.

CHAPTER SUMMARY

A competent paralegal is a paralegal who has and applies the relevant skills, attributes, and values appropriate to each matter undertaken on behalf of a client, including but not limited to (1) knowledge; (2) client service and communication; and (3) skills and judgment. You shall not undertake to represent a client in a matter unless you are familiar with the legal principles and procedures governing the applicable area of law, or are confident that you can become familiar with those legal principles and procedures in a timely and cost-effective manner (Paralegal Rule 3.01(2)).

A conflict of interest is any circumstance that may negatively affect a paralegal's ability to represent the client's best interests. Conflicts of interest may arise at any time in a client matter, as the matter evolves, new parties are added, and new circumstances or information come to light.

Because conflicts of interest may result in harm to the client, paralegals have an obligation to prospective clients, current clients, and former clients to avoid conflicts of interest and potential conflicts of interest.

Before agreeing to act for a client, you should check for conflicts of interest. You should maintain a database of all clients, their matters, and the opposing parties for this purpose.

By-law 7.1, section 22(1) requires a licensee to comply with the client identification and verification requirements set out in s. 23 whenever she is retained to provide legal services to a new or existing client on or after December 31, 2008. You do not have to identify or verify clients on matters that were in existence prior to December 31, 2008. However, if you are retained in a new or related matter for any of those clients on or after December 31, 2008, you must comply with the client identification and verification requirements in Part III of By-law 7.1.

The duty of confidentiality obliges you and your associates and employees to hold in strict confidence any information concerning any aspect of a client's affairs from the moment the professional relationship begins, unless disclosure is authorized by your client or required by law. The duty of confidentiality applies to clients who contact you but do not retain you, and to clients who retain you, sometimes on several client matters.

The duty of confidentiality applies to all information of any kind that you acquire from a client or on behalf of a client during the professional relationship, including information that is not specific to the matter in which you have been retained and information of which others may have knowledge.

The duty of confidentiality continues indefinitely.

You must never use confidential information for your own benefit, personal or financial, even if doing so does not harm the client.

You may disclose confidential client information to others only if you have written authority from the client to do so (express consent) or the nature of the matter requires it (implied consent).

In order to maintain good relations with the client, you must be an effective communicator. This includes advising the client during your initial contact with him that you are a paralegal, and explaining what that means; interviewing the client to find out what he wants; advising the client honestly and candidly as to the merits of his case and likely outcomes; obtaining and confirming client instructions when appropriate; and generally keeping the client informed on the progress of the matter as things occur.

When a client hires you, you should confirm the terms upon which you were hired in writing, using a retainer agreement or engagement letter. You should consider making it a term of the retainer that a money retainer will be required at the outset of the retainer, and that further money retainers will be required as the matter progresses and interim invoices are delivered to the client. The money retainer belongs to the client and should be deposited to your mixed trust account.

Money held in trust may not be transferred to your general account unless the client has received an invoice for legal fees and disbursements to that date, along with an interim reporting letter advising the client of the status of the matter. A final reporting letter will be sent out with your final account.

Whether you are using file management software or paper, a separate client file should be opened for each client. If you are handling several different matters for the same client, you should open a separate file for each matter. Each client file should be assigned its own client matter number, which will be used for file management purposes and for accounting and billing purposes. All correspondence, notes, and other documents and things connected with a particular matter should be filed in appropriate subfiles in the client file for that matter when not in use.

For each client file you open, you should have a file-specific tickler and checklist that sets out tasks to be performed along with deadlines for their completion. You should also maintain a general tickler system, setting out all important dates and deadlines on all active files, along with bring-forward reminders.

KEY TERMS

candid: forthright and sincere, able to look at both sides of an issue without bias *(p. 30)*

casual client: a client who consults you regarding a legal issue, but then decides not to proceed, or not to hire you to act as his legal representative *(p. 31)*

client: a person who consults with you and hires you to represent her in a matter or a number of matters *(p. 30)*

client identification: information obtained from the client regarding who the client is and what the client does *(p. 38)*

client matter number: a unique number assigned by the paralegal firm (or the file management software) to a particular client matter in order to identify that matter for filing, docketing, and billing purposes *(p. 48)*

client verification: obtaining documentary or other confirmation that the client is who he says he is *(p. 38)*

competent paralegal: a paralegal who has and applies the relevant skills, attributes, and values appropriate to each matter undertaken on behalf of a client *(p. 28)*

conflict of interest: any circumstance that may negatively affect a paralegal's ability to adequately represent the client's best interests *(p. 33)*

dispute: an argument or disagreement between two or more sides in which the interest of one side is in direct opposition to the interest of another side *(p. 33)*

due diligence: exercising the prudence and vigilance that a reasonable and prudent paralegal would exercise in similar circumstances *(p. 40)*

engagement letter: confirms the terms of the paralegal–client retainer, but is not signed back by the client *(p. 29)*

express consent: also known as explicit consent; written authorization from your client to disclose particular information to specified third parties *(p. 33)*

fiduciary: a person who is required to act with scrupulous good faith, honesty, and integrity for the benefit of another person *(p. 28)*

fiduciary relationship: a relationship of absolute trust and confidence between two persons, in which one person (the fiduciary) is required to act with scrupulous good faith, honesty and integrity for the benefit of another person (the beneficiary)—in the paralegal–client relationship, the paralegal is the fiduciary and the client is the beneficiary *(p. 28)*

final reporting letter: sent to the client at the conclusion of the client matter, along with the final invoice for fees and disbursements incurred since the last interim invoice—provides a summary of the client matter, steps taken, and results achieved *(p. 47)*

funds: cash, currency, securities, negotiable instruments, or other financial instruments *(p. 38)*

general account: a bank account used to pay for ongoing business expenses, such as salaries, rent, client disbursements that have not been billed, etc. *(p. 45)*

implied consent: unwritten consent to disclose confidential information because it is required by the professional relationship (e.g., disclosure to employees) or because the matter requires it (e.g., disclosure in pleadings and other documents filed with the court) *(p. 33)*

informed consent: consent based on information that is sufficient to allow the client to assess the situation and make an informed decision *(p. 35)*

interim invoice: a bill delivered to the client before the client matter is concluded—usually sent with an interim reporting letter *(p. 46)*

interim reporting letter: a letter sent to the client before the client matter is concluded, usually with an interim invoice—reports the steps taken in the client matter to that point, the results obtained, and the likely next steps *(p. 46)*

mixed trust account: a trust bank account into which money from many different clients will be deposited and held in trust, until such time as invoices are rendered on their files or you are directed by the client to pay out the money to whom the money belongs *(p. 45)*

money retainer: money paid to you by the client on account of future legal services and/or disbursements to be incurred; it is a deposit to secure your legal services *(p. 29)*

negotiable instrument: an unconditional order or promise to pay an amount of money, which can be transferred—for example, cheques or banknotes (paper money) *(p. 38)*

non-engagement letter: a letter confirming that the paralegal has declined to accept the retainer, or that the client has declined to retain the paralegal *(p. 29)*

paralegal–client retainer: the terms of the contractual arrangement between the paralegal and the client, including but not limited to the scope of the legal services to be provided, fees, billing practices, and the amount of the money retainer *(p. 29)*

private corporation: a corporation whose shares are not publicly traded—its incorporating documents (1) restrict the right to sell shares, (2) limit the number of its shareholders (excluding employees) to 50, and (3) prohibit public trading of its shares or securities; also called a closely held corporation *(p. 39)*

prospective client: a person who consults you about a legal issue but has not yet retained you *(p. 31)*

public company: a corporation whose shares are for sale to the general public—public companies are subject to rigorous disclosure requirements under securities legislation *(p. 39)*

retainer agreement: a letter confirming services to be rendered, your fee or hourly rate, any additional charges (disbursements, etc.), and any other terms of the paralegal–client relationship; more detailed than a retainer letter, and it must be signed back to you by the client *(p. 29)*

REFERENCES

Courts of Justice Act, RSO 1990, c. C-43, as amended.

Law Society of Upper Canada (LSUC), By-laws (Toronto: LSUC, 2005, as amended); available online at http://www.lsuc.on.ca.

Law Society of Upper Canada (LSUC), *Paralegal Professional Conduct Guidelines* (Toronto: LSUC, 2008, as amended) ("the Guidelines"); available online at http://www.lsuc .on.ca/paralegals/a/paralegal-professional-conduct -guidelines.

Law Society of Upper Canada (LSUC), *Paralegal Rules of Conduct* (Toronto: LSUC, 2007, as amended) ("the Paralegal Rules"); available online at http://www.lsuc.on.ca/ paralegals/a/paralegal-rules-of-conduct.

Law Society of Upper Canada (LSUC), *Practice Management Guidelines* (Toronto: LSUC, 2008); available online at http://rc.lsuc.on.ca/pdf/pmg/pmg.pdf.

Legal Aid Services Act, 1998, SO 1998, c. 26.

Limitations Act, 2002, SO 2002, c. 24, sched. B, as amended.

Rules of the Small Claims Court, O. Reg. 258/98.

REVIEW QUESTIONS

1. What is a competent paralegal?
2. What should you do if you do not think you are competent to represent a client?
3. **a.** What is a conflict of interest?
   b. How can a paralegal prevent conflicts of interest?
4. **a.** What is the duty of confidentiality?
   b. What kinds of information does it apply to?
   c. Who does it apply to?
   d. When does the duty arise and when does it end?
5. When is it permissible to disclose confidential information about a client?
6. What are the essentials of effective client communication?

7. What should you do whenever you talk to a client about her file?
8. What should you do when interviewing a client for the first time? Assume that there are no conflict issues.
9. What is a retainer agreement? What is the difference between a retainer agreement and an engagement letter?
10. What is a money retainer?
11. When may you transfer client money from the mixed trust account to the general account?
12. What are the basic principles for setting up a client file?

APPENDIX 2.1 Non-Engagement Letter (Conflict of Interest—Client Declines Retainer)

[Date]

[File number]

[Client name and address]

Dear [Client name]:

Re: [Matter name]

As we discussed during our [telephone conversation/meeting/initial consultation] on [date], a preliminary search revealed that [paralegal firm name] has a conflict of interest in this matter. We provided you with details of the conflict and asked you to decide whether you wished to consent to the retainer based on this disclosure. You have now advised that you do not wish to retain us.

Please be aware that whatever claim you have may be barred by the passage of time. Since time limitations may be critical to your case, we recommend that you immediately contact another paralegal or a lawyer for assistance regarding your matter. If you do not have another paralegal or a lawyer in mind to represent you, the Law Society maintains a directory of paralegals and lawyers at its website (http://www.lsuc.on.ca) who may be available to assist you, or you may wish to call the Law Society Referral Service at 1-800-268-8326. There is no charge for the Law Society Referral Service.

We confirm that we do not have any documents belonging to you. All documents were returned to you at the end of the initial meeting.

Although we were not able to assist you in this matter, we hope that you will consider [paralegal firm name] in the event that you require legal services in the future.

Thank you again for your interest in this firm.

Yours truly,

[Paralegal firm name]

[Signature]

[Signatory name]

Paralegal

[Adapted from the Law Society of British Columbia website (http://www.lawsociety.bc.ca) and the Law Society of Upper Canada website (http://www.lsuc.on.ca).]

APPENDIX 2.2 Non-Engagement Letter (Conflict of Interest—Paralegal Firm Declines Retainer)

[Date]

[File number]

[Client name and address]

Dear [Client name]:

Re: [Matter name]

As we discussed during our [telephone conversation/meeting/initial consultation] on [date], before [paralegal firm name] could agree to represent you in this matter, we had to investigate whether this representation could adversely affect existing or former clients' interests or whether there might be some other reason that we would be unable to adequately represent your interests.

On [date], we performed a conflict of interest check and found that our firm does indeed have a conflict of interest in this case. Unfortunately, we therefore cannot represent you and we must decline to do so in this matter.

Please be aware that whatever claim you have may be barred by the passage of time. Since time limitations may be critical to your case, we recommend that you immediately contact another paralegal or a lawyer for assistance regarding your matter. If you do not have another paralegal or a lawyer in mind to represent you, the Law Society maintains a directory of paralegals and lawyers at its website (http://www.lsuc.on.ca) who may be available to assist you, or you may wish to call the Law Society Referral Service at 1-800-268-8326. There is no charge for the Law Society Referral Service.

We confirm that we do not have any documents belonging to you. All documents were returned to you at the end of the initial meeting.

Although we were not able to assist you in this matter, we hope that you will consider [paralegal firm name] in the event that you require legal services in the future.

Thank you again for your interest in this firm.

Yours truly,

[Paralegal firm name]

[Signature]

[Signatory name]

Paralegal

[Adapted from the Law Society of British Columbia website (http://www.lawsociety.bc.ca) and the Law Society of Upper Canada website (http://www.lsuc.on.ca).]

APPENDIX 2.3   Verification of Identity (Individual)

[PARALEGAL FIRM NAME]

Paralegals

VERIFICATION OF IDENTITY

(For use where the client or third party is an individual)

Name: _____

Address (home): _____

Telephone number (home): _____

Address (business): _____

Telephone number (business): _____

Occupation(s): _____

Original Document Reviewed—Copy Attached

_____   Driver's Licence

_____   Birth Certificate

_____   Passport

_____   Other (specify type): _____

Meeting date identity verified: _____

Identity verified by: _____

Date file reviewed by paralegal: _____

Name of paralegal: _____

APPENDIX 2.4 Verification of Identity (Organization)

[PARALEGAL FIRM NAME]

Paralegals

VERIFICATION OF IDENTITY

(For use where the client or third party is an organization)

Name: _____

Address (business): _____

Telephone number (business): _____

Incorporation or Business Identification Number: _____

Place of issue of number: _____

Type of business or activity: _____

Person Authorized to Instruct

Name: _____

Position: _____

Telephone number: _____

Original Document Reviewed—Copy Attached

_____ Driver's Licence

_____ Birth Certificate

_____ Passport

_____ Other (specify type): _____

APPENDIX 2.4 Verification of Identity (Organization) *concluded*

Names and occupation(s) of directors:

[List]

Names, addresses and occupation(s) of owners or shareholders owning a 25% interest or more of the organization or shares in the organization:

[List]

Original Document Reviewed—Copy Attached

_____ Certificate of Corporate Status

_____ Annual Filings of the Organization (specify type): _____

_____ Partnership Agreement

_____ Trust Agreement

_____ Articles of Association

_____ Other (specify type): _____

Meeting date identity verified: _____

Identity verified by: _____

Date file reviewed by paralegal: _____

Name of paralegal: _____

APPENDIX 2.5   Attestation for Verification of Identity When the Client or Third Party Is Present in Canada and Is Not Instructing the Paralegal Face to Face

INSTRUCTIONS

The Attestor should photocopy the identity document being used to verify identity and ensure that it is legible, unexpired, and shows the name of the person whose identity is being verified, the number of the document, the name of the issuing authority, the date of issue, and a photograph of the person.

The Attestor will print the following attestation on the photocopy and date and sign the attestation.

I, the Attestor named below, hereby certify to [name of paralegal receiving the attestation] that I met with [name of person] on [date] and verified this person's identity by examining the original of this person's identity document, of which a photocopy is contained on this page. The photograph in the identity document is a true likeness of the said person, and to the best of my knowledge and belief the identity document that I examined is valid and unexpired.

Attested to by me at _____ , on _____ _____ , 20_____ .

Signature of Attestor: _____

Printed Name of Attestor: _____

Title or Profession of Attestor: _____

Address of Attestor for Service: _____

_____

Telephone Number of Attestor: _____

APPENDIX 2.6 Engagement Letter

[LETTERHEAD]

Client matter no. 632

June 14, 20—

Mrs. Maxine Chong
67 Harmony Avenue
Toronto, ON M4J 1J3

Dear Mrs. Chong:

Re: LeeAnn Kingman
Small Claims Court action

Further to our meeting on June 12, 20—, this will confirm that you have retained us to act in the above matter. By a tenancy agreement dated January 13, 20—, Ms. Kingman rented your basement apartment from February 1, 20— until April 17, 20—. The monthly rent was $775.00 including water, heat, and hydro. Ms. Kingman did not pay a last month's rent deposit, and during her tenancy Ms. Kingman paid no rent. As well, she harassed you and interfered with your reasonable enjoyment of the premises, causing damage to your health. Ms. Kingman vacated the premises on April 17, 20—.

You have instructed us to commence an action immediately in Small Claims Court for $25,000.00 for unpaid rent, damage to property, and pain and suffering, plus interest and costs. You have agreed to waive any amounts you might recover over and above $25,000.00 in order to bring the matter within Small Claims Court jurisdiction.

We anticipate that our representation will involve taking the following steps on your behalf. We will file a plaintiff's claim and serve the claim on the defendant. If Ms. Kingman does not file a defence within the time prescribed by the Rules of the Small Claims Court, we will request that the clerk note her in default. We may then obtain default judgment by a motion in writing for an assessment of damages or at an assessment hearing. If Ms. Kingman files a defence, we will make every effort to settle the matter, subject to your instructions. A settlement conference will be scheduled for no later than 90 days after Ms. Kingman's defence is filed. If the matter does not settle, we will prepare for and represent you at trial.

We also wish to confirm our agreement as to fees and payment. We charge $100.00 per hour for legal services. You will also be billed for any out-of-pocket expenses (also known as disbursements) that may be incurred, such as court filing fees and so on. We will advise you before incurring any extraordinary disbursements. At the moment, the only extraordinary disbursement we anticipate is the fee for your treating physician's report.

… /2

APPENDIX 2.6 **Engagement Letter** *concluded*

Chong v. Kingman
Client matter no. 632
Page 2 of 2

We will bill you approximately monthly, depending on the amount of work that is completed on your file during that period of time. The amount of time and expenses that will be required to represent you in this matter cannot be predicted at this time. However, as we discussed, if Ms. Kingman fails to file a defence and we obtain default judgment, we estimate that our total fees will not exceed $1,500.00 exclusive of disbursements. If Ms. Kingman files a defence and the matter goes to trial, we estimate that our total fees will not exceed $3,500.00 exclusive of disbursements. We are not guaranteeing that we can accomplish the work for this sum, but are representing to you that the amount appears reasonable in the circumstances. We will advise you before undertaking any procedures that will substantially increase the amount of your fees, and will obtain your instructions to proceed.

This will confirm that you have provided us with a money retainer of $1,000.00. This money has been placed in our trust account and will be applied to payment of invoices when delivered. You may be asked to provide further money retainers from time to time as the matter goes forward. As we discussed at our meeting, will you please forward copies of the tenancy agreement and the Notice of Early Termination to us as soon as possible. We will also require copies of your medical records and bills for the period of Ms. Kingman's tenancy and afterward. These documents will be returned to you when the matter is concluded.

We will make every effort to reach a settlement with Ms. Kingman in accordance with your instructions. However, we cannot guarantee success or that we will be able to reach a negotiated settlement. This will confirm that you have agreed that, if the matter does settle in your favour, the settlement funds are to be paid to us in trust and any outstanding fees or disbursements may be paid from those funds upon delivery of a final invoice. We will then pay any unused portion to you.

As I advised you, we are a paralegal firm. We are not lawyers. Paralegals are restricted to providing legal services in permissible areas of law only. You have indicated that you wish to proceed in Small Claims Court. Small Claims Court is an authorized area of practice for paralegals.

I trust that the foregoing is satisfactory. If you have any questions or concerns, please contact me.

I will try to respond to your phone calls and emails as quickly as possible. If a matter is urgent, I will make every effort to respond to you on an urgent basis.

Yours very truly,

Prior Mustafa LLP

Joseph Mustafa
Paralegal

APPENDIX 2.7   Sample Retainer Agreement

[Letterhead]

Retainer Agreement

General

[Date]

[Client name and address]

Dear [Name of client]:

Re: [Description of matter]

1. Description of Services

You have asked us, and we have agreed, to act for you in the matter described below. On [date], we [met/spoke] to discuss the scope of our firm's intended representation. We covered this subject in some detail and considered the nature of our fee arrangement. The purpose of this letter is to summarize and confirm the terms of your engagement of us.

You retain us to represent you in connection with [description of matter]. We anticipate that our representation will involve taking the following steps on your behalf:

    (a)   [Describe]

    (b)   [Describe]

    (c)   [Describe]

[Optional] At this time we have not been retained to represent you generally or in connection with any other matter. We will not be performing the following services:

    (d)   [Describe]

    (e)   [Describe]

    (f)   [Describe]

Your desired outcome and time frame for resolution of this matter is as follows:

[Describe]

We will work with you toward your desired outcome. However, all legal actions are subject to many possible variables. Accordingly, we cannot guarantee that your desired result will in fact be achieved. For us to work toward your desired outcome, it will be necessary for you to abide by the terms described in this letter.

2. Paralegals

As I advised you, we are a paralegal firm. We are not lawyers. Paralegals are restricted to providing legal services in permissible areas of law only. We are satisfied that your matter falls within an authorized area of practice for paralegals.

We expect that most of the work will be performed or supervised by myself (a partner in this firm), assisted by [name], an [associate/student] in this firm. However, we reserve the right to assign other paralegals in our firm to perform legal services if in our judgment that becomes necessary or desirable.

3. Fees

(a) Our fee will be based principally on the time spent by us on your behalf. Records of all time spent will be kept and accounts will then be prepared and sent to you periodically.

   Our hourly rates range from $[amount] for students to $[amount] for my associate to $[amount] for me.

   While we expect that our fee will be calculated on the basis of our regular hourly rates, we reserve the right to charge more in appropriate cases, such as pressing circumstances, the requirement for work outside normal business hours, exceptionally successful or efficient representation, or special demands on us.

   You will be charged GST/HST on fees and GST/HST on some disbursements.

[Option 1]

(b) The amount of time and expenses that will be required to represent you in this matter cannot be predicted at this time. However, as we discussed, the fee will be not less than $[amount] excluding disbursements. We will advise you before undertaking any procedures that will substantially increase the amount of your fees, and will obtain your instructions to proceed.

[Option 2]

(b) Based on our consideration of the materials and information you have provided to us, and assuming that there are no further developments or information that would cause us to vary our preliminary opinion and that nothing out of the ordinary is encountered in the course of completing this matter, we estimate that our fee, excluding disbursements, will be $[amount]. We are not guaranteeing that we can accomplish the work for that sum, but are representing to you that in our judgment that amount appears reasonable under the circumstances. We will advise you before undertaking any procedures that will substantially increase the amount of your fees, and will obtain your instructions to proceed.

4. Expenses and Allocated Charges (also called disbursements)

You will be responsible for reimbursing us for expenses (also called disbursements) we incur on your behalf and for office charges allocated to your file. These include long distance calls, faxes, postage, deliveries, travel expenses, photocopying, and government filing and search charges; the fees of agents who conduct investigations, searches, and registrations; and all other reasonable out-of-pocket expenses and office charges. We do not charge for staff overtime on evenings or weekends in order to meet time deadlines.

5. Interest

Payment is due on all of our accounts when rendered. If any account is not paid within 30 days, interest will be charged on the outstanding balance at a rate of [rate]% per annum from the date of the account, until paid.

6. Retainer

Before we begin work on your behalf, we require a retainer in the amount of $[amount]. The retainer will be placed in our trust account and will serve as a source of payment for all or part of our account or accounts when rendered. You will be asked to replenish the retainer from time to time. Any unused portion will be returned to you upon the completion or termination of our services.

[Optional]

7. Settlement funds

We have discussed and you have agreed that, if this matter settles in your favour, the settlement funds are to be paid to us in trust and any outstanding fees or disbursements may be paid from those funds. We will then pay any unused portion to you.

8. Termination of Legal Services

You have the right to terminate our services to you upon written notice to us.

Subject to our obligations to you to maintain proper standards of professional conduct, we reserve the right to terminate our services to you for good reasons, which include but are not limited to:

(a) if you fail to cooperate with us in any reasonable request;

(b) if our continuing to act would be unethical or impractical;

(c) if our retainer has not been paid; or

(d) if you fail to pay our accounts when rendered.

APPENDIX 2.7 **Sample Retainer Agreement** *concluded*

If you terminate our services or we withdraw, you will be responsible only for our fees and expenses up until the time we stop acting for you.

If you terminate our services or we withdraw, the following documents and information will be returned to you:

[List documents and information]

9. Agreement

You may want to have this agreement reviewed by another paralegal or a lawyer.

If you want us to proceed on the terms described above, please sign the enclosed copy of this letter in the space provided and return it to us, together with a retainer in the sum of $[amount], in the enclosed self-addressed envelope. If you decide that you do not want us to proceed on your behalf in this matter, please inform us promptly.

Yours truly,

[PARALEGAL FIRM NAME]

[Signature]

[Signatory name]

Paralegal

I have read and understand the retainer agreement, and agree to its terms.

_____   _____

      Client's signature   Date

[Adapted from the Lawyers' Professional Indemnity Company website (http://www.practicepro.ca/practice/financesbookletprecedents.asp)]

APPENDIX 2.8   Sample File Information Sheet: Chong v. Kingman

FILE INFORMATION SHEET

Court file number: SC-00-56789-00

Court: Toronto Small Claims

Short title of matter: Chong v. Kingman

Client matter number: 632   File opened: June 13, 20—

OUR CLIENT: Plaintiff   OTHER PARTY: Defendant/~~debtor~~

Full name: Maxine Chong (Mrs.)   Full name: LeeAnn Kingman

Address: 67 Harmony Avenue   Address: 48 Brimley Road, Apt. 1306
                     Toronto, Ontario   Toronto, Ontario
                     M4J 1J3   M2L 3T6

Our contact:

Telephone: 416 222 3333   Telephone:

Fax number: Fax number:

Email: Email:

PARALEGAL ASSIGNED TO FILE: REPRESENTATIVE:

Joseph Mustafa   Address:

ADDITIONAL NOTES:

APPENDIX 2.9 Checklist/Tickler: Chong v. Kingman

CHECKLIST

Title of matter:	Maxine Chong v. LeeAnn Kingman
Type of matter:	Small Claims
Client matter number:	632
Court file number:	SC-00-56789-00
Court address:	Toronto Small Claims Court 47 Sheppard Avenue East, 3rd floor Toronto, Ontario M2N 5X5
Telephone number:	416 326 3554
Fax number:	
Email:	

CHECKLIST/TICKLER

Task	Deadline	Bring forward	Date completed	By
Open file	asap	asap	June 14, 20—	P.A.
Draft claim	Limitations Act 2 years from Feb. 1, 20—	asap	June 21, 20—	J.M.
Issue claim	asap	asap	June 24, 20—	P.A.
Service claim	Dec. 24, 20—	asap	July 12, 20—	C.I.
Deadline defence	Aug. 2, 20—	Aug. 3, 20—		Other side
Note in default		Aug. 3, 20—		

APPENDIX 2.10   Express Consent to Disclose Confidential Information

AUTHORIZATION

I, [name of client], do hereby authorize [name of legal representative] of [name of firm] to release to [name or names of authorized recipients] or their legal representatives of record the following documents and other information: [particulars of permitted disclosure]

I have been advised of and understand the purpose and consequences of this disclosure.

Date: _____   Signature: _____

                                                              Client name

Date: _____   Witness: _____

                                                              Witness name

APPENDIX 2.11 Sample Final Reporting Letter

[LETTERHEAD]

Client matter no. 576

January 16, 20—

Mr. Henry Stamp
489 Champagne Avenue, Unit 22
Mississauga, ON L2M 4Z2

Dear Mr. Stamp:

Re: Stamp v. Champion
      Small Claims Court debt collection

You retained us to act for you in an action for recovery of money owing for a painting sold to Gerald Champion at the Downtown Toronto Art Fair in July 20—. Mr. Champion paid $2,100.00 to you for the painting by personal cheque. You later received notice from your bank that the cheque could not be cashed due to insufficient funds. You were also charged an administration fee by the bank. Mr. Champion did not respond to demands for payment, and we commenced a Small Claims Court action in October 20—. The matter has now settled. The settlement funds of $2,100.00 plus costs of $130.00 were paid by certified cheque into our trust account on January 10, 20—.

This will end our involvement in the matter, and we are forwarding our final invoice #543 for $1,034.35, which has been paid in full out of the settlement funds in accordance with the terms of the retainer agreement. Our trust cheque payable to you for the balance of $1,195.65 is also enclosed, along with a duplicate original of the settlement agreement dated January 5, 20— and full and final releases signed by you and Mr. Champion.

We are very pleased with this prompt resolution of the matter. If we can be of any assistance in the future, please contact us. I look forward to seeing your new work at the next Downtown Toronto Art Fair.

Yours very truly,
[PARALEGAL FIRM NAME]
[Name of paralegal signatory]
Paralegal

Enclosures: Invoice #543
Trust cheque #177
Settlement agreement dated January 5, 20— and signed releases

Acting for the Plaintiff: Preliminary Considerations

3

LEARNING OUTCOMES

After reading this chapter, you will understand:

- What to consider before commencing a Small Claims Court action

- How to find information about the defendant

- Legal jurisdiction of the Small Claims Court

- What a limitation period is, and the consequences of missing a limitation period

- Monetary jurisdiction of the Small Claims Court

- Damages

- Waiver or abandonment of the excess, and its consequences

- Territorial jurisdiction of the Small Claims Court

Introduction

A paralegal must be honest and candid when advising a client (Paralegal Rule 3.02(1)). This is true whether the client is seeking to retain you in a matter, or is a casual client seeking quick advice.

In this context, being **candid** means being forthright and sincere, and looking at both sides of each issue without bias. You must advise the client honestly and candidly of the applicable law, the client's options, possible outcomes, and possible risks. Your advice should enable the client to make informed decisions and give appropriate instructions in the matter.

When a client comes to you for advice about commencing a court proceeding, the first thing you have to determine is whether their case has any legal merit. Remember, a client's sense of personal grievance does not necessarily translate into a **cause of action**—that is, valid legal grounds for commencing a court action.

Legal merit is not the only issue to be considered when advising a client whether or not to litigate. Even if you are satisfied that your client's case has legal merit, you need to ask yourself other questions as well. If you fail to ask yourself these questions, and to answer them honestly for your client's benefit, you may end up giving your client bad advice.

Given the amount in dispute, is it cost-effective to litigate?

A party with legal representation should consider the cost of paying for that legal representation as well as court fees and other **disbursements**, and balance those expenses against the amount to be recovered. A successful party is entitled to recover her costs for legal fees and reasonable disbursements. However, a costs award does not usually reflect the total legal fees incurred.

A self-represented party should consider the cost of filing fees, as well as the "hidden costs" of litigation, such as stress and time lost from work to attend at court, and balance those "costs" against the amount being litigated.

What information does the plaintiff have about the defendant?

Useful information includes the correct spelling of the defendant's name; any aliases the defendant uses; the defendant's date of birth (confirmed by a birth certificate); the defendant's social insurance number; the defendant's driver's licence number; if the defendant owns a vehicle, the licence plate number; and so on.

If the plaintiff does not have reliable information about the correct name of the defendant, the defendant's current address, and so on, there are searches that can be carried out to obtain this information. However, the quality of your search results depends on the quality of the information you already have. A plaintiff who already knows the defendant's name, birth date, social insurance number, and driver's licence number will obtain much better results when searching for additional information about the defendant, such as the defendant's current address for service, than a plaintiff who knows little more than the defendant's name.

Is it worthwhile to seek a judgment against this particular defendant?

Assuming the defendant can be located, the next issue to consider is whether the defendant has any ability to pay a judgment, if one is obtained. A court judgment is just a worthless piece of paper if the judgment debtor is **judgment-proof**—that is, has no income or assets against which the judgment may be enforced. A **judgment debtor** is any person who owes money to another person pursuant to a court order.

When asking yourself this question, consider the effect on your client's rights if a limitation period expires, keeping in mind that a debtor's circumstances may change. A judgment that is not presently enforceable may become enforceable later on, when the debtor obtains employment or acquires assets against which the judgment can be enforced. Expiry of the limitation period for commencing an action in a particular matter means that the plaintiff will be statute-barred by the *Limitations Act, 2002* from ever making a claim against that particular defendant on those particular grounds. See the discussion of limitation periods below at pages 83–84.

Finding Out About the Defendant: Name Search

Some clients collect essential information about the persons with whom they do business before they advance money, approve a tenancy agreement, or sell a computer to that person. They already have the defendant's correct name, address, and so on, verified by documentation, when they send the file to you for collection. They may also have a consumer report, obtained with the defendant's informed, written consent, showing what other debts the defendant owes, and the defendant's credit ranking.

If the client did not collect this information in the ordinary course of business, or if it is the kind of claim where that information would not necessarily have been obtained ahead of time (for example, damage to property or personal injury), you must confirm, at a minimum, the defendant's full name correctly spelled and the defendant's correct address before commencing the action. You will need the correct spelling of the defendant's name to carry out other searches on the defendant. If you misspell a party's name, use an initial instead of a proper name, or state an incorrect name on the plaintiff's claim, you have named the wrong person and your judgment will be unenforceable against the real defendant. You will have to take immediate steps to correct the error by amending the claim under Rule 12, which will result in delay and additional expense.

Name Search: Individual Defendant

If the plaintiff knows the defendant's driver's licence number, or the vehicle identification number or plate number of the defendant's vehicle, you can search online at the Service Ontario website for additional information about the defendant. Search fees are payable online by credit card. Search results are not certified and are delivered online only.

Because of privacy considerations, the following searches will not provide you with the residential address of the defendant unless you are an authorized requester. An **authorized requester** is a person who has applied to and has been approved by the ministry for that designation, and is registered as an authorized requester with the ministry. Paralegal licensees may apply to become authorized requesters because paralegals carry out work for legal purposes related to the justice system, including:

- service of legal documents;
- locating persons in connection with claims, litigation, and motor vehicle collisions; and
- debt collection.

Note that "debt collection" is restricted to debts owed to road-toll authorities, financial institutions, government agencies including courts, and municipal and private parking authorities.

TABLE 3.1 Ministry of Transportation Searches

SEARCH	GOOGLE	REQUIREMENT	RESULT
Three-Year Statement of Driving Record	Uncertified driver's record Ontario	Defendant's driver's licence number	• Driver's name • Driver's address (authorized requesters only) • Driver's date of birth • Driver's gender • Driver's height • Three-year history of convictions, discharges, and other actions
Vehicle Identification Number (VIN)	Uncertified vehicle records Ontario	Vehicle identification number	• Owner's name • Owner's address (authorized requesters only) • Vehicle make, model, colour, and mileage • Plate number and registration date
Licence Plate—Recent Owner	Uncertified vehicle records Ontario	Licence plate number	• Owner's name • Owner's address (authorized requesters only) • Vehicle make, model, colour, and mileage • Plate number and registration date

Online Searches

There are a number of online resources you can use to search for information about the defendant. In many cases you need the correct name and/or a current telephone number. Some sites require payment of a fee before full search results will be disclosed. Websites and the services they provide evolve over time. The following comments are as of this writing.

Canada411 (http://www.canada411.ca): If you know the correct name of the person you are looking for, you can search for his address and telephone number. Your search may turn up multiple results. You can do a reverse search by telephone number if the telephone number is listed. Your search will be unsuccessful if you are searching using an unlisted landline or cellphone number.

Pipl (http://www.pipl.com): For individuals and businesses, you can search by name, phone number, or email address and location, but depending on the search parameters, the search results may be either inaccurate or unwieldy. You can also do reverse telephone searches using listed numbers as well as unlisted landline or cell-phone numbers. For unlisted landline numbers, a reverse search of the telephone number will get you the name and location of the caller if it is a business. A reverse search of an unlisted cellphone number belonging to an individual will get you the location of the owner but not the name or address.

CallTruth (http://www.calltruth.com): You can do reverse telephone searches using listed numbers as well as unlisted landline or cellphone numbers. For unlisted landline numbers, a reverse search will get you the name and location of the caller if it is a business. A reverse search of a cellphone number belonging to an individual will get you the location of the owner but not the name. Additional information (address, social media data, and so on) is available for a fee.

Name Search: Business Defendants

To name a business defendant correctly, you must first find out what form of business organization the defendant uses. The three types of business entities you will most commonly encounter in Small Claims Court are sole proprietorships, partnerships, and corporations. They must be properly identified on the plaintiff's claim.

Sole Proprietorships (Rule 5.06)

A **sole proprietorship** is an unincorporated business owned and run by one individual. There is no legal separation between the owner and the business—the business has no separate legal existence from the owner. This means that the business cannot sue or be sued, nor can it enter into contracts. It is the owner who enters into contracts and assumes all liability for the business. The owner is personally responsible for paying the debts of the business.

If the plaintiff is a sole proprietor operating under a business name, you may commence litigation on behalf of the plaintiff using the plaintiff's business name (Rule 5.06(1)).

If the defendant is a sole proprietor operating under a business name, you should name the defendant using the owner's name, carrying on business under the business name; and name the business using the registered business name as an additional party on a separate Form 1A.1. By naming both the individual owner and the name of the business, the plaintiff preserves her right to enforce her judgment against the assets of both the owner and the business.

Under the Ontario *Business Names Act*, a business that carries on business in Ontario using a name other than that of its owner or owners must register the business name with the Companies and Personal Property Security Branch of the Ministry of Government Services. Searches can be carried out personally by attending at the Companies Branch office at 393 University Avenue, Toronto, Ontario M5G 2M2. Searches can also be carried out online at the Service Ontario website. Because site names change constantly, try Googling "business name search Ontario." This will provide you with links to the Service Ontario website, as well as commercial online search services such as Cyberbahn. Online searches are an efficient and inexpensive way of obtaining the information you require. In the case of a sole proprietorship, the business name search will provide you with the registered business name and the name of the sole proprietor carrying on business under that name.

Partnerships (Rule 5)

A **partnership** is an unincorporated business that is formed by two or more persons with the objective of making a profit. Like a sole proprietorship, a partnership has no separate legal existence from its owners, the partners. In a general partnership, the partners are jointly and severally liable for all debts, obligations, and liabilities of the partnership. If the defendant is a partnership, you may search for its correct business name under the Ontario *Business Names Act*. The business name search will also provide you with the names of the partners. If you wish to enforce your judgment against the partnership business itself and all persons who were partners at the material time, you may obtain the names of the partners by serving a notice requiring the partnership to disclose immediately in writing the names and addresses of all partners constituting the partnership at the time specified in the notice. If a partner's current address is unknown, the last-known address must be disclosed (Rule 5.04). The firm will be served with the plaintiff's claim. Each named partner will be served with the plaintiff's claim and a notice to alleged partner (Rule 5.03(1)).

Corporations

A **corporation** is a separate legal entity from its owners, the shareholders. This arrangement is intended to protect the corporation's shareholders from risks, obligations, and liabilities incurred by the corporation. Because the personal assets of the shareholders are not available to satisfy debts, obligations, and liabilities incurred by the corporation, a court order obtained against the corporation must be enforced against the assets of the corporation.

Words such as "Inc.," "Incorporated," "Corporation," "Ltd.," or "Limited" indicate a corporate entity.

Whether they are governmental, public, or private, corporations are legal persons who can sue and be sued. Like any other party to a proceeding, corporations must be identified by their correct name on the plaintiff's claim.

Before commencing an action against a corporation, you should conduct a business name search to ensure that you are suing the corporation using its correct name. Some corporations register a unique business name at the time that they become incorporated, and then carry on business under their registered name. A corporation that has a registered name is sometimes called a "named company." Other corporations register a name at the time that they become incorporated, and then carry on business under a trade name.

Often, corporations use the registration number assigned by Companies Branch at the time they become incorporated, and then carry on business under a different name. A corporation that uses its registration number as its legal name is sometimes called a "numbered company." The registration number must be used in conjunction with other words. For example, the name of a numbered company incorporated under the Ontario *Business Corporations Act* might look something like this:

1234567 Ontario Limited. If a numbered company is carrying on business under a business name, a business name search will tell you the correct name of the numbered company.

When you have confirmed the corporate defendant's name by means of the business name search, you may use other searches to find out additional information, if required. For example, if you need to know whether the corporation is still in existence or has been dissolved, you may request a certificate of status. To obtain accurate information about a corporate defendant, including its registered corporate name, the registered office address, its officers and directors, and so on, you may wish to consider carrying out a Corporation Profile Report.

Corporate searches and business name searches can be done in person at the Companies Branch, or online at the Ministry of Government Services website or using an online commercial search service such as Cyberbahn.

Finding Out About the Defendant's Financial Circumstances

There are a number of searches that may assist you in determining whether the defendant has any current income or assets against which a judgment can be enforced. The following list is not exhaustive.

Credit Bureau Search—Consumers

When deciding which searches to conduct and what you require before conducting those searches, you should consider the *Personal Information Protection and Electronic Documents Act* (PIPEDA). PIPEDA is federal legislation that applies to personal information collected, used, or disclosed by private sector organizations in the course of commercial activities. An exception is made for organizations operating in provinces with substantially similar provincial legislation. Because Ontario does not have substantially similar legislation, PIPEDA applies in Ontario.

PIPEDA sets up procedures for the collection, use, and disclosure of personal information. These procedures are intended to give individuals control over how their personal information is handled in the private sector. An organization is responsible for the protection of personal information and the fair handling of it at all times, both within the organization and in dealings with third parties.

Paralegal firms are engaged in commercial activity in Ontario; therefore, PIPEDA applies to the provision of legal services. You must implement a privacy policy and procedures for any personal information you gather about individuals in the course of your business (including information about debtors) in compliance with PIPEDA requirements.

This means you must:

- obtain the consent of people whose personal information you collect, use, or disclose, except in a few specific and limited circumstances;
- use or disclose people's personal information only for the purpose for which they gave consent;

- even with consent, limit collection, use, and disclosure of personal information to purposes that a reasonable person would consider appropriate under the circumstances;
- permit individuals to see the personal information that your business holds about them, and to correct any inaccuracies; and
- advise people whose personal information you collect of procedures to follow if they believe their rights have been violated.

To comply with PIPEDA, consumer reporting agencies (also known as credit bureaus) require their members to obtain express (written) consent for the collection of credit information. The *Consumer Reporting Act* requires that no person shall obtain or request a consumer report without first giving written notice to the consumer (s. 10(2)). The written consent must specify the purposes for which the consent can be used.

Paralegals may become members of a consumer reporting agency such as Equifax or Trans-Union because paralegals provide legal services to the public for a fee and are therefore considered creditors. If you have obtained the written consent of the defendant, you may request a credit report online. A consumer credit report contains, among other things, the following information:

- The consumer's name, address, and other contact information.
- The consumer's credit history, based on reports made by creditors that are on the consumer's file, along with credit ratings assigned by those creditors. A credit rating of R0 means no information. A credit rating of R9 indicates an unpaid debt that has gone to collection.
- The consumer's credit score in a range from 300 to 900, which is intended to indicate how likely a consumer is to repay a debt. A score of 300 means that the consumer is a poor credit risk. A score of 660 to 724 is considered good. A score of 725 and above is very good to excellent.

Credit Bureau Search—Businesses

When requesting a commercial credit report, make sure that you have the correct name for the business you are searching. A commercial credit report contains, among other things, the following information:

- The date of the report, the legal and business names of the business, its address and telephone number.
- Company history, including name changes and information about officers and directors, if available.
- A summary of lawsuits, liens, and judgments for a five-year period.
- An analysis of payment performance.
- A commercial credit score and payment index score.

Execution Search

A judgment creditor with an unpaid judgment against the defendant may register that judgment as an execution by filing a writ of seizure and sale of land with the Sheriff's Office in any district or county in Ontario where the judgment creditor believes the defendant lives, owns property, or carries on business. A **judgment creditor** is a person who has obtained judgment against a person and is seeking to enforce the judgment. An execution search of the defendant's name will provide information about the claim numbers, dates, and amounts of all outstanding judgments against debtors in the county or district with that name and the creditors who filed them. Execution searches can be carried out in person at the Sheriff's Office in a particular county or district; or they may be conducted online through websites such as Cyberbahn. Online searches may be conducted on a county-specific or province-wide basis.

If your execution search turns up outstanding executions against a person who you are satisfied is your defendant, this will tell you that there are other creditors out there with whom the proceeds of an enforcement against the defendant's income or assets, if any, may have to be shared. Your client should be advised of this.

Personal Property Security Act Search

Property is either **real property**—that is, tangible property that is immovable (land, houses, etc.), **personal property**—that is, tangible property that is movable (vehicles, home entertainment centres, computers, books, stocks and bonds, business inventory, etc.), or **intellectual property**—that is, intangible property with value. An outstanding loan against personal property such as a motor vehicle is called a **chattel mortgage.** The **chattel mortgagee** (the holder of the loan) may register its interest in the personal property under the *Personal Property Security Act* (PPSA). Registration of the chattel mortgagee's interest under the PPSA means that, if the debtor defaults on the loan, the chattel mortgagee has the right to seize and sell the property to satisfy the balance owing. That chattel mortgagee's right to seize and sell the property on default is subject to certain statutory exemptions. See, for example, the *Consumer Protection Act, 2002*, s. 25, which states:

No repossession after two-thirds paid except by leave of court

25(1) Where a consumer under a future performance agreement has paid two-thirds or more of his or her payment obligation as fixed by the agreement, any provision in the agreement, or in any security agreement incidental to the agreement, under which the supplier may retake possession of or resell the goods or services upon default in payment by the consumer is not enforceable except by leave obtained from the Superior Court of Justice.

Powers of court

(2) Upon an application for leave under subsection (1), the court may, in its discretion, grant leave to the supplier or refuse leave or grant leave upon such terms and conditions as the court considers advisable.

If you are aware that the defendant owns personal property, such as a motor vehicle, a PPSA search will tell you whether there are any security interests registered against that personal property. If there is a secured creditor with a registered security interest in the personal property, your client's chances of recovering some part or all of his judgment by seizing and selling the personal property are slim to nil. The rights of the secured creditor in the personal property will take priority over those of ordinary creditors.

Bankruptcy Search

A person who has declared bankruptcy turns over most of her rights to deal with her property, real or personal, to the trustee in bankruptcy, who administers the bankrupt's estate. Secured creditors may realize their interest in the property against which their interest has been secured (by way of a charge against land or a PPSA registration) outside of the bankruptcy. If there is money left after they have realized on their security, they must turn the surplus over to the trustee. If there is a deficiency—that is, there is still money owing after they have seized and sold the secured property—they may file a claim as ordinary creditors in the bankruptcy.

A bankruptcy search may be done online at the website of the Office of the Superintendent of Bankruptcy (http://www.osb.ic.gc.ca). You may also use online search services such as Cyberbahn. If the search reveals that your defendant has made a proposal or declared bankruptcy, you should advise your client immediately. Existing court proceedings are stayed by a bankruptcy. In order to recover some part of what is owed from the bankrupt's estate, creditors (including judgment creditors) must file a proof of claim with the trustee. Judgment creditors rank with ordinary creditors in a bankruptcy, and generally recover very little.

Does Small Claims Court Have Jurisdiction?

Jurisdiction is the lawful authority of a court. In Ontario, jurisdiction is established by the *Courts of Justice Act* and by the common law.

Before commencing an action in Small Claims Court, you must determine whether it falls within the jurisdiction of the court. In this discussion, jurisdiction will be broken down into three categories: legal, monetary, and territorial.

Legal Jurisdiction

General

Legal jurisdiction is the lawful authority of a court to deal with certain types of matters and to prescribe certain types of remedies.

Section 23 of the *Courts of Justice Act* states the jurisdiction of the Small Claims Court:

23(1) The Small Claims Court,

(a) has jurisdiction in any action for the payment of money where the amount claimed does not exceed the prescribed amount exclusive of interest and costs; and

(b) has jurisdiction in any action for the recovery of possession of personal property where the value of the property does not exceed the prescribed amount.

At present, the prescribed amount is $25,000.00 (*Small Claims Court Jurisdiction and Appeal Limit*, s. 1). As a civil trial court, Small Claims Court has legal jurisdiction in a wide range of matters, so long as those matters also fall within its monetary jurisdiction.

Some examples of cases that Small Claims Court may hear are:

- actions for money loaned and not repaid;
- actions for services rendered and not paid for;
- actions for goods sold and received and not paid for;
- actions for wrongful dismissal or constructive dismissal where the damages sought fall within the court's monetary jurisdiction;
- actions for damage suffered in tort—for example, damage to property or personal injury;
- actions for unpaid rent for residential premises, where the defaulting tenant has vacated the premises at the time the action is commenced; and
- actions for recovery of property with a value of $25,000.00 or less.

Remedies

Section 23 of the *Courts of Justice Act* confers authority on the Small Claims Court to make orders for payment of money up to $25,000.00 exclusive of interest and costs and delivery of property with a value up to $25,000.00 exclusive of interest and costs.

Section 96(1) of the *Courts of Justice Act* states: "Courts shall administer concurrently all rules of equity and the common law." Section 96(3) of the *Courts of Justice Act* states that "[o]nly the Court of Appeal and the Superior Court of Justice, exclusive of the Small Claims Court, may grant equitable relief, unless otherwise provided." Section 96(3) appears to limit the application of s. 96(1) to courts other than the Small Claims Court.

An issue that has been debated in court decisions since the Small Claims Court was continued as a branch of what is now the Superior Court of Justice in 1989 is whether the Small Claims Court has jurisdiction to grant **equitable relief**. See, for example, *936464 Ontario Ltd. v. Mungo Bear Ltd.*, in which the plaintiff sought to recover payment for services rendered that did not form part of the original written contract with the defendant. At trial, the judge noted that there was no written contract for those services, but awarded damages to the plaintiff based on *quantum meruit*. **Quantum meruit** is a doctrine that allows the court to order payment for services provided to another without a written contract. If the person seeking payment can prove (1) that services were provided to the other party; (2) that the recipient accepted those services; (3) that the services had value; and (4) that the recipient knew that the service provider expected payment for those services, the court will imply a contract.

The defendant appealed the judgment of the trial court. One of the grounds for the defendant's appeal was that the Small Claims Court did not have jurisdiction to grant equitable relief. At the hearing of the appeal, Heeney J. for the Divisional Court concluded that *quantum meruit* is a quasi-contractual remedy, not an equitable remedy, and that, therefore, the Small Claims Court has jurisdiction to grant this remedy. Heeney J. then went on to consider the language of the *Courts of Justice Act*, and concluded that the Small Claims Court could deal with common law and equitable claims that did not exceed its monetary jurisdiction, but restricted the equitable relief that could be granted by the court to payments of money. Therefore, even if *quantum meruit* was an equitable remedy, because the relief granted was for the payment of money, the Small Claims Court as a court of equity had jurisdiction to grant it.

The issue was considered by the Ontario Court of Appeal in *Grover v. Hodges*. The Court of Appeal concluded as follows (at paragraphs 47 to 49):

> In the report by Ontario Civil Justice Review, *First Report of the Civil Justice Review* (Toronto: *Ontario Civil Justice Review*, 1995), the authors noted the following. "Frequently referred to as the 'people's court,' today's Small Claims Court in Ontario is seen as the one place where a private citizen can have ready and inexpensive access to civil justice." The Small Claims Court is more hospitable to the ever-increasing number of self-represented litigants. Procedures are simpler in the Small Claims Court; matters are decided in a summary way under relaxed rules of evidence. There are limits on the costs that may be recovered by a successful party in the Small Claims Court. These features contribute to an increase in the accessibility of our system of justice.
>
> Interpreting the words of the *Courts of Justice Act* in such a way as to restrict the jurisdiction of the Small Claims Court in a manner that would preclude it from awarding equitable relief in resolving claims properly before it would run counter to this important objective.
>
> It follows that the interpretation of the *Courts of Justice Act* provisions relevant to the jurisdiction of the Small Claims Court that is in keeping with the wording of the Act and is consistent with the intent of the legislature, apparent not only from the legislative amendments but also from the rationale behind establishing the Court itself, *is that the Small Claims Court has jurisdiction to award legal or equitable relief where the relief requested is a monetary payment under the limit of $25,000 or the return of personal property valued within that limit.* [Emphasis added.]

BOX 3.1 Small Claims Court Legal Jurisdiction

Example 1

The plaintiff sues the defendant, a well-known national newspaper, for libel in Small Claims Court. The plaintiff alleges that a story published by the defendant is false and has injured the plaintiff's reputation. At trial, the judge finds in favour of the plaintiff (that is, the plaintiff wins). The judge awards the plaintiff $3,000.00 in damages for libel, plus costs. The judge also orders that the defendant publish a full apology and retraction (withdrawal) of the libel within 60 days of the date of the judgment if requested by the plaintiff to do so. The defendant pays the damages and costs, but appeals the part of the order compelling the defendant to publish an apology and retraction. On appeal, the defendant argues that Small Claims Court has no legal jurisdiction to make an order compelling performance of a specific act.

Referring to *Grover v. Hodges*, what is the result?

Example 2

Your neighbour decides to build a fence between her backyard and yours. The posts are being driven when you check your lot survey. You realize that the proposed fence line is six inches inside your property line. You need to stop your neighbour quickly. Can Small Claims Court make an order that she stop building the fence?

Referring to *Grover v. Hodges*, what is the result?

Example 3

While you are away from home on a three-week vacation, your neighbour decides to build a fence between her backyard and yours. By the time you get home, the fence is completed. You think the fence looks ugly and cheap, and you are angry because your neighbour did not consult you before putting it up. When you check your lot survey, you realize that the fence line is six inches inside your property's boundary line. You want the fence to be torn down. Can Small Claims Court make an order compelling your neighbour to tear down the fence?

Referring to *Grover v. Hodges*, what is the result?

Limitation Periods

A limitation period is a deadline prescribed by statute for commencing a proceeding or doing some other thing, such as preserving a legal right. In Ontario, the *Limitations Act, 2002* establishes a general limitation period for commencing a claim of not later than two years from the day on which the claim was discovered. If your client discovers that someone has done him an actionable harm, but waits more than two years from the date of discovering the harm before starting a claim, he is barred by s. 4 of the *Limitations Act, 2002* from doing so. In other words, after the limitation period has expired, he is statute-barred from bringing the action. To be **statute-barred** means that a person is prevented by the governing statute from asserting his legal rights.

Limitation periods established by statutes other than the *Limitations Act, 2002* are of no force and effect unless the statute is listed in the Schedule to s. 19 of the Act.

The *Limitations Act, 2002* (s. 2) does not apply to certain types of actions:

> **2**(1) This Act applies to claims pursued in court proceedings other than,
>
>   (a) proceedings to which the *Real Property Limitations Act* applies;
>
>   (b) proceedings in the nature of an appeal, if the time for commencing them is governed by an Act or rule of court;

(c) proceedings under the *Judicial Review Procedure Act*;

(d) proceedings to which the *Provincial Offences Act* applies;

(e) proceedings based on the existing aboriginal and treaty rights of the aboriginal peoples of Canada which are recognized and affirmed in section 35 of the *Constitution Act, 1982*; and

(f) proceedings based on equitable claims by aboriginal peoples against the Crown.

Note that the general limitation period begins to run from the time the harm is discovered, not from the time the harm is done.

The limitation period established by s. 4 of the *Limitations Act, 2002* does not run during any period during which the person with the claim is

- a minor and is not represented by a litigation guardian in relation to the claim (*Limitations Act, 2002*, s. 6); or

- is incapable of commencing a proceeding in respect of the claim because of his or her physical, mental, or psychological condition, and is not represented by a litigation guardian in relation to the claim (*Limitations Act, 2002*, s. 7).

BOX 3.2 Commencing the Action: Statutory Notice Periods

The *Limitations Act, 2002*, s. 4 provides that the two-year limitation period begins to run from the date that the claim is discovered—that is, from the date that the legal wrong that is the basis for the action is discovered by the injured party, not from the date the wrong is actually committed.

Other statutes may state additional requirements for commencing an action. Where a claimant suffers damage as a result of failure to repair a provincial highway, s. 33(4) of the *Public Transportation and Highway Improvement Act* provides that no action for damages shall be brought unless notice in writing is given to the minister within 10 days from the date of the injury. The statute also provides that if the 10 days' notice is not given or is given late, a judge may permit the action to proceed if satisfied that the claimant has a reasonable excuse and that the Crown is not prejudiced by the claimant's failure to comply.

Section 5(1) of the *Libel and Slander Act* states that no action for libel in a newspaper or in a broadcast lies unless the plaintiff has, within six weeks after the alleged libel has come to the plaintiff's knowledge, given the defendant written notice of the matter complained of. Section 7(1) of the *Proceedings Against the Crown Act* states that no action for a claim shall be commenced against the Crown unless the claimant has, at least 60 days before the commencement of the action, served on the Crown a notice of the claim containing particulars of the basis for the claim.

Always remember to check the relevant legislation with respect to notice periods when diarizing for approaching deadlines in a client matter.

Monetary Jurisdiction

Section 23 of the *Courts of Justice Act* and O. Reg. 626/00 confer authority on the Small Claims Court to make orders for payment of money not exceeding $25,000.00 exclusive of interest and costs and delivery of property with a value not exceeding $25,000.00 exclusive of interest and costs.

Quantifying Damages

When advising a client about commencing a Small Claims Court proceeding, you must determine whether the claim falls within the court's monetary jurisdiction. This means that you must assess how much money is owing to your client, based on the facts as you know them, and the applicable law.

Quantifying damages means determining all of the different kinds of damage or harm your client has suffered because of another's alleged wrongdoing, and assigning a money value to that damage. At trial, the money value assigned must be supported by the evidence.

In contract law, the purpose of an award of damages is to compensate the innocent party for financial losses suffered as a result of the breach of contract—that is, to put the innocent party in the position she would have been in had the contract been performed. The damages resulting from a breach of contract (including non-payment of a debt) can usually be determined with some certainty by referring to the terms of the contract.

In tort law, damages are more difficult to determine. The value of some damages flowing from the harm may be easy to quantify—for example, medical expenses, and loss of income if the victim was unable to work for a period of time due to the injury. Other categories of damage flowing from the harm are more difficult to assign a money value to.

When advising a prospective client about a claim, you must be careful to ascertain the different types of damage the client may have suffered as a result of the alleged wrongdoing. If it appears that the client should bring the action in another court, based on the extent of the damage suffered, you should so advise the client. If the client decides to bring the action in another court, you should consider sending the client a non-engagement letter confirming the client's reasons for declining the retainer, advising of any approaching limitation periods, and urging them to seek the assistance of a lawyer.

Categories of Damages

Special damages (also known as **liquidated damages**) are specific monetary amounts whose value may be established by documents proving a debt or other fixed amount, or by an arithmetical calculation. Special damages may not require valuation by a court, so long as the plaintiff produces sufficient documentation to prove the amount claimed.

A claim that is wholly for special or liquidated damages is called a **liquidated claim**. An example of a liquidated claim is a debt collection where the amount owing is supported by documentary evidence and is not disputed by the defendant.

General damages (also known as **unliquidated damages**) are amounts that are not fixed and quantifiable based on objective evidence. General damages must be assessed by the court based on all of the evidence and on criteria established by other court decisions. Some examples of actions where general damages may be claimed are actions for personal injury, defamation, and, in some cases, wrongful dismissal.

General damages are intended to compensate the plaintiff for pecuniary and non-pecuniary loss. **Pecuniary damages** are damages awarded for losses that can be estimated in monetary terms. In the case of a chronic injury, for example, pecuniary damages might be awarded to the plaintiff for loss of future earning capacity, and cost of future care. **Non-pecuniary damages** are damages awarded for types of harm that are real and serious, but difficult to assign a monetary value to. Examples of types of non-pecuniary damages are:

- physical and mental pain and suffering;
- loss of amenities of life—that is, loss of the ability to engage in and enjoy certain activities as a result of the harm suffered; or
- loss of expectation of life—that is, loss of the pleasure of normal living as a result of the harm suffered.

Both special (liquidated) and general (unliquidated) damages may be claimed in the same action.

In addition to the above heads of damages, courts may award aggravated damages and/or punitive damages to a successful plaintiff. **Aggravated damages** are intended to compensate the plaintiff for harm or distress suffered as a result of egregious bad faith on the part of the defendant. **Punitive damages** are preventive, not compensatory. They are intended to discourage the repetition of undesirable conduct. A defendant will be ordered to pay punitive damages to the plaintiff where the defendant has knowingly engaged in wrongful acts that are so malicious or outrageous that they are deserving of punishment. (See *Richard v. Times Inc.* and *Honda Canada Inc. v. Keays.*)

Mitigation of Damages

An injured party has a duty of taking all reasonable steps to mitigate the loss or harm caused by the wrongdoer. Failure to take such reasonable steps debars the injured party from claiming any part of the damage that is the result of his neglect to take such steps (see *Asamera Oil Corp. v. Seal Oil and General Corp.*, at p. 661). For example, an employee is dismissed by an employer without reasonable notice or pay in lieu of reasonable notice. The employee (plaintiff) sues the employer for damages for wrongful dismissal. The plaintiff's claim alleges that the circumstances of his dismissal make it impossible for the employee to find other comparable employment. Question: Can the employee do nothing with a view to increasing his damages? Answer: No. The employee cannot contribute to his own losses. Pending final disposition of the matter by way of a settlement or adjudication, he must make diligent attempts to seek and find other employment, and keep a detailed record of those attempts for evidentiary purposes. Failure to do so will reduce the amount of damages to which he is entitled.

BOX 3.3 Identifying and Quantifying Damages

The Fact Situation

The plaintiff was injured when she slipped and fell down icy steps as she was leaving a friend's house after a party. She broke her right wrist and suffered extensive bruising, especially to her lower back. As a result of the fall, she experiences recurrent back pain.

The plaintiff is a self-employed 28-year-old bicycle courier, who works year-round in downtown Toronto. Her annual gross income is $24,000.00. As a result of her injuries, she was unable to work for three months. She had to pay for prescriptions for painkillers for the pain from the fall and, later, for the recurrent pain in her back. To date, these prescriptions have cost her $286.47. She has kept the receipts.

During the time that she was off work, she was wholly dependent on her partner for support. So far, physiotherapy has cost her $1,500.00. Her partner loaned her money to pay that amount.

She has now been back at work for three months. She has worked hard to get back into shape and get her income back up to where it was before her injuries, but for the first month she made only $1,500.00, and for the last two months she made only $1,800.00. Her wrist is still weak and her back still causes her pain. She is not sure that she can continue to work as a bicycle courier. Her treating physician has advised her to continue with the painkillers and the physiotherapy.

Identifying Damages

The plaintiff may claim special damages based on loss of income and out-of-pocket expenses connected to the injury, and general damages, both pecuniary and non-pecuniary.

Quantifying Damages

CATEGORY OF DAMAGES	DAMAGE SUFFERED	DESCRIPTION OF DAMAGES
Special Damages	Loss of income before return to work	The plaintiff lost three months of income at a monthly rate (gross) of $2,500.00, for a total of $7,500.00 owing.
	Loss of income after return to work	As a consequence of her time off work because of the injury, the plaintiff's monthly income was reduced by $1,000.00 (first month back at work) and $1,400.00 (second and third months back at work), for a total of $2,400.00 owing. Given the nature of her injuries, it appears that these losses may continue.
	Medical expenses	The plaintiff may claim her prescription costs ($286.47) and the costs of physiotherapy ($1,500.00), for a total of $1,786.47 to the date of the claim. Her treating physician has recommended that the medication and physiotherapy continue, so these expenses may continue to accrue from the date of the claim to the date of final resolution of the matter, and thereafter into the future.

continued . . .

Quantifying Damages continued

CATEGORY OF DAMAGES	DAMAGE SUFFERED	DESCRIPTION OF DAMAGES
General Damages: Pecuniary	Loss of future income	If the plaintiff's back injury turns out to be chronic, she may be unable to continue work as a bicycle courier or, if she does continue, she may suffer a permanent diminution in her annual earnings. She is a young woman. Whether and in what amount she can recover damages on this ground will depend on a range of factors, including her age, what other employment skills she currently has or can acquire, the availability of other employment, and how long it would reasonably take her to find other employment in her salary range.
	Cost of future care	If the back injury is chronic, she may require pain medication and physiotherapy indefinitely.
General Damages: Non-Pecuniary	Pain and suffering	Must be quantified based on medical and other evidence.
	Loss of amenities	Must be quantified based on the plaintiff's lifestyle before the injury. If she was an active, athletic person before the injury, and it can be proven that the injury will prevent her from engaging in her usual sports and other activities, she may recover damages on this ground.

The plaintiff's total special damages at this point are $11,686.47. If she wants to bring the claim in Small Claims Court, her total claim, including general damages and excluding interest and costs, will be capped at $25,000.00. Because the claims for loss of future income, cost of future care, pain and suffering, and loss of amenities cannot easily be valued at this point, she should consider bringing her action in the Superior Court of Justice.

The plaintiff's partner may have grounds for a dependant's claim under Part V of the *Family Law Act*. If he wishes to advance his claim, he should consider retaining separate legal representation.

Closing question

Has the defendant mitigated her damages? Please refer to the fact situation above when answering this question.

What If the Amount Owing Is More than $25,000.00?

Small Claims Court provides a summary, expeditious, and inexpensive forum for the recovery of comparatively modest sums of money. But what if a plaintiff is trying to recover $26,000.00 from a debtor? Or $28,500.00? Must the plaintiff pay a lawyer to commence an action in the Superior Court of Justice because the amount she is owed is two or three thousand dollars over the Small Claims Court monetary jurisdiction?

In this situation, the plaintiff has two options. She may consider commencing the action under the Rule 76—Simplified Procedure in the Superior Court of Justice, in which case she must hire a lawyer if she prefers to have legal representation. Or she may waive the right to claim any amount owing over and above the monetary jurisdiction of Small Claims Court, in order to bring the action in Small Claims Court.

SUPERIOR COURT OF JUSTICE RULE 76—SIMPLIFIED PROCEDURE

Rule 76—Simplified Procedure of the *Rules of Civil Procedure* governs actions for recovery of money amounts of $100,000.00 or less, exclusive of interest and costs, or recovery of property valued at $100,000.00 or less. The purpose of Rule 76 is similar to that of Small Claims Court—to provide a simple, fast, inexpensive way of obtaining judgments in matters within the court's jurisdiction.

Paralegals are not allowed to appear in the Superior Court of Justice, except for Small Claims Court. Parties to proceedings in the Superior Court of Justice may represent themselves, or be represented by a lawyer. A litigant who is not comfortable with Superior Court of Justice forms and procedures will require the assistance of a lawyer.

Table 3.2 provides a comparison of the filing fees for common steps in an action and enforcement in Small Claims Court and the Superior Court of Justice.

WAIVING OR ABANDONING THE EXCESS

In some cases, litigants with claims that fall outside the Small Claims Court monetary jurisdiction may wish to proceed in Small Claims Court anyway. They may prefer to represent themselves, in a court whose procedures are user-friendly for the self-represented. They may be able to afford legal representation, but would prefer to be represented by a paralegal in a court with inexpensive, expeditious procedures.

TABLE 3.2 Court Fees in the Small Claims Court and the Superior Court of Justice

STEP IN THE PROCEEDING	SMALL CLAIMS COURT	SUPERIOR COURT OF JUSTICE
Claim	$75.00 (infrequent claimant) $145.00 (frequent claimant)	$181.00
Defence	$40.00	$144.00
Defendant's claim	$75.00	n/a
Statement of defence and counterclaim adding a party	n/a	$181.00
Default judgment	$35.00 (infrequent claimant) $50.00 (frequent claimant)	$127.00
Notice of motion	$40.00	$127.00
Notice of return of motion	n/a	$127.00
Fixing date for trial	$100.00 (infrequent claimant) $130.00 (frequent claimant)	n/a
Trial record (first time only)	n/a	$337.00
Summons to witness	$19.00	$22.00
Witness fees and allowances (non-professionals)	$6.00 per attendance plus mileage	$50.00 per attendance plus mileage
Writ of delivery, writ of seizure and sale, or notice of examination	$35.00	n/a
Writ of execution	n/a	$55.00
Notice of garnishment	$100.00	$115.00 (includes filing with sheriff)

Plaintiffs who commence Small Claims Court actions for amounts that exceed the court's monetary jurisdiction must waive (or abandon) the excess in their claim. **Waiving the excess** means that they give up their right to claim any money owing above the $25,000.00 Small Claims Court limit, in order to bring the matter within Small Claims Court monetary jurisdiction—that is, to preserve their right to bring the action in Small Claims Court. On the plaintiff's claim (Form 7A), the total amount claimed in the request for relief should be $25,000.00. In the body of the claim, the plaintiff must state the total actually owing. The plaintiff must also state that he is waiving any amounts owing over and above $25,000.00 to bring the matter within the monetary jurisdiction of the Small Claims Court.

If a plaintiff is suing someone who owes him more than $25,000.00, and he chooses to waive the excess in order to bring the matter within the Small Claims Court monetary jurisdiction, he loses the right to claim the waived amount forever. He cannot abandon the excess in one proceeding, and then, after that proceeding has been resolved (whether by settlement or by adjudication), try to claim the waived amount in a subsequent proceeding. By his waiver, he has permanently abandoned any legal right to the excess.

BOX 3.4 Waiver of Excess

Background: The defendant owes the plaintiff $27,500.00, on account of a personal loan the plaintiff made to the defendant. The plaintiff makes several demands for payment, by email and by leaving messages on the defendant's voicemail. The defendant fails to make any payments on the loan. The plaintiff commenced an action against the defendant in Small Claims Court, waiving any amounts owing over $25,000.00 to bring the matter within the Small Claims Court jurisdiction. The defendant (who is out of province) fails to deliver a defence, and the plaintiff obtains a default judgment for $25,000.00 plus interest and costs.

The plaintiff waits a few months, and then commences a second action, this time for the $2,500.00 she waived in the first proceeding. Again, the defendant (who is still out of province) fails to deliver a defence. The plaintiff obtains a second default judgment for $2,500.00 plus interest and costs. Is the second judgment enforceable against the defendant?

Discussion: No. The plaintiff has no legal entitlement to money to which she has waived her rights, and the court has no authority to enter judgment with respect to an amount outside its monetary jurisdiction. The second judgment has no force and effect and if the defendant, on his return to Ontario, makes a motion to have the judgment set aside, he will succeed. Any steps taken to enforce the second judgment will also be set aside, and the plaintiff will be ordered to return those moneys to the defendant. The defendant may also be awarded costs.

The defendant remains liable to pay the judgment of $25,000.00 plus interest and costs awarded to the plaintiff in the first proceeding, unless he has valid defences that he can raise, in which case he should obtain a court order setting aside that judgment as well.

The client's consent to the waiver must be informed. Depending on the amount being waived, you may wish to consider recommending that the client obtain independent legal advice from a lawyer regarding the advantages and potential cost of proceeding in the Superior Court of Justice. The client's instructions to waive the excess and proceed in Small Claims Court should be confirmed in writing by the client.

A sample plaintiff's claim containing the language of waiver can be found in Appendix 3.1 to this chapter.

MULTIPLE ACTIONS

Rule 6.02 of the *Rules of the Small Claims Court* states that an action shall not be divided into two or more actions in order to bring it within Small Claims Court monetary jurisdiction. In other words, you cannot use **action splitting** to circumvent the court's monetary jurisdiction.

Action splitting is sometimes attempted where the defendant owes money on a **running account**. A running account is an account where the defendant is a regular customer who charges purchases against a standard account number on an ongoing basis. The defendant makes payments against the account from time to time (usually on a monthly basis), as invoices are received. A common consumer example would be a credit card account; but many other commercial relationships also involve running accounts (for example, suppliers and wholesalers or retailers).

Where a plaintiff engages in action splitting in order to circumvent the Small Claims Court monetary jurisdiction, a defendant may make a motion to the court for an order **quashing** the actions on grounds that they are based on the same set of facts or transactions. An action that has been quashed is null and void, and cannot proceed any further. The order quashing the actions will be without prejudice to the plaintiff's right to bring the action in the proper court, or to abandon the excess and bring the action in Small Claims Court. The defendant should have her costs of the motion. Rule 15.07 states that the costs of a motion, excluding disbursements, shall not exceed $100.00 unless the court orders otherwise because there are special circumstances. If bad faith can be shown on the part of the plaintiff by a defendant on a motion to quash based on action splitting contrary to Rule 6.02, the defendant should request costs in excess of $100.00 on grounds that the plaintiff's bad faith constitutes special circumstances justifying a higher costs award.

BOX 3.5 What Not to Do—Action Splitting

Your client, P Inc., is owed $30,000.00 on account of supplies and services provided to D Ltd. over the past five months. P Inc. bills D Ltd. on a monthly basis. The following invoices have not been paid:

Invoice number	Date	Amount
01234-1	January 1, 20—	$9,005.00
01234-2	February 1, 20—	$8,065.00
01234-3	March 1, 20—	$4,345.00
01234-4	April 1, 20—	$3,555.00
01234-5	May 1, 20—	$5,030.00

P Inc. does not want to pay a lawyer to collect the amount owing in the Superior Court of Justice. P Inc. commences two different actions in Small Claims Court to collect the amount owing. In Claim No. 2005, P Inc. seeks recovery of $17,070.00 on account of invoices 01234-1 and 01234-2. In Claim No. 2006, P Inc. seeks recovery of $12,930.00 on account of invoices 01234-3, 01234-4, and 01234-5.

D Ltd. is unrepresented, and raises no objection.

The two matters go to trial, and P Inc. is awarded judgment in both matters by a deputy judge. The deputy judge states his jurisdictional concerns in his reason for judgment.

D Ltd. seeks legal advice and decides to appeal the two decisions. At the hearing of the appeal, P Inc. argues that action splitting is a mere procedural irregularity, which should be allowed pursuant to Rules 1.03 and 2.01 of the *Rules of the Small Claims Court*. Rule 1.03 provides for a liberal interpretation of the *Rules of the Small Claims Court* in the interest of securing a just, expeditious, and inexpensive determination in every proceeding. Rule 2.01 permits a court to waive technical compliance with the rules, including Rule 6.02, in the interests of justice.

The appeal judge does not accept these arguments. He observes that Rules 1.03 and 2.01 cannot be interpreted to permit the court to give itself jurisdiction it does not have. He allows D Ltd.'s appeal and sets aside the judgments in Claim No. 2005 and Claim No. 2006 without prejudice to P Inc.'s right to bring an action for the amount owing in the Superior Court of Justice. He orders P Inc. to pay D Ltd.'s costs of the appeal fixed at $2,000.00.

(Adapted from *Traditional Air Systems Inc. v. Custom Gas Heating Ltd.*)

BRINGING A MOTION TO A JUDGE TO HAVE THE ACTION TRANSFERRED FROM SMALL CLAIMS COURT TO THE SUPERIOR COURT OF JUSTICE PURSUANT TO THE COURTS OF JUSTICE ACT, S. 110

Where a proceeding or a step in a proceeding is brought or taken in the wrong court, it may be transferred to the proper court, and shall be continued as if it had been commenced in that court (*Courts of Justice Act*, s. 110). This procedure is intended to be used where a party has, due to inadvertence, brought a proceeding in the wrong court.

Section 110(1) states that a proceeding or a step in a proceeding brought before the wrong court *may* be transferred or adjourned to the proper court. In other words, the transfer is **discretionary**, not **mandatory**. Where an action is discretionary, the court *may* make up its own mind about a particular matter, giving due regard to all relevant factors. Where an action is mandatory, the court *must* do something if certain preconditions exist.

A s. 110 ruling on a transfer of a matter from Small Claims Court to the Superior Court of Justice must be obtained on a motion to a judge of the Superior Court of Justice. A judge sitting in Small Claims Court has no jurisdiction to make an order under s. 110, even if the parties consent to the order. Their consent cannot confer jurisdiction upon a Small Claims Court judge (see *Maple Lodge Farms Ltd. v. Penny Lane Fruit Market Inc.*).

The factors the court must consider in exercising its discretion under s. 110(1) are the merits of the matter, whether the other party will suffer undue prejudice, and whether the moving party has acted expeditiously to correct its error (*Dunnington v. 656956 Ontario Ltd.*, paras. 2 to 4). Where the court hearing the motion is satisfied that the matter to be transferred has no merit, the court may refuse to order that it be transferred to the proper court and order costs to the opposing party (*Dunnington*, paras. 5 and 6).

In cases where the Superior Court of Justice lacks statutory jurisdiction under s. 110, it may exercise its **inherent jurisdiction** to control its own process when transferring a matter improperly brought in Small Claims Court to the Superior Court of Justice. Inherent jurisdiction refers to intrinsic judicial powers possessed by the court that are essential for the administration of justice. When invoking inherent jurisdiction, a court will pay due regard to the paramount consideration of doing justice while ensuring the most expeditious and least expensive resolution of every case on its merits (*Maple Lodge Farms*, para. 23).

Territorial Jurisdiction

Territorial jurisdiction is the geographical area where a court is authorized to conduct hearings and make orders that are binding on litigants. Territorial jurisdiction is governed by Rule 6.01 of the *Rules of the Small Claims Court*:

> **6.01**(1) An action shall be commenced,
>   (a) in the territorial division,
>   (i) in which the cause of action arose, or
>   (ii) in which the defendant or, if there are several defendants, in which any one of them resides or carries on business; or
>   (b) at the court's place of sitting that is nearest to the place where the defendant or, if there are several defendants, where any one of them resides or carries on business.
>   (2) An action shall be tried in the place where it is commenced, but if the court is satisfied that the balance of convenience substantially favours holding the trial at another place than those described in subrule (1), the court may order that the action be tried at that other place.
>   (3) If, when an action is called for trial or settlement conference, the judge finds that the place where the action was commenced is not the proper place of trial, the court may order that the action be tried in any other place where it could have been commenced under this rule.
>   **6.02** A cause of action shall not be divided into two or more actions for the purpose of bringing it within the court's jurisdiction.

Determining Where the Cause of Action Arose

In some cases, it will be easy to decide where the event giving rise to the action occurred. For example, let's say that you operate a lawn care and landscaping service in Milton. A Milton resident asks you to maintain her lawn and garden for three months while she is away on a business trip. You quote her a price of $2,100.00. She pays you a $500.00 deposit. When she returns to Milton, she refuses to pay the balance, alleging various deficiencies.

In this case, you carry on business in Milton. The defendant lives in Milton. The contract was entered into in Milton, and the breach of contract (refusal to pay the balance owing) took place in Milton. If you decide to sue, the court with territorial jurisdiction is the Milton Small Claims Court.

Similarly, if someone causes damage to property, the cause of action arises where the property is located, and the action may be commenced in the Small Claims Court with territorial jurisdiction for that geographical area.

In some cases, it will not be perfectly clear where the cause of action arose, particularly if you are acting for the plaintiff. This is often the case with breach of contract, particularly with distance contracts that are entered into by telephone or Internet, because it is not clear where the contract was made. If you are unsure about where the cause of action arose, and the contract is silent as to the applicable law in the event of breach, you should commence the action in the Small Claims Court with territorial jurisdiction in the geographical area where the defendant resides or carries on business; or, if there are multiple defendants, where one of them resides or carries on business.

Balance of Convenience (Rule 6.01(2))

The general rule is that a matter shall be tried in the place where it is commenced. However, if the court is satisfied that the balance of convenience substantially favours holding the trial at some place other than those described in Rule 6.01(1), the court may make an order to that effect.

Note that this rule applies to the trial of the matter only. A party seeking to have the **venue** (or place) of the trial moved to another territorial division under Rule 6.01(2) would do so by bringing a motion pursuant to Rule 15. Procedures on a motion are discussed in Chapter 7.

The balance of convenience is a common-law test. A court hearing a Rule 6.01(2) motion will look at the following factors when determining whether the balance of convenience favours changing the trial's venue: the number of witnesses to be called by each party, the distance those witnesses and the parties must travel to get to the place of the trial, and the expenses connected with that attendance. The court must balance the prejudice to one party of allowing the trial to proceed at the chosen venue, against the prejudice to the other party if the trial is moved to a new venue. The Supreme Court of Canada has stated that "a party whose case has a real and substantial connection with a forum has a legitimate claim to the advantages that that forum provides" (see *Amchem Products Inc. v. British Columbia (Workers' Compensation Board)*, at pp. 920-21).

Rule 6.01(3) Order

If an action is called for a trial or a settlement conference, and the judge finds that the place where the action was commenced is not the proper place of trial, the court may make an order that the action be tried in any other place with jurisdiction under Rule 6.01.

It appears that the judge appearing on the settlement conference or at trial may raise the issue herself, based on her reading of the file, or it may be raised by one of the parties during discussion at the settlement conference or as an informal pretrial motion.

Note that the order is discretionary. Even if the judge is satisfied that the action was brought in the wrong territorial jurisdiction, she is not compelled to make an order changing the place of the trial. For example, if the parties agree that the trial should take place in the court where the action was commenced, the judge may endorse the file to that effect.

Finding Your Court

Court addresses may be searched at the Ministry of the Attorney General website (http://www.attorneygeneral.jus.gov.on.ca).

CHAPTER SUMMARY

You should advise clients honestly and candidly about the merits of their case. If the defendant appears to be judgment-proof, the client should be advised of this before litigation is commenced. Carefully consider the effect on your client's rights if a limitation period expires, and keep in mind that a debtor's circumstances may change.

The client's matter must fall within Small Claims Court jurisdiction. At present, Small Claims Court has jurisdiction to award legal or equitable relief where the relief requested is a monetary payment for an amount not exceeding $25,000.00 exclusive of interest and costs, or for the return of personal property with a value not exceeding $25,000.00 exclusive of interest and costs.

A claim for more than $25,000.00 exclusive of interest and costs may be brought in Small Claims Court, so long as the claimant waives, or abandons, the excess. A claimant who is seeking damages of more than $25,000.00 may not split her claim into two or more actions in order to fall within the Small Claims Court monetary jurisdiction.

Quantifying damages means determining all of the different kinds of damage or harm your client has suffered because of another's alleged wrongdoing, and assigning a money value to that damage. At trial, the money value assigned must be supported by the evidence.

Special damages (also known as liquidated damages) are specific monetary amounts whose value may be established by documents proving a debt or other fixed amount. Special damages may not require valuation by a court, so long as the plaintiff produces sufficient documentation to prove the amount claimed.

A claim that is wholly for special or liquidated damages is called a liquidated claim. An example of a liquidated claim is a debt collection where the amount owing is supported by documentary evidence and is not disputed by the defendant.

General damages (also known as unliquidated damages) are amounts that are not fixed and quantifiable based on objective evidence. General damages must be assessed by the court based on all of the evidence and on criteria established by other court decisions. Some examples of actions where general damages may be claimed are actions for personal injury, defamation, and, in some cases, wrongful dismissal.

An injured party has a duty to take all reasonable steps to mitigate the loss or harm caused by the wrongdoer. Failure to take such reasonable steps debars the injured party from claiming any part of the damage that is a result of his failure to mitigate his damages.

A Small Claims Court action must be commenced in the territorial division where the cause of action arose, or where a defendant lives or carries on business, or at the court's place of sitting that is closest to where a defendant lives or carries on business. An action shall be tried in the place where it is commenced, unless the court is satisfied that the balance of convenience substantially favours holding the trial in another place, in which case the court may order that the action be tried at that other place.

KEY TERMS

action splitting: dividing an action into two or more actions in order to bring it within the Small Claims Court monetary jurisdiction *(p. 91)*

aggravated damages: damages intended to compensate the plaintiff for harm or distress suffered as a result of egregious bad faith on the part of the defendant *(p. 86)*

authorized requester: a person who has applied to and has been approved by the ministry for that designation, and is registered as an authorized requester with the ministry *(p. 74)*

candid: forthright and sincere, able to look at both sides of an issue without bias *(p. 72)*

cause of action: the factual and legal grounds for seeking a remedy from a court *(p. 72)*

chattel mortgage: a loan that is secured against personal property; in Ontario, such security interests are registered under the *Personal Property Security Act* *(p. 79)*

chattel mortgagee: one who holds a loan secured against personal property or chattels *(p. 79)*

corporation: a separate legal entity from its owners—the shareholders *(p. 76)*

disbursements: the out-of-pocket expenses of a legal proceeding; these include court filing fees, charges for service of documents, photocopying charges, postage, etc. *(p. 72)*

discretionary: where an action is discretionary, the court may make up its own mind about a particular matter, giving due regard to all relevant factors *(p. 92)*

equitable relief: remedies other than money damages; for example, an order compelling a person to do something (specific performance) or to stop doing something (injunction) *(p. 81)*

general damages: damages for pain and suffering caused by injury or harm, and for future losses and expenses, such as future care costs and loss of future income; general damages cannot be quantified precisely, but they must be itemized and explained to the extent that it is possible to do so; also referred to as unliquidated damages *(p. 86)*

inherent jurisdiction: judicial powers that are essential for the administration of justice *(p. 93)*

intellectual property: intangible property with value— for example, copyright, patents, trademarks *(p. 79)*

judgment creditor: a person who has obtained judgment against a person and is seeking to enforce the judgment *(p. 79)*

judgment debtor: any person who owes money to another person pursuant to a court order *(p. 73)*

judgment-proof: having no income or assets against which a judgment may be enforced *(p. 73)*

liquidated claim: claim for a debt or fixed amount of money that does not require valuation by a court *(p. 86)*

liquidated damages: a specific amount of money that may be established by unpaid invoices, NSF cheques, or other documentation proving a debt or fixed amount; also called special damages *(p. 85)*

mandatory: where an action is mandatory, the court must do something if certain preconditions exist; the court has no choice *(p. 92)*

non-pecuniary damages: damages awarded for types of harm that are real and serious, but difficult to assign a money value to *(p. 86)*

partnership: an unincorporated business that is formed by two or more persons with the objective of making a profit *(p. 76)*

pecuniary damages: damages awarded for losses that can be estimated in money terms *(p. 86)*

personal property: property that has value, and is tangible and movable *(p. 79)*

punitive damages: preventive, not compensatory, these damages are intended to discourage the repetition of undesirable conduct *(p. 86)*

quantifying damages: calculating damages—that is, determining all of the different kinds of damage or injury that a party has suffered because of another's wrongdoing, and assigning money values to the different kinds of damage, based on the evidence *(p. 85)*

quantum meruit: an equitable doctrine that allows the court to imply a contract in certain circumstances and order payment for services provided pursuant to the implied contract *(p. 81)*

quash: to declare something null and void, and of no legal force and effect *(p. 91)*

real property: property that has value, and is tangible and immovable *(p. 79)*

running account: an account where a regular customer charges purchases against a standard account number on an ongoing basis; the defendant makes payments against the account from time to time (usually on a monthly basis) *(p. 91)*

sole proprietorship: an unincorporated business owned and run by one individual *(p. 75)*

special damages: damages that compensate the plaintiff for all losses, including out-of-pocket expenses connected with the injury or harm, up to the date of the trial; can usually be calculated fairly precisely; also referred to as liquidated damages *(p. 85)*

statute-barred: to be prevented by the terms of a statute from commencing an action to assert your legal rights *(p. 83)*

unliquidated damages: *see* general damages *(p. 86)*

venue: the place where a trial is held *(p. 94)*

waiving the excess: in a plaintiff's claim or defendant's claim, giving up the right to claim any money owing above $10,000.00 (exclusive of interest and costs), in order to bring the matter within Small Claims Court monetary jurisdiction *(p. 90)*

REFERENCES

936464 Ontario Ltd. v. Mungo Bear Ltd., [2003] OJ No. 3795 (Div. Ct.).

Amchem Products Inc. v. British Columbia (Workers' Compensation Board), [1993] 1 SCR 897, at 920.

Andrews v. Grand & Toy Alberta Ltd., [1978] SCJ No. 6.

Asamera Oil Corp. v. Seal Oil and General Corp., [1979] 1 SCR 633.

Business Corporations Act, RSO 1990, c. B.16.

Business Names Act, RSO 1990, c. B.17.

Collection Agencies Act, RSO 1990, c. C.14.

Construction Lien Act, RSO 1990, c. C.30.

Consumer Protection Act, 2002, SO 2002, c. 30.

Consumer Reporting Act, RSO 1990, c. C.33.

Courts of Justice Act, RSO 1990, c. C.43.

Dunnington v. 656956 Ontario Ltd. (1991), 6 CPC (3d) 298, 89 DLR (4th) 607, 9 OR (3d) 124, 54 OAC 345, 1991 CarswellOnt 464 (Div. Ct.).

Family Law Act, RSO 1990, c. F.3.

Family Law Rules, O. Reg. 114/99.

Financial Consumer Agency of Canada, Understanding Your Credit Report and Credit Score; available online at http://www.fcac-acfc.gc.ca.

Grover v. Hodges, [2011] OJ No. 310 (CA).

Honda Canada Inc. v. Keays, [2008] SCJ No. 40.

Law Society of Upper Canada (LSUC), *Paralegal Rules of Conduct* (Toronto: LSUC, 2007, as amended); available online at http://www.lsuc.on.ca.

Libel and Slander Act, RSO 1990, c. L.12.

Limitations Act, 2002, SO 2002, c. 24, sched. B.

Maple Lodge Farms Ltd. v. Penny Lane Fruit Market Inc., 1997 CarswellOnt 4306, [1997] OJ no. 4401 (QL), at paras. 18 and 19 (Gen. Div.).

Office of the Privacy Commissioner of Canada, Commissioner's Findings under the *Personal Information Protection and Electronic Documents Act* (PIPEDA), PIPEDA Case Summary #2006-340, *Law firms collected credit reports without consent*. http://www.priv.gc.ca/cf-dc/2006/340_20060502_e.cfm.

Personal Information Protection and Electronic Documents Act, SC 2000, c. 5.

Personal Property Security Act, RSO 1990, c. P.10.

Proceedings Against the Crown Act, RSO 1990, c. P.27.

Public Transportation and Highway Improvement Act, RSO 1990, c. P.50.

Richard v. Times Inc., [2012] SCJ No. 8.

Rules of Civil Procedure, RRO 1990, Reg. 194.

Rules of the Small Claims Court, O. Reg. 258/98.

Small Claims Court Jurisdiction and Appeal Limit, O. Reg. 626/00.

Traditional Air Systems Inc. v. Custom Gas Heating Ltd. (1995), 86 OAC 72, 1995 CarswellOnt 1793 (Div. Ct.).

REVIEW QUESTIONS

1. What is a judgment-proof defendant?

2. What steps must you take before collecting personal information about individuals in the course of your paralegal practice?

3. Briefly describe the following searches and the information they provide.

   a. Credit bureau search

   b. Execution search

   c. *Personal Property Security Act* search

   d. Bankruptcy search

4. a. You decide to build a wooden privacy fence between your neighbour's backyard and yours, so that you will no longer have to look at his collection of 42 brightly painted garden gnomes. You check the local by-law to ensure that your fence complies with height restrictions and so on. The posts are being driven when Mr. Gnomemeister approaches you. "I don't want you to build a fence. It's not neighbourly," he says. You reply that you have done everything according to local by-laws. "Oh yeah?" says Mr. Gnomemeister. "Well, I don't care what the by-laws say. I'm going to get a Small Claims Court order to stop you."

   Can Small Claims Court order you to stop building the fence? Give reasons for your answer.

   b. The day after the episode described above, your neighbour, Mr. Gnomemeister, goes away for a two-week vacation. He sends you a postcard from Tuscany: "Weather beautiful, food delicious, landscape sublime. See you in court when I get back." While he is away, you finish building your fence.

When Mr. Gnomemeister gets home, the fence is finished. One evening while you are sitting in your backyard enjoying your privacy, he climbs up on a concrete toadstool and yells at you over the top of the fence, "This fence is ugly and cheap looking. It's an eyesore. I'm going to get a Small Claims Court order making you tear it down!"

Can Small Claims Court make an order compelling you to tear down the fence? Give reasons for your answer.

5. **a.** What is a limitation period? What is the general rule in Ontario concerning limitation periods?

b. What happens if you wait until after the limitation period has expired to start an action?

6. **a.** What are special damages? Give an example.

b. What are general damages? Give an example.

7. Plaintiff wishes to collect $31,500.00 from Defendant for unpaid invoices on a running account.

a. Plaintiff wants to keep her costs down by collecting the amount owing in Small Claims Court. Is the claim within the Small Claims Court monetary jurisdiction?

b. What must Plaintiff do to bring the claim in Small Claims Court?

c. What steps should you as her paralegal adviser take?

8. Plaintiff lives and carries on business out of her home in Brampton. Defendant lives in Toronto and works in Markham. The contract between Plaintiff and Defendant was signed in Toronto, and the breach of contract occurred in Toronto. Where should Plaintiff commence her action? Give reasons for your answer, referring to the *Rules of the Small Claims Court*.

APPENDIX 3.1 Parrish v. Thurston: Plaintiff's Claim with Waiver of Excess

ONTARIO

Superior Court of Justice
Cour supérieure de justice

Plaintiff's Claim
Demande du demandeur
Form / *Formule* 7A Ont. Reg. No. / *Règl. de l'Ont.* : 258/98

Seal / *Sceau*

Brampton	SC-00-45678-00
Small Claims Court / *Cour des petites créances de*	Claim No. / *N° de la demande*
7755 Hurontario Street	
Brampton, Ontario	
L6W 4T6	
Address / *Adresse*	
905 456 4700	
Phone number / *Numéro de téléphone*	

Plaintiff No. 1 / *Demandeur n° 1*

☐ Additional plaintiff(s) listed on attached Form 1A.
Le ou les demandeurs additionnels sont mentionnés sur la formule 1A ci-jointe.

☐ Under 18 years of age.
Moins de 18 ans.

Last name, or name of company / *Nom de famille ou nom de la compagnie*		
Parrish		
First name / *Premier prénom*	Second name / *Deuxième prénom*	Also known as / *Également connu(e) sous le nom de*
Maxwell		
Address (street number, apt., unit) / *Adresse (numéro et rue, app., unité)*		
c/o Prior Mustafa LLP		
City/Town / *Cité/ville*	Province	Phone no. / *N° de téléphone*
Postal code / *Code postal*		Fax no. / *N° de télécopieur*
Representative / *Représentant(e)*		LSUC # / *N° du BHC*
Prior Mustafa LLP Attn: Marie Prior		######
Address (street number, apt., unit) / *Adresse (numéro et rue, app., unité)*		
22 County Court Boulevard		
City/Town / *Cité/ville*	Province	Phone no. / *N° de téléphone*
Brampton	ON	905 111 2222
Postal code / *Code postal*		Fax no. / *N° de télécopieur*
A1A 2B3		905 111 2233

Defendant No. 1 / *Défendeur n° 1*

☐ Additional defendant(s) listed on attached Form 1A.
Le ou les défendeurs additionnels sont mentionnés sur la formule 1A ci-jointe.

☐ Under 18 years of age.
Moins de 18 ans.

Last name, or name of company / *Nom de famille ou nom de la compagnie*		
Thurston		
First name / *Premier prénom*	Second name / *Deuxième prénom*	Also known as / *Également connu(e) sous le nom de*
Frank		
Address (street number, apt., unit) / *Adresse (numéro et rue, app., unité)*		
45 Labrador Court, Suite 103		
City/Town / *Cité/ville*	Province	Phone no. / *N° de téléphone*
Toronto	ON	416 333 4444
Postal code / *Code postal*		Fax no. / *N° de télécopieur*
M3C 4D5		
Representative / *Représentant(e)*		LSUC # / *N° du BHC*
Address (street number, apt., unit) / *Adresse (numéro et rue, app., unité)*		
City/Town / *Cité/ville*	Province	Phone no. / *N° de téléphone*
Postal code / *Code postal*		Fax no. / *N° de télécopieur*

SCR 7.01-7A (June 1, 2009 / *1er juin 2009*) CSD

APPENDIX 3.1   Parrish v. Thurston: Plaintiff's Claim with Waiver of Excess   *continued*

FORM / *FORMULE* 7A   PAGE 2   SC-00-45678-00
                                                                    Claim No. / *N° de la demande*

REASONS FOR CLAIM AND DETAILS / *MOTIFS DE LA DEMANDE ET PRÉCISIONS*

Explain what happened, including where and when. Then explain how much money you are claiming or what goods you want returned.
Expliquez ce qui s'est passé, en précisant où et quand. Ensuite indiquez la somme d'argent que vous demandez ou les biens dont vous demandez la restitution, explication à l'appui.

If you are relying on any documents, you **MUST** attach copies to the claim. If evidence is lost or unavailable, you **MUST** explain why it is not attached.
*Si vous vous appuyez sur des documents, vous **DEVEZ** en annexer des copies à la demande. Si une preuve est perdue ou n'est pas disponible, vous **DEVEZ** expliquer pourquoi elle n'est pas annexée.*

What happened?   See Schedule A attached and forming part of this claim
Where?
When?

Que s'est-il passé?
Où?
Quand?

Continued on next page / *Suite à la page suivante*

FORM / *FORMULE* 7A   PAGE 3   SC-00-45678-00
                                                                  Claim No. / *N° de la demande*

How much?	$	....25,000.00.....................	
Combien?		(Principal amount claimed / *Somme demandée*)	$

☐ ADDITIONAL PAGES ARE ATTACHED BECAUSE MORE ROOM WAS NEEDED.
   DES FEUILLES SUPPLÉMENTAIRES SONT ANNEXÉES EN RAISON DU MANQUE D'ESPACE.

The plaintiff also claims pre-judgment interest from 12%   under:
Le demandeur demande aussi des intérêts   (Date)   *conformément à :*
antérieurs au jugement de

(Check only   ☐ the *Courts of Justice Act*
one box /   *la* Loi sur les tribunaux judiciaires
Cochez une
seule case)   ☒ an agreement at the rate of 12   % per year
                      un accord au taux de   % par an

and post-judgment interest, and court costs.
et des intérêts postérieurs au jugement, ainsi que les dépens.

Prepared on: November 1   , 20 --   _____
Fait le :   (Signature of plaintiff or representative / *Signature du*
                                                         demandeur/de la demanderesse ou du/de la représentant(e))

Issued on: _____ , 20 ____   _____
Délivré le :   (Signature of clerk / *Signature du greffier*)

CAUTION TO DEFENDANT:	**IF YOU DO NOT FILE A DEFENCE** (Form 9A) with the court within twenty (20) calendar days after you have been served with this Plaintiff's Claim, judgment may be obtained without notice and enforced against you. Forms and self-help materials are available at the Small Claims Court and on the following website: www.ontariocourtforms.on.ca.
AVERTISSEMENT AU DÉFENDEUR :	*SI VOUS NE DÉPOSEZ PAS DE DÉFENSE (formule 9A) auprès du tribunal au plus tard vingt (20) jours civils après avoir reçu signification de la présente demande du demandeur, un jugement peut être obtenu sans préavis et être exécuté contre vous. Vous pouvez obtenir les formules et la documentation à l'usage du client à la Cour des petites créances et sur le site Web suivant : www.ontariocourtforms.on.ca.*

APPENDIX 3.1 **Parrish v. Thurston: Plaintiff's Claim with Waiver of Excess** *continued*

Schedule A

1. The plaintiff claims:

   (a) $25,000.00;

   (b) Pre- and post-judgment interest on the amount owing at a rate of 12% per annum commencing September 1, 20— until such time as all amounts owing are paid in full, in accordance with a promissory note dated March 1, 20— signed by Frank Thurston;

   (c) In the alternative, pre- and post-judgment interest in accordance with the *Courts of Justice Act*;

   (d) His costs of this action; and

   (e) Such further and other relief as this Honourable Court deems just.

2. The plaintiff at all material times resided in the City of Brampton in the Province of Ontario.

3. The defendant at all material times resided in the City of Brampton in the Province of Ontario. On or about October 1, 20—, the defendant moved to 45 Labrador Court, Suite 103, in the City of Toronto in the Province of Ontario.

4. Pursuant to a promissory note dated March 1, 20—, the plaintiff loaned to the defendant the sum of $27,000.00.

5. Particulars of the note are as follows:

   By his signature hereto, the undersigned FRANK THURSTON acknowledges receipt of the sum of TWENTY-SEVEN THOUSAND DOLLARS ($27,000.00), paid by Maxwell Parrish to Frank Thurston on today's date. The entire principal amount shall be due and payable in full on September 1, 20—. In the event of default by Frank Thurston, interest shall accrue at a rate of 12% per annum until such time as all amounts owing are paid in full or judgment is obtained, and post-judgment interest shall accrue on the judgment amount at a rate of 12% per annum until such time as the judgment is paid in full.

6. The defendant failed to pay the amount owing pursuant to the note on the due date of September 1, 20—.

7. In spite of repeated requests for payment, the defendant failed to make any payment whatsoever on account of the amount owing.

8. The plaintiff waives his right to claim any amounts owing over and above $25,000.00 to bring this action within the jurisdiction of this Honourable Court.

[Note: In a real proceeding, photocopies of any documents upon which the plaintiff intends to rely, including the promissory note dated March 1, 20— and any demand letters sent to the defendant, would be attached to the claim.]

Acting for the Plaintiff: Commencing the Action

4

LEARNING OUTCOMES

After reading this chapter, you will understand:

- Quantifying damages
- Pre- and post-judgment interest
- Naming other parties
- Joint and several liability
- Parties under disability
- Ethical advocacy
- Rules of pleading
- Service of a plaintiff's claim and other documents
- Amending a pleading

Introduction

When you have satisfied yourself that your client has a cause of action, and that Small Claims Court is the proper court in which to commence the action, the next step is to draft the plaintiff's claim. The **plaintiff's claim** (Form 7A) is the court document that sets out the names of the parties and their addresses for service, the amount of the claim, any other relief being sought, and the allegations of fact in support of the claim. It is essential that the information in the claim be complete and accurate. Parties must be properly named, and their addresses should be correct to the best of your knowledge. The amount owing should be properly calculated. The allegations in support of the claim should be set out in an organized narrative that includes all the facts the plaintiff relies on in support of the claim. These allegations of fact (also known as particulars) should be sufficient to allow the defendant to know the case that she has to respond to.

The proceeding is commenced when the plaintiff's claim, together with a copy for each named party including the defendant, is taken to the office of the Small Claims Court with territorial jurisdiction, and issued by the clerk. The claim is issued when the clerk dates, signs, and seals it, and assigns a court file number ("Claim No." on the Form 7A). The court file number assigned by the clerk is the unique identifier for that court proceeding in that territorial jurisdiction. It must appear on all documents filed in the proceeding. The plaintiff has six months from the date of issuing the claim to serve the other parties. In appropriate circumstances, the court may extend the time for service.

Calculating Damages

Quantifying, or calculating, damages was discussed in Chapter 3, in the context of deciding whether your client's case falls within the Small Claims Court monetary jurisdiction. When calculating damages, you must determine all of the different kinds of damage or harm that the plaintiff has suffered because of the defendant's alleged wrongdoing. There must be **causation** between the damage claimed and the defendant's actions—in other words, for damages to be awarded to the plaintiff, the evidence must establish that the harm or loss suffered by the plaintiff resulted from the defendant's actions or negligence. For **special damages** (also called **liquidated damages**), you should be able to calculate the amounts owing with some precision, based on the documentary evidence and/or an arithmetical calculation. The money values assigned must be supported by the allegations of fact in the plaintiff's claim, by the documentary evidence attached to the plaintiff's claim or disclosed later on in the proceeding to other parties, and by the evidence at trial.

Calculating Damages

In a claim for a debt or fixed amount (also known as a **liquidated claim**), the amount owing may be proven by documents such as unpaid invoices, a credit card agreement, or a promissory note, or calculated using an arithmetical formula. A

promissory note is a promise to pay that is signed and dated by the debtor. It should contain, at a minimum, the following terms: the names of the payor and the debtor; the amount advanced to the debtor and the date on which it was advanced; and the terms of the loan, including payment terms, interest rates, penalties on default, and so on. So long as there is undisputed documentary evidence supporting the amount claimed, the amount of a liquidated claim does not require valuation by a court based on additional evidence.

General damages (also known as **unliquidated damages**) are amounts that are not fixed and quantifiable based on objective evidence. General damages must be assessed by the court based on all of the evidence and on criteria established by other court decisions. Some examples of actions where general damages may be claimed are actions for personal injury, defamation, and, in some cases, wrongful dismissal.

General damages are intended to compensate the plaintiff for pecuniary and non-pecuniary loss. **Pecuniary damages** are damages awarded for losses that can be estimated in money terms. In the case of a chronic injury, for example, pecuniary damages might be awarded to the plaintiff for loss of future earning capacity, and cost of future care. **Non-pecuniary damages** are damages awarded for types of harm that are real and serious, but difficult to assign a money value to. Examples of types of non-pecuniary damages are:

- physical and mental pain and suffering
- loss of amenities of life—that is, loss of the ability to engage in and enjoy certain activities as a result of the harm suffered
- loss of expectation of life—that is, loss of pleasure of normal living as a result of the harm suffered.

Both special (liquidated) and general (unliquidated) damages may be claimed in the same action.

BOX 4.1 Dante v. Herrero: Calculating Damages

Fact Situation

You work for Prior Mustafa LLP, 22 County Court Boulevard, Brampton, Ontario A1A 2B3 TEL: 905 111 2222 FAX: 905 111 2233.

Your client is Francesca Dante. Ms. Dante lives at 98 Calendar Court, Mississauga, Ontario X2X 3Y4 TEL: 905 222 3333.

On December 1, 20—, Ms. Dante loaned $4,000.00 to her best friend, Suzanne Herrero. Ms. Herrero lives at 105 Morton Avenue, Mississauga, Ontario L2X 4Y5. The loan is secured by a promissory note dated December 1, 20— signed by Ms. Herrero. The terms of the note are as follows:

By her signature hereto, the undersigned SUZANNE HERRERO acknowledges receipt of the sum of FOUR THOUSAND DOLLARS ($4,000.00), paid by Francesca Dante to Suzanne Herrero on today's date. Interest shall be payable on said sum at a rate of 12% per annum, commencing December 1, 20—. The entire principal amount plus interest thereon shall be due and payable in full on March 1, 20—. In the event of default by Suzanne Herrero, interest shall continue to accrue on the principal amount at a rate of 12% per annum until such time as all amounts owing are paid in full or judgment is obtained, and post-judgment interest shall accrue on the judgment amount, including costs, at a rate of 12% per annum until such time as the amount owing is paid in full.

On March 1, 20—, Ms. Herrero gave Ms. Dante a cheque in the amount of $4,120.00, on account of the principal owing of $4,000.00 plus three months' interest of $120.00. Ms. Dante received a notice from her bank that the cheque had been returned because of insufficient funds.

Ms. Dante comes to see you on March 27, 20—. She has phoned and emailed Ms. Herrero several times to demand payment, but has received no response. She wants to commence an action against Ms. Herrero for the amount owing.

Calculating Damages

This is a straightforward case of an unpaid loan of money. Fortunately, Ms. Dante had the good sense to write down the terms of the loan in the promissory note signed by Ms. Herrero. When calculating the amount owing, all you have to do is refer to the terms of the note.

In a Small Claims Court proceeding, the plaintiff's claim will be drafted and issued long before the matter actually gets to trial. When drafting the plaintiff's claim, you should plead all special damages that you know of at that time. The documentary disclosure attached to the plaintiff's claim should support the special damages claimed. The original documents should be filed in the documents subfile of the client file. You will need them as evidence at trial. If you do not have original documents, photocopies may be admitted as evidence by the court at trial so long as the presiding judge is satisfied as to their authenticity (*Courts of Justice Act*, s. 27(5)).

As the matter progresses, the plaintiff may become entitled to additional special damages. You should advise the other side and provide ongoing documentary disclosure in support of any additional special damages claimed. If the matter goes to trial, all written statements, documents, and records upon which you intend to rely at trial must be served on the other parties no later than 30 days before the trial date in the notice of trial (Rule 18.02(1) of the *Rules of the Small Claims Court*).

General damages are more speculative in nature. To the extent that it is possible, they must be calculated, itemized, and explained based on the evidence and accepted criteria established in the jurisprudence.

BOX 4.2 Chong v. Kingman: Calculating Damages

Fact Situation

You work for Prior Mustafa LLP, 22 County Court Boulevard, Brampton, Ontario A1A 2B3 TEL: 905 111 2222 FAX: 905 111 2233. Your client is Mrs. Maxine Chong. Mrs. Chong is a 62-year-old widow who lives alone. Her children are both married. They live in Alberta and British Columbia. She has a legal basement apartment in her house at 67 Harmony Avenue, Toronto, Ontario M4J 1J3. After her last tenant left, she did not rent out the apartment for almost a year; but when she received a notice of property tax increase from the municipality, she decided she needed the income to supplement her existing income.

Pursuant to a residential tenancy agreement (apartment lease) dated January 13, 20—, Mrs. Chong agreed to lease the basement apartment to LeeAnn Kingman, for a tenancy commencing February 1, 20— at a monthly rent of $775.00, including water, heat, and hydro. Ms. Kingman did not pay a last month's rent deposit. She told Mrs. Chong she had just found a new job after several months of unemployment and was trying to put her life back together. She seemed like a nice person and Mrs. Chong felt sorry for her. Mrs. Chong accepted Ms. Kingman's personal cheque for the first month's rent, and told her to pay the last month's rent when she had the money.

Ms. Kingman's rent cheque for February 1 was returned for insufficient funds. When Mrs. Chong asked her for a replacement cheque, Ms. Kingman became extremely abusive. She screamed and shouted and ended up slamming the apartment door in Mrs. Chong's face. That evening, she played music very loud until one o'clock in the morning. Mrs. Chong could not sleep. She was afraid the neighbours would complain to the police. When she pounded on the floor to get the music to stop, Ms. Kingman pounded back, screaming abuse and obscenities. Eventually, she turned the music off, but for the rest of the night there were sounds of banging and crashing from the basement. Mrs. Chong was terrified. "She had access to my washer, my dryer, my furnace, the fuse box, everything, down there," she tells you. "I thought she would set the house on fire."

Ms. Kingman never paid the February rent. When Mrs. Chong tried to approach her about it, she became extremely abusive. On several occasions, she came upstairs and stood outside Mrs. Chong's kitchen door, which opened onto the side entrance that Ms. Kingman used. She would pound on the door and scream. She would threaten to report Mrs. Chong to the Ontario Human Rights Tribunal for abuse and discrimination.

Ms. Kingman did not pay the rent for March. Mrs. Chong did nothing because she was afraid of how Ms. Kingman might react. She felt as if she did not own her house any more. There was always loud music, banging, and shouting from the basement, especially from around midnight until two or three o'clock in the morning.

Mrs. Chong began keeping the kitchen door locked. She could not sleep and she lost her appetite. She suffered from headaches and anxiety attacks. If she went out, she dreaded going home. Her physician prescribed medication for anxiety and insomnia.

When Ms. Kingman did not pay the April rent, Mrs. Chong called her daughter, Alice, in Penticton. When Alice heard about the situation, she said, "I'm catching the next plane to Toronto."

Alice arrived late on April 15. On April 16, she got in touch with your office. You drafted and served a Form N4—Notice to End a Tenancy Early for Non-Payment of Rent on Ms. Kingman. On April 17, Ms. Kingman vacated the apartment, taking the keys to the side entrance and the basement apartment with her. She left the basement apartment in a filthy state. It cost Mrs. Chong $1,059.00 to have a contractor come in to clean it, replace the carpet, repair the damage, and repaint. She had to pay a locksmith $125.00 to rekey the locks.

Alice stayed long enough to find Mrs. Chong a reliable, quiet tenant for the basement apartment. The new tenant moved in on June 1. There have been no more problems. Mrs. Chong has stopped taking anxiety medication, although she continues to have anxiety attacks. She still needs medication to sleep. "I've suffered so much," she says. "It's too much for a woman of my age to put up with someone like that."

On her tenancy application, Ms. Kingman stated that she is employed by a local non-governmental organization at a salary of $36,500.00 per year. You have confirmed that she is still employed by this organization. You have advised Mrs. Chong of this. She has instructed you to commence a Small Claims Court action against Ms. Kingman.

Calculating Damages—Special Damages

Mrs. Chong's special damages for all losses and out-of-pocket expenses connected to Ms. Kingman's wrongdoing are set out in the table below. Photocopies of documentation supporting these amounts should be attached to the plaintiff's claim.

If Mrs. Chong continues to incur special damages (such as additional prescription costs) as the matter progresses, you must advise the other side and produce documentary evidence in support of the additional special damages claimed as early as possible in the proceeding, and no later than 30 days before the trial date in the notice of trial (Rule 18.02(1)). If her claim includes future special damages (such as prescription costs) that will be incurred after the trial date, you must disclose this to the other side as well. There must be evidence to support this claim at trial.

Calculating Damages—General Damages

Mrs. Chong's claim for general damages is intended to compensate her for current and future pain, suffering, and loss of enjoyment of life connected with Ms. Kingman's tenancy. Because of the speculative nature of general damages, you should ask for total damages (including the amount owing for special damages as of the date of issuing the claim) in the amount of $25,000.00. This will give the court some room to award Mrs. Chong general damages as well as current and future special damages, if proven.

When drafting Mrs. Chong's claim, you must consider the different grounds upon which she may recover general damages. Based on the evidence, what types of pecuniary damages may she claim, if any? What types of non-pecuniary damages is she entitled to, if any? The plaintiff's claim should contain allegations of fact supporting the different types of damages sought to be recovered.

CATEGORY OF SPECIAL DAMAGES	AMOUNT OWING	SUPPORTING DOCUMENTATION
Loss of income: unpaid rent	Three months of unpaid rent at $775.00 per month = $2,325.00	• Residential tenancy agreement dated January 13, 20— • Form N4—Notice to End a Tenancy Early for Non-Payment of Rent
Cost of prescriptions	$183.47	Pharmacist invoices
Cost of repairs	$1,059.00	Invoice from contractor, marked Paid
Rekeying locks	$125.00	Invoice from locksmith, marked Paid
Cost of drafting and serving N4	$300.00	Invoice from Prior Mustafa LLP
Total as of date of issuing plaintiff's claim	$3,992.47	

Pre- and Post-judgment Interest

When there is no agreement stating otherwise, pre- and post-judgment interest is determined in accordance with the *Courts of Justice Act*, ss. 127 to 130:

Definitions

127(1) In this section and in sections 128 and 129,

"bank rate" means the bank rate established by the Bank of Canada as the minimum rate at which the Bank of Canada makes short-term advances to banks listed in Schedule I to the *Bank Act* (Canada);

"date of the order" means the date the order is made, even if the order is not entered or enforceable on that date, or the order is varied on appeal, and in the case of an order directing a reference, the date the report on the reference is confirmed;

"postjudgment interest rate" means the bank rate at the end of the first day of the last month of the quarter preceding the quarter in which the date of the order falls, rounded to the next higher whole number where the bank rate includes a fraction, plus 1 per cent;

"prejudgment interest rate" means the bank rate at the end of the first day of the last month of the quarter preceding the quarter in which the proceeding was commenced, rounded to the nearest tenth of a percentage point;

"quarter" means the three-month period ending with the 31st day of March, 30th day of June, 30th day of September or 31st day of December.

Calculation and publication of interest rates

(2) After the first day of the last month of each quarter, a person designated by the Deputy Attorney General shall forthwith,

(a) determine the prejudgment and postjudgment interest rate for the next quarter; and

(b) publish in the prescribed manner a table showing the rate determined under clause (a) for the next quarter and the rates determined under clause (a) or under a predecessor of that clause for all the previous quarters during the preceding 10 years.

Regulations

(3) The Attorney General may, by regulation, prescribe the manner in which the table described in clause (2)(b) is to be published.

Prejudgment interest

128(1) A person who is entitled to an order for the payment of money is entitled to claim and have included in the order an award of interest thereon at the prejudgment interest rate, calculated from the date the cause of action arose to the date of the order.

Exception for non-pecuniary loss on personal injury

(2) Despite subsection (1), the rate of interest on damages for non-pecuniary loss in an action for personal injury shall be the rate determined by the rules of court made under clause 66(2)(w).

Special damages

(3) If the order includes an amount for past pecuniary loss, the interest calculated under subsection (1) shall be calculated on the total past pecuniary loss at the end of each six-month period and at the date of the order.

Exclusion

(4) Interest shall not be awarded under subsection (1),

   (a) on exemplary or punitive damages;

   (b) on interest accruing under this section;

   (c) on an award of costs in the proceeding;

   (d) on that part of the order that represents pecuniary loss arising after the date of the order and that is identified by a finding of the court;

   (e) with respect to the amount of any advance payment that has been made towards settlement of the claim, for the period after the advance payment has been made;

   (f) where the order is made on consent, except by consent of the debtor; or

   (g) where interest is payable by a right other than under this section.

Postjudgment interest

129(1) Money owing under an order, including costs to be assessed or costs fixed by the court, bears interest at the postjudgment interest rate, calculated from the date of the order.

Interest on periodic payments

(2) Where an order provides for periodic payments, each payment in default shall bear interest only from the date of default.

Interest on orders originating outside Ontario

(3) Where an order is based on an order given outside Ontario or an order of a court outside Ontario is filed with a court in Ontario for the purpose of enforcement, money owing under the order bears interest at the rate, if any, applicable to the order given outside Ontario by the law of the place where it was given.

Costs assessed without order

(4) Where costs are assessed without an order, the costs bear interest at the postjudgment interest rate in the same manner as if an order were made for the payment of costs on the date the person to whom the costs are payable became entitled to the costs.

Other provision for interest

(5) Interest shall not be awarded under this section where interest is payable by a right other than under this section.

Discretion of court

130(1) The court may, where it considers it just to do so, in respect of the whole or any part of the amount on which interest is payable under section 128 or 129,

   (a) disallow interest under either section;

   (b) allow interest at a rate higher or lower than that provided in either section;

   (c) allow interest for a period other than that provided in either section.

Idem

(2) For the purpose of subsection (1), the court shall take into account,

(a) changes in market interest rates;

(b) the circumstances of the case;

(c) the fact that an advance payment was made;

(d) the circumstances of medical disclosure by the plaintiff;

(e) the amount claimed and the amount recovered in the proceeding;

(f) the conduct of any party that tended to shorten or to lengthen unnecessarily the duration of the proceeding; and

(g) any other relevant consideration.

Pre-judgment interest accrues on the amount claimed commencing on the date of default and ending on the date of judgment. **Post-judgment interest** accrues on the judgment amount—that is, the amount, including costs, awarded to a successful party by a court—until such time as all amounts owing have been paid in full.

The **date of default** is the date the cause of action arose—that is, the date the plaintiff discovered the harm giving rise to the action. The **cause of action** is the factual and legal grounds for seeking a remedy from a court. In an action for recovery of a debt, the date of default will be the date that the defendant failed to make a payment of money.

Page 3 of the plaintiff's claim (Form 7A) (shown in Figure 4.3) requests prejudgment interest from the date of default in accordance with the *Courts of Justice Act* or an agreement. If there is no written agreement, or if the written agreement is silent as to the rate of interest that applies in the event of a default, then pre- and post-judgment interest may be claimed at the rates set out in s. 127(1) of the *Courts of Justice Act*. Pre- and post-judgment interest rates are published quarterly online in the Court Services link at the website of the Attorney General for Ontario (http:// www.attorneygeneral.jus.gov.on.ca).

If you are asking for pre-judgment interest in accordance with a written agreement (such as a credit card agreement or a promissory note), you must check that box and state the contractual interest rate.

Note that, under s. 130 of the *Courts of Justice Act*, a court may, where it considers it just to do so, in respect of the whole or any part of the amount on which interest is payable under s. 128 or 129,

(a) disallow interest under either section;

(b) allow interest at a rate higher or lower than that provided in either section;

(c) allow interest for a period other than that provided in either section.

What If the Date the Cause of Action Arose Cannot Easily Be Determined?

In liquidated claims, such as an action for recovery of a debt, the date of default is usually easy to determine, because the event that triggers the cause of action is failure to pay by the defendant. In **unliquidated claims**, the acts of wrongdoing giving rise to the cause of action may accrue over a period of time. For example, in *Chong v. Kingman* (the details of which are set out in Box 4.2 above), the defendant, Ms. Kingman,

FIGURE 4.1 Plaintiff's Claim: Pre- and Post-judgment Interest (Form 7A)

FORM / *FORMULE* 7A	**PAGE 3**

Claim No. / *N° de la demande*

How much? $ ....
Combien? (Principal amount claimed / *Somme demandée*) $

☐ ADDITIONAL PAGES ARE ATTACHED BECAUSE MORE ROOM WAS NEEDED.
DES FEUILLES SUPPLÉMENTAIRES SONT ANNEXÉES EN RAISON DU MANQUE D'ESPACE.

The plaintiff also claims pre-judgment interest from _____ under:
Le demandeur demande aussi des intérêts (Date) *conformément à :*
antérieurs au jugement de

(Check only ☐ the *Courts of Justice Act*
one box / *la* Loi sur les tribunaux judiciaires
Cochez une
seule case) ☐ an agreement at the rate of _____ % per year
un accord au taux de % par an

and post-judgment interest, and court costs.
et des intérêts postérieurs au jugement, ainsi que les dépens.

Prepared on: _____ , 20 _____ _____
Fait le : (Signature of plaintiff or representative / *Signature du*
demandeur/de la demanderesse ou du/de la représentant(e))

Issued on: _____ , 20 _____ _____
Délivré le : (Signature of clerk / *Signature du greffier*)

defaulted on the rent over a period of three months. The defendant's other wrongful acts took place at intervals during the period of her tenancy. Because these wrongful acts took place over time, the types and severity of the damage allegedly suffered by Mrs. Chong changed.

When dealing with this type of situation, you should consider using the date of the first wrongful act by the defendant as the date when pre-judgment interest commences for purposes of filling out page 3 of the plaintiff's claim.

Naming Parties to the Proceeding

Introduction

When completing the plaintiff's claim, you must name all parties to the proceeding by their complete legal name or names, along with their contact information. When you are naming the plaintiff, consider your duty of confidentiality under Paralegal Rule 3.02. Do not state the plaintiff's address, telephone number, and so on, even though the other party or parties may have knowledge of that information, or can easily look it up online. See Appendix 4.3.

If you are representing more than one plaintiff, any additional plaintiffs must be listed on an additional parties form (Form 1A). If there is more than one defendant, any additional defendants must be listed on an additional parties form. When naming a self-represented party who is a co-plaintiff or a defendant, you must state the party's correct name, properly spelled, and the party's correct address for service, along with telephone and fax numbers if you have them. When naming a represented party who is a co-plaintiff or a defendant, you must state their correct legal name or names, along with the firm name, address, and other contact information of their representative.

Naming Individual Defendants

The complete legal names of individual defendants must be stated on the claim, spelled in their correct form. Never use an initial instead of a proper name. For example, Brian Allan Green should be named as Brian Allan Green, not as Brian A. Green or B.A. Green. If you misspell a defendant's name, or state an incorrect name, you have named the wrong person, and your judgment will be unenforceable against the person you intended to sue. You will have to take steps to correct the error by amending the claim under Rule 12, resulting in additional expense and delay.

If an individual defendant uses more than one name, you should include all of them on the plaintiff's claim. The Form 7A contains an "Also known as" field for this purpose. All names used by the defendant must be spelled correctly. In the plaintiff's claim, reasons must be provided for the plaintiff's allegation that the defendant uses two or more names.

You must make best efforts to ensure that correct, current addresses for all defendants are stated on the plaintiff's claim. Some clients collect essential information about the persons with whom they do business before they advance money, approve a tenancy agreement, or sell a computer to that person. They already have the defendant's correct name, address, and so on, verified by documentation, when they approach you about commencing an action. They may also have a consumer report, obtained with the defendant's informed, written consent, showing what other debts the defendant owes, and the defendant's credit ranking.

If the client did not collect this information in the ordinary course of business, or if it is the kind of claim where that information would not necessarily have been obtained ahead of time (for example, damage to property or personal injury), you must confirm, at a minimum, the defendant's full name correctly spelled and the defendant's correct address for purposes of completing the plaintiff's claim.

If the defendant owns a vehicle or has a driver's licence, and you know the defendant's driver's licence number, or the plate number or vehicle identification number of the vehicle, you can obtain the defendant's name and other information online at the ServiceOntario website by requesting an uncertified three-year statement of driving record or uncertified vehicle records. If you are an authorized requester, your search results will provide the address of the current owner of the vehicle. Search fees are payable online by credit card.

There are a number of online resources you can use to search for information about the defendant. In many cases you need the correct name and/or a current telephone number. Some sites require payment of a fee before full search results will be disclosed. Websites and the services they provide evolve over time. See Chapter 3 at page 73 for a detailed discussion of some of these services.

Naming Business Defendants

Sole Proprietorships (Rule 5.06)

A **sole proprietorship** is an unincorporated business owned and operated by one individual with the objective of making a profit. There is no legal separation between the owner and the business—the business has no separate legal existence from the owner. This means that the business cannot sue or be sued, nor can it enter into contracts. It is the owner who enters into contracts and assumes all liability for the business. The owner is personally responsible for paying the debts of the business.

If the plaintiff is a sole proprietorship operating under a business name, you may commence litigation on behalf of the plaintiff using the plaintiff's business name (Rule 5.06(1)).

If the defendant is a sole proprietorship operating under a business name, you should name the defendant using the owner's name, carrying on business under the business name; and name the business using the registered business name as an additional party on a separate Form 1A.1. By naming both the individual owner and the name of the business, the plaintiff preserves her right to enforce her judgment against the assets of both the owner and the business.

Alternatively, you may name the business as the defendant on the plaintiff's claim using its correct business name and address. To preserve the plaintiff's right to enforce her judgment against the assets of both the owner and the business, in the claim you should request an order that the judgment be enforceable personally against the owner as proprietor of the business. You may then serve the claim on the proprietor along with a Notice to Alleged Partner (Form 5A) (Rules 5.03(1), 5.06(2)).

Under the Ontario *Business Names Act*, a business that carries on business in Ontario using a name other than that of its owner or owners must register the business name with the Companies and Personal Property Security Branch of the Ministry of Government Services. In the case of a sole proprietorship, the business name search will provide you with the registered business name and the name of the sole proprietor carrying on business under that name. Business name searches can be carried out online at the ServiceOntario website, or by using a commercial online search service such as Cyberbahn.

BOX 4.3 Naming a Defendant Who Is a Sole Proprietor

Fact Situation

Plaintiff wishes to commence an action for unpaid invoices against an unincorporated business owned by Benvenuto Cellini, operating under the business name of Ben's Funeral Monuments. On page 1 of the plaintiff's claim (Form 7A), the defendant may be named as: Benvenuto Cellini, carrying on business as Ben's Funeral Monuments. On a separate Form 1A.1, the defendant will be named as Ben's Funeral Monuments.

Alternatively, Plaintiff may name the defendant on the plaintiff's claim as Ben's Funeral Monuments. To preserve his right to enforce the judgment against the assets of both Benvenuto Cellini and Ben's Funeral Monuments, in the claim Plaintiff should request an order that the judgment be enforceable personally against the owner as proprietor of the business. Plaintiff may then serve the claim on Benvenuto Cellini along with a Notice to Alleged Partner (Form 5A).

Partnerships (Rule 5)

GENERAL

A **partnership** is an unincorporated business that is owned and operated by two or more persons with the objective of making a profit. Like a sole proprietorship, a partnership has no separate legal existence from its owners, the partners. In a general partnership, the partners are jointly and severally liable for all debts, obligations, and liabilities of the partnership. **Joint and several liability** means that each partner in a general partnership is personally liable to the full extent of any debt, obligation, or liability incurred by other partners or partnership employees or agents acting in the ordinary course of the partnership business.

Partners may allocate liability among themselves and specify other terms and conditions of the partnership by means of a **partnership agreement**. However, the partnership agreement is binding only upon the partners themselves as parties to the agreement. If Rule 5.03 (discussed below) is complied with, a successful plaintiff may enforce her judgment against the assets of any or all of the partners in a general partnership, plus any assets of the partnership firm.

Different rules apply to a limited partnership formed under the *Limited Partnerships Act*. In a limited partnership, some partners are general partners, and some partners are limited partners. A limited partner is not liable for the obligations of the limited partnership except in respect of the value of money and other property the limited partner contributes to the limited partnership.

COMMENCING AN ACTION AGAINST A PARTNERSHIP

A partnership that is a plaintiff may commence a proceeding using the firm name of the partnership (Rule 5.01).

A proceeding against a defendant that is a partnership may be commenced using the firm name of the partnership (Rule 5.01). You may confirm the correct business name of the partnership under the Ontario *Business Names Act*. The business name search will also provide you with the names of the partners.

In a proceeding where the firm name is used to name the defendant partnership, any court order will be made using the firm name, and is enforceable against the firm's property only—that is, the assets of the business, as opposed to those of the individual partners (Rule 5.05(1)). If the plaintiff serves the persons who were partners at the material time with copies of the plaintiff's claim, along with notices to alleged partners (Form 5A), she may then enforce any judgment against the assets of the partnership firm and the assets of all partners so served (Rules 5.03 and 5.05(2)).

If a proceeding is commenced against a partnership using the firm name, the partnership's defence shall be delivered in the firm name and no person who admits being a partner at any material time may defend the proceeding separately, except with leave of the court (Rule 5.02).

In this context, the material time is the time at which the cause of action arose—that is, the time period when the partnership engaged in the actions that are the basis for the claim. How does the plaintiff find out the names of the partners in the partnership at the material time? Rule 5.04(1) states that any party, including the plaintiff, may serve a notice requiring the partners to disclose immediately in writing the names and addresses of all partners belonging to the partnership at the time specified in the notice (Rule 5.04(1)).

A person who has been served with a notice to alleged partner is deemed to have been a partner at the material time unless the person delivers a defence separately from the defence of the partnership firm, denying having been a partner at the material time (Rule 5.03(2)).

You will find a sample Form 5A—Notice to Alleged Partner at Appendix 4.1.

Corporations

GENERAL

A corporation is a separate legal entity from its owners, the shareholders. This arrangement is intended to protect the corporation's shareholders from risks, obligations, and liabilities incurred by the corporation in the course of doing business. Because the personal assets of the shareholders are not available to satisfy debts, obligations, and liabilities incurred by the corporation, a court order obtained against a corporation must be enforced against the assets of the corporation.

Corporations may be private or public. The shares of a private corporation (also known as a closely held corporation) are held by a small group of people who usually know each other, such as family members. The shares of private corporations are not traded on public stock exchanges.

Public corporations offer their shares for sale to the public on stock exchanges. Generally speaking, their purpose is the same as that of privately held companies— that is, to run a business or businesses for profit.

Governmental organizations may also form corporations. For example, municipalities are usually incorporated.

Words such as "Inc.," "Incorporated," "Corporation," "Ltd.," or "Limited" indicate a corporate entity.

Whether they are governmental, public, or private, corporations are legal persons who can sue and be sued. Like any other party to a proceeding, corporations must be identified by their correct name on the plaintiff's claim.

BACKGROUND SEARCHES

Some corporations register a unique business name at the time that they become incorporated, and then carry on business under their registered corporate name. A corporation that has a registered name is sometimes called a "named company."

A corporation may use the registration number assigned by the Companies Branch at the time it is incorporated. A corporation that uses its registration number in its registered corporate name is sometimes called a "numbered company." The registration number must be used in conjunction with other words. For example, the name of a numbered company under the Ontario *Business Corporations Act*, might look something like this: 123456 Ontario Limited.

Both named and numbered companies may carry on business under a business name. To obtain the name of the person who registered the business name, you should carry out a *Business Names Act* search. If the person turns out to be a named or numbered company carrying on business under a business name, you can obtain further information about the corporate owner by means of a corporate profile search. The corporate profile search will confirm the registered corporation name, current and expired business names, head office address, names of officers and directors, and so on.

A named company operating under a business name should be named on the plaintiff's claim using the legal corporate name and the business name. For example, a corporate defendant whose registered corporate name is Patricia's Purrfect Pets Incorporated and whose registered business name is Patz Katz & Dogz will be named on a plaintiff's claim as Patricia's Purrfect Pets Incorporated c.o.b. Patz Katz & Dogz.

A numbered company operating under a business name should be named on the plaintiff's claim using the legal corporate name and the business name. For example, a corporate defendant whose registered corporate name is 123456 Ontario Limited and whose registered business name is Flora's Fabulous Flowers will be named on a plaintiff's claim as 123456 Ontario Limited c.o.b. Flora's Fabulous Flowers.

Corporate searches and business name searches can be done in person at the Companies Branch, or online at the Ministry of Government Services website or by using an online commercial search service such as Cyberbahn.

BOX 4.4 Who Is the Defendant?

Example 1

Nekea Marshall and Vladimir Oblomov are the sole owners and shareholders of a numbered company, 334445 Ontario Inc. 334445 Ontario Inc. owns a pet grooming and boarding facility, whose business name is Camp Happy Puppy. Ms. Marshall and Mr. Oblomov run Camp Happy Puppy.

Plaintiff boards her English sheepdog, Gerald, at Camp Happy Puppy for two weeks while she is away in Europe on business. When she gets back from Europe and goes to pick up Gerald, she finds him cowering in his cage. He seems depressed and nervous. When she gets him home, he refuses to eat, and she notices that he is limping. The next day, she takes Gerald to the vet. The vet examines Gerald, and tells Plaintiff that he appears to have been in at least one fight, which caused the injury to his leg. There are also other bites that are still healing. "They're hard to see because of all the hair," the vet says. "But some of them are infected. We'll put him on antibiotics, and keep him here for a couple of days, under observation."

In the end, some surgery is required. The vet's services cost Plaintiff $1,155.00.

Plaintiff wants to sue Camp Happy Puppy for the cost of the vet bill and for recovery of the boarding costs, on grounds that Gerald's injuries were a direct result of the negligence or carelessness of Camp Happy Puppy, its agents and employees, and that, while in Camp Happy Puppy's care, Gerald did not experience the safe, healthy environment that Camp Happy Puppy advertised.

WHO IS THE DEFENDANT?

Camp Happy Puppy is the business name of a business owned by 334445 Ontario Inc. As owner, 334445 Ontario Inc. is liable for any wrongdoing or negligence on the part of Camp Happy Puppy and its agents or employees.

Although they own the numbered company, Nekea Marshall and Vladimir Oblomov cannot be added as co-defendants, because they are not co-owners of the business itself. 334445 Ontario Inc. is the owner of the business.

Example 2

Plaintiff loans $8,000.00 to 445556 Ontario Inc., a corporation whose president and sole shareholder is Plaintiff's cousin, Ahmed Kabir. The money is intended to help Cousin Ahmed out with some cash-flow problems he has been having with his restaurant, Avocado Bistro. 445556 Ontario Inc. is the owner of Avocado Bistro. Before she advances the money to 445556 Ontario Inc., Plaintiff requires Cousin Ahmed to sign a personal guarantee for the loan.

The numbered company fails to make any payments on account of the loan, in spite of Plaintiff's repeated demands. Plaintiff wants to commence a Small Claims Court proceeding to recover the amount owing.

WHO IS THE DEFENDANT?

445556 Ontario Inc. is the recipient of the loan, and will therefore be named as the defendant on the plaintiff's claim. Plaintiff should consider obtaining a corporate profile report to confirm the company's registered corporate name, its head office address (for purposes of service), its officers and directors, its date of registration, and so on. The corporate profile search will also confirm that 445556 Ontario Inc. registered Avocado Bistro as its business name under the *Business Names Act*. 445556 Ontario Inc. will be named on the claim as "445556 Ontario Inc. c.o.b. Avocado Bistro."

Can Cousin Ahmed be added as a co-defendant in his capacity as president and sole shareholder of 445556 Ontario Inc.? No, he cannot. The general rule is that directors and shareholders of a corporation are not parties to a proceeding against a corporation, who is a separate legal person from its managers and owners.

Can Cousin Ahmed be added as a co-defendant in any capacity? Yes, he can be added as a co-defendant in his capacity as guarantor of the loan. His name and address for service will appear on the additional parties form (Form 1A).

The plaintiff's claim must state Plaintiff's grounds for adding Cousin Ahmed as a co-defendant, and a photocopy of the guarantee should be attached to the claim.

Party Under Disability (Rule 4)

What Is a Party Under Disability?

The definition of "disability" is found at Rule 1.02(1).

1.02(1) In these rules, …

"disability," where used in respect of a person or party, means that the person or party is,

(a) a minor,

(b) mentally incapable within the meaning of section 6 or 45 of the *Substitute Decisions Act, 1992* in respect of an issue in the proceeding, whether the person or party has a guardian or not, or

(c) an absentee within the meaning of the *Absentees Act*.

A person or party will be deemed to be under disability in the following circumstances:

1. The person is a minor. A minor is a person under the age of majority. The age of majority in Ontario is 18 years of age.

2. The person is mentally incapable. A person may lack capacity with respect to managing property or personal care, or both. A person is incapable of managing property if the person is not able to understand information that is relevant to making a decision in the management of his or her property, or is not able to appreciate the reasonably foreseeable consequences of a decision or lack of decision (*Substitute Decisions Act, 1992*). A person is incapable of personal care if the person is not able to understand information that is relevant to making a decision concerning his or her own health care, nutrition, shelter, clothing, hygiene or safety, or is not able to appreciate the reasonably foreseeable consequences of a decision or lack of decision (*Substitute Decisions Act, 1992*, s. 45).

3. The person is an absentee as defined in s. 1 of the *Absentees Act*. An absentee means a person who, having had his or her usual place of residence or domicile in Ontario, has disappeared, whose whereabouts is unknown, and as to whom there is no knowledge as to whether he or she is alive or dead.

Parties under disability are not necessarily physically or psychologically disabled (although they may be both). The disability is legal. Persons under disability are considered to lack legal capability to perform certain acts—for example, to understand legal advice and make informed decisions based on that understanding. For this reason, a **litigation guardian** must be appointed to act on behalf of a person under disability.

There is one exception to the general rule that a person under disability must have a litigation guardian. Rule 4.01(2) provides that a minor may sue for any sum not exceeding $500.00 as if he or she were of full age.

The limitation period for commencing an action established by s. 4 of the *Limitations Act, 2002* does not run during any period during which the plaintiff is

- a minor and is not represented by a litigation guardian in relation to the claim (*Limitations Act, 2002*, s. 6); or
- is incapable of commencing a proceeding in respect of the claim because of his or her physical, mental, or psychological condition, and is not represented by a litigation guardian in relation to the claim (*Limitations Act, 2002*, s. 7).

A person under disability may not be noted in default for failure to file a defence within the prescribed time except with leave of the court (Rule 11.01(2)).

If an action has been brought against a person under disability and the action has not been defended by a litigation guardian, the court may **set aside** the noting of default or any judgment against the person under disability on such terms as are just, and may set aside any step that has been taken to enforce the judgment (Rule. 4.06).

The Role of a Litigation Guardian

A litigation guardian is a competent person who undertakes to commence or continue a legal proceeding on behalf of a person under disability. The relationship between a litigation guardian and the person under disability on whose behalf the litigation guardian acts is that of a fiduciary and beneficiary. The duties of a litigation guardian are to attend diligently to the interests of the person under disability and take all reasonably necessary steps to protect those interests, including commencing and conducting a defendant's claim if necessary (Rule 4.04(1)).

A litigation guardian is not a legal representative for the person under disability; rather, the litigation guardian is advised by the legal representative and makes decisions in the proceeding on behalf of and in the best interest of the person under disability.

Any person who is not under disability may be a litigation guardian for a plaintiff or defendant (Rule 4.03(1)). Rule 4.03(2) sets out the following guidelines for determining who may be a litigation guardian.

Person Under Age of Majority

If the plaintiff or defendant is a minor in an action to which s. 4.01(2) (claim for sum not exceeding $500.00) does not apply, the litigation guardian shall be

- the minor's parent, or
- a person with lawful custody of the minor, or
- another suitable person.

If none of the above are available and able to act, the Children's Lawyer shall be the litigation guardian.

Person Who Is Mentally Incapable

If the plaintiff or defendant is mentally incapable and has a guardian with authority to act as litigation guardian in the proceeding, then the guardian shall be the litigation guardian.

If the party under disability is mentally incapable and does not have a guardian with authority to act as litigation guardian in the proceeding, but has a power of attorney with authority to act as litigation guardian in the proceeding, then the attorney shall be the litigation guardian. A **power of attorney** is a document authorizing an individual to act on another person's behalf in a legal or business matter. The person authorized to act pursuant to the power of attorney is called the **attorney**.

If the party under disability is mentally incapable and has neither a guardian with authority to act as litigation guardian in the proceeding nor an attorney under a power of attorney with that power, then a suitable person who has no interest contrary to that of the incapable person may be the litigation guardian. If no such person is available and able to act, the public guardian and trustee shall be the litigation guardian.

Absentee

If the plaintiff or defendant is an absentee, then the committee of his or her estate appointed under the *Absentees Act* shall be the litigation guardian. A **committee** is a person appointed by the court to manage the property of an absentee.

If no committee has been appointed, a suitable person who has no interest contrary to that of the absentee may be the litigation guardian. If no such person is available to act, then the public guardian and trustee shall be the litigation guardian.

BOX 4.5 What Is the Children's Lawyer?
What Is the Public Guardian?

The Office of the Children's Lawyer and the Office of the Public Guardian and Trustee are divisions of the Ministry of the Attorney General.

The Office of the Children's Lawyer provides legal representation for children under the age of 18 in various matters, including custody and access disputes, child protection matters, estate matters, and civil litigation.

The Office of the Public Guardian and Trustee performs a wide range of activities. Among other things, it safeguards the legal, personal, and financial interests of incapable people who have no one else who is authorized to do so. The Public Guardian may act as a litigation guardian or legal representative for individuals involved in lawsuits who lack sufficient capacity to give proper instructions to a lawyer or to make informed decisions.

More information about the services provided by the Office of the Public Guardian and Trustee and the Office of the Children's Lawyer is available at the Attorney General's website (http://www.attorneygeneral.jus.gov.on.ca).

Litigation Guardians—Procedural Matters

Acting on Behalf of a Plaintiff Under Disability

Where a proceeding is commenced or continued by a litigation guardian acting on behalf of a plaintiff under disability, the plaintiff should be named in the plaintiff's claim as follows:

[name of person under disability], a person under disability, by [his/her] litigation guardian, [name of litigation guardian].

For example, if Collette Desbarais is a minor whose mother, Antoinette Desbarais, is acting as her litigation guardian, the plaintiff would be named on the plaintiff's claim as follows:

Collette Desbarais, a person under disability, by her litigation guardian, Antoinette Desbarais.

The box beside "Under 18 years of age" should be checked.

At the time of filing the claim or as soon as possible afterward, Antoinette Desbarais as litigation guardian for Collette Desbarais must file a consent in Form 4A in accordance with Rule 4.01(3). The Form 4A consent contains the following:

- the nature of the disability;
- in the case of a minor, the minor's birth date;
- a description of the relationship, if any, between the litigation guardian and the person under disability;
- a statement that the litigation guardian has no interest in the proceeding contrary to that of the person under disability;
- an acknowledgment that the litigation guardian is aware of his or her liability to pay personally any costs awarded against the litigation guardian or against the person under disability; and
- the name of the litigation guardian's legal representative, if any, along with confirmation that the legal representative has written authority to act in the proceeding.

The consent must be signed in the presence of a witness.

See Appendix 4.2 to this chapter for a precedent Form 4A—Consent to Act as Litigation Guardian.

Where the Children's Lawyer or the Public Guardian acts as litigation guardian for a plaintiff under disability, no consent is required (Rule 4.04(2)).

Acting on Behalf of Defendant Under Disability

A proceeding against a person under disability shall be defended by a defendant's litigation guardian (Rule 4.02(1)). If it appears to the court that a defendant who does not have a litigation guardian is a person under disability, the court may appoint any person who has no interest in the proceeding contrary to that of the defendant as the defendant's litigation guardian. Before making such an appointment, the court must give the proposed litigation guardian notice (Rule 4.02(3)).

The defendant's litigation guardian shall file a consent in Form 4A with the defence. The consent must be signed in the presence of a witness.

Where the Children's Lawyer or the Public Guardian acts as litigation guardian for a defendant under disability, no consent is required (Rule 4.04(2)).

Other Procedural Issues

REMOVING OR REPLACING A LITIGATION GUARDIAN

The duties of a litigation guardian are to attend diligently to the interests of the person under disability and take all steps reasonably necessary to protect those interests, including commencing and conducting a defendant's claim (Rule 4.04(1)).

The court may remove or replace a litigation guardian at any time (Rule 4.05).

SETTLEMENT REQUIRES COURT'S APPROVAL

The court must approve any settlement of a claim by or against a person under disability. If the court has not approved the settlement, it is not binding on the person under disability (Rule 4.07).

Although the rule does not contain explicit language to this effect, it is arguable that Rule 4.07 applies to a settlement of a claim by or against a person under disability, regardless of whether a court proceeding has actually been commenced, so long as the settlement amount falls within the Small Claims Court legal and monetary jurisdiction. See Rule 7.08(1) of the *Rules of Civil Procedure*, which states that "[n]o settlement of a claim made by or against a person under disability, whether or not a proceeding has been commenced in respect of the claim, is binding on the person without the approval of a judge."

Rule 7.08(3) of the *Rules of Civil Procedure* states that "[w]here an agreement for the settlement of a claim made by or against a person under disability is reached before a proceeding is commenced in respect of the claim, approval of a judge shall be obtained on an application." Applications are not available under the *Rules of the Small Claims Court*. However, if settlement is reached in a matter that is within Small Claims Court jurisdiction where a party to the settlement is a person under disability and a Small Claims Court proceeding has not yet been commenced, you should consider seeking judicial review and approval of the settlement by a judge of the Small Claims Court.

MONEY PAID INTO AND OUT OF COURT

Any money payable to a person under disability pursuant to a court order or a settlement shall be paid into court, unless the court orders otherwise. A judge shall order the terms upon which the money is to be paid out or otherwise disposed of (Rule 4.08(1)).

The court may order that money payable to a person under disability under an order or settlement shall be paid directly to the person. If the court orders that the money be paid directly to the person under disability, the payor is discharged of liability to the extent of the amount paid (Rule 4.08(2)).

Payment into court means that the money is deposited to a bank account designated by the Accountant of the Superior Court of Justice for that purpose. The money will be held in court until an order is made by the court that it be paid out, and to whom. This is called **payment out of court**.

The Accountant of the Superior Court of Justice is responsible for accepting payments into court, and paying money or other assets held by the Accountant on behalf of other persons out of court in accordance with court orders of the Superior Court of Justice, or otherwise as required by law.

Rule 22 sets out detailed procedures for payment of money into and out of court.

The Rule 22 procedure for payment of money into and out of court does not apply where money is paid into court in the following circumstances (Rule 22.02):

1. where a defendant makes an admission of liability and a proposal for terms of payment of part or all of the amount claimed under Rule 9.03;
2. under an offer to settle a claim in return for the payment of money; or
3. for the enforcement under Rule 20 of an order for payment or recovery of money, including enforcement by garnishment.

The Rule 22 procedure for payment of money into and out of court applies where:

1. a statute or a rule of the court requires a party to pay money into court;
2. a party to the proceeding is under disability; or
3. a judge orders a person to pay money into court, and the Rule 22.02 exemptions do not apply.

An example of a statutory provision requiring payment of money into court is s. 24 of the *Repair and Storage Liens Act*. For example, where a person refuses to pay a bill for repairs to her vehicle, the mechanic who performed the repairs may claim a lien against the vehicle and refuse to surrender possession of the vehicle to its owner. If the owner wishes to dispute the lien, the owner shall pay into court the full amount claimed by the lien claimant, subject to any offer of settlement, and the vehicle shall be released to its owner unless the lien claimant files an objection with the court (*Repair and Storage Liens Act*, ss. 24(1), (4), (5), and (6)).

Where a party to an action is a person under disability, Rule 22 will apply in conjunction with Rule 4.08.

PAYMENT OF MONEY INTO COURT (RULE 22.03)

A party who is paying money into court must first prepare and file (Rule 22.03(2)):

1. If the payment into court is under a statutory provision or rule, a written request for payment into court that includes the payor's name, address, and the claim number, and that refers to the provision or rule requiring payment into court.
2. If the payment into court is pursuant to a court order, a written request for payment into court that includes the payor's name, address, and the claim number, with a copy of the court order bearing the court's seal attached.

If the money is being paid into court for a person under disability, the written request must provide the person's name, date of birth, address, and telephone number. You must state whether the person under disability is a minor or a mentally incapable person, and provide the name and address of the person's litigation guardian.

A written request to pay money into or out of court may be made using a Request to Pay Money into or out of Court, as of this writing available online at: http://www.ontariocourtforms.on.ca/english/other-documents-related-to-scc. You will find a Request to Pay Money into or out of Court at Appendix 4.3 to this chapter.

Cheques or money orders should be made payable to the Accountant of the Superior Court of Justice.

You may file a request to pay money into court with the clerk at the location where the claim was commenced. Upon receiving the request, the clerk shall provide you with four copies of a Direction to Receive Funds, addressed to the bank where the deposit is to be made, and specifying the account into which the money is to be paid (Rule 22.03(3)). The clerk shall forward the documents to the Accountant (Rule 22.03(4)).

If you file the request to pay money into court in person with the Accountant at the Accountant's office at 595 Bay Street in Toronto, the Accountant shall provide you with four copies of a Direction to Receive Funds, addressed to the bank where the party may make the deposit, and specifying the account into which the money is to be paid (Rule 22.03(3)).

The Direction to Receive Funds form shall state the name of the bank where you can pay the money in, and the information the bank needs to accept the deposit. Upon receiving the Direction to Receive Funds, you shall pay the money into the specified bank account in accordance with the direction (Rule 22.03(5)). When you go to make payment at the bank stated in the Direction to Receive Funds, you shall provide the bank teller with the Direction to Receive Funds and the payment. When the deposit has been processed, the bank teller will either provide you with a receipt (Rule 22.03(6)) or stamp your copies of the Direction to Receive Funds.

You may mail the request to pay money into court with the payment to (Rule 22.03(7)):

> The Accountant of the Superior Court of Justice
> 595 Bay Street, 8th Floor
> Toronto, ON M5G 2M6

A request to pay money into court received by mail shall include the party's name and mailing address (Rule 22.03(7)).

When the payment is processed, the Accountant's office will mail you a receipt (Rule 22.03(8)).

Immediately after receiving a receipt or stamped direction from the bank, or a receipt from the Accountant's office, a party who has paid money into court shall send to every other party a copy of the receipt or stamped direction, and file a copy with the court (Rule 22.03(9)).

PAYMENT OF MONEY OUT OF COURT (RULE 22.04)

Money may only be paid out of court under an order (Rule 22.04(1)).

A payment out of court pursuant to a court order may be requested by:

- any party who is entitled to the payment out of court pursuant to the order;
- the Office of the Children's Lawyer or the Public Guardian and Trustee; or
- a party who was a minor and has now attained the age of majority.

A person who is entitled to payment out of court pursuant to a court order shall file with the Accountant (Rule 22.04(2)):

1. a Request to Pay Money into or out of Court form, with a supporting affidavit; and
2. a copy of the order for payment out of court bearing the court's seal.

If the person seeking the payment out of court is the Children's Lawyer or the Public Guardian and Trustee (Rule 22.04(3)):

1. the written request for payment out of court does not need to be in the form of a Request to Pay Money into or out of Court, and a supporting affidavit is not required; and
2. a single written request dealing with more than one proceeding may be filed.

If the party requesting the payment out of court is a minor who has attained the age of majority, the money was being held by the court until the person became 18 years of age, and the person is entitled to the money in court under an order, the Accountant will provide to the person (Rule 22.04(4)):

1. a written request for payment out of court; and
2. an affidavit proving the party's identity and that the party has attained the age of majority.

The Accountant will send these forms in the mail, along with instructions for their completion.

If the requirements for Rules 22.04(2) and (4) are met, the Accountant shall pay the money to the person named in the order for payment out of court, and the payment shall include any accrued interest, unless the court orders otherwise (Rule 22.04(5)).

Ethical Advocacy

When representing a client in a Small Claims Court proceeding, you must comply with the *Paralegal Rules of Conduct* and the *Paralegal Professional Conduct Guidelines*.

Paralegal Rule 4, which governs advocacy, applies to all appearances and proceedings before the Small Claims Court.

Duty to Clients, Tribunals, and Others (Paralegal Rules 4.01(1) to (4) and (7))

The paralegal advocate must balance a number of duties.

When acting as an advocate, you shall represent your client honourably and resolutely within the limits of the law. At the same time, you shall treat other licensees and the tribunal before which you are appearing with candour, fairness, courtesy, and respect (Paralegal Rule 4.01(1)), and you shall encourage public respect for, and try to improve, the administration of justice (Paralegal Rule 6.01(1)).

You have a duty to represent your client fearlessly and resolutely. Paralegal Rule 4 does not require you to assist an opposing party or raise matters that are harmful to your client's case, unless the Paralegal Rules state otherwise. Paralegal Rule 4 does place limits on how you may conduct yourself when acting as advocate in a Small Claims Court proceeding. Your professional obligations to other parties, other licensees, the court, and the administration of justice are paramount.

Paralegal Rule 4.01(4) sets out the following requirements for paralegal advocates:

(a) The paralegal shall raise fearlessly every issue, advance every argument, and ask every question, however distasteful, that the paralegal thinks will help the client's case.

(b) The paralegal shall try to obtain for the client the benefit of every remedy and defence authorized by law. A **remedy** is a method of enforcing a right, or preventing or compensating for a wrong.

(c) A paralegal shall never give up or abandon a client's legal rights without the client's informed consent. This Paralegal Rule applies to the client's legal rights generally, and refers specifically to an available defence under a statute of limitations. A statutory limitation period is a period of time established by a statute for commencing a proceeding. When the statutory limitation period has expired, any proceeding against your client is statute-barred—that is, it is stopped by the expiry of the statutory limitation period. Limitation periods were discussed in Chapter 3.

Informed consent is consent based on information that is sufficient to allow the client to assess the situation and make an informed decision.

(d) A paralegal shall avoid and discourage the client from:

- Resorting to frivolous and vexatious objections. An **objection** is an argument by a party that a particular piece of evidence, line of questioning, or other matter is improper or illegal and should not be allowed by the court. A **frivolous and vexatious objection** is an objection that has no legal merit and is made to annoy, harass, or embarrass the other side.

- Trying to gain advantage from mistakes or oversights by the other side that do not go to the **merits of the case**. The merits of the case are the legal principles upon which a party's assertion of rights is based. A mistake or oversight that does not go to the merits of the case does not affect a party's legal rights.
- Using tactics designed merely to delay or harass the other side.

Regarding Paralegal Rule 4.01(4)(d), Guideline 12 recommends that a paralegal should not engage in rude or disruptive conduct before a tribunal, or ill-mannered correspondence, language, or behaviour toward opposing parties or their advocates. See also Paralegal Rule 7.01(3), which states that when providing legal services, a paralegal shall not communicate, in writing or otherwise, with a client, another licensee, or any other person in a manner that is abusive, offensive, or otherwise inconsistent with the proper tone of a professional communication from a paralegal.

The Paralegal and the Tribunal Process (Paralegal Rule 4.01(5))

Abuse of Tribunal Process: Malicious Proceedings (Paralegal Rule 4.01(5)(a))

A paralegal shall not abuse the process of the tribunal by commencing or continuing to act in proceedings that, although legal, are clearly motivated by malice on the part of the client and are brought solely for the purpose of injuring the other party (Paralegal Rule 4.01(5)(a)). Proceedings that have no merit waste the time of the tribunal and its officers, and do not further the cause of justice (Guideline 12).

BOX 4.6 Abuse of Tribunal Process

Fact Situation

A prospective client wishes to commence a Small Claims Court proceeding. Based on what she tells you and the documents she produces, you do not think she is entitled to what she says she wants. Throughout the consultation, she speaks of the person against whom she wishes to commence the proceeding in disparaging terms, with contempt and anger.

Question: Should you accept the retainer?

Discussion: A paralegal shall be honest and candid when advising a client (Paralegal Rule 3.02). You must look at both sides of each issue without bias. You must advise the client honestly and candidly of the applicable law, the client's options, possible outcomes, and possible risks. Your advice should enable the client to make informed decisions and give appropriate instructions in the matter.

You should advise the client that, in your opinion, the proceeding has no legal merit, giving her your reasons. If she disregards your advice and insists on going forward, consider whether she is motivated solely by malice.

If you are satisfied that she is motivated solely by malice, you should decline the retainer. You should send her a non-engagement letter, confirming that you have decided to decline the retainer. You should advise her of any approaching limitation periods. You should confirm that any documents in your possession have been returned to her.

Question: What are the consequences of going forward with the proceeding?

Discussion: You will be in breach of Paralegal Rule 4.01(5)(a), which prohibits paralegals from starting or continuing actions that have no merit and are brought solely to harm the other party. In this case, you have concluded that the proceeding has no merit, and you believe that the client's motives are malicious. Unmeritorious proceedings waste the time of the tribunal and its officers, and do not further the cause of justice.

Misleading the Tribunal (Paralegal Rules 4.01(5)(c), (d), and (h))

A paralegal must ensure that neither the paralegal nor the client misleads the tribunal. To arrive at an appropriate decision, the tribunal must receive everything that is relevant to the issues to be decided in a matter (Guideline 12). If the tribunal is mistaken about or misunderstands some aspect of the facts or the law in a case, the paralegal should do what is necessary to correct the mistake or misunderstanding.

A paralegal shall not knowingly attempt to deceive a tribunal or influence the course of justice by (Paralegal Rule 4.01(5)(c)):

- offering false evidence,
- misstating facts or law,
- presenting or relying upon a false or deceptive affidavit,
- suppressing something that should be disclosed, or
- otherwise assisting in any deception, crime, or illegal conduct.

BOX 4.7 What Is an Affidavit?

An **affidavit** is a written statement of facts that is confirmed under oath or by affirmation by the person making the affidavit. The person making the affidavit is called the **deponent**.

The content of an affidavit is evidence. Swearing or affirming a false or deceptive affidavit or assisting another person to do so with intent to mislead is an offence contrary to s. 131 of the *Criminal Code*.

You must represent your client fearlessly and resolutely, but you shall not knowingly engage in dishonest conduct that misleads the tribunal and others in order to protect your client or gain an advantage for your client.

A paralegal shall not deliberately refrain from informing the tribunal of any binding authority that the paralegal considers to be directly on point and that has not been mentioned by an opponent (Paralegal Rule 4.01(5)(d)). **Binding authority** (also known as binding precedent) is a judicial decision by a higher court that must be followed by lower courts.

A paralegal shall not knowingly misstate the contents of a document, the testimony of a witness, the substance of an argument, or the provisions of a statute or similar authority (Paralegal Rule 4.01(5)(h)). The tribunal must be able to rely upon correct information when reviewing a case and arriving at a decision.

BOX 4.8 Binding Authority (Paralegal Rule 4.01(5)(d))

Fact Situation

You represent the defendant in a Small Claims Court proceeding. During some last-minute online research before the trial, you find a very recent appellate decision that is unfavourable to your client and favourable to the plaintiff. The decision is binding on the Small Claims Court. There are some minor legal and factual differences between the matter dealt with in the appellate decision and the matter before the court.

To your surprise, during submissions, the licensee representing the plaintiff does not refer to the decision.

Are you required to inform the court of a binding authority that is unfavourable to your client's case?

Discussion

You are required to represent your client resolutely and honourably within the limits of the law, while treating the tribunal and other licensees with candour, fairness, courtesy, and respect, and upholding the high ethical standards of the paralegal profession (Paralegal Rule 4.01(1)). You are not required to assist an adversary or advance matters that may harm your client's case, unless the Paralegal Rules provide otherwise (Paralegal Rule 4.01(3)).

You must balance your duty to your client with your duty to treat the tribunal and other licensees with candour and fairness. Your opponent has not mentioned the appellate decision. You may not deliberately refrain from informing the tribunal of the appellate decision if you think the principles stated in the decision are relevant and applicable to this case, regardless of the minor legal and factual differences. You must consider whether the court is likely to arrive at an inappropriate decision if it does not know about the decision.

Improperly Influencing the Tribunal (Paralegal Rules 4.01(5)(e) and (g))

Judges and deputy judges must be fair, impartial, independent, and neutral. A judge's decision-making must not be influenced by private or partisan interests, which may give rise to actual bias or to an appearance of bias in favour of a particular person.

A paralegal shall not appear before a judge if the paralegal, the paralegal's partner, a paralegal employed by the paralegal's firm, or the paralegal's client has a business or personal relationship with the adjudicator that either affects the judge's impartiality or may reasonably appear to affect the judge's impartiality (Paralegal Rule 4.01(5)(e)).

A paralegal shall not attempt or allow anyone else to attempt, directly or indirectly, to influence the decision or action of a tribunal or its officers in any case or matter except by open persuasion as an advocate (Paralegal Rule 4.01(5)(g)).

BOX 4.9 Offering False Evidence

Fact Situation

You are acting for the plaintiff in an action in Small Claims Court. The defendant failed to file a defence within the prescribed time, and has been noted in default. You have prepared a motion in writing for an assessment of damages, and a supporting affidavit.

When the client reviews the supporting affidavit, she objects to several statements because they are harmful to her case. "If the judge reads this, I'll get less money," she says. "Why should I say anything that's going to take money out of my pocket? I never would have told you that stuff if I'd known you were going to use it against me. I want you to leave it out completely, or change it to say something that will get me what I'm asking for."

The client provided the material to you during a telephone conversation just after the defendant was noted in default. You phoned her because you wanted to clarify some issues before you got started on the supporting affidavit. You took detailed notes of what she said, and went over them with her before ending the call. The statements in the affidavit accurately reflect your notes of the conversation. The statements contain information that is relevant to issues in the matter.

The client is correct that the material is harmful to her case. You did not obtain her consent to disclose the harmful information in the supporting affidavit.

Question: Is the harmful material confidential?

Discussion: You have a duty to hold all client information in strict confidence, unless disclosure is expressly or impliedly authorized by the client or required by law (Paralegal Rule 3.03(1)). You have neither implied nor express consent to disclose this information.

Question: Is disclosure required by law?

Discussion: Unless otherwise provided by the Paralegal Rules, you are not required to assist an adversary or advance matters that harm your client's case (Paralegal Rule 4.01(3)).

In this case, there is no adversary. The defendant has been noted in default, and is not entitled to notice of the motion for an assessment of damages. However, the court file is public, and its contents, including the affidavit supporting the motion for an assessment of damages, are available to the defendant, should he decide at some point to come forward and dispute the matter. If the harmful material is included in the affidavit, it may come to the attention of the defendant.

In cases where you are dealing with a self-represented party and the matter is uncontested, you should consider taking particular care to ensure that the tribunal has all the information necessary to come to an appropriate conclusion.

The client is not disputing the truth of the harmful statements, and you have taken careful steps to confirm their accuracy. Her concern is the harmful effect that their disclosure may have on her case.

The only material that the judge will have before her on the motion is the material that you file with the court. The harmful material is accurate, and relevant to issues in the case. If the material is deleted from the affidavit, you are knowingly attempting to deceive a tribunal and influence the course of justice by relying upon a deceptive affidavit and suppressing information that ought to be disclosed, contrary to Paralegal Rule 4.01(5)(c). You are knowingly deceiving the tribunal because you are not providing all the information that the judge will need to properly review the matter and arrive at an appropriate decision. You are knowingly attempting to influence the course of justice because you are suppressing relevant material in order to obtain a more favourable result for your client.

You are knowingly assisting or permitting the client to do something that is dishonest and dishonourable, contrary to Paralegal Rule 4.01(5)(b).

You must carefully weigh your duties of confidentiality and loyalty to the client against your duty to the tribunal and the administration of justice, keeping in mind your obligations under Paralegal Rules 4.01(4) and (5).

Question: Should you alter the harmful material so that it is favourable to your client's case?

Discussion: If you change the material to make it favourable to your client, the supporting affidavit will contain false statements. If you alter evidence you know to be true in order to gain an advantage for your client, you are knowingly attempting to deceive the tribunal and influence the course of justice by offering false evidence, relying upon a false or deceptive affidavit, and assisting in a crime, contrary to Paralegal Rule 4.01(5)(c). You are knowingly deceiving the tribunal because you are knowingly relying upon false evidence in support of the motion. You are knowingly attempting to influence the course of justice, because you are offering evidence you know to be false in order to obtain a more favourable result for your client.

You are knowingly assisting or permitting the client to do something that is dishonest and dishonourable, contrary to Paralegal Rule 4.01(5)(b).

Giving false evidence (spoken or written) under oath with intent to mislead is an offence contrary to s. 131 of the *Criminal Code*.

Question: What next?

Discussion: You should advise the client that you have a duty to provide the tribunal with everything it needs to arrive at an effective, appropriate decision. You cannot suppress or alter relevant evidence to obtain a more favourable result for her, nor can you assist her in swearing an affidavit you know to be false. You should advise her that swearing a false affidavit with intent to mislead is an offence. If she persists in her instructions, you may be required to withdraw from representation pursuant to Paralegal Rule 3.08.

Guideline 12 states that the only appropriate way to influence the decision of a court or other tribunal is by appearing before the court in the presence of, or on notice to, other parties, offering appropriate evidence in support of your client's case, and making persuasive submissions based upon applicable legal principles, unless a rule of the Small Claims Court permits or requires otherwise.

You should never communicate directly with a judge or deputy judge in the absence of other parties, unless a rule of the Small Claims Court permits you to do so (Guideline 12).

Dishonest Conduct (Paralegal Rules 4.01(5)(b), (c), and (f))

A paralegal shall not knowingly assist or permit the client to do anything that the paralegal considers to be dishonest or dishonourable (Paralegal Rule 4.01(5)(b)).

A paralegal shall not knowingly attempt to deceive a tribunal or influence the course of justice by offering false evidence (including false or deceptive affidavits), misstating facts or law, suppressing relevant information, or otherwise assisting in any deception, crime, or illegal conduct (Paralegal Rule 4.01(5)(c)).

A paralegal shall not knowingly assert a fact to be true when its truth cannot reasonably be supported by the evidence, or as a matter of which notice may be taken by the tribunal (Paralegal Rule 4.01(5)(f)).

BOX 4.10   Judicial Notice

What is meant by "a matter of which notice may be taken by the tribunal" (Paralegal Rule 4.01(5)(f))? This is known in the courts as **judicial notice**. Judges may notice, or accept as true, certain notorious facts (that is, matters of common knowledge) without hearing evidence and without inquiry. Other lesser-known facts (for example, matters that can be checked in a standard reference work and are not easily disputed) may be judicially noticed after inquiry.

Disclosure of Documents (Paralegal Rule 4.01(6))

Where the rules of a court or other tribunal require the parties to produce documents, a paralegal advocate:

1. shall explain to the client the necessity of making full disclosure of all documents relating to any matter in issue, and the duty to answer any proper question relating to any issue in the action to the best of his knowledge, information, or belief;

2. shall assist the client in fulfilling his obligation to make full disclosure; and

3. shall not make frivolous requests for production of documents or frivolous demands for information.

Timely, complete, and accurate disclosure lets the parties know the case they have to meet. It promotes settlement because it allows each party to assess the strengths and weaknesses of her own case and those of opposing parties. It also makes the hearing process more effective and fair (Guideline 12).

The *Rules of the Small Claims Court* require early and ongoing disclosure by all parties. This should be explained to the client at the initial consultation, and confirmed in the retainer agreement or engagement letter. See Rules 7.01(2)2, 9.02(1)2, 10.01(4)2, 13.03(2), and 13.05(2)(a)(vi).

Drafting the Plaintiff's Claim

What Are Pleadings?

Pleadings are the documents filed at the commencement of a proceeding in which the parties state the allegations of fact on which they rely in support of their claim or defence. In a Small Claims Court proceeding, the documents that make up the pleadings are the plaintiff's claim, the defence, the defendant's claim, and the defence to the defendant's claim. These are the documents in which the parties plead, or present, their case—thus the name pleadings.

It is important to remember that a pleading is made up of allegations of fact—that is, a series of assertions that have not yet been proven. In a Small Claims Court proceeding, an allegation of fact that is in dispute—that is, an allegation that one party says is true and the other party says is not true—does not become a fact, or the "truth," until the following process has been completed. The party making the allegation gives evidence in support of the allegation at trial. The opposing party may test the evidence during cross-examination, and/or give evidence intended to prove that the allegation is not true. The Small Claims Court judge, who is the finder of fact, accepts one party's evidence over that of the other party, on a balance of probabilities. An allegation of fact that is accepted by a judge as true, based on the evidence, then becomes a fact, or the "truth," for legal purposes.

A pleading is a piece of advocacy. When drafting a pleading you must make the strongest possible case for your client. This does not mean that you should misrepresent the facts as you know them, based on what your client has told you. You must ensure that there is some evidentiary basis for the allegations you are making. Instead, it means emphasizing the strengths of your client's case, without making false statements or misrepresentations. It is up to your opponent to expose the weaknesses in your client's case—you have no obligation to assist him or her.

When you are interviewing a client, you will find that they tell you a lot of things that may or may not be relevant to their case. Relevant statements are allegations that go toward establishing a legal basis for the relief your client is claiming. When going over your notes of the client interview, keep the following questions in mind:

- What does the client want?
- What do I need to say to support the client's case?
- Which client statements support the client's case?
- Which client statements do not support the client's case?
- Which client statements are completely irrelevant to any issue that I am aware of in the client's case at this stage of the proceeding?

BOX 4.11 Drafting a Plaintiff's Claim: What Is Relevant?

Fact Situation

You work for Prior Mustafa LLP, 22 County Court Boulevard, Brampton, Ontario A1A 2B3 TEL: 905 111 2222 FAX: 905 111 2233.

Your client is Juliette Greco. Ms. Greco is an attractive woman in her late thirties who works as a buyer for a large department store. She is very well dressed, and does not wear a wedding ring. She lives at 126 George Court, Brampton, Ontario L1X 2V4 TEL: 905 791 2234. In April 20—, she loaned $5,000.00 to her neighbour, James Hardwick, who lives at 128 George Court, Brampton, Ontario L1X 2V4 TEL: 905 791 3333. She has come to see you because he failed to pay the money back.

She has been neighbours with the Hardwick family for five years, since she moved into her house at 126 George Court. Until recently, she considered them to be her friends. She allowed the Hardwick boys (James and Charles) to swim in her pool in the summers, and occasionally she had the entire family (James, Pamela, and the two boys) over for a barbecue. She also attended a few parties at the Hardwick house. She felt sorry for James and Pamela. James is "kind of dumb," to use Juliette's own words, and Pamela has a big mouth and a bad temper.

From conversations with Pamela, Juliette knew the Hardwicks were having financial problems last spring. So when James came to her and asked her for a loan of $5,000.00, she agreed, but took the precaution of having him sign a promissory note, dated April 1, 20—. Under the terms of the note, he was supposed to pay the entire amount back on or before August 2, 20—. Juliette has a duplicate original of the promissory note.

When James failed to pay the money back, Juliette phoned him a couple of times. Pamela answered, and was extremely rude on the phone, so after that Juliette sent a couple of letters, asking for the money to be repaid. The letters are dated August 15, 20— and September 15, 20—. She sent the letters by registered mail. She has copies of the letters and the registration slips.

Juliette seems to be quite upset by what has happened. She says that she used to sit out by the pool on summer evenings when she got home from work, but whenever Pamela is in her own backyard and sees Juliette next door, Pamela makes loud, rude remarks about her. Now she is reluctant to use her backyard or her pool. Finally, she recently found dog feces on her driveway. She believes the Hardwick boys put them there.

Juliette wants to sue James for the unpaid $5,000.00 plus interest as provided in the promissory note.

What is the nature of Ms. Greco's claim? In other words, what does Ms. Greco want?

According to the last paragraph in the fact situation, Ms. Greco wants the money owing plus interest pursuant to the promissory note signed by James Hardwick on April 1, 20—. In other words, this is a debt collection.

What are the relevant facts? In other words, what facts need to be stated in the plaintiff's claim to support Ms. Greco's case?

This is a debt collection. Only those facts that relate to the debt are relevant. Relevant facts would include the amount of the loan, the terms of the loan agreement (if there is one), the circumstances of default, whether there have been any demands for payment, and whether there have been any payments on account of the balance owing.

The fact situation has been duplicated below, with the relevant facts emphasized in bold type. A brief explanation of why the facts are relevant follows each paragraph.

Your client is Juliette Greco. Ms. Greco is an attractive woman in her late thirties who works as a buyer for a large department store. She is very well dressed, and does not wear a wedding ring. **She lives at 126 George Court, Brampton, Ontario L1X 2V4 TEL: 905 791 2234. In April 20—, she loaned $5,000.00 to her neighbour, James Hardwick, who lives at 128 George Court, Brampton, Ontario L1X 2V4 TEL: 905 791 3333. She has come to see you because he failed to pay the money back.**

You need the correct names and addresses of the parties in order to correctly fill out the plaintiff's claim. You need the correct name and address of the defendant, James Hardwick, because this establishes Small Claims Court territorial jurisdiction under Rule 6. As well, you will need this information when enforcing the judgment. The information about the amount of the loan, the date the money was advanced, and the default in payment goes to establishing the basis for the claim.

She has been neighbours with the Hardwick family for five years, since she moved into her house at 126 George Court. Until recently, she considered them to be her friends. She allowed the Hardwick boys (James and Charles) to swim in her pool in the summers, and occasionally she had the entire family (James, Pamela, and the two boys) over for a barbecue. She also attended a few parties at the Hardwick house. She felt sorry for James and Pamela. James is "kind of dumb," to use Juliette's own words, and Pamela has a big mouth and a bad temper.

Nothing in this paragraph is relevant in the context of a debt collection.

From conversations with Pamela, Juliette knew the Hardwicks were having financial problems last spring. **So when James came to her and asked her for a loan of $5,000.00, she agreed, but took the precaution of having him sign a promissory note, dated April 1, 20—. Under the terms of the note, he was supposed to** pay **the entire amount back on or before August 2, 20—. Juliette has a duplicate original of the promissory note.**

Ms. Greco's motives for advancing the money are irrelevant to any legal issue in the case. The existence of the promissory note and the fact that Ms. Greco has a duplicate original are relevant because the note provides documentary evidence of the loan and its terms.

When James failed to pay the money back, Juliette phoned him a couple of times. Pamela answered, and was extremely rude on the phone, so after that **Juliette sent a couple of letters, asking for the money to be repaid. The letters are dated August 15, 20— and September 15, 20—. She sent the letters by registered mail. She has copies of the letters and the registration slips.**

This information is relevant because it establishes that Ms. Greco has made demands, both spoken and written, for payment of the debt. Also, she has documentary evidence to back this up.

Juliette seems to be quite upset by what has happened. She says that she used to sit out by the pool on summer evenings when she got home from work, but whenever Pamela is in her own backyard and sees Juliette next door, Pamela makes loud, rude remarks about her. Now she is reluctant to use her backyard or her pool. Recently, she found dog feces on her driveway. She believes the Hardwick boys put them there.

Nothing in this paragraph is relevant in the context of a debt collection.

Juliette wants to sue James for the unpaid $5,000.00 plus interest as provided in the promissory note.

This information is relevant because it tells you what your client wants.

When you have decided what the relevant facts are, you have to turn them into a persuasive narrative, which is carefully organized for maximum clarity. Sometimes, as in the case of a simple debt collection, this will be easy to do. In other cases, the narrative will be more complex, and will require careful thought, editing, and re-writing.

Small Claims Court Rules 7.01(2)(ii), 9.02(1), and 10.01(4) require that the grounds for a claim or defence be stated in concise and non-technical language with a reasonable amount of detail. Use plain, everyday language and simple sentence structures with active verbs whenever possible.

Consider using precedents. **Precedent documents** are legal documents that are used as guides for drafting subsequent documents with a similar purpose. The sample letters at Appendixes 2.1, 2.2, 2.6, and 2.7 of Chapter 2 are examples of precedent documents. They can be used as guides for writing certain types of correspondence, but you must adapt the language to different client situations. Similarly, the claim at Appendix 3.1 of Chapter 3 can be used as a guide if you are drafting a claim for a plaintiff in a similar situation.

You should develop a databank of precedent documents for use when providing legal services, keeping in mind your duty of confidentiality under Paralegal Rule 3.03. The databank should be updated on a regular basis.

Rules of Pleading

Rule 7.01 of the *Rules of the Small Claims Court* sets out the requirements for a plaintiff's claim. Some of these requirements have been incorporated into Form 7A. These include:

- the full names of the parties and the capacity in which they are suing or are being sued (see the discussion above about parties under disability);
- the name, address, telephone number, fax number, and Law Society of Upper Canada registration number of the licensee representing the plaintiff; or
- if the plaintiff is self-represented, the name, address, telephone number, and fax number (if any) of the plaintiff; and
- the address where the plaintiff believes the defendant may be served.

The plaintiff's claim must also set out, in concise and non-technical language, the nature of the claim, with reasonable certainty and detail, including the date, place and nature of the events on which the claim is based, and the amount of the claim and relief requested. There is space for these particulars at pages 2 and 3 of Form 7A, or you may wish to use a separate schedule that is attached to and forms part of the claim.

Although it is not required by the *Rules of the Small Claims Court*, licensees should consider setting out the particulars of the plaintiff's claim in a Schedule A, which is separate from but forms part of Form 7A. The Schedule A should be formatted in accordance with the requirements of Rule 4 of the *Rules of Civil Procedure*. The text should be 12 point, and it should be double spaced, with a left-hand margin of about 40 millimetres (1½ inches). The text may be printed on both sides of the paper.

The first paragraph of the Schedule A should contain a **prayer or claim for relief**—that is, a paragraph setting out the particulars of the damages claimed, pre- and post-judgment interest, and any other relief to which the plaintiff is entitled. The pleading should then set out, in consecutively numbered paragraphs, the allegations of fact upon which the claim is based. Use plain, everyday language, simple sentence structure, and active verbs whenever possible.

When drafting the pleading, also consider Rule 25.06 of the *Rules of Civil Procedure*, excerpted in part below.

RULES OF PLEADING—APPLICABLE TO ALL PLEADINGS

Material Facts

25.06(1) Every pleading shall contain a concise statement of the material facts on which the party relies for the claim or defence, but not the evidence by which those facts are to be proved.

Pleading Law

(2) A party may raise any point of law in a pleading, but conclusions of law may be pleaded only if the material facts supporting them are pleaded.

. . .

Inconsistent Pleading

(4) A party may make inconsistent allegations in a pleading where the pleading makes it clear that they are being pleaded in the alternative.

(5) An allegation that is inconsistent with an allegation made in a party's previous pleading or that raises a new ground of claim shall not be made in a subsequent pleading but by way of amendment to the previous pleading.

. . .

Documents or Conversations

(7) The effect of a document or the purport of a conversation, if material, shall be pleaded as briefly as possible, but the precise words of the document or conversation need not be pleaded unless those words are themselves material.

Nature of Act or Condition of Mind

(8) Where fraud, misrepresentation, breach of trust, malice or intent is alleged, the pleading shall contain full particulars, but knowledge may be alleged as a fact without pleading the circumstances from which it is to be inferred.

Claim for Relief

(9) Where a pleading contains a claim for relief, the nature of the relief claimed shall be specified and, where damages are claimed,

(a) the amount claimed for each claimant in respect of each claim shall be stated; and

(b) the amounts and particulars of special damages need only be pleaded to the extent that they are known at the date of the pleading, but notice of any further amounts and particulars shall be delivered forthwith after they become known and, in any event, not less than ten days before trial.

Rule 25.06 provides useful general guidelines for pleading in a Small Claims Court action. However, keep in mind that Rule 25.06 is designed for pleadings in the Superior Court of Justice, where there are procedures for pretrial discovery that are unavailable in the Small Claims Court. In a Small Claims Court action, the matter goes straight from close of pleadings to settlement conference. You should therefore consider taking a more detailed approach when drafting a Small Claims Court pleading, so that other parties know the case they have to answer. And whether you are acting for a plaintiff or a defendant, you shall comply with the obligation of early and ongoing disclosure of documents by all parties set out in the *Rules of the Small Claims Court*. See Rules 7.01(2)2, 9.02(1)2, 10.01(4)2, 13.03(2), and 13.05(2)(a)(vi). See also Paralegal Rule 4.01(6).

See Appendix 4.4 to this chapter for a sample plaintiff's claim, based on the fact situation in *Greco v. Hardwick* above. Refer also to the precedent plaintiff's claim in Appendix 3.1 to Chapter 3. In both cases, the claim is based on a promissory note.

See Appendix 4.5 for a sample plaintiff's claim based on the fact situation in *Chong v. Kingman* at Box 4.2 above.

Documentary Disclosure

The plaintiff must disclose any documents upon which she is relying in support of her claim by attaching photocopies of the documents to each copy of the claim (Rule 7.01(2)2). Early disclosure serves two purposes: (1) it gives the defendant notice of the evidence in support of the claim, and (2) it promotes negotiation and settlement.

Issuing the Plaintiff's Claim

The proceeding is commenced when the plaintiff's claim is taken to the office of the Small Claims Court with territorial jurisdiction, and issued by the court clerk. Under Rule 7.03, the plaintiff's claim is issued when the clerk dates, signs, and seals it, and assigns a court file number. On the forms, the court file number is described as the "Claim No."

When a court file number has been assigned to a proceeding, all subsequent court documents filed in that proceeding must bear the same court file number.

The original plaintiff's claim (with photocopies of any documentary evidence attached) is sealed, dated and signed, and filed by the clerk in the court file opened for that particular proceeding. The plaintiff will receive a photocopy of the sealed claim. The photocopy of the issued claim should be filed in the pleadings subfile in the client file.

The plaintiff is required to provide a copy of the claim for each defendant. All defendant copies must be stamped by the clerk. This eliminates the possibility of procedural irregularity.

> **BOX 4.12 Reminder: Court Fees**
>
> An infrequent claimant is anyone who files fewer than 10 Small Claims Court claims in a Small Claims Court office on or after January 1 in any calendar year. Infrequent claimants are charged $75.00 to file a plaintiff's claim.
>
> A frequent claimant is anyone who files 10 or more claims in a Small Claims Court office on or after January 1 in any calendar year. A frequent claimant is charged $145.00 per claim.
>
> A plaintiff may file 10 or more Small Claims Court claims in any calendar year without losing infrequent claimant status, so long as fewer than 10 claims are filed in any one particular court office. For example, let us say that in 20— the plaintiff files 6 claims in Brampton Small Claims Court, 8 claims in Newmarket Small Claims Court, and 5 claims in Cambridge Small Claims Court, for a total of 19 claims filed in that year. The plaintiff still qualifies for infrequent claimant status in those court offices, because fewer than 10 claims were filed in each one.

The plaintiff is responsible for serving the sealed and dated plaintiff's claim, along with attached documentary disclosure, on the defendant or defendants (Rule 7.03(2)).

Service of the Plaintiff's Claim

Service means delivery of a legal document to another party in the proceeding. Service of the plaintiff's claim must take place within six months of the date it is issued (Rule 8.01(2)). The time may be extended by court order, either before or after the six-month period has expired, on a motion to the court by the plaintiff.

The claim may be served personally (Rules 8.01(1) and 8.02) or by an alternative to personal service (Rule 8.03). **Personal service** means that a copy of the issued claim is personally delivered to the defendant by the plaintiff herself or by a person authorized by the plaintiff to do so (such as a process server) in accordance with the procedures set out in Rule 8.02. The requirements for proper personal service vary, depending on who the defendant is.

Alternatives to personal service may be used where the defendant has a lawyer who has been instructed to accept service; where personal service has been attempted but has been unsuccessful, for one reason or another (for example, where the defendant is avoiding service); and where it is otherwise permitted by Rule 8.

Personal Service (Rule 8.02)

For proper personal service to take place, a copy of the plaintiff's claim (or any other document required by the Rules to be personally served) must be handed over to the defendant (if the defendant is an individual) or to the defendant's designated representative (such as the defendant's litigation guardian, if the defendant is a party under disability).

The requirements for valid personal service vary, depending on who is being served. Valid personal service on an individual is different from valid personal service on a municipality, a corporation, or a partnership. You should review Rule 8.02 before attempting personal service yourself or giving instructions to an employee or agent to do so.

Personal Service on an Individual

Rule 8.02(a) provides that personal service of a document on an individual other than a person under disability is made by leaving a copy of the document with the individual.

THE AFFIDAVIT OF SERVICE

Service of any document required to be served in accordance with Rule 8 is proven by an affidavit of service. The deponent in the affidavit of service is the person who carried out the service, and thus has personal knowledge of how service was effected. The affidavit of service will be sworn by the deponent in the presence of a commissioner of oaths. The original of the affidavit of service is filed with the court, and a copy goes into your pleadings subfile. It is your proof of service of a document, who served it, the date of service, and the manner of service.

BOX 4.13 Personal Service on an Individual (Rule 8.02(a))

Refer to the fact situation in *Greco v. Hardwick* in Box 4.11 above at pages 137–138. Claire Ivory is a process server employed by Prior Mustafa LLP, the paralegals for the plaintiff, Juliette Greco. Claire has been asked to serve the plaintiff's claim on the defendant, James Hardwick. On the evening of November 8, 20—, she goes to the Hardwick residence at 128 George Court, Brampton, Ontario L1X 2V4. She knocks on the door. James Hardwick answers the door. Claire asks him if he is James Hardwick. He says yes. Claire says, "I am serving a plaintiff's claim on you in *Greco v. Hardwick*." She hands him the claim, and he takes it. This takes place at 7:30 p.m.

As Claire turns to go back to her car, James Hardwick glances at the front page of the claim. He swears, flings the claim down on the front step, goes in the house, and slams the door.

Issue: Has valid personal service of the plaintiff's claim taken place?

Discussion: Yes. Claire obtained confirmation that the person who answered the door was the named defendant, James Hardwick. She identified the document being served, and left a copy with him. The fact that James then lost his temper and threw the claim on the ground without reading it does not invalidate service.

BOX 4.14 Affidavit of Service—Personal Service on an Individual

In the *Greco v. Hardwick* fact situation discussed above, Claire Ivory is the person who **effected service** (or carried out service) of the plaintiff's claim on the defendant, James Hardwick. She will be the deponent in the affidavit of service of the plaintiff's claim, which will now be completed, sworn, and filed with the court.

A Small Claims Court defendant has 20 days from the date of service of the plaintiff's claim to deliver a defence (Rule 9.01(1)), failing which there may be adverse procedural consequences for the defendant. The affidavit of service of Claire Ivory, when filed with the court, is proof that personal service took place, and is also proof about when the 20-day period for James Hardwick to file a defence began to run.

When a plaintiff's claim has been served, you should diarize it in your checklist-tickler for a date that is 20 days (counting holidays and weekends) after the date of service. When the 20-day period has expired, you or your assistant should follow up with the court to find out whether a defence has been filed. If no defence has been filed, you should file a request to clerk to note the defendant in default and, in the case of an unliquidated claim, to sign a default judgment against the defendant (Rules 11.01 and 11.02).

See Appendix 4.6 to this chapter for a sample affidavit of service of the plaintiff's claim, based on the fact situation in *Greco v. Hardwick* above.

Personal Service on Other Persons

Rule 8.02 also sets out the requirements for valid personal service on legal persons such as parties under disability, municipalities, corporations, the federal and provincial Crowns, etc. See Table 4.1 for details of personal service on various entities. The most important thing to remember about service is that its rules are complex, and no one can remember them all. If you cannot remember, do not guess. Read Rule 8.

Alternatives to Personal Service (Rule 8.03)

Alternative methods of service may be used where the party being served has a lawyer with instructions to accept service of documents, or where personal service has been attempted and has failed, or is not feasible for various reasons. The defendant may have moved without the plaintiff's knowledge. In the case of a corporation, the address of the head office or principal place of business on record with the Companies Branch may be out of date. In other cases, a defendant may actively be avoiding service.

For a plaintiff's claim or a defendant's claim, acceptable alternatives to personal service are:

- Service at place of residence (Rule 8.03(2))
- Corporation—Service by mail or courier (Rule 8.03(3))
- Acceptance of service by lawyer (Rule 8.03(5))
- Service on individual by registered mail or courier (Rule 8.03(7))

Alternative to Personal Service—Service at Place of Residence (Rules 8.03(2) and (4))

Where a party has already tried to serve personally a document at an individual's place of residence and for any reason personal service cannot be effected, the document may be served by leaving a sealed copy addressed to the individual at the place of residence with anyone who appears to be an adult member of the same household. On the same day or the following day, another copy of the document must be mailed or sent by courier to the individual at that address.

TABLE 4.1 Personal Service (Rule 8.02)

WHO IS BEING SERVED	WITH WHOM THE DOCUMENT MAY BE LEFT	WHERE PERSONAL SERVICE IS EFFECTED
Individual (Rule 8.02(a))	The named individual	Not specified
Municipality (Rule 8.02(b))	The chair, mayor, warden, reeve, clerk, or deputy clerk of the municipality	Not specified
Corporation (Rule 8.02(c))	An officer, director, or agent of the corporation	Not specified
	A person who appears to be in control or management of a place of business of the corporation	Any place of business of the corporation
Board or commission (Rule 8.02(d))	A member or officer of the board or commission	Not specified
Person outside Ontario carrying on business in Ontario (Rule 8.02(e))	Anyone carrying on business in Ontario for the person	Not specified
Federal Crown (Rule 8.02(f))	The Deputy Attorney General of Canada	Not specified
	The chief executive officer of the agency in whose name the proceedings are taken	Not specified
Provincial Crown (Rule 8.02(g))	A solicitor in the Crown Law Office (Civil Law) of the Ministry of the Attorney General	The Crown Law Office (Civil Law) of the Ministry of the Attorney General
Absentee (Rule 8.02(h))	The absentee's committee, if one has been appointed	Not specified
	If not, with the Public Guardian and Trustee	The Office of the Public Guardian and Trustee
Minor (Rule 8.02(i))	The minor *and*, if the minor lives with a parent or other person having care and lawful custody, the parent or person with lawful custody	Not specified
Mentally incapable person (Rule 8.02(j))	In order of preference, a guardian or an attorney acting under validated power of attorney for personal care with authority to act in the proceeding	Not specified
	If the above does not apply, the mentally incapable person *and* an attorney under a power of attorney with authority to act in the proceeding	Not specified
	If the above does not apply, the mentally incapable person *and* the Public Guardian and Trustee	Not specified
Partnership (Rule 8.02(k)) NOTE: If any one or more of the partners is a corporation, refer to Rule 8.02(c)	Any one or more of the partners (see Rule 5)	Not specified
	A person who appears to be in control or management of the principal place of business of the partnership	At the principal place of business of the partnership
Sole proprietorship (Rule 8.02(l))	The sole proprietor	Not specified
	A person who appears to be in control or management of the principal place of business of the sole proprietorship	At the principal place of business of the sole proprietorship

Service under Rule 8.03(2) is effective the fifth day after the day the document is mailed or the day the courier verifies delivery (Rule 8.03(4)), or, if the last day falls on a holiday, on the next business day. The 20-day period (including holidays) for delivering a defence begins to run after the 5-day period has elapsed.

Alternative to Personal Service—Service on a Corporation (Rules 8.03(3) and (4))

All corporations incorporated under the Ontario *Business Corporations Act* are required to register their particulars, including officers, shareholders, and addresses of the head office and/or principal places of business, with the Companies and Personal Property Security Branch (Companies Branch) of the Ministry of Government Services.

Corporations incorporated under the *Canada Business Corporations Act* or under the laws of other countries, provinces, or territories are required to record the name and address of their lawyer for service in Ontario with the Ministry of Government Services.

Where these records are out of date, service of a document on an Ontario corporation may be made by mailing or sending by courier a copy of the document to the corporation at the last address recorded with the Ministry of Government Services, and by mailing or sending by courier a copy of the document to each director of the corporation as recorded at the Ministry of Government Services, at the director's last-known address recorded with the ministry.

In the case of an extra-provincial corporation, where the attorney for service in Ontario cannot be found at the last address recorded with the ministry, service may be made on the corporation by mailing or sending by courier a copy of the document to the attorney for service in Ontario at the last address recorded with the Ministry of Government Services, and by mailing or sending by courier a copy of the document to each director of the corporation as recorded at the Ministry of Government Services, at the director's last-known address recorded with the ministry.

Service is effective on the fifth day after the day the document is mailed or the day the courier verifies delivery (Rule 8.03(4))), or, if the last day falls on a holiday, on the next business day. The 20-day period (including holidays) for delivering a defence begins to run after the 5-day period has elapsed.

Alternative to Personal Service—Acceptance of Service by Lawyer (Rules 8.03(5) and (6))

Where a party has a lawyer of record, a document that would otherwise need to be served personally on that party in accordance with Rule 8.02 may instead be served on the lawyer of record or an employee in the lawyer's office. For service to be valid, the lawyer must have instructions to accept service, and the lawyer or employee accepting service must endorse the document or a copy of the document with acceptance of service and the date of the acceptance (Rule 8.03(5)). By so doing, the lawyer or an employee in the lawyer's office is deemed to represent to the court that he or she has the client's instructions to accept service (Rule 8.03(6)).

If you are serving the lawyer of record under Rule 8.03(5), you must give your process server two copies of the document being served. One will be left with the lawyer or the lawyer's employee. The other will be stamped with an acceptance of service. When the lawyer or the lawyer's employee accepts service of the document, they shall complete and sign the acceptance of service on your copy of the document. The acceptance of service proves service in the same way that an affidavit of service does. A copy of the endorsement should be put in your pleadings subfile, and the original should be filed with the court office with an affidavit of service.

Alternative to Personal Service—Service of Claim on an Individual by Registered Mail or Courier to Individual at the Individual's Place of Residence (Rules 8.03(7) and (8))

This rule is restricted to service of a plaintiff's claim or defendant's claim on an individual against whom the claim is made. The claim may be served by registered mail or by courier at the individual's place of residence, but service is valid only if the individual's signature or that of any person who appears to be a member of the same household verifying receipt of the copy is obtained (Rule 8.03(7)). Service under Rule 8.03(7) is effective on the date on which receipt of the copy of the claim is verified by signature, evidenced by a delivery confirmation provided by Canada Post or the commercial courier, as the case may be (Rule 8.03(8)).

Other Methods of Service

Substituted Service (Rule 8.04)

Sometimes prompt service of a claim by personal service or by an alternative to personal service cannot be carried out because the other party cannot be located or is actively avoiding service, or for other reasons. In these circumstances, the plaintiff may make a motion to the court for an **order for substituted service**—that is, an order permitting the plaintiff to serve the claim in a manner that is not strictly in accordance with the Rules.

Before granting an order for **substituted service**, the court must be satisfied that it is impractical to effect prompt service of the claim personally or by an alternative to personal service. The person requesting the order may be required to demonstrate that all reasonable steps have been taken to serve the other party personally or by an alternative to personal service, without success.

If the order is granted, it will specify what steps the plaintiff must take to comply with the requirements for substituted service. Unless the court orders otherwise, the plaintiff must serve a copy of the order for substituted service along with the claim.

Service Outside Ontario (Rule 8.05)

If the defendant is outside Ontario, the plaintiff may incur extra expense trying to effect service of the claim. In a costs award to the plaintiff, the court may include any reasonable costs incurred by the plaintiff in effecting service on an out-of-province defendant.

Service by Mail (Rule 8.07)

A document that may be served by mail may be sent by regular letter mail or registered mail to the last address of the person or the person's lawyer or paralegal that is known to the sender (Rule 8.07(1)(b)). If the court clerk is serving a document by mail, the document may be mailed to the last address on file with the court (Rule 8.07(1)(a)).

Service by mail becomes effective five days from the date of mailing (Rule 8.07(2)), unless the five-day period ends on a holiday, in which case, service takes effect on the next business day.

Rule 8.07(2) does not apply when a claim is served by mail under Rule 8.03(7)—Service of Claim on an individual by mail or courier at the individual's place of residence (Rule 8.07(3)).

Service by Courier (Rule 8.07.1)

A document to be served by courier must be sent by means of a commercial courier to the last address of the person or the person's lawyer or paralegal that is on file with the court or known to the sender.

Service takes effect five days after the date that the courier confirms delivery of the document (Rule 8.07.1(2)). The five-day period excludes holidays and must end on a business day.

Rule 8.07.1(2) does not apply when a claim is served by courier under Rule 8.03(7)—Service of claim on an individual by mail or courier at the individual's place of residence (Rule 8.07.1(3)).

Service by Fax (Rule 8.08)

Service by fax is deemed to be effective on the date of the faxing, if faxing took place before 5:00 p.m. on a business day (Rule 8.08(1)(a)). In any other case, service by fax becomes effective on the next business day (Rule 8.08(1)(b)). In other words, if you serve the other party by fax at or after 5:00 p.m. on a business day, service is effective on the next business day. If you serve the other party by fax on a holiday (as defined in Rule 1.02), service is effective on the next business day.

The original of the fax transmission sheet, confirming the fax number of the recipient and the date and time that service took place, should be attached to the affidavit of service filed with the court. Your file copy of the affidavit of service by fax should have a copy of the fax transmission sheet attached.

If the document that you are serving contains 16 or more pages, including the cover page, it must be faxed outside regular business hours unless you have the other party's consent to fax it between 8:00 a.m. and 5:00 p.m. (Rule 8.08(2)).

Service of Other Documents

Table 4.2 lists the documents that must be served personally or by an alternative to personal service.

The court clerk shall serve the following documents:

- A defence (including a defence to a defendant's claim), by mail or by fax (Rule 8.01(3))
- A default judgment, by mail or by fax (Rule 8.01(4))
- An assessment order made on a motion in writing for an assessment of damages, by mail if the moving party provides a stamped, self-addressed envelope with the notice of motion (Rule 8.01(5))
- A settlement conference order by mail or by fax to all parties that did not attend the settlement conference (Rule 8.01(6))

The following documents shall be served personally, by an alternative to personal service, by mail, or by courier:

- Notice of garnishment and affidavit for enforcement request, on the debtor (Rule 8.01(8)(a))
- Notice of garnishment and garnishee's statement, on the garnishee (Rule 8.01(8)(b))
- Notice of garnishment hearing (Rule 8.01(9))
- Notice of examination (Rule 8.01(10))
- Financial statement (Rule 8.01(11))

Any document that is not referred to above or in Table 4.2 may be served by mail, by courier, by fax, personally, or by an alternative to personal service, unless the court orders otherwise (Rule 8.01(14)).

TABLE 4.2 Documents That Shall Be Served Personally (Rule 8.01) or by an Alternative to Personal Service

DOCUMENT	MANNER OF SERVICE	TIME FOR SERVICE
Plaintiff's claim (Form 7A)	• Personal (Rule 8.01(1)) • Alternative to personal service (Rule 8.03(1)) • Substituted service (with leave of court) (Rule 8.04)	Six months from date of issuance, unless court order extends the time (Rule 8.01(2))
Defendant's claim (Form 10A)	• Personal (Rule 8.01(1)) • Alternative to personal service (Rule 8.03(1)) • Substituted service (with leave of court) (Rule 8.04)	Six months from date of issuance, unless court order extends the time (Rule 8.01(2))
Summons to witness (Form 18A)	• Personal (Rule 8.01(7))	At least 10 days before the hearing date
Notice of contempt hearing	• Personal (Rule 8.01(13))	At least 7 days before the hearing date

Notice of Change of Address (Rule 8.09)

Rule 8.09 requires that a party whose address for service has changed shall serve notice of the change on the court and other parties within seven days after the change takes place.

There is no form for a notice of change of address. However, best practice requires that it should be in writing and it should be sent to all other parties and filed with the clerk. The court may order that proof of service be filed by way of an affidavit of service (Rule 8.09(2)).

Failure to Receive Document (Rule 8.10)

Sometimes a document is served in accordance with Rule 8 or a court order for substituted service, but the person on whom it was deemed to be served does not receive it, or finds out about it at some time later than when it was served or deemed to have been served. A person who fails to receive a document in the above circumstances may make a motion to set aside the consequences of default, for an extension of time, or in support of a request for an adjournment, raising failure to receive the document or late receipt of the document, as the case may be, as a ground for granting the relief sought.

Amendment of Pleading (Rule 12)

General

If you make a mistake on a pleading, you are permitted to correct it by Rule 12.01(1), which provides that a plaintiff's or defendant's claim, or a defence to a plaintiff's or defendant's claim, may be **amended** (that is, changed or corrected or otherwise altered). Any changes or additions must be underlined on the pleading, and deletions or other changes should be identified. The amended pleading must be marked "Amended," filed with the clerk, and served on all parties, including parties in default (Rules 12.01(1) and (2)). An amended pleading may be served personally, by an alternative to personal service, by mail, by courier, or by fax (Rule 8.01(14)).

An amended pleading may be filed and served at any time up until at least 30 days before the original trial date, unless the court on motion allows a shorter notice period (Rule 12.01(3)(a)), or a request for clerk's order on consent under Rule 11.2.01(1) allowing a shorter notice period is obtained.

Where a person is added as a party at trial, the court may order that service of the claim be dispensed with (Rule 12.01(4)).

A party who is served with an amended pleading is not required to amend their own claim or defence, as the case may be (Rule 12.01(5)).

Motion to Strike Out or Amend a Document (Rule 12.02)

On a motion by a party, the court may strike out (delete) or amend (revise) all or part of a document if either or both of the following apply.

1. Part or all of the document should be struck out or amended because it discloses no reasonable cause of action or defence (Rule 12.02(1)(a)). A plaintiff's or defendant's claim must contain allegations of fact that support some lawful ground for requesting relief. For example, if your neighbour has a noisy party every weekend that keeps you awake until three o'clock in the morning, it may be irritating and disruptive and a reason for calling the police. However, your neighbour's parties become grounds for commencing a civil action for damages only if your neighbour or her guests cause damage to your property, and/or their behaviour negatively affects your psychological or physical health or that of your family in a way that can be documented by medical evidence, and/or your neighbour's conduct or that of her guests causes some other actionable damage.

   A defence must contain allegations of fact that support some lawful ground for denying the relief requested in the claim. If someone sues you for money, it is not a defence to say that you owe the money, but you need time to pay. That is an admission.

2. Part or all of the document should be struck out or amended because it may delay or make it difficult to have a fair trial, or is inflammatory, a waste of time, a nuisance, or an abuse of the court's process (Rules 12.02(1)(b) and (c)). These rules apply to claims or defences that contain allegations that are difficult to prove, unfair, insulting, or defamatory to other parties, and that cannot be supported by the evidence. The court may amend the allegations if there are any grounds for doing so.

On a motion where any or all of Rules 12.02(1)(a), (b), and (c) apply, the court may make an order for the following under Rule 12.02(2):

1. In the case of a claim, order that an action be stayed (stopped) or dismissed (as having no legal merit);

2. In the case of a defence, order that the defence be struck (dismissed as having no legal merit) and grant judgment for the other party; and/or

3. Impose such terms as are just (for example, costs to the successful party).

In an action where the parties are self-represented and/or unsophisticated, Rule 12.02(2) should be applied with caution. A claim should be dismissed or a defence struck only if it is perfectly clear that the flaws in pleading indicate the absence of a cause of action, not a lack of familiarity with legal principles.

CHAPTER SUMMARY

When you have satisfied yourself that Small Claims Court has jurisdiction to try your client's matter, you must set about commencing the action. The first step is to identify and quantify your client's damages. A claim that is wholly for special or liquidated damages is called a liquidated claim. In a liquidated claim for a debt or fixed amount of money, you will use the contract between the parties, unpaid invoices, and so on, to determine the amount owing. General damages (also known as unliquidated damages) are amounts that are not fixed and quantifiable based on objective evidence. General damages are more speculative in nature.

On the plaintiff's claim, other parties to the action must be properly named, in accordance with the applicable rules. If the plaintiff does not have complete or accurate information, you should take appropriate steps to ensure that you have the correct names and addresses for both individual and business defendants.

The plaintiff's claim should set out all of the factual allegations in support of the relief the plaintiff is claiming in an orderly narrative using concise, non-technical language and the dates, places, and nature of the occurrences on which the claim is based.

Copies of any documents upon which you intend to rely should be attached to the plaintiff's claim.

A proceeding is commenced when the plaintiff's claim, together with a copy for each defendant, is taken to the office of the Small Claims Court with territorial jurisdiction, and issued by the clerk. The claim is issued when the clerk dates, signs, and seals it, and assigns a court file number. The plaintiff's claim should be served personally (Rule 8.02) or by an alternative to personal service (Rule 8.03) on all defendants within six months after the date of issue. The court may extend the time for service in appropriate circumstances.

If prompt service of the claim personally or by an alternative to personal service is impractical, the court may make an order for substituted service (Rule 8.04).

A plaintiff's or defendant's claim or a defence may be amended by filing a copy marked "Amended" with the clerk and by serving copies on all other parties, including parties in default.

On a motion by a party, the court may strike out or amend a claim or a defence if it discloses no reasonable cause of action or defence, may delay or make it difficult to have a fair trial, or is inflammatory, a waste of time, a nuisance, or an abuse of the court's process (Rule 12.02).

KEY TERMS

affidavit: a written statement of facts that is confirmed under oath or by affirmation by the person making the affidavit *(p. 131)*

alternative to personal service: alternative method of delivery of a legal document to another party in a proceeding; may be used when the party being served has a lawyer with instructions to accept service of documents or when personal service has been attempted and has failed *(p. 142)*

amend: to change or correct a pleading, with the object of improving it or making it more complete *(p. 150)*

attorney: person authorized to act pursuant to a power of attorney *(p. 123)*

binding authority: a judicial decision by a higher court that must be followed by lower courts (also known as binding precedent) *(p. 132)*

causation: for damages to be awarded to the plaintiff, the evidence must establish that the harm or loss suffered by the plaintiff resulted from the defendant's actions or negligence *(p. 106)*

cause of action: the factual and legal grounds for seeking a remedy from a court *(p. 113)*

committee: a person appointed by the court to manage the property of an absentee *(p. 123)*

date of default: the date the cause of action arose *(p. 113)*

deponent: the person who makes an affidavit *(p. 131)*

effect service: carry out or perform valid service of a document *(p. 143)*

frivolous and vexatious objection: an objection that has no legal merit and is made to annoy, harass, or embarrass the other side *(p. 129)*

general damages: damages for pain and suffering caused by injury or harm, and for future losses and expenses, such as future care costs and loss of future income; general damages cannot be quantified precisely, but they must be itemized and explained to the extent that it is possible to do so; also referred to as unliquidated damages *(p. 107)*

joint and several liability: form of liability where each partner is liable for any amount up to the full amount of any judgment obtained against the partnership *(p. 117)*

judicial notice: matters of common knowledge (also referred to as "notorious facts") that a judge may accept as true without hearing evidence and without inquiry—lesser known facts (for example, matters that can be checked in a standard reference work and are not easily disputed) may be judicially noticed after inquiry *(p. 135)*

liquidated claim: claim for a debt or fixed amount of money that does not require valuation by a court *(p. 106)*

liquidated damages: a specific amount of money that may be established by unpaid invoices, NSF cheques, or other documentation proving a debt or fixed amount; also called special damages *(p. 106)*

litigation guardian: a competent person who undertakes to direct a legal proceeding on behalf of a person under disability *(p. 121)*

merits of the case: the legal principles upon which a party's assertion of rights is based *(p. 130)*

non-pecuniary damages: damages awarded for types of harm that are real and serious, but difficult to assign a money value to *(p. 107)*

objection: an argument by a party that a particular piece of evidence, line of questioning, or other matter is improper or illegal and should not be allowed by the court *(p. 129)*

order for substituted service: a court order permitting the plaintiff to serve the claim in a manner that is not set out in the Rules *(p. 147)*

partnership: an unincorporated business that is formed by two or more persons with the objective of making a profit *(p. 117)*

partnership agreement: a contract that allocates liability among the partners, and specifies other terms and conditions of the partnership; binding only on the parties to the agreement *(p. 117)*

party under disability: in Small Claims Court, a person or party who is (a) a minor, (b) mentally incapable within the meaning s. 6 or 45 of the *Substitute Decisions Act*, *1992*, or (c) an absentee within the meaning of the *Absentees Act* *(p. 121)*

payment into court: money paid to the accountant of the Superior Court of Justice pursuant to a court order, to be paid out to creditors or other parties in accordance with a court order *(p. 125)*

payment out of court: when money paid into court is paid out by the accountant of the Superior Court of Justice, in accordance with a court order *(p. 125)*

pecuniary damages: damages awarded for losses that can be estimated in money terms *(p. 107)*

personal service: personal delivery of a copy of a document (e.g., an issued plaintiff's claim) to another party in accordance with the procedures set out in Rule 8.02; the requirements for personal service vary, depending upon who the other party is (e.g., an individual, a corporation, a municipality, etc.) *(p. 142)*

plaintiff's claim: the document that sets out the names of the parties and their addresses for service, the amount of the claim, any other relief being sought, and the allegations of fact in support of the claim *(p. 106)*

pleadings: the documents filed at the commencement of a proceeding, in which the parties plead, or state, the allegations of fact on which they rely in support of their case; in a Small Claims Court proceeding, the pleadings are the plaintiff's claim, the defence, the defendant's claim, and the defence to the defendant's claim, if any *(p. 136)*

post-judgment interest: interest that accrues on the judgment amount, including costs, or on any outstanding balances, until such time as any balance owing has been paid in full *(p. 113)*

power of attorney: a document authorizing an individual to act on another person's behalf in a legal or business matter *(p. 123)*

prayer or claim for relief: the first paragraph in a claim, setting out in separate subparagraphs particulars of the damages, interest, and other relief that the plaintiff thinks she is entitled to *(p. 140)*

precedent document: a legal document that is used as a template or guide for drafting subsequent documents with a similar purpose *(p. 139)*

pre-judgment interest: interest that accrues on the amount determined to be owing commencing with the date of default and ending with the date of judgment *(p. 113)*

promissory note: a promise to pay that is signed and dated by the debtor; it should contain the following terms: the names of the payor and the debtor, the amount advanced to the debtor, and the date on which it was advanced, and the terms of the loan, including payment terms, interest rates, penalties on default, if any, etc. *(p. 107)*

remedy: a method of enforcing a right, or preventing or compensating for a wrong *(p. 129)*

service: delivery of a legal document to another party in a proceeding *(p. 142)*

set aside: to declare a court order or procedural step to be of no force and effect *(p. 122)*

sole proprietorship: an unincorporated business owned and run by one individual *(p. 116)*

special damages: damages that compensate the plaintiff for all losses, including out-of-pocket expenses connected with the injury or harm, up to the date of the trial; can usually be calculated fairly precisely *(p. 106)*

substituted service: an order permitting the plaintiff to serve the claim in a manner that is not strictly in accordance with the Rules *(p. 147)*

unliquidated claim: claim for an indefinite amount that must be valued by the court based on the evidence *(p. 113)*

unliquidated damages: an amount that is not fixed and specified, which must be determined by the court based on the evidence *(p. 107)*

REFERENCES

Absentees Act, RSO 1990, c. A.3.
Business Corporations Act, RSO 1990, c. B.16.
Business Names Act, RSO 1990, c. B.17.
Canada Business Corporations Act, RSC 1985, c. C-44.
Courts of Justice Act, RSO 1990, c. C.43.
Criminal Code, RSC 1985, c. C-46.
Law Society of Upper Canada (LSUC), *Paralegal Professional Conduct Guidelines* (Toronto: LSUC, 2008, as amended); available online at http://www.lsuc.on.ca.
Law Society of Upper Canada (LSUC), *Paralegal Rules of Conduct* (Toronto: LSUC, 2007, as amended); available online at http://www.lsuc.on.ca.
Limitations Act, 2002, SO 2002, c. 24, sched. B.
Limited Partnerships Act, RSO 1990, c. L.16.

Office of the Public Guardian and Trustee, The Accountant of the Superior Court of Justice (Queen's Printer for Ontario, 2007); available online at http://www .attorneygeneral.jus.gov.on.ca/english/family/pgt/ ascj.pdf.
Repair and Storage Liens Act, RSO 1990, c. R.25.
Rules of Civil Procedure, RRO 1990, Reg. 194.
Rules of the Small Claims Court, O. Reg. 258/98.
Small Claims Court Guide to Procedures—Guide to Money Paid Into Court (Queen's Printer for Ontario, 2009); available online at http://www.attorneygeneral .jus.gov.on.ca/english/courts/guides/ Guide_to_Money_Paid_into_Court_EN.pdf.
Substitute Decisions Act, 1992, SO 1992, c. 30.

DRAFTING EXERCISE

Dante v. Herrero—Drafting a Claim Using Precedent Documents

Review the fact situation in *Dante v. Herrero* in Box 4.1 at page 107. Referring to the precedents for a claim for money owed pursuant to an unpaid promissory note in Appendix 3.1 (*Parrish v. Thurston*) and Appendix 4.4 (*Greco v. Hardwick*), draft a plaintiff's claim (Form 7A). The claim will be prepared on April 3, 20—, and issued on the same date. Do not fill in the date of issuing on the Form 7A—the court clerk will do that when the claim is issued. The court file number (claim number) is SC-06638-00.

The claim is served personally on Ms. Herrero at her home address on April 5, 20— by Martin Bruni of Brampton, Ontario. Complete an affidavit of service (Form 8A). The affidavit of service will be sworn on April 7, 20—.

REVIEW QUESTIONS

When answering the following questions, please refer to any rules or statutory authority upon which you are relying.

1. What are special damages?

2. What are general damages?

3. On a plaintiff's claim, how do you name each of the following?

   a. An individual defendant

   b. An individual defendant who uses more than one name

   c. A corporate defendant

   d. A sole proprietorship

   e. A partnership

4. What is joint and several liability?

5. What is a person under disability?

6. What is a litigation guardian?

7. What are pleadings?

8. What are the rules for service of a claim?

9. You draft a plaintiff's claim, naming one defendant. After the claim has been issued and personally served on the defendant, you discover that you spelled the defendant's name wrong, and that you need to add a second defendant. What must you do?

APPENDIX 4.1 Notice to Alleged Partner (Form 5A)

ONTARIO

Superior Court of Justice
Cour supérieure de justice

Notice to Alleged Partner
Avis au prétendu associé

Form / *Formule* 5A Ont. Reg. No. / *Régl. de l'Ont.* : 258/98

Brampton

Small Claims Court / *Cour des petites créances de*

7755 Hurontario Street
Brampton, Ontario
L6W 4T6

Address / *Adresse*

905 456 4700

Phone number / *Numéro de téléphone*

SC-00-33445-00

Claim No. / *N° de la demande*

BETWEEN / *ENTRE*

Amrita Chakravarty

Plaintiff(s) / *Demandeur(s)/demanderesse(s)*

and / *et*

Complete Home Renovations

Defendant(s) / *Défendeur(s)/défenderesse(s)*

TO:
DESTINATAIRE :

Name of alleged partner / *Nom du (de la) prétendu(e) associé(e)*   **Franklin Butler**
Street and number / *Numéro et rue*   **455 Lonsdale Court**
City, province, postal code / *Ville, province, code postal*   **Mississauga, Ontario X2X 3Y4**

YOU ARE ALLEGED TO HAVE BEEN A PARTNER on _____, 20 _____
IL EST ALLÉGUÉ QUE VOUS ÉTIEZ UN(E) ASSOCIÉ(E) le

(or during the period) **June 1**_____, 20 -- to **October 31**_____, 20 --
(ou pendant la période du)   *au*

in the partnership/business of **Complete Home Renovations**_____,
de la société en nom collectif/l'entreprise de   (Firm name / *Raison sociale*)

a party named in this proceeding.
désignée comme partie à l'instance.

IF YOU WISH TO DENY THAT YOU WERE A PARTNER at any material time, you must defend this proceeding separately from the partnership, denying that you were a partner at the material time. If you fail to do so, you will be deemed to have been a partner on the date (or during the period) set out above.
SI VOUS SOUHAITEZ NIER QUE VOUS ÉTIEZ UN(E) ASSOCIÉ(E) *à l'époque en cause, vous devez présenter dans l'instance une défense distincte de celle de la société en nom collectif, selon laquelle vous niez avoir été un(e) associé(e) à cette époque. À défaut de ce faire, vous serez réputé(e) avoir été une(e) associé(e) à la date (ou pendant la période) susmentionnée.*

CAUTION: **AN ORDER AGAINST THE PARTNERSHIP MAY BE ENFORCED AGAINST YOU PERSONALLY** if you are deemed to have been a partner, if you admit that you were, or if the court finds that you were at the material time.
AVERTISSEMENT : *UNE ORDONNANCE CONTRE LA SOCIÉTÉ EN NOM COLLECTIF PEUT ÊTRE EXÉCUTÉE CONTRE VOUS PERSONNELLEMENT si vous êtes réputé(e) avoir été un(e) associé(e), si vous admettez ce fait ou si le tribunal conclut que vous étiez un(e) associé(e) à l'époque en cause.*

_____, 20 _____   _____
                                       (Signature of plaintiff or representative / *Signature du demandeur/de la demanderesse ou du/de la représentant(e)*)

SCR 5.03-5A (June 1, 2009 / *1er juin 2009*) CSD

APPENDIX 4.2 Consent to Act as Plaintiff's Litigation Guardian (Form 4A)

ONTARIO

Superior Court of Justice
Cour supérieure de justice

Consent to Act as Litigation Guardian
Consentement pour agir en qualité de tuteur à l'instance
Form / *Formule* 4A Ont. Reg. No. / *Règl. de l'Ont.* : 258/98

Brampton
Small Claims Court / *Cour des petites créances de*
7755 Hurontario Street
Brampton, Ontario
L6W 4T6
Address / *Adresse*

905 456 4700
Phone number / *Numéro de téléphone*

SC-00-44556-00
Claim No. / *N° de la demande*

BETWEEN / ENTRE

Collette Desbarais

Plaintiff(s) / *Demandeur(s)/demanderesse(s)*

and / et

Emma Good

Defendant(s) / *Défendeur(s)/défenderesse(s)*

My name is
Je m'appelle

And I live at
et j'habite à

Name / *Nom*
Antoinette France Desbarais

Street and number / *Numéro et rue*
15 Tranquillity Court

City, province, postal code / *Ville, province, code postal*
Brampton, Ontario A1B 2C3

Phone number and fax number / *Numéro de téléphone et numéro de télécopieur*
905 333 5555

1. I consent to act as litigation guardian in this action for the
   Je consens à agir à titre de tuteur à l'instance dans la présente action au nom du

   ☒ plaintiff, named **Collette Desbarais**
   demandeur suivant :   (Name of plaintiff / *Nom du demandeur/de la demanderesse*)

   (Check one box only. / Cochez une seule case.*)*

   and I acknowledge that I may be personally responsible for any costs awarded against me or against this person.
   et je reconnais que je peux être tenu(e) personnellement responsable des dépens auxquels moi-même ou cette personne pourrions être condamné(e)s.

   ☐ defendant, named _____ .
   défenseur suivant :   (Name of defendant / *Nom du défendeur/de la défenderesse*)

2. The above-named person is under the following disability:
   La personne susmentionnée est incapable parce qu'elle est :

   ☒ a minor whose birth date is **December 12, 2003**   .
   un mineur dont la date de naissance est le   (State date of birth of minor / *Indiquez la date de naissance du mineur*)

   (Check appropriate box(es). / Cochez la ou les cases appropriées.*)*

   ☐ mentally incapable within the meaning of Section 6 or Section 45 of the *Substitute Decisions Act, 1992* in respect of an issue in a proceeding.
   mentalement incapable au sens de l'article 6 ou 45 de la Loi de 1992 sur la prise de décisions au nom d'autrui à l'égard d'une question dans une instance.

   ☐ an absentee within the meaning of the *Absentees Act.*
   une personne absente au sens de la Loi sur les absents.

SCR 4.01-4.02-4A (June 1, 2009 / *1ᵉʳ juin 2009*) CSD

APPENDIX 4.2 **Consent to Act as Plaintiff's Litigation Guardian (Form 4A)** *concluded*

FORM / *FORMULE* **4A**   **PAGE 2**   SC-00-44556-00

Claim No. / *N° de la demande*

3. My relationship to the person under disability is:
Mon lien de parenté avec l'incapable est le suivant :
(State your relationship to the person under disability. / Indiquez votre lien de parenté avec l'incapable.)

mother

4. I have no interest in this action contrary to that of the person under disability.
Je n'ai dans la présente action aucun intérêt opposé à celui de l'incapable.

5. I am
Je

(Check one box only. / Cochez une seule case.)

☒ represented and have given written authority to   **Joseph Mustafa**

(Name of lawyer/agent with authority to act in this proceeding / *Nom de l'avocat/du mandataire autorisé à agir dans la présente instance*)

suis représenté(e) et j'ai autorisé par écrit :

of **Prior Mustafa LLP, 22 County Court Boulevard, Brampton, Ontario A1A 2B3**
de   (Address for service / *Adresse aux fins de signification*)

TEL: 905 111 2222 FAX: 905 111 2233

(Phone number and fax number / *Numéro de téléphone et numéro de télécopieur*)

to act in this proceeding.
à agir dans la présente instance.

☐ not represented by a lawyer/agent.
ne suis pas représenté(e) par un avocat/un mandataire.

_____ , 20 _____

(Signature of litigation guardian consenting / *Signature du tuteur à l'instance qui consent*)

_____

(Signature of witness / *Signature du témoin*)

Joseph Mustafa

(Name of witness / *Nom du témoin*)

NOTE: Within seven (7) calendar days of changing your address for service, notify the court and all other parties in writing.
REMARQUE : *Dans les sept (7) jours civils qui suivent tout changement de votre adresse aux fins de signification, veuillez en aviser par écrit le tribunal et les autres parties.*

SCR 4.01-4.02-4A (June 1, 2009 / *1er juin 2009*) CSD

APPENDIX 4.3 Request to Pay Money Into or Out of Court

Ontario   Ministry of the Attorney General   Court Services Division   **Request to Pay Money into or out of Court**

Court File No. _____

To the Accountant of the Superior Court of Justice or the Clerk of the Small Claims Court:

My name is _____ .
(Full name)

I live at _____ .
(Address (street and number, unit, municipality, province, and postal code))

I wish to have money: ☐ paid into court. I have completed Section A below.
                  ☐ paid out of court. I have completed Section B below.

Section A: Request to pay money into court

☐ I am paying money into court under the following statute or court rule: _____
                                                                  (List the statute or court rule, including the section number)

☐ I am paying money into court because a judge ordered me to. A copy of the court order stamped with the court's red seal is attached.

If you are paying money into court for a person under disability, please complete the following:

I am paying money into court for: _____, **born on** _____ ,
                                    (Name of person under disability)   (MM/DD/YYYY)

who lives at: _____ ,
                   (Address (street and number, unit, municipality, province, and postal code))

telephone number: _____ .
                     (xxx) xxx-xxxx

S/he is: ☐ a minor (under the age of 18).   ☐ a mentally incapable person.

Her/his litigation guardian is: _____
                                      (Name of litigation guardian)

_____
(Address (street and number, unit, municipality, province, and postal code))

_____   _____
           Signature   Date

* A request to pay into court does not need to be sworn/affirmed before a commissioner for taking affidavits.

Section B: Request to have money paid out of court and supporting affidavit

I ask that $ _____ be paid out to: ☐ me, as ordered by the court (payment will be sent to the address above), or

                                        ☐ _____ , **who lives at**
                                                 (Name of other person named in court order)

_____
(Address (street and number, unit, municipality, province, and postal code))

A copy of the court order stamped with the court's red seal is attached.

I swear/affirm that the time allowed for an appeal has ended and no appeal is pending.

Sworn/Affirmed before me at _____
                                          (Municipality)

in _____
             (Province, state or country)   _____
                                                   Signature

on _____ , 20 _____ _____
                                   Commissioner for taking affidavits   (This form is to be signed in front of a lawyer, justice of the peace, notary public or commissioner for taking affidavits.)
                               (Type or print name below if signature is illegible.)

WARNING: IT IS AN OFFENCE UNDER THE *CRIMINAL CODE* TO KNOWINGLY SWEAR OR AFFIRM A FALSE AFFIDAVIT.

Request to Pay Money into or out of Court (rev. 01/13) CSD

APPENDIX 4.4   Greco v. Hardwick: Plaintiff's Claim for Liquidated Damages (Form 7A)

ONTARIO

Superior Court of Justice
Cour supérieure de justice

Plaintiff's Claim
Demande du demandeur
Form / *Formule* 7A Ont. Reg. No. / *Règl. de l'Ont.* : 258/98

Seal / *Sceau*

Brampton
Small Claims Court / *Cour des petites créances de*
7755 Hurontario Street
Brampton, Ontario
L6W 4T6
Address / *Adresse*

905 456 4700
Phone number / *Numéro de téléphone*

SC-00-34065-00
Claim No. / *N° de la demande*

Plaintiff No. 1 / *Demandeur n° 1*

☐ Additional plaintiff(s) listed on attached Form 1A.
Le ou les demandeurs additionnels sont mentionnés sur la formule 1A ci-jointe.

☐ Under 18 years of age.
Moins de 18 ans.

Last name, or name of company / *Nom de famille ou nom de la compagnie*		
Greco		
First name / *Premier prénom*	Second name / *Deuxième prénom*	Also known as / *Également connu(e) sous le nom de*
Juliette		
Address (street number, apt., unit) / *Adresse (numéro et rue, app., unité)*		
c/o Prior Mustafa LLP		
City/Town / *Cité/ville*	Province	Phone no. / *N° de téléphone*
Postal code / *Code postal*		Fax no. / *N° de télécopieur*
Representative / *Représentant(e)*		LSUC # / *N° du BHC*
Prior Mustafa LLP Attention: Paralegal name		**######**
Address (street number, apt., unit) / *Adresse (numéro et rue, app., unité)*		
22 County Court Boulevard		
City/Town / *Cité/ville*	Province	Phone no. / *N° de téléphone*
Brampton	**Ontario**	**905 111 2222**
Postal code / *Code postal*		Fax no. / *N° de télécopieur*
		905 111 2233
A1A 2B3		

Defendant No. 1 / *Défendeur n° 1*

☐ Additional defendant(s) listed on attached Form 1A.
Le ou les défendeurs additionnels sont mentionnés sur la formule 1A ci-jointe.

☐ Under 18 years of age.
Moins de 18 ans.

Last name, or name of company / *Nom de famille ou nom de la compagnie*		
Hardwick		
First name / *Premier prénom*	Second name / *Deuxième prénom*	Also known as / *Également connu(e) sous le nom de*
James		
Address (street number, apt., unit) / *Adresse (numéro et rue, app., unité)*		
128 George Court		
City/Town / *Cité/ville*	Province	Phone no. / *N° de téléphone*
Brampton	**Ontario**	**905 791 3333**
Postal code / *Code postal*		Fax no. / *N° de télécopieur*
L1X 2V4		
Representative / *Représentant(e)*		LSUC # / *N° du BHC*
Address (street number, apt., unit) / *Adresse (numéro et rue, app., unité)*		
City/Town / *Cité/ville*	Province	Phone no. / *N° de téléphone*
Postal code / *Code postal*		Fax no. / *N° de télécopieur*

SCR 7.01-7A (June 1, 2009 / *1er juin 2009*) CSD

APPENDIX 4.4 **Greco v. Hardwick: Plaintiff's Claim for Liquidated Damages (Form 7A)** *continued*

FORM / *FORMULE* **7A** PAGE 2 SC-00-34065-00
 Claim No. / *N° de la demande*

REASONS FOR CLAIM AND DETAILS / *MOTIFS DE LA DEMANDE ET PRÉCISIONS*

Explain what happened, including where and when. Then explain how much money you are claiming or what goods you want returned.
Expliquez ce qui s'est passé, en précisant où et quand. Ensuite indiquez la somme d'argent que vous demandez ou les biens dont vous demandez la restitution, explication à l'appui.

If you are relying on any documents, you **MUST** attach copies to the claim. If evidence is lost or unavailable, you **MUST** explain why it is not attached.
*Si vous vous appuyez sur des documents, vous **DEVEZ** en annexer des copies à la demande. Si une preuve est perdue ou n'est pas disponible, vous **DEVEZ** expliquer pourquoi elle n'est pas annexée.*

What happened? See Schedule A attached and forming part of this claim
Where?
When?

Que s'est-il
passé?
Où?
Quand?

SCR 7.01-7A (June 1, 2009 / *1er juin 2009*) CSD Continued on next page / *Suite à la page suivante*

APPENDIX 4.4 **Greco v. Hardwick: Plaintiff's Claim for Liquidated Damages (Form 7A)** *continued*

FORM / *FORMULE* 7A PAGE 3 SC-00-34065-00

Claim No. / *N° de la demande*

How much? $ 5,000.00
Combien? (Principal amount claimed / *Somme demandée*) $

☒ ADDITIONAL PAGES ARE ATTACHED BECAUSE MORE ROOM WAS NEEDED.
DES FEUILLES SUPPLÉMENTAIRES SONT ANNEXÉES EN RAISON DU MANQUE D'ESPACE.

The plaintiff also claims pre-judgment interest from August 2, 20-- under:
Le demandeur demande aussi des intérêts (Date) *conformément à :*
antérieurs au jugement de

(Check only one box / Cochez une seule case)

☐ the *Courts of Justice Act*
la Loi sur les tribunaux judiciaires

☒ an agreement at the rate of 10 % per year
un accord au taux de % *par an*

and post-judgment interest, and court costs.
et des intérêts postérieurs au jugement, ainsi que les dépens.

Prepared on: November 2 , 20 --
Fait le : (Signature of plaintiff or representative / *Signature du demandeur/de la demanderesse ou du/de la représentant(e)*)

Issued on: , 20
Délivré le : (Signature of clerk / *Signature du greffier*)

CAUTION TO DEFENDANT:	**IF YOU DO NOT FILE A DEFENCE** (Form 9A) with the court within twenty (20) calendar days after you have been served with this Plaintiff's Claim, judgment may be obtained without notice and enforced against you. Forms and self-help materials are available at the Small Claims Court and on the following website: www.ontariocourtforms.on.ca.
AVERTISSEMENT AU DÉFENDEUR :	***SI VOUS NE DÉPOSEZ PAS DE DÉFENSE*** (formule 9A) *auprès du tribunal au plus tard vingt (20) jours civils après avoir reçu signification de la présente demande du demandeur, un jugement peut être obtenu sans préavis et être exécuté contre vous. Vous pouvez obtenir les formules et la documentation à l'usage du client à la Cour des petites créances et sur le site Web suivant : www.ontariocourtforms.on.ca.*

SCR 7.01-7A (June 1, 2009 / *1ᵉʳ juin 2009*) CSD

Schedule A

1. The plaintiff claims:

   (a) $5,000.00;

   (b) Pre- and post-judgment interest at a rate of 10% per annum from the date of default until such time as any amounts owing are paid in full in accordance with the terms of the promissory note dated April 1, 20—;

   (c) In the alternative, pre- and post-judgment interest in accordance with the *Courts of Justice Act*;

   (d) Her costs of this action; and

   (e) Such further and other relief as this Honourable Court deems just.

2. The plaintiff is an individual residing in the City of Brampton in the Province of Ontario.

3. The defendant is an individual residing at 128 George Court in the City of Brampton in the Province of Ontario.

4. Pursuant to a promissory note dated April 1, 20—, the plaintiff loaned the defendant the sum of $5,000.00. According to the terms of the note, the entire sum was to be repaid in full by the defendant on or before August 2, 20—. In the event of default, interest became due and owing on the balance owing at a rate of 10% per annum from the date of default until such time as all amounts owing were paid in full.

5. The defendant failed to pay the amount owing on or before August 2, 20—.

6. In spite of repeated demands for payment, both spoken and written, the defendant has failed to pay anything whatsoever on account of the amount owing to the plaintiff.

Attached documents:

Promissory note signed by James Hardwick dated April 1, 20—

Letter dated August 15, 20— from Juliette Greco to James Hardwick and registration slip

Letter dated September 15, 20— from Juliette Greco to James Hardwick and registration slip

APPENDIX 4.5 Chong v. Kingman: Plaintiff's Claim for Unliquidated Damages (Form 7A)

ONTARIO

Superior Court of Justice
Cour supérieure de justice

Plaintiff's Claim
Demande du demandeur
Form / *Formule* 7A Ont. Reg. No. / *Règl. de l'Ont.* : 258/98

Toronto

Small Claims Court / *Cour des petites créances de*
47 Sheppard Avenue East
Toronto, Ontario
M2N 5X5

Seal / *Sceau*

SC-00-56789-00

Claim No. / *N° de la demande*

Address / *Adresse*

416 326 3554

Phone number / *Numéro de téléphone*

☐ Additional plaintiff(s) listed on attached Form 1A. *Le ou les demandeurs additionnels sont mentionnés sur la formule 1A ci-jointe.*	☐ Under 18 years of age. *Moins de 18 ans.*

Plaintiff No. 1 / *Demandeur n° 1*

Last name, or name of company / *Nom de famille ou nom de la compagnie*		
Chong		
First name / *Premier prénom* **Maxine**	Second name / *Deuxième prénom*	Also known as / *Également connu(e) sous le nom de*
Address (street number, apt., unit) / *Adresse (numéro et rue, app., unité)* **c/o Prior Mustafa LLP**		
City/Town / *Cité/ville*	Province	Phone no. / *N° de téléphone*
Postal code / *Code postal*		Fax no. / *N° de télécopieur*
Representative / *Représentant(e)* **Prior Mustafa LLP Attention: Paralegal name**		LSUC # / *N° du BHC* **######**
Address (street number, apt., unit) / *Adresse (numéro et rue, app., unité)* **22 County Court Boulevard**		
City/Town / *Cité/ville* **Brampton**	Province **Ontario**	Phone no. / *N° de téléphone* **905 111 2222**
Postal code / *Code postal* **A1A 2B3**		Fax no. / *N° de télécopieur* **905 111 2233**

☐ Additional defendant(s) listed on attached Form 1A. *Le ou les défendeurs additionnels sont mentionnés sur la formule 1A ci-jointe.*	☐ Under 18 years of age. *Moins de 18 ans.*

Defendant No. 1 / *Défendeur n° 1*

Last name, or name of company / *Nom de famille ou nom de la compagnie*		
Kingman		
First name / *Premier prénom* **LeeAnn**	Second name / *Deuxième prénom*	Also known as / *Également connu(e) sous le nom de*
Address (street number, apt., unit) / *Adresse (numéro et rue, app., unité)* **48 Brimley Road, Apt. 1306**		
City/Town / *Cité/ville* **Toronto**	Province **Ontario**	Phone no. / *N° de téléphone* **416 444 5555**
Postal code / *Code postal* **L2L 3T6**		Fax no. / *N° de télécopieur*
Representative / *Représentant(e)*		LSUC # / *N° du BHC*
Address (street number, apt., unit) / *Adresse (numéro et rue, app., unité)*		
City/Town / *Cité/ville*	Province	Phone no. / *N° de téléphone*
Postal code / *Code postal*		Fax no. / *N° de télécopieur*

SCR 7.01-7A (June 1, 2009 / *1er juin 2009*) CSD

APPENDIX 4.5   Chong v. Kingman: Plaintiff's Claim for Unliquidated Damages (Form 7A)   *continued*

FORM / *FORMULE* **7A**   **PAGE 2**   SC-00-56789-00
                                                                    Claim No. / *N° de la demande*

REASONS FOR CLAIM AND DETAILS / *MOTIFS DE LA DEMANDE ET PRÉCISIONS*

Explain what happened, including where and when. Then explain how much money you are claiming or what goods you want returned.
Expliquez ce qui s'est passé, en précisant où et quand. Ensuite indiquez la somme d'argent que vous demandez ou les biens dont vous demandez la restitution, explication à l'appui.

If you are relying on any documents, you **MUST** attach copies to the claim. If evidence is lost or unavailable, you **MUST** explain why it is not attached.
*Si vous vous appuyez sur des documents, vous **DEVEZ** en annexer des copies à la demande. Si une preuve est perdue ou n'est pas disponible, vous **DEVEZ** expliquer pourquoi elle n'est pas annexée.*

What happened?   See Schedule A attached and forming part of this claim
Where?
When?

Que s'est-il
passé?
Où?
Quand?

SCR 7.01-7A (June 1, 2009 / *1er juin 2009*) CSD   Continued on next page / *Suite à la page suivante*

FORM / *FORMULE* 7A   PAGE 3   SC-00-56789-00

Claim No. / *N° de la demande*

How much? $ 25,000.00
Combien?   (Principal amount claimed / *Somme demandée*) $

☒   ADDITIONAL PAGES ARE ATTACHED BECAUSE MORE ROOM WAS NEEDED.
DES FEUILLES SUPPLÉMENTAIRES SONT ANNEXÉES EN RAISON DU MANQUE D'ESPACE.

The plaintiff also claims pre-judgment interest from February 1, 20--   under:
Le demandeur demande aussi des intérêts   (Date)   *conformément à :*
antérieurs au jugement de

(Check only   ☒ **the *Courts of Justice Act***
one box /   *la* **Loi sur les tribunaux judiciaires**
Cochez une
seule case)   ☐ an agreement at the rate of _____ % per year
                    un accord au taux de   % par an

and post-judgment interest, and court costs.
et des intérêts postérieurs au jugement, ainsi que les dépens.

Prepared on: June 24 _____ , 20 -- _____
Fait le :   (Signature of plaintiff or representative / *Signature du*
                                               demandeur/de la demanderesse ou du/de la représentant(e))

Issued on: _____ , 20 _____ _____
Délivré le :   (Signature of clerk / *Signature du greffier*)

CAUTION TO DEFENDANT: **IF YOU DO NOT FILE A DEFENCE** (Form 9A) with the court within twenty (20) calendar days after you have been served with this Plaintiff's Claim, judgment may be obtained without notice and enforced against you. Forms and self-help materials are available at the Small Claims Court and on the following website: www.ontariocourtforms.on.ca.

AVERTISSEMENT AU DÉFENDEUR : *SI VOUS NE DÉPOSEZ PAS DE DÉFENSE (formule 9A) auprès du tribunal au plus tard vingt (20) jours civils après avoir reçu signification de la présente demande du demandeur, un jugement peut être obtenu sans préavis et être exécuté contre vous. Vous pouvez obtenir les formules et la documentation à l'usage du client à la Cour des petites créances et sur le site Web suivant : www.ontariocourtforms.on.ca.*

SCR 7.01-7A (June 1, 2009 / *1ᵉʳ juin 2009*) CSD

Schedule A

1. The plaintiff claims:

    (a) $25,000.00;

    (b)   Pre- and post-judgment interest in accordance with the *Courts of Justice Act*;

    (c)   Her costs of this action; and

    (d)   Such further and other relief as this Honourable Court deems just.

2. The plaintiff resides in the City of Toronto in the Province of Ontario.

3. At all material times the defendant resided in Toronto, Ontario. She currently resides at 48 Brimley Road, Apt. 1306, Toronto, Ontario L2L 3T6.

4. Pursuant to a residential tenancy agreement dated January 13, 20—, the plaintiff agreed to rent the basement apartment in the plaintiff's home at 67 Harmony Avenue, Toronto, Ontario to the defendant. The tenancy commenced February 1, 20— at a monthly rent of $775.00, including water, heat, and hydro. The defendant did not pay a last month's rent deposit.

5. The basement apartment at 67 Harmony Avenue is a legal basement apartment with a separate entrance. The plaintiff, who is an elderly widow, occupies the main floor.

6. The defendant's personal cheque for the February, 20— rent was returned due to insufficient funds. When the plaintiff asked the defendant for a replacement cheque, the defendant became extremely abusive. The February rent was never paid. The defendant also failed to pay the rent for March and April, 20—.

7. The plaintiff made repeated requests for payment of the rent owing. Whenever the plaintiff approached the defendant about collecting the rent, the defendant became extremely abusive. She screamed and shouted. She slammed doors, and played loud music until late in the night.

8. On several occasions, the defendant stood outside the plaintiff's kitchen door, which opens onto the side entrance for the basement apartment. She pounded on the door and screamed obscenities and threats.

9. The defendant kept the plaintiff awake at night, playing loud music and making banging and crashing sounds in the basement. This behaviour would start around midnight and continue until two or three o'clock in the morning. The plaintiff was afraid the neighbours would complain to the police.

10. The defendant's behaviour terrified the plaintiff. The defendant had access to the plaintiff's washer, dryer, furnace, and fuse box, all of which were also in the basement. The plaintiff feared that the defendant would cause damage or start a fire.

11. The plaintiff began to keep the kitchen door locked. She could not sleep and she lost her appetite. She suffered from headaches and anxiety attacks. If she went out, she dreaded going home. Her physician prescribed medication for anxiety and sleep medication.

12. When the defendant failed to pay the April rent, the plaintiff phoned her daughter in British Columbia and told her about the situation. The plaintiff's daughter flew to Toronto, arriving on April 15. On April 16, the plaintiff and her daughter sought legal assistance. A notice of early termination for non-payment of rent was served on the defendant on April 16.

13. The defendant vacated the apartment on April 17. She took the keys with her, and left the basement apartment in a filthy state.

14. It cost the plaintiff $1,059.00 to have a contractor come in to clean the apartment, replace the carpet, repair the damage, and repaint. The plaintiff had to pay a locksmith $125.00 to rekey the locks.

15. On June 1, 20— the apartment was rented to a new tenant. There have been no problems with the current tenant.

16. The plaintiff was in excellent health before the events described above. She has now stopped taking anxiety medication, but she continues to have anxiety attacks and suffer from loss of appetite. She cannot sleep without medication.

17. As of the date of preparing this claim, the plaintiff is claiming special damages of $3,992.47, calculated as follows:

    Loss of income — unpaid rent

3 months × $775.00	$2,325.00
Medication	183.47
Cost of repairs	1,059.00
Rekey locks	125.00
Invoice for consultation, drafting and serving N4	300.00
Total as of June 15, 20—	$3,992.47

18. The balance of the claim is for general damages for pain, suffering, and mental distress suffered by the plaintiff as a direct result of the defendant's conduct.

Attached documents:

Tenancy agreement dated January 13, 20—

Prescriptions for medication and invoices for payment to the date of the plaintiff's claim

Invoice from contractor for repairs

Invoice from locksmith

Invoice from Prior Mustafa LLP for residential tenancy services

APPENDIX 4.6 Greco v. Hardwick: Affidavit of Service (Form 8A)

ONTARIO

Superior Court of Justice
Cour supérieure de justice

Affidavit of Service
Affidavit de signification

Form / *Formule* 8A Ont. Reg. No. / *Régl. de l'Ont.* : 258/98

Brampton	SC-00-34065-00
Small Claims Court / *Cour des petites créances de*	Claim No. / *N° de la demande*
7755 Hurontario Street	
Brampton, Ontario	
L6W 4T6	
Address / *Adresse*	

905 456 4700

Phone number / *Numéro de téléphone*

BETWEEN / *ENTRE*

Juliette Greco

Plaintiff(s) / *Demandeur(s)/demanderesse(s)*

and / *et*

James Hardwick

Defendant(s) / *Défendeur(s)/défenderesse(s)*

My name is Claire Ivory
Je m'appelle   (Full name / *Nom et prénoms*)

I live in Brampton, Ontario
J'habite à   (Municipality & province / *Municipalité et province*)

and I swear/affirm that the following is true:
et je déclare sous serment/j'affirme solennellement que les renseignements suivants sont véridiques :

1. **I served** James Hardwick _____ , on November 8 _____ , 20 -- ,
   J'ai signifié à   (Full name of person/corporation served / *Nom et prénoms*   , *le*   (Date)
                        de la personne/nom au complet de la personne morale
                        qui a reçu la signification)

   at 128 George Court, Brampton, Ontario L1X 2V4
   au   (Address (street and number, unit, municipality, province) / *Adresse (numéro et rue, unité, municipalité, province)*)

   which is ☒ the address of the person's home
   soit   *l'adresse du domicile de la personne*

   ☐ the address of the corporation's place of business
        l'adresse du lieu de travail de l'établissement de la personne morale

   ☐ the address of the person's or corporation's representative on record with the court
        l'adresse du/de la représentant(e) de la personne ou de la personne morale figurant au
        dossier du tribunal

   ☐ the address on the document most recently filed in court by the party
        l'adresse figurant sur le document déposé le plus récemment au tribunal par la partie

   ☐ the address of the corporation's attorney for service in Ontario
        l'adresse du fondé de pouvoir de la personne morale aux fins de signification en Ontario

   ☐ other address: _____
        autre adresse :   (Specify. / *Précisez.*)

   with the plaintiff's claim
   ce qui suit :   (Name(s) of document(s) served / *Titre(s) du ou des documents signifiés*)

SCR 8.06-8A (November 1, 2009 / *1er novembre 2009*) CSD

APPENDIX 4.6   Greco v. Hardwick: Affidavit of Service (Form 8A) *continued*

FORM / *FORMULE* **8A**   **PAGE 2**   SC-00-34065-00
                                                                        Claim No. / *N° de la demande*

2. I served the document(s) referred to in paragraph one by the following method:
   J'ai signifié le ou les documents mentionnés au numéro un de la façon suivante :
   (Tell how service took place by checking appropriate box(es).)
   (Indiquez la façon dont la signification a été effectuée en cochant la ou les cases appropriées.)

Personal service / *Signification à personne*
- ☒ leaving a copy with the person.
  en laissant une copie à la personne.
- ☐ leaving a copy with the _____ of the corporation.
  en laissant une copie au/à la   *(Office or position / Charge ou poste)*   *de la personne morale.*
- ☐ leaving a copy with: _____
  en laissant une copie à :   *(Specify person's name and office or position. / Indiquez le nom de la personne ainsi que sa charge ou son poste.)*

Service at place of residence / *Signification au domicile*
- ☐ leaving a copy in a sealed envelope addressed to the person at the person's place of residence with a person who appeared to be an adult member of the same household, and sending another copy of the same document(s) to the person's place of residence on the same day or the following day by:
  en laissant une copie au domicile de la personne, dans une enveloppe scellée adressée à celle-ci, auprès d'une personne habitant sous le même toit qui semblait majeure et en envoyant une autre copie du ou des mêmes documents au domicile de la personne le même jour ou le jour suivant :
  - ☐ regular lettermail.
    par courrier ordinaire.
  - ☐ registered mail.
    par courrier recommandé.
  - ☐ courier.
    par messagerie.

Service by registered mail / *Signification par courrier recommandé*
- ☐ registered mail.
  par courrier recommandé.
  (If a copy of a plaintiff's claim or defendant's claim was served by registered mail, attach a copy of the Canada Post delivery confirmation showing the signature of the person being served to this affidavit.)
  (Si une copie de la demande du demandeur ou de la demande du défendeur a été signifiée par courrier recommandé, annexez au présent affidavit une copie de la confirmation de livraison remise par Postes Canada sur laquelle figure la signature du destinataire de la signification.)

Service by courier / *Signification par messagerie*
- ☐ courier.
  par messagerie.
  (If a copy of a plaintiff's claim or defendant's claim was served by courier, attach a copy of the courier's delivery confirmation showing the signature of the person being served to this affidavit.)
  (Si une copie de la demande du demandeur ou de la demande du défendeur a été signifiée par messagerie, annexez au présent affidavit une copie de la confirmation de livraison remise par le service de messagerie sur laquelle figure la signature du destinataire de la signification.)

Service on lawyer / *Signification à l'avocat*
- ☐ leaving a copy with a lawyer who accepted service on the person's behalf.
  en laissant une copie avec l'avocat qui a accepté la signification au nom de la personne.
  (Attach a copy of the document endorsed with the lawyer's acceptance of service.)
  (Annexez une copie du document, sur lequel l'avocat a inscrit qu'il a accepté la signification.)

Service by regular lettermail / *Signification par courrier ordinaire*
- ☐ regular lettermail.
  par courrier ordinaire.

SCR 8.06-8A (November 1, 2009 / *1er novembre 2009*) CSD   **Continued on next page /** *Suite à la page suivante*

APPENDIX 4.6   Greco v. Hardwick: Affidavit of Service (Form 8A) *concluded*

FORM / *FORMULE* 8A	PAGE 3	SC-00-34065-00
		Claim No. / *N° de la demande*

Service by fax /
Signification par télécopie

☐ fax sent at _____ at the following fax number: _____
par télécopie (Time / *heure*) *au numéro de télécopieur suivant :* (Fax number / *numéro de télécopieur*)
envoyée à

Service to last known address of corporation or attorney for service, and to the directors /
Signification à la dernière adresse connue de la personne morale ou de son fondé de pouvoir aux fins de signification et aux administrateurs

☐ mail/courier to corporation or attorney for service at last known address recorded with the Ministry of Government Services, and
d'une part, par la poste/par messagerie à la personne morale ou à son fondé de pouvoir aux fins de signification, à la dernière adresse connue figurant dans les dossiers du ministère des Services gouvernementaux;

☐ mail/courier to each director, as recorded with the Ministry of Government Services, as set out below:
d'autre part, par la poste/par messagerie à chaque administrateur mentionné dans les dossiers du ministère des Services gouvernementaux et dont le nom et l'adresse sont indiqués ci-dessous :

Name of director / Nom de l'administrateur	Director's address as recorded with the Ministry of Government Services (street & number, unit, municipality, province) / Adresse de l'administrateur figurant dans les dossiers du ministère des Services gouvernementaux (numéro et rue, unité, municipalité, province)

(Attach separate sheet for additional names if necessary. / *Joignez au besoin une feuille séparée s'il y a d'autres noms à ajouter.*)

Substituted service /
Signification indirecte

☐ substituted service as ordered by the court on _____, 20 _____
par signification indirecte ordonnée par le tribunal le (Date)

☐ as follows: (Give details.)
comme suit : (*Précisez.*)

Sworn/Affirmed before me at **Brampton**
Déclaré sous serment/Affirmé solennellement devant moi à (Municipality / *municipalité*)

in **Ontario**
en/à/au (Province, state, or country / *province, État ou pays*)

on **November 10** , 20 **--**
le

_____
Commissioner for taking affidavits
Commissaire aux affidavits
(Type or print name below if signature is illegible.)
(*Dactylographiez le nom ou écrivez-le en caractères d'imprimerie ci-dessous si la signature est illisible.*)

_____
Signature
(This form is to be signed in front of a lawyer, justice of the peace, notary public or commissioner for taking affidavits.)
(*La présente formule doit être signée en présence d'un avocat, d'un juge de paix, d'un notaire ou d'un commissaire aux affidavits.*)

SCR 8.06-8A (November 1, 2009 / *1er novembre 2009*) CSD

Acting for the Plaintiff: Default Proceedings

5

LEARNING OUTCOMES

After reading this chapter, you will understand:

- The time for filing a defence

- Noting in default and default judgment

- The consequences of being noted in default

- When to file an affidavit for jurisdiction

- Obtaining default judgment for a liquidated claim

- Calculating pre-judgment interest

- Obtaining default judgment for an unliquidated claim

- Motion for set aside of a noting in default

- Dismissal of an action as abandoned

- Discontinuance of an undefended action

Introduction

A Small Claims Court proceeding is commenced when the plaintiff's claim is issued by the clerk. The claim is issued when the clerk dates, signs, and seals it, and assigns a court file number. Copies for all named defendants will be sealed by the clerk and returned to the plaintiff for service. The plaintiff has six months from the date of starting the action to serve the plaintiff's claim on the defendant. Best practice requires that the defendant be served with the plaintiff's claim as soon as practicable after the action is commenced.

When the defendant or any other party has been served with the plaintiff's claim, the details of service (including date, time, place, and manner of service) should be noted on the client file, and an affidavit of service should be prepared. The person whose evidence is contained in an affidavit is called a **deponent**. The deponent for an affidavit of service is the person who **effected service**—that is, served the document on the defendant. The deponent of the affidavit of service must attest to the truth of its contents in the presence of a commissioner of oaths. It is an offence to swear a false affidavit.

A defendant who has been served with a plaintiff's claim has 20 days from the date that service becomes effective to file a defence with the court office. The plaintiff's paralegal should note the deadline for filing a defence on the checklist/tickler in the client file. If no defence is filed with the court by the deadline, the defendant should be noted in default. To note a defendant in default, the plaintiff's paralegal files the affidavit of service with the court office, along with a request to the clerk to note the defendant in default (Form 9B). A defendant who has been noted in default cannot file a defence or take any other procedural steps, except to bring a motion to set aside the noting in default.

In a liquidated claim, the plaintiff's paralegal may also request that the clerk sign a default judgment (Form 11B). In an unliquidated claim, where all defendants have been noted in default, you may make a motion for an assessment of damages based on affidavit evidence proving the amount of the claim, or request an assessment hearing to determine the amount owing to the plaintiff.

A default judgment may be enforced against a defendant under Rule 20.

Review: Liquidated and Unliquidated Damages

In a claim that is wholly for an unpaid debt or liquidated amount (also known as a liquidated claim), the amount owing is a specific amount of money that may be established by unpaid invoices, a loan agreement, or other documentation proving a debt or fixed amount, or it may be calculated using a simple arithmetical formula.

Determining the amount of a liquidated claim is straightforward. You look at the documentary or other evidence to determine how much money the defendant owes the plaintiff. Interest may be determined based on the interest rate stated in the debt instrument—that is, the document that sets out particulars of the debt, including principal, interest, how interest is to be calculated, terms of payment, and so on. If no interest rate was agreed on, interest may be determined using the rates published pursuant to s. 127(2) of the *Courts of Justice Act*. A table of these interest rates can be found on the Attorney General's website. Calculating interest is discussed below at pages 181–188.

Liquidated damages (also known as special damages) do not require valuation by a court, so long as there is objective evidence such as documentation to support the amount claimed.

If all or part of a claim is for an unliquidated amount (also known as general damages), the amount owing cannot be determined based on objective evidence. Instead, it must be determined by the court based on all of the evidence, applying previous court decisions in which these types of damages have been quantified.

Noting a Defendant in Default

Time for Filing a Defence

General

The time for filing a defence with the court varies, depending on how the defendant was served with the claim.

You should diarize the deadline for the defendant to file a defence on every plaintiff's file you open. File management software should automatically calculate procedural and other deadlines on electronic client files and notify you as deadlines approach. If you do not use file management software, you should note approaching deadlines and tickler reminders on your desk calendar and on the checklist/tickler in the client file.

On the day after the deadline for the defendant to file a defence expires, you should contact the court office to find out whether a defence has been filed. If no defence has been filed, the affidavit of service should be filed along with a request to clerk (Form 9B) asking the clerk to note the defendant in default. If the claim is for a debt or liquidated amount, you may also arrange for the clerk to sign a default judgment (Form 11B). These procedures are discussed in more detail below.

Personal Service on the Defendant (Rule 8.01)

A defendant who has been personally served with a plaintiff's claim has 20 days from the date of service to file a defence with the court office (Small Claims Court Rule 9.01(1)). Holidays and weekends are included when counting the 20 days, but if the period ends on a holiday or weekend, then the last day for filing the defence is the next business day. (Note that under the *Rules of the Small Claims Court*, the definition of "holiday" includes any Saturday or Sunday.)

Alternatives to Personal Service (Rule 8.03)

If the defendant is served with the plaintiff's claim by an alternative to personal service, the time for delivering a defence varies, depending on the manner of service. See Table 5.1 below.

TABLE 5.1 Time for Delivering a Defence to a Plaintiff's Claim or Defendant's Claim

TYPE OF SERVICE	RULE	METHOD OF SERVICE	TIME FOR DELIVERING DEFENCE	RULE
Personal service	8.01(1), 8.02	Personal service	20 days from date of service (including holidays and ending on a business day)	9.01(1)
Alternative to personal service: service on person's lawyer	8.03(5)	Leaving a copy with the lawyer or an employee in the lawyer's office (acceptance of service must be endorsed on a copy of the document)	20 days from date of service (including holidays and ending on a business day)	9.01(1)
Alternative to personal service: service at individual's place of residence	8.03(2)	(a) Handing document in sealed envelope addressed to individual to apparently adult member of same household; and (b) On the same day or following day, serving the document by mail or by courier	5 days after date of mailing or date that delivery by courier is verified (excluding holidays and ending on a business day) *plus* 20 days (including holidays and ending on a business day)	8.03(4) 9.01(1)
Alternative to personal service: Ontario corporation	8.03(3)	(a) Service by mail or courier to address of head office or principal place of business; and (b) Service by mail or courier to each director at that director's address on record with Ministry of Government Services	5 days after date of mailing or date that delivery by courier is verified (excluding holidays and ending on a business day) *plus* 20 days (including holidays and ending on a business day)	8.03(4) 9.01(1)
Alternative to personal service: corporation outside Ontario	8.03(3)	(a) Service by mail or courier to the attorney for service in Ontario; and (b) Service by mail or courier to each director at that director's address on record with Ministry of Government Services	5 days after date of mailing or date that delivery by courier is verified (excluding holidays and ending on a business day) *plus* 20 days (including holidays and ending on a business day)	8.03(4) 9.01(1)
Alternative to personal service: service by registered mail or courier to individual at individual's place of residence	8.03(7)	Sending a copy by registered mail or by courier to the individual's place of residence	20 days (including holidays and ending on a business day) from the day the individual or member of individual's household verifies receipt of the claim by signature, as shown in delivery confirmation provided by Canada Post or the commercial courier	9.01(1) 8.03(8)
Substituted service	8.04	Awarded by court order where it is impractical to carry out service personally or by an alternative to personal service	By court order	

BOX 5.1 Calculating Time for Delivery of a Defence

Refer to Table 5.1 when reading the following examples.

Example One: Personal Service (Rules 8.01(1) and 8.02)

Ahmed B. is the defendant. Ahmed B. is personally served with a plaintiff's claim at his home at 7:35 p.m. on July 4, 20—. The deadline for filing a defence is 20 days from July 4, including holidays and weekends. Ahmed B. must file the defence on or before July 24, 20—, or, if July 24 falls on a holiday, on the next business day thereafter.

Example Two: Alternative to Personal Service: Service at Individual's Place of Residence (Rule 8.03(2))

Ellen F. is the defendant. An attempt is made to effect personal service at Ellen F.'s place of residence, but Ellen F. is not home. The plaintiff's claim, in a sealed envelope with Ellen F.'s name and address on it, is left with an adult member of Ellen F.'s household at 2:35 p.m. on September 6, 20—. On September 7, 20—, the document is given to Commercial Couriers. Commercial Couriers verifies delivery of the document at Ellen F.'s place of residence at 3:00 p.m. on September 7, 20—.

Service by courier takes effect five days after verification of delivery. Service becomes effective on September 12, 20—, unless September 12 is a holiday, in which case, service becomes effective on the next business day.

The time for filing a defence is determined by adding 20 days to September 12. The last day for filing a defence is October 2, unless October 2 falls on a holiday, in which case, the last day for filing a defence is the next business day.

Example Three: Alternative to Personal Service: Service by Registered Mail or by Courier at Individual's Place of Residence (Rules 8.03(7) and 8.07.1)

Gaetan L. is the defendant. The plaintiff's claim is served on Gaetan L. by registered mail at his place of residence.

Service by this method takes effect when Gaetan L. (or, if Gaetan L. is not available, any person who appears to be a member of the same household) verifies receipt of the copy of the claim on the Canada Post delivery confirmation. The deadline for filing a defence is 20 days after the date of verification.

If Gaetan L. or another member of his household does not sign the delivery confirmation, this method of service is not valid.

Example Four: Substituted Service (Rule 8.04)

If a party satisfies the court that it is not practical to effect prompt service of a claim personally or by an alternative to personal service, the court may make an order for substituted service.

Substituted service takes effect as stated in the court order.

Default Proceedings (Rule 11)

What Is Noting in Default?

If a defendant to a plaintiff's claim or a defendant's claim fails to file a defence to all or part of the claim within the prescribed time, an opposing party may file an affidavit of service proving service of the claim with the court and request that the clerk note the party in default (Rule 11.01(1)). The notation is made on the court file. A person under disability may not be noted in default under Rule 11.01(1) except with leave of the court (Rule 11.01(2)).

What Are the Consequences of Being Noted in Default?

A defendant who has been noted in default cannot file a defence or take any other procedural step without the plaintiff's consent or a court order (Rule 11.05(1)). The only exception is a motion for set aside of the noting in default under Rules 11.06 and 15. Motions for set aside will be discussed in more detail later in this chapter.

Other parties may take any step in the proceeding without the consent of a defendant who has been noted in default (Rule 11.05(2)).

A defendant noted in default is not entitled to notice of any step taken by other parties in the proceeding and does not have to be served with any document except the following:

1. default judgment (Rules 11.02(3) and 8.01(4));
2. amendment of claim or defence (Rule 12.01);
3. motion after judgment is signed (Rule 15.01(6)); and
4. documents in enforcement proceedings against a debtor under Rule 20.

A defendant who has been noted in default is at a serious procedural disadvantage. If your client has been noted in default, you should take immediate steps to have the noting in default set aside, either on consent or by a motion under Rule 11.06.

Who May Be Noted in Default?

GENERAL RULE (RULE 11.01(1))

Any defendant in a plaintiff's claim who fails to file a defence within the time prescribed by the Rules may be noted in default.

Any defendant in a defendant's claim who fails to file a defence to the defendant's claim within the time prescribed by the Rules may be noted in default.

PERSON UNDER DISABILITY (RULES 11.01(2) AND 4.06)

A person under disability who fails to deliver a defence within the time prescribed by the Rules may not be noted in default, except with **leave of the court** (Rule 11.01(2)). Leave of the court means permission of the court to do (or not do) something. Leave of the court is usually obtained on motion by the party seeking leave. A party who wishes to note a person under disability in default must make a motion to the court for an order permitting them to do so.

In some cases the clerk may be unaware that a party in default is a person under disability. If the person under disability is noted in default and/or default judgment is signed against her in error, the court may set aside the noting in default, the default judgment if one has been signed, and any step that has been taken to enforce the judgment, on **such terms as are just** (Rule 4.06).

BOX 5.2 Such Terms as Are Just

Rule 4.06 states that a noting in default and default judgment signed against a person under disability, as well as any steps to enforce the judgment, may be set aside on such terms as are just. This means that the court examines the conduct of the parties, any prejudice to a party as a result of the order for set aside, and any prejudice to the defendant caused by the noting in default (and default judgment, if any), and imposes conditions and/or awards costs accordingly.

A party who is aware or who suspects that an opposing party is a person under disability should not take any steps under Rule 11 without first notifying the court and seeking direction.

DEFENDANTS WHO HAVE BEEN SERVED OUTSIDE THE COURT'S TERRITORIAL JURISDICTION

Territorial jurisdiction was discussed in Chapter 3. It is the geographical area where a court is authorized to conduct hearings and make orders that are binding on litigants. Territorial jurisdiction is governed by Small Claims Court Rule 6.01.

A plaintiff may commence an action

- in the territorial division where the cause of action arose—that is, where the event giving rise to the action occurred (Rule 6.01(1)(a)(i));
- in the territorial division where the defendant lives (Rule 6.01(1)(a)(ii));
- in the territorial division where the defendant carries on business (Rule 6.01(1)(a)(ii)); or
- if there are several defendants, in the territorial jurisdiction where one of them lives or carries on business (Rule 6.01(1)(b)).

If there is only one defendant, and that defendant was served with the claim outside the court's territorial jurisdiction, the clerk will not note the defendant in default until the plaintiff proves by affidavit for jurisdiction (Form 11A) submitted to the clerk or by evidence given before a judge that the action was properly brought in the court's territorial jurisdiction (Rule 11.03(3)).

If there is more than one defendant and all defendants have been served outside the court's territorial jurisdiction, the clerk will not note the defendants in default until the plaintiff proves by affidavit for jurisdiction submitted to the clerk or by evidence given before a judge that the action was properly brought in the court's territorial jurisdiction (Rule 11.03(3)).

If the clerk is not satisfied by the affidavit for jurisdiction that the action was properly brought in a territorial division, the plaintiff may be required to present evidence that the action was properly brought in that territorial division before a judge.

Liquidated Claims (Rule 11.02)

General

Where a defendant has failed to file a defence within the time prescribed by the Rules and the claim is for a debt or liquidated amount, the clerk may note the defendant in default and sign a default judgment, including interest if claimed, against the defendant, so long as there are no issues of territorial jurisdiction pursuant to Rule 11.01(3).

BOX 5.3 Joint and Several Liability

Joint and several liability means that two or more persons are liable for the full amount of a debt or other amount of money owed.

Examples include co-holders of a credit card, co-signers on a debt, the mortgagor(s) and guarantor(s) on a mortgage, and co-owners of property where a person suffers injury.

When you are acting for a plaintiff, you must ensure that you name as defendants everyone who is potentially liable for the amount owing. This protects the plaintiff, because if successful, he has a range of persons against whom he can enforce the judgment (that is, from whom he can collect his money). If one defendant has no ability to pay or is otherwise judgment-proof, the plaintiff can enforce the judgment against the income and assets of any other defendant(s) who are jointly and severally liable.

An agreement among co-defendants allocating liability for a debt is enforceable only among the co-defendants themselves. It is not binding on the plaintiff as creditor, because the plaintiff is not a party to the agreement.

Where default judgment has been signed against a defaulting defendant in a claim for a debt or liquidated amount, the plaintiff may proceed against any co-defendants not in default for the full amount of the claim (Rule 11.02(2)).

Where part of the claim is for a liquidated amount and part is for an unliquidated amount, the clerk may note a defendant who has not filed a defence within the prescribed time in default and sign a default judgment against the defaulting defendant for the liquidated part of the claim. The plaintiff may also proceed against any co-defendants not in default for the liquidated part of the claim. The plaintiff may proceed against any co-defendants not in default for the full amount of the unliquidated portion of the claim (Rule 11.02(2)). The plaintiff may obtain default judgment against a defaulting defendant for the unliquidated portion of a claim by way of a motion in writing for an assessment of damages (Rule 11.03(2)(a)) or an assessment hearing (Rule 11.03(2)(b)) only if all defendants have been noted in default. If all defendants have not been noted in default, liability for the unliquidated portion of the claim must be determined at trial (Rule 11.03(7)).

Rule 11.02(1) states that if a defendant has been noted in default, the clerk *may* sign default judgment in respect of a claim or any part of a claim for a debt or liquidated demand in money, not that the clerk *shall* sign default judgment. In other words, the clerk has some discretion. In an undefended action where liquidated damages are claimed, the clerk may be uncertain of the amount owing. In such cases, the clerk may decline to sign default judgment.

Procedure for Obtaining Default Judgment in a Liquidated Claim

To obtain default judgment in a liquidated claim, you must complete and file the following forms:

1. An affidavit of service (Form 8A) proving service of the plaintiff's claim on the defendant;

2. A request to clerk (Form 9B) requesting that the defendant be noted in default and that the clerk sign default judgment against the defendant;

3. If the defendant was served outside the court's territorial division, an affidavit for jurisdiction (Form 11A); and

4. A draft default judgment (Form 11B) naming the defendant and stating the amount of the debt, pre-judgment interest from the date the cause of action arose to the date of preparation of the draft default judgment, costs, and the post-judgment interest rate.

The pre- and post-judgment interest rates will be those stated in the debt instrument. If there is no debt instrument, the pre- and post-judgment interest rates will be those published pursuant to s. 127(2) of the *Courts of Justice Act*. The costs stated on the draft default judgment will be the court fees for issuing the claim and the default judgment. As of this writing, the fee for issuing a claim by an infrequent claimant is $75.00. The fee for issuing a claim by a frequent claimant is $100.00. The fee for entering a default judgment for an infrequent claimant is $35.00. The fee for a frequent claimant is $50.00. The definition of "frequent claimant" can be found at O. Reg. 432/93 to the *Administration of Justice Act*. Definitions of "infrequent claimant" and "frequent claimant" can also be found at the end of Chapter 1 and in the Glossary to this text.

Calculating Interest Owing

Pre- and Post-judgment Interest

There are two types of interest available to a successful party in a Small Claims Court proceeding—pre-judgment interest and post-judgment interest. **Pre-judgment interest** accrues on the amount determined to be owing commencing with the date the cause of action arose and ending with the date of judgment. **Post-judgment interest** runs on the judgment amount, including pre-judgment interest and costs, or on any outstanding balance, until such time as all amounts owing have been paid in full. Post-judgment interest will be discussed in more detail in Chapter 11.

If there is a debt instrument (such as a credit card agreement or a promissory note), you should calculate the pre-judgment interest owing using the interest rate set out in the agreement. If there is no agreement setting out the rate of interest that applies in the event of a default, then pre- and post-judgment interest rates must be determined in accordance with the *Courts of Justice Act*, using the rates published pursuant to O. Reg. 339/07. Current tables of post-judgment and pre-judgment interest rates can be found on the Ministry of the Attorney General's website.

At page 2 of the default judgment (Form 11B), you are asked to fill in the amount the plaintiff is claiming, plus pre-judgment interest owing on that amount from the date that interest begins to accrue on the amount owing, to the present date. In the case of a draft judgment, this would be the date the draft default judgment is prepared. See Figure 5.1.

FIGURE 5.1   Default Judgment (Form 11B)

DEFAULT JUDGMENT IS GIVEN against the following defendant(s):
UN JUGEMENT PAR DÉFAUT EST RENDU contre le ou les défendeurs suivants :

Last name, or name of company / *Nom de famille ou nom de la compagnie*		
First name / *Premier prénom*	Second name / *Deuxième prénom*	Also known as / *Également connu(e) sous le nom de*

Last name, or name of company / *Nom de famille ou nom de la compagnie*		
First name / *Premier prénom*	Second name / *Deuxième prénom*	Also known as / *Également connu(e) sous le nom de*

Last name, or name of company / *Nom de famille ou nom de la compagnie*		
First name / *Premier prénom*	Second name / *Deuxième prénom*	Also known as / *Également connu(e) sous le nom de*

☐   Additional defendant(s) listed on attached page (*list in same format*).
Défendeur(s) additionnel(s) mentionné(s) sur une feuille annexée (énumérez-les en suivant le même format).

THE DEFENDANT(S) MUST PAY to the plaintiff(s) the following sums:
LE OU LES DÉFENDEURS DOIVENT VERSER au(x) demandeur(s) les sommes suivantes :

(A)   **DEBT** (principal amount claimed minus any payments received since the plaintiff's claim was issued) $ _____
        LA CRÉANCE (somme demandée moins tout paiement reçu depuis la délivrance $
        de la demande du demandeur)

(B)   **PRE-JUDGMENT INTEREST** calculated
        LES INTÉRÊTS ANTÉRIEURS AU JUGEMENT calculés

        on the sum of $ _____   at the rate of _____ %
        sur la somme de   *$ au taux de*   *pour cent*

        per annum from _____ , 20 ___ , to _____ , 20 ___ ,
        par an du   *au*

        being _____ days. $ _____
        soit   *jours.* $

FIGURE 5.2 Undefended Action: Claim for Debt or Liquidated Amount

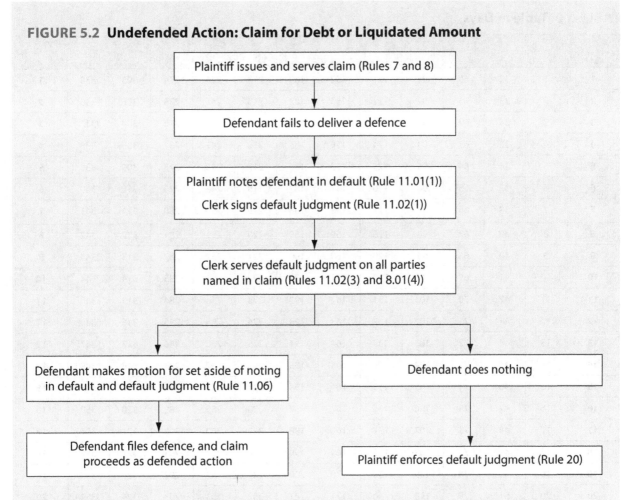

NOTE: Where there are multiple defendants, the plaintiff may note those who fail to defend in default and have a default judgment signed against them, and proceed against the defendant(s) who have filed a defence for all or part of the claim (Rule 11.02(2)).

Where there is a written agreement outlining the terms of the debt, the date that interest begins to accrue on the amount owing will depend on the terms of the agreement.

Where there is nothing in writing about the terms of the debt, the date that interest begins to accrue on the amount owing will be the date the cause of action arose— that is, the date that the defendant defaulted by failing to pay back part or all of the amount owing.

The end date will be the date the draft default judgment is prepared.

When calculating the number of days during which pre-judgment interest accrues, remember to exclude the first day of the period and include the last day of the period. This happens automatically if you use a table of days to calculate the number of days in a time period. You will find a table of days at Table 5.2.

TABLE 5.2 **Table of Days**

DAY OF MONTH	JAN	FEB	MAR	APR	MAY	JUNE	JULY	AUG	SEPT	OCT	NOV	DEC	DAY OF MONTH
1	1	32	60	91	121	152	182	213	244	274	305	335	1
2	2	33	61	92	122	153	183	214	245	275	306	336	2
3	3	34	62	93	123	154	184	215	246	276	307	337	3
4	4	35	63	94	124	155	185	216	247	277	308	338	4
5	5	36	64	95	125	156	186	217	248	278	309	339	5
6	6	37	65	96	126	157	187	218	249	279	310	340	6
7	7	38	66	97	127	158	188	219	250	280	311	341	7
8	8	39	67	98	128	159	189	220	251	281	312	342	8
9	9	40	68	99	129	160	190	221	252	282	313	343	9
10	10	41	69	100	130	161	191	222	253	283	314	344	10
11	11	42	70	101	131	162	192	223	254	284	315	345	11
12	12	43	71	102	132	163	193	224	255	285	316	346	12
13	13	44	72	103	133	164	194	225	256	286	317	347	13
14	14	45	73	104	134	165	195	226	257	287	318	348	14
15	15	46	74	105	135	166	196	227	258	288	319	349	15
16	16	47	75	106	136	167	197	228	259	289	320	350	16
17	17	48	76	107	137	168	198	229	260	290	321	351	17
18	18	49	77	108	138	169	199	230	261	291	322	352	18
19	19	50	78	109	139	170	200	231	262	292	323	353	19
20	20	51	79	110	140	171	201	232	263	293	324	354	20
21	21	52	80	111	141	172	202	233	264	294	325	355	21
22	22	53	81	112	142	173	203	234	265	295	326	356	22
23	23	54	82	113	143	174	204	235	266	296	327	357	23
24	24	55	83	114	144	175	205	236	267	297	328	358	24
25	25	56	84	115	145	176	206	237	268	298	329	359	25
26	26	57	85	116	146	177	207	238	269	299	330	360	26
27	27	58	86	117	147	178	208	239	270	300	331	361	27
28	28	59	87	118	148	179	209	240	271	301	332	362	28
29	29		88	119	149	180	210	241	272	302	333	363	29
30	30		89	120	150	181	211	242	273	303	334	364	30
31	31		90		151		212	243		304		365	31

For leap years, February 29 becomes day 60, and the numbers in the table are increased by 1 for all following days.

Calculating Pre-judgment Interest Under the Courts of Justice Act

Interest under the *Courts of Justice Act* is always calculated as simple interest.

To determine the *time period* for calculating pre-judgment interest, go to s. 128(1), which states that pre-judgment interest runs from the *date the cause of action arose* to the *date of the court order*.

To determine the *rate of interest*, you must go to the definition "prejudgment interest rate" in s. 127(1). The s. 127(1) definition states that the interest rate for prejudgment interest under the *Courts of Justice Act* is the bank rate for the quarter preceding the quarter in which the court proceeding was commenced.

A quarter is a three-month period. There are four quarters in any year:

- First quarter: January, February, March.
- Second quarter: April, May, June.
- Third quarter: July, August, September.
- Fourth quarter: October, November, December.

A proceeding is commenced on the day you issue the plaintiff's claim. If you commence the proceeding in October, during the fourth quarter (that is, October to December) of a year, then the applicable pre-judgment interest rate under the *Courts of Justice Act* is the interest rate for the preceding quarter—that is, the rate for the third quarter of that year. If you commence the proceeding in the first quarter (that is, January to March) of a year, then the applicable pre-judgment interest rate under the *Courts of Justice Act* is the interest rate for the fourth, or last, quarter of the preceding year.

To calculate pre-judgment interest, use the following steps:

1. Pre-judgment interest rate: The critical date is the *day the proceeding was commenced*. The pre-judgment interest rate will be the rate for the quarter before the quarter in which the proceeding was commenced.

2. Time period for pre-judgment interest: The *start date* is the day the cause of action arose (in a debt collection, the date of default in payment). The *end date* is the date of judgment.

3. Calculate **per diem interest: Per diem** means per day. For this calculation, you will need the *principal amount*, and the *pre-judgment interest rate expressed as a decimal*. Multiply the principal amount by the interest rate expressed as a decimal, and divide by 365 (days in year). This will give you the amount of interest that accrues per day.

4. Calculate the number of days from the date the cause of action arose to the date of judgment: For this calculation, a table of days is helpful. See Table 5.2. Find the number of the date of judgment and the number of the date the cause of action arose. From the number of the date of judgment, subtract the number of the date the cause of action arose.

5. Determine total pre-judgment interest to date of judgment: Multiply the per diem interest (calculated at step 3) by the number of days (calculated at step 4). This will give you the amount of pre-judgment interest that has accrued to the date of judgment.

Service of Default Judgment (Rule 11.02(3))

The clerk is responsible for serving the default judgment on all parties named in the claim (Rule 11.02(3)). Service is by mail or fax (Rule 8.01(4)) to the address or fax number on file with the court. See also Rules 8.07 and 8.08.

Exception to Rule 11.02

A **defendant's claim** is a claim made by a defendant against any party named in the plaintiff's claim, including the plaintiff or a co-defendant, or against a third party not named in the plaintiff's claim. Defendant's claims will be discussed in more detail in Chapter 6.

A party who wishes to dispute the defendant's claim may do so by filing a defence with the clerk, with enough copies for all parties or persons against whom the defendant's claim is made (Rule 10.03(1)). The deadline for doing so is 20 days after service of the defendant's claim (see Table 5.1 above).

If a party to a defendant's claim fails to deliver a defence within the time set out in the Rules, they may be noted in default (Rule 11.01(1)). However, judgment against a defaulting party to a defendant's claim can be obtained only on a motion or at trial (Rule 11.04). The clerk cannot sign a default judgment against a defaulting party to a defendant's claim.

BOX 5.4 Calculating Pre-judgment Interest

■ **Pre-judgment Interest—Courts of Justice Act**

You represent a plaintiff in an action for recovery of $4,000.00 loaned by the plaintiff to the defendant. There is no written agreement as to the terms of the loan. However, the plaintiff has a written receipt signed by the defendant acknowledging receipt of the money and stating that the full amount will be repaid on or before August 1, 2009. The defendant failed to make the payment.

The claim is commenced on September 3, 2009.

Step One: Determine the pre-judgment interest rate

Because there is no written loan agreement, the plaintiff must use the pre-judgment interest rate set out in the *Courts of Justice Act*. The critical date for determining the pre-judgment interest rate is the *date the action was commenced*.

In this case, the claim is commenced on September 3, 2009—that is, the third quarter of 2009. So the pre-judgment interest rate will be the bank rate for the second quarter of 2009—that is, 1.3%.

Step Two: Determine the period of time for pre-judgment interest

The defendant is served with the claim on September 7, 2009. The defendant fails to file a defence within the time prescribed by the Rules. The defendant is noted in default. The draft default judgment is dated September 30.

Pursuant to s. 128(1), pre-judgment interest is calculated from the date the cause of action arose, if that date can be determined. In the fact situation above, the date the cause of action arose is the date that the defendant failed to pay the money owing—that is, August 1, 2009. The end date for pre-judgment interest is the date the draft default judgment is prepared—that is, September 30, 2009.

Using the table of days (Table 5.2), find the number for August 1 (213) and the number for September 30 (273). The number of days from the date of default to the date of judgment = 273 − 213 = 60 days.

Step Three: Calculate the per diem interest

Calculate per diem interest using the following steps:

- Convert the interest rate to a decimal. To do this, you divide the interest rate by 100.
- Multiply the amount owing by the interest rate expressed as a decimal.
- Divide the result by the number of days in a year—that is, 365.

Using the pre-judgment interest rate of 1.3% from Step One, and following the above steps:

- Convert 1.3% to a decimal:
  1.3 ÷ 100 = 0.013
- Multiply the amount owing by the interest rate expressed as a decimal:
  0.013 × $4,000 = $52.00
- Divide the result by the number of days in a year:
  $52.00 ÷ 365 = $0.14 per day in interest.

Step Four: Calculate the amount of interest that has accrued from August 1, 2009 to September 30, 2009

The interest that accrues from August 1, 2009 to September 30, 2009: 60 days × $0.14 per day = $8.40.

▪ Pre-judgment Interest—Debt Instrument

Review the plaintiff's claim in *Parrish v. Thurston* at Appendix 3.1 in Chapter 3. The plaintiff's claim is prepared and issued on November 1, 20—. On November 3, 20—, the claim is served at the defendant's place of residence by leaving a copy in a sealed envelope addressed to the defendant with a person who appears to be an adult member of the same household, and on the same day mailing another copy of the document to the defendant at the defendant's place of residence. Judy Cordero of Brampton, Ontario effects service.

What is the deadline for filing a defence?

The defendant was served pursuant to Rule 8.03(2). Service becomes effective 5 days after the date of mailing (Rule 8.03(4))—that is, on November 8. The defendant has 20 days from November 8 to file a defence.

Assume that November 28 does not fall on a holiday. The defendant, Frank Thurston, fails to file a defence on or before November 28. On December 1, the plaintiff's paralegal, Marie Prior, prepares the documents for noting the defendant in default and obtaining default judgment.

What documents must be filed with the court?

The defendant was served in Toronto, where he now lives. The action was commenced in Brampton. Ms. Prior must prepare and file:

- an affidavit for jurisdiction (Form 11A);
- an affidavit of service (Form 8A);
- a request to clerk (Form 9B) to note the defendant in default and sign default judgment; and
- a draft default judgment (Form 11B).

The default judgment is referred to as a "draft" because it has not yet been entered—that is, signed, dated, and sealed by the clerk. In this case, because this is a liquidated claim, the clerk may also sign default judgment against the defendant.

The plaintiff is an infrequent claimant, so the fee for commencing the claim is $75.00, and the fee for entering the default judgment is $35.00.

Calculating Interest in Accordance with the Terms of a Debt Instrument

Note that, because the monetary jurisdiction of Small Claims Court is $25,000.00, you are entitled to calculate pre-judgment interest on that amount only, even though the principal amount owing pursuant to the promissory note is $27,000.00. When the plaintiff agrees to waive the excess in the plaintiff's claim, that waiver includes any interest owing on the excess.

STEP ONE: DETERMINE THE PRE-JUDGMENT INTEREST RATE

The pre-judgment interest rate is the interest rate stated in the promissory note—that is, 12% per year.

STEP TWO: DETERMINE THE PERIOD OF TIME FOR PRE-JUDGMENT INTEREST

In this case, both the interest rate and the start date for pre-judgment interest are governed by the terms of the promissory note. The note states that the entire principal amount is payable in full on September 1, 20—; failing which, pre-judgment interest at a rate of 12% starts to accrue. The defendant failed to pay the amount owing on September 1, so September 1 is the start date for pre-judgment interest of 12% per year.

The end date is the date the draft default judgment is prepared—that is, December 1, 20—.

Using the table of days (Table 5.2), find the number (from 1 to 365) for the start date (in this case, the date of default, September 1), and subtract that number from the number for the end date (in this case, December 1, the date when the draft default judgment is prepared).

The start date, September 1, is the 244th day of the year. The end date, December 1, is the 335th day of the year.

- 335 – 244 = 91 days

Note that subtraction automatically excludes the first day and includes the last day, so you do not have to worry about that.

STEP THREE: CALCULATE THE PER DIEM INTEREST

Remember the steps for per diem interest:

- Convert the interest rate from a percentage to a decimal. To do this, you divide the interest rate by 100.

- Multiply the amount owing by the interest rate expressed as a decimal.

- Divide the result by the number of days in a year—that is, 365.

The interest rate set out in the promissory note is 12% per year.

- Convert 12% to a decimal: $12 \div 100 = 0.12$

- Multiply the amount owing by the interest rate expressed as a decimal: $0.12 \times \$25,000 = \$3,000$

- Divide the result by the number of days in a year: $\$3,000 \div 365 = \$8.219$ per day in interest.

STEP FOUR: CALCULATE THE AMOUNT OF PRE-JUDGMENT INTEREST THAT HAS ACCRUED FROM SEPTEMBER 1, 20— TO DECEMBER 1, 20—

Using the contractual rate of interest of 12%, the pre-judgment interest that accrues from September 1, 20— to December 1, 20— is:

- 91 days $\times$ \$8.219 per day = \$747.93

Costs: In this case, the plaintiff is an infrequent claimant. Disbursements and expenses in the matter to the date of the default judgment are as follows:

- Issue claim: $ 75.00
- Enter default judgment: 35.00
                             $110.00

The plaintiff should claim costs of $110.00.

See Appendix 5.1 to this chapter for the completed forms.

Unliquidated Claims (Rule 11.03)

A defendant who fails to deliver a defence to a plaintiff's or defendant's claim for an unliquidated amount may be noted in default pursuant to Rule 11.01(1). However, the plaintiff may obtain a default judgment only if all defendants have been noted in default (Rule 11.03(1)). If there is only one defendant in an unliquidated claim, and that defendant has been noted in default, then Rule 11.03 applies and the plaintiff may obtain a default judgment. If there are two or more defendants in an unliquidated claim, and one defendant has been noted in default, but the others have filed defences, then Rule 11.03(1) does not apply, and the matter must go forward to a settlement conference and, if necessary, a trial (Rule 11.03(7)).

Obtaining Default Judgment in an Unliquidated Claim

The clerk cannot sign default judgment in an unliquidated claim. In an action for an unliquidated amount where all defendants in the proceeding have been noted in default, a plaintiff may obtain default judgment by (Rule 11.03(2)):

(a) filing a notice of motion and supporting affidavit (Form 15A) requesting a motion in writing for an assessment of damages, setting out the reasons why the motion should be granted, and attaching any relevant documents; or

(b) filing a request to clerk (Form 9B) requesting that an assessment hearing be arranged.

BOX 5.5 When Does Rule 11.03 Apply?

Example One

Plaintiff sues Defendant 1, Defendant 2, and Defendant 3 for an unliquidated amount. All three defendants were served outside the court's territorial division.

Defendants 1 and 2 file defences within the time permitted by the Rules. Defendant 3 does not.

CAN PLAINTIFF NOTE DEFENDANT 3 IN DEFAULT?

Yes, Plaintiff can note Defendant 3 in default (Rule 11.01(1)). Plaintiff must file:

- an affidavit of service (Form 8A) proving service on Defendant 3;
- an affidavit for jurisdiction (Form 11A) because all three defendants were served outside the court's territorial division (Rule 11.01(3)); and
- a request to clerk (Form 9B) to note Defendant 3 in default.

CAN PLAINTIFF OBTAIN A DEFAULT JUDGMENT AGAINST DEFENDANT 3, USING THE PROCEDURES SET OUT IN RULE 11.03?

No, Plaintiff cannot use the procedures in Rule 11.03 to obtain a default judgment against Defendant 3. This is an unliquidated claim. Plaintiff can obtain a default judgment against Defendant 3 only if all the defendants in the action have been noted in default. In this case, Defendants 1 and 2 have filed defences in accordance with the Rules. Therefore, all defendants in the action have not been noted in default, and Rule 11.03 does not apply.

Plaintiff will proceed to a settlement conference under Rule 13 and, if necessary, to trial under Rule 17 (Rule 11.03(7)).

Example Two

Plaintiff sues Defendant for an unliquidated amount. Defendant fails to deliver a defence within the time permitted by the Rules.

CAN PLAINTIFF NOTE DEFENDANT IN DEFAULT?

Yes, Plaintiff can note Defendant in default (Rule 11.01(1)). Plaintiff must file:

- an affidavit of service (Form 8A) proving service on Defendant, if it has not already been filed with the court office, and
- a request to clerk (Form 9B) to note Defendant in default.

CAN PLAINTIFF OBTAIN A DEFAULT JUDGMENT AGAINST DEFENDANT?

Yes, Plaintiff can obtain a default judgment against Defendant in these circumstances. This is an unliquidated claim. There is only one defendant, and that defendant has been noted in default. Therefore, all the defendants have been noted in default, and Plaintiff may obtain a default judgment using one of the methods set out in Rule 11.03(2).

Motion in Writing for an Assessment of Damages (Rule 11.03(2)(a))

A **motion** is an application to a judge to obtain an order directing that some kind of relief be granted to the party making the motion. The party who makes a motion is called the **moving party**. The party against whom a motion is made is called the **responding party**, because he responds to the moving party's motion. The moving party may be a plaintiff or a defendant. Motions may be made at any time in a proceeding, if a court order is required to resolve an issue. Small Claims Court motions are governed by Rule 15. The form used on a motion is a notice of motion and supporting affidavit (Form 15A).

The notice of motion sets out the relief requested. In part B at page 3 of Form 15A there is a separate section for a motion in writing for an assessment of damages.

An **assessment of damages** is a calculation of the money damages owed to the plaintiff by the defaulting defendant(s). The evidence in support of a motion in writing for an assessment of damages is presented in the supporting affidavit. On a motion in writing for an assessment of damages or at an assessment hearing, the plaintiff is not required to prove liability against a defendant noted in default. A defendant who has failed to respond to a claim is assumed to admit the truth of what is claimed. However, the plaintiff is required to prove the amount of the claim (Rule 11.03(5)).

An affidavit is written evidence that must be sworn by the deponent in the presence of a commissioner of oaths. The deponent is the person who makes the affidavit. The affidavit sets out the evidence proving the amount of the claim. The evidence in the affidavit is written in the first person singular (I, me, my), set out in separate, numbered paragraphs. If a document is relied on in support of the motion, a photocopy of the document will be attached to the affidavit as an exhibit. The truth of its contents will be attested to in the body of the affidavit. Exhibits are stamped, dated, and signed by the commissioner of oaths at the time the affidavit is sworn.

There must be adequate evidence before the judge reading the motion and affidavit to satisfy her that the plaintiff is entitled to the damages claimed. If the judge is not satisfied with the written evidence in support of the motion, she may order that (1) a further affidavit be provided, or (2) the assessment of damages be determined at an assessment hearing (Rule 11.03(3)).

Because the motion is in writing, attendance in person by the plaintiff or the plaintiff's representative on a motion in writing for an assessment of damages is not required. However, you must confirm a hearing date for the motion to be scheduled before a judge with the court clerk. The judge will make her decision based on the written material filed, so long as that material is adequate to prove the damages claimed.

The judge's order will be served by the clerk on the moving party or the moving party's paralegal or lawyer if a stamped, self-addressed envelope is provided with the motion materials (Rules 11.03(6) and 8.01(5)).

BOX 5.6 Motion for an Assessment of Damages (Rule 11.03(2)(a))

Review the fact situation in *Chong v. Kingman* set out in Chapter 4 in Box 4.2 at pages 108–110, as well as the sample plaintiff's claim in Appendix 4.5.

The plaintiff's claim in *Chong v. Kingman* was issued on June 24, 20—. The claim was personally served on the defendant by Claire Ivory of Mississauga, Ontario on June 24, 20—.

The defendant, Ms. Kingman, fails to file a defence within the prescribed time.

In *Chong v. Kingman*, the plaintiff is claiming both special (liquidated) and general (unliquidated) damages. Mrs. Chong's paralegal, Marie Prior, must file a request to clerk to note the defendant in default. She will request that the clerk sign default judgment with respect to the liquidated part of the claim. She will also request an assessment of damages by a motion in writing for a judgment for the unliquidated portion of the claim. The following documents must be prepared and filed for the noting in default and default judgment for the liquidated part of the claim:

- an affidavit of service (Form 8A) proving service on LeeAnn Kingman;

- a request to clerk (Form 9B) to note LeeAnn Kingman in default and sign default judgment against her for the unliquidated portion of the claim; and

- a draft default judgment (Form 11B).

Marie Prior must confirm a hearing date for the motion to be scheduled before a judge with the court clerk. Marie Prior will then draft and file a notice of motion in writing for an assessment of damages and a supporting affidavit (Form 15A). As of this writing, the court fee for filing a motion is $40.00.

When filing the notice of motion and supporting affidavit, Marie Prior will provide the clerk with a stamped, self-addressed envelope so that the clerk can mail the order made on the motion to her.

See Appendix 5.2 at the end of this chapter for examples of the documents to be filed on the motion in writing for an assessment of damages in *Chong v. Kingman*.

Assessment Hearing (Rule 11.03(2)(b))

If a plaintiff in an undefended claim for an unliquidated amount wishes to have an assessment hearing, he may file an affidavit of service of the claim (Form 8A), if one has not already been filed, and a request to clerk (Form 9B) to have the hearing scheduled (Rule 11.03(2)(b)). See Figure 5.3. All defendants must be noted in default before an assessment hearing can be requested (Rule 11.03(1)). If one or more defendants have filed a defence, the plaintiff must proceed to a settlement conference and, if necessary, to trial (Rule 11.03(7)).

The fee for fixing a date for an assessment hearing is $100.00 for an infrequent claimant, and $130.00 for a frequent claimant.

The clerk will fix a date for the hearing and send a notice of hearing to the plaintiff (Rule 11.03(4)).

An assessment hearing proceeds like a trial (Rule 11.03(4)), except that the defendant is not present. The only issue before the court is how much money the defendant owes the plaintiff (Rule 11.03(5)), because a defendant who has failed to respond to a claim is assumed to admit the truth of what is claimed. You must put before the court all relevant evidence, including documentary evidence, which will assist the judge to assign a monetary value to the damage suffered.

Documents and written statements may be received in evidence, in accordance with Rule 18.02(1) and s. 27 of the *Courts of Justice Act*, so long as the content is relevant to the subject-matter of the proceeding and is not unduly repetitious. The plaintiff may take the stand.

For a detailed discussion of procedures at trial and on assessment hearings, see Chapter 9.

FIGURE 5.3 Request to Clerk for an Assessment Hearing (Form 9B)

ONTARIO
Superior Court of Justice
Cour supérieure de justice

Request to Clerk
Demande au greffier
Form / *Formule* 9B Ont. Reg. No. / *Règl. de l'Ont.* : 258/98

Ottawa
Small Claims Court / *Cour des petites créances de*
161 Elgin Street, 2nd Floor
Ottawa, Ontario
K2P 2K1
Address / *Adresse*
613 239 1560
Phone number / *Numéro de téléphone*

SC-00-14156-00
Claim No. / *N° de la demande*

BETWEEN / *ENTRE*

Sidney Carton
Plaintiff(s) / *Demandeur(s)/demanderesse(s)*

and / *et*

Max Robespierre
Defendant(s) / *Défendeur(s)/défenderesse(s)*

TO THE CLERK OF THE Ottawa **SMALL CLAIMS COURT:**
AU GREFFIER DE LA COUR DES PETITES CRÉANCES DE
(Name of Small Claims Court location / *Emplacement de la Cour des petites créances*) :

My name is Sidney Carton **and I request that the clerk of the court:**
Je m'appelle (Name of party/representative / *Nom de la partie ou du/de la représentant(e)*) ***et je demande au greffier du tribunal de faire ce qui suit :***

(Check appropriate box(es). / Cochez la ou les cases appropriées.*)*

☒ note defendant(s) **Max Robespierre**
constater le ou les défendeurs (Name of defendant(s) / *Nom du/de la/des défendeur(s)/défenderesse(s)*)

in default for failing to file a Defence (Form 9A) within the prescribed time period [R. 11.01(1)].
en défaut pour n'avoir pas déposé de défense (formule 9A) dans le délai prescrit [par. 11.01 (1)].

☒ schedule an assessment hearing (all defendants have been noted in default) [R. 11.03(2)(b)].

Motion to Set Aside Noting in Default (Rule 11.06)

The court may set aside a noting in default or default judgment against a party, and any steps that have been taken to enforce a default judgment, on such terms as are just, if the party makes a motion to set aside. The court must be satisfied that

- the moving party has a meritorious defence;
- the moving party has a reasonable explanation for the default; and
- the motion is made as soon as is reasonably possible in all of the circumstances.

A defendant's motion for set aside is made on notice to the plaintiff. The plaintiff must be served with a copy of the motion and supporting affidavit, and any other material on which the defendant intends to rely at the hearing of the motion. The plaintiff or plaintiff's paralegal or lawyer may appear at the motion and make submissions as to why the order for set aside should not be granted, with reference to the conditions set out at Rule 11.06.

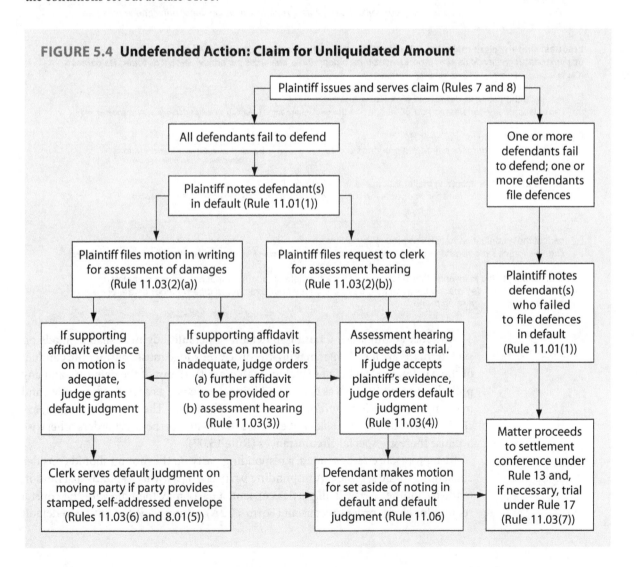

FIGURE 5.4   Undefended Action: Claim for Unliquidated Amount

FIGURE 5.5 Request for Clerk's Order on Consent (Form 11.2A)

FORM / *FORMULE* 11.2A   PAGE 2   SC-00-14156-00
                                                                 Claim No. / *N° de la demande*

TO THE PARTIES:
AUX PARTIES :

THIS REQUEST IS FILED BY: Max Robespierre
LA PRÉSENTE DEMANDE EST DÉPOSÉE PAR :   (Name of party / *Nom de la partie*)

I state that:
Je déclare que :

☒ Each party has received a copy of this form.
   Chaque partie a reçu une copie de la présente formule.

☒ No party that would be affected by the order is under disability.
   Aucune partie sur laquelle l'ordonnance aurait une incidence n'est incapable.

☒ This form has been signed and consented to by all parties, including any parties to be added, deleted or substituted.
   Toutes les parties, y compris celles qui doivent être jointes, radiées ou substituées, ont signé la présente formule et y ont consenti.

I request that the clerk make the following order(s) on the consent of all parties:
Je demande au greffier de rendre l'ordonnance ou les ordonnances suivantes sur consentement de toutes les parties :
(Check appropriate boxes. / *Cochez les cases appropriées.*)

☒ set aside the noting in default of Max Robespierre
   l'annulation de la constatation du défaut de   (Name of defendant(s) / *Nom du/de la/des défendeur(s)/défenderesse(s)*)

☐ set aside Default Judgment against _____
   l'annulation du jugement par défaut prononcé contre   (Name of defendant(s) / *Nom du/de la/des défendeur(s)/défenderesse(s)*)

☐ restore to the list the following matter that was dismissed under Rule 11.1: (Specify.)
   la réinscription au rôle de l'affaire suivante qui a été rejetée aux termes de la règle 11.1 :   (Précisez.)

☐ cancel the examination hearing regarding _____
   l'annulation de l'interrogatoire concernant   (Name of person to be examined / *Nom de la personne qui doit être interrogée*)

☐ with respect to the following step(s) taken to enforce the default judgment that are not yet completed:
   à l'égard de la ou des mesures suivantes qui ont été prises pour exécuter le jugement par défaut et qui ne sont pas encore menées à terme :

An order setting aside a noting in default or default judgment shall be made on such terms as are just. When making the order, the judge must consider the conduct of the parties, the legal issues (including the merits, if any, of the defence), and any prejudice to a party (such as delay or additional expense) as a result of the order, and may impose conditions and/or award costs accordingly. The costs of a motion, exclusive of disbursements, shall not exceed $100.00 unless the court orders otherwise because there are special circumstances (Rule 15.07).

In appropriate circumstances, a responding party on the motion should consider consenting to the set aside. A responding party is a party who responds to a motion made by another party. If all parties consent, a party may then file with the court a request for clerk's order on consent (Form 11.2A) setting aside the noting in default or default judgment. Note that there is a provision for an award of costs to be paid by one party to another party or other parties on the Form 11.2A. However, there is no provision on the Form 11.2A or in Rule 11.2.01, which governs a request for clerk's order on consent, for other terms of the consent, such as a reasonable deadline for a defence to be filed with the court.

If there are additional terms that are not covered by Form 11.2A, the parties should draft their own consent in writing containing all of the agreed-upon terms and file it with the court. The terms of the consent can then be endorsed on the file and taken out as an order to be signed by a judge.

Abandonment (Rule 11.1)

Where no steps are taken to advance a matter, the clerk is authorized by Rule 11.1 to make an order dismissing the action as abandoned.

In an undefended proceeding, the clerk shall make an order dismissing the action as abandoned if all of the following conditions apply, unless the court orders otherwise (Rule 11.1.01(1)):

1. More than 180 days have passed since the date the claim was issued or the date of an order extending the time for service of the claim.

2. No defence has been filed.

3. The action has not been disposed of by order and has not been set down for trial.

4. The clerk has given 45 days' notice to the plaintiff that the action will be dismissed as abandoned.

In a defended proceeding, the clerk shall make an order dismissing the action as abandoned if all of the following conditions apply, unless the court orders otherwise (Rule 11.1.01(2)):

1. More than 150 days have passed since the date the first defence was filed.

2. All settlement conferences under Rule 13 have been held.

3. The action has not been disposed of by order and has not been set down for trial.

4. The clerk has given 45 days' notice to all parties to the action that the action will be dismissed as abandoned.

The above conditions apply to proceedings commenced after July 1, 2006. Rules 11.1.01(3) and (4) set out transitional provisions for actions commenced before July 1, 2006.

If terms of settlement in Form 14D signed by all parties have been filed, the action will not be dismissed as abandoned by the clerk (Rule 11.1.01(5)). If the defence contains an admission of liability and proposal of terms of payment, the action will not be dismissed as abandoned by the clerk (Rule 11.1.01(6)).

The clerk shall serve a copy of an order made under Rules 11.1.01(1) and (4)(a) (undefended action) on the plaintiff, and a copy of an order made under Rules 11.1.01(2) and (4)(b) (defended action) on all parties to the action.

Discontinuance (Rule 11.3)

A plaintiff may discontinue a claim against a defendant who fails to file a defence to all or part of the claim within the time prescribed by the Rules. To discontinue an undefended claim, the plaintiff shall (Rule 11.3.01(1)):

(a) serve a notice of discontinued claim (Form 11.3A) on all defendants who were served with the claim; and

(b) file the notice with proof of service.

A notice of discontinued claim may be served personally, by an alternative to personal service, by mail, by courier, or by fax (Rule 8.01(14)).

The discontinuance of a claim is not a defence to a subsequent action on the matter, unless an order granting leave to discontinue the claim states otherwise (Rule 11.3.02).

A claim may not be discontinued by or against a person under disability except with permission from the court (Rule 11.3.01(2)).

CHAPTER SUMMARY

A defendant who has been personally served with a plaintiff's claim has 20 days from the date that service becomes effective to file a defence with the court office. The date that service becomes effective varies, depending on the manner of service.

If a defendant fails to deliver a defence within the time prescribed for doing so, the plaintiff may request that the clerk note the defendant in default. If the action is for a liquidated amount, the plaintiff may also request that the clerk sign default judgment against the defendant. A default judgment may be enforced by the plaintiff under Rule 20.

In an unliquidated claim, the plaintiff may note a defendant in default if the defendant fails to file a defence within the prescribed time. If all defendants have been noted in default, the plaintiff may then elect to make a motion in writing for an assessment of damages, or to have an assessment hearing.

A defendant who has been noted in default cannot file a defence or take any other procedural step without the plaintiff's consent or a court order (Rule 11.05(1)). The only exception is a motion for set aside of the noting in default and default judgment under Rules 11.06 and 15.

Other parties may take any step in the proceeding without the consent of a defendant who has been noted in default (Rule 11.05(2)).

A defendant noted in default is not entitled to notice of any step taken by other parties in the proceeding and does not have to be served with any document except the following:

1. default judgment (Rules 11.02(3) and 8.01(4));
2. amendment of claim or defence (Rule 12.01);
3. motion after judgment (Rule 15.01(6)); and
4. documents in enforcement proceedings against a debtor under Rule 20.

A defendant who has a good defence and a reasonable explanation for the default may make a motion under Rule 11.06 for an order setting aside the noting in default and default judgment, if one has been entered, as well as other relief. A motion for set aside is made on notice to the plaintiff. The plaintiff must be served with a copy of the notice of motion and supporting affidavit, as well as any other materials on which the defendant intends to rely at the hearing of the motion. On a contested motion for set aside, the plaintiff or plaintiff's paralegal or lawyer shall appear at the motion and make submissions as to why the order for set aside should not be granted.

In appropriate circumstances, a responding party should consider consenting to the set aside. If all parties consent, a party may then file with the court a request for clerk's order on consent (Form 11.2A) setting aside the noting in default or default judgment.

KEY TERMS

assessment of damages: a determination of the money damages owed to the plaintiff by the defaulting defendant(s); may be done by a motion in writing or by an assessment hearing *(p. 190)*

defendant's claim: a claim by a defendant against any party named in the plaintiff's claim, including the plaintiff or a co-defendant, or against a third party not named in the plaintiff's claim *(p. 186)*

deponent: the person who makes an affidavit *(p. 174)*

effect service: carry out or perform valid service of a document *(p. 174)*

leave of the court: permission from the court, by way of a court order, to do something; usually obtained on motion by a party *(p. 178)*

motion: an application to a court or a judge for the purpose of obtaining an order directing that some kind of relief be granted to the party making the motion *(p. 190)*

moving party: the party in a proceeding who makes a motion *(p. 190)*

per diem: per day (Latin) *(p. 185)*

per diem interest: the amount of interest that accrues per day on money owed *(p. 185)*

post-judgment interest: interest that accrues on the judgment amount, including costs, or on any outstanding balances, until such time as any balance owing has been paid in full *(p. 181)*

pre-judgment interest: interest that accrues on the amount determined to be owing commencing with the date of default and ending with the date of judgment *(p. 181)*

responding party: a party who answers or responds to a motion made by another party *(p. 190)*

such terms as are just: the court looks at the conduct of the parties, the legal issues, and the potential prejudice to the parties as a result of a particular court order, and imposes conditions and/or awards costs accordingly *(p. 179)*

REFERENCES

Administration of Justice Act, RSO 1990, c. A.6.

Courts of Justice Act, RSO 1990, c. C.43.

Law Society of Upper Canada (LSUC), *Paralegal Rules of Conduct* (Toronto: LSUC, 2007, as amended); available online at http://www.lsuc.on.ca.

Publication of Postjudgment and Prejudgment Interest Rates, O. Reg. 339/07.

Rules of the Small Claims Court, O. Reg. 258/98.

Small Claims Court—Fees and Allowances, O. Reg. 432/93.

DRAFTING EXERCISE

Dante v. Herrero—Noting Defendant in Default

This is a continuation of the drafting exercise in Chapter 4.

Review the fact situation in *Dante v. Herrero* in Box 4.1 at page 107 and the drafting exercise at page 154 of Chapter 4. The plaintiff's claim was prepared and issued on April 3, 20—. The claim number is SC-00-06638-00. The amount claimed was $4,000.00 plus pre-judgment interest commencing December 1, 20— at a rate of 12% per year, in accordance with the promissory note signed by Ms. Herrero.

The claim was personally served on the defendant on April 5, 20—. Assume that the affidavit of service has been filed with the court.

The deadline for filing a defence is 20 days from the date of service—in other words, April 25, 20—. The defendant fails to file a defence on or before that date.

Please draft a request to clerk (Form 9B) dated April 27, 20— to have the defendant noted in default, and default judgment signed (Form 11B). The Form 11B default judgment will also be dated April 27, 20—. Calculate pre-judgment interest owing from December 1, 20— to that date.

Calculate your costs. Your costs to the date of default judgment are the fee for issuing the claim and the fee for entering default judgment against the defendant. You will find a Small Claims Court fee schedule at the Attorney General's website (http://www.attorneygeneral.jus.gov.on.ca).

The post-judgment interest rate is 12% per year, in accordance with the promissory note.

REVIEW QUESTIONS

When answering the following questions, please refer to any rules or statutory authority upon which you are relying.

1. Calculate the deadline for delivering a defence in each of the following situations. Refer to Table 5.1 and Rule 8 for assistance.

   a. The defendant is personally served with the plaintiff's claim on November 1, 20—.

   b. The defendant is served with the plaintiff's claim at her place of residence on November 1, 20—. The document is handed to an apparently adult member of her household, and couriered to her the next day. The courier company verifies delivery on November 2, 20—.

   c. The defendant is an individual who is served with the plaintiff's claim by registered mail to his last-known address on August 1, 20—. There is no verification of receipt.

2. What is noting in default?

3. Who may be noted in default?

4. What are the consequences of being noted in default?

5. When may a person under disability be noted in default?

6. When should an affidavit for jurisdiction be filed?

7. How do you obtain a default judgment in a claim for a debt or liquidated amount?

8. How do you obtain default judgment in a claim for an unliquidated amount?

9. When may a defendant make a motion for set aside of the noting in default and default judgment (if any)?

APPENDIX 5.1   Parrish v. Thurston: Default Judgment (Liquidated Amount) Affidavit of Service (Form 8A)

ONTARIO

Superior Court of Justice
Cour supérieure de justice

Affidavit of Service
Affidavit de signification

Form / *Formule* 8A Ont. Reg. No. / *Règl. de l'Ont.* : 258/98

Brampton

Small Claims Court / *Cour des petites créances de*
7755 Hurontario Street
Brampton, Ontario
L6W 4T6

Address / *Adresse*

905 456 4700

Phone number / *Numéro de téléphone*

SC-00-45678-00

Claim No. / *N° de la demande*

BETWEEN / *ENTRE*

Maxwell Parrish

Plaintiff(s) / *Demandeur(s)/demanderesse(s)*

and / *et*

Frank Thurston

Defendant(s) / *Défendeur(s)/défenderesse(s)*

My name is Judy Cordero
Je m'appelle   (Full name / *Nom et prénoms*)

I live in Brampton, Ontario
J'habite à   (Municipality & province / *Municipalité et province*)

and I swear/affirm that the following is true:
et je déclare sous serment/j'affirme solennellement que les renseignements suivants sont véridiques :

1. **I served** Frank Thurston   , on November 3   , 20 -- ,
   J'ai signifié à   (Full name of person/corporation served / *Nom et prénoms*   , *le* _____ (Date)
                          de la personne/nom au complet de la personne morale
                          qui a reçu la signification)

   at 45 Labrador Court, Suite 103, Toronto, Ontario M3C 4D5
   au   (Address (street and number, unit, municipality, province) / *Adresse (numéro et rue, unité, municipalité, province)*)

   which is   ☒ the address of the person's home
   soit   *l'adresse du domicile de la personne*

   ☐ the address of the corporation's place of business
   l'adresse du lieu de travail de l'établissement de la personne morale

   ☐ the address of the person's or corporation's representative on record with the court
   l'adresse du/de la représentant(e) de la personne ou de la personne morale figurant au dossier du tribunal

   ☐ the address on the document most recently filed in court by the party
   l'adresse figurant sur le document déposé le plus récemment au tribunal par la partie

   ☐ the address of the corporation's attorney for service in Ontario
   l'adresse du fondé de pouvoir de la personne morale aux fins de signification en Ontario

   ☐ other address: _____
   autre adresse :   (Specify. / *Précisez.*)

   with   the plaintiff's claim
   ce qui suit :   (Name(s) of document(s) served / *Titre(s) du ou des documents signifiés*)

SCR 8.06-8A (November 1, 2009 / *1ᵉʳ novembre 2009*) CSD

APPENDIX 5.1   Parrish v. Thurston: Default Judgment (Liquidated Amount) Affidavit of Service (Form 8A)   *continued*

FORM / *FORMULE* 8A	PAGE 2	SC-00-45678-00
		Claim No. / *N° de la demande*

2. **I served the document(s) referred to in paragraph one by the following method:**
   J'ai signifié le ou les documents mentionnés au numéro un de la façon suivante :
   (Tell how service took place by checking appropriate box(es).)
   (Indiquez la façon dont la signification a été effectuée en cochant la ou les cases appropriées.)

Personal service / *Signification à personne*

☐ leaving a copy with the person.
   en laissant une copie à la personne.

☐ leaving a copy with the _____ of the corporation.
   en laissant une copie au/à la (Office or position / *Charge ou poste*) *de la personne morale.*

☐ leaving a copy with: _____
   en laissant une copie à : (Specify person's name and office or position. / *Indiquez le nom de la personne ainsi que sa charge ou son poste.*)

Service at place of residence / *Signification au domicile*

☒ leaving a copy in a sealed envelope addressed to the person at the person's place of residence with a person who appeared to be an adult member of the same household, and sending another copy of the same document(s) to the person's place of residence on the same day or the following day by:
   en laissant une copie au domicile de la personne, dans une enveloppe scellée adressée à celle-ci, auprès d'une personne habitant sous le même toit qui semblait majeure et en envoyant une autre copie du ou des mêmes documents au domicile de la personne le même jour ou le jour suivant :

   ☐ regular lettermail.
      par courrier ordinaire.

   ☐ registered mail.
      par courrier recommandé.

   ☒ courier.
      par messagerie.

Service by registered mail / *Signification par courrier recommandé*

☐ registered mail.
   par courrier recommandé.
   (If a copy of a plaintiff's claim or defendant's claim was served by registered mail, attach a copy of the Canada Post delivery confirmation showing the signature of the person being served to this affidavit.)
   (Si une copie de la demande du demandeur ou de la demande du défendeur a été signifiée par courrier recommandé, annexez au présent affidavit une copie de la confirmation de livraison remise par Postes Canada sur laquelle figure la signature du destinataire de la signification.)

Service by courier / *Signification par messagerie*

☐ courier.
   par messagerie.
   (If a copy of a plaintiff's claim or defendant's claim was served by courier, attach a copy of the courier's delivery confirmation showing the signature of the person being served to this affidavit.)
   (Si une copie de la demande du demandeur ou de la demande du défendeur a été signifiée par messagerie, annexez au présent affidavit une copie de la confirmation de livraison remise par le service de messagerie sur laquelle figure la signature du destinataire de la signification.)

Service on lawyer / *Signification à l'avocat*

☐ leaving a copy with a lawyer who accepted service on the person's behalf.
   en laissant une copie avec l'avocat qui a accepté la signification au nom de la personne.
   (Attach a copy of the document endorsed with the lawyer's acceptance of service.)
   (Annexez une copie du document, sur lequel l'avocat a inscrit qu'il a accepté la signification.)

Service by regular lettermail / *Signification par courrier ordinaire*

☐ regular lettermail.
   par courrier ordinaire.

   Continued on next page / *Suite à la page suivante*

APPENDIX 5.1 Parrish v. Thurston: Default Judgment (Liquidated Amount) Affidavit of Service (Form 8A) *concluded*

FORM / *FORMULE* 8A   PAGE 3   SC-00-45678-00

Claim No. / *N° de la demande*

| Service by fax / *Signification par télécopie* | ☐ fax sent at _____ at the following fax number: _____ *par télécopie envoyée à* (Time / *heure*) *au numéro de télécopieur suivant :* (Fax number / *numéro de télécopieur*) |

Service to last known address of corporation or attorney for service, and to the directors / *Signification à la dernière adresse connue de la personne morale ou de son fondé de pouvoir aux fins de signification et aux administrateurs <fr>*

☐ mail/courier to corporation or attorney for service at last known address recorded with the Ministry of Government Services, and
d'une part, par la poste/par messagerie à la personne morale ou à son fondé de pouvoir aux fins de signification, à la dernière adresse connue figurant dans les dossiers du ministère des Services gouvernementaux;

mail/courier to each director, as recorded with the Ministry of Government Services, as set out below:
d'autre part, par la poste/par messagerie à chaque administrateur mentionné dans les dossiers du ministère des Services gouvernementaux et dont le nom et l'adresse sont indiqués ci-dessous :

Name of director / *Nom de l'administrateur*	Director's address as recorded with the Ministry of Government Services (street & number, unit, municipality, province) / *Adresse de l'administrateur figurant dans les dossiers du ministère des Services gouvernementaux (numéro et rue, unité, municipalité, province)*
_____	_____
_____	_____
_____	_____
_____	_____
_____	_____

(Attach separate sheet for additional names if necessary. /
Joignez au besoin une feuille séparée s'il y a d'autres noms à ajouter.)

| Substituted service / *Signification indirecte* | ☐ substituted service as ordered by the court on _____ , 20 ____ , *par signification indirecte ordonnée par le tribunal le* (Date) as follows: (Give details.) *comme suit :* (*Précisez.*) |

Sworn/Affirmed before me at **Brampton**
Déclaré sous serment/Affirmé   (Municipality / *municipalité*)
solennellement devant moi à

in **Ontario**
en/à/au   (Province, state, or country / *province, État ou pays*)

on **November 10**   , 20 **--** _____
le   Commissioner for taking affidavits
                                                    Commissaire aux affidavits
                                                    (Type or print name below if signature is illegible.)
                                                    (*Dactylographiez le nom ou écrivez-le en caractères d'imprimerie ci-dessous si la signature est illisible.*)

_____
Signature
(This form is to be signed in front of a lawyer, justice of the peace, notary public or commissioner for taking affidavits.)
(*La présente formule doit être signée en présence d'un avocat, d'un juge de paix, d'un notaire ou d'un commissaire aux affidavits.*)

SCR 8.06-8A (November 1, 2009 / *1er novembre 2009*) CSD

APPENDIX 5.1   Affidavit for Jurisdiction (Form 11A)

ONTARIO

Superior Court of Justice   **Affidavit for Jurisdiction**
Cour supérieure de justice   *Affidavit établissant la compétence*
                                                           Form / *Formule* 11A Ont. Reg. No. / *Régl. de l'Ont.* : 258/98

Brampton	SC-00-45678-00
Small Claims Court / *Cour des petites créances de*	Claim No. / *N° de la demande*

7755 Hurontario Street

Brampton, Ontario

L6W 4T6
Address / *Adresse*

905 456 4700
Phone number / *Numéro de téléphone*

BETWEEN / *ENTRE*

                                    Maxwell Parrish
                                                           Plaintiff(s) / *Demandeur(s)/demanderesse(s)*

                                    and / *et*

                                    Frank Thurston
                                                           Defendant(s) / *Défendeur(s)/défenderesse(s)*

My name is Marie Prior
Je m'appelle   (Full name / *Nom et prénoms*)

I live in Brampton, Ontario
J'habite à   (Municipality & province / *Municipalité et province*)

and I swear/affirm that the following is true:
et je déclare sous serment/j'affirme solennellement que les renseignements suivants sont véridiques :

1. In this action, I am the
   Dans la présente action, je suis le/la

   ☐ plaintiff
      demandeur/demanderesse

   ☒ representative of the plaintiff(s) Maxwell Parrish
      représentant(e) du/de la/des   (Name of plaintiff(s) / *Nom du/de la/des demandeur(s)/demanderesse(s)*)
      demandeur(s)/demanderesse(s)

2. I make this affidavit in support of the plaintiff's request to note the defendant(s) in default, where all the defendants have been or will be served outside the court's territorial division [R. 11.01 (3)].
   Je fais le présent affidavit à l'appui de la demande du demandeur de faire constater le ou les défendeurs en défaut étant donné que tous les défendeurs ont reçu ou recevront la signification en dehors de la division territoriale du tribunal [par. 11.01 (3)].

SCR 11.01-11A (June 1, 2009 / *1er juin 2009*) CSD

APPENDIX 5.1   Affidavit for Jurisdiction (Form 11A)   *concluded*

FORM / *FORMULE* 11A   PAGE 2   SC-00-45678-00

                                                                        Claim No. / *N° de la demande*

3. The plaintiff is entitled to proceed with this action in this territorial division because this is:
   Le demandeur a le droit de poursuivre cette action dans cette division territoriale parce que :

   ☒ where the event (cause of action) took place.
      l'événement (cause d'action) a eu lieu dans cette division territoriale.

   ☐ where the defendant lives or carries on business.
      le défendeur réside dans cette division territoriale ou y exploite une entreprise.

   ☐ the court nearest to the place where the defendant lives or carries on business [R. 6.01].
      c'est dans cette division territoriale que se trouve le greffe du tribunal qui est le plus près de l'endroit où le défendeur réside ou exploite une entreprise. [règle 6.01].

Sworn/Affirmed before me at **Brampton**
Déclaré sous serment/Affirmé   (Municipality / *municipalité*)
solennellement devant moi à

in **Ontario**
en/à/au   (Province, state or country / *province, État ou pays*)

                                                                        Signature

on **December 1**   , 20 --   (This form is to be signed in front of a
le   lawyer, justice of the peace, notary public
                              Commissioner for taking affidavits   or commissioner for taking affidavits.)
                              Commissaire aux affidavits   (*La présente formule doit être signée en
                              (Type or print name below if signature is présence d'un avocat, d'un juge de paix,
                                          illegible.)   d'un notaire ou d'un commissaire aux
                              (*Dactylographiez le nom ou écrivez-le en   affidavits.*)
                              caractères d'imprimerie ci-dessous si la
                                    signature est illisible.*)

WARNING:	**IT IS AN OFFENCE UNDER THE *CRIMINAL CODE* TO KNOWINGLY SWEAR OR AFFIRM A FALSE AFFIDAVIT.**
AVERTISSEMENT :	*FAIRE SCIEMMENT UN FAUX AFFIDAVIT CONSTITUE UNE INFRACTION AU CODE CRIMINEL.*

SCR 11.01-11A (June 1, 2009 / *1er juin 2009*) CSD

APPENDIX 5.1   Request to Clerk (Form 9B)

ONTARIO

Superior Court of Justice
Cour supérieure de justice

Request to Clerk
Demande au greffier

Form / *Formule* 9B Ont. Reg. No. / *Règl. de l'Ont.* : 258/98

Brampton

Small Claims Court / *Cour des petites créances de*
7755 Hurontario Street
Brampton, Ontario
L6W 4T6

Address / *Adresse*

905 456 4700

Phone number / *Numéro de téléphone*

SC-00-45678-00

Claim No. / *N° de la demande*

BETWEEN / *ENTRE*

Maxwell Parrish

Plaintiff(s) / *Demandeur(s)/demanderesse(s)*

and / *et*

Frank Thurston

Defendant(s) / *Défendeur(s)/défenderesse(s)*

TO THE CLERK OF THE Brampton   **SMALL CLAIMS COURT:**
AU GREFFIER DE LA COUR   (Name of Small Claims Court location / *Emplacement de la*
DES PETITES CRÉANCES DE   *Cour des petites créances)* :

My name is Marie Prior   **and I request that the clerk of the court:**
Je m'appelle   (Name of party/representative / *Nom de la partie ou du/de la*   *et je demande au greffier du tribunal*
                            représentant(e))   *de faire ce qui suit :*

(Check appropriate box(es). / Cochez la ou les cases appropriées.*)*

☒   note defendant(s) Frank Thurston
    constater le ou les défendeurs   (Name of defendant(s) / *Nom du/de la/des défendeur(s)/défenderesse(s))*

    in default for failing to file a Defence (Form 9A) within the prescribed time period [R. 11.01(1)].
    en défaut pour n'avoir pas déposé de défense (formule 9A) dans le délai prescrit [par. 11.01 (1)].

☐   schedule an assessment hearing (all defendants have been noted in default) [R. 11.03(2)(b)].
    fixer la date d'une audience d'évaluation (tous les défendeurs ont été constatés en défaut) [alinéa
    11.03 (2) b)].

☐   schedule a terms of payment hearing because I dispute the defendant's proposed terms of payment
    contained in the Defence (Form 9A) [R. 9.03(3)].
    fixer la date d'une audience relative aux modalités de paiement parce que je conteste les modalités de
    paiement proposées par le défendeur dans la défense (formule 9A) [par. 9.03 (3)].

☐   schedule a trial [R. 16.01(1)(b)].
    fixer une date de procès [alinéa 16.01 (1) b)].

SCR 4-9-11-14-16-9B (June 1, 2009 / *1er juin 2009*) CSD

APPENDIX 5.1 Request to Clerk (Form 9B) *concluded*

FORM / *FORMULE* 9B   PAGE 2   SC-00-45678-00

Claim No. / *N° de la demande*

☐ accept payment in the amount of $ _____ into court
accepter que le paiement de   (Amount / *montant*) $ *soit consigné au tribunal,*

   ☐ according to an order of the court, dated _____ , 20 ____ .
   conformément à une ordonnance du tribunal datée du

   ☐ for a person under disability according to an order or settlement dated
   au nom d'un incapable, conformément à une ordonnance ou à une transaction datée du

   _____ , 20 ____ [R. 4.08(1)].
                            [par. 4.08 (1)].

   ☐ pursuant to the attached written offer to settle, dated _____ , 20 ____ [R. 14.05(2)].
   aux termes de l'offre de transaction écrite ci-jointe datée du   *[par. 14.05 (2)].*

   ☐ according to the following legislation:
   conformément à la disposition législative suivante :

   _____
   (Name of statute or regulation and section / *Titre de la loi ou du règlement et mention de l'article*)

☒ Other: (Specify.)
   Autre :   *(Précisez.)*

   Enter default judgment against Frank Thurston

December 1 _____ , 20 -- _____

                              (Signature of party or representative / *Signature de la partie ou du/de la*
                              représentant(e))

CAUTION:	To obtain an assessment of damages, all defendants must be noted in default. If one or more defendants has filed a defence, the matter must proceed to a settlement conference. To bring a motion in writing for an assessment of damages, file a Notice of Motion and Supporting Affidavit (Form 15A). You can get forms at court offices or online at www.ontariocourtforms.on.ca.
AVERTISSEMENT :	*Pour obtenir une évaluation des dommages-intérêts, tous les défendeurs doivent être constatés en défaut. Si un ou plusieurs défendeurs ont déposé une défense, l'affaire doit passer à l'étape de la conférence en vue d'une transaction. Pour présenter une motion par écrit en vue d'une évaluation des dommages-intérêts, déposez un avis de motion et affidavit à l'appui (formule 15A). Vous pouvez obtenir les formules aux greffes des tribunaux ou en ligne à l'adresse www.ontariocourtforms.on.ca.*

APPENDIX 5.1   Default Judgment (Form 11B)

ONTARIO

Superior Court of Justice
Cour supérieure de justice

Default Judgment
Jugement par défaut
Form / *Formule* 11B Ont. Reg. No. / *Règl. de l'Ont.* : 258/98

Seal / *Sceau*

Brampton
Small Claims Court / *Cour des petites créances de*
7755 Hurontario Street
Brampton, Ontario
L6W 4T6
Address / *Adresse*

905 456 4700
Phone number / *Numéro de téléphone*

SC-00-45678-00
Claim No. / *N° de la demande*

Plaintiff No. 1 / *Demandeur n° 1*   ☐ Additional plaintiff(s) listed on attached Form 1A.
Le ou les demandeurs additionnels sont mentionnés sur la formule 1A ci-jointe.

Last name, or name of company / *Nom de famille ou nom de la compagnie*		
Parrish		
First name / *Premier prénom*	Second name / *Deuxième prénom*	Also known as / *Également connu(e) sous le nom de*
Maxwell		
Address (street number, apt., unit) / *Adresse (numéro et rue, app., unité)*		
c/o Prior Mustafa LLP		
City/Town / *Cité/ville*	Province	Phone no. / *N° de téléphone*
Postal code / *Code postal*		Fax no. / *N° de télécopieur*
Representative / *Représentant(e)*		LSUC # / *N° du BHC*
Prior Mustafa LLP Attention: Marie Prior		**######**
Address (street number, apt., unit) / *Adresse (numéro et rue, app., unité)*		
22 County Court Boulevard		
City/Town / *Cité/ville*	Province	Phone no. / *N° de téléphone*
Brampton	**Ontario**	**905 111 2222**
Postal code / *Code postal*		Fax no. / *N° de télécopieur*
A1A 2B3		**905 111 2233**

Defendant No. 1 / *Défendeur n° 1*   ☐ Additional defendant(s) listed on attached Form 1A.
Le ou les défendeurs additionnels sont mentionnés sur la formule 1A ci-jointe.

Last name, or name of company / *Nom de famille ou nom de la compagnie*		
Thurston		
First name / *Premier prénom*	Second name / *Deuxième prénom*	Also known as / *Également connu(e) sous le nom de*
Frank		
Address (street number, apt., unit) / *Adresse (numéro et rue, app., unité)*		
45 Labrador Court, Suite 103		
City/Town / *Cité/ville*	Province	Phone no. / *N° de téléphone*
Toronto	**Ontario**	**416 333 4444**
Postal code / *Code postal*		Fax no. / *N° de télécopieur*
M3C 4D5		
Representative / *Représentant(e)*		LSUC # / *N° du BHC*
Address (street number, apt., unit) / *Adresse (numéro et rue, app., unité)*		
City/Town / *Cité/ville*	Province	Phone no. / *N° de téléphone*
Postal code / *Code postal*		Fax no. / *N° de télécopieur*

SCR 11.02-11B (June 1, 2009 / *1er juin 2009*) CSD

APPENDIX 5.1 Default Judgment (Form 11B) *continued*

NOTICE TO THE DEFENDANT(S):
AVIS AU(X) DÉFENDEUR(S) :
(Check one box only. / Cochez une seule case.)

☒ You have been noted in default according to Rule 11.01.
    vous avez été constaté(e) en défaut aux termes de la règle 11.01.

☐ You have defaulted in your payment according to Rule 9.03(2)(b), pursuant to
    vous n'avez pas effectué vos paiements aux termes de l'alinéa 9.03 (2) b), conformément à/au

_____ dated _____ , 20 _____ ,
         (Name of document / *Titre du document*)   *daté(e) du*

and 15 days have passed since you were served with a Notice of Default of Payment (Form 20L).
et 15 jours se sont écoulés depuis qu'un avis de défaut de paiement vous a été signifié (formule 20L).

DEFAULT JUDGMENT IS GIVEN against the following defendant(s):
UN JUGEMENT PAR DÉFAUT EST RENDU contre le ou les défendeurs suivants :

Last name, or name of company / *Nom de famille ou nom de la compagnie*		
Thurston		
First name / *Premier prénom*	Second name / *Deuxième prénom*	Also known as / *Également connu(e) sous le nom de*
Frank		

Last name, or name of company / *Nom de famille ou nom de la compagnie*		
First name / *Premier prénom*	Second name / *Deuxième prénom*	Also known as / *Également connu(e) sous le nom de*

Last name, or name of company / *Nom de famille ou nom de la compagnie*		
First name / *Premier prénom*	Second name / *Deuxième prénom*	Also known as / *Également connu(e) sous le nom de*

☐ Additional defendant(s) listed on attached page (*list in same format*).
    Défendeur(s) additionnel(s) mentionné(s) sur une feuille annexée (énumérez-les en suivant le même format).

THE DEFENDANT(S) MUST PAY to the plaintiff(s) the following sums:
LE OU LES DÉFENDEURS DOIVENT VERSER au(x) demandeur(s) les sommes suivantes :

(A) **DEBT** (principal amount claimed minus any payments received since the plaintiff's
claim was issued) $ 25,000.00
    LA CRÉANCE (somme demandée moins tout paiement reçu depuis la délivrance $
    de la demande du demandeur)

(B) **PRE-JUDGMENT INTEREST** calculated
    LES INTÉRÊTS ANTÉRIEURS AU JUGEMENT calculés

on the sum of $ ____25,000.00____ at the rate of __12__ %
sur la somme de   *$ au taux de*   *pour cent*

per annum from __September 1__ , 20 -- , to __December 1__ , 20 -- ,
par an du   *au*

being __91__   days. $ 747.93
soit   *jours.* $

APPENDIX 5.1 Default Judgment (Form 11B) *concluded*

FORM / *FORMULE* **11B** PAGE 3 SC-00-45678-00
Claim No. / *N° de la demande*

(C) **COSTS** to date $ _____ 110.00
  LES DÉPENS à ce jour $

  TOTAL $ _____ 25,857.93
  $

This judgment bears post-judgment interest at **12** _____ % per annum commencing this date.
Le présent jugement porte des intérêts postérieurs *pour cent à partir de la date du présent jugement.*
au jugement calculés au taux annuel de

_____ , 20 ____   _____
  (Signature of clerk / *Signature du greffier*)

CAUTION TO DEFENDANT:	**YOU MUST PAY THE AMOUNT OF THIS JUDGMENT DIRECTLY TO THE PLAINTIFF(S) IMMEDIATELY.** Failure to do so may result in additional post-judgment interest and enforcement costs.
AVERTISSEMENT AU DÉFENDEUR :	*VOUS DEVEZ VERSER DIRECTEMENT AU(X) DEMANDEUR(S) LE MONTANT DÛ AUX TERMES DU PRÉSENT JUGEMENT IMMÉDIATEMENT, à défaut de quoi d'autres intérêts postérieurs au jugement et dépens de l'exécution forcée pourront vous être imputés.*

APPENDIX 5.2   Chong v. Kingman: Motion for an Assessment of Damages
Affidavit of Service (Form 8A)

ONTARIO

Superior Court of Justice
Cour supérieure de justice

Affidavit of Service
Affidavit de signification

Form / *Formule* 8A Ont. Reg. No. / *Règl. de l'Ont.* : 258/98

Toronto

Small Claims Court / *Cour des petites créances de*
45 Sheppard Avenue East
Toronto, Ontario
M2N 5X5

Address / *Adresse*

416 326 3554

Phone number / *Numéro de téléphone*

SC-00-56789-00

Claim No. / *N° de la demande*

BETWEEN / *ENTRE*

Maxine Chong

Plaintiff(s) / *Demandeur(s)/demanderesse(s)*

and / *et*

LeeAnn Kingman

Defendant(s) / *Défendeur(s)/défenderesse(s)*

My name is   Claire Ivory
Je m'appelle   (Full name / *Nom et prénoms*)

I live in   Mississauga, Ontario
J'habite à   (Municipality & province / *Municipalité et province*)

and I swear/affirm that the following is true:
et je déclare sous serment/j'affirme solennellement que les renseignements suivants sont véridiques :

1. **I served**   LeeAnn Kingman   , on   June 24   , 20 -- ,
   J'ai signifié à   (Full name of person/corporation served / *Nom et prénoms*   , *le*   (Date)
   de la personne/nom au complet de la personne morale
   qui a reçu la signification)

   at   **48 Brimley Road, Apt. 1306, Toronto, Ontario M2L 3T6**
   au   (Address (street and number, unit, municipality, province) / *Adresse (numéro et rue, unité, municipalité, province)*)

   which is   ☒ the address of the person's home
   soit   *l'adresse du domicile de la personne*

   ☐ the address of the corporation's place of business
   l'adresse du lieu de travail de l'établissement de la personne morale

   ☐ the address of the person's or corporation's representative on record with the court
   *l'adresse du/de la représentant(e) de la personne ou de la personne morale figurant au
   dossier du tribunal*

   ☐ the address on the document most recently filed in court by the party
   l'adresse figurant sur le document déposé le plus récemment au tribunal par la partie

   ☐ the address of the corporation's attorney for service in Ontario
   l'adresse du fondé de pouvoir de la personne morale aux fins de signification en Ontario

   ☐ other address:
   autre adresse :   (Specify. / *Précisez.*)

   with   the plaintiff's claim
   ce qui suit :   (Name(s) of document(s) served / *Titre(s) du ou des documents signifiés*)

SCR 8.06-8A (November 1, 2009 / *1er novembre 2009*) CSD

APPENDIX 5.2   Chong v. Kingman: Motion for an Assessment of Damages Affidavit of Service (Form 8A)   *continued*

FORM / *FORMULE* 8A   **PAGE 2**   SC-00-56789-00
                                                          Claim No. / *N° de la demande*

2. I served the document(s) referred to in paragraph one by the following method:
J'ai signifié le ou les documents mentionnés au numéro un de la façon suivante :
(Tell how service took place by checking appropriate box(es).)
(Indiquez la façon dont la signification a été effectuée en cochant la ou les cases appropriées.)

Personal service /
Significa-tion à personne

☒ leaving a copy with the person.
en laissant une copie à la personne.

☐ leaving a copy with the _____ of the corporation.
en laissant une copie au/à la   (Office or position / *Charge ou poste*)   *de la personne morale.*

☐ leaving a copy with: _____
en laissant une copie à :   (Specify person's name and office or position. / *Indiquez le nom de la personne ainsi que sa charge ou son poste.*)

Service at place of residence /
Significa-tion au domicile

☐ leaving a copy in a sealed envelope addressed to the person at the person's place of residence with a person who appeared to be an adult member of the same household, and sending another copy of the same document(s) to the person's place of residence on the same day or the following day by:
en laissant une copie au domicile de la personne, dans une enveloppe scellée adressée à celle-ci, auprès d'une personne habitant sous le même toit qui semblait majeure et en envoyant une autre copie du ou des mêmes documents au domicile de la personne le même jour ou le jour suivant :

☐ regular lettermail.
par courrier ordinaire.

☐ registered mail.
par courrier recommandé.

☐ courier.
par messagerie.

Service by registered mail /
Significa-tion par courrier recom-mandé

☐ registered mail.
par courrier recommandé.
(If a copy of a plaintiff's claim or defendant's claim was served by registered mail, attach a copy of the Canada Post delivery confirmation showing the signature of the person being served to this affidavit.)
(Si une copie de la demande du demandeur ou de la demande du défendeur a été signifiée par courrier recommandé, annexez au présent affidavit une copie de la confirmation de livraison remise par Postes Canada sur laquelle figure la signature du destinataire de la signification.)

Service by courier /
Significa-tion par messa-gerie

☐ courier.
par messagerie.
(If a copy of a plaintiff's claim or defendant's claim was served by courier, attach a copy of the courier's delivery confirmation showing the signature of the person being served to this affidavit.)
(Si une copie de la demande du demandeur ou de la demande du défendeur a été signifiée par messagerie, annexez au présent affidavit une copie de la confirmation de livraison remise par le service de messagerie sur laquelle figure la signature du destinataire de la signification.)

Service on lawyer /
Significa-tion à l'avocat

☐ leaving a copy with a lawyer who accepted service on the person's behalf.
en laissant une copie avec l'avocat qui a accepté la signification au nom de la personne.
(Attach a copy of the document endorsed with the lawyer's acceptance of service.)
(Annexez une copie du document, sur lequel l'avocat a inscrit qu'il a accepté la signification.)

Service by regular lettermail /
Significa-tion par courrier ordinaire

☐ regular lettermail.
par courrier ordinaire.

SCR 8.06-8A (November 1, 2009 / *1er novembre 2009*) CSD   **Continued on next page / *Suite à la page suivante***

...

APPENDIX 5.2   Chong v. Kingman: Motion for an Assessment of Damages Affidavit of Service (Form 8A) *concluded*

FORM / *FORMULE* 8A   PAGE 3   SC-00-56789-00
                                                                 Claim No. / *N° de la demande*

Service by fax / *Signification par télécopie*
☐ fax sent at _____ at the following fax number: _____
par télécopie envoyée à   (Time / *heure*)   *au numéro de télécopieur suivant :*   (Fax number / *numéro de télécopieur*)

Service to last known address of corporation or attorney for service, and to the directors / *Signification à la dernière adresse connue de la personne morale ou de son fondé de pouvoir aux fins de signification et aux administrateurs <fr>*

☐ mail/courier to corporation or attorney for service at last known address recorded with the Ministry of Government Services, and
d'une part, par la poste/par messagerie à la personne morale ou à son fondé de pouvoir aux fins de signification, à la dernière adresse connue figurant dans les dossiers du ministère des Services gouvernementaux;

mail/courier to each director, as recorded with the Ministry of Government Services, as set out below:
d'autre part, par la poste/par messagerie à chaque administrateur mentionné dans les dossiers du ministère des Services gouvernementaux et dont le nom et l'adresse sont indiqués ci-dessous :

Name of director / *Nom de l'administrateur*	Director's address as recorded with the Ministry of Government Services (street & number, unit, municipality, province) / *Adresse de l'administrateur figurant dans les dossiers du ministère des Services gouvernementaux (numéro et rue, unité, municipalité, province)*

(Attach separate sheet for additional names if necessary. / *Joignez au besoin une feuille séparée s'il y a d'autres noms à ajouter.*)

Substituted service / *Signification indirecte*
☐ substituted service as ordered by the court on _____ , 20 ____ ,
par signification indirecte ordonnée par le tribunal le   (Date)

as follows: (Give details.)
comme suit : *(Précisez.)*

Sworn/Affirmed before me at **Brampton**
Déclaré sous serment/Affirmé solennellement devant moi à   (Municipality / *municipalité*)

in **Ontario**
en/à/au   (Province, state, or country / *province, État ou pays*)

on **July 15** _____ , 20 **--**
le
                    Commissioner for taking affidavits
                    Commissaire aux affidavits
                    (Type or print name below if signature is illegible.)
                    (Dactylographiez le nom ou écrivez-le en caractères d'imprimerie ci-dessous si la signature est illisible.)

                    Signature
                    (This form is to be signed in front of a lawyer, justice of the peace, notary public or commissioner for taking affidavits.)
                    (La présente formule doit être signée en présence d'un avocat, d'un juge de paix, d'un notaire ou d'un commissaire aux affidavits.)

SCR 8.06-8A (November 1, 2009 / *1er novembre 2009*) CSD

APPENDIX 5.2 Request to Clerk (Form 9B)

ONTARIO

Superior Court of Justice
Cour supérieure de justice

Request to Clerk
Demande au greffier
Form / *Formule* 9B Ont. Reg. No. / *Régl. de l'Ont.* : 258/98

Toronto
Small Claims Court / *Cour des petites créances de*
45 Sheppard Avenue
Toronto, Ontario
M2N 5X5
Address / *Adresse*

416 326 3554
Phone number / *Numéro de téléphone*

SC-00-56789-00
Claim No. / *N° de la demande*

BETWEEN / *ENTRE*

Maxine Chong

Plaintiff(s) / *Demandeur(s)/demanderesse(s)*

and / *et*

LeeAnn Kingman

Defendant(s) / *Défendeur(s)/défenderesse(s)*

TO THE CLERK OF THE Toronto **SMALL CLAIMS COURT:**
AU GREFFIER DE LA COUR (Name of Small Claims Court location / *Emplacement de la*
DES PETITES CRÉANCES DE *Cour des petites créances)* :

My name is Marie Prior **and I request that the clerk of the court:**
Je m'appelle (Name of party/representative / *Nom de la partie ou du/de la* *et je demande au greffier du tribunal*
représentant(e)) *de faire ce qui suit :*

(Check appropriate box(es). / Cochez la ou les cases appropriées.)

☒ note defendant(s) LeeAnn Kingman
constater le ou les défendeurs (Name of defendant(s) / *Nom du/de la/des défendeur(s)/défenderesse(s))*

in default for failing to file a Defence (Form 9A) within the prescribed time period [R. 11.01(1)].
en défaut pour n'avoir pas déposé de défense (formule 9A) dans le délai prescrit [par. 11.01 (1)].

☐ schedule an assessment hearing (all defendants have been noted in default) [R. 11.03(2)(b)].
fixer la date d'une audience d'évaluation (tous les défendeurs ont été constatés en défaut) [alinéa *11.03 (2) b)].*

☐ schedule a terms of payment hearing because I dispute the defendant's proposed terms of payment contained in the Defence (Form 9A) [R. 9.03(3)].
fixer la date d'une audience relative aux modalités de paiement parce que je conteste les modalités de *paiement proposées par le défendeur dans la défense (formule 9A) [par. 9.03 (3)].*

☐ schedule a trial [R. 16.01(1)(b)].
fixer une date de procès [alinéa 16.01 (1) b)].

SCR 4-9-11-14-16-9B (June 1, 2009 / *1er juin 2009*) CSD

APPENDIX 5.2 **Request to Clerk (Form 9B)** *concluded*

FORM / *FORMULE* 9B   **PAGE 2**   SC-00-56789-00
                                                                   Claim No. / *N° de la demande*

☐ accept payment in the amount of $ _____ into court
   accepter que le paiement de   (Amount / *montant*)   *$ soit consigné au tribunal,*

   ☐ according to an order of the court, dated _____ , 20 ____ .
      conformément à une ordonnance du tribunal datée du

   ☐ for a person under disability according to an order or settlement dated
      au nom d'un incapable, conformément à une ordonnance ou à une transaction datée du

      _____ , 20 ____ [R. 4.08(1)].
                                 [par. 4.08 (1)].

   ☐ pursuant to the attached written offer to settle, dated _____ , 20 ____ [R. 14.05(2)].
      aux termes de l'offre de transaction écrite ci-jointe datée du   *[par. 14.05 (2)].*

   ☐ according to the following legislation:
      conformément à la disposition législative suivante :

      _____
      (Name of statute or regulation and section / *Titre de la loi ou du règlement et mention de l'article*)

☐ Other: (Specify.)
   Autre :   *(Précisez.)*

July 15 _____ , 20 --   _____
                                    (Signature of party or representative / *Signature de la partie ou du/de la*
                                    représentant(e))

CAUTION:	To obtain an assessment of damages, all defendants must be noted in default. If one or more defendants has filed a defence, the matter must proceed to a settlement conference. To bring a motion in writing for an assessment of damages, file a Notice of Motion and Supporting Affidavit (Form 15A). You can get forms at court offices or online at www.ontariocourtforms.on.ca.
AVERTISSEMENT :	*Pour obtenir une évaluation des dommages-intérêts, tous les défendeurs doivent être constatés en défaut. Si un ou plusieurs défendeurs ont déposé une défense, l'affaire doit passer à l'étape de la conférence en vue d'une transaction. Pour présenter une motion par écrit en vue d'une évaluation des dommages-intérêts, déposez un avis de motion et affidavit à l'appui (formule 15A). Vous pouvez obtenir les formules aux greffes des tribunaux ou en ligne à l'adresse www.ontariocourtforms.on.ca.*

SCR 4-9-11-14-16-9B (June 1, 2009 / *1er juin 2009*) CSD

APPENDIX 5.2   Notice of Motion and Supporting Affidavit (Form 15A)

ONTARIO

Superior Court of Justice
Cour supérieure de justice

Notice of Motion and Supporting Affidavit
Avis de motion et affidavit à l'appui
Form / *Formule* 15A Ont. Reg. No. / *Régl. de l'Ont.* : 258/98

Toronto	SC-00-56789-00
Small Claims Court / *Cour des petites créances de*	Claim No. / *N° de la demande*
45 Sheppard Avenue East	
Toronto, Ontario	
M2N 5X5	
Address / *Adresse*	
416 326 3554	
Phone number / *Numéro de téléphone*	

Plaintiff No. 1 / *Demandeur n° 1*   ☐ Additional plaintiff(s) listed on attached Form 1A.
Le ou les demandeurs additionnels sont mentionnés sur la formule 1A ci-jointe.

Last name, or name of company / *Nom de famille ou nom de la compagnie*		
Chong		
First name / *Premier prénom*	Second name / *Deuxième prénom*	Also known as / *Également connu(e) sous le nom de*
Maxine		
Address (street number, apt., unit) / *Adresse (numéro et rue, app., unité)*		
c/o Prior Mustafa LLP		
City/Town / *Cité/ville*	Province	Phone no. / *N° de téléphone*
Postal code / *Code postal*		Fax no. / *N° de télécopieur*
Representative / *Représentant(e)*		LSUC # / *N° du BHC*
Prior Mustafa LLP Attention: Marie Prior		**######**
Address (street number, apt., unit) / *Adresse (numéro et rue, app., unité)*		
22 County Court Boulevard		
City/Town / *Cité/ville*	Province	Phone no. / *N° de téléphone*
Brampton	**Ontario**	**905 111 2222**
Postal code / *Code postal*		Fax no. / *N° de télécopieur*
A1A 2B3		**905 111 2233**

Defendant No. 1 / *Défendeur n° 1*   ☐ Additional defendant(s) listed on attached Form 1A.
Le ou les défendeurs additionnels sont mentionnés sur la formule 1A ci-jointe.

Last name, or name of company / *Nom de famille ou nom de la compagnie*		
Kingman		
First name / *Premier prénom*	Second name / *Deuxième prénom*	Also known as / *Également connu(e) sous le nom de*
LeeAnn		
Address (street number, apt., unit) / *Adresse (numéro et rue, app., unité)*		
48 Brimley Road, Apt. 1306		
City/Town / *Cité/ville*	Province	Phone no. / *N° de téléphone*
Toronto	**Ontario**	**416 444 5555**
Postal code / *Code postal*		Fax no. / *N° de télécopieur*
L2L 3T6		
Representative / *Représentant(e)*		LSUC # / *N° du BHC*
Address (street number, apt., unit) / *Adresse (numéro et rue, app., unité)*		
City/Town / *Cité/ville*	Province	Phone no. / *N° de téléphone*
Postal code / *Code postal*		Fax no. / *N° de télécopieur*

SCR 15.01-15A (June 1, 2009 / *1ᵉʳ juin 2009*) CSD

APPENDIX 5.2 Notice of Motion and Supporting Affidavit (Form 15A) *continued*

FORM / *FORMULE* 15A   PAGE 2   SC-00-56789-00

Claim No. / *N° de la demande*

THIS COURT WILL HEAR A MOTION on August 1 _____ , 20 -- , **at** 9:30 a.m. _____ ,
LE TRIBUNAL PRÉCITÉ ENTENDRA UNE MOTION le   , *à*   (Time / *heure*)

or as soon as possible after that time, at 45 Sheppard Avenue East, Toronto, Ontario M2N 5X5
ou dès que possible par la suite à/au   (Address of court location and courtroom number / *Adresse du tribunal et numéro de la salle d'audience*)

Complete Part A or Part B below, then complete the affidavit in support of motion on page 3. / *Remplissez la partie A ou la partie B ci-dessous. Remplissez ensuite l'affidavit à l'appui de la motion à la page 3.*

A.
     This motion will be made in person
     by _____ ,
     La motion sera présentée en personne par :   (Name of party / *Nom de la partie*)

     for the following order : / *en vue d'obtenir l'ordonnance suivante :*

☐   the court's permission to extend time to (Specify)
    l'autorisation du tribunal de proroger le délai pour *(Précisez)*

☐   set aside default judgment and noting in default.
    l'annulation du jugement par défaut et la constatation du défaut.

☐   set aside noting in default.
    l'annulation de la constatation du défaut.

☐   permission to file a Defence.
    l'autorisation de déposer une défense.

☐   permission to file a Defendant's Claim.
    l'autorisation de déposer une demande du défendeur.

☐   terminate garnishment and/or withdraw writ(s).
    la mainlevée de la saisie-arrêt ou le retrait d'un ou de plusieurs brefs, ou les deux.

☐   Other:
    Autre :

☒   **ADDITIONAL PAGES ARE ATTACHED BECAUSE MORE ROOM WAS NEEDED.**
    DES FEUILLES SUPPLÉMENTAIRES SONT ANNEXÉES EN RAISON DU MANQUE D'ESPACE.

☒   **DOCUMENTS ARE ATTACHED.**
    PIÈCES JOINTES.

NOTE:	**IF YOU FAIL TO ATTEND AN IN-PERSON MOTION,** an order may be made against you, with costs, in your absence. If you want to attend the motion by telephone or video conference, complete and file a Request for Telephone or Video Conference (Form 1B). If the court permits it, the clerk will make the necessary arrangements and notify the parties [R. 1.07(5)].
REMARQUE :	*SI VOUS NE VOUS PRÉSENTEZ PAS EN PERSONNE À L'AUDITION DE LA MOTION, une ordonnance peut être rendue contre vous en votre absence, avec dépens. Si vous voulez assister à l'audition de la motion par conférence téléphonique ou vidéoconférence, remplissez et déposez la Demande de conférence téléphonique ou vidéoconférence (formule 1B). Si le tribunal l'autorise, le greffier prendra les dispositions nécessaires et en avisera les parties [par. 1.07 (5)].*

APPENDIX 5.2 Notice of Motion and Supporting Affidavit (Form 15A) *continued*

FORM / *FORMULE* 15A   PAGE 3   SC-00-56789-00
                                                               Claim No. / *N° de la demande*

B. This motion in writing for an assessment of damages is made by
La présente motion par écrit en vue d'une évaluation des dommages-intérêts est présentée par

Maxine Chong
                    (Name of plaintiff / *Nom du demandeur/de la demanderesse*)

who asks the court for an order assessing damages against
qui demande au tribunal de rendre une ordonnance d'évaluation des dommages-intérêts contre

LeeAnn Kingman
                    (Name of defendant(s) / *Nom du/de la/des défendeur(s)/défenderesse(s)*)

who have/has been noted in default.
qui a/ont été constaté(e)(s) en défaut.

AFFIDAVIT IN SUPPORT OF MOTION / *AFFIDAVIT À L'APPUI DE LA MOTION*

My name is Maxine Chong
Je m'appelle   (Full name / *Nom et prénoms*)

I live in Toronto, Ontario
J'habite à   (Municipality & province / *Municipalité et province*)

I swear/affirm that the following is true:
Je déclare sous serment/j'affirme solennellement que les renseignements suivants sont véridiques :

Set out the facts in numbered paragraphs. If you learned a fact from someone else, you must give that person's name and state that you believe that fact to be true.
Indiquez les faits sous forme de dispositions numérotées. Si vous avez pris connaissance d'un fait par l'entremise d'une autre personne, vous devez indiquer le nom de cette personne et déclarer que vous croyez que ce fait est véridique.

See Schedule A attached and forming part of this affidavit

SCR 15.01-15A (June 1, 2009 / *1ᵉʳ juin 2009*) CSD   **Continued on next page / *Suite à la page suivante***

APPENDIX 5.2 Notice of Motion and Supporting Affidavit (Form 15A) *continued*

FORM / *FORMULE* 15A   PAGE 4   SC-00-56789-00
                                                                 Claim No. / *N° de la demande*

AFFIDAVIT IN SUPPORT OF MOTION, continued / *AFFIDAVIT À L'APPUI DE LA MOTION, suite*
See Schedule A attached and forming part of this affidavit

If more space is required, attach and initial extra pages. / Si vous avez besoin de plus d'espace, annexez une ou des feuilles
supplémentaires et paraphez-les.

Sworn/Affirmed before me at **Brampton**
Déclaré sous serment/Affirmé   (Municipality / *municipalité*)
solennellement devant moi à

in **Ontario**
en/à/au   (Province, state or country / *province, État ou pays*)

on **July 15**   , 20 --
le   Commissioner for taking affidavits
                                            Commissaire aux affidavits
                                            (Type or print name below if signature is illegible.)
                                            (*Dactylographiez le nom ou écrivez-le en*
                                            caractères d'imprimerie ci-dessous si la
                                            signature est illisible.)

                                                            Signature
                                            (This form is to be signed in front of a
                                            lawyer, justice of the peace, notary public
                                            or commissioner for taking affidavits.)
                                            (*La présente formule doit être signée en*
                                            présence d'un avocat, d'un juge de paix,
                                            d'un notaire ou d'un commissaire aux
                                            affidavits.)

WARNING: IT IS AN OFFENCE UNDER THE *CRIMINAL CODE* TO KNOWINGLY SWEAR OR
                  AFFIRM A FALSE AFFIDAVIT.
AVERTISSEMENT : *FAIRE SCIEMMENT UN FAUX AFFIDAVIT CONSTITUE UNE INFRACTION AU CODE*
                  CRIMINEL.

SCR 15.01-15A (June 1, 2009 / *1er juin 2009*) CSD

Schedule A

1. I, Maxine Chong, am the plaintiff in this action and have personal knowledge of the following.

2. I am a 62-year-old widow. I live alone. My children are both married. My son lives in Alberta, and my daughter lives in British Columbia. Both of them try to stay in touch with me, but they are busy people with families.

3. I have a fixed income, consisting of my pension, and some income from savings and investments. My main asset is my house. There is a legal basement apartment in the basement, but after my husband died I stopped renting it out, because I was not comfortable with having strangers in the house. Last year, I had to do some repairs to the roof. Then I received a notice of reassessment from the municipality, advising me that my taxes were being increased. I decided to start renting the basement apartment again, because I needed the extra income.

4. Pursuant to a tenancy agreement dated January 13, 20—, I agreed to rent the basement apartment in my home to the defendant for $775.00 per month commencing on February 1, 20—. A true copy of the agreement is attached as Exhibit 1.

5. The basement apartment is a self-contained, one-bedroom apartment with access to the side entrance of the house. I occupy the main floor. The washer, dryer, furnace and fuse box are in the basement, accessible from the basement apartment. The door to my kitchen opens onto the side entrance to the house and the stairs down to the basement.

6. The defendant's rent cheque for February 1 was returned for insufficient funds. A true copy of the notice from my bank is attached as Exhibit 2. When I asked her for a replacement cheque, the defendant became extremely abusive. She screamed at me and then slammed the apartment door in my face. I was very disturbed and frightened, and went back upstairs.

7. That evening, the defendant played music very loudly until one o'clock in the morning. I could not sleep. I was afraid the neighbours would complain to the police. Because of her earlier behaviour, I did not want to confront her in person. Around midnight, I pounded on the floor to get the music to stop. The defendant pounded back, screaming abuse and obscenities. Eventually, the defendant turned the music off, but for the rest of the night there were sounds of banging and crashing from

APPENDIX 5.2   **Notice of Motion and Supporting Affidavit (Form 15A)**   *continued*

the basement. I was terrified. The defendant had access to my washer, dryer, furnace and the fuse box. I feared that she would cause damage or set the house on fire.

8. The defendant never paid the February rent. When I tried to approach her about it, she became extremely abusive.

9. On several occasions in February, the defendant came upstairs and stood outside my kitchen door, which opened onto the side entrance that the defendant used. She would pound on the door and scream. She would threaten to report me to the Ontario Human Rights Commission for abuse and discrimination.

10. The defendant did not pay the rent for March. This caused me considerable financial and personal stress. I did nothing because I was afraid of how the defendant might react. I felt as if I did not own my house any more. Whenever the defendant was at home, there was loud music, banging, and shouting from the basement, especially from around midnight until two or three o'clock in the morning. True copies of my bank statements for February and March are attached as Exhibits 3 and 4.

11. I began keeping the kitchen door locked. I could not sleep and I lost my appetite. I suffered from headaches and anxiety attacks. If I went out, I dreaded going home. My physician prescribed medication for anxiety and to help me sleep. A true copy of a prescription for medication for anxiety is attached as Exhibit 5. A true copy of a prescription for medication for insomnia is attached as Exhibit 6. A true copy of an invoice from Phillips Pharmacy dated February 21, 20— in the amount of $183.47 is attached as Exhibit 7.

12. When the defendant did not pay the April rent, I was desperate. I called my daughter, Alice, in Penticton. Alice arrived late on April 5. On April 6, we got in touch with a paralegal firm specializing in residential tenancies law. The paralegal firm drafted and served a Form N4—Notice to End a Tenancy Early for Non-Payment of Rent on the defendant. A true copy of the Form N4 is attached as Exhibit 8. A true copy of an invoice dated April 18 from Prior Mustafa LLP is attached as Exhibit 9.

13. On April 17, the defendant vacated the apartment, taking the keys to the side entrance and the basement apartment with her. She left the basement apartment in a damaged, filthy state. I had to pay $1,059.00 to have the apartment cleaned, the damage repaired, and the carpet replaced. A true copy of an invoice from Magic Carpets and Walls is attached as Exhibit 10. I had to pay a locksmith $125.00 to rekey the apartment door and the side entrance to my house. A true copy of an invoice from Safety First Keys and Locks is attached as Exhibit 11.

14. My daughter stayed long enough to help me find me a reliable, quiet tenant for the basement apartment. The new tenant moved in on June 1. There have been no more problems.

15. I am sixty-two years old. I have lived on my own and managed my own affairs for nine years, since my husband died. I was in excellent health and spirits before the defendant moved into my house. I have always been very independent, which is why it took me so long to seek help from my family. I prefer to handle things myself, but I could not handle this situation.

16. Since the defendant moved out, I have stopped taking medication for anxiety, although I continue to have severe anxiety attacks and I still suffer from loss of appetite. I am frequently depressed. I am no longer as active physically as I was before the events described above. I cannot sleep without medication. Without it, the anxiety attacks wake me up in the night, and I lie there perspiring and shaking. My physician has advised me that the medication I am taking may be addictive over the long term, but there is no other way I can get to sleep.

17. As of the date this claim was issued, I claimed special damages of $3,992.47, calculated as follows:

Loss of income—unpaid rent (3 months × $775.00)	$2,325.00
Medication	183.47
Costs of repairs to basement apartment	1,059.00
Cost to rekey locks	125.00
Cost of drafting and serving N4	300.00
Total as of June 24, 20—	$3,992.47

18. Since then, I have incurred additional expenses for medication in the amount of $116.17. A true copy of an invoice from Phillips Pharmacy dated July 3, 20—is attached as Exhibit 12.

19. The balance of the claim is for general damages for physical and mental pain, suffering and distress that I experienced as a direct result of the defendant's deliberate or negligent conduct. A true copy of my treating physician's report is attached as Exhibit 13. A true copy of an invoice dated July 11, 20— in the amount of $565.00 for the physician's report is attached as Exhibit 14.

Exhibits to the affidavit: [Note that a real affidavit would have photocopies of documents stamped as exhibits, and dated and signed by the commissioner of oaths, attached to it. You will find a sample Exhibit 1 on the next page.]

Exhibit 1   Photocopy of tenancy agreement dated January 13, 20—

Exhibit 2   Photocopy of notice of NSF cheque dated February 16, 20—

Exhibit 3   Photocopy of February 20— bank statement

Exhibit 4   Photocopy of March 20— bank statement

Exhibit 5   Photocopy of prescription for medication for anxiety

Exhibit 6   Photocopy of prescription for medication for insomnia

Exhibit 7   Photocopy of invoice from Phillips Pharmacy in the amount of $183.47

Exhibit 8   Photocopy of N4—Notice to end tenancy early for non-payment of rent

Exhibit 9   Photocopy of invoice from Prior Mustafa LLP in the amount of $300.00

Exhibit 10   Photocopy of invoice from Magic Carpets and Walls in the amount of $1,059.00

Exhibit 11   Photocopy of invoice from Safety First Keys and Locks in the amount of $125.00

Exhibit 12   Photocopy of invoice from Phillips Pharmacy in the amount of $116.17

Exhibit 13   Photocopy of treating physician's report

Exhibit 14   Photocopy of invoice for treating physician's report in the amount of $565.00

APPENDIX 5.2 Sample Exhibit 1

Residential Tenancy Agreement (Ontario)

THIS AGREEMENT made the 13th day of January, 20—

BETWEEN:

Maxine Chong

67 Harmony Avenue, Toronto, Ontario M4J 1J3

("the Landlord")

and

LeeAnn Kingman

("the Tenant")

The rental premises are a legal self-contained one-bedroom apartment at 67 Harmony Avenue, Toronto Ontario M4J 1J3. The term of the tenancy shall be a 12-month period commencing 1 February 20—and ending 31 January 20—. The monthly rent shall be $775.00 inclusive of heat and hydro, payable on the first day of each and every month for the duration of the tenancy.

The Tenant shall have reasonable access to the laundry facilities in the basement at 67 Harmony Avenue, Toronto, Ontario.

The Landlord shall provide and maintain the premises in a good state of repair and fit for habitation and complying with municipal health, safety and maintenance standards.

The Tenant is responsible for the ordinary cleanliness of the premises and for the repair of damage caused by the willful or negligent conduct of the Tenant or persons permitted on the premises by the Tenant.

Signed: _____Maxine Chong_____ Dated: _____January 13, 20—_____

Signed: _____LeeAnn Kingman_____ Dated: _____Jan. 13, 20—_____

Acting for the Defendant

6

LEARNING OUTCOMES

After reading this chapter, you will understand:

- The time for filing a defence
- When to dispute the entire claim
- When to make a proposal of terms of payment
- Procedure for making a proposal of terms of payment
- Rules of pleading for a defence
- What a defendant's claim is used for
- Rules of pleading for a defendant's claim

Introduction

A defendant who is served personally with the plaintiff's claim has 20 days from the date of service to file a defence with the court.

If the defendant is served by an alternative to personal service, the time for filing a defence will vary, depending on how the plaintiff's claim is served. See Table 5.1 at page 176 for the time periods for delivering a defence to a plaintiff's or defendant's claim.

A defendant who wishes to make a claim against the plaintiff or any other person may issue a defendant's claim within 20 days after filing the defence, unless the court orders otherwise.

The court clerk will serve the defence on all other parties. The plaintiff by defendant's claim is responsible for serving the defendant's claim. The defendant's claim must be served personally or by an alternative to personal service.

A defendant who has been noted in default and/or had default judgment signed against him may make a motion for an order setting aside the noting in default and other relief. The motion should be made as soon as is reasonably possible in all of the circumstances. The supporting affidavit must provide a reasonable explanation for the default, and satisfy the court that the defendant has a meritorious defence.

Defendant Not in Default

General

The defendant should bring the plaintiff's claim with her to the initial consultation. If she intends to dispute all or part of the claim, she should also bring originals of any documents she intends to rely on in her defence. The original documents should be placed in the documents subfile for the client matter. Copies of the documents will be attached to the defence, in accordance with a defendant's obligation of early and ongoing disclosure (Rule 9.02(1)2).

As early as possible in the matter, you must find out when your client was served, because this tells you how much time you have left to file the defence. The general rule is that a defendant has 20 days from the date of being served to file a defence. This is not a big window, so you should diarize for expiry of the period and ensure that you draft and file the defence promptly upon being retained.

If the plaintiff is represented, you should contact the plaintiff's lawyer or paralegal and advise her that you are in the process of obtaining instructions. If the initial contact with the defendant does not take place until the time for filing a defence has expired or almost expired, you should contact the plaintiff or the plaintiff's legal representative and request an extension of time.

Professional courtesy requires that, if asked to do so, a party's legal representative should seek their client's instructions to consent to a brief extension of the deadline for delivering a defence, if they have been made aware that the defendant is taking reasonable steps to defend the action and there is no prejudice to the client. See Paralegal Rule 7.01(2). The consent to an extension of time for filing the defence should be confirmed in writing and should state a deadline for filing the defence. The consent should be filed with the court (Rule 3.02(2)).

If the defendant does not contact you until the time for filing the defence has almost expired, and the plaintiff refuses to consent to a reasonable extension of the time for filing the defence, you must make a motion to the court for an order extending the deadline for filing a defence, pursuant to Rule 3.02(1).

If the client declines to retain you, or you decline the retainer on grounds of a conflict of interest or for some other reason, you must advise the client in the non-engagement letter of the procedural consequences of failing to file a defence within the prescribed time, and suggest that he seek other legal representation. If the client has grounds for a defendant's claim, he should also be advised that the limitation period for a defendant's claim begins to run on the day the plaintiff's claim was served.

Drafting the Defence

General

During the initial consultation, you must go over the substance of the plaintiff's claim carefully with your client. The defence (Form 9A) gives the defendant a number of options (see Figure 6.1). You must determine which of these options is appropriate in your client's case:

1. dispute the entire claim;
2. admit liability for the claim and make a proposal of terms of payment of the amount claimed; or
3. admit liability for part of the claim, make a proposal of terms of payment of that part of the claim, and defend the remainder of the claim.

If all or part of the plaintiff's claim is disputed, the defence should state the material facts the defendant is relying on in concise non-technical language with a reasonable amount of detail (Rule 9.02(1)1). Copies of any documents upon which the defendant intends to rely shall be attached (Rule 9.02(1)2). Note that the obligation to disclose under Rule 9.02 is mandatory.

If the plaintiff is self-represented, the grounds for the claim are not likely to comply with formal rules for drafting pleadings. They may consist of nothing more than five or six handwritten sentences. This does not mean that the self-represented plaintiff does not have a good cause of action, and you should still go over the claim carefully with the defendant, with a view to drafting a persuasive defence.

Defendant Disputes All or Part of the Claim

For the overall structure of a disputed action, see Figure 6.2.

Small Claims Court Rule 9 does not require the allegations in support of a full or partial defence to be typed and double-spaced, and set out in separate, numbered paragraphs in a schedule to the Form 9A. Rule 9 requires only that the defence contain contact information for the defendant or the defendant's agent or lawyer; the

FIGURE 6.1 Disputing the Plaintiff's Claim

FORM / *FORMULE* 9A **PAGE 2**

Claim No. / *N° de la demande*

THIS DEFENCE IS BEING FILED ON BEHALF OF: (Name(s) of defendant(s))
LA PRÉSENTE DÉFENSE EST DÉPOSÉE AU NOM DE : (Nom du/de la ou des défendeur(s)/défenderesse(s))

and I/we: (Check as many as apply)
et je/nous : (Cochez la ou les cases qui s'appliquent)

☐ Dispute the claim made against me/us.
conteste/contestons la demande présentée contre moi/nous.

☐ Admit the full claim and propose the following terms of payment:
reconnais/reconnaissons être redevable(s) de la totalité de la demande et propose/proposons les modalités de paiement suivantes :

$_____ per _____ commencing _____ , 20 ___ .
(Amount / *Montant*) *$ par* (Week/month / *semaine/mois*) *à compter du*

☐ Admit part of the claim in the amount of $_____ and propose the following terms of payment:
reconnais/reconnaissons être redevable(s) (Amount / *Montant*) *$ et propose/proposons les modalités de*
d'une partie de la demande, soit *paiement suivantes :*

$_____ per _____ commencing _____ , 20 ___ .
(Amount / *Montant*) *$ par* (Week/month / *semaine/mois*) *à compter du*

REASONS FOR DISPUTING THE CLAIM AND DETAILS:
MOTIFS DE CONTESTATION DE LA DEMANDE ET PRÉCISIONS :

Explain what happened, including where and when. Explain why you do not agree with the claim made against you.
Expliquez ce qui s'est passé, en précisant où et quand. Expliquez pourquoi vous contestez la demande présentée contre vous.

If you are relying on any documents, you **MUST** attach copies to the Defence. If evidence is lost or unavailable, you **MUST** explain why it is not attached.
*Si vous vous appuyez sur des documents, vous **DEVEZ** en annexer des copies à la défense. Si une preuve est perdue ou n'est pas disponible, vous **DEVEZ** expliquer pourquoi elle n'est pas annexée.*

What happened?
Where?
When?
Que s'est-il passé?

reasons why the defendant disputes all or part of the plaintiff's claim, stated in concise non-technical language with a reasonable amount of detail (Rule 9.02(1)1); and disclosure of any documents upon which the defence is based (Rule 9.02(1)2). This is appropriate for a court intended to be user-friendly for the self-represented.

Nevertheless, you, as a professional paralegal, should use professional standards when drafting pleadings. The grounds for the defence should be set out in a separate schedule attached to and forming part of the defence. The schedule should begin with **admissions** and **denials** (if the claim is drafted in such a way as to permit this), and should then set out, in separate, numbered paragraphs, the allegations of material fact on which the defendant relies.

FIGURE 6.2   **Small Claims Court Procedure: Defendant Disputes Claim**

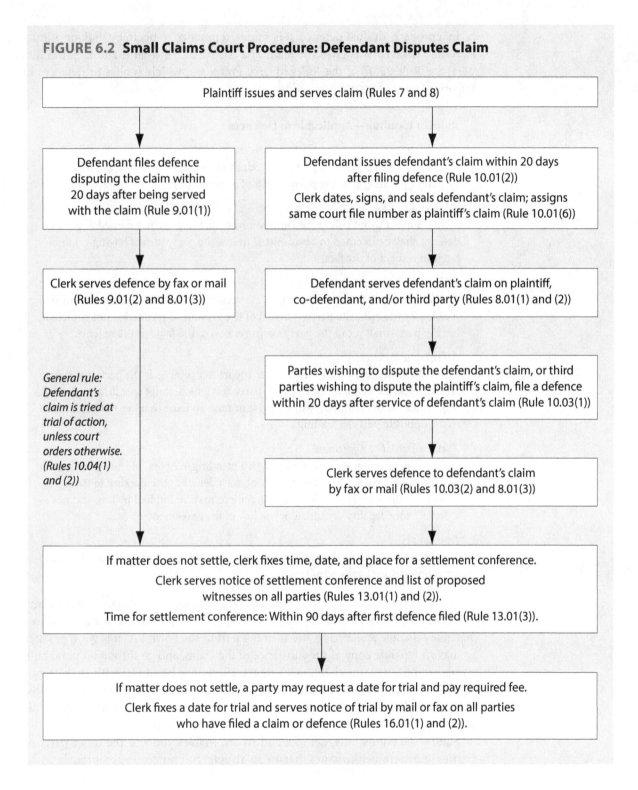

In a properly drafted defence, it is standard practice to begin by making admissions and denials. This gives the plaintiff a "snapshot" of what is and is not in dispute. See Rule 25.07 of the *Rules of Civil Procedure*, which applies to defences in Superior Court of Justice proceedings:

Rules of Pleading—Applicable to Defences

Admissions

25.07(1) In a defence, a party shall admit every allegation of fact in the opposite party's pleading that the party does not dispute.

Denials

(2) Subject to subrule (6), all allegations of fact that are not denied in a party's defence shall be deemed to be admitted unless the party pleads having no knowledge in respect of the fact.

Different Version of Facts

(3) Where a party intends to prove a version of the facts different from that pleaded by the opposite party, a denial of the version so pleaded is not sufficient, but the party shall plead the party's own version of the facts in the defence.

Affirmative Defences

(4) In a defence, a party shall plead any matter on which the party intends to rely to defeat the claim of the opposite party and which, if not specifically pleaded, might take the opposite party by surprise or raise an issue that has not been raised in the opposite party's pleading.

Effect of Denial of Agreement

(5) Where an agreement is alleged in a pleading, a denial of the agreement by the opposite party shall be construed only as a denial of the making of the agreement or of the facts from which the agreement may be implied by law, and not as a denial of the legality or sufficiency in law of the agreement.

Damages

(6) In an action for damages, the amount of damages shall be deemed to be in issue unless specifically admitted.

If the plaintiff's claim has been drafted by a licensee, the substance of the claim should be set out in double-spaced, numbered paragraphs on the Form 7A or in a separate schedule attached to and forming part of the Form 7A. It is good practice to make a separate copy of the substance of the claim, and go through it paragraph by paragraph with your client, marking the allegations he admits with an A, the allegations he denies with a D, and the allegations that are true but incomplete with a P (for partial admission). If appropriate, you should also consider marking the allegations that the defendant has no knowledge of with an NK.

Stating the admissions, denials, and so on, enables you and the other party or parties to determine the issues that are in dispute, and proceed appropriately.

BOX 6.1   How Much Should the Defendant Admit?

The defendant should admit any allegations in the plaintiff's claim that are not in dispute. An admission is just an admission of one particular allegation of fact. It has the effect of narrowing the issues in the matter. It is not an admission of liability for the claim as a whole nor is it an admission of partial liability for purposes of page 2 of the Form 9A. The defendant is simply letting the plaintiff and the court know that he acknowledges the truth of certain things the plaintiff has alleged, while reserving his right to defend against other allegations.

Denials by themselves do not constitute a defence. In addition to admissions, denials, and alternative versions of the facts, the defendant should plead all matters that support the **theory of the defence**—the defendant's legal grounds for disputing the plaintiff's claim. A defendant's legal grounds for disputing a plaintiff's claim are also referred to as **affirmative defences**.

BOX 6.2   Drafting the Defence: What Is Relevant?

Fact Situation

The plaintiff, Juliette Greco, loaned James Hardwick $5,000.00 pursuant to a promissory note dated April 1, 20—. The entire amount was due and owing on or before August 2, 20—. Mr. Hardwick defaulted in payment. Ms. Greco commenced a claim for the amount owing on November 2, 20—. The plaintiff's claim was personally served on Mr. Hardwick on November 8, 20—.

Discussion: In the paragraphs below, the fact situation according to Mr. Hardwick is given with the relevant facts emphasized in bold type. A brief explanation of why the facts are relevant follows each paragraph.

> You work for Paxton Limones PC, 82 Main Street, Suite 11, Brampton, Ontario L1N 2P3 TEL: 905 888 9999 FAX: 905 888 0000.
>
> Your client is James Hardwick. **James lives at 128 George Court in Brampton. He was recently served with a claim for $5,000.00 plus interest by the plaintiff, Juliette Greco, who is his neighbour and who lives at 126 George Court.**

This information has procedural relevance, but it is not relevant for purposes of drafting the defence.

The information is relevant because it is an admission by the defendant that he received the claim. Your next question should be, when and how was he served? You need to know in order to decide whether the deadline for delivering a defence is approaching or has passed. If the deadline has passed, you should contact the court immediately to find out if he has been noted in default.

> **James tells you that he asked Juliette for the money last spring** because she had always been friendly with them, and seemed like a nice person. She had the Hardwick family over for supper a few times, and let their sons use her pool. He needed the money to pay off some old credit card debts.
>
> When **he borrowed the money**, he thought he would be getting a lot more back on his income tax refund than he ended up getting. That is why **he signed the promissory note agreeing to the August 2, 20— repayment date**. If he had known he was going to be audited and end up paying tax, he would never have signed the note on those terms.

The action is a liquidated claim for collection of a debt. The bold pieces above are relevant to the defence, because they are admissions that James asked for and accepted the money, and signed the promissory note. Therefore, none of those allegations by the plaintiff are in dispute.

James's motives for asking for and accepting the money are irrelevant to any issue in this action. His family's relationship with the plaintiff, and his personal opinion as to Juliette's "niceness" or otherwise, would ordinarily be irrelevant in a defence to a debt collection. However, insofar as these allegations may lend credibility to James's claim that Juliette agreed to accept services in lieu of a cash payment, they may be relevant in this matter.

> As soon as he got the tax reassessment from the Canada Revenue Agency, **he spoke to Juliette about his situation, and offered to do chores**

around her house and yard instead of paying her cash. She seemed to be pleased with this arrangement. The agreement was that he would perform general yard maintenance (including some late-season snow removal and spring yard clean-up), take care of the pool, and take care of her pets (including walking the dog twice a day and cleaning up after him) for the rest of the summer, and that would take care of the loan. He insists that Juliette agreed to this, although he never got anything from her in writing. He thought a written agreement was unnecessary, because they were friends.

This information is relevant because, if it can be proven, it establishes (1) that upon defaulting in payment of the note, James took prompt action to remedy the default; (2) that the remedy proposed by James was providing services in lieu of cash payment; and (3) the terms of the spoken agreement between the parties. In his defence and defendant's claim, James is relying upon a quasi-contractual doctrine called "*quantum meruit.*" **Quantum meruit** is a doctrine that allows the court to order payment for services provided to another without a written contract. The court will imply a contract if the person seeking payment can prove (1) that services were provided to the other party; (2) that the recipient accepted those services; (3) that the services had value; and (4) that the recipient knew that the service provider expected payment for those services.

Some of the information is personal opinion (for example, the last sentence), but it goes to establishing the "neighbourly" relationship and provides plausible grounds for the informal arrangement for provision of services in lieu of payment between the plaintiff and the defendant.

More detail is required about the nature and extent of the services performed. Also, the defendant will have to provide estimates from contractors or some other form of evidence as to the monetary value of those services.

When Juliette went away on a couple of trips, she left James with her house key and the code to the security system, so that he could get into the house while she was away. He completed all the work they had agreed upon. Then he got a letter from her by registered mail in August, demanding payment of the promissory note. He

didn't know what was going on, and when he tried to speak to Juliette about it, she got very impatient and would not answer his questions.

Juliette having given her house key and security code to James supports his allegation that his services were accepted by Juliette and performed with her knowledge and consent.

The allegation that he completed all the work agreed on goes to proving that he complied with the terms of their agreement, as does his request for an explanation when she sent him the first demand letter.

James's wife, Pamela, was the one who opened the letter from Juliette demanding payment. She was furious. One evening when they were having a few drinks with friends in the backyard, they said some things they probably shouldn't have. Juliette must have overheard, because shortly after that she left a message on their answering machine telling the boys not to use her pool. **That was when James stopped doing any work for her. Shortly after that, he got another letter, demanding payment.**

This is relevant because it provides the approximate date at which he stopped providing services (mid-August).

The demand letters may also go to establishing the plaintiff's breach of the terms of the alleged agreement. This will have to be expressed in neutral terms in the defendant's claim.

James thinks it's all a "woman problem." He thinks Pamela was jealous of Juliette, and Juliette was resentful of Pamela because Pamela has a husband and two children, and she doesn't. **He reckons he performed at least $6,000.00 worth of unpaid work for Juliette since he signed the promissory note.**

The value of the services performed is relevant if it is supported by the evidence. The defendant will have to obtain and produce objective evidence of the value of the work done—for example, qualified contractors' estimates of what they would charge for comparable work.

If, as James alleges, the value of the services provided by James is greater than the amount he owes Juliette, he may have grounds for a defendant's claim against Juliette.

Drafting the Defence

Go back and read the fact situation and discussion in *Greco v. Hardwick* in Chapter 4 at pages 137–138 at Box 4.11. Also read the plaintiff's claim in *Greco v. Hardwick* in Appendix 4.4.

Now, assume that you have been retained to act for the defendant, James Hardwick (see Box 6.2).

When going over the plaintiff's claim and client notes in Box 6.2 above, you must decide which allegations in the plaintiff's claim are wholly or partially admitted by the defendant, and which are wholly or partially denied. You must determine whether the plaintiff has made any allegations that would not be within the knowledge of the defendant. Such allegations, if any, should be designated as "no knowledge." You must also determine whether the defendant should allege an alternative version of certain allegations of fact in the plaintiff's claim.

Excerpts from the plaintiff's pleading are reproduced below. Each is followed by a discussion of how you should consider dealing with that allegation when drafting the defence.

Schedule A

1. The plaintiff claims:
    (a) $5,000.00;
    (b) Pre- and post-judgment interest at a rate of 10% per annum from the date of default until such time as any amounts owing are paid in full in accordance with the terms of the promissory note dated April 1, 20—;
    (c) In the alternative, pre- and post-judgment interest in accordance with the *Courts of Justice Act*;
    (d) Her costs of this action; and
    (e) Such further and other relief as this Honourable Court deems just.

The request for relief does not contain allegations of fact. It does not have to be admitted or denied.

2. The plaintiff is an individual residing in the City of Brampton in the Province of Ontario.

Admit. The plaintiff's address is not in dispute.

3. The defendant is an individual residing at 128 George Court in the City of Brampton in the Province of Ontario.

Admit. The defendant's address is not in dispute.

4. Pursuant to a promissory note dated April 1, 20—, the plaintiff loaned the defendant the sum of $5,000.00. According to the terms of the note, the entire sum was to be repaid in full by the defendant on or before August 2, 20—. In the event of default, interest became due and owing on the balance owing at a rate of 10% per annum from the date of default until such time as all amounts owing were paid in full.

Admit. James does not dispute that he signed the note, nor does he dispute its terms.

5. The defendant failed to pay the amount owing on or before August 2, 20—.

6. In spite of repeated demands for payment, both spoken and written, the defendant has failed to pay anything whatsoever on account of the amount owing to the plaintiff.

What about these two paragraphs? Why does James believe that, although he took the money, he should not have to pay it back? What is the substance of his defence to the plaintiff's claim for money?

James should consider a partial admission, accompanied by an alternative version of the facts. James should consider admitting that he failed to pay the amount owing back in cash but allege that (1) he provided services to the plaintiff; (2) that the plaintiff accepted those services; (3) that the services had value; and (4) that the plaintiff knew that he was providing the services in lieu of paying cash for the amount owing under the promissory note.

James's defence is reproduced in Appendix 6.1 to this chapter.

Filing and Service of the Defence

The defence must be filed with the clerk within 20 days of service of the plaintiff's claim. You must file the original of the defence plus copies for all other parties with the clerk (Rule 9.01(1) of the *Rules of the Small Claims Court*).

If the defence is based in whole or in part on a document, a copy of the document shall be attached to each copy of the defence. If the document is not available, the defence shall state the reason why the document is not attached (Rule 9.02(1)2). Note that the Rule 9.02 obligation to disclose is mandatory.

As of this writing, the court fee for filing a defence is $40.00.

The clerk will serve all parties with the defence by mail or fax (Rules 9.01(2) and 8.01(3)).

When Should You Make a Proposal of Terms of Payment?

A good defence is a defence that has legal merit and that can be supported by the evidence.

Many Small Claims Court cases are for the collection of an unpaid debt of some kind. The range of defences to a claim for money are limited. For example, it is not a defence to say, "Yes, I owe the plaintiff the money, but I can't afford to pay her back right now." Inability to pay does not, by itself, absolve a debtor from liability for a debt.

As a paralegal licensee, you have a professional duty to encourage compromise and settlement if it can be achieved without prejudice to your client. See Rule 3.02(5) of the *Paralegal Rules of Conduct*. If you are advising a defendant who does not have a good defence to all or part of a claim, you should encourage your client to make a proposal of terms of payment. Page 2 of Form 9A gives the defendant the option of making a proposal of terms of payment for all or part of the plaintiff's claim (see Figure 6.1 at page 228). If the defendant makes a proposal of terms of payment for part of the plaintiff's claim, the other part of the claim remains in dispute. The factual grounds for the partial dispute must be clearly stated in the schedule to the defence. Copies of any documentary evidence on which you intend to rely in support of the partial dispute should be attached to the defence.

Before advising a client to file a partial dispute, you must be satisfied that there are legal grounds for the partial dispute, and that there is evidence to support it.

See Figure 6.3 for an overview of what happens when a defendant admits all or partial liability.

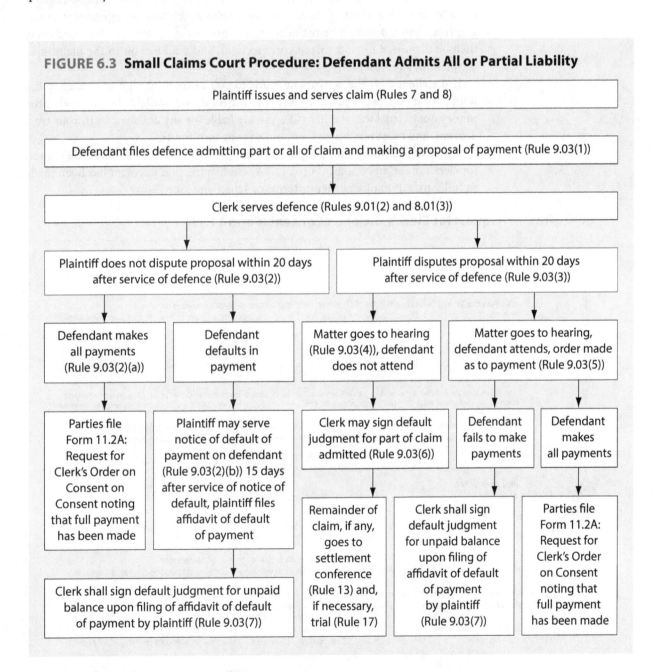

FIGURE 6.3 Small Claims Court Procedure: Defendant Admits All or Partial Liability

Plaintiff issues and serves claim (Rules 7 and 8)

Defendant files defence admitting part or all of claim and making a proposal of payment (Rule 9.03(1))

Clerk serves defence (Rules 9.01(2) and 8.01(3))

Plaintiff does not dispute proposal within 20 days after service of defence (Rule 9.03(2))

Plaintiff disputes proposal within 20 days after service of defence (Rule 9.03(3))

Defendant makes all payments (Rule 9.03(2)(a))

Defendant defaults in payment

Matter goes to hearing (Rule 9.03(4)), defendant does not attend

Matter goes to hearing, defendant attends, order made as to payment (Rule 9.03(5))

Parties file Form 11.2A: Request for Clerk's Order on Consent on Consent noting that full payment has been made

Plaintiff may serve notice of default of payment on defendant (Rule 9.03(2)(b)) 15 days after service of notice of default, plaintiff files affidavit of default of payment

Clerk may sign default judgment for part of claim admitted (Rule 9.03(6))

Defendant fails to make payments

Defendant makes all payments

Clerk shall sign default judgment for unpaid balance upon filing of affidavit of default of payment by plaintiff (Rule 9.03(7))

Remainder of claim, if any, goes to settlement conference (Rule 13) and, if necessary, trial (Rule 17)

Clerk shall sign default judgment for unpaid balance upon filing of affidavit of default of payment by plaintiff (Rule 9.03(7))

Parties file Form 11.2A: Request for Clerk's Order on Consent noting that full payment has been made

Proposal of Terms of Payment—No Dispute by Plaintiff (Rules 9.03(1) and (2))

Lump-Sum Payment

A defendant who admits liability for all or part of the claim may choose to pay the entire amount admitted to be owing in one lump-sum payment, instead of in installments. Settlement funds payable by your client to another party may be paid to you in trust by certified cheque if there is a term in the retainer agreement or engagement letter to that effect. If there is no such term in the retainer agreement or engagement letter, it should be included in the minutes of settlement. The funds may then be deposited to your mixed trust account, and paid by you to the plaintiff or the plaintiff's representative.

If the client pays the settlement funds to you in trust by regular cheque, put a hold period on the cheque to ensure that the funds are available before paying the money out of trust to the other side. You are liable for any deficiencies in your trust account, and must reimburse them out of your own funds.

If the entire amount owing is paid by a lump-sum payment, you may file a request for clerk's order on consent (Form 11.2A) confirming that payment has been made in full satisfaction of an order or terms of settlement. See Figure 6.4.

FIGURE 6.4 Request for Clerk's Order on Consent (Form 11.2A)

FORM / *FORMULE* 11.2A **PAGE 3**

Claim No. / *N° de la demande*

☐ withdraw the Writ of Seizure and Sale of Personal Property issued against: (Name of debtor(s)
le retrait du bref de saisie-exécution de biens meubles délivré contre : (*Nom du/de la/des débiteur(s)/débitrice(s)*)

and directed to the bailiff of the :
et adressé à l'huissier de (Small Claims Court location / *Emplacement de la Cour des petites créances*)

(Provide instructions about what is to be done with any proceeds held by the clerk of the court or property that has been seized by the bailiff. / *Donnez des instructions sur ce qu'il faut faire de tout produit de la vente détenu par le greffier du tribunal ou de tout bien saisi par l'huissier.*)

☐ terminate the Notice of Garnishment or Notice of Renewal of Garnishment issued against:
la fin de l'avis de saisie-arrêt ou de l'avis de renouvellement de la saisie-arrêt délivré contre :

(Name of debtor(s) / *Nom du/de la/des débiteur(s)/débitrice(s)*)

and directed to :
et adressé à (Name of garnishee / *Nom du tiers saisi*)

(Provide instructions about what is to be done with any money held by the clerk of the court. / *Donnez des instructions sur ce qu'il faut faire de toute somme d'argent détenue par le greffier du tribunal.*)

☐ note that payment has been made in full satisfaction of an order or terms of settlement
le constat qu'un paiement intégral a été effectué en exécution d'une ordonnance ou des conditions de la transaction

☐ dismiss the: ☐ Plaintiff's Claim ☐ Defendant's Claim
le rejet de la : demande du demandeur demande du défendeur

☐ costs in the amount of $ ______ , to be paid to ______
le versement de (Amount / *Montant*) *$ au titre des dépens à* (Name of party(ies) / *Nom de la ou des parties*)

______ by ______
par (Name of party(ies) / *Nom de la ou des parties*)

Installment Payments

If the client admits liability for all or part of the claim but cannot afford to pay the amount admitted to be owing in one lump-sum payment, she may propose paying in installments.

When advising a client who wishes to pay in installments, you should be careful to make the proposed terms of payment realistic. Find out what the client's after-tax income is and what her other expenses (housing, food, child care, and so on) are before recommending a payment amount. If the agreed-upon installment amount is too high, it sets the defendant up for failure.

Because installment payments take place over time, you should advise your client to keep records of all payments made, in the form of cancelled cheques, bank statements, or signed receipts, so that there is documentary evidence of what has been paid in the event that a dispute over payment arises.

Default of Payment

If the plaintiff does not dispute the defendant's proposal of terms of payment within 20 days after service of the defence, the proposal is deemed to be accepted and the defendant is required to make the payments as if the proposal were a court order (Rules 9.03(2)(a) and 9.03(3)).

> ### BOX 6.3 Nguyen v. Mirren—Sample Proposal of Terms of Payment
>
> France Nguyen advanced $3,000.00 to Mavis Mirren on January 1, 20—. The parties agreed that interest would be charged on the money at a rate of 7% per year, and that the entire amount plus interest would be paid in full on or before June 1, 20—. Ms. Mirren failed to pay the amount owing on or before June 1, 20—. After several demands for payment, Ms. Nguyen commenced an action in Newmarket Small Claims Court for the amount owing. Ms. Mirren was served with the plaintiff's claim on July 20, 20—.
>
> On July 28, 20—, Ms. Mirren filed a defence with a proposal for payment of the entire amount owing in installments of $300.00 per month, payable on the first day of each month. See Appendix 6.4 for the proposal of terms of payment in *Nguyen v. Mirren*.

If the defendant defaults on any payment, the plaintiff may serve the defendant with a notice of default of payment (Form 20L). If the defendant does not pay within 15 days after service of the notice of default of payment, the plaintiff may file an affidavit of default of payment (Form 20M) with the court. The affidavit of default states the following:

1. that the defendant failed to make a payment in accordance with the proposal;
2. the amount paid by the defendant and the unpaid balance; and
3. that 15 days have passed since the defendant was served with a notice of default of payment.

The affidavit of service of the notice of default of payment should be filed with the court along with the affidavit of default of payment.

On the filing of the affidavit of default and the affidavit of service of the notice of default, the clerk shall sign judgment for the unpaid balance of the undisputed amount. The judgment may be enforced against the defendant under Rule 20.

BOX 6.4 Nguyen v. Mirren—Default of Payment

See Box 6.3 above, and Appendix 6.4. The defence was served on the plaintiff by mail on August 1, 20—. As of August 27, the plaintiff had failed to file a dispute. The defendant made two payments, one on September 1 and one on October 1, each in the amount of $300.00. She defaulted on the November payment.

See Appendix 6.5 for examples of a notice of default of payment (Form 20L), an affidavit of default of payment (Form 20M) with detailed calculation of the amount owing, and a default judgment (Form 11B).

Pre-judgment interest was discussed in Chapter 5 at pages 185–188. For the affidavit of default of payment (Form 20M), note that when calculating interest owing, you are required to adjust the amount owing from time to time as payments are received. See Figure 6.5 below, and the detailed calculation of the amount owing attached to the Form 20M at Appendix 6.5.

FIGURE 6.5 Affidavit of Default of Payment (Form 20M)

4. The unpaid balance is calculated as follows:
Le solde impayé est calculé de la façon suivante :

(A) **DEBT** (amount of judgment) $ _____
   LA CRÉANCE (montant du jugement) $

(B) **PRE-JUDGMENT INTEREST** calculated
   LES INTÉRÊTS ANTÉRIEURS AU JUGEMENT calculés

   on the sum of $ _____   at the rate of _____ %
   sur la somme de $ *au taux de*   *pour cent*

   per annum from _____ , 20 ____ to _____ , 20 ____ ,
   par an du   *au*

   being _____ days. $ _____
   soit   *jours.* $

> **NOTE:** Calculation of interest is always on the amount owing from time to time as payments are received. This is true for both pre-judgment and post-judgment interest. Attach a separate sheet setting out how you calculated the total amount of any pre/post-judgment interest.
>
> **REMARQUE :** *Les intérêts doivent toujours être calculés sur la somme due. Le calcul doit tenir compte des paiements reçus de temps à autre. Ceci s'applique autant aux intérêts antérieurs au jugement qu'aux intérêts postérieurs au jugement. Annexez une feuille distincte indiquant comment vous avez calculé le montant total des intérêts antérieurs et postérieurs au jugement.*

SCR 9.03-20M (June 1, 2009 / *1ᵉʳ juin 2009*) CSD

Continued on next page / *Suite à la page suivante*

Proposal of Terms of Payment—Dispute by Plaintiff (Rules 9.03(3) to (7))

The plaintiff may refuse to accept the defendant's proposal of terms of payment by filing a request to clerk for a terms of payment hearing (Form 9B) within 20 days after service of the defence (Rule 9.03(3)). See Figure 6.6.

On receiving a request for a terms of payment hearing, the clerk shall fix a date and time for the hearing and serve a notice of hearing on the parties by mail or by fax. When fixing the date, the clerk must allow for a reasonable notice period from the date the request is received (Rule 9.03(4)).

If the defendant is an individual, the clerk is also required to serve a financial information form (Form 20I) on the defendant (Rule 9.03(4.2)). The defendant is required to complete the financial information form and serve it on the plaintiff before the terms of payment hearing (Rules 9.03(4.2) and (4.3)). The financial information form *shall not* be filed with the court.

A blank financial information form can be found in Appendix 6.6 to this chapter. The form is intended to give the plaintiff information about the defendant's financial situation, her ability to pay the amount owing, whether she has any assets against which a judgment can be enforced, and so on.

The terms of payment hearing is not a formal trial. It is more in the nature of a settlement conference—in other words, an informal meeting with the object of working out terms of payment that are acceptable to the plaintiff and payable by the defendant.

BOX 6.5 How Reliable Is a Financial Information Form (Form 20I)?

The financial information form is not sworn under oath. Rule 9 says nothing about providing documentation to support the information stated on the form. The usefulness of the Form 20I as a source of reliable information about the defendant/debtor's financial circumstances is, therefore, open to question.

A terms of payment hearing may be heard by a referee or "other person" (someone other than a judge or deputy judge). A **referee** is a non-judge who is authorized by Rule 21.01 to preside at terms of payment hearings. Both the plaintiff and the referee or other person may question the defendant about the information provided on the Form 20I. An adjournment may be ordered if the contents of the financial information form are incomplete, or if documentation is required to support its contents.

If the defendant does not appear at the hearing, the plaintiff may file a request to clerk (Form 9B) and default judgment for the part of the claim that has been admitted, and the clerk may sign a default judgment against the defendant for the part of the claim that has been admitted (Rule 9.03(6)). The default judgment for that part of the claim is served by the clerk on all parties named in the claim by mail or fax (Rule 8.01(4)).

FIGURE 6.6 Request to Clerk for Terms of Payment Hearing (Form 9B)

ONTARIO

Superior Court of Justice
Cour supérieure de justice

Request to Clerk
Demande au greffier
Form / *Formule* 9B Ont. Reg. No. / *Règl. de l'Ont.* : 258/98

Small Claims Court / *Cour des petites créances de* _____   Claim No. / *N° de la demande* _____

Address / *Adresse* _____

Phone number / *Numéro de téléphone* _____

BETWEEN / *ENTRE*

_____
Plaintiff(s) / *Demandeur(s)/demanderesse(s)*

and / *et*

_____
Defendant(s) / *Défendeur(s)/défenderesse(s)*

TO THE CLERK OF THE
AU GREFFIER DE LA COUR
DES PETITES CRÉANCES DE   (Name of Small Claims Court location / *Emplacement de la Cour des petites créances*) :   **SMALL CLAIMS COURT:**

My name is _____   **and I request that the clerk of the court:**
Je m'appelle   (Name of party/representative / *Nom de la partie ou du/de la représentant(e)*)   *et je demande au greffier du tribunal de faire ce qui suit :*

(Check appropriate box(es). / Cochez la ou les cases appropriées.)

☐ note defendant(s) _____
   constater le ou les défendeurs   (Name of defendant(s) / *Nom du/de la/des défendeur(s)/défenderesse(s)*)

   in default for failing to file a Defence (Form 9A) within the prescribed time period [R. 11.01(1)].
   en défaut pour n'avoir pas déposé de défense (formule 9A) dans le délai prescrit [par. 11.01 (1)].

☐ schedule an assessment hearing (all defendants have been noted in default) [R. 11.03(2)(b)].
   fixer la date d'une audience d'évaluation (tous les défendeurs ont été constatés en défaut) [alinéa 11.03 (2) b)].

☐ schedule a terms of payment hearing because I dispute the defendant's proposed terms of payment
   contained in the Defence (Form 9A) [R. 9.03(3)].
   fixer la date d'une audience relative aux modalités de paiement parce que je conteste les modalités de paiement proposées par le défendeur dans la défense (formule 9A) [par. 9.03 (3)].

If both parties appear, they may make submissions as to the defendant's ability to pay and in what amount, and an order may be made by the referee as to terms of payment by the defendant (Rule 9.03(5)).

Unless the referee specifies otherwise in the order as to terms of payment, if the defendant fails to make payments in accordance with the order, the plaintiff may file an affidavit of default of payment stating the amount paid and the balance owing, and the clerk shall sign judgment for the amount owing (Rule 9.03(7)).

Are There Grounds for a Defendant's Claim?

General

A defendant's claim is governed by Rule 10 of the *Rules of the Small Claims Court.*

A defendant may make a claim:

1. against the plaintiff (Rule 10.01(1)(a)); or

2. against any other person, including a co-defendant or a third party who is not named in the plaintiff's claim, based on a transaction or occurrence relied on by the plaintiff, or related to the plaintiff's claim (Rule 10.01(1)(b)); or

3. against the plaintiff and any other person in accordance with Rule 10.01(1)(b).

In the Rules, the term "defendant's claim" encompasses several different scenarios in terms of who is making a claim against whom.

In addition to defending in the plaintiff's claim, the defendant may make a claim back over against the plaintiff. In *Greco v. Hardwick*, discussed above, Juliette Greco commenced a plaintiff's claim against James Hardwick for the amount of $5,000.00 owing under a promissory note that James Hardwick failed to pay. In his defence, James Hardwick alleges that he provided services to Ms. Greco with a value of $5,990.00, with the understanding that the value of those services would be set off against the amount owing under the note. In his defendant's claim against Ms. Greco, Mr. Hardwick claims the difference of $990.00 between the alleged value of the services he provided and the amount due under the note. A claim by a defendant back over against a plaintiff is called a **counterclaim**.

A defendant may use a defendant's claim to make a claim against another defendant named in the plaintiff's claim. For example, Plaintiff commences an action against Defendants A and B on grounds that they are jointly liable for harm suffered by Plaintiff. If Defendant A believes that she also suffered harm as a result of the actions of Defendant B, Defendant A may file a defence denying liability in Plaintiff's action, and commence a defendant's claim against Defendant B based on her grounds for believing that she has suffered harm as a result of Defendant B's actions. A claim by a defendant over against a co-defendant is called a **crossclaim**.

A defendant may use a defendant's claim to make a claim against a person not named in the plaintiff's claim, if the defendant thinks that person is liable for some part or all of the damage suffered by the plaintiff. A claim by a defendant against a person not named in the plaintiff's claim is called a **third-party claim**. A **third party** is a person who is not a party to an agreement or transaction, or who has not been named in a plaintiff's claim, but who may have rights or obligations with respect to the agreement or transaction, or whose presence is necessary to enable the court to adjudicate effectively on the issues in the proceeding.

For example, Plaintiff commences an action against Defendant for damages in tort. Defendant believes that Third Party is responsible for the damage. In his defence, Defendant must name Third Party as a person who is wholly or partly liable for the harm suffered by Plaintiff. By naming Third Party as a defendant in the defendant's claim, Defendant joins Third Party in Plaintiff's action. If Defendant is held liable for the harm to Plaintiff, Defendant may claim **contribution and indemnity** from Third Party, if the evidence supports such a claim. Contribution means the shifting of responsibility for loss or damage from one party to another (in this case, from Defendant to Third Party), and indemnity means the obligation to make good any losses suffered by the plaintiff (in this case, the obligation of Third Party to make good the loss or damage suffered by Plaintiff, insofar as that loss or damage is proven to be attributable to Third Party).

A defendant's claim may be made against a plaintiff and/or a co-defendant or co-defendants and/or a third party or third parties so long as the issues giving rise to the defendant's claim arise out of the transaction or occurrence relied upon by the plaintiff or are related to the plaintiff's claim (Rules 10.01(1)(b) and (c)).

The defendant's claim must be filed with the court within 20 days of the date on which the defence is filed, or after that time but before trial or default judgment, with leave of the court (Rule 10.01(2)). The clerk will issue the defendant's claim by dating, signing, and sealing it, and assigning it the same claim number as that on the plaintiff's claim (Rules 10.01(4)(vii) and 10.01(6)). Any documents upon which the plaintiff by defendant's claim intends to rely shall be attached to the defendant's claim (Rule 10.01(4)2).

If you are acting for a defendant with grounds for both a defence and a defendant's claim, you may file the defence and issue the defendant's claim at the same time. As of this writing, the fee for issuing a defendant's claim is $75.00. If the grounds for a defendant's claim do not come to your attention until more than 20 days after the defence has been filed, the court may order an extension of the time for issuing a defendant's claim to any time before trial or default judgment (Rule 10.01(2)(b)). If you are contemplating making a defendant's claim late in the proceeding, keep in mind the limitation period of two years from the date the plaintiff's claim was served.

On the Form 10A, the defendant and plaintiff in the plaintiff's action switch roles. The defendant becomes the plaintiff by defendant's claim, and the plaintiff becomes a defendant by defendant's claim.

The defendant's claim will be tried with the plaintiff's claim unless to do so will complicate or delay the trial of the plaintiff's claim or cause undue prejudice to any party, in which case the court may order separate trials or direct that the defendant's claim proceed as a separate action (Rule 10.04).

The defendant's claim must be served personally or by an alternative to personal service on the other parties named in the defendant's claim (Rule 8.01(1) and (2)) within six months after being issued. The court may extend the time for service.

Drafting a Defendant's Claim: What Is Relevant?

The principles for drafting a defendant's claim are the same as those for drafting a plaintiff's claim. You must review the plaintiff's claim and your notes of what the defendant said, and pick out the pieces that form a basis for the defendant's claim. You must also ensure that the defendant has provided documentary or other evidence to substantiate a claim for money.

See Box 4.11 in Chapter 4 at pages 137–138, and review the annotated client notes in *Greco v. Hardwick* at Box 6.2 at pages 231–232 of this chapter. The defendant's claim of James Hardwick is reproduced in Appendix 6.2 to this chapter.

Defence to Defendant's Claim

A plaintiff, co-defendant, and/or third party who wishes to dispute the defendant's claim may, within 20 days after service of the defendant's claim, file a defence with the clerk (Rule 10.03(1)). The party filing the defence shall attach to the defence any documents upon which the defence is based. The party shall provide copies of the defence for all other parties or persons against whom the defendant's or plaintiff's claim is made. The clerk shall serve a copy of the defence on each party by mail or by fax (Rules 10.03(2) and 8.01(3)).

If a defendant by defendant's claim fails to file a defence within the prescribed time, she may be noted in default. However, the clerk cannot sign default judgment against a defendant by defendant's claim who has been noted in default. Judgment against a defendant by defendant's claim who has been noted in default must be obtained at trial or on motion (Rules 10.05(2) and 11.04).

Summary—Defendant Not in Default

A defendant who is not in default has the following options:

1. dispute the full claim;
2. dispute part of the claim and propose terms of payment for the part that is not disputed; or
3. admit the full claim and propose terms of payment.

A defendant who disputes the full claim must file a defence within 20 days of service of the claim. If the defendant has a claim against the plaintiff or a claim against any other person (including a co-defendant or a third party not named in the plaintiff's claim based on issues related to the plaintiff's claim), the defendant must also issue a defendant's claim within 20 days of filing the defence.

The clerk will serve the defence. The defendant is responsible for serving the defendant's claim on all parties named in the defendant's claim by personal service or by an alternative to personal service (Rule 8.01(1)).

A defendant who disputes part of the plaintiff's claim must file a defence for the disputed portion of the claim. The defendant must indicate on the Form 9A that she does not dispute the remainder of the claim, and make a proposal of terms of payment. The defendant may pay the undisputed part of the plaintiff's claim by a lump-sum payment of the full amount that is not in dispute, or she may propose payment by installments. If the plaintiff does not dispute the defendant's proposal of terms of payment within 20 days after service of the defence, the plaintiff is deemed to accept the terms of the proposal and the defendant may make payment in accordance with the terms of the proposal as if it were a court order.

A defendant who admits the entire claim must file a defence indicating the non-dispute and proposing terms of payment. If the plaintiff does not dispute the defendant's proposal of terms of payment within 20 days after service of the defence, the plaintiff is deemed to accept the terms of the proposal and the defendant may make payment in accordance with the terms of the proposal as if it were a court order.

A plaintiff who receives a proposal of terms of payment may dispute the proposed terms and request a terms of payment hearing. This must be done within 20 days after service of the defence proposing terms of payment. The clerk will schedule a hearing and serve all parties by mail or fax. An individual defendant will be required to complete a financial information form and serve it on the plaintiff before the hearing. The defendant shall not file the financial information form with the court.

At the terms of payment hearing, the referee or another person may make an order as to terms of payment by the defendant, or order an adjournment if further information as to the defendant's financial status is required.

Defendant Noted in Default

A defendant who has been noted in default should bring the plaintiff's claim with him to the client interview, along with the default judgment if one has been entered, and any **enforcement documents** that he has been served with. Enforcement documents are notices of steps taken by the plaintiff/creditor or ordered by the court to enforce the judgment. For example, a debtor may receive notice of a garnishment of his employment income by service of a notice of garnishment. Other examples of enforcement documents are a notice of garnishment hearing, a notice of examination of debtor, and a notice of contempt hearing. Enforcement of orders will be discussed in Chapter 11.

The procedural consequences of being noted in default are significant. A defendant who has been noted in default is not entitled to file a defence or take any other steps in the proceeding, except making a motion to set aside the noting in default and default judgment, if any, without leave (permission) of the court or the plaintiff's consent (Rule 11.05(1)).

Any step in the proceeding may be taken without the consent of a defendant who has been noted in default (Rule 11.05(2)).

A defendant who has been noted in default is not entitled to notice of any step in the proceeding taken by other parties, except the following (Rule 11.05(3)):

1. service of default judgment (Rule 11.02(3));
2. amendment of claim or defence (Rule 12.01);
3. motion after judgment (Rule 15.01(6)); and
4. post-judgment enforcement proceedings against a debtor (Rule 20).

As is the case whenever your client is a defendant, the first thing you have to do is go over the plaintiff's claim with him, and satisfy yourself that he has a good defence and a reasonable explanation for the default. You should then contact the other side to see if they will consent to a setting aside of the noting in default, the default judgment (if any), and any steps taken to enforce the judgment under Rule 20. If they are willing to consent, a consent for clerk's order (Form 11.2B) may be completed, signed by both parties or their paralegals or lawyers, and filed with the court. The defendant may then file a defence by a deadline agreed on by the parties. A consent by the parties for an extension of the time for filing a defence should be in writing, should state any relevant deadlines, and should be filed with the court (Rule 3.02(2)).

If the plaintiff does not consent to a clerk's order setting aside the noting in default, you must make a motion to the court for an order setting aside the noting in default and any other appropriate relief. Motions, including motions for set aside of a noting in default, will be discussed in more detail in Chapter 7.

CHAPTER SUMMARY

A defendant who was served personally with the plaintiff's claim has 20 days from the date of service to file a defence with the court. If the defendant was served by an alternative to personal service, the time for filing a defence will vary, depending on when service becomes effective.

A defendant may dispute the full claim, or admit all or part of the claim and make a proposal of terms of payment. Where only part of the claim is admitted, a defence must be filed with respect to the part in dispute. The defence or partial defence should state all the facts the defendant is relying on in brief sentences using non-technical language. Copies of any documents the defendant intends to rely on should be attached to the defence.

Defendants named in a defendant's claim must file defences within 20 days of service of the defendant's claim. If they fail to do so and are noted in default, judgment against them may only be obtained at trial or on a motion for judgment. The clerk may not sign judgment against a defendant who is in default in a defendant's claim.

If the defendant admits all or part of the claim and makes a proposal of terms of payment on the defence (Form 9A), the plaintiff has 20 days from service of the defence to dispute the proposal. If the plaintiff does not dispute the proposal during the 20-day period, the plaintiff is deemed to accept the proposal, and the defendant may begin making payments as if the proposal were a court order. If the defendant defaults in payment, the plaintiff may serve a notice of default of payment on the defendant. When 15 days have passed after service of the notice of default of payment, the plaintiff may file an affidavit of default of payment with the court, and the clerk shall sign default judgment against the defendant for the part of the claim that was admitted. Any part of the claim that was disputed will go to settlement conference and, if necessary, to trial.

The plaintiff may dispute the defendant's proposal of terms of payment within 20 days from service of the defence and request a terms of payment hearing. The clerk will serve a notice of terms of payment hearing on all parties. The clerk will also serve individual defendants with a financial information form, which must be completed by the defendant and served on the plaintiff before the hearing. The financial information form shall not be filed with the court.

If the defendant does not attend at the terms of payment hearing, the clerk may sign judgment for the part of the claim that has been admitted upon filing by the plaintiff of a request to clerk and default judgment.

If the defendant attends at the hearing, the court may hear submissions from both parties and make an order for terms of payment. If the defendant fails to make a payment, the plaintiff may file an affidavit of default of payment with the court, and the clerk shall sign judgment against the defendant for the part of the claim that was admitted upon filing by the plaintiff of a request to clerk and default judgment.

The defendant may make a claim against the plaintiff, or against any other person (including a co-defendant or a third party who is not named in the plaintiff's claim), or against the plaintiff and any other person, based on a transaction or occurrence relied on by the plaintiff or related to the plaintiff's claim. This is called a defendant's claim. On the defendant's claim, the defendant becomes the plaintiff by defendant's claim, and the plaintiff becomes the defendant by defendant's claim. The defendant's claim must be issued within 20 days of the date on which the defence is filed, unless the court extends the time. The court file number assigned to the defendant's claim will be the same as that assigned to the plaintiff's claim. The limitation period for commencing a defendant's claim starts to run on the date the plaintiff's claim is served on the defendant.

KEY TERMS

admission: a voluntary acknowledgement by a party that an allegation of fact made by another party is true—in other words, that the allegation is not in dispute *(p. 228)*

affirmative defences: a defendant's legal grounds for disputing the plaintiff's claim *(p. 231)*

contribution and indemnity: the transferring of responsibility for loss or damage from one party to another, and the corresponding obligation of the party to whom responsibility has been transferred to make good on any losses suffered by the transferor *(p. 242)*

counterclaim: a claim by a defendant back over against the plaintiff *(p. 241)*

crossclaim: a claim by a defendant over against a co-defendant *(p. 241)*

denial: an assertion by a party that an allegation of fact made by another party is not true—in other words, that the allegation is disputed *(p. 228)*

enforcement document: a document issued by the clerk at the request of a creditor in an affidavit for enforcement request—e.g., a notice of garnishment, a writ of seizure and sale of land, and so on *(p. 244)*

quantum meruit: an equitable doctrine that allows the court to imply a contract in certain circumstances and order payment for services provided pursuant to the implied contract *(p. 232)*

referee: a non-judge who is authorized by the Rules to preside at terms of payment hearings *(p. 239)*

theory of the defence: the defendant's grounds for disputing the plaintiff's claim *(p. 231)*

third party: person who is not a party to an agreement or transaction, but who may have rights or obligations with respect to the agreement or transaction, or whose presence is necessary to enable the court to adjudicate effectively on the issues in the proceeding *(p. 241)*

third-party claim: a claim by a defendant against a person not named in the plaintiff's claim *(p. 241)*

REFERENCES

Courts of Justice Act, RSO 1990, c. C.43.
Rules of Civil Procedure, RRO 1990, Reg. 194.
Rules of the Small Claims Court, O. Reg. 258/98.

IN-CLASS EXERCISE

Excellent Fences v. Renoir—Defence and Defendant's Claim

You work for: Prior Mustafa LLP
22 County Court Boulevard
Brampton, Ontario A1A 2B3

TEL: 905-111-2222   FAX: 905-111-2233

Your client is: Ms. Jeanne Renoir
78 Calculator Crescent
Milton, Ontario L2M 1S4

TEL: 905-880-9999

One week ago, on January 9, 20—, Ms. Renoir was served with the attached plaintiff's claim. Please read the plaintiff's claim. Then review Ms. Renoir's comments, which follow the plaintiff's claim. Draft a defence and defendant's claim for Ms. Renoir. Date the defence and defendant's claim January 15, 20—. Make a list of the documents you would need to attach to the defendant's claim as part of your documentary disclosure pursuant to Rule 10.01(4)2.

IN-CLASS EXERCISE Form 7A

ONTARIO

Superior Court of Justice
Cour supérieure de justice

Plaintiff's Claim
Demande du demandeur

Form / *Formule* 7A Ont. Reg. No. / *Régl. de l'Ont.* : 258/98

Seal / *Sceau*

Milton

Small Claims Court / *Cour des petites créances de*
491 Steeles Ave. E.
Milton, Ontario
L9T 1Y7
Address / *Adresse*

905 878 4165
Phone number / *Numéro de téléphone*

SC-00-87649-00
Claim No. / *N° de la demande*

Plaintiff No. 1 / *Demandeur n° 1*

☐ Additional plaintiff(s) listed on attached Form 1A.
Le ou les demandeurs additionnels sont mentionnés sur la formule 1A ci-jointe.

☐ Under 18 years of age.
Moins de 18 ans.

Last name, or name of company / *Nom de famille ou nom de la compagnie*		
Excellent Fences Inc.		
First name / *Premier prénom*	Second name / *Deuxième prénom*	Also known as / *Également connu(e) sous le nom de*
Address (street number, apt., unit) / *Adresse (numéro et rue, app., unité)*		
c/o Franklin Kafka PC		
City/Town / *Cité/ville*	Province	Phone no. / *N° de téléphone*
Postal code / *Code postal*		Fax no. / *N° de télécopieur*
Representative / *Représentant(e)*		LSUC # / *N° du BHC*
Franklin Kafka PC Attention: Frank Kafka		**######**
Address (street number, apt., unit) / *Adresse (numéro et rue, app., unité)*		
1238 Hausmann Boulevard, Suite 2		
City/Town / *Cité/ville*	Province	Phone no. / *N° de téléphone*
Milton	**Ontario**	**905 663 4444**
Postal code / *Code postal*		Fax no. / *N° de télécopieur*
L6V 8Z9		**905 663 5555**

Defendant No. 1 / *Défendeur n° 1*

☐ Additional defendant(s) listed on attached Form 1A.
Le ou les défendeurs additionnels sont mentionnés sur la formule 1A ci-jointe.

☐ Under 18 years of age.
Moins de 18 ans.

Last name, or name of company / *Nom de famille ou nom de la compagnie*		
Renoir		
First name / *Premier prénom*	Second name / *Deuxième prénom*	Also known as / *Également connu(e) sous le nom de*
Jeanne	**Marie**	**Jean Renoir**
Address (street number, apt., unit) / *Adresse (numéro et rue, app., unité)*		
78 Calculator Crescent		
City/Town / *Cité/ville*	Province	Phone no. / *N° de téléphone*
Milton	**Ontario**	**905 880 9999**
Postal code / *Code postal*		Fax no. / *N° de télécopieur*
L2M 1S4		
Representative / *Représentant(e)*		LSUC # / *N° du BHC*
Address (street number, apt., unit) / *Adresse (numéro et rue, app., unité)*		
City/Town / *Cité/ville*	Province	Phone no. / *N° de téléphone*
Postal code / *Code postal*		Fax no. / *N° de télécopieur*

SCR 7.01-7A (June 1, 2009 / *1ᵉʳ juin 2009*) CSD

FORM / *FORMULE* **7A**   **PAGE 2**   SC-00-87649-00

Claim No. / *N° de la demande*

REASONS FOR CLAIM AND DETAILS / *MOTIFS DE LA DEMANDE ET PRÉCISIONS*

Explain what happened, including where and when. Then explain how much money you are claiming or what goods you want returned.
Expliquez ce qui s'est passé, en précisant où et quand. Ensuite indiquez la somme d'argent que vous demandez ou les biens dont vous demandez la restitution, explication à l'appui.

If you are relying on any documents, you **MUST** attach copies to the claim. If evidence is lost or unavailable, you **MUST** explain why it is not attached.
*Si vous vous appuyez sur des documents, vous **DEVEZ** en annexer des copies à la demande. Si une preuve est perdue ou n'est pas disponible, vous **DEVEZ** expliquer pourquoi elle n'est pas annexée.*

What happened?   See Schedule A attached and forming part of this claim
Where?
When?

Que s'est-il
passé?
Où?
Quand?

SCR 7.01-7A (June 1, 2009 / *1ᵉʳ juin 2009*) CSD   **Continued on next page /** *Suite à la page suivante*

IN-CLASS EXERCISE **Form 7A** *continued*

FORM / *FORMULE* 7A   PAGE 3   SC-00-87649-00
                                                                     Claim No. / *N° de la demande*

How much? $ .... 3,523.00 ....
Combien?   (Principal amount claimed / *Somme demandée*) $

☒ ADDITIONAL PAGES ARE ATTACHED BECAUSE MORE ROOM WAS NEEDED.
   DES FEUILLES SUPPLÉMENTAIRES SONT ANNEXÉES EN RAISON DU MANQUE D'ESPACE.

The plaintiff also claims pre-judgment interest from September 1, 20--   **under:**
Le demandeur demande aussi des intérêts   (Date)   *conformément à :*
antérieurs au jugement de

(Check only   ☐ the *Courts of Justice Act*
one box /   *la* Loi sur les tribunaux judiciaires
Cochez une
seule case)   ☒ an agreement at the rate of 10   **% per year**
                      un accord au taux de   **% par an**

and post-judgment interest, and court costs.
et des intérêts postérieurs au jugement, ainsi que les dépens.

Prepared on: January 7   , 20 --
Fait le :   (Signature of plaintiff or representative / *Signature du*
                                                          demandeur/de la demanderesse ou du/de la représentant(e))

Issued on: _____   , 20 _____
Délivré le :   (Signature of clerk / *Signature du greffier*)

CAUTION TO DEFENDANT:	**IF YOU DO NOT FILE A DEFENCE** (Form 9A) with the court within twenty (20) calendar days after you have been served with this Plaintiff's Claim, judgment may be obtained without notice and enforced against you. Forms and self-help materials are available at the Small Claims Court and on the following website: www.ontariocourtforms.on.ca.
AVERTISSEMENT AU DÉFENDEUR :	*SI VOUS NE DÉPOSEZ PAS DE DÉFENSE (formule 9A) auprès du tribunal au plus tard vingt (20) jours civils après avoir reçu signification de la présente demande du demandeur, un jugement peut être obtenu sans préavis et être exécuté contre vous. Vous pouvez obtenir les formules et la documentation à l'usage du client à la Cour des petites créances et sur le site Web suivant : www.ontariocourtforms.on.ca.*

SCR 7.01-7A (June 1, 2009 / *1er juin 2009*) CSD

Schedule A

1. The plaintiff claims:

   (a) The liquidated amount of $3,523.00;

   (b) Pre- and post-judgment interest at a rate of 10% per year, in accordance with a contract dated April 30, 20— between the parties;

   (c) In the alternative, pre- and post-judgment interest in accordance with the *Courts of Justice Act*;

   (d) Its costs of this action; and

   (e) Such further and other relief as this Honourable Court deems just.

2. The plaintiff is a corporation incorporated under the laws of Ontario carrying on business as a landscape designer.

3. The defendant resides at 78 Calculator Crescent, Milton, Ontario L2M 1S4.

4. By a contract dated April 30, 20—, the plaintiff and the defendant agreed that the plaintiff should provide the following services to the defendant:

   (1) Build a privacy fence across the bottom of her lot (approximately 50 feet in length), no gate, pressure-treated wood, privacy lattice, 6'0" in height, all posts to be properly anchored and finished with finials;

   (2) Build a gate on the east side of the house at the top of the garden between neighbour's fence and house, posts to be properly anchored and finished with finials;

   (3) Build a privacy fence at the top of the lot with gate (approximately 15 feet in length), pressure-treated wood, privacy lattice, 6'0" in height, all posts to be properly anchored and finished with finials.

5. The total cost of the above services was $4,123.00 including applicable taxes.

6. The defendant paid a deposit of $600.00 at the time of signing the contract on April 30, 20—. In spite of repeated demands, no further payment has been received from the defendant since the job was completed.

7. All services under the contract were completed in a good and workmanlike fashion by September 1, 20—.

8. The amount owing as of this date is $3,523.00 plus interest at a rate of 10% per year in accordance with the terms of the contract dated April 30, 20—.

9. The defendant uses both "Jeanne Renoir" and "Jean Renoir" as her name. The name on her personal cheque is Jeanne Renoir, and she signed the cheque using that name. The name she uses on her business cards is Jean Renoir.

Attached document:

Copy of contract dated April 30, 20— signed by Bill Withers for the plaintiff and Jeanne Renoir

IN-CLASS EXERCISE Defendant's Comments

Ms. Renoir admits the contents of paragraphs 2 and 3 of the plaintiff's claim.

She admits that she signed a contract with the plaintiff dated April 30, 20— on the terms stated in paragraphs 4 and 5.

She denies the contents of paragraphs 7 and 8.

With respect to the contents of paragraph 6, she admits that she paid a deposit of $600.00 at the time of signing the contract. She denies that any further amount is owing.

The contract dated April 30, 20— stated that all work was to be completed by June 30, 20—. As of that date, the fences were only partly completed. Ms. Renoir adopts rescued greyhounds who have been retired from the track, and requires a large, secure, fenced running space for the dogs. As a direct result of the plaintiff's failure to complete the fence in accordance with the terms of the contract, Ms. Renoir had to board her dogs at a kennel from July 1 to September 17, 20—, at a cost of $2,100.00 including applicable taxes.

While boarding, one of her dogs contracted a skin infection. The cost of veterinary treatment was $517.00.

The work was not done in a good and workmanlike fashion. The contract provided that the supporting posts for the fence were to be properly anchored. Ms. Renoir discussed this with Bill Withers, owner of Excellent Fences Inc., in early June. They agreed that proper anchoring meant in-ground concrete or four-foot bolted metal anchors for the supporting posts. When the fence at the bottom of the property was partly completed, Ms. Renoir inspected it and asked the workers what was being used to anchor it, as she could see no sign of bolted metal anchors. She was assured that the posts were embedded in 12 inches of in-ground concrete.

During a high wind in early October, two of the posts at the top of the property became loose. The hinges on both gates were damaged because of the instability of the supporting posts and the fact that the bottom hinges were installed upside down. When the supporting posts began to shift in the high wind, the hinge pins fell out and the gates came loose and started banging back and forth, damaging the hardware. Ms. Renoir had to hire another contractor to correct the damage. Both gates had to be taken down, reassembled, rehinged, and rehung, at a cost of $976.00. Before this could be done, the supporting posts had to be restabilized with additional concrete, at a cost of $654.00. When the new contractor dug out the area around the supporting posts, he discovered that they were anchored in approximately six inches of concrete.

Please draft a defence and defendant's claim for Ms. Renoir. For the defendant's claim, you will ask for pre- and post-judgment interest at a rate of 10% per year in accordance with the contract dated April 30, 20—, and, in the alternative, pre- and post-judgment interest in accordance with the *Courts of Justice Act* in the prayer for relief.

APPENDIX 6.1 Greco v. Hardwick: Defence (Form 9A)

ONTARIO

Superior Court of Justice
Cour supérieure de justice

Defence / *Défense*
Form / *Formule* 9A Ont. Reg. No. / *Régl. de l'Ont.* : 258/98

Brampton	SC-00-34065-00
Small Claims Court / *Cour des petites créances de*	Claim No. / *N° de la demande*
7755 Hurontario Street **Brampton, Ontario** **L6W 4T6**	
Address / *Adresse*	
905 456 4700	
Phone number / *Numéro de téléphone*	

Plaintiff No. 1 / *Demandeur n° 1*

☐ Additional plaintiff(s) listed on attached Form 1A.
Le ou les demandeurs additionnels sont mentionnés sur la formule 1A ci-jointe.

☐ Under 18 years of age.
Moins de 18 ans.

Last name, or name of company / *Nom de famille ou nom de la compagnie*		
Greco		
First name / *Premier prénom* **Juliette**	Second name / *Deuxième prénom*	Also known as / *Également connu(e) sous le nom de*
Address (street number, apt., unit) / *Adresse (numéro et rue, app., unité)* **c/o Prior Mustafa LLP**		
City/Town / *Cité/ville*	Province	Phone no. / *N° de téléphone*
Postal code / *Code postal*		Fax no. / *N° de télécopieur*
Representative / *Représentant(e)* **Prior Mustafa LLP Attention: Paralegal name**		LSUC # / *N° du BHC* **######**
Address (street number, apt., unit) / *Adresse (numéro et rue, app., unité)* **22 County Court Boulevard**		
City/Town / *Cité/ville* **Brampton**	Province **Ontario**	Phone no. / *N° de téléphone* **905 111 2222**
Postal code / *Code postal* **A1A 2B3**		Fax no. / *N° de télécopieur* **905 111 2233**

Defendant No. 1 / *Défendeur n° 1*

☐ Additional defendant(s) listed on attached Form 1A.
Le ou les défendeurs additionnels sont mentionnés sur la formule 1A ci-jointe.

☐ Under 18 years of age.
Moins de 18 ans.

Last name, or name of company / *Nom de famille ou nom de la compagnie*		
Hardwick		
First name / *Premier prénom* **James**	Second name / *Deuxième prénom*	Also known as / *Également connu(e) sous le nom de*
Address (street number, apt., unit) / *Adresse (numéro et rue, app., unité)* **c/o Paxton Limones PC**		
City/Town / *Cité/ville*	Province	Phone no. / *N° de téléphone*
Postal code / *Code postal*		Fax no. / *N° de télécopieur*
Representative / *Représentant(e)* **Paxton Limones PC Attention: Paralegal name**		LSUC # / *N° du BHC* **######**
Address (street number, apt., unit) / *Adresse (numéro et rue, app., unité)* **82 Main Street, Suite 11**		
City/Town / *Cité/ville* **Brampton**	Province **Ontario**	Phone no. / *N° de téléphone* **905 888 9999**
Postal code / *Code postal* **L1N 2P3**		Fax no. / *N° de télécopieur* **905 888 0000**

SCR 9.01-10.03-9A (June 1, 2009 / *1er juin 2009*) CSD

APPENDIX 6.1 Greco v. Hardwick: Defence (Form 9A) *continued*

FORM / *FORMULE* 9A	PAGE 2	SC-00-34065-00

Claim No. / *N° de la demande*

THIS DEFENCE IS BEING FILED ON BEHALF OF: (Name(s) of defendant(s))
LA PRÉSENTE DÉFENSE EST DÉPOSÉE AU NOM DE : (Nom du/de la ou des défendeur(s)/défenderesse(s))

James Hardwick

and I/we: (Check as many as apply)
et je/nous : (Cochez la ou les cases qui s'appliquent)

☒ Dispute the claim made against me/us.
 conteste/contestons la demande présentée contre moi/nous.

☐ Admit the full claim and propose the following terms of payment:
 reconnais/reconnaissons être redevable(s) de la totalité de la demande et propose/proposons les modalités de paiement suivantes :

 $_____ per _____ commencing _____ , 20 ___ .
 (Amount / *Montant*) *$ par* (Week/month / *semaine/mois*) *à compter du*

☐ Admit part of the claim in the amount of $_____ and propose the following terms of payment:
 reconnais/reconnaissons être redevable(s) (Amount / *Montant*) *$ et propose/proposons les modalités de*
 d'une partie de la demande, soit *paiement suivantes :*

 $_____ per _____ commencing _____ , 20 ___ .
 (Amount / *Montant*) *$ par* (Week/month / *semaine/mois*) *à compter du*

REASONS FOR DISPUTING THE CLAIM AND DETAILS:
MOTIFS DE CONTESTATION DE LA DEMANDE ET PRÉCISIONS :

Explain what happened, including where and when. Explain why you do not agree with the claim made against you.
Expliquez ce qui s'est passé, en précisant où et quand. Expliquez pourquoi vous contestez la demande présentée contre vous.

If you are relying on any documents, you **MUST** attach copies to the Defence. If evidence is lost or unavailable, you **MUST** explain why it is not attached.
*Si vous vous appuyez sur des documents, vous **DEVEZ** en annexer des copies à la défense. Si une preuve est perdue ou n'est pas disponible, vous **DEVEZ** expliquer pourquoi elle n'est pas annexée.*

What happened? See Schedule A attached and forming part of this defence
Where?
When?
Que s'est-il
passé?
Où?
Quand?

SCR 9.01-10.03-9A (June 1, 2009 / *1ᵉʳ juin 2009*) CSD   **Continued on next page / *Suite à la page suivante***

APPENDIX 6.1 **Greco v. Hardwick: Defence (Form 9A)** *continued*

FORM / *FORMULE* 9A   PAGE 3   SC-00-34065-00

                                                                      Claim No. / *N° de la demande*

Why I/we disagree See Schedule A attached and forming part of this defence
with all or part of
the claim: /

Je conteste/Nous
contestons la
totalité ou une
partie de la
demande pour les
motifs suivants :

☒ ADDITIONAL PAGES ARE ATTACHED BECAUSE MORE ROOM WAS NEEDED.
DES FEUILLES SUPPLÉMENTAIRES SONT ANNEXÉES EN RAISON DU MANQUE D'ESPACE.

Prepared on: November 15   , 20 --   _____
Fait le :   (Signature of defendant or representative /
                                                       Signature du défendeur/de la défenderesse ou du/de la représentant(e))

NOTE:	Within seven (7) calendar days of changing your address for service, notify the court and all other parties in writing.
REMARQUE :	*Dans les sept (7) jours civils qui suivent tout changement de votre adresse aux fins de signification, veuillez en aviser par écrit le tribunal et les autres parties.*

CAUTION TO PLAINTIFF(S):	If this Defence contains a proposal of terms of payment, you are deemed to have accepted the terms **unless** you file with the clerk and serve on the defendant(s) a Request to Clerk (Form 9B) for a terms of payment hearing **WITHIN TWENTY (20) CALENDAR DAYS** of service of this Defence [R. 9.03(3)].
AVERTISSEMENT AU(X) DEMANDEUR(S) :	*Si la présente défense comprend une proposition à l'égard des modalités de paiement, vous êtes réputé(e)(s) les avoir acceptées, **sauf** si vous déposez auprès du greffier et signifiez au(x) défendeur(s) une demande au greffier (formule 9B) pour la tenue d'une audience relative aux modalités de paiement **DANS LES VINGT (20) JOURS CIVILS** de la signification de la présente défense [par. 9.03 (3)].*

SCR 9.01-10.03-9A (June 1, 2009 / *1ᵉʳ juin 2009*) CSD

APPENDIX 6.1   Greco v. Hardwick: Defence (Form 9A)   *concluded*

Schedule A

1. The defendant, James Hardwick, admits the allegations contained in paragraphs 2, 3, and 4 of the plaintiff's claim.

2. With respect to paragraphs 5 and 6, the defendant admits that he failed to pay the amount owing on the due date stated in the promissory note dated April 1, 20—. The defendant states, and the fact is, that when he realized that he could not pay the amount owing in cash, he advised the plaintiff that he was unable to pay, and offered to provide services in lieu of a cash payment. The plaintiff agreed that the value of these services would be set off against any amounts owing pursuant to the promissory note dated April 1, 20—.

3. During the period from April 15, 20— to August 19, 20—, the defendant provided unpaid services to the plaintiff in the amount of $5,990.00. The services provided included general yard clean-up and maintenance, pool care and maintenance, general repairs, and pet care and clean-up. All services were provided with the plaintiff's knowledge and consent.

4. Based on current prices charged by yard maintenance and pet care contractors, the unpaid services performed by the defendant and accepted by the plaintiff in lieu of cash payment of the amount owing under the promissory note have a cash value of $5,990.00, calculated as follows:

    (a) Sixteen weeks of yard maintenance at $155.00 per week for a total of $2,480.00;

    (b) Five weeks of pet care at $250.00 per week for a total of $1,250.00;

    (c) Eleven weeks of pool maintenance at $120.00 per week for a total owing of $1,320.00; and

    (d) Miscellaneous services (mail, mending fence, attending to alarm system, painting garden shed, clearing out and disposing of dead animals, and so on) estimated $940.00.

5. The defendant asks that the plaintiff's claim be dismissed with costs payable to the defendant.

Attached documents:

Quotation of $1,850.00 for twelve weeks of general yard maintenance, including mowing, hedge trimming, pruning, and so on by Green Tree Yard and Garden Inc.

Quotation of $350.00 per week for in-house pet care from Serene Beasts Pet Services.

Quotation of $95.00 per week for general pool maintenance from Mermaids R Us.

APPENDIX 6.2 Greco v. Hardwick: Defendant's Claim (Form 10A)

ONTARIO
Superior Court of Justice
Cour supérieure de justice

Defendant's Claim
Demande du défendeur

Form / *Formule* 10A Ont. Reg. No. / *Régl. de l'Ont.* : 258/98

Brampton

Small Claims Court / *Cour des petites créances de*
7755 Hurontario Street
Brampton, Ontario
L6W 4T6

Seal / *Sceau*

SC-00-34065-00
Claim No. / *N° de la demande*

Address / *Adresse*

905 456 4700
Phone number / *Numéro de téléphone*

Plaintiff by Defendant's Claim No. 1 /
Demandeur dans la demande du défendeur n° 1

☐ Additional plaintiff(s) listed on attached Form 1A.
Le ou les demandeurs additionnels sont mentionnés sur la formule 1A ci-jointe.

☐ Under 18 years of age.
Moins de 18 ans.

Last name, or name of company / *Nom de famille ou nom de la compagnie*		
Hardwick		
First name / *Premier prénom* **James**	Second name / *Deuxième prénom*	Also known as / *Également connu(e) sous le nom de*
Address (street number, apt., unit) / *Adresse (numéro et rue, app., unité)* **c/o Paxton Limones PC**		
City/Town / *Cité/ville*	Province	Phone no. / *N° de téléphone*
Postal code / *Code postal*		Fax no. / *N° de télécopieur*
Representative / *Représentant(e)* **Paxton Limones PC Attention: Paralegal name**		LSUC # / *N° du BHC* **######**
Address (street number, apt., unit) / *Adresse (numéro et rue, app., unité)* **82 Main Street, Suite 11**		
City/Town / *Cité/ville* **Brampton**	Province **Ontario**	Phone no. / *N° de téléphone* **905 888 9999**
Postal code / *Code postal* **L1N 2P3**		Fax no. / *N° de télécopieur* **905 888 0000**

Defendant by Defendant's Claim No. 1 /
Défendeur dans la demande du défendeur n° 1

☐ Additional defendant(s) listed on attached Form 1A.
Le ou les défendeurs additionnels sont mentionnés sur la formule 1A ci-jointe.

☐ Under 18 years of age.
Moins de 18 ans.

Last name, or name of company / *Nom de famille ou nom de la compagnie*		
Greco		
First name / *Premier prénom* **Juliette**	Second name / *Deuxième prénom*	Also known as / *Également connu(e) sous le nom de*
Address (street number, apt., unit) / *Adresse (numéro et rue, app., unité)* **c/o Prior Mustafa LLP**		
City/Town / *Cité/ville*	Province	Phone no. / *N° de téléphone*
Postal code / *Code postal*		Fax no. / *N° de télécopieur*
Representative / *Représentant(e)* **Prior Mustafa LLP Attention: Paralegal name**		LSUC # / *N° du BHC* **######**
Address (street number, apt., unit) / *Adresse (numéro et rue, app., unité)* **22 County Court Boulevard**		
City/Town / *Cité/ville* **Brampton**	Province **Ontario**	Phone no. / *N° de téléphone* **905 111 2222**
Postal code / *Code postal* **A1A 2B3**		Fax no. / *N° de télécopieur* **905 111 2233**

SCR 10.01-10A (June 1, 2009 / *1ᵉʳ juin 2009*) CSD

APPENDIX 6.2   Greco v. Hardwick: Defendant's Claim (Form 10A)   *continued*

FORM / *FORMULE* **10A**   **PAGE 2**   SC-00-34065-00
                                                                         Claim No. / *N° de la demande*

REASONS FOR CLAIM AND DETAILS / *MOTIFS DE LA DEMANDE ET PRÉCISIONS*

Explain what happened, including where and when. Then explain how much money you are claiming or what goods you want returned.
Expliquez ce qui s'est passé, en précisant où et quand. Ensuite indiquez la somme d'argent que vous demandez ou les biens dont vous demandez la restitution, explication à l'appui.

If you are relying on any documents, you **MUST** attach copies to the claim. If evidence is lost or unavailable, you **MUST** explain why it is not attached.
*Si vous vous appuyez sur des documents, vous **DEVEZ** en annexer des copies à la demande. Si une preuve est perdue ou n'est pas disponible, vous **DEVEZ** expliquer pourquoi elle n'est pas annexée.*

What happened?   **See Schedule A attached and forming part of this defendant's claim**
Where?
When?
Que s'est-il passé?
Où?
Quand?

SCR 10.01-10A (June 1, 2009 / *1ᵉʳ juin 2009*) CSD   **Continued on next sheet /** *Suite à la page suivante*

APPENDIX 6.2 Greco v. Hardwick: Defendant's Claim (Form 10A) *continued*

FORM / *FORMULE* 10A   PAGE 3   SC-00-34065-00
                                                                    Claim No. / *N° de la demande*

See Schedule A attached and forming part of this defendant's claim

How much? $ .... 990.00 $
Combien?   (Principal amount claimed / *Somme demandée*)

☒ ADDITIONAL PAGES ARE ATTACHED BECAUSE MORE ROOM WAS NEEDED.
   DES FEUILLES SUPPLÉMENTAIRES SONT ANNEXÉES EN RAISON DU MANQUE D'ESPACE.

The plaintiff by defendant's claim also claims pre-judgment
interest from   August 19, 20--   under:
Le demandeur dans la demande du défendeur demande aussi des   (Date)   *conformément à :*
intérêts antérieurs au jugement à compter du

(Check only   ☒ the *Courts of Justice Act*
one box /   *la* Loi sur les tribunaux judiciaires
Cochez une
seule case)   ☐ an agreement at the rate of _____ % per year
                    un accord au taux de   % par an

and post-judgment interest, and court costs.
et des intérêts postérieurs au jugement, ainsi que les dépens.

Prepared on: November 15   , 20 --   _____
Fait le :   (Signature of plaintiff or representative / *Signature du*
                                           demandeur/de la demanderesse ou du/de la représentant(e))

Issued on: _____ , 20 ____   _____
Délivré le :   (Signature of clerk / *Signature du greffier*)

CAUTION TO DEFENDANT BY DEFENDANT'S CLAIM: *AVERTISSEMENT AU DÉFENDEUR DANS LA DEMANDE DU DÉFENDEUR :*	**IF YOU DO NOT FILE A DEFENCE** (Form 9A) with the court within twenty (20) calendar days after you have been served with this Defendant's Claim, judgment may be obtained by Defendant's Claim without notice and enforced against you. Forms and self-help materials are available at the Small Claims Court and on the following website: www.ontariocourtforms.on.ca. *SI VOUS NE DÉPOSEZ PAS DE DÉFENSE (formule 9A) auprès du tribunal au plus tard vingt (20) jours civils après avoir reçu signification de la présente demande du défendeur, un jugement peut être obtenu par suite de cette demande sans préavis et être exécuté contre vous. Vous pouvez obtenir les formules et la documentation à l'usage du client à la Cour des petites créances et sur le site Web suivant : www.ontariocourtforms.on.ca.*

SCR 10.01-10A (June 1, 2009 / *1er juin 2009*) CSD

APPENDIX 6.2 **Greco v. Hardwick: Defendant's Claim (Form 10A)** *continued*

Schedule A

1. The plaintiff by defendant's claim claims:

    (a) Damages of $990.00;

    (b) Pre- and post-judgment interest in accordance with the *Courts of Justice Act*;

    (c) His costs of this action; and

    (d) Such further and other relief as this Honourable Court deems just.

2. After the promissory note dated April 1, 20— was signed, the plaintiff by defendant's claim ("Mr. Hardwick") approached the defendant by defendant's claim ("Ms. Greco") and offered to perform services in lieu of repayment in cash. Ms. Greco agreed to accept Mr. Hardwick's services.

3. Between April 15, 20— and August 19, 20—, when he received the first demand letter by registered mail from Ms. Greco, Mr. Hardwick performed the following services.

4. Mr. Hardwick cleared the lawns and garden beds of winter debris, and prepared them for spring planting where necessary.

5. Mr. Hardwick mowed Ms. Greco's grass on a weekly basis commencing the week of May 1 and ending the week of August 21. Mr. Hardwick maintained Ms. Greco's in-ground pool. Said services included general maintenance, bi-weekly cleaning, and some mechanical repairs.

6. Mr. Hardwick performed other maintenance on Ms. Greco's property, including hedge trimming, pruning, and disposal of yard waste. Mr. Hardwick scraped and painted Ms. Greco's garden shed. Mr. Hardwick also lifted the floor of the shed to remove and dispose of the remains of dead animals.

7. Mr. Hardwick cared for Ms. Greco's dog and two cats when Ms. Greco was out of town on business. Ms. Greco travels a good deal in the course of her employment. During the period in question, she was out of town from May 20 to May 31, and from June 10 to on or about June 30. She provided Mr. Hardwick with a key to her house and the code to the security system for the times when she was away.

8. All services were performed with Ms. Greco's knowledge and consent.

9. Based on current prices charged by yard maintenance and pet care contractors, the unpaid services performed by Mr. Hardwick and accepted by Ms. Greco have a cash value of $5,990.00, calculated as follows:

    (a) Sixteen weeks of yard maintenance at $155.00 per week for a total of $2,480.00;

    (b) Five weeks of pet care at $250.00 per week for a total of $1,250.00;

    (c) Eleven weeks of pool maintenance at $120.00 per week for a total of $1,320.00; and

    (d) Miscellaneous services (mail, mending fence, attending to alarm system, painting garden shed, clearing out and disposing of dead animals, etc.) valued at $940.00.

Attached documents:

Quote of $1,850.00 for twelve weeks of general yard maintenance, including mowing, hedge trimming, pruning, etc. by Green Tree Yard and Garden Inc.

Quote of $350.00 per week for in-house pet care from Serene Beasts Pet Services.

Quote of $95.00 per week for general pool maintenance from Mermaids R Us.

APPENDIX 6.3   Greco v. Hardwick: Defence to Defendant's Claim (Form 9A)

ONTARIO

Superior Court of Justice
Cour supérieure de justice

Defence / *Défense*
Form / *Formule* 9A Ont. Reg. No. / *Régl. de l'Ont.* : 258/98

Brampton	**SC00-34065-00**
Small Claims Court / *Cour des petites créances de*	Claim No. / *N° de la demande*
7755 Hurontario Street	
Brampton, Ontario	
L6W 4T6	
Address / *Adresse*	
905 456 4700	
Phone number / *Numéro de téléphone*	

Plaintiff No. 1 / *Demandeur n° 1*   ☐ Additional plaintiff(s) listed on attached Form 1A.   ☐ Under 18 years of age.
Le ou les demandeurs additionnels sont mentionnés sur la formule 1A ci-jointe.   *Moins de 18 ans.*

Last name, or name of company / *Nom de famille ou nom de la compagnie*		
Hardwick **Plaintiff by defendant's claim**		
First name / *Premier prénom*	Second name / *Deuxième prénom*	Also known as / *Également connu(e) sous le nom de*
James		
Address (street number, apt., unit) / *Adresse (numéro et rue, app., unité)*		
c/o Paxton Limones PC		
City/Town / *Cité/ville*	Province	Phone no. / *N° de téléphone*
Postal code / *Code postal*		Fax no. / *N° de télécopieur*
Representative / *Représentant(e)*		LSUC # / *N° du BHC*
Paxton Limones PC Attention: Paralegal name		**######**
Address (street number, apt., unit) / *Adresse (numéro et rue, app., unité)*		
82 Main Street, Suite 11		
City/Town / *Cité/ville*	Province	Phone no. / *N° de téléphone*
Brampton	**Ontario**	**905 888 9999**
Postal code / *Code postal*		Fax no. / *N° de télécopieur*
L1N 2P3		**905 888 0000**

Defendant No. 1 / *Défendeur n° 1*   ☐ Additional defendant(s) listed on attached Form 1A.   ☐ Under 18 years of age.
Le ou les défendeurs additionnels sont mentionnés sur la formule 1A ci-jointe.   *Moins de 18 ans.*

Last name, or name of company / *Nom de famille ou nom de la compagnie*		
Greco **Defendant by defendant's claim**		
First name / *Premier prénom*	Second name / *Deuxième prénom*	Also known as / *Également connu(e) sous le nom de*
Juliette		
Address (street number, apt., unit) / *Adresse (numéro et rue, app., unité)*		
c/o Prior Mustafa LLP		
City/Town / *Cité/ville*	Province	Phone no. / *N° de téléphone*
Postal code / *Code postal*		Fax no. / *N° de télécopieur*
Representative / *Représentant(e)*		LSUC # / *N° du BHC*
Prior Mustafa LLP Attention: Paralegal name		**######**
Address (street number, apt., unit) / *Adresse (numéro et rue, app., unité)*		
22 County Court Boulevard		
City/Town / *Cité/ville*	Province	Phone no. / *N° de téléphone*
Brampton	**Ontario**	**905 111 2222**
Postal code / *Code postal*		Fax no. / *N° de télécopieur*
A1A 2B3		**905 111 2233**

SCR 9.01-10.03-9A (June 1, 2009 / *1ᵉʳ juin 2009*) CSD

APPENDIX 6.3   Greco v. Hardwick: Defence to Defendant's Claim (Form 9A)   *continued*

FORM / *FORMULE* 9A   PAGE 2   SC00-34065-00
_____
Claim No. / *N° de la demande*

THIS DEFENCE IS BEING FILED ON BEHALF OF: (Name(s) of defendant(s))
LA PRÉSENTE DÉFENSE EST DÉPOSÉE AU NOM DE : (Nom du/de la ou des défendeur(s)/défenderesse(s))

Juliette Greco (Defendant by defendant's claim)

and I/we: (Check as many as apply)
et je/nous : (Cochez la ou les cases qui s'appliquent)

☒ Dispute the claim made against me/us.
    conteste/contestons la demande présentée contre moi/nous.

☐ Admit the full claim and propose the following terms of payment:
    reconnais/reconnaissons être redevable(s) de la totalité de la demande et propose/proposons les modalités de paiement suivantes :

    $_____ per _____ commencing _____, 20_____.
    (Amount / *Montant*) $ par (Week/month / *semaine/mois*) *à compter du*

☐ Admit part of the claim in the amount of $_____ and propose the following terms of payment:
    reconnais/reconnaissons être redevable(s) (Amount / Montant) $ et propose/proposons les modalités de
    d'une partie de la demande, soit paiement suivantes :

    $_____ per _____ commencing _____, 20_____.
    (Amount / *Montant*) $ par (Week/month / *semaine/mois*) *à compter du*

REASONS FOR DISPUTING THE CLAIM AND DETAILS:
MOTIFS DE CONTESTATION DE LA DEMANDE ET PRÉCISIONS :

Explain what happened, including where and when. Explain why you do not agree with the claim made against you.
Expliquez ce qui s'est passé, en précisant où et quand. Expliquez pourquoi vous contestez la demande présentée contre vous.

If you are relying on any documents, you **MUST** attach copies to the Defence. If evidence is lost or unavailable, you **MUST** explain why it is not attached.
*Si vous vous appuyez sur des documents, vous **DEVEZ** en annexer des copies à la défense. Si une preuve est perdue ou n'est pas disponible, vous **DEVEZ** expliquer pourquoi elle n'est pas annexée.*

What happened?   See Schedule A attached and forming part of this defence to defendant's claim
Where?
When?
Que s'est-il passé?
Où?
Quand?

APPENDIX 6.3 **Greco v. Hardwick: Defence to Defendant's Claim (Form 9A)** *continued*

FORM / *FORMULE* 9A PAGE 3 SC00-34065-00

Claim No. / *N° de la demande*

Why I/we disagree See Schedule A attached and forming part of this defence to defendant's claim
with all or part of
the claim: /
Je conteste/Nous
contestons la
totalité ou une
partie de la
demande pour les
motifs suivants :

☒ ADDITIONAL PAGES ARE ATTACHED BECAUSE MORE ROOM WAS NEEDED.
  DES FEUILLES SUPPLÉMENTAIRES SONT ANNEXÉES EN RAISON DU MANQUE D'ESPACE.

Prepared on: November 28 , 20 --
Fait le : _____
                                         (Signature of defendant or representative /
                                 Signature du défendeur/de la défenderesse ou du/de la représentant(e))

NOTE:	Within seven (7) calendar days of changing your address for service, notify the court and all other parties in writing.
REMARQUE :	*Dans les sept (7) jours civils qui suivent tout changement de votre adresse aux fins de signification, veuillez en aviser par écrit le tribunal et les autres parties.*

CAUTION TO PLAINTIFF(S):	If this Defence contains a proposal of terms of payment, you are deemed to have accepted the terms **unless** you file with the clerk and serve on the defendant(s) a Request to Clerk (Form 9B) for a terms of payment hearing **WITHIN TWENTY (20) CALENDAR DAYS** of service of this Defence [R. 9.03(3)].
AVERTISSEMENT AU(X) DEMANDEUR(S) :	*Si la présente défense comprend une proposition à l'égard des modalités de paiement, vous êtes réputé(e)(s) les avoir acceptées, **sauf** si vous déposez auprès du greffier et signifiez au(x) défendeur(s) une demande au greffier (formule 9B) pour la tenue d'une audience relative aux modalités de paiement **DANS LES VINGT (20) JOURS CIVILS** de la signification de la présente défense [par. 9.03 (3)].*

SCR 9.01-10.03-9A (June 1, 2009 / *1er juin 2009*) CSD

Schedule A

1. With respect to paragraph 2 of the defendant's claim, the defendant by defendant's claim ("Ms. Greco") admits that shortly after signing the promissory note dated April 1, 20—, the plaintiff by defendant's claim ("Mr. Hardwick") advised her that he would not be able to pay the full amount owing on the due date of August 1, 20—. He proposed doing yard and pool maintenance in partial payment of the amount owing, and paying what he could in cash installments commencing on the due date. Ms. Greco agreed to this arrangement.

2. With respect to paragraphs 3, 4, 5, 6, and 8, Ms. Greco admits that Mr. Hardwick performed the services stated during the period from April 15 to August 19, 20—. In past years, she has always hired Glenn Woods Garden Services to maintain the yard and pool. The annual fee charged to her by Glenn Woods for lawn care, landscaping, and pool maintenance from April 15 to October 15 has always been in the range of $1,500.00. Before agreeing to accept his services, Ms. Greco obtained Mr. Hardwick's assurance that the charge for his services would be in that range. She also advised him that her acceptance of these services would constitute partial payment only of the amount due on the note. She accepted his services instead of those of Glenn Woods for one summer only on those terms.

3. The garden shed required a fresh coat of stain only. It did not have to be scraped and painted. Ms. Greco's nephew offered to do the work for free.

4. With respect to the contents of paragraph 7, Ms. Greco states and the fact is that Mr. Hardwick's children have often cared for her pets when she was away on business trips. She always leaves the key and security code with Mr. Hardwick or his wife so that the boys can get into her house to feed the cats and dog, clean the litter box, change the water, and let the dog out. The dog is elderly and arthritic, and does not need to be walked.

5. Ms. Greco has never been charged for this assistance in the past. Her nephew or nieces would have taken care of the animals for nothing while she was gone. They have done so in the past, when the Hardwick children were unable to help out.

6. On August 1, 20—, Ms. Greco approached Mr. Hardwick and asked when she could start expecting payments on the amount still owing on the note. Mr. Hardwick said he would pay $500.00 on or before August 10, 20—. When she received no payment, Ms. Greco sent the first demand letter, dated August 15, 20—.

7. With respect to paragraph 9, Ms. Greco states and the fact is that the values assigned by Mr. Hardwick to the services provided are grossly inflated. She asks that the defendant's claim be dismissed with costs to Ms. Greco.

Attached documents:

20— invoice from Glenn Woods Garden Services in the amount of $1,455.00, marked "Paid in full"

20— invoice from Glenn Woods Garden Services in the amount of $1,450.00, marked "Paid in full"

20— invoice from Glenn Woods Garden Services in the amount of $1,550.00, marked "Paid in full"

APPENDIX 6.4 Nguyen v. Mirren: Defence with Proposal of Terms of Payment (Form 9A)

ONTARIO

Superior Court of Justice
Cour supérieure de justice

Defence / *Défense*
Form / *Formule* 9A Ont. Reg. No. / *Règl. de l'Ont.* : 258/98

Newmarket

Small Claims Court / *Cour des petites créances de*
50 Eagle Street West
Newmarket, Ontario
L3Y 6B1

Address / *Adresse*

905 853 4809

Phone number / *Numéro de téléphone*

SC-0098865-00

Claim No. / *N° de la demande*

Plaintiff No. 1 / *Demandeur n° 1*

☐ Additional plaintiff(s) listed on attached Form 1A.
Le ou les demandeurs additionnels sont mentionnés sur la formule 1A ci-jointe.

☐ Under 18 years of age.
Moins de 18 ans.

Last name, or name of company / *Nom de famille ou nom de la compagnie*		
Nguyen		
First name / *Premier prénom* **France**	Second name / *Deuxième prénom*	Also known as / *Également connu(e) sous le nom de*
Address (street number, apt., unit) / *Adresse (numéro et rue, app., unité)* **c/o Prior Mustafa LLP**		
City/Town / *Cité/ville*	Province	Phone no. / *N° de téléphone*
Postal code / *Code postal*		Fax no. / *N° de télécopieur*
Representative / *Représentant(e)* **Prior Mustafa LLP Attention: Paralegal name**		LSUC # / *N° du BHC* **######**
Address (street number, apt., unit) / *Adresse (numéro et rue, app., unité)* **22 County Court Boulevard**		
City/Town / *Cité/ville* **Brampton**	Province **Ontario**	Phone no. / *N° de téléphone* **905 111 2222**
Postal code / *Code postal* **A1A 2B3**		Fax no. / *N° de télécopieur* **905 111 2233**

Defendant No. 1 / *Défendeur n° 1*

☐ Additional defendant(s) listed on attached Form 1A.
Le ou les défendeurs additionnels sont mentionnés sur la formule 1A ci-jointe.

☐ Under 18 years of age.
Moins de 18 ans.

Last name, or name of company / *Nom de famille ou nom de la compagnie*		
Mirren		
First name / *Premier prénom* **Mabel**	Second name / *Deuxième prénom*	Also known as / *Également connu(e) sous le nom de*
Address (street number, apt., unit) / *Adresse (numéro et rue, app., unité)* **89 Oliver Crescent, Unit 442**		
City/Town / *Cité/ville* **Newmarket**	Province **Ontario**	Phone no. / *N° de téléphone* **905 222 3333**
Postal code / *Code postal* **E1H 2F2**		Fax no. / *N° de télécopieur*
Representative / *Représentant(e)*		LSUC # / *N° du BHC*
Address (street number, apt., unit) / *Adresse (numéro et rue, app., unité)*		
City/Town / *Cité/ville*	Province	Phone no. / *N° de téléphone*
Postal code / *Code postal*		Fax no. / *N° de télécopieur*

SCR 9.01-10.03-9A (June 1, 2009 / *1ᵉʳ juin 2009*) CSD

APPENDIX 6.4   Nguyen v. Mirren: Defence with Proposal of Terms of Payment (Form 9A)   *continued*

FORM / *FORMULE* 9A   PAGE 2   SC-0098865-00
_____
                                                                         Claim No. / *N° de la demande*

THIS DEFENCE IS BEING FILED ON BEHALF OF: (Name(s) of defendant(s))
LA PRÉSENTE DÉFENSE EST DÉPOSÉE AU NOM DE :   (Nom du/de la ou des défendeur(s)/défenderesse(s))

Mabel Mirren
_____

and I/we: (Check as many as apply)
et je/nous :   (Cochez la ou les cases qui s'appliquent)

☐   Dispute the claim made against me/us.
      conteste/contestons la demande présentée contre moi/nous.

☒   Admit the full claim and propose the following terms of payment:
      reconnais/reconnaissons être redevable(s) de la totalité de la demande et propose/proposons les
      modalités de paiement suivantes :

      $ _____300.00_____ per **month**_____   commencing **September 1**_____ , 20 **--** .
              (Amount / *Montant*)   *$ par*   (Week/month / *semaine/mois*)   *à compter du*

☐   Admit part of the claim in the amount of $ _____   and propose the following terms of payment:
      reconnais/reconnaissons être redevable(s)   (Amount / *Montant*)   *$ et propose/proposons les modalités de*
      d'une partie de la demande, soit   *paiement suivantes :*

      $ _____ per _____   commencing _____ , 20 _____ .
              (Amount / *Montant*)   *$ par*   (Week/month / *semaine/mois*)   *à compter du*

REASONS FOR DISPUTING THE CLAIM AND DETAILS:
MOTIFS DE CONTESTATION DE LA DEMANDE ET PRÉCISIONS :

Explain what happened, including where and when. Explain why you do not agree with the claim made against you.
Expliquez ce qui s'est passé, en précisant où et quand. Expliquez pourquoi vous contestez la demande
présentée contre vous.

If you are relying on any documents, you **MUST** attach copies to the Defence. If evidence is lost or unavailable,
you **MUST** explain why it is not attached.
*Si vous vous appuyez sur des documents, vous **DEVEZ** en annexer des copies à la défense. Si une preuve est*
*perdue ou n'est pas disponible, vous **DEVEZ** expliquer pourquoi elle n'est pas annexée.*

What happened?   n/a
Where?
When?
Que s'est-il
passé?
Où?
Quand?

APPENDIX 6.4 Nguyen v. Mirren: Defence with Proposal of Terms of Payment (Form 9A) *concluded*

FORM / *FORMULE* 9A   PAGE 3   SC-0098865-00
                                                                                        Claim No. / *N° de la demande*

Why I/we disagree with all or part of the claim: /

Je conteste/Nous contestons la totalité ou une partie de la demande pour les motifs suivants :

☐ ADDITIONAL PAGES ARE ATTACHED BECAUSE MORE ROOM WAS NEEDED.
DES FEUILLES SUPPLÉMENTAIRES SONT ANNEXÉES EN RAISON DU MANQUE D'ESPACE.

Prepared on: July 28 _____ , 20 -- _____
Fait le :   (Signature of defendant or representative /
                                                   Signature du défendeur/de la défenderesse ou du/de la représentant(e))

NOTE:	Within seven (7) calendar days of changing your address for service, notify the court and all other parties in writing.
REMARQUE :	*Dans les sept (7) jours civils qui suivent tout changement de votre adresse aux fins de signification, veuillez en aviser par écrit le tribunal et les autres parties.*

CAUTION TO PLAINTIFF(S):	If this Defence contains a proposal of terms of payment, you are deemed to have accepted the terms **unless** you file with the clerk and serve on the defendant(s) a Request to Clerk (Form 9B) for a terms of payment hearing **WITHIN TWENTY (20) CALENDAR DAYS** of service of this Defence [R. 9.03(3)].
AVERTISSEMENT AU(X) DEMANDEUR(S) :	*Si la présente défense comprend une proposition à l'égard des modalités de paiement, vous êtes réputé(e)(s) les avoir acceptées, **sauf** si vous déposez auprès du greffier et signifiez au(x) défendeur(s) une demande au greffier (formule 9B) pour la tenue d'une audience relative aux modalités de paiement **DANS LES VINGT (20) JOURS CIVILS** de la signification de la présente défense [par. 9.03 (3)].*

SCR 9.01-10.03-9A (June 1, 2009 / *1er juin 2009*) CSD

APPENDIX 6.5 Nguyen v. Mirren: Notice of Default of Payment by Defendant (Form 20L)

ONTARIO

Superior Court of Justice
Cour supérieure de justice

Notice of Default of Payment
Avis de défaut de paiement
Form / *Formule* 20L Ont. Reg. No. / *Régl. de l'Ont.* : 258/98

Newmarket
Small Claims Court / *Cour des petites créances de*
50 Eagle Street West
Newmarket, Ontario
L3Y 6B1

SC-00-98865-00
Claim No. / *N° de la demande*

Address / *Adresse*

905 853 4809
Phone number / *Numéro de téléphone*

BETWEEN / *ENTRE*

France Nguyen

Plaintiff(s)/Creditor(s) / *Demandeur(s)/demanderesse(s)/Créancier(s)/créancière(s)*

and / *et*

Mabel Mirren

Defendant(s)/Debtor(s) / *Défendeur(s)/défenderesse(s)/Débiteur(s)/débitrice(s)*

TO: Mabel Mirren
DESTINATAIRE(S) :   (Name of defendant(s)/debtor(s) / *Nom du/de la/des défendeur(s)/défenderesse(s)/débiteur(s)/débitrice(s)*)

TAKE NOTICE that you defaulted in your payment(s) to
VEUILLEZ PRENDRE NOTE que vous n'avez pas effectué le ou les paiements que vous deviez verser à

France Nguyen

(Name of plaintiff(s)/creditor(s) / *Nom du/de la/des demandeur(s)/demanderesse(s)/créancier(s)/créancière(s)*)

(Check appropriate box. / Cochez la case appropriée.)

☐ under an order for periodic payment, dated _____ , 20 _____ .
   en vertu d'une ordonnance prescrivant des versements périodiques datée du

According to Rule 20.02(4) of the *Rules of the Small Claims Court*, the order for periodic payment terminates on the day that is 15 days after the creditor serves the debtor with this notice, unless before that date, a Consent (Form 13B) is filed in which the creditor waives the default.
Conformément au paragraphe 20.02 (4) des Règles de la Cour des petites créances, *l'ordonnance prescrivant des versements périodiques prend fin le 15ᵉ jour qui suit la signification par le créancier au débiteur du présent avis, sauf si, avant cette date, le créancier dépose le consentement (formule 13B) dans lequel il renonce à la constatation du défaut.*

☒ under a proposal of terms of payment in the Defence (Form 9A) dated July 28 _____ , 20 -- .
   en vertu d'une proposition à l'égard des modalités de paiement dans la défense (formule 9A) datée du

According to Rule 9.03(2)(c) the clerk may sign judgment for the unpaid balance of the undisputed amount on the day that is 15 days after the plaintiff serves the defendant with this notice.
Conformément à l'alinéa 9.03 (2) c), le greffier peut consigner un jugement relativement au solde impayé de la somme non contestée le 15ᵉ jour qui suit la signification par le demandeur au défendeur du présent avis.

SCR 20.02-20L (June 1, 2009 / *1ᵉʳ juin 2009*) CSD

APPENDIX 6.5 Nguyen v. Mirren: Notice of Default of Payment by Defendant (Form 20L) *concluded*

FORM / *FORMULE* 20L   PAGE 2   SC-00-98865-00
                                                                   Claim No. / *N° de la demande*

You can get forms and self-help materials at the Small Claims Court or online at: www.ontariocourtforms.on.ca.
Vous pouvez obtenir les formules et la documentation à l'usage du client auprès de la Cour des petites créances
ou en ligne à l'adresse : www.ontariocourtforms.on.ca.

NOTE TO DEFENDANT/DEBTOR: / *REMARQUE AU DÉFENDEUR/DÉBITEUR :*

If you / *Si, selon le cas :*

- failed to make payments but intend to do so; or
  vous n'avez pas effectué de paiements mais vous avez l'intention de le faire;

- made payments but the payments were not received by the creditor;
  vous avez effectué des paiements mais le créancier ne les a pas reçus;

contact the plaintiff/creditor to make payment arrangements or correct the reason for non-receipt of payments.
You may obtain the plaintiff/creditor's written consent (Form 13B may be used) to waive the default and file it with
the court within 15 days of being served with this notice. Failure to do so may result in the following:
communiquez avec le demandeur/créancier pour prendre les dispositions de paiement ou pour régler le motif de la
non-réception des paiements. Vous pouvez obtenir le consentement écrit du demandeur/créancier (vous pouvez utiliser
la formule 13B) pour renoncer à la constatation du défaut et le déposer au tribunal dans les 15 jours de la signification
du présent avis. Si vous ne le faites pas, vous pourriez subir l'une ou l'autre des conséquences suivantes :

- in the case of default under a proposal of terms of payment in the Defence (Form 9A), the plaintiff may
  obtain default judgment for the unpaid balance of the undisputed amount; or
  si vous n'effectuez pas les paiements conformément aux modalités de paiement proposées dans la
  défense (formule 9A), le demandeur pourra obtenir un jugement par défaut relativement au solde impayé
  de la somme non contestée;

- in the case of default under an order for periodic payment, the order will terminate and the creditor may take
  other steps to enforce the order.
  si vous n'effectuez pas les paiements conformément à une ordonnance prescrivant des versements
  périodiques, l'ordonnance prendra fin et le créancier pourra prendre d'autres mesures en vue de
  l'exécution forcée de l'ordonnance.

November 5   , 20 --
                                          _____
                                          (Signature of plaintiff/creditor or representative / *Signature du demandeur/de*
                                          la demanderesse/du créancier/de la créancière ou du/de la représentant(e))
                                          Prior Mustafa LLP
                                          22 County Court Boulevard
                                          Brampton, Ontario A1A 2B3
                                          TEL: 905 111 2222
                                          Attention: Paralegal name
                                          (Name, address and phone number of plaintiff/creditor or representative /
                                          Nom, adresse et numéro de téléphone du demandeur/de la
                                          demanderesse/du créancier/de la créancière ou du/de la représentant(e))

SCR 20.02-20L (June 1, 2009 / *1er juin 2009*) CSD

APPENDIX 6.5 Nguyen v. Mirren: Affidavit of Default of Payment by Defendant (Form 20M)

ONTARIO
Superior Court of Justice
Cour supérieure de justice

Affidavit of Default of Payment
Affidavit de défaut de paiement
Form / *Formule* 20M Ont. Reg. No. / *Régl. de l'Ont.* : 258/98

Newmarket
Small Claims Court / *Cour des petites créances de*

SC-00-98865-00
Claim No. / *N° de la demande*

50 Eagle Street West
Newmarket, Ontario
Address / *Adresse*

905 853 4809
Phone number / *Numéro de téléphone*

BETWEEN / *ENTRE*

France Nguyen
Plaintiff(s)/Creditor(s) / *Demandeur(s)/demanderesse(s)/Créancier(s)/créancière(s)*

and / *et*

Mabel Mirren
Defendant(s)/Debtor(s) / *Défendeur(s)/défenderesse(s)/Débiteur(s)/débitrice(s)*

My name is   **France Nguyen**
Je m'appelle   (Full name / *Nom et prénoms*)

I live in   **Newmarket, Ontario**
J'habite à   (Municipality & province / *Municipalité et province*)

and I swear/affirm that the following is true:
et je déclare sous serment/j'affirme solennellement que les renseignements suivants sont véridiques :

1. In this action, I am the
Dans la présente action, je suis le/la

(Check one box only. / *Cochez une seule case.*)

☒ plaintiff/creditor.
demandeur/demanderesse/créancier/créancière.

☐ representative of the plaintiff(s)/creditor(s)
représentant(e) du/de la/des demandeur(s)/demanderesse(s) ou du/de la/des créancier(s)/créancière(s)

(Name of plaintiff(s)/creditor(s) / *Nom du/de la/des demandeur(s)/demanderesse(s) ou du/de la/des créancier(s)/créancière(s)*)

2. To date, I have received from the defendant(s)/debtor(s) $ ____600.00____ , the last payment being made
À ce jour, j'ai reçu du ou des défendeurs/débiteurs   (Amount / *Montant*) $, soit le dernier paiement ayant

on or about ____October 1____ , 20 __ .
été effectué le ou vers le

3. I make this affidavit in support of a request that:
Je fais le présent affidavit à l'appui d'une demande visant à :

(Check appropriate box and complete paragraph. / *Cochez la case appropriée et remplissez le point.*)

☒ the clerk of the court issue a Default Judgment (Form 11B) [R. 9.03(2)(c)]. The defendant(s)
enjoindre au greffier du tribunal de rendre un jugement par défaut (formule 11B) [alinéa 9.03 (2) c)].
Le ou les défendeurs

Mabel Mirren
(Name(s) of defendant(s) / *Nom du/de la/des défendeur(s)/défenderesse(s)*)

failed to make payment in accordance with the proposed terms of payment in the Defence
n'ont pas effectué les paiements conformément aux modalités de paiement proposées dans la défense

(Form 9A) dated ____July 28____ , 20 __ and fifteen (15) days have passed since the
(formule 9A) datée du   *et quinze (15) jours se sont écoulés depuis*

defendant was served with a Notice of Default of Payment (Form 20L) at the following address(es):
la signification de l'avis de défaut de paiement au défendeur (formule 20L) à l'adresse (aux adresses)
suivante(s) :

(Address(es) of defendant(s) / *Adresse(s) du/de la/des défendeur(s)/défenderesse(s)*)

SCR 9.03-20M (April 11, 2012 / *11 avril 2012*) CSD

APPENDIX 6.5 Nguyen v. Mirren: Affidavit of Default of Payment by Defendant (Form 20M)

continued

FORM / *FORMULE* 20M	PAGE 2	SC-00-98865-00
		Claim No. / *N° de la demande*

☐ the clerk of the court issue a Default Judgment (Form 11B) [R. 9.03(7)]. The defendant(s)
enjoindre au greffier du tribunal de rendre un jugement par défaut (formule 11B) [par. 9.03 (7)]. Le ou les défendeurs

_____

(Name of defendant(s) / *Nom du/de la/des défendeur(s)/défenderesse(s)*)

failed to make payment in accordance with the terms of payment order
n'ont pas effectué les paiements conformément à l'ordonnance relative aux modalités de paiement

(Check appropriate box and complete paragraph. / Cochez la case appropriée et remplissez le point.)

dated _____, 20 _____ .
datée du

☐ I may enforce the judgment [R. 20.02(3)]. The debtor(s)
m'autoriser à exécuter le jugement [par. 20.02 (3)]. Le ou les débiteurs

_____

(Name(s) of debtor(s) / *Nom du/de la/des débiteur(s)/débitrice(s)*)

failed to make payment in accordance with the order for periodic payment dated
n'ont pas effectué les paiements conformément à l'ordonnance prescrivant des versements périodiques datée du

_____, 20 _____ , and fifteen (15) days have passed since the debtor(s) has/have
et quinze (15) jours se sont écoulés depuis la signification de

been served with a Notice of Default of Payment (Form 20L) at the following address(es):
l'avis de défaut de paiement (formule 20L) au ou aux débiteurs à l'adresse (aux adresses) suivante(s) :

_____

(Address(es) of debtor(s) / *Adresse(s) du/de la/des débiteur(s)/débitrice(s)*)

A Consent (Form 13B) in which the creditor waives the default has not been filed.
Un consentement (formule 13B) dans lequel le créancier renonce à la constatation du défaut n'a pas été déposé.

4. The unpaid balance is calculated as follows:
   Le solde impayé est calculé de la façon suivante :

(A) **DEBT** $ _____ 3,000.00
    LA CRÉANCE $

(B) **PRE-JUDGMENT INTEREST** calculated
    LES INTÉRÊTS ANTÉRIEURS AU JUGEMENT calculés

on the sum of $ _____ 3,000.00 _____ at the rate of _____ 7.0 _____ %
sur la somme de $ au taux de   pour cent

per annum from **January 1** _____ , 20 -- to **November 27** _____ , 20 -- ,
par an du   au

being _____ 330 _____ days. $ _____ 191.40
soit   jours. $

> **NOTE:** Calculation of interest is always on the amount owing from time to time as payments are received. This is true for both pre-judgment and post-judgment interest. Attach a separate sheet setting out how you calculated the total amount of any pre/post-judgment interest.
>
> **REMARQUE :** *Les intérêts doivent toujours être calculés sur la somme due. Le calcul doit tenir compte des paiements reçus de temps à autre. Ceci s'applique autant aux intérêts antérieurs au jugement qu'aux intérêts postérieurs au jugement. Annexez une feuille distincte indiquant comment vous avez calculé le montant total des intérêts antérieurs et postérieurs au jugement.*

SUBTOTAL (amount of judgment) $ 3,191.40
TOTAL PARTIEL (*montant du jugement*) $

APPENDIX 6.5 Nguyen v. Mirren: Affidavit of Default of Payment by Defendant (Form 20M)

concluded

FORM / *FORMULE* 20M	PAGE 3	SC-00-98865-00
		Claim No. / *N° de la demande*

(C) **COSTS** to date of judgment
     LES DÉPENS à la date du jugement
          $ 135.00
          $

(D) **TOTAL AMOUNT OF PAYMENTS RECEIVED FROM DEBTOR**
     after judgment (if any)   (minus) $ 600.00
     LE MONTANT TOTAL DES PAIEMENTS REÇUS DU DÉBITEUR   *(moins)* $
     après le jugement (le cas échéant)

(E) **POST-JUDGMENT INTEREST** to date calculated
     LES INTÉRÊTS POSTÉRIEURS AU JUGEMENT à ce jour, calculés

     on the sum of $ _____   at the rate of _____ %
     sur la somme de $ *au taux de*   *pour cent*

     per annum from _____ , 20 ___ to _____ , 20 ___ ,
     par an du   *au*

     being _____ days. $ 0
     soit   *jours.* $

(F) **SUBSEQUENT COSTS** incurred after judgment (including the cost of serving
     the Notice of Default of Payment (Form 20L)) $ 95.00
     LES DÉPENS SUBSÉQUENTS engagés après le jugement (y compris le coût de $
     signification de l'avis de défaut de paiement (formule 20L))

                        TOTAL DUE $ 2,821.40
                        SOLDE DÛ $

Sworn/Affirmed before me at   **Brampton**
Déclaré sous serment/Affirmé   (Municipality / *municipalité*)
solennellement devant moi à

in _____   **Ontario**
en/à/au   (Province, state, or county / *province, État ou pays*)
                         Signature
                    (This form is to be signed in front of a
on **November 27** , 20 --   lawyer, justice of the peace, notary public
le   or commissioner for taking affidavits.)
          Commissioner for taking affidavits   (*La présente formule doit être signée en*
           Commissaire aux affidavits   *présence d'un avocat, d'un juge de paix,*
          (Type or print name below if signature is *d'un notaire ou d'un commissaire aux*
                illegible.)   *affidavits.*)
          (*Dactylographiez le nom ou écrivez-le en*
          caractères d'imprimerie ci-dessous si la
          signature est illisible.)

WARNING:	IT IS AN OFFENCE UNDER THE *CRIMINAL CODE* TO KNOWINGLY SWEAR OR AFFIRM A FALSE AFFIDAVIT.
AVERTISSEMENT :	*FAIRE SCIEMMENT UN FAUX AFFIDAVIT CONSTITUE UNE INFRACTION AU* CODE CRIMINEL.

SCR 9.03-20M (April 11, 2012 / *11 avril 2012*) CSD

APPENDIX 6.5   Nguyen v. Mirren (Form 20M): Adjusted Calculation of Amount Owing

Principal $3,000.00

Interest   7.0% per year (simple interest)

Convert interest rate to a decimal = $7 \div 100 = 0.07$

Calculate per diem interest = $(3,000.00 \times 0.07) \div 365 = \$0.58$ per diem

Calculate interest on $3,000.00 from January 1 to September 1 (date of first payment):

Time period = September 1 (244) – January 1 (1) = 243 days

Interest = 243 days × $0.58 per day = $140.94

Amount owing as of September 1   = $3,000.00 + $140.94

                                                        = $3,140.94

MINUS September 1 payment   300.00

BALANCE OWING $2,840.94

Calculate interest to October 1 (date of second payment):

Time period = September 1 to October 1 = [274] – [244] = 30 days

Interest = 30 days × $0.58 per day   = $17.40

Amount owing as of October 1   = $2,840.94 + $17.40

                                                  = $2,858.34

MINUS October 1 payment   300.00

BALANCE OWING $2,558.34

Interest calculated from October 1 (date of last payment) to November 27 (date of preparing affidavit of default of payment):

Time period = 331 – 374 = 57 days

Interest = 57 days × $0.58 = $33.06

Amount owing as of June 4   = $2,558.34 + $33.06

                                                = $2,591.40

APPENDIX 6.5   Nguyen v. Mirren: Default Judgment (Form 11B)

ONTARIO

Superior Court of Justice
Cour supérieure de justice

Seal / *Sceau*

Default Judgment
Jugement par défaut
Form / *Formule* 11B Ont. Reg. No. / *Règl. de l'Ont.* : 258/98

Newmarket	SC-00-98865-00
Small Claims Court / *Cour des petites créances de*	Claim No. / *N° de la demande*
50 Eagle Street West	
Newmarket, Ontario	
L3Y 6B1	
Address / *Adresse*	
905 853 4809	
Phone number / *Numéro de téléphone*	

Plaintiff No. 1 / *Demandeur n° 1*   ☐ Additional plaintiff(s) listed on attached Form 1A.
Le ou les demandeurs additionnels sont mentionnés sur la formule 1A ci-jointe.

Last name, or name of company / *Nom de famille ou nom de la compagnie*		
Nguyen		
First name / *Premier prénom*	Second name / *Deuxième prénom*	Also known as / *Également connu(e) sous le nom de*
France		
Address (street number, apt., unit) / *Adresse (numéro et rue, app., unité)*		
c/o Prior Mustafa LLP		
City/Town / *Cité/ville*	Province	Phone no. / *N° de téléphone*
Postal code / *Code postal*		Fax no. / *N° de télécopieur*
Representative / *Représentant(e)*		LSUC # / *N° du BHC*
Prior Mustafa LLP Attention: Paralegal name		**######**
Address (street number, apt., unit) / *Adresse (numéro et rue, app., unité)*		
22 County Court Boulevard		
City/Town / *Cité/ville*	Province	Phone no. / *N° de téléphone*
Brampton	**Ontario**	**905 111 2222**
Postal code / *Code postal*		Fax no. / *N° de télécopieur*
A1A 2B3		**905 111 2233**

Defendant No. 1 / *Défendeur n° 1*   ☐ Additional defendant(s) listed on attached Form 1A.
Le ou les défendeurs additionnels sont mentionnés sur la formule 1A ci-jointe.

Last name, or name of company / *Nom de famille ou nom de la compagnie*		
Mirren		
First name / *Premier prénom*	Second name / *Deuxième prénom*	Also known as / *Également connu(e) sous le nom de*
Mabel		
Address (street number, apt., unit) / *Adresse (numéro et rue, app., unité)*		
89 Oliver Crescent, Unit 442		
City/Town / *Cité/ville*	Province	Phone no. / *N° de téléphone*
Newmarket	**Ontario**	**905 222 3333**
Postal code / *Code postal*		Fax no. / *N° de télécopieur*
E1H 2F2		
Representative / *Représentant(e)*		LSUC # / *N° du BHC*
Address (street number, apt., unit) / *Adresse (numéro et rue, app., unité)*		
City/Town / *Cité/ville*	Province	Phone no. / *N° de téléphone*
Postal code / *Code postal*		Fax no. / *N° de télécopieur*

SCR 11.02-11B (September 1, 2010 / *1ᵉʳ septembre 2010*) CSD

APPENDIX 6.5 **Nguyen v. Mirren: Default Judgment (Form 11B)** *continued*

FORM / *FORMULE* 11B   **PAGE 2**   SC-00-98865-00
                                                                        Claim No. / *N° de la demande*

NOTICE TO THE DEFENDANT(S):
AVIS AU(X) DÉFENDEUR(S) :
(*Check one box only.* / *Cochez une seule case.*)

☐ You have been noted in default according to Rule 11.01.
   vous avez été constaté(e) en défaut aux termes de la règle 11.01.

☒ You have defaulted in your payment according to Rule 9.03(2)(b), pursuant to
   vous n'avez pas effectué vos paiements aux termes de l'alinéa 9.03 (2) b), conformément à/au

   a proposal of terms of payment in the Defence (Form 9A)   dated **July 28**   , 20 -- ,
                    (Name of document / *Titre du document*)   *daté(e) du*

   and 15 days have passed since you were served with a Notice of Default of Payment (Form 20L).
   et 15 jours se sont écoulés depuis qu'un avis de défaut de paiement vous a été signifié (formule 20L).

DEFAULT JUDGMENT IS GIVEN against the following defendant(s):
UN JUGEMENT PAR DÉFAUT EST RENDU *contre le ou les défendeurs suivants :*

Last name, or name of company / *Nom de famille ou nom de la compagnie*		
Mirren		
First name / *Premier prénom*	Second name / *Deuxième prénom*	Also known as / *Également connu(e) sous le nom de*
Mabel		

Last name, or name of company / *Nom de famille ou nom de la compagnie*		
First name / *Premier prénom*	Second name / *Deuxième prénom*	Also known as / *Également connu(e) sous le nom de*

Last name, or name of company / *Nom de famille ou nom de la compagnie*		
First name / *Premier prénom*	Second name / *Deuxième prénom*	Also known as / *Également connu(e) sous le nom de*

☐ Additional defendant(s) listed on attached page (*list in same format*).
   Défendeur(s) additionnel(s) mentionné(s) sur une feuille annexée (énumérez-les en suivant le même format).

THE DEFENDANT(S) MUST PAY to the plaintiff(s) the following sums:
LE OU LES DÉFENDEURS DOIVENT VERSER *au(x) demandeur(s) les sommes suivantes :*

(A) **DEBT** (principal amount claimed minus any payments received since the plaintiff's
   claim was issued) $ 2,400.00
   LA CRÉANCE *(somme demandée moins tout paiement reçu depuis la délivrance* $
   de la demande du demandeur)

(B) **PRE-JUDGMENT INTEREST** calculated
   LES INTÉRÊTS ANTÉRIEURS AU JUGEMENT *calculés*

   on the sum of $ 3,000.00   at the rate of   **7.0**   %
   sur la somme de   *$ au taux de*   *pour cent*

   per annum from   **January 1**   , 20 -- , to **November 27**   , 20 -- ,
   par an du   *au*

   being   **330**   days. $ 191.40
   soit   *jours.* $

APPENDIX 6.5   Nguyen v. Mirren: Default Judgment (Form 11B)   *concluded*

FORM / *FORMULE* 11B	PAGE 3	SC-00-98865-00
		Claim No. / *N° de la demande*

(C) **COSTS** to date (including the cost of issuing this judgment) $ _____ 230.00

 LES DÉPENS à ce jour (dont les frais afférents à la prononciation $
 du présent jugement)

TOTAL $ _____ 2,821.40

$

This judgment bears post-judgment interest at   **7.0**   % per annum commencing this date.
Le présent jugement porte des intérêts postérieurs   pour cent à partir de la date du présent jugement.
au jugement calculés au taux annuel de

_____ , 20 ____   _____

(Signature of clerk / *Signature du greffier*)

CAUTION TO DEFENDANT:	**YOU MUST PAY THE AMOUNT OF THIS JUDGMENT DIRECTLY TO THE PLAINTIFF(S) IMMEDIATELY.** Failure to do so may result in additional post-judgment interest and enforcement costs.
AVERTISSEMENT AU DÉFENDEUR :	*VOUS DEVEZ VERSER DIRECTEMENT AU(X) DEMANDEUR(S) LE MONTANT DÛ AUX TERMES DU PRÉSENT JUGEMENT IMMÉDIATEMENT, à défaut de quoi d'autres intérêts postérieurs au jugement et dépens de l'exécution forcée pourront vous être imputés.*

APPENDIX 6.6 Financial Information Form (Form 20I)

FINANCIAL INFORMATION FORM
FORMULE DE RENSEIGNEMENTS FINANCIERS
Form / *Formule* 20I Ont. Reg. No. / *Régl. de l'Ont.* : 258/98

This form is to be completed by the debtor and served on the creditor.
La présente formule doit être remplie par le débiteur et signifiée au créancier.

This form is not to be filed in the court file.
Cette formule ne doit pas être déposée au dossier du greffe.

MONTHLY INCOME *REVENU MENSUEL*		MONTHLY EXPENSES *DÉPENSES MENSUELLES*	
Employer(s) _____ *Employeur(s)*		Rent/Mortgage *Loyer/Hypothèque*	$ _____ $
Employer(s) _____ *Employeur(s)*		Maintenance/Support Payments *Versements d'aliments*	$ _____ $
Net salary *Salaire net*	$ _____ $	Property taxes *Impôts fonciers*	$ _____ $
Commissions *Commissions*	$ _____ $	Utilities (heat, water & light) *Services d'utilité publique (chauffage, eau et éclairage)*	$ _____ $
Tips and gratuities *Pourboires et gratifications*	$ _____ $	Phone *Téléphone*	$ _____ $
Employment insurance *Prestations d'assurance-emploi*	$ _____ $	Cable *Câblodistribution*	$ _____ $
Pension income *Revenu de pension*	$ _____ $	House/Tenant insurance *Assurance-habitation /assurance de responsabilité locative*	$ _____ $
Investment income *Revenu de placements*	$ _____ $	Life insurance *Assurance-vie*	$ _____ $
Rental income *Revenu de location*	$ _____ $	Food *Nourriture*	$ _____ $
Business income *Revenu tiré d'une entreprise*	$ _____ $	Childcare/Babysitting *Garderie/gardiennage d'enfants*	$ _____ $
Child tax benefit *Prestation fiscale pour enfants*	$ _____ $	Motor vehicle (lease or loan) *Véhicule automobile (location à bail ou prêt)*	$ _____ $
Maintenance *(if any)* *Aliments* (le cas échéant)	$ _____ $	(licence, insurance, fuel & maintenance) *(permis, assurance, essence et entretien)*	$ _____ $
Monthly income of other adult household members *Revenu mensuel des autres membres adultes du ménage*	$ _____ $	Transportation (public) *Transports (en commun)*	$ _____ $
Other *Autre*	$ _____ $		
Income assistance *Aide au revenu*	$ _____ $		
INCOME TOTAL *REVENU TOTAL*	$ _____ $	EXPENSES TOTAL *DÉPENSES TOTALES*	$ _____ $

Continued on next page / *Suite à la page suivante*

APPENDIX 6.6   Financial Information Form (Form 20I) *concluded*

FORM / *FORMULE* **20I**   **PAGE 2**

MONTHLY DEBTS
DETTES MENSUELLES

Credit card(s) payments *(please specify):*
Paiements de carte(s) de crédit (Veuillez préciser.)

_____ $ _____ $

_____ $ _____ $

_____ $ _____ $

Bank or finance company loan payments *(please specify):*
Remboursement de prêt(s) d'une banque ou d'une compagnie de financement (Veuillez préciser.)

_____ $ _____ $

_____ $ _____ $

Department store(s) payments *(please specify):*
Versements à un ou des grands magasins (Veuillez préciser.)

_____ $ _____ $

_____ $ _____ $

DEBTS TOTAL $ _____
DETTES TOTALES $ _____

VALUE OF ASSETS
VALEUR DES AVOIRS

Real estate equity $ _____
Valeur nette réelle des biens immobiliers $

  Market value $ _____
  Valeur marchande $

  Mortgage balance $ _____
  Solde de l'hypothèque $

Automobile equity $ _____
Valeur nette réelle des véhicules automobiles $

  Make and year _____
  Marque et année

  Loan balance $ _____
  Solde du/des prêts $

Bank or other account balance(s)
(include RRSP's) $ _____
Solde de compte(s) bancaire(s) ou autre(s) compte(s) $
(Incluez les REÉR.)

Stocks & bonds $ _____
Actions et obligations $

Life insurance (cash value) $ _____
Assurance-vie (valeur de rachat) $

Money owing to you $ _____
Sommes qui vous sont dues $

Name of debtor _____
Nom du débiteur/de la débitrice

Personal property $ _____
Biens meubles $

Cash $ _____
Argent comptant $

Other $ _____
Autre $

TOTAL VALUE OF ASSETS $ _____
VALEUR TOTALE DES AVOIRS $

SCR 9.03-20.10-20I (January 25, 2006 / *25 janvier 2006*) CSD

Motions

7

LEARNING OUTCOMES

After reading this chapter, you will understand:

- When to use a request for clerk's order on consent

- What a motion is

- What a supporting affidavit is used for

- What an exhibit is

- Time for service and filing of a motion

- *Ex parte* motions

- Motions on notice

- Motions in writing for an assessment of damages

What Is a Motion?

General

A motion is a procedural step that is usually taken while the action is still going forward. On a motion before trial, the party making the motion is requesting **interim relief**—that is, a judge's order resolving an issue in the action that cannot wait until a settlement conference or trial. You may also use a motion to resolve an issue that arises after trial, if the trial judge made a purely arithmetical error in calculating the amount of the judgment, or if there is relevant evidence that was not available to a party at the time of the original trial and could not reasonably have been expected to be available at that time (Rule 17.04).

Motions are governed by Rule 15 of the *Rules of the Small Claims Court*. The form used on a motion is a notice of motion and supporting affidavit (Form 15A).

Any party to an action may make a motion. It does not matter whether you are a plaintiff or a defendant—you have the right to make a motion to the court if you require the court's assistance in resolving an issue. The party making the motion is called the **moving party**, regardless of whether that party is a plaintiff or a defendant. The other party is called the **responding party**, because that party answers, or responds to, the motion.

Judges may make a wide range of orders on a motion. These orders are intended to help the parties resolve issues and move the proceeding along.

For example, a plaintiff who has been unable to serve the plaintiff's claim personally or by an alternative to personal service on a defendant may make a motion to obtain directions from the judge as to an acceptable form of substituted service. If the plaintiff can demonstrate to the court that good faith efforts have been made to comply with Rule 8, and that it is impractical to effect prompt service of the claim personally or by an alternative to personal service, the court may allow substituted service (Rule 8.04).

No Further Motions Without Leave of the Court (Rule 15.04)

Generally, it is up to a party or the party's representative to determine whether it is necessary to bring a motion before the court. However, motions are intended to be used in good faith. That is, they are intended to expedite the action, not slow it down while adding to another party's legal expenses.

Motions that are brought for the sole purpose of harassing another party—that is, delaying the action while adding to another party's costs—abuse the court's process and bring the administration of justice into disrepute. (This type of procedural abuse used to be called **motioning the other party to death**.) Rule 15.04 provides that if the court is satisfied that a party has tried to delay the action, add to its costs, or otherwise abuse the court's process by making numerous motions without merit, the court may, on a motion by the party being harassed, make an order prohibiting the other party from making any further motions in the action without leave of the court.

Request for Clerk's Order on Consent (Rule 11.2, Form 11.2A)

Depending on the nature of the relief sought, before making a motion you should consider contacting the other party or parties to see whether they will consent to the relief you are seeking. If they are willing to do so, you may file a request for clerk's order on consent (Form 11.2A) confirming the terms of the order. The request for clerk's order on consent must be signed by all parties, including added, deleted, or substituted parties. It must state that each party has received a copy of the request, and that no party that would be affected by the order is under disability (Rule 11.2.01(1)2).

If the above conditions are met, the clerk shall, on the filing of a request for clerk's order on consent, make an order granting the relief sought, including costs, if the relief sought is (Rule 11.2.01(1)1):

    i. amending a claim or defence less than 30 days before the originally scheduled trial date,

    ii. adding, deleting or substituting a party less than 30 days before the originally scheduled trial date,

    iii. setting aside the noting in default or default judgment against a party and any specified step to enforce the judgment that has not yet been completed,

    iv. restoring a matter that was dismissed as abandoned under rule 11.1 to the list,

    v. noting that payment has been made in full satisfaction of a judgment or terms of settlement, or

    vi. dismissing an action.

The clerk shall serve a copy of an order made under Rule 11.2.01(1) on any party who requests it and provides a stamped, self-addressed envelope (Rule 11.2.01(2)).

Where an order is made under Rule 11.2.01(1)1(iii) to set aside a specified step to enforce the judgment under Rule 20 and the enforcement step has not been completed, a party shall file a copy of the order at each court location where the enforcement step has been requested (Rule 11.2.01(4)).

BOX 7.1 Reminder: Parties Under Disability

Rule 1.02(1) states that "disability," where used in respect of a person or party, means that the person or party is (a) a minor, (b) mentally incapable within the meaning of s. 6 or 45 of the *Substitute Decisions Act, 1992*, or (c) an absentee within the meaning of the *Absentees Act*. Special procedures for parties under disability are set out at Rule 4. Parties under disability are discussed in Chapter 4.

The clerk may refuse to make an order on consent under Rule 11.2.01(1). If the clerk refuses to make the order requested, the clerk shall serve a copy of the request for clerk's order on consent, with reasons for the refusal, on all parties (Rule 11.2.01(3)). The matter will then have to be resolved by a judge.

You will find a sample request for clerk's order on consent at Appendix 7.1 to this chapter.

Notice of Motion and Supporting Affidavit (Form 15A)

The form that is used on a motion is a notice of motion and supporting affidavit (Form 15A).

The notice of motion states:

- the parties and their legal representatives, if any;
- the date, time, and location (including courtroom number) of the hearing of the motion; and
- the order sought by the moving party.

Supporting Affidavit

An affidavit is a written statement of facts and evidence upon which a party to a motion relies. The person making the affidavit is called the **deponent**. In Small Claims Court, all affidavits have the same structure. An affidavit begins with a **preamble**, in which the person making the affidavit identifies herself, states the municipality and province in which she lives, and swears or affirms that the contents of the affidavit are true. The **body of the affidavit** contains the facts and evidence in support of the relief sought on the motion, stated in the first person (I, me, my, and so on). The affidavit concludes with a **jurat,** which contains the place and date the affidavit was sworn, the signature of the deponent, and the signature of the commissioner of oaths in whose presence the deponent swears or affirms the truth of the contents of the affidavit. True copies of any documents upon which the deponent intends to rely at the hearing of the motion must be identified in the body of the affidavit and attached to the affidavit as **exhibits**.

On a Small Claims Court motion, the supporting affidavit, which forms part of the Form 15A, will contain the written statement of facts and evidence upon which the moving party relies in support of the motion. The supporting affidavit on a motion tells the deponent's story about why an order is needed and why it should be granted by the court. True copies of any documents that the moving party intends to rely upon at the hearing of the motion must be identified in the body of the affidavit and attached to the supporting affidavit as exhibits.

Rule 15 of the *Small Claims Court Rules* does not specifically address formal requirements for affidavits. You may wish to consider using a separate schedule attached to and forming part of the Form 15A when drafting a supporting affidavit. With respect to formatting and other issues, you should also consider Rule 4.06 of the *Rules of Civil Procedure*, excerpted below:

AFFIDAVITS
Format

4.06(1) An affidavit used in a proceeding shall,

(a) [deleted];

(b) be expressed in the first person;

(c) state the full name of the deponent and, if the deponent is a party or a lawyer, officer, director, member or employee of a party, shall state that fact;

(d) be divided into paragraphs, numbered consecutively, with each paragraph being confined as far as possible to a particular statement of fact; and

(e) be signed by the deponent and sworn or affirmed before a person authorized to administer oaths or affirmations.

Contents

(2) An affidavit shall be confined to the statement of facts within the personal knowledge of the deponent or to other evidence that the deponent could give if testifying as a witness in court, except where these rules provide otherwise.

The statements made in the affidavit should, for the most part, be within the personal knowledge of the deponent. **Statements of information and belief** are acceptable, so long as the source of the information and the fact of the deponent's belief in its truth are specified in the affidavit. See Rule 39.01(4) of the *Rules of Civil Procedure*, excerpted below:

Contents—Motions

(4) An affidavit for use on a motion may contain statements of the deponent's information and belief, if the source of the information and the fact of the belief are specified in the affidavit.

The contents of the supporting affidavit must be sworn or affirmed in the same manner as oral (spoken) evidence given on the witness stand—that is, the deponent (in this case, the moving party) must swear or affirm the truth of the contents of the affidavit in the presence of a commissioner of oaths.

Exhibits

Copies of any documents relied on in support of the motion must be identified in the body of the affidavit and attached to the supporting affidavit as exhibits.

The supporting affidavit should identify the document that is attached as an exhibit in sufficient detail. Documents should be identified by the type of document (contract, invoice, cancelled cheque, and so on), the date of the document, the name of the signatory or signatories if any, and any other relevant details. A **signatory** is someone who signs a document. Exhibits should be identified as they occur in the narrative, and copies should be stamped as exhibits and attached to the affidavit in the same order. The deponent must attest to the fact that the copy is a **true copy**— that is, an accurate copy of the original document.

BOX 7.2   What Is a Statement of Information and Belief?

The role of the deponent of an affidavit is the same as the role of a witness who takes the stand and gives evidence under oath at trial, except that the evidence in the affidavit is written, and the evidence at trial is usually spoken.

The general rule is that a witness can give evidence only about matters within her personal knowledge. That rule is relaxed for a deponent of a supporting affidavit on a motion. She is allowed to state, as a fact, information not within her personal knowledge that she has received from another individual or some other source— that is, make statements of information and belief.

A statement of information and belief must be identified as such, by naming the source of the information and the fact that the deponent believes the statement to be true.

When to use a statement of information and belief: The defendant is served with a plaintiff's claim on May 1, 20—. She has a good defence, but does not seek legal representation until May 23, 20—, when she is already out of time for filing a defence. Her paralegal contacts the plaintiff's paralegal by telephone and email on May 23 to advise the plaintiff's paralegal that he has been retained and will require a short extension of the deadline for filing a defence. The plaintiff's paralegal does not respond. When the defendant's paralegal attempts to file the defence on May 25, he is advised by the court clerk that the defendant was noted in default on May 24.

If the matter cannot be resolved on consent, a motion for an order setting aside the default must be brought by the defendant. The defendant will be the deponent in the supporting affidavit. The excerpt below from her supporting affidavit contains examples of statements of information and belief:

3. I am advised by my paralegal, Joseph Mustafa, and believe that he contacted the plaintiff's paralegal, Frances Douglas, by telephone and email on May 23, 20— to advise Ms. Douglas that I had retained him and to request a short extension of the deadline for filing a defence. A true copy of the email dated May 23, 20— is attached as Exhibit 1.

4. Ms. Douglas did not respond to Mr. Mustafa's telephone call and email. I am advised by Mr. Mustafa and believe that when he tried to file my defence on May 25, 20—, he was informed that I had been noted in default on May 24, 20—.

The deponent has no personal knowledge of the events described in paragraphs 3 and 4 above—she was not present when her paralegal tried to contact the plaintiff's paralegal on May 23, 20—, she only knows about Ms. Douglas's failure to respond because Mr. Mustafa told her about it, and she was not present when Mr. Mustafa attempted to file her defence. Her affidavit indicates this by using the language of information and belief—"I am advised by [name of informant] and believe that …"—specifying the source of the deponent's information, and that she believes the information to be true.

In the body of the affidavit, a document to be attached as an exhibit will be identified using language along the following lines:

4. Pursuant to a residential tenancy agreement dated January 13, 20—, I agreed to rent the basement apartment in my home at 67 Harmony Avenue, Toronto, Ontario to the defendant. The tenancy commenced February 1, 20— at a monthly rent of $775.00, including water, heat, and hydro. A true copy of the tenancy agreement dated January 13, 20— is attached as Exhibit 1.

Each exhibit to the original affidavit is stamped. The exhibits are dated and signed by the commissioner of oaths at the same time the affidavit is sworn or affirmed by the deponent. Once sworn or affirmed, exhibits form part of the affidavit, and may be referred to during argument on the motion.

Exhibit stamps may be purchased from a legal stationer such as Dye & Durham, or they may be computer-generated. The standard language of an exhibit stamp is as follows:

This is Exhibit 1
to the affidavit of Om Chandra Prakash
sworn before me at Brampton, Ontario
on November 14, 20—
Ruth Prawer
A commissioner etc.

Perjury

The deponent of an affidavit has the same moral duty to tell the truth as a witness who takes the stand at trial and swears or affirms that in his testimony to the court he will tell the truth, the whole truth, and nothing but the truth.

A deponent who knowingly swears or affirms a false affidavit commits **perjury**. Perjury is a criminal offence. Everyone who commits perjury is guilty of an indictable offence and liable to imprisonment for a term not exceeding 14 years.

See page 4 of the Form 15A, excerpted below. See also the *Criminal Code*, ss. 131 and 132.

FIGURE 7.1 Warning: Perjury (Form 15A)

Types of Motions

General

In Small Claims Court, there are three types of motions:

1. a motion without notice to other parties (also called an **ex parte motion**);
2. a motion on notice to other parties; and
3. a motion in writing for an assessment of damages in an unliquidated claim where all defendants have been noted in default (discussed in Chapter 5).

Motion Without Notice (Rule 15.03)

A motion without notice (also known as an *ex parte* motion) is a motion made without notifying the other parties to the action—that is, without serving the motion materials on other parties or giving them any other notice that the motion is being brought.

In Small Claims Court, motions without notice are permitted if the nature or circumstances of the motion make notice unnecessary or not reasonably possible (Rule 15.03(1)). You must prepare proper motion materials in accordance with Rule 15.01(1) and file a copy with the court. If you appear before a judge on an *ex parte* motion, be prepared to make submissions to the judge as to why the motion should be allowed to proceed without notice to other parties. If the judge decides that notice to the other parties is required, you must follow the procedures for a motion on notice, discussed below.

If you are representing the moving party on an *ex parte* motion, you must ensure that the motion materials filed by the moving party with the court make full and fair disclosure of all material facts upon which the moving party is relying. A paralegal shall not knowingly attempt to deceive a tribunal or influence the course of justice by misstating facts or law, presenting or relying upon a deceptive affidavit, or suppressing what ought to be disclosed (Rule 4.01 of the *Paralegal Rules of Conduct*).

A party who obtains an order on a motion without notice must serve the order, along with a copy of the notice of motion and supporting affidavit, on all other parties within five days after the order is signed (Rule 15.03(2)). Service is by mail, by courier, by fax, by personal service, or by an alternative to personal service, unless the court orders otherwise (Rule 8.01(14)).

Any party affected by the *ex parte* order may make a motion to **set aside** (cancel or have declared null and void) or **vary** (change the terms of) the order, within 30 days after service (Rule 15.03(3)).

On a responding party's motion to set aside or vary an *ex parte* order, any failure by the moving party to make full and fair disclosure of all material facts reasonably within the moving party's knowledge in the material filed in support of the motion without notice should be raised as a ground for setting aside the order. The *Rules of the Small Claims Court* are silent on this issue, but you may argue by analogy with reference to Rule 1.03(2) of the *Rules of the Small Claims Court,* and Rule 39.01(6) of the *Rules of Civil Procedure*. Rule 39.01(6) is excerpted below:

Full and Fair Disclosure on Motion or Application Without Notice

(6) Where a motion or application is made without notice, the moving party or applicant shall make full and fair disclosure of all material facts, and failure to do so is in itself sufficient ground for setting aside any order obtained on the motion or application.

Motion on Notice (Rule 15.01)

When drafting your motion materials, you must contact the court clerk or the court scheduling office to obtain a date and time for hearing the motion (Rule 15.01(2)). The date, time, and location (including the room number of the courtroom where the motion will be heard) must be stated on the notice of motion at the top of page 2.

Before contacting the clerk to set a date, you should consider contacting all other parties, including self-represented parties, to obtain a range of dates when they will be available to attend on the motion. That way, a responding party has no excuse for requesting an **adjournment** of the motion—that is, putting it off to a later date— because he or his representative is unavailable on the hearing date.

A motion shall not be adjourned at a party's request before the hearing date unless the written consent of all parties is filed when the request is made, unless the court orders otherwise (Rule 15.05).

The notice of motion and the supporting affidavit shall be served at least seven days before the hearing date on all parties who have filed a claim and any defendant who has not been noted in default (Rule 15.01(3)(a)). The notice of motion and supporting affidavit shall be filed with the court with proof of service at least three days before the hearing of the motion (Rule 15.01(3)(b)).

The notice of motion and supporting affidavit may be served by personal service, an alternative to personal service, mail, courier, or fax, unless the court orders otherwise (Rule 8.01(14)). Keep in mind that you must count the seven-day minimum notice period from the date service becomes effective. This will vary depending on the type of service, so carefully review Rule 8 if you are unsure about how much time you have before the hearing date to get the motion served and filed.

A party who has been served with motion materials may respond to the moving party's motion by serving an affidavit in response (Form 15B) on every party who has filed a claim or defence. An affidavit in response contains the facts and evidence (including documents) that the responding party intends to rely on when opposing the motion. The affidavit in response must be filed, with proof of service, at least two days before the hearing date for the motion (Rule 15.01(4)).

The moving party may serve a supplementary affidavit on every party who has filed a claim or defence and file it with proof of service at least two days before the hearing date (Rule 15.01(5)). A supplementary affidavit may be used to respond to an affidavit filed by a responding party, and/or to put additional evidence before the court for use on the motion.

Motion After Judgment Has Been Signed (Rules 17.04 and 15.01(6))

If a motion is made after judgment has been signed (that is, after default judgment has been signed or the court has made a final order), the motion materials must be served on all parties, including parties who have been noted in default (Rule 15.01(6)). See also Rule 11.05(3)3.

BOX 7.3 Sample Motion Materials: Motion for Set Aside of Default Judgment (Parrish v. Thurston)

Background

The following is a summary of what has happened so far.

On March 1, 20—, the plaintiff, Maxwell Parrish, loaned Frank Thurston $27,000.00. Mr. Thurston signed a promissory note dated March 1, 20— acknowledging that he had received the money, and promising to pay it back in full on September 1, 20—. The note provided that, in the event of default, interest at a rate of 12 percent per annum would accrue on any outstanding balance commencing September 1, 20— and continuing until such time as all amounts owing were paid in full.

Mr. Thurston failed to pay the amount owing on September 1, 20—. A demand letter dated October 13, 20— was sent to Mr. Thurston by the plaintiff's paralegal. A plaintiff's claim was issued on November 1, 20— in Brampton Small Claims Court for $25,000.00 plus pre-judgment interest in accordance with the promissory note dated March 1, 20—. The plaintiff waived the amount owing over and above the Small Claims Court monetary jurisdiction.

New Developments

Service of the plaintiff's claim took place on November 3, 20—. The defendant failed to file a defence within the prescribed time. Default judgment was signed on December 1, 20—.

Mr. Thurston receives the default judgment in the mail on December 8, 20—. He immediately contacts Anna Limones at Paxton Limones PC, 82 Main Street, Suite 11, Brampton, Ontario L1N 2P3 TEL: 905 888 9999 FAX: 905 888 0000 for legal advice. Mr. Thurston tells Ms. Limones that he did not receive the plaintiff's claim.

Mr. Thurston's story is that he lost his job on June 15, 20—. To save on expenses, he moved in with some friends at the address on the plaintiff's claim in September, but it did not work out. He moved back home to Brampton in early October. He received the default judgment because it was forwarded to his Brampton address by Canada Post. He has no idea what happened to the plaintiff's claim. When he tried to get in touch with a former roommate at the Labrador Court address, the number was out of service.

By the time the amount owing under the note became due on September 1, Mr. Thurston had been looking for work for two months, with no luck. The market for his type of work is very competitive, and he decided that he should set aside the money he had saved from his employment earnings and freelance work to be used if he was still unemployed when his employment insurance benefits ran out.

Mr. Thurston says he phoned Mr. Parrish several times in July and August and left voicemails advising him that he had lost his job and would not be able to pay off the note until he found another one. Mr. Parrish did not return his calls.

On December 1, 20—, Mr. Thurston found another job, with an annual salary of $39,000.00. He wants to make a motion to set aside the noting in default and default judgment. If the motion is granted, he wants to file a defence making a proposal of terms of payment.

Mr. Thurston's notice of motion and supporting affidavit are at Appendix 7.2 to this chapter.

Hearing of the Motion

Method of Hearing (Rule 15.02(1))

A motion may be heard in a number of ways, depending on the relief being asked for and the technology available. Rule 15.02(1) states that a motion may be heard:

1. In person. The parties or their representatives attend at court before a judge to argue the motion.

2. By telephone or video conference if telephone or video conference facilities are available at the court. A party must file a request for telephone or video conference (Form 1B) giving reasons for the request. When deciding whether or not to grant the request, the judge shall consider the balance of convenience between the party requesting the telephone or video conference and any party who opposes it; plus any other relevant matter (Rule 1.07(3)).

   If the court makes an order directing a telephone or video conference, the court shall make the necessary arrangements and notify the parties (Rule 1.07(4)).

   A judge presiding at a proceeding or a step in a proceeding may set aside or vary an order directing a telephone or video conference (Rule 1.07(5)).

3. By a motion in writing for an assessment of damages. In an action where all defendants have been noted in default, the plaintiff may obtain judgment for the unliquidated portion of a claim by filing a motion in writing for an assessment of damages (Rule 11.03(2)(a)). A date must be obtained from the court for the motion to be scheduled before a judge. The attendance of the parties is not required (Rule 15.02(2)). The order made on a motion in writing for an assessment of damages is called an **assessment order**. An assessment order shall be served by the clerk to the moving party if the moving party provides a stamped, self-addressed envelope with the notice of motion (Rule 8.01(5)). Although there is nothing in Rule 8 or Rule 12 specifically addressing service of an assessment order on the defendant, presumably the order will be served by the clerk on the defendant in the same manner as a default judgment signed by the clerk in a liquidated claim (see Rules 8.01(4) and 11.02(3)).

4. By any other method that the judge determines is fair and reasonable. This is in keeping with the general principle stated in Rule 1.03(1) that the Rules shall be liberally construed to secure the just, most expeditious, and least-expensive determination of every proceeding on its merits in accordance with s. 25 of the *Courts of Justice Act*.

Arguing a Motion in Person or by Telephone or Video Conference (Rules 15.02(1)(a) and (b))

The procedure on a motion on notice to be argued in person is very different from the procedure at a trial.

At a trial, the witnesses for the plaintiff and the defendant take the stand, give sworn evidence in support of the claim or defence, and are cross-examined by the other side.

When all the evidence has been heard and tested by cross-examination, the plaintiff and defendant, or their legal representatives, make submissions as to the order the court should make, with reference to the evidence and any applicable court decisions. The judge then summarizes the findings of fact (that is, the parts of the evidence that the judge accepts as true on a balance of probabilities), applies legal principles to those findings of fact, and makes an order.

When a motion is argued in person, the parties or their representatives are required to be present at the court at the time stated on the notice of motion, and to wait until their matter is called. You should consider arriving early. When the matter is called, the parties or their representatives take their places at the counsel tables

FIGURE 7.2 What Does the Courtroom Look Like?

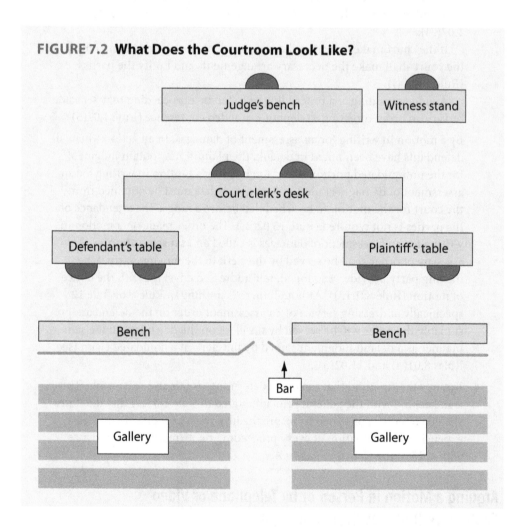

facing the judge's bench. The moving party or her representative speaks first. Usually the moving party's submissions to the judge will consist of a brief summary of what she is asking for, and arguments as to why the court should grant the order, with reference to the evidence in the supporting affidavit, the exhibits attached, and any relevant law. **Submissions** are legal arguments made to the judge for her consideration when deciding whether or not to grant the relief requested.

The other party or parties then present arguments as to why the order should not be granted, with reference to any materials they have filed.

During submissions, the judge may ask questions or seek clarification from the party making submissions from time to time.

Having heard the parties' submissions, the judge makes an order. The judge may give brief reasons for the order. The judge will write the order on the endorsement record. The successful party may obtain a copy of the endorsement from the court clerk.

Where the technology is available, the same procedure will be followed on a motion by telephone or video conference.

Motion in Writing for an Assessment of Damages (Rules 11.03(2)(a) and 15.02(1)(c))

A motion in writing for an assessment of damages may be made where (1) all or part of the claim is for an unliquidated amount; (2) all defendants have been served with the claim; (3) none of the defendants have filed a defence within the time required; and (4) all defendants have been noted in default. Keep in mind that, in many cases, there will be only one defendant in an unliquidated claim in Small Claims Court. If that defendant goes into default, the plaintiff may note the defendant in default and make a motion in writing for an assessment of damages.

A date must be obtained from the court for the motion to be scheduled before a judge. The attendance of the parties is not required (Rule 15.02(2)). An assessment order shall be served by the clerk to the moving party if the moving party provides a stamped, self-addressed envelope with the notice of motion (Rule 8.01(5)). Although there is nothing in Rule 8 or Rule 12 specifically addressing service of an assessment order on the defendant, presumably the order will be served by the clerk on the defendant in the same manner as a default judgment signed by the clerk in a liquidated claim (see Rules 8.01(4) and 11.02(3)).

In an unliquidated claim where one or more defendants have filed a defence, a plaintiff requiring an assessment of damages against a defendant noted in default shall proceed to a settlement conference under Rule 13 and, if necessary, to trial in accordance with Rule 17 (Rule 11.03(7)).

Motions in writing for an assessment of damages were discussed in detail in Chapter 5 at pages 190–191. A sample motion for an assessment of damages can be found at Appendix 5.2.

CHAPTER SUMMARY

A motion is used to obtain a judge's order or direction resolving an issue in the action that cannot wait until final resolution by trial or settlement.

A motion is not always necessary to determine an issue. Where all parties (including added, deleted, or substituted parties) consent, an issue may be resolved by a request for clerk's order on consent (Form 11.2A), so long as the relief sought falls within Rule 11.2.01(1)1. The request for clerk's order on consent must be signed by all parties (including added, deleted, or substituted parties). It must state that all parties have received a copy of the request, and that no party who would be affected by the order is under disability.

Motions are governed by Rule 15. The form filed on a motion is a notice of motion and supporting affidavit (Form 15A).

Any party to an action may make a motion. The party making the motion is called the moving party. The other party or parties are called responding parties.

The notice of motion sets out the time, date, and place where the motion will be heard, and the relief being asked for on the motion. The supporting affidavit contains the written evidence in support of the motion. Any documents to be relied upon in support of the motion will be identified in the body of the affidavit and attached to the affidavit as exhibits.

A motion without notice (also known as an *ex parte* motion) is a motion made without notifying the other party or parties. A motion without notice may be made if the nature and circumstances of the motion make notice unnecessary or not reasonably possible. The party making the motion must serve a copy of the order and the motion materials on every party affected by the order within five days after the order is signed. A party affected by an order made on an *ex parte* motion may make a motion to set aside or vary the order within 30 days of being served with the order.

Where a motion is on notice to the other party or parties, the moving party must contact the clerk to obtain a date and time for hearing the motion before serving the motion materials. It is advisable to contact the other party or parties and agree on some mutually convenient dates before contacting the clerk.

The motion materials must be served on all parties, except a defendant who has been noted in default, at least seven days before the hearing date, and filed with proof of service at least three days before the hearing date.

A responding party may serve an affidavit in response and file it, with proof of service, at least two days before the hearing date.

The moving party may serve a supplementary affidavit and file it, with proof of service, at least two days before the hearing date.

A motion on notice may be heard in person, or by telephone or video conference where those facilities are available, or by any other method that a judge determines is fair and reasonable in the circumstances.

KEY TERMS

adjournment: putting a court procedure, such as a motion, settlement conference, or trial, off to a later date (*p. 291*)

assessment order: an assessment order is an order made by a judge on a motion in writing for an assessment of damages in an unliquidated claim where all defendants have been noted in default (*p. 293*)

body of the affidavit: contents comprise the facts and evidence in support of the relief sought (*p. 286*)

deponent: the person who makes an affidavit (*p. 286*)

***ex parte* motion**: a motion made without notice to other parties (*p. 290*)

exhibit: an original document that is material to an issue in the action; it must be identified by a witness with personal knowledge of its contents, which may be referred to in her spoken evidence; it is then marked as an exhibit by the court clerk and placed in the court file as part of the evidence (*p. 286*)

interim relief: judge's order resolving an issue in the action that cannot wait until a settlement conference or trial (*p. 284*)

jurat: conclusion of affidavit with place and date of where affidavit sworn, signature of deponent, and signature of commissioner of oaths (*p. 286*)

motioning the other party to death: using motions to delay the action, add to the costs of other parties, or otherwise abuse the process of the court *(p. 284)*

moving party: the party in a proceeding who makes a motion *(p. 284)*

perjury: swearing or affirming a statement (including a document) that you know is not true; perjury is a criminal offence *(p. 289)*

preamble: in an affidavit, statement identifying the person making the affidavit, the municipality and province in which that person lives, and an affirmation that the contents of the affidavit are true *(p. 286)*

responding party: a party who answers or responds to a motion made by another party *(p. 284)*

set aside: to declare a court order or procedural step to be of no force and effect *(p. 290)*

signatory: someone who signs a document *(p. 287)*

statement of information and belief: in a supporting affidavit, a statement of information that the deponent received from another person or source, and that the deponent believes to be true *(p. 287)*

submissions: legal arguments made to a judge for her consideration when deciding whether the relief requested by a party should be granted *(p. 295)*

true copy: an accurate copy of an original document *(p. 287)*

vary a court order: to change the terms of a court order *(p. 290)*

REFERENCES

Absentees Act, RSO 1990, c. A.3.
Courts of Justice Act, RSO 1990, c. C.43.
Criminal Code, RSC 1985, c. C-46.
Law Society of Upper Canada (LSUC), *Paralegal Rules of Conduct* (Toronto: LSUC, 2007, as amended); available online at http://www.lsuc.on.ca.

Rules of Civil Procedure, RRO 1990, Reg. 194.
Rules of the Small Claims Court, O. Reg. 258/98.
Substitute Decisions Act, 1992, SO 1992, c. 30.

IN-CLASS EXERCISE
Dante v. Herrero—Motion to Set Aside Default Judgment

Background

Francesca Dante loaned $4,000.00 to her best friend, Suzanne Herrero, on December 1, 20—. The loan is secured by a promissory note dated December 1, 20— signed by Ms. Herrero. The terms of the note are as follows:

By her signature hereto, the undersigned SUZANNE HERRERO acknowledges receipt of the sum of FOUR THOUSAND DOLLARS ($4,000.00), paid by Francesca Dante to Suzanne Herrero on today's date. Interest shall be payable on said sum at a rate of 12 percent per annum, commencing December 1, 20—. The entire principal amount plus interest thereon shall be due and payable in full on March 1, 20—. In the event of default by Suzanne Herrero, interest shall continue to accrue at a rate of 12 percent per annum until such time as all amounts owing are paid in full or judgment is obtained, and post-judgment interest shall accrue on the judgment amount, including costs, at a rate of 12 percent per annum until such time as the amount owing is paid in full.

On March 1, 20—, Ms. Herrero gave Ms. Dante a cheque in the amount of $4,120.00, on account of the principal and interest then owing. The cheque was returned due to insufficient funds.

Ms. Dante commenced a claim for $4,000.00 plus interest at a rate of 12 percent per year commencing December 1, 20— in claim number SC-00-06638-00 on April 3, 20—.

Ms. Herrero was personally served with the plaintiff's claim on April 5, 20—. She failed to file a defence within the prescribed time. On April 27, 20—, the plaintiff obtained default judgment.

See also Chapter 4, Box 4.1 at page 107, and the drafting exercise at Chapter 4, page 154 and Chapter 5, page 198.

New Developments

Ms. Herrero receives the default judgment in the mail on May 3, 20—.

She immediately contacts Paxton Limones PC, 82 Main Street, Suite 11, Brampton, Ontario L1N 2P3 TEL: 905-888-9999 FAX: 905-888-0000 for legal advice.

According to Ms. Herrero, shortly after signing the note dated December 1, 20—, she had some unexpected expenses, and realized that she would not be able to pay the whole amount back in full on the due date of March 1, 20—. She phoned and emailed Ms. Dante several times during January and February to discuss repaying the loan in installments. Ms. Dante insisted that the money be paid in full on March 1. "I need that money for other things!" she told Ms. Herrero during a telephone conversation in early February. She did not respond to Ms. Herrero's email messages.

Frustrated, Ms. Herrero mailed Ms. Dante the cheque dated March 1, 20— for $4,120.00, knowing that it would probably be returned for insufficient funds. She did not return Ms. Dante's phone calls and emails because she was tired of arguing with Ms. Dante about a situation she could not change.

When she was served with the plaintiff's claim, she was so angry she tossed it in a drawer and forgot about it. She realizes now that that was not a very sensible thing to do.

Her telephone number and email address have not changed. She cannot understand why Ms. Dante did not just get in touch with her to talk about payment terms. "We used to be friends, you know," she said. "I don't know what's up with Francesca all of a sudden."

Please draft a notice of motion and supporting affidavit for Ms. Herrero. You are seeking an order for set aside of the noting in default and other relief. Refer to the precedent motion and affidavit at Appendix 7.2 for assistance in completing the documents. Keep in mind that the documents at Appendix 7.2 are precedents only—they should be used as a guideline, not copied word for word.

The motion is scheduled for May 21, 20— at 9:30 a.m. at Courtroom 10B at Brampton Small Claims Court. The notice of motion and supporting affidavit are prepared on May 7, 20—. The affidavit will be sworn on the same date.

REVIEW QUESTIONS

1. What is a motion? What is it used for?

2. **a.** What is the party who makes a motion called?

   b. What is the other party called?

   c. Can a defendant make a motion?

3. What form is served and filed on a motion? Please cite the applicable rule.

4. A plaintiff wishes to use a request for clerk's order on consent to obtain an order amending the claim and adding a party. The added party refuses to sign the request for clerk's order on consent. Can the plaintiff obtain her order using a request for clerk's order on consent? Cite the applicable rule.

5. A defendant wishes to use a request for clerk's order on consent to obtain an order amending the defence. The plaintiff is a party under disability. Can the defendant obtain the order using a request for clerk's order on consent? Cite the applicable rule.

6. What is the person who makes an affidavit called?

7. What is the supporting affidavit that forms part of the Form 15A notice of motion used for on a motion?

8. What are submissions?

9. What are exhibits? How is an exhibit identified in an affidavit?

10. What is a motion without notice and when may it be made? Please refer to any relevant rule or rules.

11. **a.** Must the moving party on a motion without notice file proper motion materials?

    b. What are the obligations of a party who obtains an order on a motion without notice? Please refer to any relevant rule or rules.

12. Give a brief description of the procedure at the hearing of a motion on notice that is being heard in person.

APPENDIX 7.1 Chakravarty v. Complete Home Renovations: Request for Clerk's Order on Consent (Form 11.2A)

ONTARIO
Superior Court of Justice
Cour supérieure de justice

Request for Clerk's Order on Consent
Demande d'ordonnance du greffier sur consentement
Form / *Formule* 11.2A Ont. Reg. No. / *Régl. de l'Ont.* : 258/98

Brampton
Small Claims Court / *Cour des petites créances de*
7755 Hurontario Street
Brampton, Ontario
L6W 4T6
Address / *Adresse*

905 456 4700
Phone number / *Numéro de téléphone*

SC-00-80011-00
Claim No. / *N° de la demande*

Plaintiff No. 1 / *Demandeur n° 1*

☐ Additional plaintiff(s) listed on attached Form 1A.
Le ou les demandeurs additionnels sont mentionnés sur la formule 1A ci-jointe.

Last name, or name of company / *Nom de famille ou nom de la compagnie*		
Chakravarty		
First name / *Premier prénom* **Amrita**	Second name / *Deuxième prénom*	Also known as / *Également connu(e) sous le nom de*
Address (street number, apt., unit) / *Adresse (numéro et rue, app., unité)* **c/o Prior Mustafa LLP**		
City/Town / *Cité/ville*	Province	Phone no. / *N° de téléphone*
Postal code / *Code postal*		Fax no. / *N° de télécopieur*
Representative / *Représentant(e)* **Prior Mustafa LLP Attention: Paralegal name**		LSUC # / *N° du BHC* **######**
Address (street number, apt., unit) / *Adresse (numéro et rue, app., unité)* **22 County Court Boulevard**		
City/Town / *Cité/ville* **Brampton**	Province **Ontario**	Phone no. / *N° de téléphone* **905 111 2222**
Postal code / *Code postal* **A1A 2B3**		Fax no. / *N° de télécopieur* **905 111 2233**

Defendant No. 1 / *Défendeur n° 1*

☐ Additional defendant(s) listed on attached Form 1A.
Le ou les défendeurs additionnels sont mentionnés sur la formule 1A ci-jointe.

Last name, or name of company / *Nom de famille ou nom de la compagnie*		
Complete Home Renovations Inc.		
First name / *Premier prénom*	Second name / *Deuxième prénom*	Also known as / *Également connu(e) sous le nom de*
Address (street number, apt., unit) / *Adresse (numéro et rue, app., unité)* **455 Lonsdale Court**		
City/Town / *Cité/ville* **Mississauga**	Province **Ontario**	Phone no. / *N° de téléphone* **905 123 4444**
Postal code / *Code postal* **X2X 3Y4**		Fax no. / *N° de télécopieur* **905 123 5555**
Representative / *Représentant(e)*		LSUC # / *N° du BHC*
Address (street number, apt., unit) / *Adresse (numéro et rue, app., unité)*		
City/Town / *Cité/ville*	Province	Phone no. / *N° de téléphone*
Postal code / *Code postal*		Fax no. / *N° de télécopieur*

NOTE: This request must be signed by all parties and anyone being added, deleted or substituted.
REMARQUE : *La présente demande doit être signée par toutes les parties et par toute personne qui est jointe, radiée ou substituée.*

SCR 11.2.01-11.2A (June 1, 2009 / *1er juin 2009*) CSD

APPENDIX 7.1 Chakravarty v. Complete Home Renovations:
Request for Clerk's Order on Consent (Form 11.2A) *continued*

FORM / *FORMULE* 11.2A   **PAGE 2**   SC-00-80011-00
_____
                                                           Claim No. / *N° de la demande*

TO THE PARTIES:
AUX PARTIES :

THIS REQUEST IS FILED BY: Complete Home Renovations Inc.
LA PRÉSENTE DEMANDE EST DÉPOSÉE PAR :   (Name of party / *Nom de la partie*)

I state that:
Je déclare que :

☒ Each party has received a copy of this form.
   Chaque partie a reçu une copie de la présente formule.

☒ No party that would be affected by the order is under disability.
   Aucune partie sur laquelle l'ordonnance aurait une incidence n'est incapable.

☒ This form has been signed and consented to by all parties, including any parties to be added, deleted or
   substituted.
   *Toutes les parties, y compris celles qui doivent être jointes, radiées ou substituées, ont signé la présente
   formule et y ont consenti.*

I request that the clerk make the following order(s) on the consent of all parties:
Je demande au greffier de rendre l'ordonnance ou les ordonnances suivantes sur consentement de toutes les parties :
(Check appropriate boxes. / Cochez les cases appropriées.)

☒ set aside the noting in default of **Complete Home Renovations Inc.**
   l'annulation de la constatation du défaut de   (Name of defendant(s) / *Nom du/de la/des défendeur(s)/défenderesse(s)*)

☐ set aside Default Judgment against
   l'annulation du jugement par défaut prononcé contre   (Name of defendant(s) / *Nom du/de la/des
                                                                  défendeur(s)/défenderesse(s)*)

☐ restore to the list the following matter that was dismissed under Rule 11.1: (Specify.)
   la réinscription au rôle de l'affaire suivante qui a été rejetée aux termes de la règle 11.1 :   (Précisez.)
_____

☐ cancel the examination hearing regarding _____
   l'annulation de l'interrogatoire concernant   (Name of person to be examined / *Nom de la personne qui doit être interrogée*)

☐ with respect to the following step(s) taken to enforce the default judgment that are not yet completed:
   *à l'égard de la ou des mesures suivantes qui ont été prises pour exécuter le jugement par défaut et qui ne
   sont pas encore menées à terme :*

   ☐ withdraw the Writ of Seizure and Sale of Land issued against: (Name of debtor(s))
      le retrait du bref de saisie-exécution de biens-fonds délivré contre : (Nom du/de la/des débiteur(s)/débitrice(s))

   and directed to the sheriff of the _____ :
   et adressé au shérif de   (Name of county/region in which the sheriff(enforcement office) is located / *Nom du
                                      comté/de la région où se trouve le shérif (bureau de l'exécution)*)
   _____
   (Provide instructions about what is to be done with any proceeds held or property seized by the sheriff. / *Donnez des instructions
   sur ce qu'il faut faire de tout produit de la vente détenu ou bien saisi par le shérif.*)

APPENDIX 7.1 Chakravarty v. Complete Home Renovations: Request for Clerk's Order on Consent (Form 11.2A) *continued*

FORM / *FORMULE* 11.2A PAGE 3 SC-00-80011-00

Claim No. / *N° de la demande*

☐ withdraw the Writ of Seizure and Sale of Personal Property issued against: (Name of debtor(s))
le retrait du bref de saisie-exécution de biens meubles délivré contre : *(Nom du/de la/des débiteur(s)/débitrice(s))*

and directed to the bailiff of the :
et adressé à l'huissier de (Small Claims Court location / *Emplacement de la Cour des petites créances*)

(Provide instructions about what is to be done with any proceeds held by the clerk of the court or property that has been seized by the bailiff. / *Donnez des instructions sur ce qu'il faut faire de tout produit de la vente détenu par le greffier du tribunal ou de tout bien saisi par l'huissier.*)

☐ terminate the Notice of Garnishment or Notice of Renewal of Garnishment issued against:
la fin de l'avis de saisie-arrêt ou de l'avis de renouvellement de la saisie-arrêt délivré contre :

(Name of debtor(s) / *Nom du/de la/des débiteur(s)/débitrice(s)*)

and directed to :
et adressé à (Name of garnishee / *Nom du tiers saisi*)

(Provide instructions about what is to be done with any money held by the clerk of the court. / *Donnez des instructions sur ce qu'il faut faire de toute somme d'argent détenue par le greffier du tribunal.*)

☐ note that payment has been made in full satisfaction of an order or terms of settlement
le constat qu'un paiement intégral a été effectué en exécution d'une ordonnance ou des conditions de la transaction

☐ dismiss the: ☐ Plaintiff's Claim ☐ Defendant's Claim
le rejet de la : *demande du demandeur* *demande du défendeur*

☒ costs in the amount of $ 300.00 , to be paid to **Amrita Chakravarty**
le versement de (Amount / *Montant*) *$ au titre des dépens à* (Name of party(ies) / *Nom de la ou des parties*)

by **Complete Home Renovations Inc.**
par (Name of party(ies) / *Nom de la ou des parties*)

The originally scheduled trial date is less than 30 days away and I request that the clerk make the following order(s) on the consent of all parties and any person to be added or substituted :
La date du procès fixée à l'origine tombe dans moins de 30 jours et je demande au greffier de rendre l'ordonnance ou les ordonnances suivantes sur consentement de toutes les parties et de toute personne qui doit être jointe ou substituée :
(Check appropriate boxes. / *Cochez les cases appropriées.*)

☐ amend a Plaintiff's Claim issued on , 20 .
la modification de la demande d'un demandeur délivrée le
(Attach two (2) copies of the amended Plaintiff's Claim. / *Annexez deux (2) copies de la demande du demandeur modifiée.*)

☐ amend a Defence filed on , 20 .
la modification d'une défense déposée le
(Attach two (2) copies of the amended Defence. / *Annexez deux (2) copies de la défense modifiée.*)

APPENDIX 7.1 Chakravarty v. Complete Home Renovations: Request for Clerk's Order on Consent (Form 11.2A) *continued*

FORM / *FORMULE* 11.2A　　　　　PAGE 4　　　　　SC-00-80011-00

Claim No. / *N° de la demande*

☐ amend a Defendant's Claim issued on _____ , 20 ____ .
la modification de la demande d'un défendeur délivrée le
(Attach two (2) copies of the amended Defendant's Claim. / Annexez deux (2) copies de la demande du défendeur modifiée.)

☐ add _____
la jonction de　　　　　　　　(Name of party / *Nom de la partie*)

to the　☐ Plaintiff's Claim　　　☐ Defendant's Claim
à la　　*demande du demandeur*　　　*demande du défendeur*

as a　☐ defendant　　　☐ Plaintiff
à titre de　*défendeur/défenderesse*　*demandeur/demanderesse*

☐ delete _____
la radiation de　　　　　　　(Name of party / *Nom de la partie*)

from the　☐ Plaintiff's Claim　　☐ Defendant's Claim
de la　　*demande du demandeur*　　*demande du défendeur*

☐ substitute _____
la substitution à　　　　　　(Name of party / *Nom de la partie*)

with _____
de　　　　　　　　　　(Name of party / *Nom de la partie*)

in the　☐ Plaintiff's Claim　　☐ Defendant's Claim
dans la　*demande du demandeur*　*demande du défendeur*

December 15 _____ , 20 --　　　　　_____ , 20 ____

(Signature of party consenting / *Signature de la partie qui consent*)　　(Signature of party consenting / *Signature de la partie qui consent*)

Amrita Chakravarty　　　　**Franklin Butler for Complete Home Renovations Inc.**
(Name of party consenting / *Nom de la partie qui consent*)　　(Name of party consenting / *Nom de la partie qui consent*)

(Signature of witness / *Signature du témoin*)　　(Signature of witness / *Signature du témoin*)

Paralegal name　　　　**Witness name**
(Name of witness / *Nom du témoin*)　　(Name of witness / *Nom du témoin*)

_____ , 20 ____　　　　_____ , 20 ____

(Signature of party consenting / *Signature de la partie qui consent*)　　(Signature of party consenting / *Signature de la partie qui consent*)

(Name of party consenting / *Nom de la partie qui consent*)　　(Name of party consenting / *Nom de la partie qui consent*)

(Signature of witness / *Signature du témoin*)　　(Signature of witness / *Signature du témoin*)

(Name of witness / *Nom du témoin*)　　(Name of witness / *Nom du témoin*)

SCR 11.2.01-11.2A (June 1, 2009 / *1er juin 2009*) CSD　　Continued on next page / *Suite à la page suivante*

APPENDIX 7.1 Chakravarty v. Complete Home Renovations: Request for Clerk's Order on Consent (Form 11.2A) *concluded*

DISPOSITION: *The clerk of the court will complete this section.*
DÉCISION : Le greffier du tribunal remplit cette partie.

☐ order to go as asked
ordonnance de procéder comme il a été demandé

☐ order refused because:
ordonnance refusée pour les motifs suivants :

_____, 20 _____   _____
                                              (Signature of clerk / *Signature du greffier*)

APPENDIX 7.2 Parrish v. Thurston: Motion for Set Aside of Noting in Default and Default Judgment (Form 15A)

ONTARIO

Superior Court of Justice
Cour supérieure de justice

Notice of Motion and Supporting Affidavit
Avis de motion et affidavit à l'appui
Form / *Formule* 15A Ont. Reg. No. / *Régl. de l'Ont.* : 258/98

Brampton Small Claims Court / *Cour des petites créances de* **7755 Hurontario Street** **Brampton, Ontario** **L6W 4T6** Address / *Adresse* **905 456 4700** Phone number / *Numéro de téléphone*	**SC-00-45678-00** Claim No. / *N° de la demande*

Plaintiff No. 1 / *Demandeur n° 1* ☐ Additional plaintiff(s) listed on attached Form 1A.
Le ou les demandeurs additionnels sont mentionnés sur la formule 1A ci-jointe.

Last name, or name of company / *Nom de famille ou nom de la compagnie* **Parrish**		
First name / *Premier prénom* **Maxwell**	Second name / *Deuxième prénom*	Also known as / *Également connu(e) sous le nom de*
Address (street number, apt., unit) / *Adresse (numéro et rue, app., unité)* **c/o Prior Mustafa LLP**		
City/Town / *Cité/ville*	Province	Phone no. / *N° de téléphone*
Postal code / *Code postal*		Fax no. / *N° de télécopieur*
Representative / *Représentant(e)* **Prior Mustafa LLP Attention: Marie Prior**		LSUC # / *N° du BHC* ######
Address (street number, apt., unit) / *Adresse (numéro et rue, app., unité)* **22 County Court Boulevard**		
City/Town / *Cité/ville* **Brampton**	Province **Ontario**	Phone no. / *N° de téléphone* **905 111 2222**
Postal code / *Code postal* **A1A 2B3**		Fax no. / *N° de télécopieur* **905 111 2233**

Defendant No. 1 / *Défendeur n° 1* ☐ Additional defendant(s) listed on attached Form 1A.
Le ou les défendeurs additionnels sont mentionnés sur la formule 1A ci-jointe.

Last name, or name of company / *Nom de famille ou nom de la compagnie* **Thurston**		
First name / *Premier prénom* **Frank**	Second name / *Deuxième prénom*	Also known as / *Également connu(e) sous le nom de*
Address (street number, apt., unit) / *Adresse (numéro et rue, app., unité)* **c/o Paxton Limones PC**		
City/Town / *Cité/ville*	Province	Phone no. / *N° de téléphone*
Postal code / *Code postal*		Fax no. / *N° de télécopieur*
Representative / *Représentant(e)* **Paxton Limones PC Attention: Anna Limones**		LSUC # / *N° du BHC* ######
Address (street number, apt., unit) / *Adresse (numéro et rue, app., unité)* **82 Main Street, Suite 11**		
City/Town / *Cité/ville* **Brampton**	Province **Ontario**	Phone no. / *N° de téléphone* **905 888 9999**
Postal code / *Code postal* **L1N 2P3**		Fax no. / *N° de télécopieur* **905 888 0000**

SCR 15.01-15A (June 1, 2009 / *1er juin 2009*) CSD

APPENDIX 7.2   Parrish v. Thurston: Motion for Set Aside of Noting in Default and Default Judgment (Form 15A) *continued*

FORM / *FORMULE* 15A   PAGE 2   SC-00-45678-00

Claim No. / *N° de la demande*

THIS COURT WILL HEAR A MOTION on   December 21   , 20 -- , at   9:30 a.m.   ,
LE TRIBUNAL PRÉCITÉ ENTENDRA UNE MOTION le   , *à*   (Time / *heure*)

or as soon as possible after that time, at   7755 Hurontario Street, Brampton, Ontario, Courtroom 7A
ou dès que possible par la suite à/au   (Address of court location and courtroom number / *Adresse du tribunal et numéro de la salle d'audience*)

Complete Part A or Part B below, then complete the affidavit in support of motion on page 3. / *Remplissez la partie A ou la partie B ci-dessous. Remplissez ensuite l'affidavit à l'appui de la motion à la page 3.*

A.   This motion will be made in person by   Frank Thurston   ,
La motion sera présentée en personne par :   (Name of party / *Nom de la partie*)

for the following order : / *en vue d'obtenir l'ordonnance suivante :*

☒   the court's permission to extend time to   (Specify)
l'autorisation du tribunal de proroger le délai pour   (Précisez)

file a defence   .

☒   set aside default judgment and noting in default.
l'annulation du jugement par défaut et la constatation du défaut.

☐   set aside noting in default.
l'annulation de la constatation du défaut.

☒   permission to file a Defence.
l'autorisation de déposer une défense.

☐   permission to file a Defendant's Claim.
l'autorisation de déposer une demande du défendeur.

☐   terminate garnishment and/or withdraw writ(s).
la mainlevée de la saisie-arrêt ou le retrait d'un ou de plusieurs brefs, ou les deux.

☒   Other:
Autre :
Costs of this motion to be paid by the plaintiff to the defendant.

☒   ADDITIONAL PAGES ARE ATTACHED BECAUSE MORE ROOM WAS NEEDED.
DES FEUILLES SUPPLÉMENTAIRES SONT ANNEXÉES EN RAISON DU MANQUE D'ESPACE.

☐   DOCUMENTS ARE ATTACHED.
PIÈCES JOINTES.

NOTE:	IF YOU FAIL TO ATTEND AN IN-PERSON MOTION, an order may be made against you, with costs, in your absence. If you want to attend the motion by telephone or video conference, complete and file a Request for Telephone or Video Conference (Form 1B). If the court permits it, the clerk will make the necessary arrangements and notify the parties [R. 1.07(5)].
REMARQUE :	*SI VOUS NE VOUS PRÉSENTEZ PAS EN PERSONNE À L'AUDITION DE LA MOTION, une ordonnance peut être rendue contre vous en votre absence, avec dépens. Si vous voulez assister à l'audition de la motion par conférence téléphonique ou vidéoconférence, remplissez et déposez la Demande de conférence téléphonique ou vidéoconférence (formule 1B). Si le tribunal l'autorise, le greffier prendra les dispositions nécessaires et en avisera les parties [par. 1.07 (5)].*

SCR 15.01-15A (June 1, 2009 / *1er juin 2009*) CSD   Continued on next page / *Suite à la page suivante*

APPENDIX 7.2 Parrish v. Thurston: Motion for Set Aside of Noting in Default and Default Judgment (Form 15A) *continued*

Claim No. / *N° de la demande*

B.   This motion in writing for an assessment of damages is made by
La présente motion par écrit en vue d'une évaluation des dommages-intérêts est présentée par

(Name of plaintiff / *Nom du demandeur/de la demanderesse*)

who asks the court for an order assessing damages against
qui demande au tribunal de rendre une ordonnance d'évaluation des dommages-intérêts contre

(Name of defendant(s) / *Nom du/de la/des défendeur(s)/défenderesse(s)*)

who have/has been noted in default.
qui a/ont été constaté(e)(s) en défaut.

AFFIDAVIT IN SUPPORT OF MOTION / *AFFIDAVIT À L'APPUI DE LA MOTION*

My name is Frank Thurston
Je m'appelle   (Full name / *Nom et prénoms*)

I live in Brampton, Ontario
J'habite à   (Municipality & province / *Municipalité et province*)

I swear/affirm that the following is true:
Je déclare sous serment/j'affirme solennellement que les renseignements suivants sont véridiques :

Set out the facts in numbered paragraphs. If you learned a fact from someone else, you must give that person's name and state that you believe that fact to be true.
Indiquez les faits sous forme de dispositions numérotées. Si vous avez pris connaissance d'un fait par l'entremise d'une autre personne, vous devez indiquer le nom de cette personne et déclarer que vous croyez que ce fait est véridique.

See Schedule A attached and forming part of this affidavit

APPENDIX 7.2   Parrish v. Thurston: Motion for Set Aside of Noting in Default and Default Judgment (Form 15A)   *continued*

FORM / *FORMULE* 15A   PAGE 4   SC-00-45678-00
                                                             Claim No. / *N° de la demande*

AFFIDAVIT IN SUPPORT OF MOTION, continued / *AFFIDAVIT À L'APPUI DE LA MOTION, suite*

See Schedule A attached and forming part of this affidavit

If more space is required, attach and initial extra pages. / Si vous avez besoin de plus d'espace, annexez une ou des feuilles supplémentaires et paraphez-les.

Sworn/Affirmed before me at **Brampton**
Déclaré sous serment/Affirmé   (Municipality / *municipalité*)
solennellement devant moi à

in **Ontario**
en/à/au   (Province, state or country / *province, État ou pays*)

on **December 9**   , 20 --   _____
le   Commissioner for taking affidavits
                                  Commissaire aux affidavits
                                  (Type or print name below if signature is illegible.)
                                  (Dactylographiez le nom ou écrivez-le en caractères d'imprimerie ci-dessous si la signature est illisible.)

Signature
(This form is to be signed in front of a lawyer, justice of the peace, notary public or commissioner for taking affidavits.)
(La présente formule doit être signée en présence d'un avocat, d'un juge de paix, d'un notaire ou d'un commissaire aux affidavits.)

WARNING: IT IS AN OFFENCE UNDER THE *CRIMINAL CODE* **TO KNOWINGLY SWEAR OR AFFIRM A FALSE AFFIDAVIT.**
AVERTISSEMENT : FAIRE SCIEMMENT UN FAUX AFFIDAVIT CONSTITUE UNE INFRACTION AU CODE CRIMINEL.

SCR 15.01-15A (June 1, 2009 / *1er juin 2009*) CSD

Schedule A

1. I am the defendant in this action and have personal knowledge of the following.

2. On March 1, 20—, the plaintiff loaned me $27,000.00 pursuant to a promissory note of the same date. Under the terms of the note, the entire amount was due in full on September 1, 20—. Interest at a rate of 12% per annum began to accrue in the event of default of payment on September 1, 20—. Interest continues to accrue until such time as any amounts owing pursuant to the note are paid in full. A true copy of the promissory note dated March 1, 20— is attached as Exhibit 1.

3. When I borrowed the money, I was employed full-time by XRZ Networks Inc. at an annual salary of $40,000.00. I was also doing freelance work. I used the money to pay some business debts and purchase necessary equipment and supplies for my business. I anticipated that I would be able to pay the full amount back on the due date, with the proceeds from a couple of the freelance projects.

4. My employment with XRZ Networks Inc. was terminated abruptly on June 15, 20—. I immediately began seeking other employment, but the market for my type of work is very competitive, and the results of my job search were disappointing. Because of the uncertainty about when I would find paid employment, I decided to use my employment insurance benefits for my living expenses, and set aside the money that I had saved from my employment earnings and freelance work to be used if I was still unemployed when my benefits ran out.

5. I phoned Mr. Parrish several times in July and August and left voicemails advising him that I had lost my job and would not be able to pay the amount due on the note on September 1. He did not return my calls.

APPENDIX 7.2   Parrish v. Thurston: Motion for Set Aside of Noting in Default and Default Judgment (Form 15A)   *continued*

6. I am advised by my paralegal, Anna Limones, and believe that according to the affidavit of service in the court file, the plaintiff's claim was served on November 3, 20— by leaving a copy with one of my former roommates at Unit 103, 45 Labrador Court and delivering another copy to that address by courier. I did not receive the plaintiff's claim. I lived at the Labrador Court address for a brief period in September 20—. I moved back to Brampton in early October. I have been living at my parents' home in Brampton since then.

7. I received the default judgment dated December 1, 20— because it was forwarded to my Brampton address by Canada Post. When I received the default judgment, I promptly sought legal assistance. I have tried to contact a former roommate at the Labrador Court address to find out what happened with the plaintiff's claim, but the number is out of service.

8. On December 1, 20—, I found full-time employment, at an annual salary of $39,000.00. I am in a position to pay the amount claimed by the plaintiff in installments. I wish to file a defence with a proposal of terms of payment.

By his signature hereto, the undersigned FRANK THURSTON acknowledges receipt of the sum of TWENTY-SEVEN THOUSAND DOLLARS ($27,000.00), paid by Maxwell Parrish to Frank Thurston on today's date. The entire principal amount shall be due and payable in full on September 1, 20—. In the event of default by Frank Thurston, interest shall accrue at a rate of 12% per annum until such time as all amounts owing are paid in full or judgment is obtained, and post-judgment interest shall accrue on the judgment amount at a rate of 12% per annum until such time as the judgment is paid in full.

Date: *March 1, 20—*

Signed: *Frank Thurston*
Frank Thurston

This is Exhibit 1
to the affidavit of Frank Thurston
sworn before me at Brampton, Ontario
on December 9, 20—

Anna Limones

A commissioner etc.

Offers to Settle and Settlement Conferences

8

LEARNING OUTCOMES

After reading this chapter, you will understand:

- The duty to encourage compromise and settlement

- Restrictions on disclosure of settlement discussions

- When and how to make or accept an offer to settle

- How to finalize settlement

- The consequences of failing to comply with the terms of settlement

- The costs consequences of failing to accept an offer to settle

- The purpose of the settlement conference

- The role of the court at the settlement conference

Introduction

A paralegal has a professional duty to advise and encourage a client to compromise and settle a dispute if settlement can be achieved on a reasonable basis.

The *Rules of the Small Claims Court* also encourage considering compromise and settlement from the outset of a proceeding. Defendants are encouraged to settle by Rule 9.03, which states that a defendant may admit liability for all or part of the amount claimed and make a proposal of terms of payment in the defence filed with the court. If the plaintiff does not dispute the defendant's proposal within 20 days of service of the defence, the proposal of terms of payment is deemed to be accepted and the defendant may begin paying money into court in accordance with its terms, as if it were a court order.

Rule 14—Offer to Settle sets up a detailed process for making and accepting offers to settle as the action goes forward from the pleadings stage. Rule 14.01.1 states that an offer, an acceptance, and a notice of withdrawal of offer shall be in writing. There are court forms that may be used for each of these steps (Forms 14A, 14B, and 14C). There is also a court form for recording the terms of a settlement in writing (Form 14D).

The parties are given a further opportunity to come to an agreement at the settlement conference. The Small Claims Court settlement conference is intended, among other things, to narrow and resolve the issues and to facilitate settlement of the action (Rule 13.03(1)).

The parties may continue to negotiate settlement up until any time before a final disposition of the matter. Depending on the result obtained at trial, there may be adverse costs consequences for a party who does not accept an offer to settle that is made seven or more days before the trial and remains open until the trial. See Rule 14.07, discussed below.

The Professional Duty to Encourage Settlement

The *Paralegal Rules of Conduct* (the "Paralegal Rules") and the *Paralegal Professional Conduct Guidelines* (the "Guidelines") impose a professional obligation on paralegals to encourage compromise and settlement. Paralegal Rule 3.02(5) states that a paralegal shall advise and encourage a client to compromise or settle a dispute whenever it is possible to do so on a reasonable basis.

Compromise and Settlement

The costs of legal proceedings are not just monetary. There is also a certain amount of wear and tear on the parties and on others associated with the matter. Litigation tends to keep alive grievances and ill-feeling that might otherwise dissipate over time. It can be very stressful, and it is often time-consuming. **Compromise and settlement** (also called "compromising your damages") means that the parties to a dispute agree to waive some part of what is owing or to make other concessions in order to resolve a matter without the additional costs, delay, and uncertainty of continuing a legal proceeding.

You should encourage your client to make an offer to settle as early as possible in a proceeding (Paralegal Guideline 7, paragraphs 5–7). Before making an offer to settle, you should discuss possible terms with your client, and obtain his informed instructions as to what those terms should be. You should confirm those instructions in writing. You should allow the other party reasonable time for review and acceptance of the offer.

When you receive an offer to settle from another party, you should review the offer with your client. You should explain its terms, and the implications of accepting or refusing the offer or making a counter-offer. Whatever your recommendation, you should explain your reasons to the client and ensure that the client understands them. The client's instructions should be confirmed in writing.

In a negotiation, a person making an offer is called an **offeror.** A person receiving an offer is called an **offeree.**

Negotiating Settlement (Rule 14)

General

A settlement agreement in a court action is a contract that is intended to bring the litigation to an end, so long as the parties perform its terms.

As with any contract, for a settlement agreement to be legally binding, there must be an offer, acceptance, and **consideration**. Consideration is something that causes a party to enter into a contract or agreement. It has been defined as "some right, interest, profit or benefit accruing to the one party, or some forbearance, detriment, loss or responsibility given, suffered or undertaken by the other" (see *Currie v. Misa*).

Consent by the parties to the terms of the settlement agreement must be *informed*—that is, the parties must have enough information about what they are signing and any risks or benefits to themselves to make an intelligent decision about whether or not to sign. There must be no **duress** or **misrepresentation**. Duress is threatening someone or otherwise forcing her to agree to something she would not have agreed to without the threat or use of force. Misrepresentation is giving an inaccurate, untrue, or incomplete version of the facts—in the case of a settlement, an inaccurate or incomplete version of the terms or implications of the agreement, with the result that one or more of the parties signing does not have a real understanding of the potential risks or disadvantages of what he is agreeing to.

BOX 8.1 What Exactly Is Consideration?

Consideration is a legal concept deriving from the 19th-century common law of contract. You will find a list of things that the courts have called consideration below. The list is not exhaustive.

Note: A **promisor** is a person who makes a promise. A **promisee** is a person who benefits from a promise.

Consideration may be:

- a right bargained for by the promisee;

- indirect benefits to the promisor;

- liability or risk assumed, right relinquished, disadvantage experienced, or change of legal status by promisee, so long as the detriment is at the promisor's request; or

- 10 peppercorns (Lord Denning).

Contract law also applies to the negotiation itself. You must know the rules of offer and acceptance, and when they add up to an agreement.

To begin with, you need to know the difference between an **offer** and an **invitation to treat**. An offer contains all essential terms. If an offer is accepted, the result is a binding contract that can be performed. An invitation to treat, on the other hand, is intended to do nothing more than open up negotiations. An invitation to treat lacks at least some essential terms, such as a fixed amount of money to be paid, terms of payment, and so on.

BOX 8.2 Invitation to Treat

A common example of an invitation to treat is an advertisement of a house for resale in a newspaper or on the Internet. There are pictures of the house, along with a brief description of its best features, and, in some cases, a price. In most housing markets, it is understood that the description is intended to emphasize the house's best features (and may not be accurate), that the price (whether or not it is advertised) is negotiable, and that closing the deal will be subject to certain conditions, including conveyance of clear title to the land and, in some cases, a satisfactory report by a building inspector. In other words, the advertisement is designed to invite negotiation with potential purchasers—it is not a firm offer.

Table 8.1 is a basic outline of the law of offer and acceptance. Keep in mind that contracts or settlement agreements are often the result of prolonged negotiation.

When negotiating a settlement with opposing parties, you must negotiate in good faith—that is, with a view to achieving a settlement that both parties can live with, so long as that result can be achieved without prejudice to your client. Negotiation is about ascertaining the goals of the parties, and working toward an agreement that will achieve those goals. When negotiating, you should represent your client's interests resolutely and fearlessly, but that does not mean trying to hammer the other party into the ground. This is why a settlement negotiation is also called *compromise* and settlement—because a settlement cannot be achieved unless both parties compromise, or make trade-offs, in order to achieve their own goals and avoid the expense, stress, and uncertain outcomes of litigation.

Negotiating settlement with self-represented parties presents unique challenges. The self-represented party must understand that you are acting exclusively in the interests of your own client. Unsophisticated individuals will sometimes mistake politeness and professionalism for sympathy with their own case. You must be very careful not to encourage this misconception, and you must be very careful also not to say anything to a self-represented party that could be mistaken for legal advice. See Paralegal Rule 4.05, excerpted below:

4.05 When a paralegal is dealing on a client's behalf with an unrepresented person, the paralegal shall,

(a) urge the unrepresented person to obtain independent representation;

(b) take care to see that the unrepresented person is not proceeding under the impression that his or her interests will be protected by the paralegal; and

(c) make clear to the unrepresented person that the paralegal is acting exclusively in the interests of the client and accordingly his or her comments may be partisan.

TABLE 8.1 Negotiating an Agreement

ACTION	RESPONSE	LEGAL RESULT
• Party A makes an invitation to treat or negotiate	• Party B responds	• Negotiation begins; may or may not result in a binding contract
• Party A makes an offer containing all the essential terms, including the offer's expiry date	• Party B does not respond	• Offer expires on the date stated in the offer*
• Party A makes an offer containing all the essential terms • No expiry date	• Party B does not respond	• Party A may withdraw the offer by serving notice of withdrawal of offer (Form 14C) on Party B*
• Party A makes an offer containing all the essential terms, including expiry date	• Party B rejects the offer	• Party A's offer becomes void when it is rejected
• Party A makes an offer containing all the essential terms, including expiry date	• Party B accepts the offer before it expires	• The parties have a binding agreement
• Party A makes an offer containing all the essential terms, including expiry date	• Party B makes a counter-offer containing all the essential items before the offer expires	• If Party A accepts Party B's counter-offer, there is a binding agreement • If Party A does not accept Party B's counter-offer before it expires, there is no deal and negotiations end or start all over again with a new offer by one of the parties

* Exception: A defendant makes a proposal of terms of payment in the defence (Form 9A). If the plaintiff does not dispute the proposal within 20 days, the plaintiff is deemed to have accepted the proposal, and the defendant may commence making the payments as if the proposal were a court order.

Offer to Settle (Form 14A)

General

An offer to settle, an acceptance of an offer to settle, and a withdrawal of an offer to settle shall be made in writing (Rule 14.01.1(1)). An offer to settle may be made in Form 14A. An acceptance of an offer to settle may be made in Form 14B. A withdrawal of an offer to settle may be made in Form 14C.

There are some exceptions to the requirement that an acceptance of an offer to settle shall be in writing. For example, a defendant's proposal of terms of payment in a defence is deemed to be accepted if the plaintiff does not dispute the proposal within 20 days of service (see Rule 9.03 and discussion below). If an offer by a plaintiff to settle a claim in return for a payment of money by a defendant includes a term that the money is to be paid into court, the defendant may accept the offer only by paying the money into court and notifying the plaintiff of the payment (Rule 14.05(2)).

An offer to settle may be made at any time (Rule 14.02(1)).

An offer to settle does not have to be made using Form 14A. However, it must be in writing, and it must be signed and dated by the party making the offer or her legal representative.

Never make an offer to settle on a client's behalf without first discussing the offer with your client, and ensuring that the client understands the risks and benefits of the offer, and agrees to its terms. You should confirm the client's instructions in writing.

Terms of an Offer to Settle

When drafting an offer to settle on behalf of your client, you must remember that, if it is accepted, it becomes a binding agreement between the parties, to be confirmed by the terms of settlement. You must take care to include all essential terms for performance of the agreement. At a minimum, the offer to settle should include the following:

1. The settlement amount, including interest and costs, if any.

2. How the settlement amount is to be paid.

   a. If the settlement amount is to be paid by lump sum (one payment), that should be stated in the offer, along with the manner of payment (for example, bank draft or certified cheque, or by credit card to the trust account of the offeror's legal representative), to whom the payment should be directed, and the date by which the payment is to be paid. If the settlement funds are to be paid into your trust account, the offer should state that the money is to be paid to you in trust.

   b. If the settlement amount is to be paid in installments, the offer to settle should state the amount, frequency, start date for payment, due date thereafter, how payments are to be made (for example, by postdated cheques, bank drafts, etc.).

   c. If the settlement amount is to be paid into court, the offer should include a term to that effect. See Rules 14.05(2) and (3), and discussion below.

3. If interest is accruing on the settlement amount, the interest rate, the document authorizing the interest rate, if any (loan agreement, promissory note, and so on), and how interest is calculated.

4. A date after which the offer is no longer available for acceptance. If no such term is stated in the offer, you must serve a notice of withdrawal of offer on the other side if you wish to withdraw it. Where an offer contains a date after which it can no longer be accepted, it is deemed to be withdrawn on the day after that date if it has not been accepted (Rule 14.03(2)).

5. If the offer is not made in Form 14A, it should state that, in the event of a default in payment, the defaulting party will be deemed to consent to a court order for the amount owing plus costs. The amount of costs payable on default should be reasonable and should be specified in the offer. If the offer does not contain such a term, or if the offer is made in Form 14A, Rule 14.06 will apply in the event of a default. Rule 14.06 states that if a party to an accepted offer to settle fails to comply with its terms, the party not in default may (a) make a motion to the court for judgment in terms of the accepted offer; or (b) continue the proceeding as if there had been no offer to settle.

BOX 8.3 When May You Pay Yourself Out of Settlement Funds Held in Your Trust Account?

You are permitted to pay outstanding legal fees and disbursements out of settlement funds held in your trust account to the credit of a client matter if:

- the settlement funds are payable to the client;
- you discussed the arrangement with the client at the initial consultation and confirmed it in writing in the retainer agreement or engagement letter;
- all parties have signed full and final releases; and
- you deliver a final invoice for fees and disbursements to the client before moving the money from your trust account to your general account.

The balance remaining should be paid to the client unless the client has directed you to do otherwise in writing. If you are paying the balance by trust cheque, it should be delivered with the final reporting letter and invoice.

In no circumstances may you pay yourself from settlement funds held in your trust account on behalf of the client to be paid to another party.

Terms Set Out in the Rules

Many of the terms that should be contained in an offer to settle are stated in the Rules. This means that, if a party fails to include an important term in the offer (such as the deadline for accepting the offer), the Rules will fill in the gaps. This protects self-represented parties who are not accustomed to drafting offers to settle or terms of settlement.

Here are the terms set out in the Rules:

1. Withdrawal of offer (Rule 14.03(1)): If the offer does not state a date and time when the offer is no longer available for acceptance, the party making the offer may withdraw the offer at any time before acceptance by serving a notice of withdrawal (Form 14C).

2. Deemed withdrawal (Rule 14.03(2)): If the offer contains a deadline for acceptance, and it is not accepted on or before that date, it is deemed to be withdrawn on the day after the stated deadline. The Form 14A offer to settle contains a term stating the date after which the offer is no longer available for acceptance. All the party making the offer has to do is fill in the date.

3. No acceptance of offer after court has disposed of the claim (Rule 14.03(3)): Disposition of a claim happens when the court makes a final order in the matter. Offers to settle may remain open until the court makes a final order.

    Rule 14.05(1) complements Rules 14.03(1), (2), and (3). Rule 14.05(1) states that an offer to settle may be accepted by serving acceptance of the offer on the party who made it at any time before the offer is withdrawn, or the court disposes of the action. An acceptance of offer must be in writing (Rule 14.01.1(1)), and may be made using Form 14B.

4. Payment into court (Rules 14.05(2) and (3)): A plaintiff's offer to settle may include a term that the money shall be paid into court. If the defendant pays the money into court and notifies the plaintiff, that is deemed to be acceptance of the plaintiff's offer (Rule 14.05(2)). The defendant's notification to the plaintiff of payment of money into court should be in writing.

    A request to clerk (Form 9B) may be completed when money is paid into court. A copy of the offer to settle should be attached when payment into court is made pursuant to the offer. See Figure 8.1. If the payment into court is to or for a person under disability or is made pursuant to a statutory provision, a request to pay money into or out of court must be completed. See Appendix 4.3 in Chapter 4 at page 159.

    If a defendant offers to pay money to a plaintiff to settle a claim, the plaintiff may make it a term of acceptance that the defendant pay the settlement amount into court. When paying the money into court, the defendant must complete and file a request to clerk (Form 9B), with a copy of the plaintiff's acceptance attached. If the defendant fails to pay the money into court, it is deemed to be a default, and the plaintiff may make a motion to the court for judgment in the terms of the accepted offer, or continue the proceeding as if there had been no offer to settle (Rules 14.05(3) and 14.06).

5. Costs (Rule 14.05(4)): A written offer to settle should always include a term as to costs. If the offer is silent as to costs, Rule 14.05(4) applies. Rule 14.05(4) restricts a costs award to disbursements—that is, the offering party's out-of-pocket expenses, such as court filing fees. Rule 14.05(4) does not address legal fees that must be paid by a party who is represented.

    If an accepted offer to settle does not deal with costs, a plaintiff who accepts a defendant's offer to settle is entitled to disbursements assessed to the date the plaintiff was served with the offer (Rule 14.05(4)(a)). If the accepted offer was made by the plaintiff, the plaintiff is entitled to disbursements assessed to the date that the notice of acceptance of offer was served (Rule 14.05(4)(b)).

You will find a sample of an offer to settle in Form 14A in Appendix 8.1 to this chapter.

FIGURE 8.1 Request to Clerk: Payment of Money into Court Pursuant to a Written Offer to Settle (Form 9B)

FORM / *FORMULE* 9B **PAGE 2**

____
Claim No. / *N° de la demande*

☐ accept payment in the amount of $ ____________ into court
accepter que le paiement de (Amount / *montant*) *$ soit consigné au tribunal,*

☐ according to an order of the court, dated ____________, 20 ____.
conformément à une ordonnance du tribunal datée du

☐ for a person under disability according to an order or settlement dated
au nom d'un incapable, conformément à une ordonnance ou à une transaction datée du

____________, 20 ____ [R. 4.08(1)].
[par. 4.08 (1)].

☐ pursuant to the attached written offer to settle, dated ____________, 20 ____ [R. 14.05(2)].
aux termes de l'offre de transaction écrite ci-jointe datée du *[par. 14.05 (2)].*

☐ according to the following legislation:
conformément à la disposition législative suivante :

____.
(Name of statute or regulation and section / *Titre de la loi ou du règlement et mention de l'article*)

☐ Other: (Specify.)
Autre : *(Précisez.)*

____________, 20 ____ ____________________
(Signature of party or representative / *Signature de la partie ou du/de la représentant(e)*)

CAUTION:	To obtain an assessment of damages, all defendants must be noted in default. If one or more defendants has filed a defence, the matter must proceed to a settlement conference. To bring a motion in writing for an assessment of damages, file a Notice of Motion and Supporting Affidavit (Form 15A). You can get forms at court offices or online at www.ontariocourtforms.on.ca.
AVERTISSEMENT :	*Pour obtenir une évaluation des dommages-intérêts, tous les défendeurs doivent être constatés en défaut. Si un ou plusieurs défendeurs ont déposé une défense, l'affaire doit*

BOX 8.4 Why Is a Term About Payment of Costs Important in a Plaintiff's Offer to Settle?

Plaintiff commences a claim for $10,000.00 plus pre- and post-judgment interest of 12% on February 1, 20—. Plaintiff is an infrequent claimant, who has retained a paralegal as its representative. The court fee for issuing the claim is $75.00.

Defendant files a defence and serves a defendant's claim for $2,500.00. Plaintiff files a defence to defendant's claim. The court filing fee for the defence to defendant's claim is $40.00.

Plaintiff makes a written offer to settle for $7,000.00, which is served on Defendant on April 4, 20—. Defendant accepts the offer.

If there is no term as to costs in the plaintiff's offer to settle, what is the plaintiff entitled to under Rule 14.05(4)(b)?

Plaintiff is entitled to the total disbursements assessed to the date the offer was served—that is, an amount not exceeding $100.00 for preparation of the plaintiff's claim (Rule 19.01(4)), $75.00 for issuing the plaintiff's claim, $40.00 for filing the defence to defendant's claim, and an amount not exceeding $60.00 for each person served with the claim (Rule 19.01(3)).

If there is a term as to costs in the plaintiff's offer to settle, what is the plaintiff entitled to?

If Defendant accepts the offer to settle, the costs payable become a term of the settlement. The amount of costs, exclusive of disbursements, shall not exceed the maximum stated in s. 29 of the *Courts of Justice Act*—that is, 15 percent of the amount claimed. In this case, the amount claimed was $10,000.00. Plaintiff may ask for costs in any amount up to 15 percent of $10,000.00—that is, $1,500.00, exclusive of disbursements.

Accepting an Offer

An offer may be accepted at any time before the deadline for acceptance stated in the offer. If there is no deadline for acceptance stated in the offer, it may be accepted at any time up until a notice of withdrawal is served.

Regardless of whether informal, spoken negotiations have been going on, both offer and acceptance shall be in writing. If you are acting for the party making the offer, you must discuss the risks and advantages of making the offer with your client; obtain informed, written instructions from the client as to the terms of the offer; and if appropriate arrange for the client to review and approve the written offer before it is forwarded to the other side. If you are acting for the party accepting the offer, you must review the offer with your client; discuss the risks and advantages of accepting the offer; and obtain informed, written instructions to accept or reject the offer, or to make a counter-offer.

You will find a sample of an acceptance of offer to settle in Form 14B at Appendix 8.2 to this chapter. You will find a sample of terms of settlement in Form 14D at Appendix 8.3 to this chapter.

Failure to Comply with Accepted Offer (Rule 14.06)

If a party to an accepted offer to settle made in Form 14A fails to comply with the terms of the offer, the other party may

1. make a motion to the court for judgment according to the terms of the accepted offer (Rule 14.06(a)); or

2. continue with the proceeding as if there had been no offer to settle (Rule 14.06(b)).

Deadline for Acceptance of Offer

When making an offer to settle, it is standard practice to include a term stating the deadline for acceptance of the offer. If it is not accepted, the offer is deemed to have been withdrawn on the day after that date. The Form 14A—Offer to Settle contains a term to this effect. See Figure 8.2.

If an offer to settle does not state a date after which it is no longer available for acceptance, then the party making the offer may withdraw the offer at any time before it is accepted, by serving a notice of withdrawal of an offer to settle on the party to whom it was made. A withdrawal of an offer to settle must be in writing. A withdrawal of an offer to settle may be made in Form 14C.

When May Settlement Discussions Be Disclosed to a Judge? (Rule 14.04)

The general rule is that settlement discussions, including offers to settle, should never be disclosed to a judge at any stage of the action, subject to the exceptions discussed below. The assumption is that a judge who is aware of settlement discussions may develop a bias against a party he perceives as being unreasonable, which will prevent him from being an impartial adjudicator.

There are two exceptions to the rule that settlement discussions shall not be disclosed to judges:

1. Settlement negotiations and offers to settle may be revealed to the judge who presides at a settlement conference. This encourages free and frank discussion of the issues and promotes settlement of the matter, which is one of the objectives of a settlement conference. See the discussion of Rule 13.02 below.

2. Settlement negotiations and offers to settle may be raised after the trial judge has made a final decision at trial (Rule 14.04). At that point, the reasonableness of a party's conduct in failing to accept an offer to settle may be considered by the judge when making an order as to costs.

FIGURE 8.2 **Offer to Settle (Form 14A)**

FORM / *FORMULE* 14A   PAGE 2

_____
Claim No. / *N° de la demande*

3.   This offer to settle is available for acceptance until _____ , 20 -- .
      L'acceptation de la présente offre de transaction peut se faire jusqu'au

This offer to settle may be accepted by serving an acceptance of offer to settle (Form 14B may be used) on the
party who made it, at any time before it is withdrawn or before the court disposes of the claim to which the offer
applies [R. 14.05(1)]. You can get forms at court offices or online at www.ontariocourtforms.on.ca.
*La présente offre de transaction peut être acceptée en signifiant une acceptation de l'offre de transaction (la
formule 14B peut être utilisée) à la partie qui l'a faite, avant que l'offre ne soit retirée ou avant que le tribunal ne
décide la demande qui en fait l'objet [par. 14.05 (1)]. Vous pouvez obtenir des formules aux greffes des
tribunaux ou en ligne à l'adresse www.ontariocourtforms.on.ca.*

_____ , 20 --   _____
                                           (Signature of party or representative making offer / *Signature de la partie ou
                                           du/de la représentant(e)*)

                                           _____
                                           (Name, address and phone number of party or representative / *Nom,
                                           adresse et numéro de téléphone de la partie ou du/de la représentant(e)*)

Costs Consequences of Failure to Accept an Offer to Settle (Rule 14.07)

Before discussing Rule 14.07, it will be useful to review what legal costs mean, and
the general rule with respect to awards of costs.

> ### BOX 8.5 Review: What Are Costs?
>
> Costs are money amounts that the court orders one party to pay to another party,
> as reimbursement for legal fees and disbursements. Costs are awarded in addition
> to any other relief that may be ordered.
>
> The general rule is that costs are awarded to the **successful party**, to reimburse
> the successful party for expenses incurred in the course of the proceeding. These
> expenses include the party's representation fees, plus disbursements for out-of-
> pocket expenses such as court fees, witness fees, expert reports, and so on.

Rule 14.07 sets out special rules for costs awards to parties who refuse to accept reasonable offers to settle made prior to the trial. These special rules are set out in Table 8.2.

The costs awards set out in Rule 14.07 are discretionary—that is, the court may choose to follow Rule 14.07 or not, depending on the circumstances.

How does Rule 14.07 play out in terms of real money? The first thing to remember is that Rule 14.07 will apply only after there has been a trial. This means it must be read together with Rule 19.

Rule 19.01(1) states that a successful party is entitled to have his reasonable disbursements, including the cost of preparing a plaintiff's or defendant's claim or a defence, effecting service, and expenses for travel, accommodation, photocopying, and experts' reports, paid by the unsuccessful party, unless the court orders otherwise.

The amount assessed for preparing a plaintiff's or defendant's claim or a defence shall not exceed $100.00 (Rule 19.01(4)). The amount assessed for effecting service shall not exceed $60.00 for each person served unless the court is of the opinon that there are special circumstances that justify assessing a greater amount (Rule 19.01(3)).

Rule 19.04 states that, if the successful party is represented by a lawyer, student-at-law, or agent, the court may allow a reasonable representation fee at trial or at an assessment hearing. Rule 19.02 states that any power under Rule 19 to award costs is subject to s. 29 of the *Courts of Justice Act*, which limits an award of costs, exclusive

TABLE 8.2 Rule 14.07—Costs Consequences of Failure to Accept Offer to Settle

RULE NUMBER	PARTY MAKING OFFER	CONDITIONS	RESULT AT TRIAL	POTENTIAL COSTS CONSEQUENCES
14.07(1)	• Plaintiff makes offer to defendant	• Offer made at least 7 days before the trial • Offer is not withdrawn before the trial • Defendant does not accept offer	• Plaintiff obtains a judgment that is as favourable as or more favourable than the terms of the offer	• Costs awarded to *plaintiff* • Court *may* award costs to successful plaintiff equal to twice the costs of the action (exclusive of disbursements) • Rule 14.07(1) costs award is *discretionary*, not mandatory. • Court may consider the reasonableness of defendant in failing to accept plaintiff's offer to settle when deciding whether Rule 14.07(1) should be applied
14.07(2)	• Defendant makes offer to plaintiff	• Offer made at least 7 days before the trial • Offer is not withdrawn before the trial • Plaintiff does not accept offer	• Plaintiff obtains a judgment that is as favourable as or less favourable than the terms of the offer	• Costs awarded to *defendant* • Court *may* award costs to defendant equal to twice the costs the plaintiff (as successful party) is entitled to from the date the offer was served • Rule 14.07(2) costs award is *discretionary*, not mandatory • Court may consider the reasonableness of plaintiff in failing to accept defendant's offer to settle when deciding whether Rule 14.07(2) should be applied

of disbursements, to not more than 15 percent of the amount claimed or the value of the property sought to be recovered unless the court considers it necessary in the interests of justice to penalize a party or a party's representative for unreasonable behaviour in the proceeding.

The Settlement Conference (Rule 13)

General

A settlement conference is an informal meeting before a judge, deputy judge, or referee. A referee is a non-judge who is authorized by Rule 21.01(1)(b) to conduct settlement conferences. A referee shall not make a final decision at a settlement conference, but shall report her findings and recommendations to the court (Rule 21.01(2)).

A settlement conference must be held in every defended action—that is, every action where at least one party disputes another party's claim (Rule 13.01(1)). The court clerk is responsible for setting the date for the settlement conference (Rule 13.01(2)). The settlement conference must be held within 90 days after the first defence is filed (Rule 13.01(3)). If there is only one defendant, the settlement conference must be held within 90 days after the sole defendant files her defence with the court.

The clerk is required to send each party a blank list of proposed witnesses (Form 13A) along with the notice of settlement conference (Rule 13.01(2)).

BOX 8.6 How Does Rule 14.07 Work?

Plaintiff's offer to settle (Rule 14.07(1)): Plaintiff commences an action against Defendant for $4,000.00. Plaintiff is represented by a paralegal. Defendant is self-represented. Plaintiff makes an offer to settle for $3,500.00 including costs. The offer is made 30 days before the trial date, and has not expired or been withdrawn at the time the trial commences. Defendant, who is self-represented, does not accept the offer.

Having heard the evidence at trial, the court awards Plaintiff $3,800.00 and requests submissions as to costs.

All issues of liability and the relief to be granted have now been determined, with the exception of costs. The parties may now disclose any offers to settle or related negotiations to the trial judge (Rule 14.04). Plaintiff is the successful party and is entitled to her costs, including a reasonable representation fee.

As well, there was a plaintiff's offer to settle that was not accepted. When making submissions as to an appropriate award of costs, Plaintiff's paralegal may refer to Rule 14.07(1). The Rule 14.07(1) criteria are met—that is, Plaintiff obtained a judgment that is more favourable than the terms of the offer; the offer was

made at least seven days before the trial; and the offer was not withdrawn and did not expire before the trial. Therefore, subject to s. 29 of the *Courts of Justice Act*, the court may award Plaintiff an amount not exceeding twice her costs of the action.

Applying s. 29 of the *Courts of Justice Act* and Rule 19.04, Plaintiff is entitled to a maximum representation fee of 15 percent of the amount claimed of $4,000.00—that is, $600.00. When awarding costs for representation fees, the court cannot exceed this amount (Rule 19.02), unless the court considers it necessary in the interests of justice to penalize Defendant or Defendant's representative for unreasonable behaviour in the proceeding (*Courts of Justice Act*, s. 29).

Several courts have ruled that failure to accept a reasonable offer to settle in circumstances where Rule 14.07 applies is unreasonable behaviour in the proceeding triggering the exception to the 15 percent cap on costs set out in s. 29, and have awarded double costs pursuant to Rule 14.07, accordingly. See *Melara-Lopez v. Richarz*, wherein the court stated, quoting Deputy Judge Winny in *Beatty v. Reitzel Insulation Co.*:

[80] In my view, the cost consequences of a party's failure to accept a reasonable offer should be meaningful consequences if they are to encourage settlements in a meaningful way. To interpret s. 29 as if it were a de facto bar or effective cap on the operation of SCCR 14.07 is undesirable and unwarranted based on the legislative text and purpose and the need for a reasonable and just rule dealing with the cost consequences of offers to settle in this court. It would tend to undermine the court's discretion to impose cost consequences where parties inflate or exaggerate their claims and will encourage parties to claim unreasonable amounts by allowing them to do so without fear of any real cost consequences.

[81] I find that the proviso in *Courts of Justice Act* s. 29, dealing with penalizing a party for unreasonable behaviour should be applicable in conjunction with a party's failure to accept a reasonable offer to settle under SCCR 14.07. If a party fails to accept a reasonable offer to settle and that rule is triggered, then the party is deemed to have behaved unreasonably. That unreasonable behaviour should permit SCCR 14.07 to operate in tandem with the court's discretion under the proviso in s. 29.

[82] Accordingly, SCCR 14.07 can be applied to award double costs even if the double amount exceeds the 15% *prima facie* limit under s. 29.

In *Melara-Lopez v. Richarz*, the defendant made an offer to settle before the action was commenced. In this case, Plaintiff made an offer to settle, which meets the criteria of Rule 14.07, and was not accepted by Defendant, but that offer was made 30 days before the trial date, and Defendant was self-represented. The court may consider both of these factors when making its decision about whether the offer justifies an exception to s. 29 of the *Courts of Justice Act* that would trigger an order of double costs under Rule 14.07.

Defendant's offer to settle (Rule 14.07(2)): Plaintiff commences an action against Defendant for $3,300.00. Defendant makes an offer to settle for $2,500.00. The offer is made immediately after the settlement conference, and has not expired at the time the trial commences.

At trial, both Plaintiff and Defendant are represented by paralegals. After hearing the evidence, the court awards Plaintiff $2,200.00 and requests submissions as to costs.

All issues of liability and the relief to be granted have now been determined, with the exception of costs. The parties may now disclose any offers to settle or related negotiations to the trial judge (Rule 14.04). Ordinarily, Plaintiff as the successful party would be entitled to her costs, including a reasonable representation fee not exceeding 15 percent of the amount claimed of $3,300.00—that is, $495.00 (*Courts of Justice Act*, s. 29). However, there was a defendant's offer to settle that was not accepted. The Rule 14.07(2) criteria triggering costs in favour of the defendant are met—that is, Plaintiff obtained a judgment that is less favourable than the terms of Defendant's offer; the offer was made at least seven days before the trial; and the offer was not withdrawn and did not expire before the trial. When making submissions as to an appropriate award of costs, Defendant's paralegal may refer to Rule 14.07(2), and also to *Melara-Lopez v. Richarz*.

Applying the *Melara-Lopez v. Richarz* rule, Defendant may request double costs from the date the offer to settle was served. The court may order costs to Defendant in an amount up to $990.00 if the court is satisfied that Plaintiff's refusal to accept Defendant's offer was unreasonable in the proceeding.

In Conclusion: Advise your client about Rule 14.07 and s. 29 of the *Courts of Justice Act*. If it is possible to do so without prejudice to your client, encourage compromise and settlement on a reasonable basis. Make a reasonable offer to settle early and leave it open. If the matter goes to trial and it is appropriate to do so, keep Rule 14.07 and the *Melara-Lopez v. Richarz* rule in mind when you are making submissions as to costs.

As part of your preparation for making submissions as to a costs award in a matter, you should consider preparing a **bill of costs**. A bill of costs is an itemized list of a party's representation fees and disbursements, supported by documentation such as dockets, copies of invoices, and so on. A bill of costs is not required by the *Rules of the Small Claims Court*, but you may refer to the format of Form 57A Bill of Costs of the *Rules of Civil Procedure*, which is used when assessing fees and disbursements in the Superior Court of Justice. You will find a sample bill of costs at Appendix 9.3 in Chapter 9 at page 398.

Purposes of a Settlement Conference

As its name indicates, the primary purpose of a settlement conference is to promote settlement of the action, where appropriate. The rule that a settlement conference shall be scheduled by the clerk within 90 days of the filing of the first defence is intended to promote early settlement in matters where that is possible. Where settlement is not possible, or is not possible at the time when the settlement conference is held, according to Rule 13.03(1), the settlement conference may be used to:

- resolve or narrow the issues in the action;
- expedite a final resolution of the action;
- encourage settlement of the action;
- assist the parties in preparation for trial; and
- provide full disclosure between the parties of the relevant facts and evidence.

Because the settlement conference is intended to promote settlement, the parties and their legal representatives must be able to discuss all issues freely and frankly (Rule 13.03(3)). Free and frank discussion includes disclosing any settlement discussions that have taken place to that point. Thereafter, except as otherwise provided in the Rules or with the consent of the parties, the matters discussed at the settlement conference, including disclosure of settlement negotiations to that date, shall not be disclosed to others until after the action has been disposed of (Rule 13.03(4)).

Preparing for a Settlement Conference

Disclosure

The general rule in Small Claims Court actions is that full and fair disclosure should take place as early as possible in the proceeding. Early disclosure lets the parties know the case they have to meet, and promotes early settlement because it helps them to assess the strengths and weaknesses of their own case and that of their opponent.

See Rules 7.01(2), 9.02(2), and 10.01(4)2, which require that copies of all documents on which a claim or defence is based be attached to the claim or defence. If a document is unavailable, the claim or defence shall state the reason why the document is not attached.

Rule 13.03(2) sets out an additional disclosure requirement. At least 14 days before the date of the settlement conference, each party or his legal representative shall serve the other parties with copies of any documents (including an expert report) that were not attached to the claim or defence, and file them with the court (Rule 13.03(2)(a)). Each party shall also serve and file a list of proposed witnesses and any other persons with knowledge of the matters in dispute in the action (Rule 13.03(2)(b)).

The court may award costs against a person who attends a settlement conference without having filed the material required by Rule 13.03(2) (Rule 13.02(7)).

Other Issues to Consider

When you receive the notice of settlement conference, you should contact your client immediately with the date, time, and location of the conference, and advise her that it is mandatory to attend the settlement conference.

If you are unable to attend on the date set for the settlement conference, you should contact the court office and request an adjournment to another date. You should consider contacting the other side to advise them that you are asking for an adjournment and request some mutually convenient dates.

When preparing for a settlement conference, you should do a thorough review of the contents of the client file, including the pleadings, disclosure, motions if any, offers to settle, counter-offers, and so on. Even if no settlement is achieved, thorough preparation for the settlement conference means more effective representation for your client at the settlement conference. It also gives you a head start on getting ready for trial.

If a person who attends a settlement conference is so ill-prepared that it frustrates the purposes of the conference set out in Rule 13.03(1) from being carried out, the court may order costs against that person (Rule 13.02(7)(a)).

When reviewing the client file in preparation for the settlement conference, consider the following (the list is not exhaustive):

- What issues are in dispute? What issues are not in dispute?
- What are the strengths of your client's case? What are its weaknesses?
- Are there any documents, written statements, or audio or visual records that you require from other parties? Prepare a list.
- Are there any documents, written statements, or audio or visual records that you have not yet provided to other parties?
- If yes, and you have the documents and so on in your possession, you should ensure that, at least 14 days before the date of the settlement conference,
  - the additional disclosure is served on all other parties, and
  - copies of the additional disclosure, along with proof of service on other parties, are filed with the court.
- If you do not yet have the documents and so on in your possession, you should prepare a list of all documents not yet disclosed, and produce the list to the court and the other party or parties at the settlement conference. The additional disclosure shall be served at least 30 days before the trial date on all parties who were served with a notice of trial.
- Who are your witnesses? At least 14 days before the date of the settlement conference, you must:
  - complete and serve a list of proposed witnesses on all other parties, and
  - file a copy of the list of proposed witnesses along with proof of service on all other parties with the court.
- When compiling your list of witnesses, keep in mind that, under Rule 18.02(1), at least 30 days before the trial date you may serve on all parties who were served with a notice of trial, a document or written statement or audio or visual record, and it shall be received in evidence, unless the trial judge orders otherwise. Opposing parties who wish to cross-examine the witness or author of the document may summon her or him as a witness under Rule 18.02(4). Persons whose written documents or statements, including

expert reports, you intend to rely upon at trial should be included on your list of proposed witnesses, although you are not required to summon them to appear in person.

- Do you require an expert report? If you have not already obtained and served an expert report on other parties in accordance with Rule 13.03(2), you shall disclose it on your list of documentary disclosure not yet in your possession. Upon obtaining it, you shall serve it at least 30 days before the trial date on all parties who were served with a notice of trial, and file proof of service with the court. See discussion above.

- Have you received a list of proposed witnesses or their documents or written statements or audio or visual records from other parties? If not, why not? Follow up with other parties or their representatives, and, if necessary, with the judge at the settlement conference. If other parties intend to rely upon documents or written statements, you will need to review those documents and written statements before the trial in order to decide whether you need to summon the author(s) for purposes of cross-examination on their contents under Rule 18.02(4).

Procedure at a Settlement Conference (Rule 13.02)

Attendance

The parties and, if they are represented, their representatives shall participate in the settlement conference, unless the court orders otherwise (Rule 13.02(1)). A party who attends must have authority to settle the matter. If a party requires another person's approval before agreeing to settlement, that party shall arrange to have telephone access to the other person throughout the conference, whether the conference takes place during or after regular business hours (Rule 13.02(2)).

It is mandatory for the parties and their legal representatives to attend the settlement conference (Rule 13.02(1)). Participation may be by personal attendance, or by telephone or video conference if those facilities are available at the court (Rules 13.02(1)(b) and 1.07). A party who wishes to conduct the settlement conference by telephone or video conference must file a request for telephone or video conference (Form 1B), stating the reasons for the request. If a judge grants the request, the court will make the necessary arrangements and notify the parties.

If a party who has received a notice of settlement conference fails to attend at the settlement conference, the court may impose appropriate sanctions, including an order requiring her to pay the other party's costs (Rule 13.02(5)(a)). The costs of a settlement conference shall not exceed $100.00 unless the court orders otherwise because there are special circumstances (Rule 13.10). The court may also order that an additional settlement conference be held (Rules 13.02(3) and (5)(b)).

Rule 13.02(6) sets out special sanctions for a non-attending defendant in the following circumstances. If a defendant

1. fails to attend a first settlement conference,
2. receives notice of an additional settlement conference, and

3. fails to attend the additional settlement conference,

the court may strike out the defence and dismiss the defendant's claim, if any, and allow the plaintiff to prove the plaintiff's claim without a trial, or make such other order as is just.

What to Bring to a Settlement Conference

You should bring with you the following:

- the *Rules of the Small Claims Court*;
- a calculator;
- your calendar to check available dates for trial;
- copies of pleadings and offers to settle (if any);
- statement of facts;
- list of disputed issues;
- list of proposed witnesses or authors of documents and written statements upon which you intend to rely at trial;
- any case law or legislation on which you intend to rely at trial, with copies for all parties and the court; and
- any disclosure not produced prior to the settlement conference, with copies for all parties and the court.

What Happens at a Settlement Conference?

A settlement conference is conducted informally. It may take place in a court office or meeting room. The parties and their representatives sit at a table with the judge or referee. It is a private meeting. No members of the public are allowed to attend.

A judge, deputy judge, or referee may conduct a settlement conference. The judge or deputy judge who conducts the settlement conference is prohibited from presiding at the trial, if any (Rule 13.08). Referees cannot make court orders or preside at trials. A referee who presides at a settlement conference shall report his findings and recommendations to the court (Rule 21.01(2)). Based on those recommendations, a judge may make any order that may be made under Rule 13.05(1) or (2).

A settlement conference judge may make recommendations to the parties on any matter relating to the conduct of the action, in order to fulfill the purposes of the settlement conference as set out in Rule 13.03(1). A recommendation is not the same thing as a court order. It is a suggestion only, with which the parties may or may not choose to comply. Among other things, the judge may make recommendations with respect to (Rule 13.04):

1. clarification and simplification of issues in the action;
2. getting rid of claims or defences that appear to be unsupported by the evidence and/or the law; and
3. admission of certain facts or documents without further proof at trial.

A settlement conference judge may make any order relating to the conduct of the action that the court could make, including but not limited to the following (Rules 13.05(1) and (2)):

1. adding or deleting parties;

2. consolidating actions (that is, taking two separate actions with the same parties and similar issues, and combining them into one action so that they can be tried together);

3. staying (or stopping) the action;

4. amending or striking out a claim or defence on grounds that it discloses no reasonable cause of action or defence, may delay or prejudice a fair trial, or has no legal merit (Rule 12.02(1));

5. staying or dismissing a claim;

6. directing production of documents;

7. changing the place of trial under Rule 6.01;

8. directing an additional settlement conference under Rule 13.02(3);

9. ordering costs; and

10. at an additional settlement conference, ordering judgment under Rule 13.02(6) against a defendant who fails to attend a first settlement conference, receives notice of an additional settlement conference, and fails to attend the additional settlement conference.

If you are acting for a defendant at a settlement conference, and you have concerns that the court where the action was commenced is not the proper place of trial, you should raise this issue at the settlement conference. You should have legal argument in support of your position prepared, along with case law in support of your argument. You should bring copies of the case law for other parties and the court. The settlement conference judge may then, if appropriate, make an order that the action be tried at another venue. See Rules 6.01(2) and (3).

If the settlement conference is conducted by a referee, a judge may make any of the above orders on the referee's recommendation.

Rule 13.05(4) states that, if all parties consent, a judge may order final judgment at a settlement conference where the matter in dispute is for an amount under the appealable limit (currently $2,500.00 exclusive of interest and costs (*Courts of Justice Act*, s. 31; O. Reg. 626/00, s. 2)). To obtain a judgment at a settlement conference in a matter to which Rule 13.05(4) applies, a party must file a consent in Form 13B signed by all parties before the settlement conference stating that they wish to obtain a final determination of the matter at the settlement conference even if a mediated settlement is not reached (Rule 13.05(4)).

Within 10 days after the judge signs a Rule 13.05(4) order at a settlement conference, the order shall be served on any parties who were not present at the settlement conference by the clerk, by mail or fax in accordance with Rule 8.01(6).

At the end of a settlement conference, the court shall prepare a memorandum on the file (Rule 13.06(1)). The memorandum summarizes the following:

1. any recommendations made under Rule 13.04;

2. the issues remaining in dispute;

3. the matters agreed on by the parties;

4. any relevant evidentiary issues; and

5. information relating to scheduling of the remaining steps in the proceeding.

The memorandum shall be filed with the clerk, who is required to give a copy to the trial judge (Rule 13.06(2)).

A judge who conducts a settlement conference in an action shall not preside at the trial of the action (Rule 13.08).

Additional Matters

After a settlement conference has been held, a claim against a party who is not in default shall not be withdrawn or discontinued by the party making the claim without the written consent of the party against whom the claim is made, or leave of the court (Rule 13.09).

At or after the settlement conference, the clerk shall provide the parties with a notice stating that one of the parties must request a trial date if the action is not disposed of within 30 days after the settlement conference, and pay the fee required for setting the action down for trial (Rule 13.07). A request to clerk (Form 9B) is used to request a trial date. As of this writing, the fee for an infrequent claimant to fix a date for a trial is $100.00. The fee for a frequent claimant to do so is $130.00.

It is the plaintiff's action, so it is the plaintiff's responsibility to move the matter forward. Rule 11.1.01(2) states that, unless the court orders otherwise, the clerk shall make an order dismissing an action as abandoned if the following conditions are satisfied:

1. More than 150 days have passed since the first defence was filed.

2. All settlement conferences required under Rule 13 have been held.

3. The action has not been disposed of by order and has not been set down for trial.

4. The clerk has given 45 days notice to all parties to the action that the action will be dismissed as abandoned.

CHAPTER SUMMARY

Paralegals have a duty to encourage their clients to settle their differences, if a reasonable outcome for the client can be achieved by negotiation.

A settlement agreement in a court action is a contract. As with any contract, there must be an offer, acceptance, and consideration. The offer and acceptance must take place without duress or misrepresentation. The *Rules of the Small Claims Court* state that an offer to settle, an acceptance of an offer to settle, and a notice of withdrawal of an offer to settle shall be made in writing (Rule 14.01.1(1)). The parties may use Forms 14A, 14B, and 14C for these purposes.

A proposal of terms of payment in a defence is the same thing as an offer to settle. If accepted by the plaintiff, or not disputed by the plaintiff within 20 days after service of the defence, it becomes a binding agreement, which has the same effect as a court order.

When drafting an offer to settle, you must take care to include all essential terms for performance of the agreement, including but not limited to the settlement amount, including interest and costs, if any; the terms of payment;

the interest rate, if interest is being paid on the outstanding balance; the date after which the offer is no longer available for acceptance; and the consequences of default in payment, including additional costs, if any.

A settlement conference must be held in every defended action. The purposes of a settlement conference are to resolve or narrow issues in the action, to expedite disposition of the action, to encourage settlement, to assist the parties in effective preparation for trial, and to ensure full disclosure between the parties of the relevant facts and evidence.

A judge who attends at a settlement conference shall not preside at trial.

Settlement negotiations may be revealed to and discussed with the judge at a settlement conference. Where the action is not settled at the settlement conference, settlement discussions may not be disclosed again until after a final order has been made at trial. At that time they may be raised as going to the issue of costs to be paid by one party to another.

KEY TERMS

bill of costs: an itemized list of a party's representation fees and disbursements supported by documentation *(p. 325)*

compromise and settlement: when a party agrees to waive some part of what is owing or make other concessions in order to resolve a matter without the additional costs, delay, and uncertainty of a court proceeding *(p. 313)*

consideration: something that causes a party to enter into a contract; sometimes, but not always, a party's expectation of profiting from or receiving a benefit from the contract *(p. 313)*

duress: threatening someone or otherwise forcing her to agree to something she would not have agreed to without the threat or use of force *(p. 313)*

invitation to treat: an invitation intended to do nothing more than open up negotiations; usually does not contain essential terms, such as a fixed amount of money to be paid, terms of payment, etc. *(p. 314)*

misrepresentation: an inaccurate, untrue, or incomplete version of the facts; in contract law, an inaccurate or incomplete description of the terms of the agreement, with the result that the person signing does not have a real understanding of what he is signing *(p. 313)*

offer: in the context of contracts, an offer containing all essential terms; if accepted, a binding contract is the result *(p. 314)*

offeree: the party receiving an offer *(p. 313)*

offeror: the party making an offer *(p. 313)*

promisee: a person who receives a promise *(p. 314)*

promisor: a person who makes a promise *(p. 314)*

successful party: the party who succeeds, or wins, at trial; it may be the plaintiff or the defendant *(p. 322)*

REFERENCES

Beatty v. Reitzel Insulation Co., [2008] OJ No. 953 (SCJ).

Courts of Justice Act, RSO 1990, c. C.43.

Currie v. Misa (1875), LR 10 Ex. 153; aff'd. 1 App. Cas. 554 (HL).

Law Society of Upper Canada (LSUC), *Paralegal Professional Conduct Guidelines* (Toronto: LSUC, 2008, as amended) ("the Guidelines"); available online at http://www.lsuc.on.ca.

Law Society of Upper Canada (LSUC), *Paralegal Rules of Conduct* (Toronto: LSUC, 2007, as amended); available online at http://www.lsuc.on.ca.

Melara-Lopez v. Richarz, [2009] OJ No. 6313 (SCJ), aff'd. [2009] OJ No. 4362 (Div. Ct.).

Rules of the Small Claims Court, O. Reg. 258/98.

REVIEW QUESTIONS

1. What is a settlement agreement in a court action?

2. What three things are needed for a settlement contract to be legally binding?

3. What is the difference between an offer and an invitation to treat?

4. Is a proposal of terms of payment in a defence the same thing as an offer to settle? If yes, why? If no, why not?

5. Name five terms that an offer to settle should include. Give brief details where necessary.

6. Name five terms that should be contained in an offer to settle, which are implied by the Rules, if they are not included in the offer to settle. Please provide the rule numbers.

7. What happens if a party to an accepted offer made in Form 14A fails to comply with the terms of the offer (in other words, fails to perform the terms of the settlement agreement)?

8. What is the general rule with respect to revealing settlement discussions to a judge? What are two exceptions to the general rule?

9. What are the costs consequences to a plaintiff to whom Rule 14.07(1) applies?

10. What are the costs consequences to a plaintiff to whom Rule 14.07(2) applies?

11. What is a settlement conference, and when must it be held?

12. What are the purposes of a settlement conference? Name five, and cite the authority for your answer.

13. What must a party disclose prior to a settlement conference? Please state the authority for your answer.

14. What are the consequences for a party of failing to attend at a settlement conference?

15. What is the role of the court at a pretrial conference?

APPENDIX 8.1 Chakravarty v. Complete Home Renovations:
Plaintiff's Offer to Settle (Form 14A)

ONTARIO

Superior Court of Justice
Cour supérieure de justice

Offer to Settle
Offre de transaction

Form / *Formule* 14A Ont. Reg. No. / *Régl. de l'Ont.* : 258/98

Brampton

Small Claims Court / *Cour des petites créances de*

**7755 Hurontario Street
Brampton, Ontario
L6W 4T6**

Address / *Adresse*

905 456 4700

Phone number / *Numéro de téléphone*

SC-00-33445-00

Claim No. / *N° de la demande*

BETWEEN / *ENTRE*

Amrita Chakravarty

Plaintiff(s) / *Demandeur(s)/demanderesse(s)*

and / *et*

Complete Home Renovations Inc.

Defendant(s) / *Défendeur(s)/défenderesse(s)*

My name is Amrita Chakravarty
Je m'appelle

(Full name / *Nom et prénoms*)

1.   In this action, I am the
     Dans la présente action, je suis le/la

   ☒   Plaintiff
       demandeur/demanderesse

   ☐   Defendant
       défendeur/défenderesse

   ☐   representative of
       représentant(e) de   (Name of party(ies) / *Nom de la ou des parties*)

2.   I offer to settle this action against Complete Home Renovations Inc.
     Je présente une offre de transaction dans cette action contre   (Name of party(ies) / *Nom de la ou des parties*)

     on the following terms: *(Set out terms in numbered paragraphs, or on an attached sheet.)*
     selon les conditions suivantes : (Indiquez les conditions sous forme de paragraphes numérotés ou sur une feuille annexée.)

     The defendant, Complete Home Renovations Inc., shall pay $2,500.00 plus costs of $400.00, for a
     total amount of $2,900.00, by certified cheque payable to Prior Mustafa LLP in Trust in full and final
     settlement of this claim.

     Said payment shall be delivered to Prior Mustafa LLP to the attention of Joseph Mustafa at or before
     12:00 noon on Friday, January 18, 20--.

SCR 14.01.1-14A (June 1, 2009 / *1ᵉʳ juin 2009*) CSD

APPENDIX 8.1 Chakravarty v. Complete Home Renovations:
Plaintiff's Offer to Settle (Form 14A)   *concluded*

FORM / *FORMULE* 14A   PAGE 2   SC-00-33445-00

Claim No. / *N° de la demande*

3.   This offer to settle is available for acceptance until **12:00 noon, January 18** , 20 **--** .
     L'acceptation de la présente offre de transaction peut se faire jusqu'au

This offer to settle may be accepted by serving an acceptance of offer to settle (Form 14B may be used) on the
party who made it, at any time before it is withdrawn or before the court disposes of the claim to which the offer
applies [R. 14.05(1)]. You can get forms at court offices or online at www.ontariocourtforms.on.ca.
*La présente offre de transaction peut être acceptée en signifiant une acceptation de l'offre de transaction (la
formule 14B peut être utilisée) à la partie qui l'a faite, avant que l'offre ne soit retirée ou avant que le tribunal ne
décide la demande qui en fait l'objet [par. 14.05 (1)]. Vous pouvez obtenir des formules aux greffes des
tribunaux ou en ligne à l'adresse www.ontariocourtforms.on.ca.*

January 3   , 20 **--**

(Signature of party or representative making offer / *Signature de la partie ou
du/de la représentant(e)*)

Prior Mustafa LLP
22 County Court Boulevard
Brampton, Ontario A1A 2B3
TEL: 905 111 2222
Attention: Joseph Mustafa

(Name, address and phone number of party or representative / *Nom,
adresse et numéro de téléphone de la partie ou du/de la représentant(e)*)

NOTE:	**IF YOU ACCEPT AN OFFER TO SETTLE, THEN FAIL TO COMPLY WITH ITS TERMS,** judgment in the terms of the accepted offer may be obtained against you on motion to the court, or the action may continue as if there has been no offer to settle [R. 14.06].
REMARQUE :	*SI VOUS ACCEPTEZ UNE OFFRE DE TRANSACTION MAIS QU'ENSUITE VOUS N'EN OBSERVEZ PAS LES CONDITIONS, un jugement suivant les conditions de l'offre acceptée peut être obtenu contre vous sur présentation d'une motion au tribunal ou l'action peut continuer comme s'il n'y avait jamais eu d'offre de transaction [règle 14.06].*

NOTE:	**IF THIS OFFER TO SETTLE IS NOT ACCEPTED, IT SHALL NOT BE FILED WITH THE COURT OR DISCLOSED** to the trial judge until all questions of liability and relief (other than costs) have been determined [R. 14.04].
REMARQUE :	*SI LA PRÉSENTE OFFRE DE TRANSACTION N'EST PAS ACCEPTÉE, ELLE NE DOIT PAS ÊTRE DÉPOSÉE AUPRÈS DU TRIBUNAL NI DIVULGUÉE au juge du procès tant que toutes les questions relatives à la responsabilité et aux mesures de redressement (à l'exclusion des dépens) n'ont pas été décidées [règle 14.04].*

SCR 14.01.1-14A (June 1, 2009 / *1er juin 2009*) CSD

APPENDIX 8.2 Chakravarty v. Complete Home Renovations:
Defendant's Acceptance of Offer to Settle (Form 14B)

ONTARIO
Superior Court of Justice
Cour supérieure de justice

Acceptance of Offer to Settle
Acceptation de l'offre de transaction
Form / *Formule* 14B Ont. Reg. No. / *Régl. de l'Ont.* : 258/98

Brampton
Small Claims Court / *Cour des petites créances de*
7755 Hurontario Street
Brampton, Ontario
L6W 4T6
Address / *Adresse*

905 456 4700
Phone number / *Numéro de téléphone*

SC-00-33445-00
Claim No. / *N° de la demande*

BETWEEN / *ENTRE*

Amrita Chakravarty

Plaintiff(s) / *Demandeur(s)/demanderesse(s)*

and / *et*

Complete Home Renovations Inc.

Defendant(s) / *Défendeur(s)/défenderesse(s)*

My name is Anna Limones
Je m'appelle   (Full name / *Nom et prénoms*)

1. In this action, I am the
   Dans la présente action, je suis le/la

   ☐ plaintiff
      demandeur/demanderesse

   ☐ defendant
      défendeur/défenderesse

   ☒ representative of **Complete Home Renovations Inc.**
      représentant(e) de   (Name of party(ies) / *Nom de la ou des parties*)

2. I accept the offer to settle from **Amrita Chakravarty**
   J'accepte l'offre de transaction faite par   (Name of party(ies) / *Nom de la ou des parties*)

   dated **January 3**   , 20 -- .
   et datée du

3. This offer to settle has not expired and has not been withdrawn.
   Cette offre de transaction n'est pas expirée et n'a pas été retirée.

January 10   , 20 --

(Signature of party or representative accepting offer / *Signature de la partie ou du/de la représentant(e) qui accepte l'offre*)
Paxton Limones PC
82 Main Street, Suite 11, Brampton, Ontario L1N 2P3
TEL: 905 888 9999
Attention: Anna Limones
(Name, address and phone number of party or representative / *Nom, adresse et numéro de téléphone de la partie ou du/de la représentant(e)*)

CAUTION:	**IF YOU ACCEPT AN OFFER TO SETTLE, THEN FAIL TO COMPLY WITH ITS TERMS,** judgment in the terms of the accepted offer may be obtained against you on motion to the Court, or this action may continue as if there has been no offer to settle [R. 14.06].
AVERTISSEMENT :	*SI VOUS ACCEPTEZ UNE OFFRE DE TRANSACTION MAIS QU'ENSUITE VOUS N'EN OBSERVEZ PAS LES CONDITIONS, un jugement suivant les conditions de l'offre acceptée peut être obtenu contre vous sur présentation d'une motion au tribunal ou la présente action peut continuer comme s'il n'y avait jamais eu d'offre de transaction [règle 14.06].*

SCR 14.01.1-14B (June 1, 2009 / *1ᵉʳ juin 2009*) CSD

APPENDIX 8.3 Terms of Settlement (Form 14D)

ONTARIO

Superior Court of Justice
Cour supérieure de justice

Terms of Settlement
Conditions de la transaction
Form / *Formule* 14D Ont. Reg. No. / *Règl. de l'Ont.* : 258/98

Brampton
Small Claims Court / *Cour des petites créances de*
7755 Hurontario Street
Brampton, Ontario
L6W 4T6
Address / *Adresse*

905 456 4700
Phone number / *Numéro de téléphone*

SC-00-33445-00
Claim No. / *N° de la demande*

BETWEEN / *ENTRE*

Amrita Chakravarty
Plaintiff(s) / *Demandeur(s)/demanderesse(s)*

and / *et*

Complete Home Renovations Inc.
Defendant(s) / *Défendeur(s)/défenderesse(s)*

We have agreed to settle this action on the following terms:
Nous avons convenu de régler la présente action selon les conditions suivantes :

1. Complete Home Renovations Inc. _____ shall pay to
    (Name of party(ies) / *Nom de la ou des parties*) *verse à*

    Amrita Chakravarty _____ the sum of
    (Name of party(ies) / *Nom de la ou des parties*) *la somme de*

    $ _____ 2,900.00 as follows as full and final settlement of the claim, inclusive of interest and costs:
    $ comme suit, à titre de transaction complète et définitive sur la demande, y compris les intérêts et les dépens :

    (Provide terms of payment such as start date, frequency, amount and duration / *Indiquez les modalités de paiement telles que la date de début des versements ainsi que leur fréquence, leur montant et leur durée.*)

    The defendant, Complete Home Renovations Inc., shall pay $2,500.00 plus costs of $400.00, for a total amount of $2,900.00, by certified cheque payable to Prior Mustafa LLP in Trust in full and final settlement of this claim.

    Said payment shall be delivered to Prior Mustafa LLP to the attention of Joseph Mustafa at or before 12:00 noon on Friday, January 18, 20--.

Put a line through any blank space and initial.
Tracez une ligne en travers de tout espace laissé en blanc et apposez vos initiales.

SCR 14D (June 1, 2009 / *1er juin 2009*) CSD

APPENDIX 8.3 **Terms of Settlement (Form 14D)** *concluded*

FORM / *FORMULE* **14D**   **PAGE 2**   SC-00-33445-00
                                                                          Claim No. / *N° de la demande*

2.   This claim (and Defendant's Claim, if any) is withdrawn.
        Cette demande (et celle du défendeur, le cas échéant) est retirée (sont retirées).

3.   If a party to these terms of settlement fails to comply, judgment in the terms of settlement may be obtained
        against that party on motion to the court or this action may continue as if there has been no settlement.
        Si une partie aux présentes conditions de la transaction n'en observe pas les conditions, un jugement
        suivant les conditions de la transaction peut être obtenu contre cette partie sur présentation d'une motion
        au tribunal ou la présente action peut continuer comme s'il n'y avait jamais eu de transaction.

4.   Provided that the terms of settlement are complied with, the parties above fully and finally release one
        another from all claims related to the facts and issues raised in this action.
        Pourvu que les conditions de la transaction soient observées, les parties susmentionnées se dégagent
        l'une et l'autre complètement et définitivement de toutes demandes liées aux faits et questions en litige
        soulevés dans la présente action.

The parties do not need to sign terms of settlement on the same day, but each must sign in the presence of his or her witness who signs a
moment later. (For additional parties' signatures, attach a separate sheet in the below format.)
Les parties ne sont pas tenues de signer les conditions de la transaction le même jour, mais chacune doit les signer en présence de son
témoin, qui les signe à son tour aussitôt après. (S'il y a lieu, annexez une autre feuille portant la signature des parties additionnelles
présentée selon le format indiqué ci-dessous.)

January 11 _____ , 20 --	January 11 _____ , 20 --
_____	_____
(Signature of party / *Signature de la partie*)	(Signature of party / *Signature de la partie*)
Amrita Chakravarty	**Complete Home Renovations Inc.**
	per: Franklin Butler
(Name of party / *Nom de la partie*)	(Name of party / *Nom de la partie*)
_____	_____
(Signature of witness / *Signature du témoin*)	(Signature of witness / *Signature du témoin*)
Joseph Mustafa	**Anna Limones**
(Name of witness / *Nom du témoin*)	(Name of witness / *Nom du témoin*)
_____ , 20 ____	_____ , 20 ____
_____	_____
(Signature of party / *Signature de la partie*)	(Signature of party / *Signature de la partie*)
_____	_____
(Name of party / *Nom de la partie*)	(Name of party / *Nom de la partie*)
_____	_____
(Signature of witness / *Signature du témoin*)	(Signature of witness / *Signature du témoin*)
_____	_____
(Name of witness / *Nom du témoin*)	(Name of witness / *Nom du témoin*)

SCR 14D (June 1, 2009 / *1er juin 2009*) CSD

Trials and Assessment Hearings

9

LEARNING OUTCOMES

After reading this chapter, you will understand:

- Requesting and conducting an assessment hearing
- Requesting a date for trial
- Requesting adjournment of a trial date
- Preparing for trial
- The consequences of a party's failure to attend
- The consequences of a witness's failure to attend
- Courtroom etiquette
- Evidence at a Small Claims Court trial
- Procedure at trial
- Introducing exhibits
- Objections
- Closing submissions
- Costs

Introduction

In an undisputed action for unliquidated damages where all defendants have been noted in default, a plaintiff may file a motion in writing for an assessment of damages, or file a request to clerk for an assessment hearing (Rule 11.03(2)). An **assessment hearing** is similar to a trial except that the defendant is not present and the only issue for the court to determine is the amount of the claim.

If a disputed action is not resolved at the settlement conference, the clerk shall provide the parties with a notice stating that one of the parties must request a trial date if the action is not disposed of within 30 days after the settlement conference, and pay the fee required for setting the action down for trial (Rule 13.07).

Any party may request that the clerk fix a date for trial by attending at the court office, filing a request to clerk (Form 9B), and paying the fee. The clerk then fixes a date for trial and serves a notice of trial on each party who has filed a claim or defence.

Before requesting a date for trial, you should consider getting a list of available dates from the court clerk, and then contacting the other parties or their representatives, if they are represented, and obtaining some mutually agreeable dates for the trial. That way, adjournments and the resulting delay and expense can be avoided.

Full and fair disclosure of the parties' evidence should have taken place at or before the settlement conference. However, if a party intends to submit as evidence at trial a document, written statement, or audio or visual record that has not already been disclosed to all parties entitled to disclosure, the party wishing to introduce the evidence must serve it on all other parties served with the notice of trial at least 30 days before the trial date. The document or record shall then be received in evidence unless the trial judge orders otherwise (Rule 18.02(1)). Written statements must be signed. Written statements or documents must provide the name, address, and telephone number of the author. If the written statement is an expert report, in addition to the name, address, and telephone number of the author, a summary of the author's qualifications must be appended to or included in the document.

If you require an adjournment of the trial date because a witness is unavailable, or you have a scheduling conflict, or for some other good reason, you should contact the court as soon as possible and request that the court adjourn the trial to a later date. Before contacting the court to request an adjournment, you should consider contacting the other parties or their representatives, if they are represented, to advise them that you are asking for an adjournment and to obtain some mutually convenient dates for rescheduling the trial.

If another party advises you that they require an adjournment, you should seek instructions from your client to consent, if the request is reasonable, sufficient notice has been given, and no prejudice to the rights of your client would result. This is in keeping with your professional duty of courtesy and good faith to licensees and others (Paralegal Rule 7.01(2)).

If you require witnesses other than your client to be present at trial, you must serve them personally with a summons to witness and with attendance money at least 10 days before the trial date (Rule 8.01(7)).

The structure of a Small Claims Court trial is the same as that of other civil trials, except that the rules of evidence are relaxed in Small Claims Court. At the commencement of the trial, the judge may request opening submissions. The plaintiff then takes the stand and gives his evidence in support of the claim. He is then cross-examined by the defendant or the defendant's representative. At the end of cross-examination, he may be re-examined with respect to any new issue raised in cross-examination.

If the plaintiff has summoned any additional witnesses to appear in person, those witnesses also take the stand, give evidence, are cross-examined, and are re-examined by the plaintiff with respect to any new issues raised in cross-examination if appropriate.

If the plaintiff has served a document, written statement, or audio or visual record that she intends to rely upon at trial upon all other parties at least 30 days before the trial date, it shall be received in evidence for the plaintiff unless the court orders otherwise (Rule 18.02(1)). A defendant or other party who has been served with a written statement or document by the plaintiff and who wishes to cross-examine the witness or author with respect to its contents may summon him or her to appear at trial for that purpose (Rule 18.02(4)).

When the plaintiff's evidence is concluded, the defendant takes the stand, gives evidence under oath, is cross-examined, and is re-examined if appropriate.

If the defendant has summoned any additional witnesses to appear in person, those witnesses also take the stand, give evidence, are cross-examined, and are re-examined by the defendant with respect to any new issues raised in cross-examination if appropriate.

If the defendant has served a document, written statement, or audio or visual record that he intends to rely upon at trial upon all other parties at least 30 days before the trial date, it shall be received in evidence for the defendant unless the court orders otherwise. A plaintiff or other party who has been served with a written statement or document by the defendant and who wishes to cross-examine the witness or author with respect to its contents may summon him or her to appear at trial for that purpose.

When the evidence for both parties is concluded, the parties or their representatives, if they are represented, may be asked to make closing submissions as to judgment.

Having heard the evidence and closing submissions, the court may give spoken reasons for judgment immediately, take a brief recess before giving its reasons and making an order, or reserve judgment and provide written or spoken reasons at a later date. The court will then ask for submissions as to costs.

An award of costs, excluding disbursements, to a successful party who is represented cannot exceed 15 percent of the amount claimed (*Courts of Justice Act*, s. 29, Rule 19.02).

A successful party who is self-represented may be awarded an amount not exceeding $500.00 as compensation for inconvenience and expense caused by another party (Rule 19.05).

If the court is satisfied that a party has unduly complicated or prolonged an action or has been unreasonable in some other way, the court may order that party to pay an amount as compensation to another party as a penalty (Rule 19.06).

A plaintiff who makes an offer to settle at least seven days before trial that is not accepted by the defendant and is not withdrawn and did not expire before the trial may request an amount of costs not exceeding twice the costs of the action if the plaintiff obtains a judgment as favourable as, or more favourable than, the terms of the offer (Rule 14.07(1)).

A defendant who makes an offer to settle at least seven days before trial that is not accepted by the plaintiff and is not withdrawn and did not expire before the trial may request an amount of costs not exceeding twice the costs awardable to a successful party from the date the offer was served if the plaintiff obtains a judgment as favourable as or less favourable than the terms of the offer (Rule 14.07(2)).

If an amount under Rule 14.07(1) or (2) is awarded to a self-represented party, the court may also award the party an amount not exceeding $500.00 as compensation for inconvenience and expense (Rule 14.07(3)).

General

Assessment Hearings

In a plaintiff's claim for unliquidated damages where all defendants have been noted in default, a plaintiff may

(a) file with the court a motion in writing for an assessment of damages and supporting affidavit, setting out the reasons why the motion should be granted and attaching any relevant documents (Rule 11.03(2)(a), Form 15A); or

(b) file a request to clerk requesting that an assessment hearing be arranged (Rule 11.03(2)(b), Form 9B).

The plaintiff may prefer to resolve the matter by way of a motion in writing, because it does not require a court attendance. On a motion in writing for an assessment of damages, the plaintiff is not required to prove liability against the defendant noted in default, but the affidavit evidence must be sufficiently detailed to prove the amount of the claim (Rule 11.03(5)). For a discussion of the affidavit evidence to be filed in support of a Rule 11.03(2)(a) motion, see Chapter 5, Box 5.6 at page 191. See also Appendix 5.2 at pages 210–223. If a judge finds that a plaintiff's affidavit is inadequate or unsatisfactory, the judge may order that a further affidavit be provided or an assessment hearing be held (Rule 11.03(3)).

> ### BOX 9.1 Application of Rule 11.03
>
> Remember that an unliquidated amount is an amount that is not fixed and specified by a document or other evidence. It must be determined by the court based on all of the evidence.
>
> Rule 11.03 does not apply unless all the defendants in a plaintiff's claim for an unliquidated amount have been noted in default. If there are multiple defendants, and one of them has delivered a defence, the plaintiff must proceed to a settlement conference under Rule 13 and if necessary to trial under Rule 17 in order to obtain a final disposition of the matter (Rule 11.03(7)). However, any defendant who has been noted in default is subject to the consequences set out in Rule 11.05.

Where part of a plaintiff's claim is for a debt or liquidated amount and part is for an unliquidated amount, and a defendant fails to file a defence within the prescribed time, the plaintiff may file proof of service and a request to clerk with the court. The clerk may note the defendant in default and sign judgment against the defendant for the part of the claim that is for a debt or liquidated amount. If all defendants have been noted in default, the procedures set out in Rule 11.03 apply to the part of the claim that is for an unliquidated amount.

An assessment hearing may be held:

1. where the plaintiff requests an assessment hearing (Rule 11.03(2)(b)); or
2. where a judge orders an assessment hearing. A judge may order an assessment hearing where the affidavit evidence filed in support of a Rule 11.03(2)(a) motion in writing is inadequate or unsatisfactory, and the judge requires spoken evidence from witnesses in order to determine the amount owing (Rule 11.03(3)(b)).

Where an assessment hearing is requested by the plaintiff or ordered by a judge, the plaintiff will be required to fix a date for the hearing. The plaintiff must complete a request to clerk (Form 9B) for an assessment hearing to be scheduled. See Figure 9.1 below. The plaintiff or his paralegal then attends at the court office to file the request to clerk and pay the fee. As of this writing, the fee for fixing a date for an assessment hearing for an infrequent claimant is $100.00. The fee for a frequent claimant is $130.00.

An assessment hearing is like a trial (Rule 11.03(4)), except that the defendant is not present, and, as with a motion in writing for an assessment of damages, the plaintiff is not required to prove liability against a defendant noted in default, because the defendant by her default is deemed to admit liability (Rule 11.03(5)). The only issue before the court is how much money the defendant owes the plaintiff.

A judge or deputy judge will preside at an assessment hearing. Section 27 of the *Courts of Justice Act* applies to an assessment hearing, so the court may admit as evidence at the hearing and act upon any oral testimony and any document or other thing so long as the evidence is relevant to the subject matter of the proceeding and is not unduly repetitious. You should prepare for an assessment hearing by marshalling all of the evidence, documentary and otherwise, in support of the amount claimed. Generally, only the plaintiff will be required to attend. However, if you intend to call any witnesses other than the plaintiff, those witnesses must be served personally with a summons to witness and attendance money at least ten days before the hearing date.

Relevant evidence may include expert reports and other documentary evidence, if appropriate, which may be entered as exhibits during spoken testimony by your witnesses. Whatever its nature, the evidence should be presented in an organized and coherent fashion. You should consider preparing a written list of your questions in advance, with notations for documents to be put in as exhibits during that person's testimony. You should also prepare your closing remarks in advance. Your closing remarks should summarize the evidence put before the court in support of the

FIGURE 9.1 Request to Clerk (Form 9B)

BETWEEN / *ENTRE*

_____
Plaintiff(s) / *Demandeur(s)/demanderesse(s)*

and / *et*

_____
Defendant(s) / *Défendeur(s)/défenderesse(s)*

TO THE CLERK OF THE _____ **SMALL CLAIMS COURT:**
AU GREFFIER DE LA COUR   (Name of Small Claims Court location / *Emplacement de la*
DES PETITES CRÉANCES DE   *Cour des petites créances*) :

My name is _____ **and I request that the clerk of the court:**
Je m'appelle   (Name of party/representative / *Nom de la partie ou du/de la*   ***et je demande au greffier du tribunal***
                              représentant(e))   ***de faire ce qui suit :***

(Check appropriate box(es). / Cochez la ou les cases appropriées.)

> *Tick this box to request a date for an assessment hearing.*

☐ note defendant(s) _____
   constater le ou les défendeurs   (Name of defendant(s) / *Nom du/de la/des défendeur(s)/défenderesse(s)*)

   in default for failing to file a Defence (Form 9A) within the prescribed time period [R. 11.01(1)].
   en défaut pour n'avoir pas déposé de défense (formule 9A) dans le délai prescrit [par. 11.01 (1)].

☐ schedule an assessment hearing (all defendants have been noted in default) [R. 11.03(2)(b)].
   fixer la date d'une audience d'évaluation (tous les défendeurs ont été constatés en défaut) [alinéa 11.03 (2) b)].

> *Tick this box to request a date for a trial.*

☐ schedule a terms of payment hearing because I dispute the defendant's proposed terms of payment
   contained in the Defence (Form 9A) [R. 9.03(3)].
   fixer la date d'une audience relative aux modalités de paiement parce que je conteste les modalités de paiement proposées par le défendeur dans la défense (formule 9A) [par. 9.03 (3)].

☐ schedule a trial [R. 16.01(1)(b)].
   fixer une date de procès [alinéa 16.01 (1) b)].

amount claimed, interest, and costs. You should have the numbers, calculations, and legal principles at your fingertips, so that you can refer to them in your submissions.

Fixing a Date for Trial (Rule 16)

General

If the action is not resolved at the settlement conference the clerk will provide the parties with a notice stating that one of the parties must request a trial date and pay the fee if the action is not disposed of within 30 days after the settlement conference (Rule 13.07).

Any party may request that the clerk fix a date for trial (Rule 16.01(1)(b)). However, it is the plaintiff's action, so, generally speaking, the plaintiff is responsible for moving the matter forward, including fixing a date for trial, unless the court orders otherwise or another party (for example, a plaintiff by defendant's claim) chooses to take this step.

When fixing a date for trial, the party or the party's legal representative must complete a request to clerk (Form 9B) for a trial date to be scheduled, and attend at the court office to file the request to clerk and pay the fee. As of this writing, the fee for fixing a trial date for an infrequent claimant is $100.00. The fee for a frequent claimant is $130.00.

The clerk then serves a notice of trial on each party who has filed a claim or defence.

What to Do When You Receive a Notice of Trial

When you receive a notice of trial, you should contact your client and advise him of the date. Tell him that his attendance is mandatory, and advise him to note the date and time in his calendar.

The notice of trial should be filed in your pleadings subfile. The trial date should be noted in your calendar, along with suitable bring-forward dates. It should also be noted in the central tickler, if you maintain one, and on the checklist/tickler in the client file.

You should review the settlement conference endorsement record to find out whether there are any directions, recommendations, or orders by the settlement conference judge that require further action. You should diarize for and ensure that any further action required by you or by other parties is completed by the deadlines stated in the Rules or in the order.

If you intend to put in as evidence at trial a document, written statement, or audio or visual record that has not already been disclosed to all parties entitled to disclosure, you should consider whether you already have the document in your possession, or need to obtain it from a witness or other person, and diarize appropriately for follow-up. Your tickler period should give you time to obtain the document if you do not already have it, and serve it on all other parties served with the notice of trial at least 30 days before the trial date, in accordance with Rule 18.02(1). If a written statement or document served on other parties earlier in the proceeding does not provide the name, telephone number, and address for service of the witness or author, or, in the case of an expert witness, a summary of credentials, as required by Rule 18.02(3), then you should serve the written statement or document again, this time with all of the required information, on all other parties at least 30 days before the trial date.

If you will require the presence of witnesses other than your client at the trial, you shall serve them personally with a summons to witness and attendance money at least ten days before the trial date (Rule 8.01(7)). If you are satisfied that the written statements and documents you have served on other parties in accordance with Rule 18.02(1) are sufficient and will be received in evidence by the court, summoning additional witnesses to appear in person at trial in support of your client's claim or defence will not be necessary.

If you intend to cross-examine the witness of another party on her written statement or document, you must serve the witness with a summons to witness and attendance money at least ten days before the trial date (Rule 8.01(7)). At the same time you shall serve all other parties who have received a notice of trial with a copy of the summons to witness (Rule 18.02(5)).

Some of the above can be done by your personal assistant, if you have one and if he is experienced and reliable. When delegating, keep in mind that you are responsible for all business entrusted to you. You must directly supervise any work delegated to non-licensees (Paralegal Rule 8.01, Guideline 18).

Adjournment of the Trial Date (Rule 17.02)

The court may postpone or adjourn a trial on such terms as are just, including the payment by one party to another of an amount as compensation for inconvenience and expense (Rule 17.02(1)). If the trial of an action has been adjourned two or more times, any further adjournment may be made only on motion with notice to all the parties who were served with the notice of trial, unless the court orders otherwise (Rule 17.02(2)).

Before requesting a date for trial, you should consider contacting the other parties or their representatives, if they are represented, and obtaining some mutually convenient dates for the trial before filing the request to clerk. You can then provide the clerk with a number of dates when all parties can attend. That way, you may avoid the delay and inconvenience of a request for an adjournment by a party who is not available on the trial date.

On receiving a request for an adjournment from another party or their representative, you should consider your duty to agree to reasonable requests concerning trial dates, adjournments, and waiver of procedural formalities and similar matters that do not prejudice the rights of your client, and advise your client accordingly (Paralegal Rule 7.01(2), Guideline 17). When deciding whether a request for an adjournment is reasonable, you should consider whether

1. the party requesting the adjournment has given you reasonable notice;
2. it is the first such request;
3. you are satisfied that they have a good reason for asking; and
4. there are any other relevant considerations, including prejudice to your client.

Never consent to an adjournment without your client's instructions to do so.

If you yourself require an adjournment of a trial date for a very good reason— you have a scheduling conflict, your client is unavailable on the scheduled date, and so on—you should advise all other parties well in advance of the trial date that you require an adjournment, and obtain some mutually convenient dates for the adjournment, if possible. You should contact the court office with your request. If a judge grants your request and orders an adjournment, the clerk will notify all parties of the new date.

BOX 9.2 Adjournments

A judge is not bound to order an adjournment just because the parties have consented to one. The consent of the parties is just one factor that a judge will consider when deciding whether to allow an adjournment. The judge will also look at whether there is a good reason for the adjournment, and whether there have been previous adjournments. See the discussion of Rule 17.02(2) above.

If the judge does not grant the request for an adjournment, the trial will go ahead on the original date. All parties should be present and ready to go on that date. A paralegal who has a scheduling conflict must make any necessary arrangements to avoid prejudicing the client.

Where an adjournment has been agreed to by the parties before the scheduled trial date, the court office should be informed so that the matter can be referred to a judge. If the judge allows the adjournment, the clerk will notify the parties of the new trial date.

Sometimes a party will, without prior notice to other parties, turn up on the trial date to request an adjournment, or send a friend to do so. If the court exercises its discretion to grant the adjournment on such terms as are just under Rule 17.02(1), the other parties should, at a minimum, receive compensation for inconvenience and expense. The other parties should consider requesting that additional terms be imposed, if appropriate.

Failure to Attend at Trial (Rule 17.01)

The consequences of failure to attend at trial, and the remedial action that may be taken by the party who failed to attend, are set out in Rule 17.01 and Table 9.1.

Evidence at Trial (Rule 18)

Application of Rule 18.01

At the trial of an undefended action, the plaintiff's case may be proved by affidavit, unless the trial judge orders otherwise (Rule 18.01).

Rule 18.01 has been carried over from the old *Rules of the Small Claims Court*, before the changes that came into effect on July 1, 2006. Before July 1, 2006, an unliquidated claim that was undefended went to trial. In those circumstances, Rule 18.01 allowed the plaintiff to prove her case by affidavit evidence, unless the trial judge ordered otherwise. Rule 11.03 of the current Rules permits a plaintiff in a claim for an unliquidated amount where all defendants have been noted in default to obtain judgment by filing a motion in writing for an assessment of damages or by requesting an assessment hearing.

Inspection of Property (Rule 17.03)

The trial judge may, in the presence of the parties or their representatives, inspect any real or personal property concerning which a question arises in the action. Real property is tangible, immovable, and has value—in other words, land, or buildings. Personal property is property that is tangible, movable, and has value—for example, vehicles, stocks, jewellery, furniture, etc. The inspection of the real or personal property must take place in the presence of the parties or their representatives.

TABLE 9.1 Failure to Attend at Trial (Rule 17.01)

WHO FAILS TO ATTEND	WHAT THE JUDGE MAY DO	OTHER ISSUES	WHAT AN ABSENT PARTY MAY DO
All parties (Rule 17.01(1))	• Strike the action off the trial list • Make such other order as is just		• Make a motion on notice to all other parties who were served with a notice of trial to have the matter restored to the trial list (Rules 1.03, 2.01, and 15)
A party (Rule 17.01(2)(a))	• Proceed with trial in party's absence • Make such other order as is just		• Make a motion for an order setting aside or varying the judgment, on such terms as are just, where (1) a judgment is obtained against the absent party, and (2) the motion is made within 30 days after the absent party becomes aware of the judgment (Rules 17.01(4) and (5)(a)); or • Make a motion for an order extending the 30-day period if there are special circumstances justifying the extension (Rules 17.01(4) and (5)(b))
Defendant (Rule 17.01(2)(b))	• Strike out defence and dismiss defendant's claim, if any • Allow plaintiff to prove the plaintiff's claim • Plaintiff is not required to prove liability against absent party but is required to prove the amount of the claim (Rule 17.01(2.1)) • Make such other order as is just	• Before making any other order, the judge must consider any issue as to proper place of trial raised under Rule 6.01(1) in the defence, and make a ruling*	• Make a motion for an order setting aside or varying the judgment, on such terms as are just, where (1) a judgment is obtained against the absent party, and (2) the motion is made within 30 days after the absent party becomes aware of the judgment (Rules 17.01(4) and (5)(a)); or • Make a motion for an order extending the 30-day period if there are special circumstances justifying the extension (Rules 17.01(4) and (5)(b))
Plaintiff (Rule 17.01(2)(c))	• Dismiss the plaintiff's action • If there is a defendant's claim, allow the defendant to prove the claim • Make such other order as is just	• Before making any other order, the judge must consider any issue as to proper place of trial raised under Rule 6.01(1) in the defence, and make a ruling*	• Make a motion for an order setting aside or varying the judgment, on such terms as are just, where (1) a judgment is obtained against the absent party, and (2) the motion is made within 30 days after the absent party becomes aware of the judgment (Rules 17.01(4) and (5)(a)); or • Make a motion for an order extending the 30-day period if there are special circumstances justifying the extension (Rules 17.01(4) and (5)(b))

* If the defence contains an allegation that the matter has been brought in the wrong court, the court must consider that allegation and rule on it before making any other order. If the court determines that the matter should have been brought in another territorial jurisdiction, then the court has no legal jurisdiction to make any order in the matter except an order moving the matter to the court with territorial jurisdiction.

Written Statements, Documents, and Records (Rule 18.02)

Disclosure—General

At every stage of a Small Claims Court action, full and fair disclosure of documents is required. The Rule 1.02 definition of "document" includes data and information in electronic form. If a plaintiff's claim is based in whole or in part on a document, the document is required to be attached to each copy of the claim. If the document is unavailable, the claim must state the reason why the document is not attached (Rule 7.01(2)2).

Similar disclosure obligations apply where a defence or defendant's claim is based in whole or in part on a document (Rules 9.02(1)2 and 10.01(4)2).

In a defended action, further disclosure is required at the settlement conference stage. At least 14 days before the date of the settlement conference, each party must serve on all other parties and file with the court (1) a copy of any document to be relied on at the trial, including an expert report, not attached to the party's claim or defence, and (2) a list of proposed witnesses and of other persons who know about the matters in dispute in the action (Rule 13.03(2)).

If the settlement conference judge is not satisfied with a party's disclosure, she may make an order directing further production of documents (Rule 13.05(2)(vi)). The order should state (1) the documents to be disclosed with reasonable specificity; (2) a deadline for completion of the additional disclosure; and (3) the consequences of failure to comply. These conditions fall within a settlement conference judge's discretion to make any order relating to the conduct of the action that the court could make, as set out in Rule 13.05(1).

Pretrial Disclosure—Documents and Written Statements (Rule 18.02)

A document or written statement or an audio or visual record that has been served, at least 30 days before the trial date, on all parties served with a trial notice, shall be received in evidence, unless the trial judge orders otherwise (Rule 18.02(1)).

Note that Rule 18.02(1) captures any documents served on other parties prior to the settlement conference pursuant to Rule 13.03(2), as well as documentary disclosure attached to and served with a pleading.

Rule 18.02(1) is an exception to the hearsay rule. Rule 18.02(1) applies to the following written statements and documents (Rule 18.02(2)):

1. The signed written statement of any witness, including the written report of an expert, to the extent that the written statement relates to facts and opinions that the witness would be permitted to testify about in person.

2. Any other document, including but not limited to
   - a hospital record or medical report made in the course of care and treatment,
   - a financial record,
   - a receipt,

- a bill,
- documentary evidence of loss of income or property damage, and
- a repair estimate.

A party who serves a written statement or document described in Rule 18.02(2) on another party shall append or include in the statement or document the name, telephone number, and address for service of the witness or author (Rule 18.02(3)(a)). If the witness or author is giving expert evidence, a summary of his or her qualifications shall also be provided (Rule 18.02(3)(b)). If a written statement or document served on other parties earlier in the proceeding does not provide all of the information required by Rule 18.02(3), then you should serve the written statement or document again, this time with all of the required information, on all other parties at least 30 days before the trial date.

The Ontario *Evidence Act* permits the following documents to be received in evidence as authentic, absent proof to the contrary (the list is not inclusive):

- books and records of banks (s. 33);
- photographic prints of a promissory note, cheque, receipt, instrument, agreement, document, plan, or other record or book of entry kept by a person (s. 34);
- electronic records (including printouts) (s. 34.1);
- business records made in the usual and ordinary course of business (s. 35); and
- medical records, including a report signed by a practitioner that is obtained by or prepared for a party to an action, or any other report of a practitioner that relates to an action (s. 52).

Summons to Witness (Rule 18.03, Form 18A)

General

The general rule with respect to evidence at trial is that a person whose evidence is material to the conduct of an action should be present at the trial to give his evidence under oath or by affirmation and be cross-examined on that evidence. In order to ensure the attendance of a witness at trial, a **summons to witness** along with attendance money is served personally on that witness. A witness who has been served with a summons to witness has a legal obligation to appear in court and give evidence under oath or affirmation. The evidence must be relevant to issues in the matter, and admissible under the applicable rules of evidence, including the hearsay rule.

Rule 18.03(1) states that a party who requires the attendance of a person in Ontario as a witness may serve the person with a summons to witness (Form 18A) requiring him or her to attend the trial at the time and place stated in the summons. Rule 18.03(2) states that the summons may also require the witness to produce at trial the documents or other things in his or her possession, control, or power relating to the matters in question in the action that are specified in the summons. This language is included in the Form 18A summons, with a space where the party serving the summons may list specific documents and things required to be produced, if known.

If a party has served documents or written statements at least 30 days before the trial date on all parties who were served with the notice of trial, the documents and statements served shall be received in evidence, unless the trial judge orders otherwise (Rule 18.02(1)). This means that a party who intends to rely at trial upon a document or written statement served in accordance with Rule 18.02(1) does not have to summon the witness or author to attend in person to give evidence as to its contents. However, a party who has been served with a written statement or document and wishes to cross-examine the witness or author may summon him or her as a witness (Rule 18.02(4)).

A summons to witness shall be served personally at least ten days before the trial date, and it must be accompanied by attendance money (Rule 8.01(7)). If the person served is the author of a written statement or document who is being summoned under Rule 18.02(4) by a party who wishes to cross-examine the witness on the contents of the written statement or document at trial, the party serving the summons to witness must also serve a copy of the summons on every other party at the same time as service of the summons (Rule 18.02(5)). Service of a summons to witness and payment of attendance money is proven by filing an affidavit of service (Form 8A) with the court (Rule 18.03(4)). Service of a copy of the summons on another party is also proven by filing an affidavit of service with the court. The summons to witness remains in effect until the attendance of the witness is no longer required (Rule 18.03(5)).

BOX 9.3 Greco v. Hardwick: Summons to Witness (Form 18A, Rule 18.02(5))

You will find the factual background and the pleadings in *Greco v. Hardwick* at Chapter 4, Box 4.11 and Appendix 4.4, and at Chapter 6, Box 6.2 and Appendixes 6.1, 6.2, and 6.3.

Background: Juliette Greco commenced an action against James Hardwick for recovery of an amount owing under a promissory note. Mr. Hardwick defended the action on grounds that in lieu of payment of the note, he had provided services to Ms. Greco with her knowledge and consent; that the services had value; and that she had benefited from the services. Mr. Hardwick also served a defendant's claim for recovery of the value of services in excess of the amount owing under the note. In her defence to defendant's claim, Ms. Greco alleged that some of the services provided by Mr. Hardwick could have been obtained at no cost from other sources, and that the values stated for yard and pool maintenance were grossly inflated. In support of her defence to defendant's claim, she relied on invoices from Glenn Woods, her service provider in previous years.

The matter went to settlement conference, but the parties failed to come to an agreement. The trial is scheduled for April 18, 20—. There has been full disclosure by both parties. As part of her disclosure prior to the settlement conference, Ms. Greco served a signed written statement by Glenn Woods attesting to what he would charge for the services provided by Mr. Hardwick.

Mr. Hardwick wishes to summon Mr. Woods for cross-examination at trial on the contents of his written statement.

At Appendix 9.1, you will find the summons to witness served on Glenn Woods by James Hardwick's paralegal, along with affidavits of service of the summons and attendance money on Glenn Woods, and of a copy of the summons to witness on the plaintiff (defendant by defendant's claim), Juliette Greco.

Attendance Money

Attendance money must be served with the summons to witness. Attendance money should be in the form of a firm cheque on your general (operating) account, payable to the witness being summoned. It is a disbursement that can be charged back to your client.

The amount of attendance money required to be paid in a Small Claims Court action is very modest. Attendance money for an ordinary witness is $6.00 per day plus mileage. If the witness is a barrister, solicitor, physician, surgeon, engineer, or veterinary surgeon who is not a party to the action and has been summoned to give evidence of a professional service rendered or to give a professional opinion, the witness money payable is $15.00 per day plus kilometres travelled per day—30 cents per kilometre in southern Ontario, and 30.5 cents per kilometre in northern Ontario (*Kilometre Allowances* regulation to the *Administration of Justice Act*). You will find the *Kilometre Allowances* regulation reproduced at Appendix E to this book.

BOX 9.4 What Is Personal Service?

Your process server goes to serve Mr. Bill Witness with a summons to witness and witness money at his place of business at 10:30 a.m. The process server enters the place of business, approaches Bill Witness, and asks, "Are you Bill Witness?" Mr. Witness says, "Yes I am." The process server hands the summons to witness and the cheque for attendance money to Mr. Witness, and says, "I am serving you with a summons to witness and attendance money."

Bill Witness glances at the summons, and says, "I'm a busy man! I don't have time for this!" He tries to hand the summons and cheque back to the process server. When she refuses to accept them, he throws them on the floor. The process server leaves.

Has personal service taken place?

Yes. The process server obtained personal identification from the person to be served, described the documents being served, and handed them to the witness. What the witness does with the documents after service is irrelevant. Any person who has been served with a summons to witness should comply with the summons. A judge may issue a warrant for the arrest of a witness who fails to comply with a summons (Rule 18.03(6)).

Failure to Attend

A witness who has been properly summoned must attend at court on the specified date and remain in attendance in accordance with the requirements of the summons to witness. If a witness who has been served with a summons to witness fails to attend or does not remain in attendance, the trial judge may issue a warrant (Form 18B) directing all police officers in Ontario to apprehend the witness anywhere in Ontario and bring him or her promptly before the court (Rule 18.03(6)).

The party who summoned the witness may assist the police in apprehending the witness by filing an identification form with the clerk (Form 20K, Rule 18.03(6.1)).

When apprehended, the witness may be detained in custody (that is, put in jail) until his or her presence is no longer required; or the judge may release the witness on such terms as are just. In either case, the witness may be ordered to pay any costs arising out of the failure to attend or to remain in attendance (Rule 18.03(7)).

You will find a sample warrant for arrest of defaulting witness and identification form at Appendix 9.2.

Abuse of Power to Summon a Witness (Rule 18.03(8))

Only persons whose evidence is material to the conduct of an action should be summoned to attend at trial. **Material evidence** is evidence that has a logical connection to an issue or issues in dispute in the action. It is evidence that, on its own or combined with other evidence, helps the trial judge to decide which party's allegations to accept as being true.

If a party summons a witness who has no material evidence to give with respect to the issues in dispute in the action, she wastes the time of the court, the other parties, and the witness. In such cases, the court may order that the party pay compensation for inconvenience and expense directly to the witness.

Interpreters

The Ministry of the Attorney General is required to provide interpreters from English to French or French to English. Interpreters in other languages must be provided by the party requiring their presence.

If a party serves a summons to witness on a witness who requires an interpreter for a language other than English or French, the party must arrange for a qualified interpreter to attend at the trial (Rule 18.03(5.1)).

A **qualified interpreter** is someone who is trained to interpret in a courtroom environment. Interpreters are not under oath when they interpret. They must provide an unbiased and accurate version of what the witness under oath is saying on the stand.

If a party does not comply with the requirement under Rule 18.03(5.1) to provide a qualified interpreter for a witness who requires an interpreter for a language other than English or French, every other party is entitled to request an adjournment of the trial, with costs (Rule 18.03(5.2)).

When Is a Summons to Witness Required in a Small Claims Court Action?

Summons to Witness Not Required

In Small Claims Court, the parties to an action are required to attend at trial, and to take the stand and give relevant evidence under oath or affirmation in support of the claim or defence.

Any witness who is not a party to the action and who is required to give evidence in the action may do so by way of a signed written statement under Rule 18.02(2). Unless the trial judge orders otherwise, the written statement shall be received in evidence, if

- the signed written statement or an appendix thereto states the name, telephone number, and address for service (and, in the case of an expert witness, a summary of qualifications) of the author of the written statement (Rule 18.02(3)); and

- the party relying on the signed written statement serves the statement on all other parties who have received a notice of trial at least 30 days before the trial date (Rule 18.02(1)).

Rule 18.02 is an exception to the hearsay rule. Rule 18.02 should be read in conjunction with s. 27 of the *Courts of Justice Act*, which states:

Evidence

   27(1) Subject to subsections (3) and (4), the Small Claims Court may admit as evidence at a hearing and act upon any oral testimony and any document or other thing so long as the evidence is relevant to the subject-matter of the proceeding, but the court may exclude anything unduly repetitious.

Idem

   (2) Subsection (1) applies whether or not the evidence is given or proven under oath or affirmation or admissible as evidence in any other court.

Idem

   (3) Nothing is admissible in evidence at a hearing,

   (a) that would be inadmissible by reason of any privilege under the law of evidence; or

   (b) that is inadmissible by any Act.

Conflicts

   (4) Nothing in subsection (1) overrides the provisions of any Act expressly limiting the extent to or purposes for which any oral testimony, documents or things may be admitted or used in evidence in any proceeding.

Copies

   (5) A copy of a document or any other thing may be admitted as evidence at a hearing if the presiding judge is satisfied as to its authenticity.

The hearsay exception stated in Rule 18.02(1) applies to the following written statements and documents (Rule 18.02):

1. The signed written statement of any witness, including the written report of an expert, to the extent that the written statement relates to facts and opinions that the witness would be permitted to testify about in person.

2. Any other document, including but not limited to
   - a hospital record or medical report made in the course of care and treatment;
   - a financial record;
   - a receipt;
   - a bill;
   - documentary evidence of loss of income or property damage; and
   - a repair estimate.

The trial judge may exclude a written statement or document, or an audio or visual record if it is (*Courts of Justice Act*, s. 27):

- irrelevant to any issue in the action;
- unduly repetitious of other evidence already filed;
- not admissible under any provincial or federal statute, such as the Ontario *Evidence Act* or the *Canada Evidence Act*; or
- privileged under the common law of privilege, which states that solicitor–client privilege (and, by analogy, paralegal–client privilege) is a right of fundamental justice to be determined by the courts, unless the client waives the privilege and the waiver is informed, voluntary, and in writing.

The trial judge may also exclude a written statement or document, or an audio or visual record,

- if to admit them would be unjust or not agreeable to good conscience (*Courts of Justice Act*, s. 25); or
- if the written statement or document relates to facts and opinions about which the witness would not be permitted to testify in person (Rule 18.02(2)1).

Summons to Witness Required

A party who has been served with a written statement or document under Rule 18.02(1) and wishes to cross-examine the witness or author may summon the witness or author by serving the person with a summons to witness (Form 18A) and attendance money (Rules 8.01(7), 18.02(4), 18.03(1)). Service of the summons and attendance money by the party or the party's licensee shall take place at least ten days before the trial date (Rule 8.01(7)). Service of the summons and attendance money on the witness or author is proven by filing with the court an affidavit of service (Form 8A).

A party who serves a summons to witness and attendance money on a witness or author pursuant to Rule 18.02(4) shall, at the time the summons is served (that is, at least ten days before the trial date), also serve a copy of the summons on every other party (Rule 18.02(5)). Service on every other party of a copy of the summons may be proven by filing with the court an affidavit of service (Form 8A).

If you have served a document, written statement, or audio or visual record on all other parties who were served with a notice of trial at least 30 days before the trial date, and you have concerns about the quality or sufficiency of its contents, you should consider serving a summons to witness and attendance money upon its author if you believe that its author has material evidence to give that is not adequately reflected by the contents of the written statement. That way, you can attempt to cure the defects in the written statement with evidence elicited during direct examination of its author.

You should always serve a summons to witness and attendance money on any person with material evidence in support of your client's claim or defence from whom a written statement has not been obtained. The person's name should be disclosed on the list of proposed witnesses and other persons with knowledge of the matters in dispute in the action (Form 13A) served on all other parties and filed with the court at least 14 days before the date of the settlement conference. If that is not possible in the circumstances (because the witness came to your attention late in the proceeding, for example), then give all other parties notice of your intention to call the witness as soon as is feasible, in keeping with your obligation of early and ongoing disclosure.

What Is an Expert Witness?

An expert witness is not the same thing as an ordinary witness. An ordinary witness is a person who has knowledge of facts or events touching on issues in the dispute, and who gives evidence under oath or affirmation about that knowledge, subject to the rules of evidence. In Small Claims Court, an ordinary witness may give evidence by way of a signed written statement pursuant to the Rule 18.02 hearsay exception.

An **expert witness** may or may not have knowledge of the facts themselves, but because of education, experience, specialization, and so on, has knowledge about an issue or issues in the action that the court does not have, because the matters in issue go beyond the range of ordinary knowledge. The expert witness gives **opinion evidence** about these issues to the court. Opinion evidence is evidence of what the expert witness thinks, believes, or infers with regard to facts and issues in the dispute.

The expert witness's opinion evidence must be relevant to issues in the action, and it must help the court understand those issues. In Small Claims Court, an expert witness may give her evidence by way of a signed written statement pursuant to the Rule 18.02 hearsay exception.

A party who serves on another party a written statement or document shall append to or include in the statement or document the name, telephone number, and address for service of the witness; and, in the case of a witness giving expert evidence, a summary of the expert witness's qualifications (Rule 18.02(3)).

The qualifications required to make a witness an expert will vary, depending on the nature of the expert evidence being given. An expert witness who is giving opinion evidence about a medical issue may provide educational qualifications, experience as a practitioner, areas of specialization, details of research, a list of published works, etc. An expert witness who is giving opinion evidence about how properly to construct a retaining wall or a concrete foundation may choose to emphasize her years of experience in building such structures, as opposed to, say, her educational qualifications.

An expert report that has been served at least 30 days before the trial date on all parties who were served with a notice of trial shall be received in evidence, unless the trial judge orders otherwise (Rule 18.02(1)). Service of the expert report is proven by filing with the court an affidavit of service (Form 8A) for each party served with the expert report.

A party who has been served with an expert report and wishes to cross-examine its author may summon the expert as a witness by serving a summons to witness (Form 18A) and attendance money on the expert, and a copy of the summons on every other party. Service on the expert and on all other parties is proven by filing with the court an affidavit of service (Form 8A) for each person served.

An expert witness's qualifications shall be stated in the written report or in an appendix to the report (Rule 18.02(3)(b)).

The admissibility of an expert report or other document that has been served on all other parties in accordance with Rule 18.02(1) is to be determined when the document is tendered at trial. If some proper basis exists to exclude the document, that should be determined without the need for cross-examination of the witness or author (see *Turner v. Kitchener (City)*). Any prejudice to another party because of failure to serve the report in accordance with Rule 18.02(1) is a factor the court will consider when determining whether to admit the report (see *Steckley v. Haid*).

If the report is admitted by the court, the admission of its contents serves as direct examination of the expert witness. An opposing party who has summoned an expert witness under Rule 18.02(4) may then cross-examine the expert witness with a view to discrediting the evidence contained in the expert report, but not with a view to discrediting the expert's qualifications (*Turner v. Kitchener (City)*, at paragraph 14):

> [T]he common law admissibility considerations for expert evidence are not applicable in the Small Claims Court in the same way as in other courts. This court's general discretion to admit or reject any given piece of evidence may result in exclusion of an expert report in unusual circumstances such as where an expert is clearly unqualified to give the opinion evidence proffered and will be of no assistance to the court, or if the opinion relies to a high degree on speculative, unreliable or unprovable factual assumptions. But it appears to me that we do not conduct *voir dires* in Small Claims Court as a precondition to admissibility of expert evidence where the expert's qualifications are challenged.

BOX 9.5 What Is an Expert Witness?

Background: Plaintiff is a homeowner who hires Careless Contractor Inc. to renovate Plaintiff's basement. The contract provides that all work is to be completed in a good and workmanlike fashion, in compliance with applicable codes and bylaws. The renovation is incomplete and shoddy. When Careless Contractor does not correct Plaintiff's list of deficiencies after repeated written demands, Plaintiff hires Fred Oliveiro of We Care About You Ltd. to repair the work done by Careless.

Mr. Oliveiro has been doing home renovations for 15 years. We Care is fully insured, and has never been the defendant in a court action by a dissatisfied customer.

Plaintiff commences an action against Careless Contractor for return of her deposit, damages for breach of contract, and the cost of reasonable repairs.

Thirty days before the settlement conference, Plaintiff serves a written statement by Mr. Oliveiro describing the deficiencies in Careless Contractor's work, what had to be done to correct those deficiencies, and the cost of the corrections. The statement includes the name, telephone number, and address for service of Mr. Oliveiro, along with a summary of his qualifications. Service is proven by filing an affidavit of service of the written statement (Form 8A) on Careless Contractor Inc. with the court office.

Discussion: Mr. Oliveiro is not an ordinary witness—that is, he has no personal knowledge of the shoddy work done by Careless Contractor. He was not standing by watching while Careless Contractor performed the deficient work. He came in after the fact, to assess what had been done wrong and perform necessary repairs.

Mr. Oliveiro has special knowledge and expertise about home renovations, based on 15 years of experience in the field. The trial judge does not have this knowledge. Mr. Oliveiro's opinion about what was wrong with the work done by Careless Contractor is relevant to the main issue in the case (failure to perform the work contracted for in a good and workmanlike manner in compliance with applicable codes and bylaws). His evidence will be helpful to the judge in making an informed decision about that issue, and any consequent damages. Therefore, Mr. Oliveiro is an expert witness.

If Careless Contractor Inc. wishes to cross-examine Mr. Oliveiro, Careless shall serve a summons to witness on Mr. Oliveiro, along with attendance money, at least ten days before the trial date (Rules 18.02(4) and 8.01(7)). A copy of the summons to witness shall also be served on Plaintiff (Rule 18.02(5)). Service is proven by filing with the court an affidavit of personal service on Mr. Oliveiro of a summons to witness along with attendance money (Rule 18.02(6)), and an affidavit of service on Plaintiff of a copy of the summons (Rule 8.01(14)).

Preparing for Trial

Pretrial Tasks: Review

Table 9.2 reviews the pretrial tasks in a defended action.

TABLE 9.2 Pretrial Tasks in a Defended Action: Review

TASK	WHO	WHEN	HOW
Compliance with order for further disclosure made by the settlement conference judge (Rule 13.05(1)(vi))	A party named in the order	• As soon as possible after the settlement conference, and before any deadline stated in the order	• Serve disclosure of documents, witnesses, etc., on other parties as set out in the order • Service proven by filing affidavit of service (Form 8A) with the court
Obtain any documents, written statements, or audio or visual records that have not already been disclosed to other parties and that a party intends to rely on at trial	Plaintiff or defendant	• As soon as possible after the settlement conference, and before the Rule 18.02(1) 30-day deadline for service expires	• Contact the witness or author • If a fee will be charged for the document or written statement, discuss with the client how the fee is to be paid—any arrangement should be confirmed in writing
Disclosure of a document or written statement or audio or visual record not already disclosed that a party intends to rely on at trial (Rule 18.02)	Plaintiff or defendant	• At least 30 days before the trial date (Rule 18.02(1))	• Service on all parties who were served with a notice of trial (Rule 18.02(1)) • May be served by mail, by courier, personally, or by an alternative to personal service • Written statement or document must include name, telephone number, and address for service of the witness or author (Rule 18.02(3)(a)) • If witness or author is giving expert evidence, the written statement or document should also include a summary of his or her qualifications (Rule 18.02(3)(b))
Summon witness or author of a written document or statement served under Rules 18.02(1) and (2)	Any party served with a written document or statement under Rules 18.02(1) and (2)	• At least 10 days before the trial date (Rule 8.01(7))	• Personal service of summons to witness plus attendance money on witness or author (Rule 8.01(7)) • Service of a copy of the summons on every other party who has received a notice of trial • Service proven by filing with the court an affidavit of service (Form 8A) on the witness and each other party

(Table 9.2 is concluded on the next page.)

TABLE 9.2 Concluded

TASK	WHO	WHEN	HOW
Summon a witness (Rule 18.03)	A party who requires the attendance of a person in Ontario to give evidence at the trial	• At least 10 days before the trial date (Rule 8.01(7)) • Note: It is good practice to serve the summons to witness well in advance of the 10-day deadline	• Personal service of summons to witness plus attendance money on witness (Rule 8.01(7)) • Service proven by filing affidavit of service with the court (Form 8A)
Offer to settle (Rule 14.01)	Plaintiff or defendant	• At any time up until after the court disposes of the action (Rule 14.03(3)) • At least 7 days before the trial commences, if you want to trigger the Rule 14.07 costs consequences	• Serve a written offer to settle (Form 14A) on the other party • File proof of service in client file

Reviewing the Client Matter

When preparing a file for a trial in a defended action, you should check your tickler system to ensure that you have complied with all deadlines for disclosure, summoning witnesses, making offers to settle, and so on. You should also ensure that other parties have met their obligations in terms of disclosure, service of a copy of a summons to witness for witnesses they intend to cross-examine under Rule 18.0(5), and so on.

You should review the pleadings, along with any witness notes and documents, and directions or comments by the settlement conference judge, to determine what evidence you need to put in. Keep in mind that an allegation in a pleading is just that—an unproven statement—unless it is supported under oath by spoken evidence or documentary evidence that is accepted by the Small Claims Court trial judge.

You should go over your client's evidence with her with a view to clarifying the issues and shaping your direct examination. You should make notes of everything that is said. You should review those notes with your client before ending the interview.

Interviewing Witnesses

General (Paralegal Rules 4.01(5), 4.02)

In the following discussion, "Paralegal Rule" means a rule in the *Paralegal Rules of Conduct*, and "Guideline" means a guideline in the *Paralegal Professional Conduct Guidelines*.

A paralegal may seek information from any potential witness in a proceeding (Paralegal Rule 4.02(1)), including witnesses appearing for opposing parties. The witness need not be summoned. When contacting witnesses, you shall be fair and honourable in your dealings with them (Guideline 12).

When contacting witnesses, you should identify yourself to the witness, and explain that you are a paralegal. You must give the witness your client's name and status in the proceeding, and ensure that the witness understands that you are acting exclusively in your client's interest.

A witness has no obligation to speak to you. If a witness tells you they do not want to talk to you, you should leave the witness alone. You are not permitted to **harass a witness** (Paralegal Rule 4.01(5)(j)).

When interviewing witnesses, you shall take care not to subvert or suppress any evidence. You shall not coach a witness to leave out evidence or to say things that are not completely true in order to benefit your client (Paralegal Rule 4.02(1)).

When interviewing witnesses, you shall take care not to procure the witness to stay out of the way—in other words, you shall not cause or persuade a witness not to give evidence at trial (Paralegal Rule 4.02(1)).

Additional restrictions on a paralegal advocate's conduct when dealing with witnesses are set out at Paralegal Rule 4.01(5), which requires that, when acting as an advocate, a paralegal shall not

- knowingly permit a witness or party to be presented in a false or misleading way, or to impersonate another;
- needlessly abuse, hector, harass, or inconvenience a witness; or
- persuade a witness not to give evidence, or encourage a witness not to attend a hearing.

Interviewing Represented Persons (Paralegal Rule 7.02)

If a person is represented by a legal practitioner in a matter, you shall not

- approach or communicate or deal with the person on the matter, or
- attempt to negotiate or compromise the matter directly with the person

except through or with the consent of the legal practitioner (Paralegal Rule 7.02(1)). A legal practitioner is the same thing as a licensee.

The two exceptions to Paralegal Rule 7.02(1) are stated at Paralegal Rules 7.02(2) and (3).

According to Rule 7.02(2), if a person is receiving legal services from a legal practitioner under a limited-scope retainer on a particular matter, you may, without the consent of the legal practitioner, approach, communicate, or deal directly with the person on the matter, unless

- you have received written notice of the limited nature of the legal services being provided by the legal practitioner, and
- the issue about which you wish to approach, communicate, or deal with the client falls within the scope of the limited retainer.

Rule 7.02(3) states that if you have no other interest in a matter, you may give a second opinion to a person who is represented by a legal practitioner with respect to that matter.

If you are acting for a party in a matter involving a corporation or organization represented by another legal practitioner, according to Paralegal Rule 7.02(4), you shall not, without the legal practitioner's consent or unless otherwise authorized or required by law, communicate, facilitate communication with, or deal with a person

- who is a director or officer, or another person who is authorized to act on behalf of the corporation or organization;
- who is likely involved in decision making for the corporation or organization or who provides advice in relation to the particular matter;
- whose act or omission may be binding on or imputed to the corporation or organization for the purposes of its liability; or
- who supervises, directs, or regularly consults with the legal practitioner and who makes decisions based on the legal practitioner's advice.

If a person described above is represented in the matter by a legal practitioner, the consent of the legal practitioner is sufficient to allow a paralegal to communicate, facilitate communication with, or deal with the person (Paralegal Rule 7.02(5)).

For purposes of Paralegal Rule 7.02(4), "organization" includes a partnership, limited partnership, association, union, fund, trust, co-operative, unincorporated association, sole proprietorship, and a government department, agency, or regulatory body.

Paralegal Rule 7.02 applies to communications with any person, whether or not a party to a formal adjudicative proceeding, contract, or negotiation, who is represented by a licensee in the matter to which the communication relates (Paralegal Rule 7.02(7)).

A paralegal is prohibited from communicating with a represented person if the paralegal has direct knowledge that the person is represented, or if the paralegal should be able to infer from the circumstances that the person is represented (Paralegal Rule 7.02(8)).

Direct Examination: Preparing Your Questions

The Rules of the Small Claims Court provide for disclosure at every stage of the action. This means that, by the time the matter gets to trial, you should have a good sense of the strengths and weaknesses of your client's case and of the opposing party's case.

The best way to make a good case for your client at trial is by thoroughly preparing your client and any other witnesses who will appear in person and by putting complete, detailed evidence on every material issue before the court, whether by way of signed written statements and documents, or by spoken evidence given under oath or by affirmation. If your documentary evidence is complete and detailed, and you use direct examination to present spoken evidence to the court as a concise, organized narrative, it is unlikely that cross-examination will do much to undermine your client's claim or defence.

BOX 9.6 Greco v. Hardwick: Preparing for Trial

The background to this matter can be found at Box 9.3 at pages 351–352. The pleadings in this action can be found in Chapter 4 at Appendix 4.4, and in Chapter 6 at Appendixes 6.1, 6.2, and 6.3.

Assume that you are the paralegal for Juliette Greco, the plaintiff (defendant by defendant's claim). The date for trial is April 18, 20—.

You are reviewing the client file to determine what evidence is required at trial to tell the judge Ms. Greco's story and convince the judge that she should get what she is asking for.

When reviewing the factual background and the pleadings, ask yourself the following questions.

QUESTION	ANSWER
1. What is the basis for Ms. Greco's action, as stated in the plaintiff's claim?	• An unpaid debt.
2. What evidence is needed to support Ms. Greco's claim?	• Evidence that money was paid to Mr. Hardwick. • Evidence that the money was not paid back to Ms. Greco.
3. What evidence do we have in the present case to support Ms. Greco's claim?	• A promissory note dated April 1, 20—. • Mr. Hardwick's admission that he took the money (see Schedule A to defence at Appendix 6.1 at page 257). • Mr. Hardwick's admission that he did not pay the money back.
4. Is that evidence sufficient?	• No. See discussion of the defendant's dispute, below.
5. What is the basis for the defendant's dispute, as stated in the defence and defendant's claim?	• That he performed services in lieu of payment, with Ms. Greco's knowledge and consent, and that she benefited from the services provided. • That these services had a value of $5,990.00, as calculated at paragraph 9 of the defendant's claim.
6. What evidence is needed to support Mr. Hardwick's dispute?	• Mr. Hardwick's evidence that he performed the services with Ms. Greco's knowledge and consent and that Ms. Greco benefited from the services provided (particulars in defendant's claim). • The estimates attached to the defendant's claim.
7. Is that evidence sufficient?	• No.
8. What is the basis for Ms. Greco's defence to defendant's claim?	• There was no written contract with respect to the services to be provided or their value. • Ms. Greco disputes the terms of the spoken contract. • Ms. Greco disputes the value assigned to the services rendered.

(Concluded on the next page.)

QUESTION	ANSWER
9. What evidence is needed to support Ms. Greco's defence to Mr. Hardwick's defendant's claim?	• There was a spoken agreement that the plaintiff by defendant's claim ("Mr. Hardwick") would perform the services for a fee in the range of the fee charged by Glenn Woods Garden Services for the same services. • The defendant by defendant's claim ("Ms. Greco") accepted the services offered by Mr. Hardwick in partial payment only of the amount due on the note. • Many of the services Mr. Hardwick or his children performed had been performed in the past for no charge. • Many of the services Mr. Hardwick or his children performed could have been completed by others for no charge. • When the note became due, Ms. Greco approached Mr. Hardwick regarding payment of the balance due on the note. • She then began sending demands for payment (see documents attached to Ms. Greco's claim). • The values assigned by Mr. Hardwick to the services performed are grossly inflated. • Glenn Woods performed identical services in the past for a fee ranging from $1,400.00 to $1,550.00.

QUESTION	Evidentiary issue	Discussion / Answer
10. Is that evidence sufficient?	Mr. Hardwick intends to rely on the estimates attached to the defendant's claim as evidence at the trial.	• We have served a signed written statement by our own witness, Glenn Woods containing evidence as to the value of services equivalent to those provided to Ms. Greco by Mr. Hardwick. • We may serve a summons to witness on the authors of the estimates relied on by Mr. Hardwick, in order to cross-examine them on their estimates and determine the extent to which their prices reflect equivalent services.
	What is a weakness in both parties' cases?	• The absence of a written contract with respect to the services to be provided by Mr. Hardwick in lieu of payment of the debt owing to Ms. Greco. When a spoken agreement is at issue in an action, the judge must make **findings as to credibility**—that is, the judge must decide whose evidence about the terms of the agreement to believe on a balance of probabilities. This makes for unpredictable outcomes.

Direct examination is the series of questions that you ask your own witnesses when they take the stand, to structure their evidence and help them tell their story clearly and concisely, so that it can be easily understood by the court. The questions you ask in direct examination provide the pieces of the witness's story. If you miss one of the pieces, or get the pieces in the wrong order, the story becomes confusing. Breaking the narrative down into an orderly progression of facts is part of the difficult art of direct examination. The best way to do this is to prepare a detailed list of the questions you need to ask in direct examination beforehand, and refer to these questions during the trial.

As you go through your list of questions in direct examination at trial, listen carefully to the witness's answers, and be prepared to depart from the script. If an answer is incomplete, ask the witness questions to clarify what he said. If a witness's answer to one question answers several other questions, cross those questions off the list.

Because the purpose of direct examination is to let the witness tell her story, you should draft your questions using open-ended questions only. With a few exceptions, those are the only questions you will be allowed to ask your witnesses in direct examination.

Open-ended, or direct, questions are questions that do not "lead" the witness—that is, they do not contain any language that implies certain facts or suggests a "correct" answer to the witness. Open-ended questions may, but do not always, use "who," "what," "when," "where," and "how."

Questions that imply the existence of certain facts or suggest a correct answer to a witness (or to the court) are called **leading questions**. Leading questions are perfectly acceptable in cross-examination, but they are only permitted in direct examination when the question concerns information that is not in dispute.

Tables 9.3 and 9.4 contain some examples of the same question, phrased as an open-ended question and as a leading question. Assume that the witness in the stand is the plaintiff, Juliette Greco.

TABLE 9.3 Greco v. Hardwick: Asking Open-Ended Questions and Leading Questions

OPEN-ENDED QUESTION	LEADING QUESTION
What is your name?	Your name is Juliette Greco?
Where do you live?	You live at 126 George Court in Brampton?
Who are your neighbours?	James and Pamela Hardwick are your neighbours?
What is their address?	They live at 128 George Court?

The leading questions in Table 9.3 *are* permissible for use in direct examination, because they are about issues that are not in dispute (in the *Greco v. Hardwick* case, the parties' names and addresses). However, keep in mind that it is good practice to use open-ended questions in direct examination whenever possible. If your witness has been prepared properly, she should have no problem telling her story without being led.

**TABLE 9.4 Greco v. Hardwick:
Asking Open-Ended Questions and Leading Questions**

OPEN-ENDED QUESTION	LEADING QUESTION
Was the money due under the promissory note paid?	James Hardwick told you he could not pay the money?
Did he discuss this with you?	James Hardwick offered to perform services in lieu of payment?
When did the discussion take place?	He made the offer shortly after signing the promissory note?
What did he say?	He offered to do yard and pool maintenance instead of paying?
Did you accept his offer?	Before accepting his offer, you obtained Mr. Hardwick's assurance that the charge for his services would be in the range of what you had been charged in past years by Glenn Woods Garden Services?
Did you discuss a price?	(See above.)

The leading questions in Table 9.4 *are not* permissible in direct examination, because they are about issues that are disputed in the action—that is, the terms of the spoken agreement between Juliette Greco and James Hardwick for performance of services instead of payment of money.

The open-ended questions in Table 9.4 let the witness tell the court her story about the issues in dispute (the terms of her unwritten agreement with James Hardwick to accept services instead of payment, including the value to be assigned to those services). With the leading questions, all the witness gets to say is "yes" or "no." In other words, the paralegal asking the questions, who is not under oath and cannot be cross-examined, is shaping the evidence.

When preparing your questions, you should note the places in the evidence where you intend to submit a document as an **exhibit**.

An exhibit is an original document that is material to an issue in the action. It must be identified by a witness with personal knowledge of its contents. The contents of the document may be referred to in the witness's spoken evidence. It is then marked as an exhibit by the court clerk and placed in the court file as part of the evidence.

In Small Claims Court, a copy of a document or any other thing may be admitted as evidence at a hearing if the presiding judge is satisfied as to its authenticity (*Courts of Justice Act*, s. 27).

Exhibits should be entered at the point in the witness's evidence where they support and confirm that evidence. That is why it is important to note their place in the evidentiary narrative when you are drafting your questions.

The procedure for entering documents as exhibits at trial is discussed below.

Cross-Examination: Preparing Your Questions

General

In direct examination, the relationship between the paralegal and the witness is usually friendly. When a paralegal puts a properly prepared witness on the stand, the paralegal should already know what the witness will say. The paralegal's questions are designed to help the witness tell the story.

Cross-examination is used to pinpoint weaknesses or inconsistencies in the testimony of another party or another party's witness. You should avoid using open-ended questions in cross-examination, because they leave the narrative in the witness's control. You should use leading questions exclusively, or as often as possible.

A successful Small Claims Court cross-examination may be very brief, because quite often there is not that much evidence that is susceptible to testing by cross-examination. The trick to successful cross-examination is to select the weaknesses in a witness's evidence that go to issues in dispute, and plan your questions carefully to explore and emphasize those weaknesses.

As with direct examination, you should prepare your questions for cross-examination ahead of time. You should listen carefully to the witness's testimony in direct examination, and take notes. Be prepared to revise and adapt your questions in response to what the witness says in direct examination and the answers the witness gives you in cross-examination.

Preparation

When you are preparing for cross-examination of another party's witnesses, the first question you should always ask yourself is: Will cross-examining this witness accomplish anything for my client's case? In a civil case, there is no absolute obligation to cross-examine. If cross-examination is unlikely to accomplish anything that assists your client's case, you should not cross-examine.

If you decide to cross-examine another's party's witness, keep in mind that if a signed written statement by that witness was served on you at least 30 days before the trial date, it is your obligation to serve a summons to witness (Form 18A) and attendance money on the author of the statement. The summons must be served personally at least ten days before the trial date (Rule 8.01(7)) and at the same time you must serve all other parties with a copy of the summons. Service is proven by filing with the court an affidavit of service for each person served.

When you summon a witness under Rule 18.02(4), there is no direct examination of that witness by the party relying upon the contents of the written statement or document. If the trial judge admits the written statement or document into evidence, the contents of the written statement or document is the evidence. When the witness is called to the stand, you will cross-examine the witness on the contents of the written statement or document only.

Whether you are planning to cross-examine on a written statement or document, or cross-examine a witness who has given direct evidence under oath, you should consider making a list of the questions you intend to ask in cross-examination ahead of time. Even though you may not use all of your prepared questions in cross-examination, preparing your questions ahead of time gives you an opportunity to review and assess possible weaknesses and ambiguities in the evidence.

Courtesy

Paralegal Rule 4.01(5)(j) states that, when acting as an advocate, a paralegal shall not needlessly abuse, hector, harass, or inconvenience a witness. A well-prepared cross-examination is just as effective if conducted in a courteous manner. An ill-prepared cross-examination will not be saved by rude or abusive conduct toward the witness.

Conclusion

When preparing your cross-examination, analyze the issues and evidence carefully. You want to target weaknesses in the other party's evidence, with a view to emphasizing the strengths of your own party's case.

When cross-examining a witness, if you do not get the answer you want to a particular question, do not get into a debate with the witness about it or engage in any other form of bullying or harassment. Use your questions to probe the issue, and then move on to your next point. Stay calm, be polite, and be thorough.

Listen carefully to the other party's evidence during direct examination. If the witness gives evidence that is consistent and credible, you may decide to change your questions, not to question the witness on certain issues, or not to question the witness at all.

Exhibits

If you intend to rely on a document at trial, you should ensure that the document has been disclosed to all other parties. If you are aware of the document when you draft your claim or defence, a copy should be attached to and served with the pleading. If you become aware of the document later in the action and you intend to rely on it at trial, you should disclose it at least 14 days before the settlement conference (Rule 13.03(2)). If that is impossible, you should disclose the document in accordance with any order or direction from the settlement conference judge or by serving it on all parties who have been served with a notice of trial at least 30 days before the trial date.

If you are putting a document in as evidence at trial, it must be introduced as an exhibit. In Small Claims Court, a copy of a document may be received in evidence so long as the presiding judge is satisfied as to its authenticity. If an original is available, it should be produced. Any document that you produce as an exhibit at trial should already have been served on all other parties.

As was noted above, when you are making your list of questions for direct examination, you should note the places in the examination where an exhibit will be introduced. As exhibits are entered, you should list them separately in the order that they are marked by the court clerk.

When introducing an exhibit, you first show the original document to the other parties if they are self-represented, or to their representatives. You should have photocopies of the document handy in case the judge and an opposing party requests one.

If the witness has personal knowledge of the document, you will show the original document to the witness, and ask him to identify it. You then question the witness with respect to those parts of the document's contents that are material to the action. When you have finished questioning him, you hand the original to the clerk, and request that the document be admitted into evidence. The trial judge may wish to examine the document, or simply order the clerk to mark it as an exhibit. The clerk will then mark the document as an exhibit and place it in the court file as part of the evidence.

An exhibit that has been identified by a sworn witness with personal knowledge of the document is marked by a number. If you plan to refer in evidence to an exhibit that will be identified by a later witness, you will ask that it be marked for identification. Exhibits for identification are marked with letters. You may request that an exhibit marked for identification be admitted into evidence when a witness who has personal knowledge of its contents takes the stand.

BOX 9.7 Greco v. Hardwick: Submitting a Document as an Exhibit

The following dialogue demonstrates how the promissory note in *Greco v. Hardwick* would be submitted as an exhibit at trial.

Plaintiff's paralegal:	What was the amount of the loan to Mr. Hardwick?
Ms. Greco:	$5,000.00.
Plaintiff's paralegal:	When was the money paid to Mr. Hardwick?
Ms. Greco:	April 1, 20—.
Plaintiff's paralegal:	Was there anything in writing with respect to the loan?
Ms. Greco:	Yes. The defendant signed a promissory note dated April 1, 20—.
Plaintiff's paralegal (to the judge):	Your Honour, I am showing the defendant's paralegal an original of a promissory note dated April 1, 20—. A photocopy of the note has already been disclosed to him.
The judge (to the defendant's paralegal):	You've received a copy of this document?
Defendant's paralegal (to the judge):	Yes, Your Honour. A photocopy of this document was attached to the plaintiff's claim. And my client has a duplicate original.

The judge (to the plaintiff's paralegal):	Proceed.
Plaintiff's paralegal (to Ms. Greco):	Can you identify this document for the court?
Ms. Greco:	Yes. It is a duplicate original of a promissory note signed by James Hardwick on April 1, 20—.
Plaintiff's paralegal:	Please tell the court about the terms of the note.
Ms. Greco:	The amount of the loan was $5,000.00. The due date was August 2, 20—. In the event of default, interest became payable at a rate of 10% per year until any balance owing was paid in full.
Plaintiff's paralegal:	When did Mr. Hardwick sign the note?
Ms. Greco:	He signed both copies of the note in my presence when I gave him the cheque for $5,000.00 on April 1, 20—. I gave him the original, and I kept the duplicate original.
Plaintiff's paralegal:	Your Honour, I would ask that the promissory note dated April 1, 20— signed by James Hardwick be marked as Exhibit 1.

The judge may then examine the document, or simply order the clerk to mark it as an exhibit.

Trial Book

When preparing for a trial, you should consider putting together a **trial book**, either digitally or in paper format. If you are using paper, your material should be organized in a three-ring binder with tabs for each section. The following is a suggestion for organization of the contents of your trial book:

- A table of contents outlining the contents of each tab.
- Opening submissions. Even if the trial judge does not request opening submissions, it is best to be prepared.

If you are acting for the plaintiff:

- For each witness for the plaintiff, your questions for direct examination with annotations for introduction of exhibits.
- For each witness for the plaintiff, your notes of evidence in cross-examination, if any, and issues for re-examination.
- For each witness for other parties, your notes of evidence during direct examination.
- For each witness for other parties, your questions for cross-examination.

If you are acting for the defendant:

- For each witness for other parties, your notes of evidence and issues arising out of direct examination.
- For each witness for other parties, your questions for cross-examination and notes of re-examination, if any.
- For each witness for the defendant, your questions for direct examination with annotations for introduction of exhibits.
- For each witness for the defendant, your notes of evidence in cross-examination, if any, and issues for re-examination.

Your trial book should also include:

- Closing submissions.
- Submissions as to interest and costs.
- Any legal authorities upon which you intend to rely, with copies for the court and other parties, and all relevant passages highlighted.
- Written statements and documents to be submitted as exhibits in order of submission.
- A list of the other party's exhibits in order of submission.
- Disclosure by other parties for your reference.

You should consider including a draft bill of costs stating disbursements and legal services to the date of trial in your trial book, for your reference if the judge asks for submissions as to costs immediately after handing down her decision. You will find a draft bill of costs for Juliette Greco, plaintiff (defendant by defendant's claim) in *Greco v. Hardwick*, in Form 57A of the *Rules of Civil Procedure* at Appendix 9.3 to this chapter. Note that the representation fee on the bill of costs is calculated in accordance with s. 29 of the *Courts of Justice Act* and Rule 19.02, and may not reflect the amount that would actually be billed to the client for a matter where there was attendance at a settlement conference and a trial.

Trial Procedure

General

When you arrive at the courthouse, you should go to the courtroom where your trial is scheduled to be heard. A **docket** will be posted outside the courtroom listing the matters to be heard that day. You should note where your matter is on the list. You should then go into the courtroom, fill out a **counsel slip**, and give it to the clerk. A counsel slip is a piece of paper that tells the court what your name is, the matter you are there on, and who you are representing. It gives the court notice that there is someone appearing on the matter.

If your client and/or any other witnesses are there, you should speak to them outside the courtroom. If the opposing party and her legal representative are there, you should greet them so that they know you are present.

When court starts, all parties will be called into the courtroom.

If you are still actively negotiating settlement with the other side, the negotiations should take place outside the courtroom. You may wish to inform the court clerk that you are outside talking, so that he can page you if your matter is called.

If there are no matters to discuss outside the courtroom, the parties, their legal representatives, and any additional witnesses should take seats in the public gallery until their matter is called.

Courtroom Etiquette

Proper Dress

Licensees should wear business attire on Small Claims Court appearances. Men should wear a suit and tie. Women should wear a suit or dress slacks with a suit jacket. Dark colours are preferable. Jewellery should be kept to a minimum.

Conduct in the Courtroom

In the courtroom, you should behave with the utmost decorum and professionalism. You should not read newspapers, chew gum, or talk to others (except very briefly in an undertone) in a courtroom where a judge is sitting. Cellphones should be turned off.

If you need to talk to your client, a witness, another party, or another party's legal representative, you should do so outside the courtroom.

The Judge

When acting as an advocate, you shall treat the judge with candour, fairness, courtesy, and respect (Paralegal Rule 4.01(1)).

You should rise when a judge enters or leaves the courtroom. You should rise whenever you address the bench or the bench addresses you. When entering or leaving a courtroom in which a judge is sitting, you should pause at the door, turn to face the bench, and bow to the bench.

Experienced judges will be aware of the applicable law in most of the cases that come before them. However, occasionally, a judge will ask you to explain a particular legal principle. If asked, you must inform her honestly and candidly about the law in question, to the best of your knowledge and ability, keeping in mind Paralegal Rule 4.01(5)(d).

Small Claims Court judges tend to play an activist role in the courtroom. At a Small Claims Court trial, the judge will often intervene in the proceeding, questioning witnesses, clarifying issues, and taking any necessary steps to ensure that a self-represented party is not denied a fair trial because of lack of familiarity with court procedure. This is an appropriate role for a trial judge to play in a court where quite often one or both parties are self-represented and unsophisticated. It is in keeping with the general mandate of the court to hear and determine in a summary way all questions of law and fact in order to secure a just, speedy, and inexpensive determination of the matter before it (*Courts of Justice Act*, s. 25; Rule 1.03(1)).

Where one party is self-represented and the other has legal representation, the trial judge's role is to ensure procedural fairness for the self-represented party, and to discourage bullying or intimidation of the self-represented party by the other party's legal representative. The judge should never give legal advice to a litigant.

Self-Represented Parties

You should treat self-represented parties with courtesy and respect.

Paralegal Rule 4.05 states that, when dealing with a self-represented person, you shall

1. urge the self-represented person to obtain independent representation;
2. ensure that the self-represented person is not proceeding under the impression that you are protecting his or her interests; and
3. make clear to the self-represented person that you are acting exclusively in the interests of your client and that your comments may be partisan.

You are not required to educate an unsophisticated, self-represented adversary as to the law. However, you do have a duty to be truthful, honest, and thorough in presenting your client's case and the law as it applies to your client's case, in order to ensure that the court is not misled.

As in other civil actions, settlement negotiations in Small Claims Court may continue right up until there is a final disposition of the matter. Negotiating a settlement with a self-represented party presents unique challenges. The self-represented party must be advised and must understand that you are acting exclusively in the best interests of your client.

If a matter involving a self-represented party settles at trial, the trial judge must review the terms of settlement. The trial judge cannot give legal advice to the self-represented party with respect to the terms of the agreement. For example, she cannot comment on whether she thinks some of the terms are unclear or unduly harsh—that amounts to giving a legal opinion. She is restricted to ensuring that the self-represented party understands the terms of settlement, and satisfying herself that the court has legal jurisdiction to make an order in accordance with the terms of settlement.

Trial Procedure

Introductions and Opening Submissions

When the matter is called, the parties take their places at the counsel tables facing the judge's bench. The plaintiff and her representative sit at the counsel table on the right facing the judge's bench. The defendant and his representative sit at the counsel table on the left facing the judge's bench.

The plaintiff's paralegal rises and introduces herself by last name and initial. The defendant's paralegal rises and introduces himself by last name and initial.

If requested to do so by the judge, the parties' representatives may then make brief opening submissions. The plaintiff's paralegal goes first, followed by the defendant's paralegal.

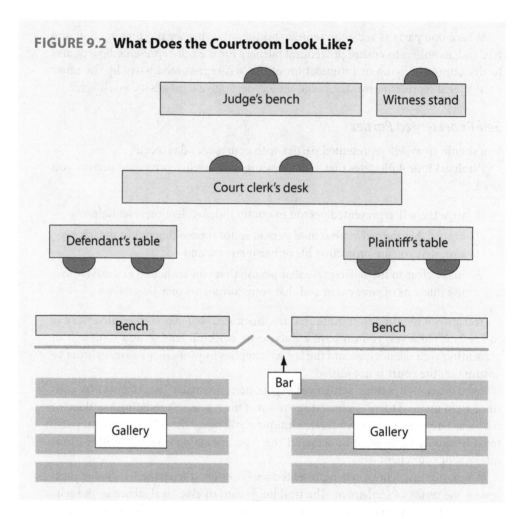

FIGURE 9.2 **What Does the Courtroom Look Like?**

Self-represented parties, through no fault of their own other than lack of legal sophistication, often mistake the purpose of opening submissions. They use the opportunity to start giving evidence and arguing their case. In matters where the parties are self-represented, busy judges with long lists often dispense with opening submissions and go straight to the evidence.

An experienced and courteous judge will always request a brief opening submission from parties who are represented. So you should always have one prepared, because, if requested, it assists the judge to focus his mind on the issues in the case before him.

In this context, a submission is an explanation of what a party wants, and a brief summary of the facts that entitle the party to get it. The word "brief" needs emphasis. The judge does not wish to listen to details at this point—that is what the evidence is for. More detailed submissions should be saved for closing argument.

The plaintiff's paralegal makes submissions first. The defendant's paralegal then makes brief submissions about the grounds for the defence and the defendant's claim, if any.

Order Excluding Witnesses

If either party has summoned non-party witnesses, before any evidence is heard, the judge should be asked to make an **order excluding witnesses**. An order excluding witnesses requires all witnesses except the parties themselves to leave the courtroom and wait outside the courtroom until they are called to give evidence themselves. The purpose of an order excluding witnesses is to prevent witnesses who have not yet taken the stand from hearing, and being influenced by, the evidence of the witnesses who take the stand ahead of them. When a witness has given his evidence and has been cross-examined, he may remain in the courtroom and hear the remainder of the case if he wishes.

An order excluding witnesses is required only when there are witnesses other than the parties giving evidence. If the plaintiff and the defendant are the only witnesses, an order excluding witnesses is not required.

Evidence

After introductions and opening submissions are finished, and, if required, an order excluding witnesses has been made, the plaintiff is invited to call her first witness. Usually, this will be the plaintiff herself. The plaintiff takes the stand, is sworn or affirmed, and gives her evidence in support of her claim during direct examination. If there is a defendant's claim, the plaintiff may give evidence in support of her defence to the defendant's claim at the same time as her evidence in support of the plaintiff's claim, if appropriate. The plaintiff's representative should consider requesting a direction from the judge regarding this before proceeding.

When direct examination is completed, the plaintiff may be cross-examined by the defendant's paralegal. If any new issues are raised in cross-examination, the plaintiff may be re-examined by her legal representative on those issues at the completion of cross-examination. The purpose of **re-examination** (also called reply or rebuttal evidence) is to clarify and, if necessary, neutralize or rebut any potentially damaging evidence brought out during cross-examination. Re-examination should be brief, and may deal only with new issues that were raised during cross-examination. It may not be used to introduce new evidence; and if either party tries to use re-examination for this purpose, the other party should object.

The same procedure applies to any other witnesses the plaintiff calls, if any. Plaintiff's witnesses who were summoned by other parties for purposes of cross-examination with respect to written statements and documents under Rule 18.02(4) are subject to cross-examination and re-examination only.

When the plaintiff and any other witnesses for the plaintiff have given their evidence, the plaintiff's case is closed. The defendant and any other witnesses for the defendant then take the stand, are sworn or affirmed, give evidence for the defence and defendant's claim (if there is one), and are cross-examined. Any new issues raised during cross-examination may be clarified or rebutted during re-examination by the defendant's representative.

When all of the defendant's evidence has been heard, the defendant's case is closed. The judge will then ask whether there is any reply. The plaintiff or a plaintiff's witness may take the stand and give reply evidence intended to rebut evidence by the defendant or a defendant's witness. The defendant has the right to respond to the rebuttal.

BOX 9.8 Objections

Objections are used to draw the court's attention to improper evidence or procedure. They should be made promptly. A paralegal who objects to a particular question or line of questioning by another licensee should raise the objection as soon as the other licensee has finished speaking, and before the witness has had a chance to answer.

Do not raise an objection unless you have reasonable grounds for doing so. Know what those grounds are, and state them when raising the objection. If you are objecting to the improper use of leading questions in direct examination by the opposing paralegal, rise and say: "Objection. My colleague is leading the witness." If you are objecting to improper use of re-examination by the opposing paralegal, rise and say: "Objection. My colleague cannot try to introduce new evidence during reply. He must restrict his questioning to evidence that is already before the court."

When you have raised an objection, the opposing party may be invited to make submissions. The judge will then make a ruling, sustaining the objection or dismissing the objection. When the judge has made that ruling, whether you agree with it or not, do not get into a debate with the judge about it. Thank the judge, and sit down.

When raising objections in Small Claims Court, keep s. 27 of the *Courts of Justice Act* in mind. Section 27 states that at a hearing, a Small Claims Court judge may admit and act on any oral testimony, document, or other thing so long as it is relevant and not unduly repetitious, regardless of whether that evidence would be admissible in any other court. In other words, in Small Claims Court, cases may be decided entirely or in part based on hearsay evidence, so long as any statutory rules with respect to evidence (as set out in the Ontario *Evidence Act*, for example) are complied with. During oral testimony, you may object to hearsay evidence, but the judge may admit the hearsay evidence unless it is irrelevant and unduly repetitious.

It is very important to keep this relaxed approach toward admissible evidence in mind when your opponent is self-represented. You have a duty to protect your client and promote your client's interests; but if you use this duty as an excuse for objecting to every mistake a self-represented party makes, it will look like harassment. Restrict your objections to the most serious errors, and be polite and respectful when making them.

Communication with Witnesses Giving Evidence (Paralegal Rule 4.03)

When preparing for a hearing, you may contact any witness, whether the witness is sympathetic to your client's cause or not. Different rules apply during a hearing. Your ability to speak to any witness who is giving testimony is restricted, to ensure that you do not influence what the witness says in the stand.

During a hearing, whether you may speak to a witness depends upon

- whether the witness gives evidence that supports your (and your client's) cause, or the cause of an opposing party, and
- what stage the witness is at in giving evidence.

A witness who gives evidence that supports your cause is called a **sympathetic witness**. A witness who gives evidence that supports an opposing party's cause is called an **unsympathetic witness**.

Whether a paralegal is representing a plaintiff, a defendant, a third party, or an accused, there are certain key stages in the process which govern what the paralegal may discuss with the witness:

- During examination-in-chief (also known as direct examination), when a paralegal examines her own witness in support of her client's case.
- Any interval between commencement of examination-in-chief and completion of examination-in-chief—if, for example, the court takes a recess before examination-in-chief of the witness has been completed.
- After the paralegal has finished examination-in-chief of the witness but before cross-examination of the witness by another licensee.
- During cross-examination of a witness by an opposing licensee.
- After an opposing licensee has finished cross-examination of the witness, but before the paralegal begins any re-examination of the witness.
- During re-examination, when the paralegal re-examines her own witness on matters arising out of the cross-examination.

Subject to the direction of the tribunal, you shall observe the rules respecting communication with witnesses giving evidence set out in Paralegal Rule 4.03(1). For a summary of these rules, see Table 9.5.

If you are uncertain whether you may speak to a witness under Paralegal Rule 4.03(1), you should obtain the consent of the opposing licensee or leave of the tribunal before entering into any discussion with a witness that might otherwise be inappropriate under the rule (Paralegal Rule 4.03(2)).

Paralegal Rule 4.03(1) applies, with necessary modifications, to examinations out of court (Paralegal Rule 4.03(3)).

Closing Submissions

When the parties' witnesses have been called, have given evidence, and have been cross-examined and re-examined, and both parties' cases are closed, the judge may ask for closing submissions from each party as to judgment. The plaintiff makes closing submissions first.

In order to be persuasive, a party's closing submission should review the issues in dispute, summarize the evidence that supports the party's claim or defence, and present arguments as to why the relief the party is seeking should be granted by the court based on that evidence and the applicable law.

TABLE 9.5 Communication with Witnesses (Paralegal Rule 4.03(1))

STAGE OF PROCEEDING	PERMITTED COMMUNICATION WITH WITNESS IN STAND			
You call the witness	**Sympathetic witness or unsympathetic witness***			**Applicable point under Rule 4.03(1)**
• Examination-in-chief conducted by you	During an interval, you may discuss anything not covered in the examination to that point.			1
• After examination-in-chief • Before cross-examination	You shall not discuss with the witness the evidence given during examination-in-chief or relating to any matter touched on during examination-in-chief.			3
• Cross-examination by opposing party	You shall have no conversation with the witness about the witness's evidence or any issue in the proceeding.			4
• After cross-examination • Before re-examination	You shall have no conversation with the witness about evidence to be dealt with on re-examination.			5
• Re-examination	During an interval, you may discuss anything not covered in the re-examination to that point.			1
Opposing party calls the witness	**Sympathetic witness**	**Applicable point under Rule 4.03(1)**	**Unsympathetic witness**	**Applicable point under Rule 4.03(1)**
• Examination-in-chief conducted by opposing party	You may discuss the witness's evidence with the witness.	–	You may discuss the witness's evidence with the witness.	2
• After examination-in-chief • Before cross-examination	You may discuss the witness's evidence with the witness.	–	You may discuss the witness's evidence with the witness.	–
• Cross-examination conducted by you	You may discuss anything not covered in the witness's evidence to that point.	7	You may discuss the witness's evidence with the witness.	6
• After cross-examination • Before re-examination	You may discuss the witness's evidence with the witness.	–	You may discuss the witness's evidence with the witness.	–
• Re-examination by opposing party	You shall have no conversation with the witness about evidence to be dealt with on re-examination.	8	You may discuss the witness's evidence with the witness.	8

* A sympathetic witness gives evidence that supports your cause; an unsympathetic witness gives evidence that supports an opposing party's cause.

You should prepare a draft closing submission in advance. Depending on the evidence at trial, you may have to alter your draft submission, but it will still provide a useful framework for your closing arguments.

If you intend to refer to case law or statute law in your closing submission, you should disclose any law to which you will be referring at trial to other parties or their representatives before the trial date. At trial, you should have enough copies in your trial book for the judge, for other parties, and for yourself. Any passages you intend to refer to during legal argument should be highlighted on all copies, and you should have the page number or paragraph references at your fingertips.

Submissions as to Costs

General

After the trial judge has made his decision and granted judgment in the matter, he will ask the parties for submissions as to costs. Costs are money amounts that the court orders one party to pay to the other party. Costs are awarded in addition to any other relief, monetary or otherwise, that may be ordered. The general rule is that costs are awarded to the successful party, to reimburse the successful party for representation fees, if any, and disbursements incurred by that party to conduct the action.

Costs were discussed in Chapter 8 at pages 322–324, in the context of offers to settle. The discussion below deals with costs awards at trial.

Disbursements

A successful party is entitled to recover all reasonable disbursements, including costs of effecting service, travel expenses, accommodation, photocopying, and experts' reports, from the unsuccessful party, unless the court orders otherwise (Rule 19.01(1)).

The clerk shall assess disbursements in accordance with the regulations to the *Administration of Justice Act* and Rules 19.01(3) and (4). The clerk's assessment is subject to review by the court. The relevant regulations are *Kilometre Allowances* and *Small Claims Court—Fees and Allowances*. Rule 19.01(3) states that the amount of disbursements assessed for effecting service shall not exceed $60.00 for each person served unless it is the court's opinion that there are special circumstances that justify assessing a greater amount. The amount of disbursements assessed for preparing a pleading shall not exceed $100.00 (Rule 19.01(4)).

Representation Fee

If the successful party is represented by a lawyer, student-at-law, or agent, the court may award the party a reasonable representation fee at trial or at an assessment hearing (Rule 19.04). The portion of a costs award that is for disbursements is intended to reimburse the successful party for out-of-pocket expenses. The portion of a costs award that is a representation fee is intended to reimburse the successful party for the cost of legal services and representation.

Any authority to award costs exclusive of disbursements—in other words, a representation fee—under Rule 19 is subject to s. 29 of the *Courts of Justice Act* (Rule 19.02). Section 29 of the *Courts of Justice Act* states that, in Small Claims Court, an award of costs, other than disbursements, shall not exceed 15 percent of the amount claimed or the value of the property sought to be recovered, unless the court considers it necessary in the interests of justice to penalize a party or a party's representative for unreasonable behaviour in the proceeding.

Section 29 limits an award of costs, other than disbursements, to 15 percent of the amount claimed, not 15 percent of the amount the court actually awards. Fifteen percent of the current Small Claims Court maximum monetary jurisdiction of $25,000.00 is $3,750.00. $3,750.00 is the maximum award of costs, other than disbursements, that the court may order to be paid to a successful party by an unsuccessful party in a Small Claims Court action, unless the exception for unreasonable behaviour by a party or a party's representative during the proceeding applies, in which case the court may make a higher costs award.

Costs Consequences of Failure to Accept an Offer to Settle (Rule 14.07(1) and (2))

If a plaintiff makes an offer to settle at least seven days before trial that is not accepted by the defendant and is not withdrawn and does not expire before the trial, the court may award the plaintiff an amount of costs not exceeding twice the costs of the action, if the plaintiff obtains a judgment as favourable as or more favourable than the terms of the offer (Rule 14.07(1)).

If a defendant makes an offer to settle at least seven days before trial that is not accepted by the plaintiff and is not withdrawn and does not expire before the trial, the court may award the defendant an amount of costs not exceeding twice the costs awardable to a successful party from the date the offer was served, if the plaintiff obtains a judgment as favourable as or less favourable than the terms of the offer (Rule 14.07(2)).

Failing to accept an offer to settle that falls within the conditions set out in Rules 14.07(1) and (2) has been deemed by the courts to be unreasonable behaviour by a party or a party's representative that triggers the exception to the general rule set out in s. 29 of the *Courts of Justice Act* limiting a costs award for a representation fee to 15 percent of the amount claimed. See *Melara-Lopez v. Richarz*, discussed in Chapter 8 at page 325. If the exception is triggered, the maximum amount of costs the court may award for a representation fee under Rule 14.07 is $2 \times 15\%$ of the amount claimed. Disbursements will be assessed and awarded in addition to the amount awarded for a reasonable representation fee.

A costs award to a self-represented party will not include a representation fee. A self-represented party who is successful at trial is entitled to a costs order for payment of her reasonable disbursements only. If a self-represented party makes an offer to settle to which Rule 14.07(1) or (2) applies, the court may award the self-represented party an amount not exceeding $500.00 as compensation for inconvenience and expense (Rule 14.07(3)), in addition to any amount payable for reasonable disbursements incurred by the self-represented party in the proceeding.

Compensation for Inconvenience and Expense (Rule 19.05)

The court may order an unsuccessful party to pay to a successful party who is self-represented an amount not exceeding $500.00 as compensation for inconvenience and expense.

Penalty (Rule 19.06)

If the court is satisfied that any party (self-represented or represented, successful or unsuccessful) has unduly complicated or prolonged an action or has otherwise acted unreasonably, the court may order the party to pay an amount as compensation to another party.

Submission as to Costs at Conclusion of the Trial

When both parties have made their closing submissions as to judgment, the judge will give her decision. She may give her reasons for judgment immediately after hearing submissions, or she may wish to **reserve judgment**—that is, take some time to review the evidence and the applicable law, and provide the parties with written or spoken reasons at a later time. After the judge has handed down her decision, she will then ask the successful party for a submission as to costs. Other parties may comment on the submission. If Rule 14.07 or Rule 19.06 applies, a party or her representative may raise Rule 14.07 or Rule 19.06 when making submissions.

If Rule 19.06 applies, any party (self-represented or represented, successful or unsuccessful) who has unduly complicated or prolonged the action or has otherwise acted unreasonably may be ordered by the court to pay compensation to another party (whether that party is self-represented or represented, successful or unsuccessful). When preparing your submission on costs, you should review Rule 19.06 if you think it may be applicable, and provide details of the party's unreasonable behaviour during the course of the action in your submission.

You should prepare your submission as to costs ahead of time. Your submission should refer to any rules of the *Small Claims Court Rules* or sections of the *Courts of Justice Act* on which you are relying, so that you are prepared for any questions the judge or another party may raise. A successful client may not recover all of her representation fees, but she is entitled to recover 15 percent of the amount claimed exclusive of disbursements under s. 29 of the *Courts of Justice Act*, and you should draft your submission on costs with that in mind. The clerk will assess proper disbursements.

When preparing your submissions as to costs, you should consider preparing a bill of costs to present to the judge and other parties. A **bill of costs** provides a calculation of the cost of legal services for purposes of determining a reasonable representation fee under the Rules and the *Courts of Justice Act*. It also contains an itemized list of all expenses and disbursements in the matter. Disbursements are assessed in accordance with the regulations to the *Administration of Justice Act* and Rules 19.01(3) and (4). For disbursements (such as photocopies or expert reports) that are not listed in the regulations, the client may not recover the full amount claimed on the bill of costs. For disbursements such as court filing fees, the client is entitled to recover the full amount.

The Small Claims Court forms do not include a bill of costs. You will find a draft bill of costs for Juliette Greco, plaintiff (defendant by defendant's claim) in *Greco v. Hardwick*, in Form 57A of the *Rules of Civil Procedure* at Appendix 9.3 to this chapter. Note that the representation fee on the bill of costs is calculated in accordance with s. 29 of the *Courts of Justice Act* and Rule 19.02, and may not reflect the amount that would actually be billed to the client for a matter where there was preparation for and attendance at a settlement conference and a trial.

CHAPTER SUMMARY

In an action for unliquidated damages where all defendants in the proceeding have been noted in default, a plaintiff may (1) file a motion in writing for an assessment of damages, with an affidavit in support setting out reasons why the motion should be granted, including details as to the amount of damages owed; or (2) request an assessment hearing.

An assessment hearing may be held:

1. where the plaintiff requests an assessment hearing (Rule 11.03(2)(b)); or

2. where a judge orders an assessment hearing. A judge will order an assessment hearing where the affidavit evidence filed in support of a Rule 11.03(2)(a) motion in writing for an assessment of damages is so inadequate or unsatisfactory that the judge requires spoken evidence from the plaintiff in order to make a decision (Rule 11.03(3)(b)).

Where an assessment hearing is requested by the plaintiff or ordered by a judge, the plaintiff will be required to fix a date for the hearing. An assessment hearing is like a trial (Rule 11.03(4)), except that the defendant is not present, and, as with a motion in writing for an assessment of damages, the plaintiff is not required to prove liability against a defendant noted in default, because the defendant by her default is deemed to admit liability (Rule 11.03(5)). The only issue before the court is how much money the defendant owes the plaintiff.

If a disputed action is not resolved at the settlement conference, the clerk shall provide the parties with a notice stating that one of the parties must request a trial date if the action is not disposed of within 30 days after the settlement conference. A party requesting a trial date shall file a request to clerk with the court office and pay the fee. The clerk will then send out a notice of trial to all parties not in default.

When you receive a notice of trial in a defended action, you should contact your client immediately and advise him of the date. The notice of trial should be filed in your pleadings subfile. The trial date should be noted in your calendar and tickler, with appropriate bring-forward dates. You should do a review of the settlement conference endorsement record, to find out whether there are any directions, recommendations, or court orders by the settlement conference judge that require further action. You should ensure that any further action required is taken.

The general rule with respect to evidence at trial is that a witness should be summoned to be present at the trial to give evidence, identify documents, and be cross-examined.

In Small Claims Court, any witness who is not a party to the action and who is required to give evidence in the action may do so by way of a signed written statement or document or an audio or visual record under Rules 18.02(1) and (2). Unless the trial judge orders otherwise, the written statement shall be received in evidence if

- the signed written statement or an appendix thereto states the name, telephone number, and address for service (and, in the case of an expert witness, a summary of qualifications) of the author of the written statement; and

- the party relying on the signed written statement serves the statement on all other parties who have received a notice of trial at least 30 days before the trial date.

A party who has been served with a written statement or document and wishes to cross-examine the witness or author may summon the witness or author by serving the person with a summons to witness (Form 18A) and attendance money (Rules 8.01(7), 18.02(4), 18.03(1)). Service of the summons and attendance money by the party or the party's licensee shall take place at least ten days before the trial date (Rule 8.01(7)).

A party who serves a summons to witness and attendance money on a witness or author shall, at the time the summons is served, serve a copy of the summons on all other parties.

If you have served a document, written statement, or audio or visual record on all other parties who were served with a notice of trial at least 30 days before the trial date, and you have concerns about the quality or sufficiency of its contents, you should consider serving a summons to witness and attendance money upon its author. That way, if the court rules that the document shall not be received in evidence, its author can be called to give evidence; or, if the document is received in evidence, you can attempt to cure its defects with evidence elicited during direct examination of its author.

You should always serve a summons to witness and attendance money on any person with material evidence in support of your client's claim or defence from whom a written statement has not been obtained.

At the courthouse on the trial date, the parties take their places at the counsel tables facing the judge's bench when the matter is called. The paralegals for the plaintiff and defendant introduce themselves, and give brief opening submissions if invited by the trial judge to do so.

If either party has summoned additional witnesses, before any evidence is heard, the judge should be asked to make an order excluding those witnesses from hearing evidence. An order excluding witnesses is required only when there are witnesses other than the parties giving evidence.

The plaintiff is then invited to call her first witness. Usually, this will be the plaintiff herself. The plaintiff takes the stand, is sworn or affirmed, and gives her evidence in support of her claim in direct examination. If there is a defendant's claim, the plaintiff should give evidence in support of her defence to the defendant's claim at the same time as her evidence in support of the plaintiff's claim, if it is appropriate to do so.

The plaintiff may be cross-examined by the defendant or the defendant's representative when direct examination is completed. If any new issues are raised in cross-examination, the plaintiff will be re-examined by her legal representative on those issues at the completion of cross-examination. The same procedure applies to any other witnesses the plaintiff calls.

When the plaintiff and her witnesses, if any, have given their evidence, the plaintiff's case is closed. The defendant and the defendant's witnesses, if any, then take the stand, are sworn or affirmed, give evidence in support of the defence and the defendant's claim, if any, and are cross-examined and, where appropriate, re-examined.

When all of the defendant's evidence has been heard, the defendant's case is closed. If the parties are represented, the judge should then request closing submissions from the parties' legal representatives.

A party's closing submission should review the issues in dispute, summarize the evidence that supports the party's claim or defence, and present arguments as to why the relief the party is seeking should be granted by the court based on that evidence. The successful party should be prepared to make submissions as to costs. The representative of the successful party should consider preparing a draft bill of costs for reference when making submissions as to costs.

KEY TERMS

assessment hearing: a hearing wherein the court determines the amount of the claim *(p. 340)*

bill of costs: an itemized list of a party's representation fees and disbursements supported by documentation *(p. 381)*

counsel slip: a form that must be filled out on a court appearance and given to the court clerk; it gives the court notice that there is someone appearing on the matter, and tells the court what your name is, the matter you are there on, and who your client is *(p. 371)*

cross-examination: questions used to pinpoint weaknesses or inconsistencies in the testimony of another party or another party's witness *(p. 367)*

direct examination: the questions that you ask your own witnesses when they take the stand to shape the evidence into a clear, concise narrative that can be easily understood by the court *(p. 365)*

docket: a list of matters to be heard on a particular day in a particular courtroom; it will be posted outside the courtroom for the date those matters are scheduled to be heard *(p. 371)*

exhibit: an original document that is material to an issue in the action; it must be identified by a witness with personal knowledge of its contents, which may be referred to in her spoken evidence; it is then marked as an exhibit by the court clerk and placed in the court file as part of the evidence *(p. 366)*

expert witness: a witness who, because of education and/or specialization, has knowledge about an issue or issues in the action that the trial judge or other trier of fact does not have; the expert witness's evidence must be helpful to the court and necessary to a proper determination of the issue(s) about which the expert witness gives an opinion *(p. 356)*

finding as to credibility: where there is conflicting evidence from witnesses, a decision by the trier of fact (the judge in a non-jury trial) about whose evidence to believe, in all of the circumstances; factors to be considered are the witness's demeanour on the witness stand, knowledge of the circumstances, and relationship to the matters in question, including any issues of bias *(p. 364)*

harass a witness: engage in conduct that is coercive or threatening toward a witness at any stage of a proceeding *(p. 361)*

leading question: a question that implies the existence of certain facts or suggests a correct answer to a witness (or to the trier of fact); the general rule is that leading questions may be used only in cross-examination of a witness *(p. 365)*

material evidence: evidence that has a logical connection to an issue or issues in dispute in the action; evidence that will assist the trier of fact to make a determination about whose allegations to believe *(p. 353)*

open-ended, or direct, question: a question that lets the witness give his own answer without prompting; a question that does not contain any language suggesting a "correct" answer to the witness *(p. 365)*

opinion evidence: in the case of an expert witness, testimony of what the expert witness thinks, believes, or infers with regard to facts in dispute *(p. 356)*

order excluding witnesses: an order that all witnesses except the parties themselves shall leave the courtroom and wait outside the courtroom until they are called to give evidence; the purpose of an order excluding witnesses is to prevent witnesses who have not yet taken the stand from hearing, and being influenced by, the evidence of the witnesses who take the stand ahead of them; required only when there are witnesses other than the parties giving evidence; if the plaintiff and the defendant are the only witnesses, an order excluding witnesses is not required *(p. 375)*

qualified interpreter: a person who is trained to interpret in a courtroom environment; interpreters are not under oath when they interpret; they must provide an unbiased and accurate version of what the witness under oath is saying on the stand *(p. 353)*

re-examination: evidence intended to clarify and, if necessary, neutralize or rebut any potentially damaging evidence brought out in cross-examination; also called "reply evidence" or "rebuttal evidence" *(p. 375)*

reserve judgment: the judge will take time to review the evidence and the applicable law and provide the parties with a written or spoken decision at a later time *(p. 381)*

summons to witness: a document compelling the attendance at trial of a person whose evidence is material to the conduct of an action *(p. 350)*

sympathetic witness: a witness who gives evidence that supports your cause *(p. 377)*

trial book: book of notes, documents, submissions, and so on prepared for and used by a party at trial, containing all important information needed at the trial in a secure and organized format *(p. 370)*

unsympathetic witness: a witness who gives evidence that supports an opposing party's cause *(p. 377)*

REFERENCES

Administration of Justice Act, RSO 1990, c. A.6.

Courts of Justice Act, RSO 1990, c. C.43.

Evidence Act, RSO 1990, c. E.23.

Kilometre Allowances, RRO 1990, Reg. 11.

Law Society of Upper Canada (LSUC), *Paralegal Professional Conduct Guidelines* (Toronto: LSUC, 2008, as amended); available online at http://www.lsuc.on.ca.

Law Society of Upper Canada (LSUC), *Paralegal Rules of Conduct* (Toronto: LSUC, 2007, as amended); available online at http://www.lsuc.on.ca.

Melara-Lopez v. Richarz, [2009] OJ No. 6313 (SCJ), aff'd. [2009] OJ No. 4362 (Div. Ct.).

Rules of the Small Claims Court, O. Reg. 258/98.

Small Claims Court—Fees and Allowances, O. Reg. 432/93.

Steckley v. Haid, [2009] OJ No. 2014 (Sm. Cl. Ct.).

Turner v. Kitchener (City), [2011] OJ No. 4803 (Sm. Cl. Ct.).

REVIEW QUESTIONS

When answering the following questions, you should note the numbers of any rules you are relying on.

1. **a.** What is an assessment hearing?

   b. When will an assessment hearing be held?

   c. What must the plaintiff prove at an assessment hearing?

2. In a defended action, who may set a date for trial? What form must be filed? What is the fee?

3. You have just received a notice of trial in Small Claims Court. You are already booked to appear on several matters in Provincial Offences Court on that date. What should you do?

4. You are acting for the defendant in a Small Claims Court matter. The plaintiff is self-represented. You receive a notice of trial. You and your client show up on the trial date. You have served all written statements and documents on the defendant at least 30 days before the trial date. You have served a summons to witness on one of the defendant's witnesses for purposes of cross-examination on his written statement. The witness is in the courtroom. You are ready to go. When the matter is called, the plaintiff's son appears in the courtroom, and requests an adjournment. The son says that his father had to leave the province suddenly to attend the funeral of an uncle. What should you ask for?

5. You are acting for the plaintiff in a Small Claims Court action in Milton. After the settlement conference, and 45 days before the trial date, your client produces documents that you have never seen before. One of them is a written statement about material issues in the matter by a witness who currently lives in Toronto. You intend to rely on these documents at trial. What should you do?

6. What is an expert witness?

7. If a party requires a witness to attend at trial in person to give evidence, what should that party do? What is the deadline for doing so?

8. What happens if a witness who has been properly summoned fails to attend?

9. Name six things that you should do when preparing for trial. Note: There are more than six things that you should do when preparing for trial, but for purposes of this question you are only required to name six.

10. What is direct examination? What sort of questions do you use in direct examination?

11. What are leading questions? When may they be used at trial?

12. In a Small Claims Court trial, what should you focus on in cross-examination?

13. **a.** What is the purpose of an objection, and how do you make an objection?

    b. I made an objection, and the judge made a ruling that was clearly wrong. What should I do?

14. **a.** When are closing submissions made?

    b. When are submissions as to costs made?

APPENDIX 9.1   Greco v. Hardwick: Summons to Witness (Form 18A)

ONTARIO

Superior Court of Justice
Cour supérieure de justice

Summons to Witness
Assignation de témoin

Form / *Formule* 18A Ont. Reg. No. / *Règl. de l'Ont.* : 258/98

Seal / *Sceau*

Brampton
Small Claims Court / *Cour des petites créances de*
7755 Hurontario Street
Brampton, Ontario
L6W 4T6
Address / *Adresse*

905 456 4700
Phone number / *Numéro de téléphone*

SC-00-34065-00
Claim No. / *N° de la demande*

BETWEEN / *ENTRE*

Juliette Greco

Plaintiff(s) / *Demandeur(s)/demanderesse(s)*

and / *et*

James Hardwick

Defendant(s) / *Défendeur(s)/défenderesse(s)*

TO: Glenn Woods
DESTINATAIRE :

(Name of witness / *Nom du témoin*)

YOU ARE REQUIRED TO ATTEND AND TO GIVE EVIDENCE IN COURT at the trial of this action on
VOUS ÊTES REQUIS(E) DE VOUS PRÉSENTER DEVANT LE TRIBUNAL POUR TÉMOIGNER *à l'instruction
de cette action le*

April 18 , 20 -- **at** 9:30 a.m. , **at**
à   (Time / *heure*)   *à/au*

7765 Hurontario Street, Brampton, Ontario L6W 4T1
(Address of court location / *Adresse du tribunal*)

and to remain until your attendance is no longer required. You may be required to return to court from time to time.
*et d'y demeurer jusqu'à ce que votre présence ne soit plus requise. Vous pourriez être requis(e) de vous
présenter à nouveau devant le tribunal à l'occasion.*

YOU ARE ALSO REQUIRED TO BRING WITH YOU AND PRODUCE AT THE TRIAL the following documents
or other things in your possession, control or power: (Identify and describe particular documents and other things required)
***VOUS ÊTES EN OUTRE REQUIS(E) D'APPORTER AVEC VOUS ET DE PRODUIRE LORS DE
L'INSTRUCTION*** *les documents ou autres objets suivants dont vous avez la garde, la possession ou le contrôle :*
(Indiquez et décrivez les documents et autres objets particuliers qui sont requis)

**Fee schedules and invoices for lawn care, landscaping and pool maintenance for four years prior to the
current year**

SCR 18.03-18A (June 1, 2009 / *1er juin 2009*) CSD

APPENDIX 9.1 **Greco v. Hardwick: Summons to Witness (Form 18A)** *concluded*

FORM / *FORMULE* 18A   PAGE 2   SC-00-34065-00

                                                              Claim No. / *N° de la demande*

and all other documents or other things in your possession, control or power relating to the action.
ainsi que tous les autres documents ou autres objets dont vous avez la garde, la possession ou le contrôle et qui se rapportent à l'action.

James Hardwick   has requested the clerk to issue this summons.

_____   *a demandé au greffier de délivrer la présente*
(Name of party / *Nom de la partie*)   *assignation.*

_____, 20 ____   _____

                                                (Signature of clerk / *Signature du greffier*)

NOTE:	THIS SUMMONS MUST BE SERVED personally, at least 10 days before the trial date, on the person to be summoned together with attendance money calculated in accordance with the Small Claims Court Schedule of Fees, which is a regulation under the *Administration of Justice Act*. To obtain a copy of the regulation, attend the nearest Small Claims Court or access the following website: www.e-laws.gov.on.ca.
REMARQUE :	*LA PRÉSENTE ASSIGNATION DOIT ÊTRE SIGNIFIÉE à personne, au moins 10 jours avant la date du procès, à la personne devant être assignée, avec l'indemnité de présence calculée conformément au barème des honoraires et frais de la Cour des petites créances qui constitue un règlement pris en application de la Loi sur l'administration de la justice. Vous pouvez obtenir un exemplaire du règlement auprès de la Cour des petites créances de votre localité ou en consultant le site Web suivant : www.lois-en-ligne.gouv.on.ca.*

CAUTION:	IF YOU FAIL TO ATTEND OR REMAIN IN ATTENDANCE AS REQUIRED BY THIS SUMMONS, A WARRANT MAY BE ISSUED FOR YOUR ARREST.
AVERTISSEMENT :	*SI VOUS NE VOUS PRÉSENTEZ PAS OU SI VOUS NE DEMEUREZ PAS PRÉSENT(E) COMME L'EXIGE LA PRÉSENTE ASSIGNATION, UN MANDAT D'ARRÊT PEUT ÊTRE DÉLIVRÉ CONTRE VOUS.*

SCR 18.03-18A (June 1, 2009 / *1er juin 2009*) CSD

APPENDIX 9.1 Greco v. Hardwick: Affidavit of Service of Summons to Witness and Attendance Money (Form 8A)

ONTARIO
Superior Court of Justice
Cour supérieure de justice

Affidavit of Service
Affidavit de signification
Form / *Formule* 8A Ont. Reg. No. / *Régl. de l'Ont.* : 258/98

Brampton
Small Claims Court / *Cour des petites créances de*
7755 Hurontario Street
Brampton, Ontario
L6W 4T6
Address / *Adresse*

905 456 4700
Phone number / *Numéro de téléphone*

SC-00-34065-00
Claim No. / *N° de la demande*

BETWEEN / *ENTRE*

Juliette Greco
Plaintiff(s) / *Demandeur(s)/demanderesse(s)*

and / *et*

James Hardwick
Defendant(s) / *Défendeur(s)/défenderesse(s)*

My name is
Je m'appelle
Neela Subramaniam
(Full name / *Nom et prénoms*)

I live in
J'habite à
Brampton, Ontario
(Municipality & province / *Municipalité et province*)

and I swear/affirm that the following is true:
et je déclare sous serment/j'affirme solennellement que les renseignements suivants sont véridiques :

1. **I served**
   J'ai signifié à
   Glenn Woods
   (Full name of person/corporation served / *Nom et prénoms de la personne/nom au complet de la personne morale qui a reçu la signification*)
   , on
   , *le*
   March 15
   (Date)
   , 20 -- ,

   at
   au
   78 Bosky Dell Crescent, Mississauga, Ontario M2N 3P4
   (Address (street and number, unit, municipality, province) / *Adresse (numéro et rue, unité, municipalité, province)*)

   which is
   soit
   ☒ the address of the person's home
   l'adresse du domicile de la personne

   ☐ the address of the corporation's place of business
   l'adresse du lieu de travail de l'établissement de la personne morale

   ☐ the address of the person's or corporation's representative on record with the court
   l'adresse du/de la représentant(e) de la personne ou de la personne morale figurant au dossier du tribunal

   ☐ the address on the document most recently filed in court by the party
   l'adresse figurant sur le document déposé le plus récemment au tribunal par la partie

   ☐ the address of the corporation's attorney for service in Ontario
   l'adresse du fondé de pouvoir de la personne morale aux fins de signification en Ontario

   ☐ other address:
   autre adresse :
   (Specify. / *Précisez.*)

   with
   ce qui suit :
   a summons to witness (Form 18A) and attendance money
   (Name(s) of document(s) served / *Titre(s) du ou des documents signifiés*)

SCR 8.06-8A (September 1, 2010 / *1er septembre* 2010) CSD

APPENDIX 9.1   Greco v. Hardwick: Affidavit of Service of Summons to Witness and Attendance Money (Form 8A) *continued*

FORM / *FORMULE* 8A   PAGE 2   SC-00-34065-00
_____
                                                              Claim No. / *N° de la demande*

2. I served the document(s) referred to in paragraph one by the following method:
    J'ai signifié le ou les documents mentionnés au numéro un de la façon suivante :
    (Tell how service took place by checking appropriate box(es).)
    (Indiquez la façon dont la signification a été effectuée en cochant la ou les cases appropriées.)

Personal service / *Significa- tion à personne*	☒	leaving a copy with the person. *en laissant une copie à la personne.*
	☐	leaving a copy with the _____ of the corporation. *en laissant une copie au/à la* (Office or position / *Charge ou poste*) *de la personne morale.*
	☐	leaving a copy with: _____ *en laissant une copie à :* (Specify person's name and office or position. / *Indiquez le nom de la personne ainsi que sa charge ou son poste.*)

Service at place of residenc e / *Significa- tion au domicile*   ☐   leaving a copy in a sealed envelope addressed to the person at the person's place of residence with a person who appeared to be an adult member of the same household, and sending another copy of the same document(s) to the person's place of residence on the same day or the following day by:
en laissant une copie au domicile de la personne, dans une enveloppe scellée adressée à celle-ci, auprès d'une personne habitant sous le même toit qui semblait majeure et en envoyant une autre copie du ou des mêmes documents au domicile de la personne le même jour ou le jour suivant :

    ☐   regular lettermail. *par courrier ordinaire.*

    ☐   registered mail. *par courrier recommandé.*

    ☐   courier. *par messagerie.*

Service by registered mail / *Significa- tion par courrier recom- mandé*   ☐   registered mail.
par courrier recommandé.
(If a copy of a plaintiff's claim or defendant's claim was served by registered mail, attach a copy of the Canada Post delivery confirmation, showing the signature verifying delivery, to this affidavit.)
(Si une copie de la demande du demandeur ou de la demande du défendeur a été signifiée par courrier recommandé, annexez au présent affidavit une copie de la confirmation de livraison remise par Postes Canada sur laquelle figure une signature qui confirme la livraison.)

Service by courier / *Significa- tion par messa- gerie*   ☐   courier.
par messagerie.
(If a copy of a plaintiff's claim or defendant's claim was served by courier, attach a copy of the courier's delivery confirmation, showing the signature verifying delivery, to this affidavit.)
(Si une copie de la demande du demandeur ou de la demande du défendeur a été signifiée par messagerie, annexez au présent affidavit une copie de la confirmation de livraison remise par le service de messagerie sur laquelle figure la signature du destinataire de la signification.)

Service on lawyer / *Significa- tion à l'avocat*   ☐   leaving a copy with a lawyer who accepted service on the person's behalf.
en laissant une copie avec l'avocat qui a accepté la signification au nom de la personne.
(Attach a copy of the document endorsed with the lawyer's acceptance of service.)
(Annexez une copie du document, sur lequel l'avocat a inscrit qu'il a accepté la signification.)

Service by regular lettermail / *Significa- tion par courrier ordinaire*   ☐   regular lettermail.
par courrier ordinaire.

SCR 8.06-8A (September 1, 2010 / *1er septembre 2010*) CSD

Continued on next page / *Suite à la page suivante*

APPENDIX 9.1 Greco v. Hardwick: Affidavit of Service of Summons to Witness and Attendance Money (Form 8A) *concluded*

FORM / *FORMULE* 8A	PAGE 3	SC-00-34065-00
		Claim No. / *N° de la demande*

Service by fax / *Significa-tion par télécopie*

☐ fax sent at _____ at the following fax number: _____
par télécopie (Time / *heure*) *au numéro de télécopieur* (Fax number / *numéro de*
envoyée à *suivant :* *télécopieur*)

Service to last known address of corporation or attorney for service, and to the directors / *Significa-tion à la dernière adresse connue de la personne morale ou de son fondé de pouvoir aux fins de signification et aux administra-teurs*

☐ mail/courier to corporation or attorney for service at last known address recorded with the Ministry of Government Services, and
d'une part, par la poste/par messagerie à la personne morale ou à son fondé de pouvoir aux fins de signification, à la dernière adresse connue figurant dans les dossiers du ministère des Services gouvernementaux;

mail/courier to each director, as recorded with the Ministry of Government Services, as set out below:
d'autre part, par la poste/par messagerie à chaque administrateur mentionné dans les dossiers du ministère des Services gouvernementaux et dont le nom et l'adresse sont indiqués ci-dessous :

Name of director / *Nom de l'administrateur*	Director's address as recorded with the Ministry of Government Services (street & number, unit, municipality, province) / *Adresse de l'administrateur figurant dans les dossiers du ministère des Services gouvernementaux (numéro et rue, unité, municipalité, province)*
_____	_____
_____	_____
_____	_____
_____	_____
_____	_____

(Attach separate sheet for additional names if necessary. /
Joignez au besoin une feuille séparée s'il y a d'autres noms à ajouter.)

Substituted service / *Significa-tion indirecte*

☐ substituted service as ordered by the court on _____ , 20 _____ ,
par signification indirecte ordonnée par le tribunal le (Date)

as follows: (Give details.)
comme suit :   (*Précisez.*)

Sworn/Affirmed before me at   **Brampton**
Déclaré sous serment/Affirmé (Municipality / *municipalité*)
solennellement devant moi à

in   **Ontario**
en/à/au (Province, state, or country / *province, État ou pays*)

on   **March 22** , 20 **--**
le _____
Commissioner for taking affidavits
Commissaire aux affidavits
(Type or print name below if signature
is illegible.)
(*Dactylographiez le nom ou écrivez-le*
en caractères d'imprimerie ci-dessous
si la signature est illisible.)

Signature
(This form is to be signed in front of a
lawyer, justice of the peace, notary public or
commissioner for taking affidavits.)
(*La présente formule doit être signée en*
présence d'un avocat, d'un juge de paix,
d'un notaire ou d'un commissaire aux
affidavits.)

SCR 8.06-8A (September 1, 2010 / *1er septembre 2010*) CSD

APPENDIX 9.1 Greco v. Hardwick: Affidavit of Service of Copy of Summons to Witness on Plaintiff's Paralegal (Form 8A)

ONTARIO

Superior Court of Justice
Cour supérieure de justice

Affidavit of Service
Affidavit de signification

Form / *Formule* 8A Ont. Reg. No. / *Règl. de l'Ont.* : 258/98

Brampton	**SC-00-34065-00**
Small Claims Court / *Cour des petites créances de*	Claim No. / *N° de la demande*
7755 Hurontario Street	
Brampton, Ontario	
L6W 4T6	
Address / *Adresse*	
905 456 4700	
Phone number / *Numéro de téléphone*	

BETWEEN / *ENTRE*

Juliette Greco

Plaintiff(s) / *Demandeur(s)/demanderesse(s)*

and / *et*

James Hardwick

Defendant(s) / *Défendeur(s)/défenderesse(s)*

My name is
Je m'appelle

Neela Subramaniam

(Full name / *Nom et prénoms*)

I live in
J'habite à

Brampton, Ontario

(Municipality & province / *Municipalité et province*)

and I swear/affirm that the following is true:
et je déclare sous serment/j'affirme solennellement que les renseignements suivants sont véridiques :

1. **I served**   Prior Mustafa LLP Attention: Marie Prior   , on   March 15   , 20 -- ,
   J'ai signifié à   (Full name of person/corporation served / *Nom et prénoms*   , *le*   (Date)
   de la personne/nom au complet de la personne morale
   qui a reçu la signification)

   at   22 County Court Boulevard, Brampton, Ontario A1A 2B3
   au   (Address (street and number, unit, municipality, province) / *Adresse (numéro et rue, unité, municipalité, province)*)

   which is   ☐ the address of the person's home
   soit   *l'adresse du domicile de la personne*

   ☐ the address of the corporation's place of business
   l'adresse du lieu de travail de l'établissement de la personne morale

   ☒ the address of the person's or corporation's representative on record with the court
   l'adresse du/de la représentant(e) de la personne ou de la personne morale figurant au dossier du tribunal

   ☐ the address on the document most recently filed in court by the party
   l'adresse figurant sur le document déposé le plus récemment au tribunal par la partie

   ☐ the address of the corporation's attorney for service in Ontario
   l'adresse du fondé de pouvoir de la personne morale aux fins de signification en Ontario

   ☐ other address:
   autre adresse :   (Specify. / *Précisez.*)

   with   a copy of a summons to witness (Form 18A) directed to Glenn Woods
   ce qui suit :   (Name(s) of document(s) served / *Titre(s) du ou des documents signifiés*)

SCR 8.06-8A (September 1, 2010 / *1er septembre 2010*) CSD

APPENDIX 9.1   Greco v. Hardwick: Affidavit of Service of Copy of Summons to Witness on Plaintiff's Paralegal (Form 8A) *continued*

FORM / *FORMULE* 8A	PAGE 2	SC-00-34065-00
		Claim No. / *N° de la demande*

2. I served the document(s) referred to in paragraph one by the following method:
J'ai signifié le ou les documents mentionnés au numéro un de la façon suivante :
(Tell how service took place by checking appropriate box(es).)
(Indiquez la façon dont la signification a été effectuée en cochant la ou les cases appropriées.)

Personal service / *Signification à personne*

☐ leaving a copy with the person.
en laissant une copie à la personne.

☐ leaving a copy with the _____ of the corporation.
en laissant une copie au/à la   (Office or position / *Charge ou poste*)   *de la personne morale.*

☐ leaving a copy with: _____
en laissant une copie à :   (Specify person's name and office or position. / *Indiquez le nom de la personne ainsi que sa charge ou son poste.*)

Service at place of residence / *Signification au domicile*

☐ leaving a copy in a sealed envelope addressed to the person at the person's place of residence with a person who appeared to be an adult member of the same household, and sending another copy of the same document(s) to the person's place of residence on the same day or the following day by:
en laissant une copie au domicile de la personne, dans une enveloppe scellée adressée à celle-ci, auprès d'une personne habitant sous le même toit qui semblait majeure et en envoyant une autre copie du ou des mêmes documents au domicile de la personne le même jour ou le jour suivant :

    ☐ regular lettermail.
    par courrier ordinaire.

    ☐ registered mail.
    par courrier recommandé.

    ☐ courer.
    par messagerie.

Service by registered mail / *Signification par courrier recommandé*

☐ registered mail.
par courrier recommandé.
(If a copy of a plaintiff's claim or defendant's claim was served by registered mail, attach a copy of the Canada Post delivery confirmation, showing the signature verifying delivery, to this affidavit.)
(Si une copie de la demande du demandeur ou de la demande du défendeur a été signifiée par courrier recommandé, annexez au présent affidavit une copie de la confirmation de livraison remise par Postes Canada sur laquelle figure une signature qui confirme la livraison.)

Service by courier / *Signification par messagerie*

☐ courier.
par messagerie.
(If a copy of a plaintiff's claim or defendant's claim was served by courier, attach a copy of the courier's delivery confirmation, showing the signature verifying delivery, to this affidavit.)
(Si une copie de la demande du demandeur ou de la demande du défendeur a été signifiée par messagerie, annexez au présent affidavit une copie de la confirmation de livraison remise par le service de messagerie sur laquelle figure la signature du destinataire de la signification.)

Service on lawyer / Signification à l'avocat

☐ leaving a copy with a lawyer who accepted service on the person's behalf.
en laissant une copie avec l'avocat qui a accepté la signification au nom de la personne.
(Attach a copy of the document endorsed with the lawyer's acceptance of service.)
(Annexez une copie du document, sur lequel l'avocat a inscrit qu'il a accepté la signification.)

Service by regular lettermail / *Signification par courrier ordinaire*

☐ regular lettermail.
par courrier ordinaire.

APPENDIX 9.1   Greco v. Hardwick: Affidavit of Service of Copy of Summons to Witness on Plaintiff's Paralegal (Form 8A) *concluded*

FORM / *FORMULE* 8A	PAGE 3	SC-00-34065-00
		Claim No. / *N° de la demande*

Service by fax /
Signification par télécopie

☒ fax sent at   **3:00 p.m.**   at the following fax number: **905 111 2233**
par télécopie *(Time / heure)*   *au numéro de télécopieur* *(Fax number / numéro de*
envoyée à   *suivant :*   *télécopieur)*

Service to last known address of corporation or attorney for service, and to the directors /
Signification à la dernière adresse connue de la personne morale ou de son fondé de pouvoir aux fins de signification et aux administrateurs

☐ mail/courier to corporation or attorney for service at last known address recorded with the Ministry of Government Services, and
d'une part, par la poste/par messagerie à la personne morale ou à son fondé de pouvoir aux fins de signification, à la dernière adresse connue figurant dans les dossiers du ministère des Services gouvernementaux;

mail/courier to each director, as recorded with the Ministry of Government Services, as set out below:
d'autre part, par la poste/par messagerie à chaque administrateur mentionné dans les dossiers du ministère des Services gouvernementaux et dont le nom et l'adresse sont indiqués ci-dessous

Name of director / *Nom de l'administrateur*	Director's address as recorded with the Ministry of Government Services (street & number, unit, municipality, province) / *Adresse de l'administrateur figurant dans les dossiers du ministère des Services gouvernementaux (numéro et rue, unité, municipalité, province)*
_____	_____
_____	_____
_____	_____
_____	_____
_____	_____

(Attach separate sheet for additional names if necessary. /
Joignez au besoin une feuille séparée s'il y a d'autres noms à ajouter.)

Substituted service /
Signification indirecte

☐ substituted service as ordered by the court on _____, 20 ____ ,
par signification indirecte ordonnée par le tribunal le   *(Date)*

as follows: (Give details.)
comme suit :   *(Précisez.)*

Sworn/Affirmed before me at   **Brampton**
Déclaré sous serment/Affirmé   *(Municipality / municipalité)*
solennellement devant moi à

in   **Ontario**
en/à/au   *(Province, state, or country / province, État ou pays)*

on   **March 22**   , 20 **--**   _____
le _____   Commissioner for taking affidavits
          Commissaire aux affidavits
          (Type or print name below if signature
          is illegible.)
          *(Dactylographiez le nom ou écrivez-le
          en caractères d'imprimerie ci-dessous
          si la signature est illisible.)*

_____
Signature
(This form is to be signed in front of a
lawyer, justice of the peace, notary public or
commissioner for taking affidavits.)
*(La présente formule doit être signée en
présence d'un avocat, d'un juge de paix,
d'un notaire ou d'un commissaire aux
affidavits.)*

APPENDIX 9.2   Warrant for Arrest of Defaulting Witness (Form 18B)

ONTARIO

Superior Court of Justice
Cour supérieure de justice

Warrant for Arrest of Defaulting Witness
Mandat d'arrêt d'un témoin défaillant
Form / *Formule* 18B Ont. Reg. No. / *Régl. de l'Ont.* : 258/98

Seal / *Sceau*

Thunder Bay
Small Claims Court / *Cour des petites créances de*
277 Camelot Street
Thunder Bay, Ontario
P7A 4B3
Address / *Adresse*

807 343 2710
Phone number / *Numéro de téléphone*

SC-00-05432-00
Claim No. / *N° de la demande*

BETWEEN / *ENTRE*

Emma Flood

Plaintiff(s) / *Demandeur(s)/demanderesse(s)*

and / *et*

Christine Michaeli

Defendant(s) / *Défendeur(s)/défenderesse(s)*

TO ALL POLICE OFFICERS IN ONTARIO AND TO THE OFFICERS OF ALL CORRECTIONAL INSTITUTIONS IN ONTARIO:
À TOUS LES AGENTS DE POLICE DE L'ONTARIO ET AUX AGENTS DE TOUS LES ÉTABLISSEMENTS CORRECTIONNELS DE L'ONTARIO :

The witness   **Anton Zupetti, also known as Andy Zupetti**
Le témoin   (Name / *Nom*)

of   **343 King's Cross Road, Thunder Bay, Ontario A2B 3C4**
de   (Address / *Adresse*)

was served with a Summons to Witness (Form 18A) to give evidence at the trial of this action, and the prescribed attendance money was paid or tendered.
a reçu signification d'une assignation de témoin (formule 18A) pour témoigner à l'instruction de la présente action, et l'indemnité de présence prescrite lui a été versée ou offerte.

The witness failed to attend or to remain in attendance at the trial, and I am satisfied that the evidence of this witness is material to this proceeding.
Le témoin ne s'est pas présenté ou n'est pas demeuré présent au procès, et je suis convaincu(e) que son témoignage est essentiel à l'instance.

YOU ARE ORDERED TO ARREST AND BRING this person before the court to give evidence in this action, and if the court is not then sitting or if the person cannot be brought before the court immediately, to deliver the person to a provincial correctional institution or other secure facility, to be admitted and detained there until the person can be brought before the court.
JE VOUS ORDONNE D'ARRÊTER CETTE PERSONNE ET DE L'AMENER devant le tribunal afin qu'elle témoigne dans l'action et, si le tribunal ne siège pas ou si la personne ne peut être amenée devant le tribunal immédiatement, de la livrer à un établissement correctionnel provincial ou à un autre établissement de garde en milieu fermé, afin qu'elle y soit admise et détenue jusqu'à ce qu'elle puisse être amenée devant le tribunal.

I FURTHER ORDER YOU TO HOLD this person in custody and to detain him/her only so long as necessary to bring this person before a court as ordered above.
JE VOUS ORDONNE EN OUTRE DE MAINTENIR cette personne sous garde et de la détenir tant et aussi longtemps qu'il sera nécessaire pour l'amener devant un tribunal, comme il est ordonné ci-dessus.

_____ , 20 _____   _____
                                      (Signature of judge / *Signature du juge*)

SCR 18.03-20.11-18B (June 1, 2009 / *1er juin 2009*) CSD

APPENDIX 9.2 Identification Form (Form 20K)

ONTARIO

Superior Court of Justice
Cour supérieure de justice

Identification Form
Formule de renseignements signalétiques
Form / Formule 20K Ont. Reg. No. / Régl. de l'Ont. : 258/98

Thunder Bay
Small Claims Court / *Cour des petites créances de*
277 Camelot Street
Thunder Bay, Ontario
P7A 4B3
Address / *Adresse*

SC-00-05432-00
Claim No. / *N° de la demande*

807 343 2710
Phone number / *Numéro de téléphone*

BETWEEN / *ENTRE*

Emma Flood
Plaintiff(s)/Creditor(s) / *Demandeur(s)/demanderesse(s)/Créancier(s)/créancière(s)*

and / *et*

Christine Michaeli
Defendant(s)/Debtor(s) / *Défendeur(s)/défenderesse(s)/Débiteur(s)/débitrice(s)*

TO HELP PROCESS A CIVIL WARRANT FOR COMMITTAL, the following information, or **as much information as is reasonably available should be provided.** This is necessary for the police to identify the person to be arrested. Without this information it will be difficult to enforce the warrant.
POUR FACILITER LA DÉLIVRANCE D'UN MANDAT DE DÉPÔT AU CIVIL, les renseignements suivants ou autant de renseignements qui sont raisonnablement disponibles devraient être fournis. Ces renseignements sont nécessaires pour que la police puisse identifier la personne à arrêter. Sans ces renseignements, il sera difficile d'exécuter le mandat.

1. Name **Zupetti**   **Anton**   **Leopold**
Nom   (Last name of individual / *Nom de famille*   (First name / *Premier prénom*)   (Second name / *Deuxième prénom*)
        du particulier)

2. Also known as names (if any) **Andy Zupetti**
Nom(s) sous lequel/lesquels la personne est également connue (le cas échéant)

3. Last known address and telephone number
Dernière adresse connue et dernier numéro de téléphone connu
343 King's Cross Road, Thunder Bay, Ontario A2B 3C4

4. (a) Date of birth *(d, m, y)* **22/04/1980**
        Date de naissance (j, m, a)

5. Physical description
Description physique

(a) Gender **M**   (b) Height **5' 8"**   (c) Weight **195**   (d) Build **stocky**
Sexe   *Taille*   *Poids*   *Corpulence*

(e) Colour of eyes **green**   (f) Hair colour **brown**   (g) Complexion **fair**
Couleur des yeux   *Couleur des cheveux*   *Teint*

(h) Clean-shaven **no (goatee)**   (i) Wears glasses **no**
Rasé de près   *Porte des lunettes*

(j) Clothing habits and tastes **casual (blue jeans and hoodies)**
Habitudes et goûts vestimentaires

SCR 20.11-20K (June 1, 2009 / *1er juin 2009*) CSD

APPENDIX 9.2 **Identification Form (Form 20K)** *concluded*

FORM / *FORMULE* 20K   **PAGE 2**   SC-00-05432-00

Claim No. / *N° de la demande*

head shaved, goatee, facial piercings, tattoos on neck,
(k) Distinguishing marks, scars, tattoos, etc. arms and upper torso
Marques distinctives, cicatrices, tatouages, etc.

(l) Other **Slight limp (right leg)**
Autre   (Specify / *Précisez*.)

6. Usual occupation **unemployed**
Profession habituelle

7. Last known place of employment **unemployed**
Dernier lieu de travail connu

8. Vehicle description
Description du véhicule

(a) Make, model and year **Honda Civic 2003**   (b) Colour **Black**
Marque, modèle et année   *Couleur*

(c) Licence plate number **BBAD 666**   Province or state **Ontario**
Numéro de la plaque d'immatriculation   *Province ou État*

(d) Driver's licence number   Province or state
Numéro du permis de conduire   *Province ou État*

(e) Distinguishing features on the vehicle (dents, car stereo, etc.)
Caractéristiques distinctives du véhicule (bosses, autoradio, etc.)

Customized, tinted glass, some rust

9. Other information
Autres renseignements

10. Photograph of the person provided in the box below, if available.
Une photographie de la personne figure dans la case ci-dessous, si elle est disponible.

The information supplied above is true to the best of my knowledge
and belief.
*Au mieux de ma connaissance et de ce que je tiens pour véridique,
les renseignements ci-dessus sont exacts.*

(Signature of party / *Signature de la partie*)

Emma Flood
(Name of party / *Nom de la partie*)

December 15   , 20 --

SCR 20.11-20K (June 1. 2009 / *1er juin 2009*) CSD

APPENDIX 9.3 Greco v. Hardwick: Draft Bill of Costs

Client matter number MP20—1214
HST number 12374 683

Courts of Justice Act

Superior Court of Justice   Claim no. SC-00-34065-00

Brampton Small Claims Court

BETWEEN:

Juliette Greco

Plaintiff (Defendant by defendant's claim)

and

James Hardwick

Defendant (Plaintiff by defendant's claim)

BILL OF COSTS

AMOUNT CLAIMED FOR FEES:

In support of the claim for fees, attach copies of dockets or other evidence.

Representation fees: 15% of the amount claimed of $5,000.00 (*Courts of Justice Act*, s. 29, Rule 19.02)	$ 750.00
HST on fees	97.50*
TOTAL FEES PLUS HST	$ 847.50

AMOUNT CLAIMED FOR DISBURSEMENTS:

In support of the claim for disbursements, attach copies of invoices or other evidence.

* Disbursements subject to HST are indicated with an asterisk.

Preparation of plaintiff's claim	$ 100.00*
Filing of plaintiff's claim (infrequent claimant)	75.00
Personal service of plaintiff's claim	50.00
Preparation of defence to defendant's claim	100.00*
Filing of defence to defendant's claim	40.00
Fix trial date (infrequent claimant)	100.00
Issue summons to witness (three witnesses—Green Tree Yard and Garden Inc., Serene Beasts Pet Services, Mermaids R Us)	57.00
Personal service of summons to witness on three witnesses	150.00
Service of copies of summons to witness (3 witnesses) on other parties who have received a notice of trial (one other party)	35.00
One-day court attendance fee for three witnesses	18.00
Mileage fee for attendance by three witnesses	
Green Tree Yard and Garden Inc. 20 km @ $.30/km	6.00
Serene Beasts Pet Services 35 km @ $.30/km	10.50
Mermaids R Us 15 km @ $.30 km	4.50
Photocopies—240 copies @ $.40 per page	96.00*

APPENDIX 9.3 Greco v. Hardwick: Draft Bill of Costs *concluded*

Client matter number MP20—1214
HST number 12374 683

TOTAL DISBURSEMENTS	$ 842.00
HST on disbursements	38.48*
TOTAL DISBURSEMENTS PLUS HST	$ 880.48
TOTAL FEES AND DISBURSEMENTS	$ 1,592.00
HST exigible	135.98*
TOTAL FEES AND DISBURSEMENTS PLUS HST	$ 1,727.98

TO: Paxton Limones PC
82 Main Street, Suite 11
Brampton, Ontario
L1N 2P3

This bill of costs is assessed and allowed at $_____ this _____ day of _____, 20—

Signature: _____

Motions for New Trial and Appeals

10

LEARNING OUTCOMES

After reading this chapter, you will understand:

- Grounds for a Rule 17.04 motion for a new trial or amendment of judgment

- Drafting and serving documents on a Rule 17.04 motion

- Appeal to the Divisional Court

Introduction

A motion pursuant to Rule 17.04 of the *Rules of the Small Claims Court* may be made in the following circumstances. If the trial judge made a purely arithmetical error in calculating the amount of damages awarded, you may make a motion requesting that the court pronounce the judgment that ought to have been given at trial and order judgment accordingly. If you discover relevant evidence that was not available at the time of the original trial and could not reasonably have been expected to be available at that time, you may make a motion for a new trial.

If a party believes that the trial judge's decision was incorrect or faulty for reasons other than those set out in Rule 17.04, the judgment must be appealed. Appeals of Small Claims Court trial decisions are governed by s. 31 of the *Courts of Justice Act*, and by Rule 61 of the *Rules of Civil Procedure*.

An appeal of a final order in a Small Claims Court action lies to the Divisional Court. The Divisional Court is the appellate branch of the Superior Court of Justice. It hears appeals in matters that involve amounts of not more than $50,000.00, exclusive of costs (*Courts of Justice Act*, s. 19(1.2)).

An appeal to the Divisional Court shall be heard in the region where the hearing of the action that led to the decision appealed from took place, unless the parties agree otherwise or the Chief Justice of the Superior Court of Justice orders otherwise because it is necessary to do so in the interests of justice (*Courts of Justice Act*, s. 20(1)).

An appeal of a Small Claims Court decision may be heard by one judge of the Superior Court of Justice (*Courts of Justice Act*, s. 21(2)(b)).

At present, paralegals are not allowed to appear on appeals in Divisional Court. Parties who choose to appeal a Small Claims Court decision must represent themselves or hire a lawyer.

Motion for a New Trial or Amendment of the Judgment (Rule 17.04)

Where there is a purely arithmetical error in the determination by the court of the amount of damages awarded, a party may make a motion for an amendment of the judgment (Rule 17.04(5)1). Where there is relevant evidence that was not available to the party at the time of the original trial and could not reasonably have been expected to be available at that time, a party may make a motion for a new trial (Rule 17.04(5)2).

A motion for a new trial or an order amending the judgment must be made within 30 days after the date the final order is made (Rule 17.04(1)). The motion is made to a Small Claims Court judge or deputy judge.

The moving party shall make a request to a court reporter to make a transcript of the reasons for judgment and any other portion of the proceeding that is relevant. The transcript can be ordered by contacting the court office. The current charge for a transcript is $3.20 per page for the first copy, and $0.55 per page for each additional copy. For a schedule of fees, see *Court Reporters and Court Monitors*, O. Reg.

587/91 to the *Administration of Justice Act*. The court reporter will notify you when the transcript is ready. The transcript will not be released to you until you have paid the court reporter's fee for the transcription.

The moving party shall serve the notice of motion and supporting affidavit, along with proof that a request has been made for a transcript of the reasons for judgment and any other portion of the proceeding that is relevant, on all parties, including parties who have been noted in default, at least seven days before the hearing date. The motion shall be filed, along with proof of service on all parties, with the court at least three days before the hearing date (Rules 15.01(3), 15.01(6), and 17.04(2)).

If available, a copy of the transcript or partial transcript shall be served on all parties who were served with the original notice of trial and filed, with proof of service, at least three days before the hearing date of the motion (Rule 17.04(3)).

If the motion is for an order amending the judgment based on an arithmetical error, the relief sought will be an order that the court pronounce the judgment that ought to have been given at trial, and order judgment accordingly (Rule 17.04(4)(a)(ii)). The supporting affidavit must contain evidence of the arithmetical error in the determination of the amount of damages awarded (Rule 17.04(5)1), as well as a calculation of the correct amount.

If the motion is for an order for a new trial on grounds of new evidence, the relief sought will be an order granting a new trial (Rule 17.04(4)(a)(i)). According to Rule 17.04(5)2, the supporting affidavit should contain facts and evidence to the effect that

- the evidence is relevant;
- the evidence was not available to the party at the time of the original trial; and
- the evidence could not reasonably have been expected to be available at that time.

On the hearing of the motion, if the moving party satisfies the court that

1. there was a purely arithmetical error in the determination of the amount of damages awarded, or
2. there is relevant evidence that was not available to the party at the time of the original trial and could not reasonably have been expected to be available at that time, the court may
   a. grant a new trial, or
   b. pronounce the judgment that ought to have been given at trial and order judgment accordingly.

Otherwise, the court shall dismiss the motion (Rule 17.04(4)(b)).

Arithmetical Error (Rule 17.04(5)1)

A purely arithmetical error is a miscalculation of the amount of damages awarded to a party—for example, a mistake in addition or subtraction. Any party may make a Rule 17.04 motion to have the error corrected.

Rule 17.04(5)1 should be used only where there is an arithmetical error in calculating the amount of the award. It should not be used to request that the judge on the motion reconsider the trial judge's decision as to the amount owing because the moving party thinks that amount is wrong for some other reason.

BOX 10.1 Greco v. Hardwick: What Is a Purely Arithmetical Error?

Background: Juliette Greco commences an action against her neighbour, James Hardwick, for $5,000.00 when he defaults in payment of a promissory note for a loan in that amount. The note provides for pre-judgment interest of 10 percent per year on the amount owing in the event of default. The due date stated in the note is August 2, 20—.

In his defence and counterclaim, James Hardwick admits that he signed the note and received the money. He states that he realized shortly after taking the money that he would not be able to pay it back on the due date. He then entered into a spoken agreement with Ms. Greco that he would perform services instead of making money payments. He performed those services, and their fair market value exceeds the amount owing under the promissory note. He has produced written quotations that the fair market value of the services provided totals $5,990.00.

In her defence to the defendant's claim, Ms. Greco disputes the value of Mr. Hardwick's services. She alleges that she could have obtained similar services for $1,500.00 from Glenn Woods of Glenn Woods Garden Services, the person who usually provides those services to her. She could have obtained other services allegedly provided by Mr. Hardwick for free.

The matter goes to trial on April 18, 20—. In his reasons for judgment, the trial judge states that he accepts Ms. Greco's evidence with respect to the value of Mr. Hardwick's services, and orders that Mr. Hardwick shall pay Ms. Greco $5,000.00 minus $1,500.00, for a total owing of $2,500.00, plus pre- and post-judgment interest at a rate of 10 percent per year in accordance with the promissory note, and costs fixed at $1,350.00 inclusive of disbursements.

The mistake is discovered by Ms. Greco's paralegal when he requests a copy of the judge's endorsement from the clerk.

Discussion: This is a purely arithmetical error. The judge clearly intended to award Ms. Greco $3,500.00, but made a mistake in his subtraction. To correct the error, a motion must be brought under Rule 17.04(1), requesting that the court amend the final order to correct the amount owing to $3,500.00, pursuant to Rules 17.04(4)(a)(ii) and 17.04(5)1. The motion must be made within 30 days after April 18, 20—.

You will find the notice of motion and supporting affidavit at Appendix 10.1 to this chapter.

Additional issue: The defendant, Mr. Hardwick, thinks the judge's decision is completely wrong, because he believes that the judge should have accepted his evidence that the services he performed were worth more than the amount owing under the note. May he make a Rule 17.04 motion to have the trial judge's error corrected?

Discussion: No. Mr. Hardwick's objections are legal and/or factual—they are not based on a simple arithmetical error. If he wishes to challenge the trial judge's order, he must do so by way of an appeal to a single judge of the Divisional Court.

New Evidence (Rule 17.04(5)2)

For a Rule 17.04 motion to succeed on this ground, the court must be satisfied that the evidence (1) is new—that is, it is evidence that the moving party did not know about at the time of the trial; (2) is relevant to the issues in the action; (3) is credible; (4) was not available to the party at the time of the original trial; and (5) could not reasonably have been expected to be available at that time.

Some examples of new evidence are:

1. a witness whose evidence is material to issues in the case, but who was not discovered until after the trial (*Applecrest Investments Ltd. v. Guardian Insurance Co.*);

2. a document that is material to issues in the action, but that is not discovered until after the trial, in spite of the moving party's diligent efforts to discover all relevant documents (*R. Clancy Heavy Equipment Sales Ltd. v. Joe Gourley Construction Ltd.*).

Appeal of a Small Claims Court Judgment

The appeal of a final order in a Small Claims Court action to the Divisional Court is governed by s. 31 of the *Courts of Justice Act* and by Rule 61 of the *Rules of Civil Procedure*. The Divisional Court is the appellate branch of the Superior Court of Justice. It hears appeals in matters that involve final orders (*Courts of Justice Act*, s. 19(1.2))

(a) for a single payment of not more than $50,000, exclusive of costs;

(b) for periodic payments that amount to not more than $50,000, exclusive of costs, in the 12 months commencing on the date the first payment is due under the order;

(c) dismissing a claim for an amount that is not more than the amount set out in clause (a) or (b); or

(d) dismissing a claim for an amount that is more than the amount set out in clause (a) or (b) and in respect of which the judge or jury indicates that if the claim had been allowed the amount awarded would have been not more than the amount set out in clause (a) or (b).

Section 31 applies to a final order in an action for the payment of money in excess of the prescribed amount, excluding costs; or for the recovery of possession of personal property exceeding the prescribed amount in value. At present, the prescribed amount is $2,500.00. See O. Reg. 626/00 to the *Courts of the Justice Act*.

In actions to which s. 31 applies, an appeal to the Divisional Court is as of right. An **appeal as of right** is an automatic right to appeal. In other words, the party making the appeal (the appellant) can do so without first applying for permission (leave) to do so from the appeal court.

At present, paralegals are not allowed to provide any form of legal services to clients with respect to Divisional Court appeals. Providing legal services includes giving legal advice on the merits of an appeal and drafting documents on the appeal.

Parties who wish to appeal a Small Claims Court order must represent themselves or hire a lawyer.

If you are a paralegal whose client wishes to appeal a final order in a Small Claims Court action, or if you are contacted by a person seeking legal advice about whether to appeal a final order in a Small Claims Court action, you should advise him to seek the services of a lawyer. You may wish to direct him to the Law Society Referral Service (1-800-268-8326) or to the Lawyer and Paralegal Directory at the Law Society website. You should consider sending the person a non-engagement letter confirming that you have declined the retainer on grounds of unauthorized practice. The non-engagement letter should advise him of any limitation periods, and suggest that he seek the services of a lawyer. You will find a sample non-engagement letter at Appendix 10.2.

CHAPTER SUMMARY

A motion for a new trial or for an amendment of the judgment (Rule 17.04 of the *Rules of the Small Claims Court*) may be made in the following circumstances. If the trial judge made a purely arithmetical error in calculating the amount of damages awarded, you may make a motion for an amendment of the judgment. If you discover relevant evidence that was not available at the time of the original trial and could not reasonably have been expected to be available at that time, you may make a motion for an amendment of the judgment or for a new trial.

The motion must be made within 30 days after the final order is made. The moving party shall serve the notice of motion and supporting affidavit, along with proof that a request has been made for a transcript of the reasons for judgment and any other portion of the proceeding that is relevant, on all parties at least seven days before the hearing date, and file it with the court at least three days before the hearing date (Rules 15.01(3), 15.01(6), and 17.04(2)). If available, copies of the transcript or partial transcript shall be served on all the parties who were served with the original notice of motion and filed, with proof of service, at least three business days before the hearing date for the motion (Rule 17.04(3)).

If the motion is for an order amending the judgment based on an arithmetical error, the supporting affidavit must show the error in calculating the judgment, as well as the correct calculation of the judgment.

If the motion is for an order for a new trial on grounds of new evidence, the evidence in the supporting affidavit should demonstrate that there is relevant evidence that was not available to the party at the time of the original trial and could not reasonably have been expected to be available at that time.

A final order in a Small Claims Court action for the payment of money in excess of $2,500.00, excluding costs, or for recovery of possession of personal property with a value exceeding $2,500.00 may be appealed to the Divisional Court. The Divisional Court is the appellate branch of the Superior Court of Justice. It hears appeals in matters that involve amounts of not more than $50,000.00, exclusive of costs. The appeal is as of right—that is, the party making the appeal has an automatic right to do so, without seeking leave from the appeal court.

At present, paralegals are not allowed to provide any form of legal services to clients with respect to Divisional Court appeals. Providing legal services includes giving legal advice on the merits of an appeal and drafting documents on the appeal. Persons who wish to appeal a Small Claims Court order must represent themselves or seek the services of a lawyer.

KEY TERMS

appeal as of right: an automatic right to appeal, without first seeking permission to do so from the appeal court *(p. 405)*

REFERENCES

Administration of Justice Act, RSO 1990, c. A.6.

Applecrest Investments Ltd. v. Guardian Insurance Co., [1992] OJ no. 1060 (Gen. Div.).

Court Reporters and Court Monitors, O. Reg. 587/91.

Courts of Justice Act, RSO 1990, c. C.43.

R. Clancy Heavy Equipment Sales Ltd. v. Joe Gourley Construction Ltd., [2001] AJ no. 638 (Alta. CA).

Rules of Civil Procedure, RRO 1990, Reg. 194.

Rules of the Small Claims Court, O. Reg. 258/98.

Small Claims Court Jurisdiction and Appeal Limit, O. Reg. 626/00.

REVIEW QUESTIONS

When answering the following questions, please cite the applicable rule or rule(s).

1. What are the grounds for making a motion under Rule 17.04?

2. What is the deadline for making a Rule 17.04 motion?

3. What documents must be served and filed in support of a Rule 17.04 motion?

4. On a motion for an amendment of judgment, what order should you seek at page 2 of the notice of motion?

5. You are a licensed paralegal. What should you do if a client or other person approaches you for advice about appealing a final order in a Small Claims Court action?

APPENDIX 10.1   Greco v. Hardwick: Motion for an Order Amending Judgment Based on Arithmetical Error (Rule 17.04) (Form 15A)

ONTARIO

Superior Court of Justice
Cour supérieure de justice

Notice of Motion and Supporting Affidavit
Avis de motion et affidavit à l'appui
Form / *Formule* 15A Ont. Reg. No. / *Régl. de l'Ont.* : 258/98

Brampton	**SC-00-34065-00**
Small Claims Court / *Cour des petites créances de*	Claim No. / *N° de la demande*
7755 Hurontario Street	
Brampton, Ontario	
L6W 4T6	
Address / *Adresse*	
905 456 4700	
Phone number / *Numéro de téléphone*	

Plaintiff No. 1 / *Demandeur n° 1*   ☐ Additional plaintiff(s) listed on attached Form 1A.
Le ou les demandeurs additionnels sont mentionnés sur la formule 1A ci-jointe.

Last name, or name of company / *Nom de famille ou nom de la compagnie*		
Greco		
First name / *Premier prénom*	Second name / *Deuxième prénom*	Also known as / *Également connu(e) sous le nom de*
Juliette		
Address (street number, apt., unit) / *Adresse (numéro et rue, app., unité)*		
c/o Prior Mustafa LLP		
City/Town / *Cité/ville*	Province	Phone no. / *N° de téléphone*
Postal code / *Code postal*		Fax no. / *N° de télécopieur*
Representative / *Représentant(e)*		LSUC # / *N° du BHC*
Prior Mustafa LLP, Attention: Paralegal name		**######**
Address (street number, apt., unit) / *Adresse (numéro et rue, app., unité)*		
22 County Court Boulevard		
City/Town / *Cité/ville*	Province	Phone no. / *N° de téléphone*
Brampton	**Ontario**	**905 111 2222**
Postal code / *Code postal*		Fax no. / *N° de télécopieur*
A1A 2B3		**905 111 2233**

Defendant No. 1 / *Défendeur n° 1*   ☐ Additional defendant(s) listed on attached Form 1A.
Le ou les défendeurs additionnels sont mentionnés sur la formule 1A ci-jointe.

Last name, or name of company / *Nom de famille ou nom de la compagnie*		
Hardwick		
First name / *Premier prénom*	Second name / *Deuxième prénom*	Also known as / *Également connu(e) sous le nom de*
James		
Address (street number, apt., unit) / *Adresse (numéro et rue, app., unité)*		
c/o Paxton Limones PC		
City/Town / *Cité/ville*	Province	Phone no. / *N° de téléphone*
Postal code / *Code postal*		Fax no. / *N° de télécopieur*
Representative / *Représentant(e)*		LSUC # / *N° du BHC*
Paxton Limones PC, Attention: Paralegal name		**######**
Address (street number, apt., unit) / *Adresse (numéro et rue, app., unité)*		
82 Main Street, Suite 11		
City/Town / *Cité/ville*	Province	Phone no. / *N° de téléphone*
Brampton	**Ontario**	**905 888 9999**
Postal code / *Code postal*		Fax no. / *N° de télécopieur*
L1N 2P3		**905 888 0000**

SCR 15.01-15A (September 1, 2010 / *1ᵉʳ septembre 2010*) CSD

FORM / *FORMULE* 15A PAGE 2 SC-00-34065-00

Claim No. / *N° de la demande*

THIS COURT WILL HEAR A MOTION on May 10 , 20 -- , at 9:30 a.m. ,
LE TRIBUNAL PRÉCITÉ ENTENDRA UNE MOTION le , à (Time / *heure*)

or as soon as possible after that time, at Courtroom 5, 7765 Hurontario Street, Brampton, Ontario
ou dès que possible par la suite à/au (Address of court location and courtroom number / *Adresse du tribunal et numéro de la salle d'audience*)

Complete Part A or Part B below, then complete the affidavit in support of motion on page 3. / *Remplissez la partie A ou la partie B ci-dessous. Remplissez ensuite l'affidavit à l'appui de la motion à la page 3.*

A. **This motion will be made in person by** Juliette Greco
La motion sera présentée en personne par : (Name of party / *Nom de la partie*)

for the following order : / *en vue d'obtenir l'ordonnance suivante :*

☐ the court's permission to extend time to (Specify)
l'autorisation du tribunal de proroger le délai pour (Précisez)

☐ set aside default judgment and noting in default.
l'annulation du jugement par défaut et la constatation du défaut.

☐ set aside noting in default.
l'annulation de la constatation du défaut.

☐ permission to file a Defence.
l'autorisation de déposer une défense.

☐ permission to file a Defendant's Claim.
l'autorisation de déposer une demande du défendeur.

☐ set aside order dismissing claim as abandoned.
l'annulation d'une demande pour cause de renonciation

☐ terminate garnishment and/or withdraw writ(s).
la mainlevée de la saisie-arrêt ou le retrait d'un ou de plusieurs brefs, ou les deux.

☒ Other:
Autre :

That the court pronounce judgment on terms that the defendant, James Hardwick, shall pay to the plaintiff, Juliette Greco, $5,000.00 minus $1,500.00, for a total owing of $3,500.00, plus pre- and post-judgment interest at a rate of 10% per year in accordance with the promissory note dated April 1, 20--, and costs fixed at $1,350.00 inclusive of disbursements.

That the court order judgment accordingly.

☒ **ADDITIONAL PAGES ARE ATTACHED BECAUSE MORE ROOM WAS NEEDED.**
DES FEUILLES SUPPLÉMENTAIRES SONT ANNEXÉES EN RAISON DU MANQUE D'ESPACE.

☐ **DOCUMENTS ARE ATTACHED.**
PIÈCES JOINTES.

NOTE: **IF YOU FAIL TO ATTEND AN IN-PERSON MOTION,** an order may be made against you, with costs, in your absence. If you want to attend the motion by telephone or video conference, complete and file a Request for Telephone or Video Conference (Form 1B). If the court permits it, the clerk will make the necessary arrangements and notify the parties [R. 1.07(5)].

REMARQUE : *SI VOUS NE VOUS PRÉSENTEZ PAS EN PERSONNE À L'AUDITION DE LA MOTION, une ordonnance peut être rendue contre vous en votre absence, avec dépens. Si vous voulez assister à l'audition de la motion par conférence téléphonique ou vidéoconférence, remplissez et déposez la Demande de conférence téléphonique ou vidéoconférence (formule 1B). Si le tribunal l'autorise, le greffier prendra les dispositions nécessaires et en avisera les parties [par. 1.07 (5)].*

SCR 15.01-15A (September 1, 2010 / *1er septembre 2010*) CSD Continued on next page / *Suite à la page suivante*

APPENDIX 10.1   Greco v. Hardwick: Motion for an Order Amending Judgment Based on Arithmetical Error (Rule 17.04) (Form 15A)   *continued*

FORM / *FORMULE* 15A	PAGE 3	SC-00-34065-00
		Claim No. / *N° de la demande*

B.   This motion in writing for an assessment of damages is made by
La présente motion par écrit en vue d'une évaluation des dommages-intérêts est présentée par

_____ ,
(Name of plaintiff / *Nom du demandeur/de la demanderesse*)

who asks the court for an order assessing damages against
qui demande au tribunal de rendre une ordonnance d'évaluation des dommages-intérêts contre

_____
(Name of defendant(s) / *Nom du/de la/des défendeur(s)/défenderesse(s)*)

who have/has been noted in default.
qui a/ont été constaté(e)(s) en défaut.

AFFIDAVIT IN SUPPORT OF MOTION / *AFFIDAVIT À L'APPUI DE LA MOTION*

My name is   Juliette Greco
Je m'appelle   (Full name / *Nom et prénoms*)

I live in   Brampton, Ontario
J'habite à   (Municipality & province / *Municipalité et province*)

I swear/affirm that the following is true:
Je déclare sous serment/j'affirme solennellement que les renseignements suivants sont véridiques :

Set out the facts in numbered paragraphs. If you learned a fact from someone else, you must give that person's name and state that you believe that fact to be true.
Indiquez les faits sous forme de dispositions numérotées. Si vous avez pris connaissance d'un fait par l'entremise d'une autre personne, vous devez indiquer le nom de cette personne et déclarer que vous croyez que ce fait est véridique.

See Schedule A attached and forming part of this affidavit

Continued on next page / *Suite à la page suivante*

FORM / *FORMULE* 15A   PAGE 4   SC-00-34065-00
                                                                 Claim No. / *N° de la demande*

AFFIDAVIT IN SUPPORT OF MOTION, continued / *AFFIDAVIT À L'APPUI DE LA MOTION, suite*
See Schedule A attached and forming part of this affidavit

If more space is required, attach and initial extra pages. / Si vous avez besoin de plus d'espace, annexez une ou des feuilles supplémentaires et paraphez-les.

Sworn/Affirmed before me at **Brampton**	
Déclaré sous serment/Affirmé (Municipality / *municipalité*)	
solennellement devant moi à	
in **Ontario**	
en/à/au (Province, state or country / *province, État ou pays*)	Signature
on **April 28** , 20 --	(This form is to be signed in front of a lawyer, justice of the peace, notary public or commissioner for taking affidavits.)
le Commissioner for taking affidavits	*(La présente formule doit être signée en présence d'un avocat, d'un juge de paix, d'un notaire ou d'un commissaire aux affidavits.)*
Commissaire aux affidavits	
(Type or print name below if signature is illegible.)	
(Dactylographiez le nom ou écrivez-le en caractères d'imprimerie ci-dessous si la signature est illisible.)	

WARNING:	**IT IS AN OFFENCE UNDER THE *CRIMINAL CODE* TO KNOWINGLY SWEAR OR AFFIRM A FALSE AFFIDAVIT.**
AVERTISSEMENT :	*FAIRE SCIEMMENT UN FAUX AFFIDAVIT CONSTITUE UNE INFRACTION AU CODE CRIMINEL.*

APPENDIX 10.1 Greco v. Hardwick: Motion for an Order Amending Judgment Based on Arithmetical Error (Rule 17.04) (Form 15A) *concluded*

Schedule A

1. I am the plaintiff in this proceeding, and as such have personal knowledge of the following.

2. At the trial of this matter on April 18, 20—, it was not disputed that I loaned $5,000.00 to the defendant pursuant to a promissory note dated April 1, 20—. The due date for the loan was August 2, 20—. In the event of any default, interest at a rate of 10% per year became due and payable on any balance outstanding. The issues before the court were:

    (a) the terms of an alleged spoken agreement between the defendant and me that the defendant should provide services in lieu of payment of the note;

    (b) the services that were provided pursuant to that alleged agreement; and

    (c) the value, if any, to be assigned to those services.

3. The defendant was present at trial, and gave evidence in support of his defence and defendant's claim.

4. Having heard all of the evidence at trial and closing submissions for both parties, Smith J. made the following order (at page 3, lines 5 to 14 of the transcript of the reasons for judgment):

    "I accept the plaintiff's evidence with respect to the value of Mr. Hardwick's services. Both Ms. Greco and Mr. Woods were credible witnesses. I do not find Mr. Hardwick's evidence with respect to the terms of the alleged agreement wholly credible; nor do I find the written estimates of the value of the services he provided credible. I value those services at $1,500.00. Order to go that the defendant, James Hardwick, shall pay to the plaintiff, Juliette Greco, $5,000.00 minus $1,500.00, for a total owing of $2,500.00, plus pre- and post-judgment interest at a rate of 10% per year in accordance with the promissory note dated April 1, 20—, and costs fixed at $1,350.00 inclusive of disbursements."

5. Upon reviewing his notes, my paralegal, Joseph Mustafa, discovered the trial judge's error in calculating the damages owing.

6. Under the terms of the court order dated April 18, 20—, the amount of damages owing to me is $5,000.00 − $1,500.00 = $3,500.00.

7. I make this affidavit in support of a motion for an order correcting the April 18, 20— judgment to state that the defendant, James Hardwick, shall pay me the amount of $3,500.00 plus pre- and post-judgment interest at a rate of 10% per year in accordance with the promissory note dated April 1, 20—, and costs fixed at $1,350.00 inclusive of disbursements, and for no other or improper purpose.

APPENDIX 10.2 Non-Engagement Letter
(Unauthorized Practice—Paralegal Firm Declines Retainer)

[Date]

[File number]

[Client name and address]

Dear [Client name]:

Re: [Matter name]

You are the defendant in Claim No. SC-00-88069-00 in London Small Claims Court. You contacted us on [date] to discuss appealing the final order of Deputy Judge Grewal dated June 3, 20—. As we discussed during our [telephone conversation/meeting/initial consultation], an appeal of a final order in a Small Claims Court action lies to the Divisional Court. We are a paralegal firm. At present, paralegals are not permitted to appear before the Divisional Court.

We therefore cannot represent you and we must decline to do so in this matter.

The time for appealing a Small Claims Court decision is 30 days after a final order is made. Since time limitations may be critical to your case, we recommend that you immediately contact a lawyer for assistance regarding your matter. If you do not have a lawyer in mind to represent you, the Law Society of Upper Canada maintains a directory of lawyers at its website (http://www.lsuc.on.ca) who may be available to assist you, or you may wish to seek assistance by calling the Law Society Referral Service at 1-800-268-8326 or accessing their online request form, available at the website. We confirm that we do not have any documents belonging to you. All documents that you produced to us have been returned to you.

Although we were not able to assist you in this matter, we hope that you will consider [paralegal firm name] in the event that you require legal services in the future.

Thank you again for your interest in this firm.

Yours truly,

[PARALEGAL FIRM NAME]

[Signature]

[Signatory name]
Licensed Paralegal

[Adapted from the Law Society of British Columbia website (http://www.lawsociety.bc.ca) and the Law Society of Upper Canada website (http://www.lsuc.on.ca).]

Enforcing Small Claims Court Judgments

11

LEARNING OUTCOMES

After reading this chapter, you will understand:

- What enforcement of a judgment is
- Types of creditors
- General powers of the court in an enforcement
- Orders for periodic payment
- Consolidation orders
- Enforcement of orders made outside of Ontario
- Calculating post-judgment interest
- Certificate of judgment
- Examination of the debtor or other person
- Contempt hearings
- Garnishment
- Seizure and sale of personal property
- Seizure and sale of land
- Delivery of personal property

Introduction

A Small Claims Court order for payment of money to an unsecured creditor is just a piece of paper unless the person who is ordered to pay the money is willing to pay, or has income or assets against which the order can be enforced.

Any lawful attempt to obtain an amount owing pursuant to a court order is called **enforcement of an order**. An order may be enforced by garnishment of debts owed by others to a debtor, or by seizing and selling the debtor's assets, or by any other lawful method. An enforcement pursuant to a writ of seizure and sale is also called an execution.

In Small Claims Court, enforcement of orders is governed by Rule 20 of the *Rules of the Small Claims Court*.

For purposes of Rule 20, a party who is entitled to enforce a Small Claims Court order for the payment or recovery of money against another person is called a **creditor**. A party against whom a Small Claims Court order for the payment or recovery of money may be enforced is called a **debtor** (Rule 20.01).

A debtor against whom there are two or more unsatisfied orders for the payment of money may make a motion to the court for a consolidation order (Rule 20.09). At the hearing of the motion, the court may make a consolidation order setting out a list of all unpaid orders, the amounts to be paid into court by the debtor under the consolidation order, and the times of payment. All payments made by the debtor are shared equally among creditors named in the consolidation order.

While the consolidation order is in force, no step to enforce the judgment may be taken or continued against the debtor by a creditor named in the order, except issuing a writ of seizure and sale of land and filing it with the sheriff.

A consolidation order terminates immediately if (1) an order for payment of money is obtained against the debtor after the date of the consolidation order for a debt incurred after the consolidation order, or (2) the debtor is in default for 21 days.

A creditor who intends to request an enforcement or a garnishment in a jurisdiction other than the jurisdiction in which the order was made may do so by filing a certificate of judgment in that jurisdiction (Rule 20.04).

A creditor who does not have current information about the income and assets of a debtor may schedule an examination of the debtor or any other person with knowledge of the financial circumstances of the debtor by requesting that the clerk of the court in the territorial division in which the debtor or other person to be examined resides or carries on business issue a notice of examination directed to the debtor or other person (Rule 20.10). The debtor or other person with knowledge of the debtor's circumstances may be examined with respect to the reason for non-payment; the debtor's income and property; the debts owed to and by the debtor; any transfers of property the debtor has made before or after a court order; the debtor's present, past, and future means to satisfy the order; whether the debtor intends to obey the order or has any reason for not doing so; and any other matter pertinent to the enforcement of the order.

A person who is served with a notice of examination shall (1) inform themselves about the matters set out in Rule 20.10(4) and be prepared to answer questions; and (2) where the debtor is an individual, complete a financial information form and serve it on the creditor requesting the examination. The financial information form shall not be filed with the court.

The examination takes place in the presence of the court. It is conducted under oath, and is recorded. When the examination is concluded, the court may make an order as to payment. While the order is in force, no step to execute the judgment may be taken, other than issuing and filing a writ of seizure and sale of land with the sheriff.

A creditor may enforce an order for the payment or recovery of money by garnishment of debts, including employment income, payable to the debtor by other persons. A creditor who wishes to enforce an order by garnishment shall file with the clerk of a court in the territorial division in which the debtor resides or carries on business an affidavit for enforcement request and, if the order was made in another territorial division, a certificate of judgment, and the clerk shall issue a notice of garnishment directed to the garnishee named in the affidavit.

The garnishee is liable to pay to the clerk any debt of the garnishee to the debtor, within 10 days after service of the notice on the garnishee or 10 days after the debt becomes payable, whichever is later.

A creditor may file with the court an affidavit for enforcement request requesting that the clerk issue to a bailiff a writ of seizure and sale of personal property and the bailiff shall enforce the writ for the amount owing, post-judgment interest, and the bailiff's fees and expenses (Rule 20.06(1)).

A writ of seizure and sale of personal property remains in force for six years after the date of its issue and for a further six years after each renewal (Rule 20.06(2)). It may be renewed before it expires by filing a request to renew a writ of seizure and sale with the bailiff.

A creditor may file with the court an affidavit for enforcement request asking that the clerk issue a writ of seizure and sale of land directed to the sheriff specified by the creditor (Rule 20.07(1)). A writ of seizure and sale of land may be registered as an execution with the sheriff in the district or county where the creditor believes that the debtor has an interest in land.

A writ of seizure and sale of land remains in force for six years from the date of its issue and for a further six years after each renewal. It may be renewed before it expires by filing a request to renew a writ of seizure and sale with the sheriff.

Where the court has made an order for the delivery of personal property, a creditor in whose favour the order was made or her representative may file with the court an affidavit for enforcement request stating that the property has not been delivered and requesting that the clerk issue a writ of delivery of personal property to a bailiff (Rule 20.05).

General

In Small Claims Court, enforcement of orders is governed by Rule 20. Orders by some other courts, tribunals, and boards for payment of $25,000.00 or less may also be enforced under Rule 20. Section 68 of the *Provincial Offences Act* states that unpaid fines levied in provincial offences proceedings may be collected by civil enforcement in Small Claims Court. Section 19 of the *Statutory Powers Procedure Act* states that a certified copy of a tribunal's decision or order in a proceeding may be filed in the Superior Court of Justice (of which Small Claims Court is a branch) by the tribunal or by a party, and on filing shall be deemed to be an order of that court and is enforceable as such.

As of this writing, the fee for receiving a process from the Ontario Court of Justice or an order or judgment as provided by statute is $25.00. Refer to the Small Claims Court fee schedule published as O. Reg. 432/93 to the *Administration of Justice Act*. You can also find the current fee schedule at the website of the Ministry of the Attorney General in the Court Services link, and at Appendix D at page 559 of this text.

Types of Creditors

In a collection, there are three types of creditors:

1. secured creditors;
2. preferred creditors; and
3. ordinary creditors (also known as unsecured creditors).

Secured Creditors

Secured creditors are creditors whose loans are secured against real or personal property of the debtor. If the debtor defaults in payment, the secured creditor may **realize on her security** under the terms of the security agreement.

The real or personal property against which the loan is pledged is known as **collateral**.

Security against land may take the form of a mortgage, a lien, a construction lien, and so on. The secured creditor's interest in the land is registered against title to the land, and shows up on a standard title search.

If the form of security is a mortgage, the person who holds the security is called the **mortgagee**. The person who receives the loan or other benefit and pledges the security is called the **mortgagor**.

In Ontario, a security interest in personal property (also known as a **chattel mortgage**) is registered by the person holding the security interest under the *Personal Property Security Act* (PPSA). The claim of the holder of a security interest registered under the PPSA takes priority over the claims of other creditors with respect to the personal property that is the security.

The right of a creditor who has registered a security interest under the PPSA to seize and sell the personal property that is the security in the event of default by a debtor is subject to s. 25 of the *Consumer Protection Act, 2002*, which states that where two-thirds of the purchase price has been paid, the vendor's right of repossession in the event of default by the purchaser is not enforceable, except with leave from the Superior Court of Justice:

No repossession after two-thirds paid except by leave of court
   25(1) Where a consumer under a future performance agreement has paid two-thirds or more of his or her payment obligation as fixed by the agreement, any

provision in the agreement, or in any security agreement incidental to the agreement, under which the supplier may retake possession of or resell the goods or services upon default in payment by the consumer is not enforceable except by leave obtained from the Superior Court of Justice.

Powers of court

(2) Upon an application for leave under subsection (1), the court may, in its discretion, grant leave to the supplier or refuse leave or grant leave upon such terms and conditions as the court considers advisable.

A **future performance agreement** is a sales contract where the purchaser takes possession of property in return for a promise to make future payments for the property to the vendor, who retains title and a right of repossession in the property until the purchase price is paid in full.

PRIORITY OF SECURED INTERESTS

The general rule with respect to security registered against land or personal property is that priority is ranked by order of the time of registration of the security, unless there is an agreement stating otherwise. For example, a mortgagee whose interest is registered chronologically first against the title to land is called a first mortgagee. The security interest of a first mortgagee will rank ahead of the interest of any second, third, or subsequent mortgagees whose mortgages are registered later, unless there is a subordination agreement between a prior mortgagee and a subsequent mortgagee stating that the prior mortgagee's interest is subordinate to that of the subsequent mortgagee.

Preferred Creditors

Preferred creditors are unsecured creditors who rank ahead of ordinary unsecured creditors in a debt collection or a bankruptcy because of priority and special rights conferred by a statute. In Ontario, s. 2 of the *Creditors' Relief Act, 2010* confers priority over ordinary unsecured creditors upon the Crown in right of Canada, support and maintenance creditors, and the Crown in right of Ontario, in that order. The federal Crown may waive its priority with respect to a judgment debt in writing, in which case the sheriff may reassign to a support or maintenance order priority over the judgment debt. A **support and maintenance creditor** is a person to whom arrears of child and/or spousal support are owed by the debtor. Section 2 is excerpted below:

No priority among execution or garnishment creditors

2(1) Except as otherwise provided in this Act, there is no priority among creditors by execution or garnishment issued by the Superior Court of Justice, the Family Court of the Superior Court of Justice and the Ontario Court of Justice. …

Exception, support or maintenance orders

(3) A support or maintenance order has the following priority over other judgment debts, other than debts owing to the Crown in right of Canada, regardless of when an enforcement process is issued or served:

1. If the maintenance or support order requires periodic payments, the order has priority to the extent of all arrears owing under the order at the time of seizure or attachment.

2. If the support or maintenance order requires the payment of a lump sum, the order has priority to the extent of any portion of the lump sum that has not been paid.

Support orders rank equally

(4) Support and maintenance orders rank equally with one another.

Priority if execution creditors include the Crown

(5) If there are no support or maintenance orders against a debtor and the Crown is an execution creditor, the priority among the execution creditors and creditors by garnishment is in the following order:

1. The Crown in Right of Canada, with respect to writs of execution filed on its behalf, with all such writs ranking equally with one another.

2. The Crown in right of Ontario with respect to writs of execution filed on its behalf, with all such writs ranking equally with one another.

3. All other creditors by execution or garnishment.

If federal Crown waives priority

(6) If the Crown in right of Canada, as represented by the Minister of Justice, provides a written waiver of the priority of the Crown in right of Canada with respect to a judgment debt for which the Crown in right of Canada would otherwise have priority, the sheriff may reassign to a support or maintenance order priority over the judgment debt, regardless of when an enforcement process is issued or served with respect to that judgment debt.

Ordinary Creditors

Ordinary creditors are unsecured creditors with no preferred status. This is the type of creditor who will often be encountered in a Small Claims Court debt collection. The amount that an ordinary creditor is able to collect on a judgment debt will depend on what assets or income, if any, the debtor possesses against which the judgment may be enforced.

General Power of the Court

Section 28 of the *Courts of Justice Act* states that the Small Claims Court may order the times and the proportions in which money payable under an order of the court shall be paid. Section 28 confers broad discretion on the court to make orders with respect to the payment of money. The court may make an order for a lump-sum payment, or for periodic payments, or for some combination thereof. A **lump-sum payment** is a one-time payment of the full amount owing or a portion thereof. **Periodic payments** are payments of fixed amounts at regular intervals until such time as all amounts owing are paid in full.

While an order for periodic payment of money pursuant to the *Courts of Justice Act*, s. 28 is in force, no step to enforce the judgment may be taken or continued against the debtor by a creditor named in the order, except issuing a writ of seizure and sale of land and filing it with the sheriff (Rule 20.02(2)).

Under Rule 20.02(1), the court may:

(a) stay the enforcement of an order of the court, for such time and on such terms as are just; and

(b) vary the times and proportions in which money payable under an order of the court shall be paid, if the court is satisfied that the debtor's circumstances have changed.

A **stay of enforcement** stops a creditor or creditors from enforcing their judgments against the debtor, for so long as the debtor complies with the terms of the court order. A stay of enforcement under Rule 20.02(2) is automatic where there is an order for periodic payment of money. Rule 20.02(1)(a) places no restrictions on the circumstances in which a stay of enforcement may be ordered by a court, although any order would be subject to the court's obligation to make orders that are just and agreeable to good conscience in accordance with s. 25 of the *Courts of Justice Act*.

Rule 20.02(1)(b) allows the court to vary, or change, the times of payment and the amounts to be paid, if the court is satisfied that the debtor's circumstances have changed. If the debtor's financial circumstances have deteriorated since the order for periodic payment was made, the court may order that the amount of a periodic payment, or the frequency of payments, or both, be reduced. If the debtor's financial circumstances have improved since the order for periodic payment was made, the court may order that the amount of the periodic payment, or the frequency of payments, or both, be increased.

Order for Periodic Payment—Default in Payment by Debtor

If the debtor fails to make a payment under an order for periodic payment, the creditor may serve the debtor with a notice of default of payment (Form 20L). A notice of default of payment may be served by mail, by courier, by fax, personally, or by an alternative to personal service, unless the court orders otherwise (Rule 8.01(14)).

An order for periodic payment terminates on the day that is 15 days after the creditor serves the debtor with the notice of default of payment, unless a consent (Form 13B) in which the creditor waives the default is filed within the 15-day period (Rule 20.02(4)).

To **waive the default** means to give up the right to terminate the order for periodic payment based on the debtor's failure to pay. A creditor may consider waiving the default if the creditor is satisfied that the debtor's failure to pay was inadvertent and the debtor will continue making payments if the order for periodic payment is left in place.

If no consent is filed within the 15-day period, the creditor may file with the court an affidavit of default of payment (Form 20M), together with a copy of the notice of default of payment and proof of service (Rule 20.02(3)). Upon termination of the order for periodic payment, a creditor may enforce her judgment by any lawful method.

Calculating Post-judgment Interest

Post-judgment interest starts to run on the total judgment amount from the date of the order. The *total judgment amount* is the money award plus pre-judgment interest plus costs (*Courts of Justice Act*, s. 129(1); Rule 3.01).

If there is a contractual interest rate, you will calculate post-judgment interest using that rate, and the method of calculating post-judgment interest set out in the contract. Section 347 of the *Criminal Code* prohibits an interest rate in excess of 60 percent:

Criminal interest rate

347(1) Despite any other Act of Parliament, every one who enters into an agreement or arrangement to receive interest at a criminal rate, or receives a payment or partial payment of interest at a criminal rate, is

(a) guilty of an indictable offence and liable to imprisonment for a term not exceeding five years; or

(b) guilty of an offence punishable on summary conviction and liable to a fine not exceeding $25,000 or to imprisonment for a term not exceeding six months or to both.

Definitions

(2) In this section,

"credit advanced" means the aggregate of the money and the monetary value of any goods, services or benefits actually advanced or to be advanced under an agreement or arrangement minus the aggregate of any required deposit balance and any fee, fine, penalty, commission and other similar charge or expense directly or indirectly incurred under the original or any collateral agreement or arrangement;

"criminal rate" means an effective annual rate of interest calculated in accordance with generally accepted actuarial practices and principles that exceeds sixty per cent on the credit advanced under an agreement or arrangement;

In Ontario, the *Payday Loans Act* prohibits interest on payday loans in excess of $21.00 per $100.00 (see *Payday Loans Act*, s. 32, and O. Reg. 98/09, s. 18(1)). Subject to the provisions above, the interest rate will be whatever the parties have agreed to in the contract.

If there is no agreement setting out the rate of interest that applies in the event of a default, then pre- and post-judgment interest rates must be determined in accordance with ss. 127 to 130 of the *Courts of Justice Act*, using the rates published pursuant to O. Reg. 339/07. Current tables of post-judgment and pre-judgment interest rates can be found at the Ministry of the Attorney General's website in the Court Services link.

Calculating Post-judgment Interest Under the Courts of Justice Act

When calculating interest under the *Courts of Justice Act*, you must read the applicable sections carefully. Section 129(1) states that money owing under an order, including costs to be assessed or costs fixed by the court, bears interest at the post-judgment interest rate, calculated from the date of the order. In other words, s. 129(1) gives you the start date for the *time period* for calculating post-judgment interest.

However, if you want to know the *rate of interest*, you must go to the definition of "post-judgment interest rate" in s. 127(1). The s. 127(1) definition states that the interest rate for post-judgment interest under the *Courts of Justice Act* is the bank rate at the end of the first day of the last month of the quarter preceding the quarter in which the date of the order falls.

A quarter is a three-month period. There are four quarters in any year:

- First quarter: January, February, March
- Second quarter: April, May, June
- Third quarter: July, August, September
- Fourth quarter: October, November, December.

If the order for payment of money is made in September, during the third quarter of the year, then the applicable post-judgment interest rate under the *Courts of Justice Act* is the interest rate for the preceding quarter—that is, the second quarter of that year. If the order for payment of money is made in February, during the first quarter of the year, then the applicable post-judgment interest rate under the *Courts of Justice Act* is the interest rate for the fourth, or last, quarter of the preceding year.

In recent years, both pre- and post-judgment interest rates have remained fixed at 1.3 and 3.0 percent, respectively; so determining the rate is easy, as long as you make sure you are referring to the correct table. However, that was not the case in the past, when pre- and post-judgment interest rates changed every quarter or two; and it may not be the case in the future. So, if you do not have a contractual interest rate, do not make assumptions. Refer to the tables at the Attorney General's website, and ensure that you apply s. 127(1) correctly when determining your pre- and post-judgment interest rates.

BOX 11.1 Calculating Post-judgment Interest Using the Courts of Justice Act

At trial on September 8, 2010, the plaintiff, who is self-represented, is awarded $7,000.00 plus pre-judgment interest of $28.86 and costs fixed at $283.00, for a total judgment amount of $7,311.86.

Calculating Post-judgment Interest

Because there is no written loan agreement, the plaintiff must use the pre- and post-judgment interest rates set out in the *Courts of Justice Act*.

Pursuant to s. 127(1) of the *Courts of Justice Act*, the post-judgment interest rate is the adjusted bank rate at the end of the first day of the last month of the quarter preceding the quarter in which the date of the order falls. In this case, the order falls in September—that is, the third quarter of 2010. So the post-judgment interest rate will be the published rate for the second quarter of 2010—that is, 2.0 percent.

Pursuant to s. 129(1), post-judgment interest is calculated from the date of the order—that is, September 8, 2010, which is also the end date for pre-judgment interest. Rule 3.01 states that, when calculating a period of time under the Rules, you shall exclude the first day and include the last day. Addition and subtraction will do that automatically.

Post-judgment interest continues to accrue until all amounts owing, including interest and subsequent costs, are paid in full. However, post-judgment interest for a specific enforcement can only be calculated to the date of preparation of the forms.

Calculation of simple interest on both pre- and post-judgment interest is on the amount owing from time to time as payments are received. After every payment, you should recalculate the per diem interest, to determine whether the per diem is being reduced as payments are applied to reduce the balance owed. See the detailed calculation of interest in Appendix 6.5 at page 276 and Appendix 11.1 at page 463.

Please note that the following calculations are for simple interest only. If there is a debt instrument, you must calculate interest in accordance with its terms.

Step One: Calculate per diem interest

Per diem means per day. **Per diem interest** is the amount of interest that accrues per day on money owed. To calculate per diem interest, you must first convert the interest rate from a percentage to a decimal.

Calculate per diem interest using the following steps.

- Convert the interest rate to a decimal by dividing the interest rate by 100.
- Multiply the amount owing by the interest rate expressed as a decimal.
- Divide the result by the number of days in a year—that is, 365.

In this case, the post-judgment interest rate under the *Courts of Justice Act* is 2.0%. Following the above steps:

- Convert 2.0% to a decimal: 2.0 ÷ 100 = 0.02
- Multiply the total judgment amount by the interest rate expressed as a decimal: 0.02 x ($7,000 + $28.86 + $283.00 = $7,311.86) = $146.24
- Divide the result by the number of days in a year: $146.24 ÷ 365 = $0.40 per day in interest.

Step Two: Calculate the number of days that have elapsed since post-judgment interest began to run

You prepare an affidavit for enforcement request (garnishment) and a notice of garnishment on September 15. You must calculate post-judgment interest to the date of preparing the affidavit for enforcement request and enforcement document. The **enforcement document** is the document that is issued pursuant to the request in the affidavit for enforcement request (in this case, a notice of garnishment).

The start date for post-judgment interest is the date the order was made—that is, September 8. The end date for purposes of this particular calculation is September 15 (although post-judgment interest will continue to accrue until all amounts owing are paid in full). Use the table of days (Table 5.2) at page 184 to calculate the number of days that elapsed between the start date and the end date for purposes of filling out the forms for this particular enforcement. Note that subtracting the number for the start date from the number for the end date automatically excludes the first day of the time period and includes the last day of the time period in compliance with Rule 3.01. If you are calculating a time period over a year-end, subtract the number for the start date in the first year from 365, and add on the number of days to the end date in the following year.

Find the number (from 1 to 365) for the start date (that is, the date the order was made—in this case, September 8), and subtract that number from the number for the date of the notice of garnishment (in this case, September 15).

September 15 is the 258th day of the year. September 8 is the 251st day of the year.

- 258 – 251 = 7 days

Step Three: Calculate the amount of post-judgment interest that has accrued from September 8, 2010 to September 15, 2010

The post-judgment interest that accrues from the date the order was made to the date the garnishment forms were prepared.

- 7 days x $0.40 per day = $2.80

Post-judgment Interest and Subsequent Costs

At each stage of a debt collection, when completing your forms, you must remember to:

- calculate the amount of post-judgment interest to the date of preparing the forms for the current enforcement; and
- accrue your subsequent costs—that is, add the costs claimed for the current enforcement step to the costs claimed for prior enforcement steps.

In this case, "costs" means the creditor's reasonable out-of-pocket expenses for enforcement of the judgment. At a minimum, you will claim the court fee for issuing the enforcement document. Examples of enforcement documents are a notice of debtor examination, a notice of garnishment, a writ of seizure and sale of land, and a writ of seizure and sale of personal property.

BOX 11.2 Parrish v. Thurston: Order for Periodic Payments—Default in Payment

Background: The plaintiff is Maxwell Parrish. Maxwell Parrish commenced an action against the defendant, Frank Thurston, in Brampton Small Claims Court Claim no. SC-00-45678-00 for recovery of an unpaid debt of $27,000.00 owing pursuant to a promissory note dated March 1, 20—. The plaintiff waived any amounts owing over and above $25,000.00 to bring the action within the monetary jurisdiction of the Small Claims Court. The defendant did not defend the claim, and default judgment for the amount owing of $25,000.00 plus pre-judgment interest of $747.93 and costs of $110.00, for a total judgment amount of $25,857.93, was signed on December 1, 20—. You will find the draft default judgment (Form 11B) at Appendix 5.1 to Chapter 5.

Mr. Thurston brought a motion for set aside of the default judgment dated December 1, 20— (see Appendix 7.2 to Chapter 7). That motion was subsequently withdrawn on the written consent of all parties.

At a debtor examination on February 14 in the following year, the court orders that Frank Thurston pay to Maxwell Parrish the amount of $400.00 per month on the first day of each and every month commencing on March 1, 20— and continuing until all amounts owing are paid in full.

Mr. Thurston makes payments on March 1 and April 1. He fails to make a payment on May 1, and does not respond to Mr. Parrish's telephone calls and emails. On May 14, Mr. Parrish's paralegal serves a notice of default of payment (Form 20L) on Mr. Thurston by regular letter mail under Rule 8.01(14). Service by mail is effective on the fifth day following the date of mailing—that is, on May 19. The 15-day period for waiver of the default ends on June 3. Mr. Parrish advises his paralegal that he does not wish to waive the default. On June 4, his paralegal files a copy of the notice of default of payment together with an affidavit of default of payment with the court.

Discussion: You will find the notice of default of payment (Form 20L) together with proof of service, an affidavit of default of payment (Form 20M), and an adjusted calculation of the amount owing at Appendix 11.1 to this chapter. On the affidavit of default of payment (Form 20M), subsequent costs include the following: fee for issuing a notice of debtor examination ($35.00), cost of effecting service of the notice of examination on Mr. Thurston ($50.00), and cost of effecting service of the notice of default of payment on Mr. Thurston ($50.00), for a total of $135.00. Note that the amounts charged for effecting service do not exceed the maximum of $60.00 stated in Rule 19.01(3).

Consolidation Order (Rule 20.09)

A consolidation order is a form of debtor relief. A debtor against whom there are two or more unsatisfied orders for payment of money may make a motion to the court for a consolidation order (Rule 20.09(1)).

A debtor who wishes to make a motion for a consolidation order shall contact the court clerk in the territorial division where the debtor lives to schedule a hearing date for the motion. The debtor must complete and file a notice of motion and supporting affidavit (Form 15A) with the court, and serve copies of the motion and supporting affidavit on all creditors named in the supporting affidavit at least seven days before the hearing date (Rule 20.09(3)).

The supporting affidavit shall include the following information (Rule 20.09(2)):

1. the names and addresses of all creditors who have obtained an order for payment of money against the debtor;

2. the amount owed to each creditor;

3. the amount of the debtor's income from all sources, identifying the sources; and

4. the debtor's current financial obligations and any other relevant facts.

When setting out the debtor's current financial obligations and any other relevant facts, the debtor may consider referring to the Financial Information Form (Form 20I) as a guide. You will find a blank Form 20I at Appendix 11.4 to this chapter.

The rule does not require documentary disclosure. However, the debtor should be prepared to produce documents in support of the affidavit evidence, either as exhibits attached to the affidavit, or to all parties at the hearing of the motion.

You will find an example of a notice of motion and supporting affidavit (Form 15A) for a consolidation order at Appendix 11.2 to this chapter.

At the hearing of the motion, the court may make a consolidation order setting out (Rule 20.09(4)):

1. a list of all unsatisfied judgments, including the date, court, and amount, and the amount unpaid;

2. the amounts to be paid into court by the debtor under the consolidation order; and

3. the times of the payments.

If the court makes a consolidation order, the total of the amounts to be paid into court by the debtor on account of the consolidation order may not exceed 20 percent of the debtor's wages as set out in s. 7 of the *Wages Act* (discussed below at Table 11.1, pages 430–431). The *Wages Act* defines "wages" as the debtor's wages after all lawful deductions—that is, the debtor's **net wages** after income tax, employment insurance premiums, Canada Pension Plan contributions, pension adjustments, and so on—have been deducted.

At the hearing of the motion, a creditor may make submissions as to the amount and times of payment (Rule 20.09(6)). All payments into a consolidation account belong to the creditors named in the consolidation order. The creditors share equally in the distribution of the money (Rule 20.09(12)). The clerk shall distribute the money paid into the consolidation account at least once every six months (Rule 20.09(13)).

While the consolidation order is in force, no step to enforce the judgment may be taken by a creditor named in the order, except issuing a writ of seizure and sale of land and filing it with the sheriff (Rule 20.09(9)).

If an order for payment of money is made against the debtor after the date of the consolidation order, for a debt incurred before the date of the consolidation order, the creditor may file a certified copy of the new order with the clerk. The creditor shall be added to the list of creditors in the consolidation order, and the creditor is entitled to share in distribution under the order from the time his name is added (Rule 20.09(7)).

A consolidation order terminates immediately if

- an order for payment of money is obtained against the debtor for a debt incurred after the date of the consolidation order (Rule 20.09(8)), or

- the debtor is in default under it for 21 days (Rule 20.09(10)).

If a consolidation order terminates, the clerk shall serve a notice of termination of consolidation order on all creditors named in the order, and no further consolidation order shall be made with respect to the debtor for one year after the date of the termination (Rule 20.09(11)). The notice of termination of consolidation order shall be served by mail or fax (Rule 20.09(11.1)).

When a consolidation order with respect to a debtor terminates under Rule 20.09(8) or 20.09(10)), a creditor may enforce an order for payment or recovery of money by any lawful means.

If payment is made in full satisfaction of the consolidation order, the debtor may, with the consent of all parties, file a request for clerk's order on consent (Form 11.2A) indicating that payment has been made in full satisfaction of the order. If the debtor cannot obtain the consent of all parties, she may make a motion for an order confirming that payment has been made in full satisfaction of the order (Rule 20.12).

BOX 11.3 Consolidation Order: Events of Termination

Scenario One

Debtor obtains a consolidation order for payments of money to Creditors One, Two, and Three on December 3, 20—. On December 20, 20—, Creditor Four obtains an order for payment of money against Debtor, for a debt incurred on August 1, 20—.

Question: Does the consolidation order dated December 3, 20— terminate because of the December 20, 20— order for payment of money in favour of Creditor Four?

Answer: No, because the debt to Creditor Four was incurred by Debtor before the date of the consolidation order (Rule 20.09(7)).

Question: Is Creditor Four entitled to share in the proceeds of the December 3 consolidation order?

Answer: Yes. Creditor Four may file a certified copy of the December 20, 20— order with the clerk, and the clerk will add Creditor Four to the consolidation order, entitling Creditor Four to share equally in any distributions from that time forward (Rule 20.09(7)).

Scenario Two

Debtor obtains a consolidation order for payments of money to Creditors One, Two, and Three on February 5, 20—. On September 13, 20—, Creditor Four obtains an order for payment of money against Debtor, for a debt incurred on May 13, 20—.

Question: Does the consolidation order dated February 5, 20— terminate because of the September 13, 20— order for payment of money in favour of Creditor Four?

Answer: Yes, because the debt to Creditor Four was incurred by Debtor after the date of the consolidation order (Rule 20.09(8)).

Question: What are the consequences of termination of the order?

Answer: The clerk shall serve a notice of termination of consolidation order on Creditors One, Two, and Three by mail or fax. No further consolidation order may be made in respect of the debtor for one year after the date of termination (Rule 20.09(11)). On termination of the order, all creditors may enforce their orders in any way they see fit.

Enforcement of Orders Made in Another Canadian Province or Territory

An order for payment of $25,000.00 or less or return of property with a value of $25,000.00 or less made by a court in another Canadian province or territory (except Quebec) may be filed in the Ontario Small Claims Court under the *Reciprocal Enforcement of Judgments Act* and enforced in Ontario as if it were an order of the Small Claims Court. The application to register the judgment may be made at any time within six years after the date of the judgment.

If the judgment debtor was not personally served with the originating process in the original action and did not appear or defend the action, reasonable notice of the application shall be given to the judgment debtor. An **originating process** is the document that commences the action. An **originating court**, or **original court**, is the court where the judgment is made. For purposes of an application under the *Reciprocal Enforcement of Judgments Act*, a **registering court** is the court in which the judgment is registered.

You must obtain permission to file the order from a judge of the Small Claims Court where you wish to file the order. You may request permission by filing a notice of motion and supporting affidavit, along with a certified copy of the order, at the Small Claims Court office where the order is to be filed.

No judgment shall be registered if the registering court is satisfied that any of the following apply:

1. the court where the order originated acted without jurisdiction;
2. the judgment debtor was a person who was neither carrying on business nor ordinarily resident within the jurisdiction of the original court, and did not voluntarily appear or otherwise submit to the jurisdiction of the court;
3. the judgment debtor, being the defendant in the proceeding, was not duly served with the originating process and did not appear, despite the fact that the judgment debtor was ordinarily resident or was carrying on business within the jurisdiction of the court or agreed to submit to the jurisdiction of the court;
4. the judgment was obtained by fraud;
5. an appeal is pending, or the judgment debtor is entitled to appeal and intends to appeal against the judgment;
6. the judgment was in respect of a cause of action which for reasons of public policy or for some other similar reason would not have been entertained by the registering court; or
7. the judgment debtor would have a good defence if an action were brought on the original judgment.

Your supporting affidavit should contain evidence that is sufficient to satisfy the registering court that none of the above conditions apply.

You do not have to attend at the motion, but you may attend if you wish. The court will notify you by mail if permission has been granted to file the order in Ontario for enforcement. There is a fee for the motion and for receiving the judgment for enforcement.

A judgment registered under the Act is of the same force and effect as if it had been made by the registering court.

Certificate of Judgment (Rule 20.04)

A creditor who has obtained an order for payment of money in one Small Claims Court territorial division and who wishes to enforce it in another territorial division may do so by filing an affidavit for enforcement request with the originating court, and paying the fee to issue a certificate of judgment. The originating court will then issue a certificate of judgment (Form 20A) directed to the clerk at the court location specified in the affidavit for enforcement request and the certificate of judgment. As of this writing, the fee for issuing a certificate of judgment is $19.00.

After it has been issued by the originating court, the certificate of judgment is filed with the court in the territorial division where you wish to enforce your order. When you file the certificate of judgment with that court, your order becomes enforceable as if it were an order of that court. The court clerk will create a new file and assign a claim number to your matter. All documents filed in that court must use the claim number assigned to the matter in that division.

You will find examples of an affidavit for enforcement request and certificate of judgment at Appendix 11.3 to this chapter.

Methods of Enforcing an Order

General (Rule 20.03)

In addition to any other lawful method of enforcing an order for payment of money, a creditor may enforce the order by:

1. a writ of seizure and sale of personal property (Rule 20.06);
2. a writ of seizure and sale of land (Rule 20.07); and
3. a garnishment (Rule 20.08).

Assets Exempt from Seizure

Certain assets of a debtor cannot be seized by the sheriff or bailiff under a writ, nor may they be garnished. Assets that can be seized or garnished are called **exigible assets**. Assets that cannot be seized or garnished are called **non-exigible assets**. See Table 11.1 on the following pages for an overview of assets that are exempt from seizure.

TABLE 11.1 Assets Exempt from Seizure or Garnishment

ASSETS	AUTHORITY	EXEMPT FROM SEIZURE	EXCEPTIONS
FEDERAL			
Pensions, Benefits	*Canada Pension Plan*, RSC 1985, c. C-8	Pension benefits	Most federal pensions may be garnished in an enforcement of a family support order (*Garnishment, Attachment and Pension Diversion Act*, RSC 1995, c. G-2). Employment insurance benefits are considered income under the *Family Responsibility and Support Arrears Enforcement Act, 1996* (SO 1996, c. 31) and are also subject to garnishment by support creditors.
	Canadian Forces Superannuation Act, RSC 1985, c. C-17	Pensions	
	Old Age Security Act, RSC 1985, c. O-9	Benefits	
	Pension Fund Societies Act, RSC 1985, c. P-8	Interest of a member in the fund of a society is exempt and cannot be assigned to a creditor or others	
	RCMP Superannuation Act, RSC 1985, c. R-11	Benefits	
	Employment Insurance Act, SC 1996, c. 23	Benefits	
	War Veterans Allowances Act, RSC 1985, c. W-3	Allowances	
Other Assets	*Indian Act*, RSC 1985, c. I-5	Real and personal property of status natives cannot be seized by a non-native creditor	
PROVINCIAL			
Wages	*Wages Act*, RSO 1990, c. W.1	80% of a person's wages. "Wages" does not include an amount that an employer is required by law to deduct from wages. The exemption amount may be increased on motion by a debtor or decreased on motion by a creditor.	Support creditors may garnish up to 50% of a person's wages.
Insurance Benefits	*Workplace Safety and Insurance Act, 1997*, SO 1997, c. 16	Benefits are not assignable.	Support creditors may garnish up to 50% of a person's benefits.
	Insurance Act, RSO 1990, c. I.8	• Where a beneficiary is designated, insurance money does not form part of the insured's estate and is not subject to claims of creditors of the insured. • If the beneficiary is a family member of the insured, the rights and interests of the insured in the insurance money and in the contract are exempt from execution or seizure.	—

ASSETS	AUTHORITY	EXEMPT FROM SEIZURE	EXCEPTIONS
Pensions, Benefits	*Compensation for Victims of Crime Act,* RSO 1990, c. C.24	Victim's compensation	—
	Ontario Works Act, 1997, SO 1997, c. 25, s. 23	Welfare benefits under *Family Benefits Act* or *Ontario Works Act, 1997*	A portion may be deducted to recover arrears of a support deduction order enforceable under the *Family Responsibility and Support Arrears Enforcement Act, 1996,* SO 1996, c. 31.
	Pension Benefits Act, RSO 1990, c. P.8	Pension benefits	A party to a domestic contract or subject to a court order may claim up to 50% of a former spouse's benefits accumulated during the spousal relationship.
Other Assets	*Execution Act,* RSO 1990, c. E.24, s. 2 NOTE: Amounts prescribed by *Exemptions,* O. Reg. 657/05 to the *Execution Act* as of the date of this writing.	• Clothing up to a certain amount ($5,650.00) • Household furniture, utensils, equipment, food, and fuel up to a certain amount ($11,300.00) • Tools and instruments ordinarily used by the debtor in the debtor's business, profession, or calling up to a certain amount ($11,300.00) • If a person earns a living through farming or agriculture, the livestock, fowl, bees, books, tools, implements, and seed ordinarily used by the debtor in the debtor's business, up to a certain amount ($28,300.00) • One motor vehicle worth less than the prescribed amount ($5,650.00)	—

Finding Out About the Debtor: Examination of Debtor or Other Person (Rule 20.10)

Arranging an Examination of Debtor

An examination of the debtor is not an enforcement. Rather, it is a very useful investigative tool to help the creditor find out about the debtor's current financial circumstances for purposes of enforcement of a judgment for payment or recovery of money.

Where there is an order for payment or recovery of money and the debtor has (1) failed to pay anything, or (2) made some payments and then stopped paying, leaving a balance owing, the creditor may request an examination of the debtor or other person with relevant information about the debtor's financial circumstances.

The creditor arranges an examination of the debtor by filing an affidavit for enforcement request, requesting that the clerk of the court where the debtor resides or carries on business issue a notice of examination (Form 20H) directed to the debtor or another person (Rule 20.10(1)). The notice of examination states the date, time, and location of the examination.

In addition to individual debtors, the following persons may be examined (Rule 20.10(5)):

1. an officer or director of a corporate debtor;
2. any partner of a debtor that is a partnership; or
3. the sole proprietor of a debtor that is a sole proprietorship.

The affidavit for enforcement request (Form 20P) shall set out (Rule 20.10(2)):

1. the date of the order and the amount awarded;
2. the territorial division where the order was made;
3. the rate of post-judgment interest payable;
4. the total amount of any payments received since the order was made; and
5. the amount owing, including post-judgment interest.

If the order was made in a territorial jurisdiction other than the jurisdiction where the debtor currently resides or carries on business, the creditor seeking the examination shall issue a certificate of judgment (Form 20A) in the originating court and file it at the court location where the examination is to be held. The court clerk at the location where the examination is to be held will then open a court file and assign a claim number for the matter in that court. The claim number assigned to the matter in that division, and the address and telephone number of the Small Claims Court in that division, shall be used for all documents filed with or issued by the court clerk in that division.

The notice of examination shall be served on the debtor or person to be examined personally as provided in Rule 8.02 or by an alternative to personal service as provided in Rule 8.03, unless a court orders otherwise (Rule 8.01(10)).

If the person to be examined is the debtor and the debtor is an individual, the creditor shall serve a blank financial information form (Form 20I) on the debtor along with the notice of examination (Rule 8.01(11)). The financial information form is for the information of the creditor only. It shall not be filed with the court.

The notice of examination and, if the debtor is an individual, the financial information form shall be served at least 30 days before the date fixed for the examination. The notice of examination shall be filed, with proof of service, at least three days before the date fixed for the examination (Rule 8.01(12)).

You will find examples of an affidavit for enforcement request (debtor examination), notice of examination, and blank financial information form at Appendix 11.4 to this chapter.

Procedure at the Examination of Debtor

The examination may be conducted in person by the creditor and the debtor, or by video conference if facilities for video conferencing are available at the court (Rules 1.07(1.1) and 20.10(5.1)). The examination is held in the presence of a judge or deputy judge. The examination shall be (Rule 20.10(6)):

1. held in the absence of the public, unless the court orders otherwise;
2. conducted under oath; and
3. recorded.

The debtor, any other persons to be examined, and any witnesses whose evidence the court considers necessary may be examined in relation to (Rule 20.10(4)):

1. the reason for non-payment;
2. the debtor's income and property;
3. the debts owed to and by the debtor;
4. the sale or transfer of any property by the debtor before or after the order was made;
5. the debtor's present, past, and future resources available to satisfy the order;
6. whether the debtor intends to pay the order or has any reason for not doing so; and
7. any other matter pertinent to enforcing the order.

A person who is served with a notice of examination shall inform himself about the matters set out above and be prepared to answer questions about them (Rule 20.10(4.1)(a)). In the case of a debtor who is an individual, the debtor shall complete the financial information form and serve it on the creditor requesting the examination, but shall not file it with the court. The financial information form shall be produced to the judge presiding at the examination hearing (Rule 20.10(4.1)(b)). The judge's copy should be returned to the debtor when the examination is concluded.

A debtor required to complete a financial information form shall bring to the examination hearing all documents that are necessary to support the information that is provided in the financial information form (Rule 20.10(4.2)). Examples of documents that may be required to be produced are pay stubs, income tax statements, bank statements or passbooks, credit card statements, deeds, mortgages, commercial or residential tenancy agreements, and so on. Although Rule 20.10(4.2) does not require it, a person who is not an individual debtor and who is required to attend an examination hearing should consider bringing to the examination all documents that are relevant to the issues stated in Rule 20.10(4).

The questions that can be asked of a debtor or other person at a debtor examination are wide-ranging, and may cover all aspects of the debtor's financial situation. For standard scripts of the questions that should be asked on an examination of a debtor, see Appendixes 11.5 (individual debtor) and 11.6 (corporate debtor). These are scripts only. The questions may be adapted, depending on the circumstances of the debtor being examined.

The creditor or the creditor's representative should take detailed notes of what is said at the examination. A debtor should also consider taking notes of the examination.

After the examination or if the debtor's consent is filed, the court may make an order as to payment (Rule 20.10(7)). While the order as to payment is in force, no step to enforce the judgment may be taken or continued against the debtor by a creditor named in the order, except to issue a writ of seizure and sale of land and file it with the sheriff (Rule 20.10(8)).

If the debtor fails to make a payment under the order, the creditor may serve the debtor with a notice of default of payment (Form 20L). A notice of default of payment may be served by mail, by courier, by fax, personally (Rule 8.02), or by an alternative to personal service (Rule 8.03), unless the court orders some other type of service (Rule 8.01(14)).

An order for periodic payment terminates on the day that is 15 days after the creditor serves the debtor with the notice of default of payment, unless a consent (Form 13B) in which the creditor waives the default is filed within the 15-day period (Rule 20.02(4)). If no consent is filed within the 15-day period, the creditor may file with the court an affidavit of default of payment (Form 20M), together with a copy of the notice of default of payment and proof of service (Rule 20.02(3)). See Appendix 11.1 to this chapter. Upon termination of the order for periodic payment, a creditor may enforce an order for payment or recovery of money by any lawful means.

Contempt Hearing (Rule 20.11)

If a person who has been served with a notice of examination attends at the examination but refuses to answer questions or produce documents or records, the court may order that person to attend before the court for a contempt hearing (Rule 20.11(1)).

If a person who has been served with a notice of examination fails to attend the examination, the court may order that person to attend before it for a contempt hearing under ss. 30(1) and (2) of the *Courts of Justice Act*:

Contempt hearing for failure to attend examination

30(1) The Small Claims Court may, in accordance with the rules of court, order a debtor or other person who is required to and fails to attend an examination respecting a default by the debtor under an order of the court for the payment or recovery of money, to attend before the court for a contempt hearing.

Finding of contempt

(2) The Small Claims Court may find a person to be in contempt of court at a hearing referred to in subsection (1), if the court is satisfied that,

(a) the person was required to attend the examination;

(b) the person was served, in accordance with the rules of court, with a notice to attend the examination;

(c) the person failed to attend the examination; and

(d) the failure to attend was wilful.

If the court makes an order for a contempt hearing, the clerk shall provide the creditor with a notice of contempt hearing setting out the time, date, and place of the hearing. The creditor shall serve the debtor or person to be examined with the notice of contempt hearing by personal service and file the affidavit of service at least seven days before the hearing (Rules 8.01(13), 20.11(3)(b)).

A person who has been ordered to attend a contempt hearing may make a motion to set aside the order. The motion may be made before or after receiving the notice of contempt hearing; but it must be made before the date of the hearing. On the motion, the court may set aside the order to attend at a contempt hearing, and order that the person attend instead at another examination under Rule 20.10 (Rule 20.11(4)).

A judge or deputy judge may order, hear, and determine a contempt hearing in the Small Claims Court (*Courts of Justice Act*, s. 30(3)). If a contempt hearing is heard and determined by a deputy judge or provincial judge who was assigned to the Provincial Court (Civil Division) immediately before September 1, 1990, the court shall not make an order that the person be imprisoned (*Courts of Justice Act*, s. 30(4)).

At a contempt hearing of a debtor or other person for refusing to answer questions or produce documents and records held under Rule 20.11(1), the court may find the person to be in contempt of court if the person fails to show cause why he should not be held in contempt for refusing to answer questions or produce documents and records (Rule 20.11(5)).

At a contempt hearing of a debtor or other person for failure to attend on an examination, a judge may find the person to be in contempt of court if the judge is satisfied (Rule 20.11(6)), *Courts of Justice Act*, s. 30(2)) that:

1. the person was required to attend the examination;
2. the person was served, in accordance with the rules of court, with a notice to attend the examination;
3. the person failed to attend the examination; and
4. the failure to attend was wilful.

If the court is satisfied that the person failed to attend because of an honest mistake or as a result of inadvertence, the court will not make a finding of contempt.

At a contempt hearing, the court may order that the person (Rule 20.11(7))

1. attend an examination under Rule 20.10;
2. be jailed for a period of not more than five days;
3. attend at an additional contempt hearing under Rule 20.11(1) or the *Courts of Justice Act*, s. 30(1); or
4. comply with any other order that the judge considers necessary or just.

If a warrant of committal is ordered under Rule 20.11(7)(b), the creditor may complete and file with the clerk an identification form (Form 20K) to assist the police in apprehending the person named in the warrant of committal. The clerk shall issue the warrant of committal (Form 20J), accompanied by the identification form if one is filed. The warrant of committal directs all police officers in Ontario to apprehend the person named in the warrant anywhere in Ontario and promptly bring the person to the nearest correctional institution.

A person who is apprehended under a warrant of committal shall be discharged from custody on order of the court or when the time set out in the warrant expires, whichever is earlier. In either case, the period of incarceration cannot exceed five days (Rules 20.11(9), 20.11(7)(b)).

The warrant of committal remains in force for 12 months after the date of its issue and may be renewed by the court on a motion by the creditor for further 12-month periods thereafter, unless the court orders otherwise (Rule 20.11(10)).You will find examples of a warrant of committal and identification form at Appendix 11.7 to this chapter.

A debtor who has been served with a notice of contempt hearing should consider seeking legal representation.

Garnishment (Rule 20.08)

A creditor may enforce an order for payment or recovery of money by garnishment of debts payable to the debtor by other persons. If a debt is payable to the debtor and to one or more co-owners, one half of the indebtedness or a greater or lesser amount specified in a court order may be garnished.

If more than six years have passed since the order for payment or recovery of money was made, a notice of garnishment may be issued only with leave of the court on motion by the creditor (Rule 20.08(2.1)). If a notice of garnishment is not issued within one year after the date on which an order granting leave to issue it was made, the order ceases to have effect and a notice of garnishment may be issued only with leave of the court on a subsequent motion (Rule 20.08(2.2)).

A notice of garnishment may be renewed before it expires by filing with the clerk of the court in which the notice was issued an affidavit for enforcement request (Form 20P) requesting renewal of the notice of garnishment, and a notice of renewal of garnishment (Form 20E.1) (Rule 20.08(5.2)). On filing of the affidavit for enforcement request and notice of renewal of garnishment, the clerk shall issue the notice of renewal of garnishment, naming as garnishee the person named in the affidavit (Rule 20.08(5.3)). The rules that apply to notices of garnishment also apply to notices of renewal of garnishment (Rule 20.08(5.4)).

Key Terms

In order to understand how a garnishment works, you must understand certain key terms and concepts.

First of all, in a garnishment, the **garnishee** is any person who owes money to the debtor. If the debtor is employed, then the employer is the garnishee, because the employer owes employment income to the debtor from time to time. If the debtor has a bank account, the bank is the garnishee, because the bank owes the debtor the money held in the bank account.

The **garnishor** is any creditor who is trying to enforce an order for payment of money by way of a garnishment.

Garnishee is a noun. Garnish is a verb (action word). A garnishor (creditor) garnishes money owed to the debtor when the garnishor seizes part or all of the money owed by the garnishee to the debtor in a garnishment.

What Can Be Garnished?

The following sources of money may be attached in a garnishment:

1. wages paid by an employer to an employee;
2. commissions and tips;
3. bank accounts, whether solely owned by the debtor, or owned jointly with other persons;
4. money paid out of an RRSP;
5. money paid from a mutual fund;
6. accounts receivable of a business debtor;
7. cash value of a life insurance policy owned by the debtor; and
8. payments to the debtor from an estate.

A creditor who does not have current information about a debtor's financial circumstances should consider conducting a debtor examination before taking any steps to enforce the order for payment or recovery of money.

Procedure on a Garnishment

A creditor who wishes to enforce an order for payment or recovery of money by way of a garnishment shall file with the clerk of a court in the territorial division in which the debtor resides or carries on business an affidavit for enforcement request (Form 20P), and a certificate of judgment (Form 20A) if the order was made in another territorial division (Rule 20.08(3)). The clerk shall issue a notice of garnishment (Form 20E) naming as garnishee the person named in the affidavit for enforcement request (Rule 20.08(4)). The notice of garnishment shall name only one debtor and one garnishee (Rule 20.08(5)).

If you are issuing notices of garnishment against a debtor for more than one garnishee, you must file an affidavit for enforcement request and a notice of garnishment for each garnishee.

The court clerk issues the notice of garnishment by signing and dating it. There is a fee for issuing each separate notice of garnishment, which is recoverable in the garnishment. The fee per notice is currently $100.00.

The clerk will return the issued notice of garnishment to you. You will then serve the garnishee (that is, the person who owes the debtor money) with a copy of the notice of garnishment and a blank garnishee's statement (Form 20F). Service is by mail, by courier, personally as provided in Rule 8.02, or by an alternative to personal service as provided in Rule 8.03 (Rule 8.01(8)(b)). If the garnishee is a financial institution, the address for service of the notice of garnishment and all further notices required to be served shall be served at the branch where the debt is payable (for example, where the debtor has a bank account) (Rule 20.08(6.2)).

You shall serve a copy of the notice of garnishment and affidavit for enforcement request on the debtor within five days of serving the notice of garnishment on the garnishee (Rule 20.08(6.1)). Service is by mail, by courier, personally as provided in Rule 8.02, or by an alternative to personal service as provided in Rule 8.03 (Rule 8.01(8)(a)).

Proof of service of the notice of garnishment and other documents on the garnishee and the debtor is by way of affidavits of service (Rule 20.08(6.3)). You should file proof of service promptly with the court. The clerk must be satisfied that proper service of the notice of garnishment has taken place before she will start making payments out of court.

The garnishment attaches a debt payable by the garnishee to the debtor at the time the notice of garnishment is served, and any debts payable within six years after the notice is served (Rule 20.08(8)). A garnishee who admits owing a debt to the debtor is liable to pay to the clerk of the court any debt of the garnishee to the debtor, up to the total amount shown in the notice of garnishment, within 10 days after service of the notice, or ten days after the debt becomes payable, whichever is later (Rule 20.08(7)).

If the garnishee does not make payments to the clerk and does not send a garnishee's statement disputing the garnishment, the creditor is entitled to an order against the garnishee for payment of the entire amount set out in the notice of garnishment, unless a court orders otherwise (Rule 20.08(17)).

If a garnishee who has been served with a notice of garnishment pays a debt attached by the notice to a person other than the clerk, the garnishee remains liable to pay the debt in accordance with the notice (Rule 20.08(18)).

If the garnishee is the debtor's employer, the amount being paid into court shall not exceed 20 percent of the debtor's wages, as set out in s. 7 of the *Wages Act* (see Table 11.1 at pages 430–431 above) (Rule 20.08(9)). The other 80 percent of the debtor's wages are exempt from garnishment, except by support or maintenance creditors, who may garnish up to 50 percent of a debtor's wages. For purposes of the *Wages Act*, the term "wages" does not include an amount that an employer is required by law to deduct from wages. In other words, the exemption applies to net wages—that is, whatever is left after such lawful deductions as income tax, EI, CPP, etc. Payments from an insurance or indemnity scheme that are intended to replace income lost because of disability are deemed to be wages, whether the scheme is administered by the employer or another person (*Wages Act*, s. 7(1.1)).

A judge may decrease the exemption on motion by the creditor, if the judge is satisfied that it is just to do so, having regard to the nature of the debt owed to the creditor, the person's financial circumstances, and any other matter the judge considers relevant (*Wages Act*, s. 7(4)). In other words, if the creditor has reason to believe that the debtor's financial circumstances have improved, the creditor may make a motion to decrease the exemption. The supporting affidavit should contain evidence, including documents attached as exhibits, demonstrating that the debtor's circumstances have improved.

A judge may increase the exemption on motion by the debtor on notice to the creditor, if the judge is satisfied that it is just to do so, having regard to the debtor's financial circumstances and any other matter the judge considers relevant (*Wages Act*, s. 7(5)). In other words, if the debtor's financial circumstances have deteriorated, the debtor may make a motion to increase the exemption. The supporting affidavit should contain evidence, including documents attached as exhibits, demonstrating that the debtor's circumstances have gotten worse.

When a garnishee starts paying money into court, the money is paid into the court's account in trust for the creditor. If proof of service on the garnishee and the debtor has been filed by the creditor, after an initial 30-day holding period for the first payment received, the clerk will begin making payments out of court to the creditor or creditors. Subsequent payments will be made as the money is received (Rule 20.08(20.1)).

If two or more creditors have filed requests for garnishment at the same court location against the same debtor, any amount paid into court under any of the notices of garnishment issued to those creditors will be divided equally among all creditors who have not been paid in full (Rule 20.08(10)).

According to Rule 20.08(20), payment of creditors will be delayed if:

1. a creditor, debtor, garnishee, co-owner of a debt, or any other interested person has requested a garnishment hearing under Rule 20.08(15);
2. a notice of motion and supporting affidavit has been filed under
   - Rule 8.10 (failure to receive document),
   - Rule 11.06 or 11.2.01(1)1(iii) (setting aside of noting in default or default judgment, if any), or
   - Rule 17.04 (motion for new trial or amendment of judgment); or
3. a request for clerk's order on consent (Form 11.2A) has been filed setting aside the noting in default or default judgment against a party or any specified step to enforce a judgment that has not yet been completed.

You will find examples of an affidavit for enforcement request (garnishment), notice of garnishment, and blank garnishee's statement at Appendix 11.8.

Reminder: In a garnishment, the creditor serves the notice of garnishment (Form 20E) and blank garnishee's statement (Form 20F) on the garnishee. Within five days after service on the garnishee, the creditor serves the affidavit for enforcement request (garnishment) (Form 20P) and notice of garnishment on the debtor.

Garnishment Hearing

A creditor, debtor, garnishee, co-owner of the debt, or any other interested party may request a garnishment hearing. A **co-owner of the debt** is a person who is entitled to part of a debt also payable to the debtor. An example of a co-owner of a debt is a person who holds a bank account jointly with the debtor.

A garnishment hearing is intended to determine the rights of persons with an interest in the debt being garnished. To set up a garnishment hearing, the person requesting the hearing shall call the court office and obtain a hearing date from the clerk. The person shall then complete the notice of garnishment hearing (Form 20Q) and serve it on the creditor, debtor, garnishee, and co-owner of the debt, if any, and any other interested persons. Service is by mail, by courier, personally as provided in Rule 8.02, or by an alternative to personal service as provided in Rule 8.03 (Rules 8.01(9), 20.08(15), 20.08(15.1)).

The notice of garnishment hearing shall be filed at the court office before the hearing date.

You will find examples of a completed garnishee's statement, notice to co-owner of debt (Form 20G) and note of garnishment hearing (Form 20Q) at Appendix 11.9 to this chapter.

At a garnishment hearing, the court may (Rule 20.08(15.2))

1. if it is alleged that the garnishee's debt to the debtor has been **assigned** or **encumbered**, order the **assignee** or **encumbrancer** to appear and state the nature and particulars of the claim;

2. determine the rights and liabilities of the garnishee, any co-owner of the debt, the debtor, and any assignee or encumbrancer;

3. vary or suspend periodic payments under a notice of garnishment; or

4. determine any other matter in relation to a notice of garnishment.

To assign a legal right or entitlement (including wages owed or the money in a bank account) is to transfer it to another person. The person who assigns the right or entitlement to another is called the assignor. The person to whom the right or entitlement is assigned is called the assignee. To encumber is to register a mortgage, lien, or other security interest against property. The person holding the security interest is called the encumbrancer.

Where an assignment of a legal right or entitlement by a debtor to a creditor or other person has the effect of prejudicing the lawful claims of other creditors, it will be subject to judicial scrutiny. Where an **encumbrance** of the debtor's property for the benefit of a creditor or other person has the effect of prejudicing the lawful claims of creditors, it will be subject to judicial scrutiny.

Payment Where a Debt Is Jointly Owned

A co-owner of a debt is a person to whom a debt is owed jointly with the debtor—for example, a person who holds a bank account jointly with the debtor.

A garnishee (that is, the person who owes money to the debtor) is required to identify any co-owners of a debt in the garnishee's statement. The garnishee shall serve a copy of the garnishee's statement on the creditor and the debtor. Service is by mail, courier or fax, personally as provided in Rule 8.02 or by an alternative to personal service as provided in Rule 8.03, unless a court orders otherwise (Rule 8.01(14)).

A creditor who is served with a garnishee's statement shall forthwith serve any co-owners of the debt named in the garnishee's statement with a notice to co-owner of debt (Form 20G) and a copy of the garnishee's statement (Rule 20.08(14)). Service is by mail, courier or fax, personally as provided in Rule 8.02 or by an alternative to personal service as provided in Rule 8.03, unless a court orders otherwise (Rule 8.01(14)).

A person who has been served with a notice to co-owner of debt must request a garnishment hearing within 30 days after the notice is sent. If she fails to do so, she loses her right to dispute the enforcement of the creditor's order for the payment of money or a payment made by the clerk (Rule 20.08(16)).

You will find a completed garnishee's statement, a notice to co-owner of debt (Form 20G), and a notice of garnishment hearing (Form 20Q) at Appendix 11.9 to this chapter.

If a debt is owed to the debtor and one or more co-owners, and (Rule 20.08(21))

- a payment of the jointly owned debt has been made to the clerk,
- no request for a garnishment hearing is made, and
- the 30-day period from service of the notice to co-owner of debt required by Rule 20.08(16) has expired,

then the creditor may file with the clerk, within 30 days after expiry of the Rule 20.08(16) notice period,

1. proof of service of the notice to co-owner; and
2. an affidavit stating that the creditor believes that no co-owner of the debt is a person under disability, and the grounds for the belief.

The affidavit required by Rule 20.08(21) may contain statements of the deponent's information and belief, specifying the source of the information and the fact of the belief (Rule 20.08(22)).

If the creditor does not file the material referred to above, the clerk shall return the money to the garnishee.

When dealing with a co-owner or co-owners of a debt in a garnishment, you should consider diarizing for the above deadlines, with appropriate tickler periods for follow-up.

Satisfaction of a Debt by Garnishment (Rule 20.08(20.2))

When the amount owing under an order that is enforced by garnishment is paid, the creditor shall immediately serve a notice of termination of garnishment (Form 20R) on the garnishee and on the clerk. You will find an example of a notice of termination of garnishment at Appendix 11.10 to this chapter.

Writ of Seizure and Sale of Personal Property (Rule 20.06)

A writ of seizure and sale of personal property (Form 20C) is used to seize **personal property** of the debtor and sell it at public auction to satisfy all or part of an order for payment of money in favour of the creditor.

The *Rules of the Small Claims Court* do not require the issuance and filing of a certificate of judgment in order to register a writ of seizure and sale of personal property in a territorial division other than the division where the order for payment or recovery of money was made. However, if you intend to enforce a writ of seizure and sale of personal property in a jurisdiction other than the jurisdiction where the order originated, you should issue a certificate of judgment in the originating jurisdiction and file it with the court office in the jurisdiction where you intend to seize and sell property.

To obtain a writ of seizure and sale of personal property, a creditor may complete and file an affidavit for enforcement request (Form 20P) requesting the clerk to issue to the bailiff of the Small Claims Court a writ of seizure and sale of personal property, and a writ of seizure and sale of personal property (Form 20C). On payment of the fee, the clerk will issue the writ of seizure and sale of personal property. As of this writing, the fee for issuing a writ of seizure and sale of personal property is $35.00. The bailiff shall enforce the writ for the amount owing, post-judgment interest, and the bailiff's reasonable fees and expenses (Rule 20.06(1)).

A writ of seizure and sale of personal property remains in force for six years from the date of its issue, and is renewable at six-year intervals thereafter (Rule 20.06(2)). It may be renewed before its expiration by filing a request to renew writ of seizure and sale (Form 20N) with the bailiff (Rule 20.06(3)). You should consider diarizing for the date a writ of seizure and sale expires, with appropriate ticklers for follow-up.

If more than six years have passed since the order for payment or recovery of money was made, a writ of seizure and sale of personal property may be issued only with leave of the court on motion by the creditor (Rule 20.06(1.1)). If the writ of seizure and sale of personal property is not issued within one year after the date on which an order granting leave to issue it was made, the order ceases to have effect and a writ of seizure and sale of personal property may be issued only with leave of the court on a subsequent motion (Rule 20.06(1.2)).

The writ of seizure and sale of personal property contains the name, address, and When the clerk has issued the writ of seizure and sale of personal property, you must file it with the enforcement office. If you wish to enforce the writ of seizure and sale of personal property, you must file a direction to enforce writ of seizure and sale of personal property (Form 20O) with the bailiff (Rule 20.06(4)). The direction to enforce provides the bailiff with detailed information about the property to be seized and its location. Before taking any steps to enforce the writ, the bailiff will require you to pay an enforcement fee and a deposit to cover anticipated expenses of enforcing the writ. These expenses may include insurance, locksmith, freight, storage, and advertising the sale of the property seized. You will also be charged for every attempt, successful or not, to enforce the writ, plus a kilometre allowance. If the initial deposit is not sufficient to cover the expenses incurred in enforcing the writ, you will be required to make an additional deposit.

If the creditor is trying to seize a motor vehicle, snowmobile, or boat, she must provide the court with the following:

- A current PPSA search and a *Repair and Storage Liens Act* search, indicating whether there are liens or security interests registered against the vehicle, and the amount of the lien or security (available at the ServiceOntario website).

- A vehicle abstract search to prove that the vehicle is owned by the debtor (available at the Ministry of Transportation website).

- In the case of a motor vehicle, an up-to-date copy of a used-vehicle information package that is not more than one week old (available at the ServiceOntario website).

If there is a security interest registered against the vehicle, an ordinary creditor who is considering seizing the vehicle should think carefully about whether it will be worthwhile to do so. The secured creditor is entitled to have any balance due on their security paid out of the proceeds of the sale before ordinary creditors take their share. There may be little or nothing left for an ordinary creditor after the secured creditor and the bailiff's fees and charges have been paid.

Certain assets of the debtor are exempt from seizure under s. 2 of the *Execution Act*:

1. clothing up to a prescribed amount (currently $5,650.00);

2. household furniture, utensils, equipment, food, and fuel up to a prescribed amount (currently $11,300.00);

3. tools and instruments ordinarily used by the debtor in the debtor's business, profession, or calling up to a prescribed amount (currently $11,300.00);

4. if a person earns a living through farming or agriculture, the livestock, fowl, bees, books, tools, implements, and seed ordinarily used by the debtor in the debtor's business, up to a prescribed amount (currently $28,300.00);

5. sufficient seed to seed all the person's land under cultivation, not exceeding 100 acres, as selected by the debtor, and 14 bushels of potatoes, and, where seizure is made between the 1st day of October and the 30th day of April, such food and bedding as are necessary to feed and bed the livestock and fowl that are exempt under s. 2 until the 30th day of April; and

6. one motor vehicle worth less than the prescribed amount (currently $5,650.00).

A sheriff or bailiff who is executing a writ of seizure and sale of personal property must comply with s. 20 of the *Execution Act*, excerpted below:

Execution of writ of seizure and sale

20(1) A sheriff acting under a writ of seizure and sale, a writ of delivery or a writ of sequestration may use reasonable force to enter land and premises other than a dwelling where he or she believes, on reasonable and probable grounds, that there is property liable to be taken in execution under the writ and may use reasonable force to execute the writ.

Idem, dwelling

(2) A sheriff acting under a writ of seizure and sale, a writ of delivery or a writ of sequestration in respect of property on premises that is used as a dwelling shall not use force to enter the dwelling or execute the writ except under the authority of an order of the court by which the writ was issued, and the court may make the order where in the opinion of the court there is reasonable and probable grounds to believe that there is property on the premises that is liable to be taken in execution under the writ.

If the personal property to be seized pursuant to the writ of seizure and sale of personal property is in a dwelling, you should consider obtaining a court order permitting the use of reasonable force by the bailiff to enter the residential premises before filing a direction to enforce writ of seizure and sale of personal property with the bailiff. A certified copy of the order should be attached to the direction to enforce.

The bailiff must be satisfied that the personal property being seized is owned by the debtor, and is free and clear of any claims by co-owners. If the debtor disputes the seizure on grounds that an asset is jointly owned by a spouse, other family member, or the debtor's business, the bailiff will refuse to seize the asset, and return the writ to you with a brief report to that effect. Where there is a title dispute, you must apply to the court for an order authorizing you to seize the asset in question. All of this takes time and money, and may prove not to be cost-effective in the context of a Small Claims Court collection.

The bailiff may refuse to seize the debtor's personal property if the bailiff is not satisfied that the value of the property when sold will exceed the costs of executing the writ of seizure and sale.

Where a debtor's personal property has been seized pursuant to a writ of seizure and sale of personal property, the bailiff must deliver an inventory of the property seized within a reasonable time after a request is made by the debtor or the debtor's agent (Rule 20.06(5)).

Personal property seized under a writ of seizure and sale shall not be sold by the bailiff unless notice of the time and place of sale has been (Rule 20.06(6)):

1. mailed at least 10 days before the sale
   a. to the creditor at the address shown on the writ, or to the creditor's lawyer or paralegal, and
   b. to the debtor at the debtor's last known address; and
2. advertised in a manner that is likely to bring it to the attention of the public.

The costs of advertising are paid for by the creditor.

The bailiff is an officer of the court, and has a duty to obtain a fair price for the personal property sold pursuant to the writ. A sale of personal property pursuant to a writ may be challenged by the debtor as an **improvident sale** if the debtor believes that the price obtained at auction does not reflect the actual value of the property. In some circumstances, it may be necessary to hire an appraiser to obtain an appraisal of the value of the property. The costs of the appraisal are paid for by the creditor.

If other creditors have filed writs of seizure and sale of personal property against the debtor in the same district or county, any proceeds of the sale remaining after the bailiff's reasonable fees and expenses for executing the writ, storage costs, the cost of an appraisal, and so on, have been paid will be shared among all creditors on a pro rata basis. A **pro rata distribution** means that the share of each creditor in the proceeds of the execution will be determined proportionately based on what the creditor is owed.

BOX 11.4 Pro Rata Distribution: How Does It Work?

Creditors A, B, and C have filed writs of seizure and sale of personal property with the bailiff in the same territorial division.

Amount owing to Creditor A	$1,000.00
Amount owing to Creditor B	2,000.00
Amount owing to Creditor C	3,000.00
Total owing	$6,000.00

Creditor A files a direction to enforce writ of seizure and sale of personal property with the sheriff. After the bailiff's reasonable fees and expenses, and all other costs associated with seizing and selling the property have been paid, there is $1,200.00 remaining for distribution.

Amount paid to Creditor A = 1/6 x 1,200 = $200.00
Amount paid to Creditor B = 2/6 x 1,200 = $400.00
Amount paid to Creditor C = 3/6 x 1,200 = $600.00

You will find examples of a writ of seizure and sale of personal property (Form 20C), and direction to enforce writ of seizure and sale of personal property (Form 20O) at Appendix 11.11 to this chapter.

Writ of Seizure and Sale of Land (Rule 20.07)

A creditor may request that the clerk issue a writ of seizure and sale of land (Form 20D) directed to the sheriff in any region where the debtor may own **real property**. Real property is property that is tangible and immovable and has value—in other words, land or buildings. The creditor's request must be supported by an affidavit for enforcement request requesting that the clerk issue a writ of seizure and sale of land. If you are filing a writ of seizure and sale of land in more than one county or district, you will need to complete an affidavit for enforcement request and a writ of seizure and sale of land for each location where the debtor may own land. There is a fee for issuing the writ (currently $35.00) and a fee for filing it with the sheriff in the division where the debtor may own land (currently $100.00). Sheriff's fees are published at O. Reg. 294/92 to the *Administration of Justice Act*.

Before considering this method of enforcement, a creditor should consider conducting a debtor examination to determine whether a debtor has an interest in land anywhere in Ontario, and, if yes, what the nature of the interest is and where the land is located.

The *Rules of the Small Claims Court* do not require issuance and filing of a certificate of judgment in order to register a writ of seizure and sale of land in a territorial division other than the division where the order for payment or recovery of money was made. However, if you intend to enforce a writ of seizure and sale of land in a jurisdiction other than the jurisdiction where the order originated, you should issue a certificate of judgment in the originating jurisdiction and file it with the court office in the jurisdiction where the debtor has an interest in land.

A writ of seizure and sale of land remains in force for six years from the date of issue, and is renewable indefinitely for further terms of six years (Rule 20.07(3)). It may be renewed before it expires by filing a request to renew a writ of seizure and sale (Form 20N) with the sheriff. You should consider diarizing for the date a writ of seizure and sale of land expires, with appropriate ticklers for follow-up.

If more than six years have passed since the order for payment or recovery of money was made, a writ of seizure and sale of land may be issued only with leave of the court on motion by the creditor (Rule 20.07(1.1)). If the writ of seizure and sale of land is not issued within one year after the date on which an order granting leave to issue it was made, the order ceases to have effect and a writ of seizure and sale of land may be issued only with leave of the court on a subsequent motion (Rule 20.07(1.2)).

A writ of seizure and sale of land that is filed with the sheriff in the district or county where the debtor has an interest in land will show up on the results of an execution search against the debtor's name in that district. A search for executions against the debtor's name will be carried out by a purchaser if the debtor sells the land, and by a mortgagee. A purchaser will require that funds be set aside out of the closing funds to pay any unsatisfied judgments registered against the debtor/vendor's name. A mortgagee will not advance funds until any unsatisfied judgments registered against the debtor/vendor's name are paid; or the mortgagee may withhold funds from the amount advanced to pay the unsatisfied judgments itself. In either event, the creditors will get paid, although they will have to wait until the land is sold or remortgaged.

A creditor who has filed a writ of seizure and sale against land has a right to direct the sheriff to seize and sell the land. The procedure for sale of land is set out at Rule 60.07 of the *Rules of Civil Procedure*, excerpted below:

Sale of Land

(17) A creditor may not take any step to sell land under a writ of seizure and sale until four months after the writ was filed with the sheriff or, where the writ has been withdrawn, four months after the writ was re-filed.

(18) No sale of land under a writ of seizure and sale may be held until six months after the writ was filed with the sheriff or, where the writ has been withdrawn, six months after the writ was re-filed.

(19) A sale of land shall not be held under a writ of seizure and sale unless notice of the time and place of sale has been,

(a) mailed to the creditor at the address shown on the writ or to the creditor's lawyer and to the debtor at the debtor's last known address, at least thirty days before the sale;

(b) published in *The Ontario Gazette* once at least thirty days before the sale and in a newspaper of general circulation in the place where the land is situate, once each week for two successive weeks, the last notice to be published not less than one week nor more than three weeks before the date of sale; and

(c) posted in a conspicuous place in the sheriff's office for at least thirty days before the sale.

(20) The notice shall set out,

(a) a short description of the property to be sold;

(b) the short title of the proceeding;

(c) the time and place of the intended sale; and

(d) the name of the debtor whose interest is to be sold.

(21) The sheriff may adjourn a sale to a later date where the sheriff considers it necessary in order to realize the best price that can be obtained in all the circumstances, and where the sale is adjourned, it may be conducted on the later date with such further notice, if any, as the sheriff considers advisable.

(22) Where notice of a sale of land under a writ of seizure and sale is published in *The Ontario Gazette* before the writ expires, the sale may be completed by a sale and transfer of the land after the writ expires.

Abortive Sale

(23) Where personal property or land seized under a writ of seizure and sale remains unsold for want of buyers, the sheriff shall notify the creditor of the date and place of the attempted sale and of any other relevant circumstances.

(24) On receipt of a notice under subrule (23), the creditor may instruct the sheriff in writing to sell the personal property or land in such manner as the sheriff considers will realize the best price that can be obtained.

A Small Claims Court creditor who is considering this method of enforcement should be referred to a real estate lawyer or to the Law Society Referral Service at 1-800-268-8326 or 416-947-3330 (within the GTA).

The sheriff is an officer of the court and has a duty to obtain a fair price for the property being sold. A debtor may challenge a sale of land on grounds of improvident sale if the debtor believes that the sale price does not reflect the value of the land.

After amounts owing to secured and preferred creditors (if any), and the sheriff's reasonable fees and expenses of the seizure and sale, have been paid from the proceeds of the sale, ordinary execution creditors who have filed writs of seizure and sale of land in that district or county will participate in any balance remaining on a pro rata basis.

You will find an example of a writ of seizure and sale of land at Appendix 11.12 to this chapter.

Delivery of Personal Property (Rule 20.05)

The Small Claims Court has jurisdiction in any action for the recovery of possession of personal property where the value of the property does not exceed the prescribed amount value of $25,000.00 (*Courts of Justice Act*, s. 23).

Section 20(2) of the *Execution Act* states that a sheriff acting under a writ of seizure and sale or a writ of delivery in respect of property on premises that is used as a dwelling shall not use force to enter the dwelling or execute the writ except under the authority of an order of the court by which the writ was issued. The court may make the order where in the opinion of the court there are reasonable and probable grounds to believe that there is property on the premises that is liable to be taken in execution under the writ.

If you are acting for the plaintiff in a claim for recovery of possession of personal property that is located in a private dwelling, ensure that, in addition to any other relief granted at trial, you obtain an order from the court authorizing the bailiff to use reasonable force to enter a private dwelling to execute a writ of delivery, if necessary, in accordance with *Execution Act*, s. 20(2).

To enforce an order for delivery of personal property, the person in whose favour an order for delivery of personal property was made may file an affidavit for enforcement request requesting that the clerk issue to a bailiff a writ of delivery of personal property, and a writ of delivery of personal property (Form 20B). Both the affidavit for enforcement request and the writ will contain the following information about the personal property: its location; the make, model, and serial number, if applicable; and distinguishing marks, if any.

The *Rules of the Small Claims Court* do not require issuance and filing of a certificate of judgment in order to register a writ of delivery in a territorial division other than the division where the order for delivery of personal property was made. However, if the personal property to be delivered is located in a division other than the division where the order was made, the person seeking its recovery must obtain a certificate of judgment from the clerk of the originating court and file it, with the affidavit for enforcement request and writ of delivery, with the clerk of the court in the division where the writ of delivery is to be enforced.

If the court order for delivery of personal property refers to items set out in the issued claim, a copy of the issued claim should be attached to the writ of delivery.

If the address provided does not clearly identify where the items are located, a detailed map showing the nearest intersection should be attached to the writ of delivery.

If an order for use of reasonable force to enter a private dwelling was made by the trial judge, the clerk must indicate that on the writ of delivery and attach a copy of the order to the writ.

The clerk will date and sign the writ of delivery and return it to the owner or the owner's representative. The original writ, with a copy of an order permitting use of reasonable force to enter a private dwelling, if any, is filed with the enforcement office, along with a copy of the affidavit for enforcement request.

As of this writing, the fee for issuing a writ of delivery is $35.00. The bailiff's charge for each attempt, whether successful or not, to enforce a writ of delivery is $36.00 plus a kilometre allowance.

When a date is set for execution of the writ, the bailiff will contact the owner. The owner is responsible for attending at the premises with the bailiff at the date and time specified. The owner is also responsible for making arrangements for removal of the items to be seized quickly and efficiently, and for paying for those arrangements, which may include:

- hiring a locksmith to gain access to the property;
- hiring a moving company or rental vehicle to remove large pieces such as furniture; and/or
- if the property must be dismantled before being removed, arranging to have people present to dismantle it quickly.

If the property referred to in a writ of delivery cannot be found or taken by the bailiff, the person in whose favour the order was made may make a motion to the court for an order directing the bailiff to seize any other personal property of the person against whom the order was made (Rule 20.05(2)). If an order is made under Rule 20.05(2), the bailiff will require a deposit in advance for storage costs. The bailiff will hold the property seized in storage until the court makes a further order for its disposition (Rule 20.05(3)). While the property is being held by the bailiff pending a further court order, the person who requested its seizure must continue to pay storage costs from time to time. If he fails to do so, the seizure will be deemed to be abandoned (Rule 20.05(4)).

You will find examples of an affidavit for enforcement request and a writ of delivery in Appendix 11.13 to this chapter.

Satisfaction of Order (Rule 20.12)

If payment has been made in full satisfaction of an order or terms of settlement,

1. where all parties consent, a party may file a request for clerk's order on consent (Form 11.2A) indicating that payment has been made in full satisfaction of the order or terms of settlement; or

2. a debtor may make a motion for an order confirming that payment has been made in full satisfaction of the order or terms of settlement.

When an amount owing under an order that is enforced by garnishment is paid, the creditor shall immediately serve a notice of termination of garnishment (Form 20R) on the garnishee and on the clerk.

CHAPTER SUMMARY

Rule 20 of the *Rules of the Small Claims Court* sets out the procedures for ordinary creditors to follow when enforcing orders for payment or recovery of money or for delivery of personal property.

A debtor against whom there are two or more unsatisfied orders for the payment of money may make a motion to the court for a consolidation order (Rule 20.09). The motion shall be served on all creditors named in the supporting affidavit at least seven days before the hearing date. At the hearing of the motion, the court may make a consolidation order setting out a list of all unsatisfied orders; the amount to be paid into court by the debtor under the consolidation order; and the times of payment. All payments into a consolidation account are shared equally among the creditors named in the consolidation order.

Payments made under a consolidation order are periodic payments. While an order for periodic payment is in effect, the only enforcement step available to creditors named in the order is to issue and file a writ of seizure and sale of land.

There are three main types of creditors: secured, preferred, and ordinary. Secured creditors are creditors whose loans are secured against real or personal property. Preferred creditors are unsecured creditors who rank ahead of ordinary unsecured creditors because of a priority conferred by statute. Ordinary creditors are unsecured creditors without preferred status. This is the type of creditor most likely to be encountered in a Small Claims Court proceeding.

A creditor who intends to enforce a judgment in another territorial division may do so by issuing a certificate of judgment in the court location where the order originated and filing it in the court location where the order is to be enforced (Rule 20.04).

A creditor who does not have current information about the income and assets of a debtor may request an examination of debtor or other person (Rule 20.10). The examination may be conducted in person or by video conference where facilities for a video conference are available. The examination shall be held in the absence of the public unless the court orders otherwise, conducted under oath, and recorded. The debtor or any other person may be examined in relation to the reason for non-payment of the debt; the debtor's income and property; other debts owed to and by the debtor; the debtor's past, present, and future means to satisfy the order; and any other matter pertinent to the enforcement of the order.

A creditor may enforce an order for payment or recovery of money by garnishment of debts payable to the debtor by other persons (Rule 20.08). If a debt is payable to the debtor and to one or more co-owners, one half of the indebtedness or a greater or lesser amount specified in a court order may be garnished.

Where more than one creditor has filed a notice of garnishment against the same debtor, all creditors share equally in any proceeds of the garnishment, regardless of how much they are actually owed.

When the amount owing under an order that is enforced by a garnishment is paid, the creditor shall immediately serve a notice of termination of garnishment on the garnishee and the clerk.

A writ of seizure and sale of personal property authorizes the bailiff to seize any personal property of the debtor, sell it by public auction, and apply the proceeds to the cost of enforcement and satisfaction of the order (Rule 20.06).

A writ of seizure and sale of personal property remains in force for six years after the date of its issue, and for a further six years after each renewal (Rule 20.06(2)).

A writ of seizure and sale of land may be filed with the sheriff in any county or region where the debtor may own land (Rule 20.07(1)). A writ of seizure and sale of land remains in force for six years after the date of its issue and for a further six years after each renewal (Rule 20.07(3)). The writ will show up on a standard execution search against the property. Before the property can be transferred, refinanced, or dealt with in any other way, the amount owing must be paid by the debtor.

An order for delivery of personal property may be enforced by a writ of delivery of personal property (Rule 20.05).

If payment is made in full satisfaction of an order, including a consolidation order, and where all parties consent, a party may file a request for clerk's order on consent indicating that payment has been made in full satisfaction of the order or terms of settlement; or the debtor may make a motion for an order confirming that payment has been made in full.

KEY TERMS

assign: to transfer a legal right or entitlement (including wages owed or the money in a bank account) to another person *(p. 440)*

assignee: a person to whom something is transferred *(p. 440)*

chattel mortgage: a loan that is secured against personal property; in Ontario, such security interests are registered under the *Personal Property Security Act* *(p. 418)*

collateral: real or personal property against which a loan is pledged *(p. 418)*

co-owner of debt: a person who is entitled to part of a debt payable to a debtor, and may assert their right to co-ownership of the debt in a garnishment of that debt *(p. 439)*

creditor: a person to whom money is owed; a person who is entitled to enforce an order for the payment of recovery of money (Rule 20.01) *(p. 416)*

debtor: a person who owes money to another person; also, a person against whom an order for the payment of money may be enforced *(p. 416)*

encumber: to mortgage or place a lien or other security interest against property *(p. 440)*

encumbrance: a security interest registered against real or personal property *(p. 440)*

encumbrancer: the person holding the lien or security interest *(p. 440)*

enforcement document: a document issued by the clerk at the request of a creditor in an affidavit for enforcement request—e.g., a notice of garnishment, a writ of seizure and sale of land, and so on *(p. 424)*

enforcement of an order: a lawful attempt to obtain an amount owing pursuant to a court order *(p. 416)*

execution of an order: see the definition for "enforcement of an order"

exigible assets: assets that can be seized or garnished *(p. 429)*

future performance agreement: a sales contract where the purchaser takes possession of property in return for a promise to make future payments for the property to the vendor, who retains title and a right of repossession in the property until the purchase price is paid in full *(p. 419)*

garnishee: a person who owes money to a debtor *(p. 436)*

garnishor: a creditor who enforces an order for payment or recovery of money by way of a garnishment *(p. 436)*

improvident sale: sale by a lender of a debtor's property for a price that does not reflect the property's market value; grounds for a debtor to challenge the sale of the property in a court *(p. 444)*

lump-sum payment: a one-time payment of the full amount owing or a portion thereof *(p. 420)*

mortgagee: a person who holds a mortgage *(p. 418)*

mortgagor: a person who is given a mortgage by a mortgagee *(p. 418)*

net wages: amount of wages after all lawful deductions *(p. 426)*

non-exigible assets: assets that cannot be seized or garnished *(p. 429)*

original court: the court where an order is made *(p. 428)*

originating court: the court where an order is made *(p. 428)*

originating process: the document that commences an action *(p. 428)*

per diem: per day (Latin) *(p. 424)*

per diem interest: the amount of interest that accrues per day on money owed *(p. 424)*

periodic payments: fixed amounts of money that must be paid at regular intervals, usually on a stated date such as the first day of each and every month *(p. 420)*

personal property: property that has value, and is tangible and movable *(p. 441)*

preferred creditor: an unsecured creditor who ranks ahead of ordinary unsecured creditors in a debt collection or a bankruptcy because of priority and special rights conferred by a statute *(p. 419)*

pro rata distribution: the share of each creditor in the proceeds of the distribution will be determined proportionately based on what the creditor is owed *(p. 444)*

real property: property that has value, and is tangible and immovable *(p. 445)*

realize on the security: when a secured creditor, upon default by a debtor, seizes and sells the property pledged as security for a debt, and applies the proceeds of the sale to the balance owing on the debt *(p. 418)*

registering court: the court in which a judgment is registered *(p. 428)*

secured creditor: a creditor whose loans are secured against real or personal property; if the debtor defaults in payment, the secured creditor may seize and sell the property, and pay the balance owing on the loan out of the proceeds of the sale, in accordance with the terms of the security agreement *(p. 418)*

stay of enforcement: stopping enforcement by creditors against a debtor for so long as the debtor complies with the terms of a court order *(p. 421)*

support and maintenance creditor: a person to whom child or spousal support is owed by a debtor *(p. 419)*

waive the default: a decision by a lender or creditor not to insist upon strict compliance by a debtor with the terms for payment of a debt or other obligation *(p. 421)*

REFERENCES

Administration of Justice Act, RSO 1990, c. A.6.
Application, O. Reg. 322/92.
Assignments and Preferences Act, RSO 1990, c. A.33.
Bank Act, SC 1991, c. 46.
Canada Pension Plan, RSC 1985, c. C-8.
Canadian Forces Superannuation Act, RSC 1985, c. C-17.
Compensation for Victims of Crime Act, RSO 1990, c. C-24.
Consumer Protection Act, 2002, SO 2002, c. 30, Sch. A.
Courts of Justice Act, RSO 1990, c. C.43.
Creditors' Relief Act, 2010, SO 2010, c. 16, Sch. 4.
Criminal Code, RSC 1985, c. C-46.
Employment Insurance Act, SC 1996, c. 23.
Execution Act, RSO 1990, c. E.24.
Exemptions, O. Reg. 657/05.
Family Benefits Act, RSO 1990, c. F.2.
Family Responsibility and Support Arrears Enforcement Act, 1996, SO 1996, c. 31.
Fraudulent Conveyances Act, RSO 1990, c. F.29.
Garnishment, Attachment and Pension Diversion Act, RSC 1995, c. G-2.
General, O. Reg. 98/09.
Indian Act, RSC 1985, c. I-5.
Insurance Act, RSO 1990, c. I-8.
Old Age Security Act, RSC 1985, c. O-9.

Ontario Works Act, 1997, SO 1997, c. 25.
Payday Loans Act, SO 2008, c. 9.
Pension Benefits Act, RSO 1990, c. P-8.
Pension Fund Societies Act, RSC 1985, c. P-8.
Personal Property Security Act, RSO 1990, c. P.10.
Provincial Offences Act, RSO 1990, c. P.33.
Publication of Postjudgment and Prejudgment Interest Rates, O. Reg. 339/07.
RCMP Superannuation Act, RSC 1985, c. R-11.
Reciprocal Enforcement of Judgments Act, RSO 1990, c. R.5.
Repair and Storage Liens Act, RSO 1990, c. R.23.
Rules of Civil Procedure, RRO 1990, Reg. 194.
Rules of the Small Claims Court, O. Reg. 258/98.
Sheriffs—Fees, O. Reg. 294/92.
Small Claims Court—Fees and Allowances, O. Reg. 432/93.
Small Claims Court Guide to Procedures: After Judgment— Guide to Getting Results (Queen's Printer for Ontario, 2009); available online at http://www.attorneygeneral.jus.gov.on.ca.
Statutory Powers Procedure Act, RSO 1990, c. S.22.
Wages Act, RSO 1990, c. W.1.
War Veterans Allowances Act, RSC 1985, c. W-3.
Workplace Safety and Insurance Act, 1997, SO 1997, c. 16.

DRAFTING EXERCISE
Dante v. Herrero—Enforcement of an Order (Garnishment)

On November 15, 20— in Brampton Small Claims Court claim number SC-00-06638-00, the plaintiff, Francesca Dante, is awarded judgment against the defendant, Suzanne Herrero, for $4,000.00 plus pre-judgment interest in the amount of $458.96 and costs fixed at $810.00.

The pre- and post-judgment interest rate is 12.0 percent. Use the table of days (Table 5.2) at page 184 to calculate post-judgment interest.

Claim number: SC-00-06638-00
Court: Brampton
Address: 7755 Hurontario Street
                Brampton, Ontario L6W 4T6
Telephone: 905 456 4700

Plaintiff: Francesca Dante
Address: c/o Prior Mustafa LLP

Representative: Prior Mustafa LLP
Attention: Joseph Mustafa
LSUC #:   ######
Address: 22 County Court Boulevard
                Brampton, Ontario A1A 2B3
Telephone: 905 111 2222
Fax: 905 111 2233

Defendant: Suzanne Herrero
Address: 105 Morton Avenue
                Mississauga, Ontario L2X 4Y5
Telephone: 905 324 8890

It has come to the creditor's attention that the debtor, Suzanne Herrero, works for XYZ Staffing Enterprises, 42 Adelaide Street West, Suite 345, Toronto, Ontario M5X 8Z9 TEL: 416 777 8888 FAX: 416 777 8899.

Draft an affidavit for enforcement request and notice of garnishment. The notice of garnishment will be directed to the clerk in the territorial division where the debtor resides. These documents should be dated December 12, 20—. Also print out two additional forms that would be required at this stage in this enforcement.

Your additional costs on the affidavit for enforcement request in the garnishment will be the fee for issuing the notice of garnishment.

You will find Small Claims Court addresses, forms, and fees at the Attorney General's website (http://www.attorneygeneral .jus.gov.on.ca).

REVIEW QUESTIONS

When answering the following questions, make a note of the numbers of any rules or other authorities in support of your answers.

1. What is enforcement of a judgment? Why is enforcement necessary?

2. If a Small Claims Court creditor needs to obtain a wide range of current information about a debtor's financial circumstances and ability to pay a judgment, what is the most efficient way of doing so?

3. Debtor has four orders for payment of money outstanding against her. Debtor is employed, but is struggling to make payments to all four creditors and pay for living expenses. What should Debtor do? Please provide details of the appropriate procedure.

4. When is a certificate of judgment used in an enforcement?

5. When should you use a writ of delivery?

6. a. Creditor obtains a judgment in Newmarket Small Claims Court. Creditor wishes to file a writ of seizure and sale of land in Toronto. What is the procedure?

   b. How does a writ of seizure and sale of land assist Creditor in enforcing her judgment?

7. a. When is a garnishment used to enforce a judgment?

   b. What are five sources of money that can be garnished?

   c. What are five sources of money that cannot be garnished by an ordinary creditor?

8. **a.** Creditor serves a notice of garnishment on the branch of the bank at which Debtor has an account. The bank account is jointly owned. How does Creditor find out that there is a co-owner of the debt?

 b. What must Creditor do upon receiving notice from the branch?

 c. What must the co-owner of the debt do if he wishes to protect his interest in the debt?

APPENDIX 11.1   Notice of Default of Payment (Form 20L)

ONTARIO

Superior Court of Justice
Cour supérieure de justice

Notice of Default of Payment
Avis de défaut de paiement

Form / *Formule* 20L Ont. Reg. No. / *Régl. de l'Ont.* : 258/98

Brampton	**SC-00-45678-00**
Small Claims Court / *Cour des petites créances de*	Claim No. / *N° de la demande*
7755 Hurontario Street	
Brampton, Ontario	
L6W 4T6	
Address / *Adresse*	
905 456 4700	
Phone number / *Numéro de téléphone*	

BETWEEN / *ENTRE*

Maxwell Parrish

Plaintiff(s)/Creditor(s) / *Demandeur(s)/demanderesse(s)/Créancier(s)/créancière(s)*

and / *et*

Frank Thurston

Defendant(s)/Debtor(s) / *Défendeur(s)/défenderesse(s)/Débiteur(s)/débitrice(s)*

TO: **Frank Thurston**
DESTINATAIRE(S) **:**   (Name of defendant(s)/debtor(s) / *Nom du/de la/des défendeur(s)/défenderesse(s)/débiteur(s)/débitrice(s)*)

TAKE NOTICE that you defaulted in your payment(s) to
VEUILLEZ PRENDRE NOTE que vous n'avez pas effectué le ou les paiements que vous deviez verser à

Maxwell Parrish

(Name of plaintiff(s)/creditor(s) / *Nom du/de la/des demandeur(s)/demanderesse(s)/créancier(s)/créancière(s)*)

(Check appropriate box. / Cochez la case appropriée.)

☒   under an order for periodic payment, dated _____ **February 14** _____ , 20 -- ___ .
en vertu d'une ordonnance prescrivant des versements périodiques datée du

According to Rule 20.02(4) of the *Rules of the Small Claims Court*, the order for periodic payment terminates on the day that is 15 days after the creditor serves the debtor with this notice, unless before that date, a Consent (Form 13B) is filed in which the creditor waives the default.
Conformément au paragraphe 20.02 (4) des Règles de la Cour des petites créances, l'ordonnance prescrivant des versements périodiques prend fin le 15ᵉ jour qui suit la signification par le créancier au débiteur du présent avis, sauf si, avant cette date, le créancier dépose le consentement (formule 13B) dans lequel il renonce à la constatation du défaut.

☐   under a proposal of terms of payment in the Defence (Form 9A) dated _____ , 20 ____ .
en vertu d'une proposition à l'égard des modalités de paiement dans la défense (formule 9A) datée du

According to Rule 9.03(2)(c) the clerk may sign judgment for the unpaid balance of the undisputed amount on the day that is 15 days after the plaintiff serves the defendant with this notice.
Conformément à l'alinéa 9.03 (2) c), le greffier peut consigner un jugement relativement au solde impayé de la somme non contestée le 15ᵉ jour qui suit la signification par le demandeur au défendeur du présent avis.

SCR 20.02-20L (June 1, 2009 / *1ᵉʳ juin 2009*) CSD

APPENDIX 11.1 Notice of Default of Payment (Form 20L) *concluded*

FORM / *FORMULE* 20L   **PAGE 2**   SC-00-45678-00
Claim No. / N° de la demande

You can get forms and self-help materials at the Small Claims Court or online at: www.ontariocourtforms.on.ca.
Vous pouvez obtenir les formules et la documentation à l'usage du client auprès de la Cour des petites créances ou en ligne à l'adresse : www.ontariocourtforms.on.ca.

NOTE TO DEFENDANT/DEBTOR: / *REMARQUE AU DÉFENDEUR/DÉBITEUR :*

If you / *Si, selon le cas :*

- failed to make payments but intend to do so; or
  vous n'avez pas effectué de paiements mais vous avez l'intention de le faire;

- made payments but the payments were not received by the creditor;
  vous avez effectué des paiements mais le créancier ne les a pas reçus;

contact the plaintiff/creditor to make payment arrangements or correct the reason for non-receipt of payments. You may obtain the plaintiff/creditor's written consent (Form 13B may be used) to waive the default and file it with the court within 15 days of being served with this notice. Failure to do so may result in the following:
communiquez avec le demandeur/créancier pour prendre les dispositions de paiement ou pour régler le motif de la non-réception des paiements. Vous pouvez obtenir le consentement écrit du demandeur/créancier (vous pouvez utiliser la formule 13B) pour renoncer à la constatation du défaut et le déposer au tribunal dans les 15 jours de la signification du présent avis. Si vous ne le faites pas, vous pourriez subir l'une ou l'autre des conséquences suivantes :

- in the case of default under a proposal of terms of payment in the Defence (Form 9A), the plaintiff may obtain default judgment for the unpaid balance of the undisputed amount; or
  si vous n'effectuez pas les paiements conformément aux modalités de paiement proposées dans la défense (formule 9A), le demandeur pourra obtenir un jugement par défaut relativement au solde impayé de la somme non contestée;

- in the case of default under an order for periodic payment, the order will terminate and the creditor may take other steps to enforce the order.
  si vous n'effectuez pas les paiements conformément à une ordonnance prescrivant des versements périodiques, l'ordonnance prendra fin et le créancier pourra prendre d'autres mesures en vue de l'exécution forcée de l'ordonnance.

May 12   , 20 --

(Signature of plaintiff/creditor or representative / *Signature du demandeur/de la demanderesse/du créancier/de la créancière ou du/de la représentant(e)*)
Prior Mustafa LLP
Attn: Marie Prior, Licensed Paralegal
22 County Court Boulevard
Brampton, Ontario A1A 2B3
TEL: 905 111 2222
FAX: 905 111 2233

(Name, address and phone number of plaintiff/creditor or representative / *Nom, adresse et numéro de téléphone du demandeur/de la demanderesse/du créancier/de la créancière ou du/de la représentant(e)*)

SCR 20.02-20L (June 1, 2009 / *1er juin 2009*) CSD

APPENDIX 11.1   Affidavit of Service (Form 8A)

ONTARIO

Superior Court of Justice
Cour supérieure de justice

Affidavit of Service
Affidavit de signification

Form / *Formule* 8A Ont. Reg. No. / *Régl. de l'Ont.* : 258/98

Brampton

Small Claims Court / *Cour des petites créances de*

7755 Hurontario Street
Brampton, Ontario
L6W 4T6

Address / *Adresse*

905 456 4700

Phone number / *Numéro de téléphone*

SC-00-45678-00

Claim No. / *N° de la demande*

BETWEEN / *ENTRE*

Maxwell Parrish

Plaintiff(s) / *Demandeur(s)/demanderesse(s)*

and / *et*

Frank Thurston

Defendant(s) / *Défendeur(s)/défenderesse(s)*

My name is   **Judy Cordero**
Je m'appelle   (Full name / *Nom et prénoms*)

I live in   **Brampton, Ontario**
J'habite à   (Municipality & province / *Municipalité et province*)

and I swear/affirm that the following is true:
et je déclare sous serment/j'affirme solennellement que les renseignements suivants sont véridiques :

1. **I served**   **Frank Thurston**   , on **May 12**   , 20 -- ,
   J'ai signifié à   (Full name of person/corporation served / *Nom et prénoms*   , *le*   (Date)
                        de la personne/nom au complet de la personne morale
                        qui a reçu la signification)

   at   **43 High River Drive, Brampton, Ontario H5T 3X4**
   au   (Address (street and number, unit, municipality, province) / *Adresse (numéro et rue, unité, municipalité, province)*)

   which is   ☒ the address of the person's home
   soit   *l'adresse du domicile de la personne*

              ☐ the address of the corporation's place of business
                 l'adresse du lieu de travail de l'établissement de la personne morale

              ☐ the address of the person's or corporation's representative on record with the court
                 l'adresse du/de la représentant(e) de la personne ou de la personne morale figurant au
                 dossier du tribunal

              ☐ the address on the document most recently filed in court by the party
                 l'adresse figurant sur le document déposé le plus récemment au tribunal par la partie

              ☐ the address of the corporation's attorney for service in Ontario
                 l'adresse du fondé de pouvoir de la personne morale aux fins de signification en Ontario

              ☐ other address: _____
                 autre adresse :   (Specify. / *Précisez.*)

   with   **a notice of default of payment**
   ce qui suit :   (Name(s) of document(s) served / *Titre(s) du ou des documents signifiés*)

SCR 8.06-8A (September 1, 2010 / *1er septembre 2010*) CSD

APPENDIX 11.1 Affidavit of Service (Form 8A) *continued*

FORM / *FORMULE* 8A   PAGE 2   SC-00-45678-00
                                                                _____
                                                                Claim No. / *N° de la demande*

2. **I served the document(s) referred to in paragraph one by the following method:**
    J'ai signifié le ou les documents mentionnés au numéro un de la façon suivante :
    (Tell how service took place by checking appropriate box(es).)
    (Indiquez la façon dont la signification a été effectuée en cochant la ou les cases appropriées.)

Personal service / *Significa-tion à personne*

☐ leaving a copy with the person.
   en laissant une copie à la personne.

☐ leaving a copy with the _____ of the corporation.
   en laissant une copie au/à la (Office or position / *Charge ou poste*) *de la personne morale.*

☐ leaving a copy with: _____
   en laissant une copie à : (Specify person's name and office or position. / *Indiquez le nom de la personne ainsi que sa charge ou son poste.*)

Service at place of residence / *Significa-tion au domicile*

☐ leaving a copy in a sealed envelope addressed to the person at the person's place of residence with a person who appeared to be an adult member of the same household, and sending another copy of the same document(s) to the person's place of residence on the same day or the following day by:
   en laissant une copie au domicile de la personne, dans une enveloppe scellée adressée à celle-ci, auprès d'une personne habitant sous le même toit qui semblait majeure et en envoyant une autre copie du ou des mêmes documents au domicile de la personne le même jour ou le jour suivant :

   ☐ regular lettermail.
      par courrier ordinaire.

   ☐ registered mail.
      par courrier recommandé.

   ☐ courier.
      par messagerie.

Service by registered mail / *Significa-tion par courrier recom-mandé*

☐ registered mail.
   par courrier recommandé.
   (If a copy of a plaintiff's claim or defendant's claim was served by registered mail, attach a copy of the Canada Post delivery confirmation, showing the signature verifying delivery, to this affidavit.)
   (Si une copie de la demande du demandeur ou de la demande du défendeur a été signifiée par courrier recommandé, annexez au présent affidavit une copie de la confirmation de livraison remise par Postes Canada sur laquelle figure une signature qui confirme la livraison.)

Service by courier / *Significa-tion par messa-gerie*

☐ courier.
   par messagerie.
   (If a copy of a plaintiff's claim or defendant's claim was served by courier, attach a copy of the courier's delivery confirmation, showing the signature verifying delivery, to this affidavit.)
   (Si une copie de la demande du demandeur ou de la demande du défendeur a été signifiée par messagerie, annexez au présent affidavit une copie de la confirmation de livraison remise par le service de messagerie sur laquelle figure la signature du destinataire de la signification.)

Service on lawyer / *Significa-tion à l'avocat*

☐ leaving a copy with a lawyer who accepted service on the person's behalf.
   en laissant une copie avec l'avocat qui a accepté la signification au nom de la personne.
   (Attach a copy of the document endorsed with the lawyer's acceptance of service.)
   (Annexez une copie du document, sur lequel l'avocat a inscrit qu'il a accepté la signification.)

Service by regular lettermail / *Significa-tion par courrier ordinaire*

☒ regular lettermail.
   par courrier ordinaire.

SCR 8.06-8A (September 1, 2010 / *1ᵉʳ septembre 2010*) CSD   **Continued on next page** / *Suite à la page suivante*

APPENDIX 11.1 **Affidavit of Service (Form 8A)** *concluded*

FORM / *FORMULE* 8A	PAGE 3	SC-00-45678-00
		Claim No. / *N° de la demande*

Service by fax /
Significa-tion par télécopie

☐ fax sent at _____ at the following fax number: _____
par télécopie (Time / *heure*) *au numéro de télécopieur* (Fax number / *numéro de*
envoyée à *suivant :* *télécopieur*)

Service to last known address of corporation or attorney for service, and to the directors /
Significa-tion à la dernière adresse connue de la personne morale ou de son fondé de pouvoir aux fins de signification et aux administra-teurs

☐ mail/courier to corporation or attorney for service at last known address recorded with the
Ministry of Government Services, and
d'une part, par la poste/par messagerie à la personne morale ou à son fondé de pouvoir aux fins
de signification, à la dernière adresse connue figurant dans les dossiers du ministère des
Services gouvernementaux;

mail/courier to each director, as recorded with the Ministry of Government Services, as set out below:
d'autre part, par la poste/par messagerie à chaque administrateur mentionné dans les dossiers du
ministère des Services gouvernementaux et dont le nom et l'adresse sont indiqués ci-dessous :

Name of director / *Nom de l'administrateur*	Director's address as recorded with the Ministry of Government Services (street & number, unit, municipality, province) / *Adresse de l'administrateur figurant dans les dossiers du ministère des Services gouvernementaux (numéro et rue, unité, municipalité, province)*
_____	_____
_____	_____
_____	_____
_____	_____

(Attach separate sheet for additional names if necessary. /
Joignez au besoin une feuille séparée s'il y a d'autres noms à ajouter.)

Substituted service /
Significa-tion indirecte

☐ substituted service as ordered by the court on _____ , 20 _____ ,
par signification indirecte ordonnée par le tribunal le (Date)

as follows: (Give details.)
comme suit : (*Précisez.*)

Sworn/Affirmed before me at **Brampton**
Déclaré sous serment/Affirmé (Municipality / *municipalité*)
solennellement devant moi à

in _____ **Ontario**
en/à/au (Province, state, or country / *province, État ou pays*)

on **May 17** , 20 -- _____
le Commissioner for taking affidavits
Commissaire aux affidavits
(Type or print name below if signature
is illegible.)
(*Dactylographiez le nom ou écrivez-le*
en caractères d'imprimerie ci-dessous
si la signature est illisible.)

_____
Signature
(This form is to be signed in front of a
lawyer, justice of the peace, notary public or
commissioner for taking affidavits.)
(*La présente formule doit être signée en*
présence d'un avocat, d'un juge de paix,
d'un notaire ou d'un commissaire aux
affidavits.)

SCR 8.06-8A (September 1, 2010 / *1ᵉʳ septembre 2010*) CSD

APPENDIX 11.1   Affidavit of Default of Payment (Form 20M)

ONTARIO
Superior Court of Justice
Cour supérieure de justice

Affidavit of Default of Payment
Affidavit de défaut de paiement
Form / Formule 20M Ont. Reg. No. / Règl. de l'Ont. : 258/98

Brampton
Small Claims Court / *Cour des petites créances de*

7755 Hurontario Street
Brampton, Ontario
L6W 4T6
Address / *Adresse*

905 456 4700
Phone number / *Numéro de téléphone*

SC-00-45678-00
Claim No. / *N° de la demande*

BETWEEN / *ENTRE*

Maxwell Parrish
Plaintiff(s)/Creditor(s) / *Demandeur(s)/demanderesse(s)/Créancier(s)/créancière(s)*

and / *et*

Frank Thurston
Defendant(s)/Debtor(s) / *Défendeur(s)/défenderesse(s)/Débiteur(s)/débitrice(s)*

My name is
Je m'appelle

Maxwell Parrish
(Full name / *Nom et prénoms*)

I live in
J'habite à

Brampton, Ontario
(Municipality & province / *Municipalité et province*)

and I swear/affirm that the following is true:
et je déclare sous serment/j'affirme solennellement que les renseignements suivants sont véridiques :

1. In this action, I am the
   Dans la présente action, je suis le/la

   (Check one box only. / Cochez une seule case.)

   ☒ plaintiff/creditor.
   demandeur/demanderesse/créancier/créancière.

   ☐ representative of the
   plaintiff(s)/creditor(s)
   *représentant(e) du/de la/des demandeur(s)/demanderesse(s)
   ou du/de la/des créancier(s)/créancière(s)*

   (Name of plaintiff(s)/creditor(s) / *Nom du/de la/des demandeur(s)/demanderesse(s) ou du/de la/des créancier(s)/créancière(s)*)

2. To date, I have received from the defendant(s)/debtor(s) $ _____ **800.00** , the last payment being made
   À ce jour, j'ai reçu du ou des défendeurs/débiteurs (Amount / *Montant*) *$, soit le dernier paiement ayant*

   on or about _____ **April 1** _____ , 20 __-- __ .
   été effectué le ou vers le

3. I make this affidavit in support of a request that:
   Je fais le présent affidavit à l'appui d'une demande visant à :

   (Check appropriate box and complete paragraph. / Cochez la case appropriée et remplissez le point.)

   ☐ the clerk of the court issue a Default Judgment (Form 11B) [R. 9.03(2)(c)]. The defendant(s)
   enjoindre au greffier du tribunal de rendre un jugement par défaut (formule 11B) [alinéa 9.03 (2) c)].
   Le ou les défendeurs

   _____
   (Name(s) of defendant(s) / *Nom du/de la/des défendeur(s)/défenderesse(s)*)

   failed to make payment in accordance with the proposed terms of payment in the Defence
   n'ont pas effectué les paiements conformément aux modalités de paiement proposées dans la défense

   (Form 9A) dated _____ , 20 _____ and fifteen (15) days have passed since the
   (formule 9A) datée du *et quinze (15) jours se sont écoulés depuis*

   defendant was served with a Notice of Default of Payment (Form 20L) at the following address(es):
   la signification de l'avis de défaut de paiement au défendeur (formule 20L) à l'adresse (aux adresses)
   suivante(s) :

   _____
   (Address(es) of defendant(s) / *Adresse(s) du/de la/des défendeur(s)/défenderesse(s)*)

SCR 9.03-20M (April 11, 2012 / *11 avril 2012*) CSD

APPENDIX 11.1 Affidavit of Default of Payment (Form 20M) *continued*

FORM / *FORMULE* 20M	PAGE 2	SC-00-45678-00
		Claim No. / *N° de la demande*

☐ the clerk of the court issue a Default Judgment (Form 11B) [R. 9.03(7)]. The defendant(s)
enjoindre au greffier du tribunal de rendre un jugement par défaut (formule 11B) [par. 9.03 (7)]. Le ou les défendeurs

_____
(Name of defendant(s) / *Nom du/de la/des défendeur(s)/défenderesse(s)*)

failed to make payment in accordance with the terms of payment order
n'ont pas effectué les paiements conformément à l'ordonnance relative aux modalités de paiement

(Check appropriate box and complete paragraph. / Cochez la case appropriée et remplissez le point.)

dated _____ , 20 _____ .
datée du

☒ I may enforce the judgment [R. 20.02(3)]. The debtor(s)
m'autoriser à exécuter le jugement [par. 20.02 (3)]. Le ou les débiteurs

Frank Thurston
_____
(Name(s) of debtor(s) / *Nom du/de la/des débiteur(s)/débitrice(s)*)

failed to make payment in accordance with the order for periodic payment dated
n'ont pas effectué les paiements conformément à l'ordonnance prescrivant des versements périodiques datée du

February 14 _____ , 20 **--** _____ , and fifteen (15) days have passed since the debtor(s) has/have
et quinze (15) jours se sont écoulés depuis la signification de

been served with a Notice of Default of Payment (Form 20L) at the following address(es):
l'avis de défaut de paiement (formule 20L) au ou aux débiteurs à l'adresse (aux adresses) suivante(s) :

43 High River Drive, Brampton, Ontario H5T 3X4
_____
(Address(es) of debtor(s) / *Adresse(s) du/de la/des débiteur(s)/débitrice(s)*)

A Consent (Form 13B) in which the creditor waives the default has not been filed.
Un consentement (formule 13B) dans lequel le créancier renonce à la constatation du défaut n'a pas été déposé.

4. The unpaid balance is calculated as follows:
Le solde impayé est calculé de la façon suivante :

(A) **DEBT** $ 25,000.00
 LA CRÉANCE $

(B) **PRE-JUDGMENT INTEREST** calculated
 LES INTÉRÊTS ANTÉRIEURS AU JUGEMENT calculés

on the sum of $ **25,000.00** at the rate of **12** %
sur la somme de $ *au taux de* *pour cent*

per annum from **September 1** , 20 **--** to **December 1** , 20 **--** ,
par an du *au*

being **91** days. $ 747.93
soit *jours.* $

> **NOTE:** Calculation of interest is always on the amount owing from time to time as payments are received. This is true for both pre-judgment and post-judgment interest. Attach a separate sheet setting out how you calculated the total amount of any pre/post-judgment interest.
>
> **REMARQUE :** *Les intérêts doivent toujours être calculés sur la somme due. Le calcul doit tenir compte des paiements reçus de temps à autre. Ceci s'applique autant aux intérêts antérieurs au jugement qu'aux intérêts postérieurs au jugement. Annexez une feuille distincte indiquant comment vous avez calculé le montant total des intérêts antérieurs et postérieurs au jugement.*

SUBTOTAL (amount of judgment) $ 25,747.93
TOTAL PARTIEL *(montant du jugement)* $

SCR 9.03-20M (April 11, 2012 / *11 avril 2012*) CSD

Continued on next page / *Suite à la page suivante*

APPENDIX 11.1   **Affidavit of Default of Payment (Form 20M)** *continued*

FORM / *FORMULE* 20M   PAGE 3   SC-00-45678-00
_____
                                                                          Claim No. / *N° de la demande*

(C) **COSTS** to date of judgment $ 110.00
     LES DÉPENS à la date du jugement $

(D) **TOTAL AMOUNT OF PAYMENTS RECEIVED FROM DEBTOR**
     after judgment (if any)   (minus) $ 800.00
     LE MONTANT TOTAL DES PAIEMENTS REÇUS DU DÉBITEUR   *(moins)* $
     après le jugement (le cas échéant)

(E) **POST-JUDGMENT INTEREST** to date calculated
     LES INTÉRÊTS POSTÉRIEURS AU JUGEMENT à ce jour, calculés

     on the sum of $ 25,857.93   at the rate of **12**   %
     sur la somme de $ *au taux de*   *pour cent*

     per annum from **December 1**   , 20 -- to **June 4**   , 20 -- ,
     par an du   *au*

     being **185**   days. $ 1,572.50
     soit   *jours.* $

(F) **SUBSEQUENT COSTS** incurred after judgment (including the cost of serving
     the Notice of Default of Payment (Form 20L)) $ 135.00
     LES DÉPENS SUBSÉQUENTS engagés après le jugement (y compris le coût de $
     signification de l'avis de défaut de paiement (formule 20L))

                                                    TOTAL DUE $ 26,765.43
                                                    SOLDE DÛ $

_____

Sworn/Affirmed before me at   **Brampton**
Déclaré sous serment/Affirmé   (Municipality / *municipalité*)
solennellement devant moi à

in   **Ontario**
en/à/au   (Province, state, or county / *province, État ou pays*)
                                                                          Signature
                                                                (This form is to be signed in front of a
on   **June 4**   , 20 --   lawyer, justice of the peace, notary public
le   or commissioner for taking affidavits.)
                            Commissioner for taking affidavits   (*La présente formule doit être signée en
                            Commissaire aux affidavits   présence d'un avocat, d'un juge de paix,
                            (Type or print name below if signature is d'un notaire ou d'un commissaire aux
                            illegible.)   affidavits.*)
                            (*Dactylographiez le nom ou écrivez-le en
                            caractères d'imprimerie ci-dessous si la
                            signature est illisible.*)

_____

WARNING:	IT IS AN OFFENCE UNDER THE *CRIMINAL CODE* TO KNOWINGLY SWEAR OR AFFIRM A FALSE AFFIDAVIT.
AVERTISSEMENT :	*FAIRE SCIEMMENT UN FAUX AFFIDAVIT CONSTITUE UNE INFRACTION AU CODE CRIMINEL.*

APPENDIX 11.1 Affidavit of Default of Payment *concluded*

Parrish v. Thurston: Adjusted Calculation of Amount Owing (Post-judgment)

Judgment amount = $25,000.00 (debt) + $747.93 (pre-judgment interest) + $110.00 (costs)

= $25,857.93

Convert interest rate to a decimal = $7 \div 100 = 0.07$

Calculate per diem interest = $(\$25,857.93 \times .12) \div 365 = \$8.50$ per diem

Post-judgment interest from December 1 to March 1 (date of first payment)

Time period = December 1 to March 1 = 30 days + 60 days = 90 days

Post-judgment interest = 90 days × $8.50 per day = $765.00

Amount owing as of March 1 = $25,857.93 + $765.00

= $26,622.93

MINUS March 1 payment   400.00

BALANCE OWING $26,222.93

Post-judgment interest to April 1 (date of second payment)

Time period = March 1 to April 1 = [91] – [60] = 31 days

Post-judgment interest = 31 days × $8.50 per day = $263.50

Amount owing as of April 1   = $26,222.93 + $263.50

= $26,486.43

MINUS April 1 payment   400.00

BALANCE OWING $26,086.43

Post-judgment interest calculated from April 1 (date of last payment) to June 4 (date of preparing affidavit of default of payment)

Time period = 64 days

Post-judgment interest = 64 days × $8.50 per day = $544.00

Amount owing as of June 4   = $26,086.43 + $544.00

= $26,630.43

APPENDIX 11.2 Notice of Motion and Supporting Affidavit (Form 15A)

ONTARIO

Superior Court of Justice
Cour supérieure de justice

Notice of Motion and Supporting Affidavit
Avis de motion et affidavit à l'appui
Form / *Formule* 15A Ont. Reg. No. / *Règl. de l'Ont.* : 258/98

Newmarket
Small Claims Court / *Cour des petites créances de*
50 Eagle Street West
Newmarket, Ontario
L3Y 6B1
Address / *Adresse*

905 853 4809
Phone number / *Numéro de téléphone*

SC-00-98865-00
Claim No. / *N° de la demande*

Plaintiff No. 1 / *Demandeur n° 1*   ☒ Additional plaintiff(s) listed on attached Form 1A.
Le ou les demandeurs additionnels sont mentionnés sur la formule 1A ci-jointe.

Last name, or name of company / *Nom de famille ou nom de la compagnie*		
Nguyen		
First name / *Premier prénom* **France**	Second name / *Deuxième prénom*	Also known as / *Également connu(e) sous le nom de*
Address (street number, apt., unit) / *Adresse (numéro et rue, app., unité)* **c/o Prior Mustafa LLP**		
City/Town / *Cité/ville*	Province	Phone no. / *N° de téléphone*
Postal code / *Code postal*		Fax no. / *N° de télécopieur*
Representative / *Représentant(e)* **Prior Mustafa LLP Attention: Paralegal name**		LSUC # / *N° du BHC* **######**
Address (street number, apt., unit) / *Adresse (numéro et rue, app., unité)* **22 County Court Boulevard**		
City/Town / *Cité/ville* **Brampton**	Province **Ontario**	Phone no. / *N° de téléphone* **905 111 2222**
Postal code / *Code postal* **A1A 2B3**		Fax no. / *N° de télécopieur* **905 111 2233**

Defendant No. 1 / *Défendeur n° 1*   ☐ Additional defendant(s) listed on attached Form 1A.
Le ou les défendeurs additionnels sont mentionnés sur la formule 1A ci-jointe.

Last name, or name of company / *Nom de famille ou nom de la compagnie*		
Mirren		
First name / *Premier prénom* **Mabel**	Second name / *Deuxième prénom*	Also known as / *Également connu(e) sous le nom de*
Address (street number, apt., unit) / *Adresse (numéro et rue, app., unité)* **89 Oliver Crescent, Unit 442**		
City/Town / *Cité/ville* **Newmarket**	Province **Ontario**	Phone no. / *N° de téléphone* **905 222 3333**
Postal code / *Code postal* **E1H 2F2**		Fax no. / *N° de télécopieur*
Representative / *Représentant(e)*		LSUC # / *N° du BHC*
Address (street number, apt., unit) / *Adresse (numéro et rue, app., unité)*		
City/Town / *Cité/ville*	Province	Phone no. / *N° de téléphone*
Postal code / *Code postal*		Fax no. / *N° de télécopieur*

SCR 15.01-15A (June 1, 2009 / *1er juin 2009*) CSD

APPENDIX 11.2 **Notice of Motion and Supporting Affidavit (Form 15A)** *continued*

FORM / *FORMULE* 15A   PAGE 2   SC-00-98865-00
Claim No. / *N° de la demande*

THIS COURT WILL HEAR A MOTION on January 11 _____ , 20 -- , at 9:30 a.m. ,
LE TRIBUNAL PRÉCITÉ ENTENDRA UNE MOTION le _____ , *à* _____ (Time / *heure*)

or as soon as possible after that time, at 50 Eagle Street West, Newmarket, Ontario, Courtroom 5A
ou dès que possible par la suite à/au   (Address of court location and courtroom number / *Adresse du tribunal et numéro de la salle d'audience*)

Complete Part A <u>or</u> Part B below, then complete the affidavit in support of motion on page 3. / *Remplissez la partie A <u>ou</u> la partie B ci-dessous. Remplissez ensuite l'affidavit à l'appui de la motion à la page 3.*

A. **This motion will be made in person by**
La motion sera présentée en personne par :   Mabel Mirren _____ ,
(Name of party / *Nom de la partie*)

for the following order : / *en vue d'obtenir l'ordonnance suivante :*

☐ the court's permission to extend time to (Specify)
l'autorisation du tribunal de proroger le délai pour (Précisez)
_____

☐ set aside default judgment and noting in default.
l'annulation du jugement par défaut et la constatation du défaut.

☐ set aside noting in default.
l'annulation de la constatation du défaut.

☐ permission to file a Defence.
l'autorisation de déposer une défense.

☐ permission to file a Defendant's Claim.
l'autorisation de déposer une demande du défendeur.

☐ terminate garnishment and/or withdraw writ(s).
la mainlevée de la saisie-arrêt ou le retrait d'un ou de plusieurs brefs, ou les deux.

☒ Other:
Autre :
Consolidation order (Rule 20.09)

☒ **ADDITIONAL PAGES ARE ATTACHED BECAUSE MORE ROOM WAS NEEDED.**
DES FEUILLES SUPPLÉMENTAIRES SONT ANNEXÉES EN RAISON DU MANQUE D'ESPACE.

☒ **DOCUMENTS ARE ATTACHED.**
PIÈCES JOINTES.

NOTE:	IF YOU FAIL TO ATTEND AN IN-PERSON MOTION, an order may be made against you, with costs, in your absence. If you want to attend the motion by telephone or video conference, complete and file a Request for Telephone or Video Conference (Form 1B). If the court permits it, the clerk will make the necessary arrangements and notify the parties [R. 1.07(5)].
REMARQUE :	*SI VOUS NE VOUS PRÉSENTEZ PAS EN PERSONNE À L'AUDITION DE LA MOTION, une ordonnance peut être rendue contre vous en votre absence, avec dépens. Si vous voulez assister à l'audition de la motion par conférence téléphonique ou vidéoconférence, remplissez et déposez la Demande de conférence téléphonique ou vidéoconférence (formule 1B). Si le tribunal l'autorise, le greffier prendra les dispositions nécessaires et en avisera les parties [par. 1.07 (5)].*

SCR 15.01-15A (June 1, 2009 / *1er juin 2009*) CSD

Continued on next page / *Suite à la page suivante*

APPENDIX 11.2 **Notice of Motion and Supporting Affidavit (Form 15A)** *continued*

FORM / *FORMULE* 15A   PAGE 3   SC-00-98865-00
                                                                 Claim No. / *N° de la demande*

B. **This motion in writing for an assessment of damages is made by**
    La présente motion par écrit en vue d'une évaluation des dommages-intérêts est présentée par

_____
                        (Name of plaintiff / *Nom du demandeur/de la demanderesse*)

who asks the court for an order assessing damages against
qui demande au tribunal de rendre une ordonnance d'évaluation des dommages-intérêts contre

_____
                        (Name of defendant(s) / *Nom du/de la/des défendeur(s)/défenderesse(s)*)

who have/has been noted in default.
qui a/ont été constaté(e)(s) en défaut.

AFFIDAVIT IN SUPPORT OF MOTION / *AFFIDAVIT À L'APPUI DE LA MOTION*

My name is Mabel Mirren
Je m'appelle   (Full name / *Nom et prénoms*)

I live in Newmarket, Ontario
J'habite à   (Municipality & province / *Municipalité et province*)

I swear/affirm that the following is true:
Je déclare sous serment/j'affirme solennellement que les renseignements suivants sont véridiques :

Set out the facts in numbered paragraphs. If you learned a fact from someone else, you must give that person's name and state that you believe that fact to be true.
Indiquez les faits sous forme de dispositions numérotées. Si vous avez pris connaissance d'un fait par l'entremise d'une autre personne, vous devez indiquer le nom de cette personne et déclarer que vous croyez que ce fait est véridique.

  See Schedule A attached and forming part of this affidavit

SCR 15.01-15A (June 1, 2009 / *1er juin 2009*) CSD   Continued on next page / *Suite à la page suivante*

APPENDIX 11.2 Notice of Motion and Supporting Affidavit (Form 15A) *continued*

FORM / *FORMULE* 15A   PAGE 4   SC-00-98865-00

Claim No. / *Nº de la demande*

AFFIDAVIT IN SUPPORT OF MOTION, continued / *AFFIDAVIT À L'APPUI DE LA MOTION, suite*
See Schedule A attached and forming part of this affidavit

If more space is required, attach and initial extra pages. / Si vous avez besoin de plus d'espace, annexez une ou des feuilles supplémentaires et paraphez-les.

Sworn/Affirmed before me at **Newmarket**
Déclaré sous serment/Affirmé   (Municipality / *municipalité*)
solennellement devant moi à

in **Ontario**
en/à/au   (Province, state or country / *province, État ou pays*)

on **December 11**   , 20 --
le

Commissioner for taking affidavits
Commissaire aux affidavits
(Type or print name below if signature is illegible.)
(Dactylographiez le nom ou écrivez-le en caractères d'imprimerie ci-dessous si la signature est illisible.)

Signature
(This form is to be signed in front of a lawyer, justice of the peace, notary public or commissioner for taking affidavits.)
(La présente formule doit être signée en présence d'un avocat, d'un juge de paix, d'un notaire ou d'un commissaire aux affidavits.)

WARNING: **IT IS AN OFFENCE UNDER THE *CRIMINAL CODE* TO KNOWINGLY SWEAR OR AFFIRM A FALSE AFFIDAVIT.**

AVERTISSEMENT : *FAIRE SCIEMMENT UN FAUX AFFIDAVIT CONSTITUE UNE INFRACTION AU CODE CRIMINEL.*

SCR 15.01-15A (June 1, 2009 / *1ᵉʳ juin 2009*) CSD

APPENDIX 11.2 **Notice of Motion and Supporting Affidavit (Form 15A)** *concluded*

Schedule A

1. I am the debtor in the following actions and as such have personal knowledge of the following.

2.

Creditor	Claim No.	Judgment Amount	Date
France Nguyen 92 Friendship Court Newmarket, Ontario L3Z 3X5	Newmarket SC-00-98865-00	$ 2,744.08	Nov. 27, 20—
National Bank of Canada MasterCard P.O. Box 4700 Rexdale, Ontario X1X 2Y3	Newmarket SC-00-98950-00	$ 5,378.48	Dec. 2, 20—
Ferndale Property Management 47 Mary Street Newmarket, Ontario L3Y 3Y4	Newmarket SC-00-98985-00	$ 2,500.00	Dec. 5, 20—
TOTAL OWING		$10,622.56	

3. My net monthly employment income is $2,478.00. I have no other sources of income.

4. My current monthly expenses are as follows:

Rent	$ 975.00
Food	500.00
Vehicle lease	250.00
Car insurance, fuel	250.00
Clothing	100.00
TOTAL	$2,075.00

5. When I have paid my living expenses in every month, I have $403.00 left with which to pay any additional expenses.

APPENDIX 11.3 Affidavit for Enforcement Request (Form 20P)

ONTARIO

Superior Court of Justice
Cour supérieure de justice

Affidavit for Enforcement Request
Affidavit relatif à une demande d'exécution forcée

Form / *Formule* 20P Ont. Reg. No. / *Règl. de l'Ont.* : 258/98

Thunder Bay

Small Claims Court / *Cour des petites créances de*

277 Camelot Street
Thunder Bay, Ontario
P7A 4B3

Address / *Adresse*

807 343 2710

Phone number / *Numéro de téléphone*

SC-00-05432-00

Claim No. / *N° de la demande*

BETWEEN / *ENTRE*

Emma Flood

Plaintiff(s)/Creditor(s) / *Demandeur(s)/demanderesse(s)/Créancier(s)/créancière(s)*

and / *et*

Christine Michaeli

Defendant(s)/Debtor(s) / *Défendeur(s)/défenderesse(s)/Débiteur(s)/débitrice(s)*

My name is Emma Flood
Je m'appelle

(Full name / *Nom et prénoms*)

I live in Thunder Bay, Ontario
J'habite à

(Municipality & province / *Municipalité et province*)

and I swear/affirm that the following is true:
et je déclare sous serment/j'affirme solennellement que les renseignements suivants sont véridiques :

1. **In this action, I am the**
   Dans la présente action, je suis le/la

   (Check one
   box only. /
   *Cochez une
   seule case.*)

   ☒ plaintiff/creditor.
   demandeur/demanderesse/créancier/créancière.

   ☐ representative of the plaintiff(s)/creditor(s).
   représentant(e) du/de la/des demandeur(s)/demanderesse(s)/créancier(s)/créancière(s).

   I make this affidavit in support of a request that the clerk of the court issue the following enforcement process(es):
   Je fais le présent affidavit à l'appui d'une demande visant à enjoindre au greffier du tribunal de délivrer l'acte ou les actes de procédure portant exécution forcée suivants :

   ☒ Certificate of Judgment (Form 20A) to the clerk of the   Sault Ste. Marie
   Certificat de jugement (formule 20A), au greffier   (Name of court where the judgment is to be filed / *Nom du tribunal*
   de la Cour des petites créances de   *où le jugement doit être déposé*)

   Small Claims Court.

   ☐ Writ of Seizure and Sale of Personal Property (Form 20C) directed to the bailiff of
   Bref de saisie-exécution de biens meubles (formule 20C) adressé à l'huissier de la Cour des petites créances de

   Small Claims Court.

   _____
   (Name of court location / *Emplacement du tribunal*)

   ☐ Writ of Seizure and Sale of Land (Form 20D) directed to the sheriff of _____
   Bref de saisie-exécution de biens-fonds (formule 20D) adressé   (Name of county/region in which the
   au shérif du/de la   enforcement office is located / *Comté/région où*
   est situé le bureau de l'exécution*)

SCR 20.04-10-20P (June 1, 2009 / *1ᵉʳ juin 2009*) CSD

APPENDIX 11.3   Affidavit for Enforcement Request (Form 20P)   *continued*

FORM / *FORMULE* 20P   **PAGE 2**   SC-00-05432-00

Claim No. / *N° de la demande*

☐ Notice of Garnishment (Form 20E)/Notice of Renewal of Garnishment (Form 20E.1).
   Avis de saisie-arrêt (formule 20E)/Avis de renouvellement de la saisie-arrêt (formule 20E.1).

   I believe that the garnishee
   Je crois que le tiers saisi
                                            (Name of garnishee / *Nom du tiers saisi*)

   at
   à/au
                                            (Address of garnishee / *Adresse du tiers saisi*)

   is indebted to the debtor or will become indebted to the debtor for the following reasons:
   est ou sera redevable d'une dette au débiteur pour les motifs suivants :

   The Notice will be served on the debtor
   L'avis sera signifié au débiteur,
                                            (Name of debtor / *Nom du débiteur/de la débitrice*)

   at
   à/au
                        (Address of debtor for service / *Adresse du débiteur/de la débitrice aux fins de signification*)

   within five days of serving it on the garnishee.
   dans les cinq jours qui suivent sa signification au tiers saisi.

☐ Notice of Examination (Form 20H).
   Avis d'interrogatoire (formule 20H).

☐ Writ of Delivery (Form 20B).
   Bref de délaissement (formule 20B).

☐ Other *(Set out the nature of your request):*
   Autre (Indiquez la nature de votre demande) :

Complete this section if you are requesting a Writ of Delivery.
Remplissez la présente section si vous demandez un bref de délaissement.

2. An order for the delivery of the following personal property:
   Une ordonnance de délaissement des biens meubles suivants :
   (According to the court order, set out a description of the property to be delivered. Identify any marks or serial numbers. / Selon l'ordonnance du tribunal, donnez la description des biens qui doivent être restitués. Indiquez toute marque d'identification ou tout numéro de série y figurant.)

APPENDIX 11.3 Affidavit for Enforcement Request (Form 20P) *continued*

FORM / *FORMULE* **20P**   **PAGE 3**   SC-00-05432-00
                                                                        Claim No. / *N° de la demande*

was made in this action against: _____
a été rendue dans l'action contre :   (Name of person against whom the order was made / *Nom de la personne contre qui*
                                                           l'ordonnance a été rendue)

on _____, 20 ____, in the _____
le _____   *à la Cour des petites*   (Name of court location where order was made / *Emplacement*
                                            créances de   *du tribunal où l'ordonnance a été rendue*)

Small Claims Court. Since the above listed personal property has not been delivered, I make this affidavit in
support of a request that the clerk of the court issue a Writ of Delivery (Form 20B) to the bailiff of the
Étant donné que les biens meubles susmentionnés n'ont pas été restitués, je fais le présent affidavit à l'appui
d'une demande visant à enjoindre au greffier du tribunal de délivrer un bref de délaissement (formule 20B) à
l'huissier de la Cour des petites créances de

_____ Small Claims Court.
              (Name of court location / *Emplacement du tribunal*)

**Complete this section if you are requesting a Certificate of Judgment, Writ of Seizure
and Sale of Personal Property, Writ of Seizure and Sale of Land, Notice of
Garnishment, Notice of Renewal of Garnishment or Notice of Examination.**
Remplissez la présente section si vous demandez un certificat de jugement, un bref de
saisie-exécution de biens meubles, un bref de saisie-exécution de biens-fonds, un avis
de saisie-arrêt, un avis de renouvellement de la saisie-arrêt ou un avis d'interrogatoire.

3. A judgment was made in this action against Christine Michaeli
   Un jugement a été rendu dans l'action contre   (Name of debtor(s) / *Nom du/de la/des débiteur(s)/débitrice(s)*)

   on December 25 _____, 20 -- in the _____
   le   *à la Cour des petites créances de*

   Thunder Bay _____ Small Claims Court
              (Name of court where judgment was made / *Nom du tribunal où le jugement a été rendu*)

   for the following sums:
   à l'égard des sommes suivantes :

   (A) **DEBT** $ 8,000.00
        LA CRÉANCE $

   (B) **PRE-JUDGMENT INTEREST** calculated
        LES INTÉRÊTS ANTÉRIEURS AU JUGEMENT calculés

        on the sum of $ _____ 8,000.00 _____ at the rate of 2.5 _____ %
        sur la somme de $ *au taux de*   *pour cent*

        per annum from February 28 _____, 20 -- to December 15 _____, 20 -- ,
        par an du   *au*

        being 290 _____ days. $ 158.90
        soit   *jours.* $

                              SUBTOTAL (Amount of Judgment) $ 8,158.90
                              TOTAL PARTIEL (montant du jugement) $

   (C) **COSTS** to date of judgment $ 235.00
        LES DÉPENS à la date du jugement $

APPENDIX 11.3   Affidavit for Enforcement Request (Form 20P) *concluded*

FORM / *FORMULE* **20P**   **PAGE 4**   SC-00-05432-00

Claim No. / *N° de la demande*

(D) **TOTAL AMOUNT OF PAYMENTS RECEIVED FROM DEBTOR**
after judgment (if any)   (minus) $
LE MONTANT TOTAL DES PAIEMENTS REÇUS DU   (moins) $
DÉBITEUR après le jugement (le cas échéant)

(E) **POST-JUDGMENT INTEREST** to date calculated
LES INTÉRÊTS POSTÉRIEURS AU JUGEMENT à ce jour, calculés

on the sum of $ _____ 8,393.90 _____ at the rate of 2.0 _____ %
sur la somme de _____ $ *au taux de* _____ *pour cent*

per annum from December 15 , 20 -- to January 23 , 20 -- ,
par an du _____ *au*

being 39 _____ days. $ 17.94
soit _____ *jours.* $

> **NOTE:** Calculation of interest is always on the amount owing from time to time as payments are received. This is true for both pre-judgment and post-judgment interest. Attach a separate sheet setting out how you calculated the total amount of any pre/post-judgment interest.
> *REMARQUE : Les intérêts doivent toujours être calculés sur la somme due. Le calcul doit tenir compte des paiements reçus de temps à autre. Ceci s'applique autant aux intérêts antérieurs au jugement qu'aux intérêts postérieurs au jugement. Annexez une feuille distincte indiquant comment vous avez calculé le montant total des intérêts antérieurs et postérieurs au jugement.*

(F) **SUBSEQUENT COSTS** incurred after judgment (including the cost of issuing
the requested enforcement(s)) $ 19.00
LES DÉPENS SUBSÉQUENTS engagés après le jugement (y compris le $
coût de la délivrance de la ou des mesures d'exécution forcée demandées)

                                                    TOTAL DUE $ 8,430.84
                                                    SOLDE DÛ $

Sworn/Affirmed before me at **Thunder Bay**
Déclaré sous serment/Affirmé   (Municipality / *municipalité*)
solennellement devant moi à

in **Ontario**
en/à/au   (Province, state or country / *province, État ou pays*)

on **January 23** , 20 --
le   Commissioner for taking affidavits
                                  Commissaire aux affidavits
                        (Type or print name below if signature is illegible.)
                        (Dactylographiez le nom ou écrivez-le en caractères
                        d'imprimerie ci-dessous si la signature est illisible.)

_____
Signature
(This form is to be signed in front of a
lawyer, justice of the peace, notary public
or commissioner for taking affidavits.)
(La présente formule doit être signée en
présence d'un avocat, d'un juge de paix, d'un
notaire ou d'un commissaire aux affidavits.)

WARNING: **IT IS AN OFFENCE UNDER THE** *CRIMINAL CODE* **TO KNOWINGLY SWEAR OR**
                    AFFIRM A FALSE AFFIDAVIT.
AVERTISSEMENT : *FAIRE SCIEMMENT UN FAUX AFFIDAVIT CONSTITUE UNE INFRACTION AU CODE*
                  CRIMINEL.

APPENDIX 11.3   Certificate of Judgment (Form 20A)

ONTARIO

Superior Court of Justice
Cour supérieure de justice

Certificate of Judgment
Certificat de jugement

Form / *Formule* 20A Ont. Reg. No. / *Régl. de l'Ont.* : 258/98

Seal / *Sceau*

Thunder Bay
Small Claims Court / *Cour des petites créances de*
277 Camelot Street
Thunder Bay, Ontario
P7A 4B3
Address / *Adresse*

807 343 2710
Phone number / *Numéro de téléphone*

SC-00-05432-00
Claim No. / *N° de la demande*

BETWEEN / *ENTRE*

Emma Flood

Creditor(s) / *Créancier(s)/créancière(s)*

and / *et*

Christine Michaeli

Debtor(s) / *Débiteur(s)/débitrice(s)*

A judgment was made in this action on <u>December 15</u>, 20 -- , **in the**
Un jugement a été rendu dans la présente action le , *à la*

Thunder Bay

(Name of court where judgment was made / *Nom de la cour où le jugement a été rendu*)

against / *contre*

Last name of debtor, or name of company / *Nom de famille du débiteur/de la débitrice ou nom de la compagnie*		
Michaeli		
First name / *Premier prénom*	Second name / *Deuxième prénom*	Third name / *Troisième prénom*
Christine		
Address / *Adresse*		

Last name of debtor, or name of company / *Nom de famille du débiteur/de la débitrice ou nom de la compagnie*		
First name / *Premier prénom*	Second name / *Deuxième prénom*	Third name / *Troisième prénom*
Address / *Adresse*		

Last name of debtor, or name of company / *Nom de famille du débiteur/de la débitrice ou nom de la compagnie*		
First name / *Premier prénom*	Second name / *Deuxième prénom*	Third name / *Troisième prénom*
Address / *Adresse*		

☐ Additional debtor(s) and also known as names are listed on attached Form 1A.1.
Le ou les débiteur(s) additionnel(s) et le ou les noms sous lesquels les débiteurs sont également connus sont mentionnés sur la formule 1A.1 ci-jointe.

SCR 20.04-20A (September 1, 2010 / *1er septembre 2010*) CSD

APPENDIX 11.3 Certificate of Judgment (Form 20A) *concluded*

FORM / *FORMULE* 20A   PAGE 2   SC-00-05432-00
                                                                  Claim No. / *N° de la demande*

Judgment was made for the following sums:
Un jugement a été rendu à l'égard des sommes suivantes :

(A) **AMOUNT OF JUDGMENT** (debt and pre-judgment interest) $ 8,158.90
    LE MONTANT DU JUGEMENT *(créance et intérêts antérieurs au jugement)* $

(B) **COSTS** to date of judgment $ 235.00
    LES DÉPENS *à la date du jugement* $

Post-judgment interest continues to accrue at   2.0   % per annum.
Les intérêts postérieurs au jugement continuent   (Interest rate /   % par an.
à courir au taux de   Taux d'intérêt)

_____ , 20 ____   _____
                                      (Signature of clerk / *Signature du greffier*)

TO THE CLERK OF THE _____ Sault Ste. Marie _____ **SMALL CLAIMS COURT:**
AU GREFFIER DE LA COUR DES PETITES   (Name of court to where the judgment is to be filed
CRÉANCES DE   / *Nom du tribunal où le jugement doit être déposé*)

The person requesting this certificate is   Emma Flood
La personne qui demande le présent certificat est   (Name of party requesting certificate / *Nom de la partie qui demande le certificat*)

                   53 Edward Street, Thunder Bay, Ontario P2B 1J3
                   (Address of party requesting certificate / *Adresse de la partie qui demande le certificat*)

SCR 20.04-20A (September 1, 2010 / *1er septembre 2010*) CSD

APPENDIX 11.4   Affidavit for Enforcement Request (Form 20P)

ONTARIO

Superior Court of Justice
Cour supérieure de justice

Affidavit for Enforcement Request
Affidavit relatif à une demande d'exécution forcée
Form / *Formule* 20P Ont. Reg. No. / *Régl. de l'Ont.* : 258/98

Sault Ste. Marie
Small Claims Court / *Cour des petites créances de*
426 Queen Street East
Sault Ste. Marie, Ontario
P6A 6W2
Address / *Adresse*

705 945 8000
Phone number / *Numéro de téléphone*

SC-00-81632-00
Claim No. / *N° de la demande*

BETWEEN / *ENTRE*

Emma Flood

Plaintiff(s)/Creditor(s) / *Demandeur(s)/demanderesse(s)/Créancier(s)/créancière(s)*

and / *et*

Christine Michaeli

Defendant(s)/Debtor(s) / *Défendeur(s)/défenderesse(s)/Débiteur(s)/débitrice(s)*

My name is Emma Flood
Je m'appelle

(Full name / *Nom et prénoms*)

I live in Thunder Bay, Ontario
J'habite à

(Municipality & province / *Municipalité et province*)

and I swear/affirm that the following is true:
et je déclare sous serment/j'affirme solennellement que les renseignements suivants sont véridiques :

1. **In this action, I am the**
   Dans la présente action, je suis le/la

   (Check one
   box only. /
   *Cochez une
   seule case.*)

   ☒ plaintiff/creditor.
   demandeur/demanderesse/créancier/créancière.

   ☐ representative of the plaintiff(s)/creditor(s).
   représentant(e) du/de la/des demandeur(s)/demanderesse(s)/créancier(s)/créancière(s).

   I make this affidavit in support of a request that the clerk of the court issue the following enforcement process(es):
   Je fais le présent affidavit à l'appui d'une demande visant à enjoindre au greffier du tribunal de délivrer l'acte ou les actes de procédure portant exécution forcée suivants :

   ☐ Certificate of Judgment (Form 20A) to the clerk of the
   *Certificat de jugement (formule 20A), au greffier
   de la Cour des petites créances de*

   (Name of court where the judgment is to be filed / *Nom du tribunal
   où le jugement doit être déposé*)

   Small Claims Court.

   ☐ Writ of Seizure and Sale of Personal Property (Form 20C) directed to the bailiff of
   Bref de saisie-exécution de biens meubles (formule 20C) adressé à l'huissier de la Cour des petites créances de

   Small Claims Court.

   (Name of court location / *Emplacement du tribunal*)

   ☐ Writ of Seizure and Sale of Land (Form 20D) directed to the sheriff of
   *Bref de saisie-exécution de biens-fonds (formule 20D) adressé
   au shérif du/de la*

   (Name of county/region in which the
   enforcement office is located / *Comté/région où
   est situé le bureau de l'exécution*)

SCR 20.04-10-20P (June 1, 2009 / *1er juin 2009*) CSD

APPENDIX 11.4 **Affidavit for Enforcement Request (Form 20P)** *continued*

FORM / *FORMULE* 20P   PAGE 2   SC-00-81632-00

Claim No. / *N° de la demande*

☐ Notice of Garnishment (Form 20E)/Notice of Renewal of Garnishment (Form 20E.1).
  Avis de saisie-arrêt (formule 20E)/Avis de renouvellement de la saisie-arrêt (formule 20E.1).

  I believe that the garnishee _____
  Je crois que le tiers saisi   (Name of garnishee / *Nom du tiers saisi*)

  at _____
  à/au   (Address of garnishee / *Adresse du tiers saisi*)

  is indebted to the debtor or will become indebted to the debtor for the following reasons:
  est ou sera redevable d'une dette au débiteur pour les motifs suivants :

  The Notice will be served on the debtor _____
  L'avis sera signifié au débiteur,   (Name of debtor / *Nom du débiteur/de la débitrice*)

  at _____
  à/au   (Address of debtor for service / *Adresse du débiteur/de la débitrice aux fins de signification*)

  within five days of serving it on the garnishee.
  dans les cinq jours qui suivent sa signification au tiers saisi.

☒ Notice of Examination (Form 20H).
  Avis d'interrogatoire (formule 20H).

☐ Writ of Delivery (Form 20B).
  Bref de délaissement (formule 20B).

☐ Other *(Set out the nature of your request)*:
  Autre (Indiquez la nature de votre demande) :

Complete this section if you are requesting a Writ of Delivery.
Remplissez la présente section si vous demandez un bref de délaissement.

2. An order for the delivery of the following personal property:
    Une ordonnance de délaissement des biens meubles suivants :
    (According to the court order, set out a description of the property to be delivered. Identify any marks or serial numbers. / Selon l'ordonnance du tribunal, donnez la description des biens qui doivent être restitués. Indiquez toute marque d'identification ou tout numéro de série y figurant.)

APPENDIX 11.4 Affidavit for Enforcement Request (Form 20P) *continued*

FORM / *FORMULE* 20P   PAGE 3   SC-00-81632-00

Claim No. / *N° de la demande*

was made in this action against: _____
a été rendue dans l'action contre :   (Name of person against whom the order was made / *Nom de la personne contre qui l'ordonnance a été rendue*)

on _____, 20 ____, in the _____
le   *à la Cour des petites*   (Name of court location where order was made / *Emplacement*
                               créances de   *du tribunal où l'ordonnance a été rendue*)

Small Claims Court. Since the above listed personal property has not been delivered, I make this affidavit in
support of a request that the clerk of the court issue a Writ of Delivery (Form 20B) to the bailiff of the
*Étant donné que les biens meubles susmentionnés n'ont pas été restitués, je fais le présent affidavit à l'appui
d'une demande visant à enjoindre au greffier du tribunal de délivrer un bref de délaissement (formule 20B) à
l'huissier de la Cour des petites créances de*

_____ Small Claims Court.
                    (Name of court location / *Emplacement du tribunal*)

**Complete this section if you are requesting a Certificate of Judgment, Writ of Seizure
and Sale of Personal Property, Writ of Seizure and Sale of Land, Notice of
Garnishment, Notice of Renewal of Garnishment or Notice of Examination.**
*Remplissez la présente section si vous demandez un certificat de jugement, un bref de
saisie-exécution de biens meubles, un bref de saisie-exécution de biens-fonds, un avis
de saisie-arrêt, un avis de renouvellement de la saisie-arrêt ou un avis d'interrogatoire.*

3. A judgment was made in this action against Christine Michaeli
   Un jugement a été rendu dans l'action contre   (Name of debtor(s) / *Nom du/de la/des débiteur(s)/débitrice(s)*)

   on December 15 , 20 -- in the _____
   le   *à la Cour des petites créances de*

   Thunder Bay _____ Small Claims Court
            (Name of court where judgment was made / *Nom du tribunal où le jugement a été rendu*)

   for the following sums:
   à l'égard des sommes suivantes :

   (A) **DEBT** $ _____ 8,000.00
       LA CRÉANCE $

   (B) **PRE-JUDGMENT INTEREST** calculated
       LES INTÉRÊTS ANTÉRIEURS AU JUGEMENT *calculés*

       on the sum of $ _____ 8,000.00 at the rate of 2.5 %
       sur la somme de   *$ au taux de*   *pour cent*

       per annum from February 28 , 20 -- to December 15 , 20 -- ,
       par an du   *au*

       being 290 _____ days. $ _____ 158.90
       soit   *jours.* $

                              SUBTOTAL (Amount of Judgment) $ 8,158.90
                              TOTAL PARTIEL (montant du jugement) $

   (C) **COSTS** to date of judgment $ _____ 235.00
       LES DÉPENS *à la date du jugement* $

Continued on next page / *Suite à la page suivante*

APPENDIX 11.4   Affidavit for Enforcement Request (Form 20P)   *concluded*

FORM / *FORMULE* 20P   PAGE 4   SC-00-81632-00
                                                                    Claim No. / *N° de la demande*

(D) **TOTAL AMOUNT OF PAYMENTS RECEIVED FROM DEBTOR**
    after judgment (if any)   (minus) $ 0
    LE MONTANT TOTAL DES PAIEMENTS REÇUS DU   *(moins)* $
    DÉBITEUR après le jugement (le cas échéant)

(E) **POST-JUDGMENT INTEREST** to date calculated
    LES INTÉRÊTS POSTÉRIEURS AU JUGEMENT à ce jour, calculés

    on the sum of $ _____8,393.90_____ at the rate of **2.0** %
    sur la somme de _____ $ *au taux de* _____ *pour cent*

    per annum from **December 15** , 20 -- to **February 1** , 20 -- ,
    par an du _____ *au*

    being **48** _____ days. $ 22.08
    soit   *jours.* $

    > **NOTE:** Calculation of interest is always on the amount owing from time to time as payments are
    > received. This is true for both pre-judgment and post-judgment interest. Attach a separate sheet
    > setting out how you calculated the total amount of any pre/post-judgment interest.
    > *REMARQUE : Les intérêts doivent toujours être calculés sur la somme due. Le calcul doit tenir
    > compte des paiements reçus de temps à autre. Ceci s'applique autant aux intérêts antérieurs au
    > jugement qu'aux intérêts postérieurs au jugement. Annexez une feuille distincte indiquant comment
    > vous avez calculé le montant total des intérêts antérieurs et postérieurs au jugement.*

(F) **SUBSEQUENT COSTS** incurred after judgment (including the cost of issuing
    the requested enforcement(s)) $ 54.00
    LES DÉPENS SUBSÉQUENTS engagés après le jugement (y compris le $
    coût de la délivrance de la ou des mesures d'exécution forcée demandées)

                                        TOTAL DUE $ 8,469.98
                                        SOLDE DÛ $

Sworn/Affirmed before me at **Thunder Bay**
Déclaré sous serment/Affirmé   (Municipality / *municipalité*)
solennellement devant moi à

in **Ontario**
en/à/au   (Province, state or country / *province, État ou pays*)

on **February 1** , 20 --
le   Commissioner for taking affidavits
                              Commissaire aux affidavits
                              (Type or print name below if signature is illegible.)
                              *(Dactylographiez le nom ou écrivez-le en caractères
                              d'imprimerie ci-dessous si la signature est illisible.)*

_____
Signature
(This form is to be signed in front of a
lawyer, justice of the peace, notary public
or commissioner for taking affidavits.)
*(La présente formule doit être signée en
présence d'un avocat, d'un juge de paix, d'un
notaire ou d'un commissaire aux affidavits.)*

WARNING: **IT IS AN OFFENCE UNDER THE *CRIMINAL CODE* TO KNOWINGLY SWEAR OR
                 AFFIRM A FALSE AFFIDAVIT.**
AVERTISSEMENT : *FAIRE SCIEMMENT UN FAUX AFFIDAVIT CONSTITUE UNE INFRACTION AU CODE
                 CRIMINEL.*

SCR 20.04-10-20P (June 1, 2009 / *1ᵉʳ juin 2009*) CSD

APPENDIX 11.4   Notice of Examination (Form 20H)

ONTARIO

Superior Court of Justice
Cour supérieure de justice

Notice of Examination
Avis d'interrogatoire

Form / Formule 20H Ont. Reg. No. / Régl. de l'Ont. : 258/98

(Seal / *Sceau*)

Sault Ste. Marie
Small Claims Court / *Cour des petites créances de*
426 Queen Street East
Sault Ste. Marie, Ontario
P6A 6W2
Address / *Adresse*

705 945 8000
Phone number / *Numéro de téléphone*

SC-00-81632-00
Claim No. / *N° de la demande*

BETWEEN / *ENTRE*

Emma Flood

Creditor(s) / *Créancier(s)/créancière(s)*

and / *et*

Christine Michaeli

Debtor(s) / *Débiteur(s)/débitrice(s)*

TO:
DESTINATAIRE :

Christine Michaeli
(Name of person to be examined / *Nom de la personne qui doit être interrogée*)

of
de/du

55A Tranquillity Boulevard, Sault Ste. Marie, Ontario P6S 1C5
(Address of person to be examined / *Adresse de la personne qui doit être interrogée*)

The creditor   Emma Flood
Le créancier   (Name of creditor / *Nom du/de la créancier/créancière*)

de

53 Edward Street
of   Thunder Bay, Ontario P2B 1J3
(Address of creditor / *Adresse du/de la créancier/créancière*)

has obtained a judgment against   Christine Michaeli   on   December 15   ,
a obtenu un jugement contre   (Name of debtor / *Nom du débiteur/de la débitrice*)   *le*

20 -- , in the   Thunder Bay   Small Claims Court.
à la Cour des petites créances de   (Name of court where judgment was made / *Nom du tribunal où le jugement a été rendu*)

According to the supporting affidavit filed by the creditor, the total due on the judgment is
Selon l'affidavit à l'appui déposé par le créancier, le solde somme due aux termes du jugement s'élève à

$ 8,469.98   .   *(This amount must match the total amount identified in the supporting affidavit.)*
(Total)   *$.*   *(Ce montant doit correspondre au montant total énoncé dans l'affidavit à l'appui.)*

This total due takes into account all money received, accrued post-judgment interest and costs to
Ce solde somme due tient compte de toutes les sommes reçues, des intérêts postérieurs au jugement courus et des dépens

this date: February 1   , 20 -- .   *(This date must match the date of the supporting affidavit.)*
à cette date :   *(Cette date doit correspondre à celle de l'affidavit à l'appui.)*

YOU ARE REQUIRED TO ATTEND AN EXAMINATION HEARING to explain how the debtor will pay this judgment and if there are any reasons for not doing so.
VOUS ÊTES REQUIS(E) DE VOUS PRÉSENTER À UN INTERROGATOIRE *pour expliquer de quelle façon le débiteur acquittera la somme due aux termes de ce jugement et s'il existe quelque motif que ce soit de ne pas le faire.*

SCR 20.10-20H (April 11, 2012 / *11 avril 2012*) CSD

Continued on next page / *Suite à la page suivante*

APPENDIX 11.4 Notice of Examination (Form 20H) *concluded*

FORM / *FORMULE* 20H   PAGE 2   SC-00-81632-00
_____
                                                                Claim No. / *N° de la demande*

THIS COURT WILL HOLD AN EXAMINATION HEARING
LE TRIBUNAL PRÉCITÉ TIENDRA UN INTERROGATOIRE

on   March 15   , 20 -- , at   9:30 a.m.   or as soon as possible after that
le   , à   (Time / *heure*)   time, at
                                                             ou dès que possible par la suite à/au

277 Camelot Street, Thunder Bay, Ontario P7A 4B3
_____
                        (Address of court location / *Adresse du tribunal*)

6H
_____
                        (Courtroom number / *Numéro de la salle d'audience*)

_____, 20 _____   _____
                                          (Signature of clerk / *Signature du greffier*)

CAUTION TO PERSON BEING EXAMINED:	If you fail to attend the examination hearing or attend and refuse to answer questions or produce documents, you may be ordered to attend a contempt hearing. At the contempt hearing, you may be found in contempt of court and the court may order you to be jailed.
AVERTISSEMENT À LA PERSONNE QUI EST INTERROGÉE :	*Si vous ne vous présentez pas à l'interrogatoire ou si vous vous présentez mais que vous refusez de répondre aux questions ou de produire des documents, le tribunal peut ordonner que vous vous présentiez à une audience pour outrage. Lors de l'audience pour outrage, vous pouvez être reconnu(e) coupable d'outrage au tribunal et le tribunal peut ordonner que vous soyez incarcéré(e).*

NOTE TO DEBTOR:	A debtor who is an individual must serve on the creditor a completed Financial Information Form (Form 20I) prior to the hearing. This form must **not** be filed with the court. The debtor must provide a completed copy of this form to the judge at the examination hearing. The debtor must also bring to the hearing documents that support the information given in this form.
REMARQUE AU DÉBITEUR :	*Le débiteur qui est un particulier doit signifier au créancier une formule de renseignements financiers remplie (formule 20I) avant l'interrogatoire. Cette formule ne doit **pas** être déposée auprès du tribunal. Le débiteur doit remettre la formule dûment remplie au juge chargé de l'audience. Le débiteur doit aussi apporter à l'audience les documents qui appuient l'information donnée sur cette formule.*

SCR 20.10-20H (April 11, 2012 / *11 avril 2012*) CSD

APPENDIX 11.4   Financial Information Form (Form 20I)

FINANCIAL INFORMATION FORM
FORMULE DE RENSEIGNEMENTS FINANCIERS

Form / *Formule* 20I Ont. Reg. No. / *Règl. de l'Ont.* : 258/98

This form is to be completed by the debtor and served on the creditor.
La présente formule doit être remplie par le débiteur et signifiée au créancier.

This form is not to be filed at the court office. The debtor must provide a completed copy of this form to the judge at the examination hearing. The debtor must also bring to the hearing documents that support the information given in this form.
Cette formule ne doit pas être déposée au bureau du tribunal. Le débiteur doit remettre la formule dûment remplie au juge chargé de l'audience. Le débiteur doit aussi apporter à l'audience les documents qui appuient l'information donnée sur cette formule.

MONTHLY INCOME *REVENU MENSUEL*		MONTHLY EXPENSES *DÉPENSES MENSUELLES*	
Employer(s) _____ *Employeur(s)*		Rent/Mortgage *Loyer/Hypothèque*	$ _____ $
Employer(s) _____ *Employeur(s)*		Maintenance/Support Payments *Versements d'aliments*	$ _____ $
Net salary *Salaire net*	$ _____ $	Property taxes *Impôts fonciers*	$ _____ $
Commissions *Commissions*	$ _____ $	Utilities (heat, water & light) *Services d'utilité publique (chauffage, eau et éclairage)*	$ _____ $
Tips and gratuities *Pourboires et gratifications*	$ _____ $	Phone *Téléphone*	$ _____ $
Employment insurance *Prestations d'assurance-emploi*	$ _____ $	Cable *Câblodistribution*	$ _____ $
Pension income *Revenu de pension*	$ _____ $	House/Tenant insurance *Assurance-habitation /assurance de responsabilité locative*	$ _____ $
Investment income *Revenu de placements*	$ _____ $	Life insurance *Assurance-vie*	$ _____ $
Rental income *Revenu de location*	$ _____ $	Food *Nourriture*	$ _____ $
Business income *Revenu tiré d'une entreprise*	$ _____ $	Childcare/Babysitting *Garderie/gardiennage d'enfants*	$ _____ $
Child tax benefit *Prestation fiscale pour enfants*	$ _____ $	Motor vehicle (lease or loan) *Véhicule automobile (location à bail ou prêt)*	$ _____ $
Maintenance *(if any)* *Aliments* (le cas échéant)	$ _____ $	(licence, insurance, fuel & maintenance) *(permis, assurance, essence et entretien)*	$ _____ $
Monthly income of other adult household members *Revenu mensuel des autres membres adultes du ménage*	$ _____ $	Transportation (public) *Transports (en commun)*	$ _____ $
Other *Autre*	$ _____ $		
Income assistance *Aide au revenu*	$ _____ $		
INCOME TOTAL *REVENU TOTAL*	$ _____ $	**EXPENSES TOTAL** *DÉPENSES TOTALES*	$ _____ $

Continued on next page / *Suite à la page suivante*

APPENDIX 11.4 Financial Information Form (Form 20I) *concluded*

FORM / *FORMULE* 20I   PAGE 2

MONTHLY DEBTS
DETTES MENSUELLES

Credit card(s) payments *(please specify)*:
Paiements de carte(s) de crédit (Veuillez préciser.)

_____ $ _____
                                        $ _____

_____ $ _____
                                        $ _____

_____ $ _____
                                        $ _____

Bank or finance company loan payments *(please specify)*:
Remboursement de prêt(s) d'une banque ou d'une compagnie de financement (Veuillez préciser.)

_____ $ _____
                                        $ _____

_____ $ _____
                                        $ _____

Department store(s) payments *(please specify)*:
Versements à un ou des grands magasins (Veuillez préciser.)

_____ $ _____
                                        $ _____

_____ $ _____
                                        $ _____

DEBTS TOTAL $ _____
DETTES TOTALES $ _____

VALUE OF ASSETS
VALEUR DES AVOIRS

Real estate equity $ _____
Valeur nette réelle des biens immobiliers $ _____

   Market value $ _____
   Valeur marchande $ _____

   Mortgage balance $ _____
   Solde de l'hypothèque $ _____

Automobile equity $ _____
Valeur nette réelle des véhicules automobiles $ _____

   Make and year _____
   Marque et année

   Loan balance $ _____
   Solde du/des prêts $ _____

Bank or other account balance(s) *(include RRSPs)* $ _____
Solde de compte(s) bancaire(s) ou autre(s) compte(s) (Incluez les REÉR.) $ _____

Stocks & bonds $ _____
Actions et obligations $ _____

Life insurance (cash value) $ _____
Assurance-vie (valeur de rachat) $ _____

Money owing to you $ _____
Sommes qui vous sont dues $ _____

Name of debtor _____
Nom du débiteur/de la débitrice

Personal property $ _____
Biens meubles $ _____

Cash $ _____
Argent comptant $ _____

Other $ _____
Autre $ _____

TOTAL VALUE OF ASSETS $ _____
VALEUR TOTALE DES AVOIRS $ _____

_____   _____
(Name / *Nom*)   (Signature)

SCR 9.03-20.10-20I (April 11, 2012 / *11 avril 2012*) CSD

APPENDIX 11.5   Examination of Individual Debtor

The following script is a list of standard questions to be used on a judgment debtor examination of an individual debtor. You will need to adapt it to the information provided by the debtor in the financial information form. When examining the debtor, remember to obtain documentary backup for as much information as possible. Any amount stated on the financial information form should be supported by documentation. Any statement made under oath during the examination should be supported by documentation, to the best of the debtor's ability to produce such documentation.

If the debtor fails to provide photocopies of documents such as a deed, mortgage/charge, apartment lease agreement, vehicle lease agreement, bank loans, or lines of credit, etc., request the judge's permission to keep and photocopy the originals, on your undertaking to return them in good order and within a reasonable time to the debtor.

PERSONAL INFORMATION

[Comments] _____

Full name: _____

Are you the same person as _____ ,

who owes money to _____ ,

according to this judgment in court file number _____ , dated _____ ?

Are the details contained in the financial information form you have provided true and complete?

☐ YES   ☐ NO _____

Do you ever use any other name(s)? ☐ YES   ☐ NO

If yes, what are they? _____

Birth date: _____ [birth certificate]

S.I.N.: _____ [social insurance card]

Home telephone: _____ Work telephone: _____

Home address: _____

Spousal status: ☐ Unmarried   ☐ Cohabiting   ☐ Married   ☐ Divorced   ☐ Separated

Name of spouse or partner (if any): _____

Dependants:

Name	Age	Relationship

APPENDIX 11.5 **Examination of Individual Debtor** *continued*

EMPLOYMENT STATUS AND INCOME

☐ Employed   ☐ Unemployed   ☐ Self-employed   ☐ Full-time   ☐ Part-time

If employed, name and address of employer: _____

_____

Name of person you report to: _____

Your position: _____ Salary: _____

[If the debtor is employed, you should ask for three recent pay stubs and tax returns for the past three years.]

Pay period: _____

Commissions, bonuses, etc.: _____

Length of time with current employer: _____

Length of time in current position: _____

Previous positions, and their duration, with this employer: _____

_____

Are you related in any way to your employer?   ☐ YES   ☐ NO

Do you have any sources of income other than employment income?   ☐ YES   ☐ NO

[If yes, obtain details and documentation. If the debtor has disclosed any other forms of income in the Monthly Income column on the file information form, confirm the amount for the record and obtain documentation or the debtor's undertaking to disclose documentation for each type of income.]

DEBTOR'S SPOUSE OR PARTNER

Full name: _____

Address: _____

Telephone: _____

☐ Employed   ☐ Unemployed   ☐ Self-employed   ☐ Full-time   ☐ Part-time

If employed, name and address of employer: _____

_____

Name of person spouse/partner reports to: _____

Spouse's/partner's position: _____

Spouse's/partner's salary:_____

[If the debtor's spouse/partner is employed, you should ask for three recent pay stubs.]

Pay period: _____

Commissions, bonuses, etc.: _____

Length of time with current employer: _____

Length of time in current position: _____

APPENDIX 11.5 **Examination of Individual Debtor** *continued*

MONTHLY EXPENSES

Rent/mortgage

☐ Lease ☐ Own Municipal address: _____

Details of ownership [copy of deed, mortgage/charge, recent mortgage statements]

Type of ownership (joint tenancy, tenant in common, etc.): _____

Date of purchase: _____

Particulars of purchase: _____ [closing letter]

Current value: _____ [market value of similar properties, recent notice of property tax assessment]

Mortgage payments

Amount: _____ When due: _____ Current balance due: _____

Do you own any other real estate? ☐ YES ☐ NO

[If yes, go through the above questions and documentary disclosure again.]

Details of leased residence [copy of tenancy agreement, plus notices of any legal rent increases]

Name of landlord/owner: _____

Address: _____

Rent: _____ Due date: _____

[If there is no tenancy agreement, ask for copies of cancelled rent cheques, money orders, receipts for cash.]

Are you related in any way to your landlord? ☐ YES ☐ NO

Who pays the rent?: _____ How is it paid?: _____

Rent arrears: ☐ YES ☐ NO If yes, amount: _____

Application to the Landlord and Tenant Board pending? ☐ YES ☐ NO

[notice of early termination, landlord application, etc.]

Other Monthly Expenses [must be supported by documentation]

For each of the following, confirm the monthly amount due and discover whether there any arrears.

Support payments: [copy of order plus three current pay stubs showing deduction]

Property taxes: [copy of recent tax bills]

Utilities, phone, cable, property insurance, etc.: [at least three recent invoices]

Motor vehicle (lease or loan): [purchase/loan documents or lease agreement]

Year, make, and model: _____

☐ Own Purchase price: _____ Balance owing on loan: _____

☐ Lease Monthly payments: _____ Balance owing: _____

APPENDIX 11.5 **Examination of Individual Debtor** *concluded*

Routine costs: [copy of most recent policy, etc.]

Insurance: _____   Plates: _____

Licence: _____   Maintenance: _____

Fuel: _____   Monthly payments (see below): _____

MONTHLY DEBTS

Credit card debts: [at least three months of statements]

Name of card: _____   Account number: _____

Amount owing: _____   Amount paid each month: _____

Bank or finance company loans: [at least three months of statements]

Particulars of debt: _____

Amount owing: _____   Amount paid each month: _____

VALUE OF ASSETS

Real estate equity (see above): _____

Automobile equity (see above): _____

Bank accounts: [statements and passbooks]

☐ Sole owner   ☐ Co-owner   Particulars: _____

Accounts receivable: [unpaid invoices or other proof of money owing]

Names and addresses of debtors and amounts owing

_____

_____

Life insurance (cash value):   [copy of policy]

Personal property:

☐ Sole owner   ☐ Co-owner   Particulars (chattel mortgage, free and clear): _____

Value: _____   Location: _____

LIST OF OTHER CREDITORS

For each creditor not mentioned above, obtain the following information:

- Name and address of creditor
- Security held (if any)
- Amount owed
- Judgment (if any), including amount and court file number

TRANSFER OF ASSETS

Assets sold within the past two years:

Obtain particulars of the sale, including purchaser, purchase price, date, etc.

[copy of contract or any other documents confirming the sale or transfer]

Assets transferred within the past two years:

Obtain terms of transfer, including transferee, date, terms of transfer, etc.

APPENDIX 11.6   Examination of Corporate Debtor

An officer or director of a corporate debtor will be examined on behalf of the corporation.

PRELIMINARY

Name: _____   Phone: _____

Address: _____

Position with the company: _____

Length of time in that position: _____

Are you an officer of [name of corporation] _____?

Are you aware of the amount owing to [name of creditor] _____,

pursuant to a judgment dated _____ , in court file number _____,

in [name of court] _____?

MINUTE BOOK

Location of minute books: _____

[Ask whether he/she will make the corporation minute books available to you if you wish to examine them.]

FINANCIAL STATEMENTS

Required for the current period: The books of accounting, general ledger, etc.

Required for the past five years:

- Particulars of revenues
- Salaries paid to officers and directors
- Loans, advances, or dividends to shareholders
- Any extraordinary expenses or revenues during the five-year period
- Whether company has returned any goods to creditors or paid creditors out of the normal course of business
- Bank statements

The company's current auditors/accountants/solicitors

Changes over the past five years

PARTICULARS OF CORPORATION

- Date of incorporation
- Original share issue (including kinds, numbers, and values of original shares)
- Original and past shareholders
- Current shareholders
- Was the corporation owned by one shareholder at any time
- Whether there is a shareholders' agreement (If yes, request that a copy be disclosed.)
- Details regarding share transfers
- Were the transferred shares paid for in full
- Original, past, and current directors and officers
- Office and premises:
  - Location
  - Owned or leased   [Request details and documentation.]
  - Did the company own the premises at any time
- Business:
  - Type of business
  - Details of the financial difficulties that caused the company to default on the debt
  - Has the company ceased to carry on business, and, if yes, on what date
- Other creditors:
  - Names and addresses of all secured creditors of the company, and the nature of their security
  - Names and addresses of all ordinary creditors of the company, including other execution creditors
  - Details of any money owed to a bank, an overdraft or bank loan; form of security held by the bank
  - Any mortgages or liens against vehicles, equipment, trade fixtures, inventory, or other assets of the company
- Corporate assets:
  - Real property
  - Motor vehicles
  - Machinery, equipment, tools, etc.
  - Inventory
  - Accounts receivable or other debts or obligations owing to the company

APPENDIX 11.7   Warrant of Committal (Form 20J)

ONTARIO

Superior Court of Justice
Cour supérieure de justice

Warrant of Committal
Mandat de dépôt

Form / *Formule* 20J Ont. Reg. No. / *Règl. de l'Ont.* : 258/98

Seal / *Sceau*

Sault Ste. Marie

Small Claims Court / *Cour des petites créances de*

**426 Queen Street East
Sault Ste. Marie, Ontario
P6A 2W2**

Address / *Adresse*

705 945 8000

Phone number / *Numéro de téléphone*

SC-00-81632-00

Claim No. / *N° de la demande*

BETWEEN / *ENTRE*

Emma Flood

Plaintiff(s) / *Demandeur(s)/demanderesse(s)*

and / *et*

Christine Michaeli

Defendant(s) / *Défendeur(s)/défenderesse(s)*

**TO ALL POLICE OFFICERS IN ONTARIO AND TO THE OFFICERS OF ALL CORRECTIONAL
INSTITUTIONS IN ONTARIO:**
*À TOUS LES AGENTS DE POLICE DE L'ONTARIO ET AUX AGENTS DE TOUS LES ÉTABLISSEMENTS
CORRECTIONNELS DE L'ONTARIO :*

THIS WARRANT IS FOR THE COMMITTAL OF / *LE PRÉSENT MANDAT EST DÉCERNÉ POUR
L'INCARCÉRATION DE*

Last name / *Nom de famille*			
Michaeli			
First name / *Premier prénom*	Second name / *Deuxième prénom*		Also known as / *Également connu(e) sous le nom de*
Christine			
Address (street number, apt., unit) / *Adresse (numéro et rue, app., unité)*			
55A Tranquillity Boulevard			
City/Town / *Cité/ville*	Province		Phone no. / *N° de téléphone*
Sault Ste. Marie	**Ontario**		**705 945 6789**
Postal code / *Code postal*			Fax no. / *N° de télécopieur*
P6S 1C5			

A Notice of Contempt Hearing was issued from this court which required
Un avis d'audience pour outrage a été délivré par le tribunal précité ordonnant à

Christine Michaeli

(Name of person required to attend contempt hearing / *Nom de la personne tenue de se présenter à l'audience pour outrage*)

to attend the sittings of this court at ____**9:30 a.m.**____ on ____**April 2**____, 20 **--** .
de se présenter aux séances du   (Time / *Heure*)   *le*   (Date)
tribunal à

At the contempt hearing, it was duly proven that the Notice of Contempt Hearing was properly served, and
*Lors de l'audience pour outrage, il a été dûment prouvé que l'avis d'audience pour outrage a été signifié en
bonne et due forme et*

SCR 20.11-20J (September 1, 2010 / *1ᵉʳ septembre 2010*) CSD

APPENDIX 11.7 **Warrant of Committal (Form 20J)** *concluded*

FORM / *FORMULE* **20J**   **PAGE 2**   SC-00-81632-00
                                                                          Claim No. / *N° de la demande*

this court found this person to be in contempt of court because he/she:
d'autre part, le tribunal a reconnu la personne susmentionnée coupable d'outrage au tribunal pour l'un des motifs suivants :

☒ wilfully failed to attend an examination hearing as required by a Notice of Examination (Form 20H), which was properly served.
elle a délibérément omis de se présenter à un interrogatoire comme l'exigeait un avis d'interrogatoire (formule 20H), qui a été signifié en bonne et due forme.

(Check appropriate box. / Cochez la case appropriée.)

☐ attended the examination hearing, refused to answer questions or produce documents or records, and failed to show cause why he/she should not be held in contempt for refusing to answer questions or produce documents or records.
elle s'est présentée à l'interrogatoire mais a refusé de répondre aux questions ou de produire des documents ou des dossiers et a omis de justifier pourquoi elle ne devrait pas être accusée pour outrage pour avoir refusé de répondre aux questions ou de produire des documents ou des dossiers.

At the contempt hearing, a judge of this court ordered this person to be committed.
Lors de l'audience pour outrage, un juge du tribunal a ordonné l'incarcération de la personne susmentionnée.

YOU ARE ORDERED to take the person named above to the nearest correctional institution and admit and
IL VOUS EST ORDONNÉ d'amener la personne susmentionnée à l'établissement correctionnel le plus proche

detain him or her there for _____ **five (5)** _____ days.
et de l'y admettre et l'y détenir pendant _____ *jours.*

This warrant expires twelve (12) months from the date of issue, unless renewed by court order. If renewed, the warrant expires twelve (12) months from the date of the renewal.
Le présent mandat expire douze (12) mois à compter de la date de sa délivrance, sauf si le tribunal le renouvelle par ordonnance. S'il est renouvelé, le mandat expire douze (12) mois à compter de la date du renouvellement.

_____ , 20 _____   _____
                                        (Signature of clerk / *Signature du greffier*)

SCR 20.11-20J (September 1, 2010 / *1ᵉʳ septembre 2010*) CSD

APPENDIX 11.7 Identification Form (Form 20K)

ONTARIO

Superior Court of Justice
Cour supérieure de justice

Identification Form
Formule de renseignements signalétiques
Form / *Formule* 20K Ont. Reg. No. / *Régl. de l'Ont.* : 258/98

Sault Ste. Marie | **SC-00-81632-00**
Small Claims Court / *Cour des petites créances de* | Claim No. / *N° de la demande*
426 Queen Street East
Sault Ste. Marie, Ontario
P6A 2W2

Address / *Adresse*

705 945 8000
Phone number / *Numéro de téléphone*

BETWEEN / *ENTRE*

Emma Flood
Plaintiff(s)/Creditor(s) / *Demandeur(s)/demanderesse(s)/Créancier(s)/créancière(s)*

and / *et*

Christine Michaeli
Defendant(s)/Debtor(s) / *Défendeur(s)/défenderesse(s)/Débiteur(s)/débitrice(s)*

TO HELP PROCESS A CIVIL WARRANT FOR COMMITTAL, the following information, or **as much information as is reasonably available should be provided**. This is necessary for the police to identify the person to be arrested. Without this information it will be difficult to enforce the warrant.
POUR FACILITER LA DÉLIVRANCE D'UN MANDAT DE DÉPÔT AU CIVIL, les renseignements suivants ou autant de renseignements qui sont raisonnablement disponibles devraient être fournis. Ces renseignements sont nécessaires pour que la police puisse identifier la personne à arrêter. Sans ces renseignements, il sera difficile d'exécuter le mandat.

1. Name   **Michaeli**   **Christine**
     Nom   (Last name of individual / *Nom de famille du particulier*)   (First name / *Premier prénom*)   (Second name / *Deuxième prénom*)

2. Also known as names (if any)   n/a
     Nom(s) sous lequel/lesquels la personne est également connue (le cas échéant)

3. Last known address and telephone number
     Dernière adresse connue et dernier numéro de téléphone connu
     55A Tranquillity Boulevard
     Sault Ste. Marie, Ontario P6S 1C5   **TEL: 705 945 6789**

4. (a) Date of birth *(d, m, y)*   **24 April 1988**
         Date de naissance (j, m, a)

5. Physical description
     Description physique

     (a) Gender **female**   (b) Height **5' 7"**   (c) Weight **160 lbs**   (d) Build **heavy set**
         Sexe   *Taille*   *Poids*   *Corpulence*

     (e) Colour of eyes **blue**   (f) Hair colour **black**   (g) Complexion **fair**
         Couleur des yeux   *Couleur des cheveux*   *Teint*

     (h) Clean-shaven **n/a**   (i) Wears glasses **No**
         Rasé de près   *Porte des lunettes*

     (j) Clothing habits and tastes   **Goth**
         Habitudes et goûts vestimentaires

SCR 20.11-20K (June 1, 2009 / *1er juin 2009*) CSD

APPENDIX 11.7 Identification Form (Form 20K) *concluded*

FORM / *FORMULE* **20K**   **PAGE 2**   SC-00-81632-00
                                                              Claim No. / *N° de la demande*

(k) Distinguishing marks, scars, tattoos, etc.   **multiple piercings, scorpion tattoo on upper right arm**
   Marques distinctives, cicatrices, tatouages, etc.

(l) Other   **Loud, distinctive laugh**
   Autre   (Specify / *Précisez.*)

6. Usual occupation   **Sales clerk, wait person, fashion designer**
   Profession habituelle

7. Last known place of employment   **The Portal (bar/night club), Thunder Bay, Ontario**
   Dernier lieu de travail connu

8. Vehicle description
   Description du véhicule

(a) Make, model and year   **n/a**   (b) Colour
   Marque, modèle et année   *Couleur*

(c) Licence plate number   Province or state
   Numéro de la plaque d'immatriculation   *Province ou État*

(d) Driver's licence number   Province or state
   Numéro du permis de conduire   *Province ou État*

(e) Distinguishing features on the vehicle (dents, car stereo, etc.)
   Caractéristiques distinctives du véhicule (bosses, autoradio, etc.)

9. Other information
   Autres renseignements

10. Photograph of the person provided in the box below, if available.
   Une photographie de la personne figure dans la case ci-dessous, si elle est disponible.

The information supplied above is true to the best of my knowledge and belief.
Au mieux de ma connaissance et de ce que je tiens pour véridique, les renseignements ci-dessus sont exacts.

(Signature of party / *Signature de la partie*)

Emma Flood

(Name of party / *Nom de la partie*)

April 5   , 20 --

APPENDIX 11.8   Affidavit for Enforcement Request (Form 20P)

ONTARIO

Superior Court of Justice
Cour supérieure de justice

Affidavit for Enforcement Request
Affidavit relatif à une demande d'exécution forcée
Form / *Formule* 20P Ont. Reg. No. / *Régl. de l'Ont.* : 258/98

Sault Ste. Marie
Small Claims Court / *Cour des petites créances de*
426 Queen Street East
Sault Ste. Marie, Ontario
P6A 2W2
Address / *Adresse*

705 945 8000
Phone number / *Numéro de téléphone*

SC-00-81632-00
Claim No. / *N° de la demande*

BETWEEN / *ENTRE*

Emma Flood
Plaintiff(s)/Creditor(s) / *Demandeur(s)/demanderesse(s)/Créancier(s)/créancière(s)*

and / *et*

Christine Michaeli
Defendant(s)/Debtor(s) / *Défendeur(s)/défenderesse(s)/Débiteur(s)/débitrice(s)*

My name is
Je m'appelle

Victor Oblomov
(Full name / *Nom et prénoms*)

I live in
J'habite à

Sault Ste. Marie, Ontario
(Municipality & province / *Municipalité et province*)

and I swear/affirm that the following is true:
et je déclare sous serment/j'affirme solennellement que les renseignements suivants sont véridiques :

1. **In this action, I am the**
    Dans la présente action, je suis le/la

    (Check one box only. / *Cochez une seule case.*)

    ☐ plaintiff/creditor.
    demandeur/demanderesse/créancier/créancière.

    ☒ representative of the plaintiff(s)/creditor(s).
    représentant(e) du/de la/des demandeur(s)/demanderesse(s)/créancier(s)/créancière(s).

    I make this affidavit in support of a request that the clerk of the court issue the following enforcement process(es):
    Je fais le présent affidavit à l'appui d'une demande visant à enjoindre au greffier du tribunal de délivrer l'acte ou les actes de procédure portant exécution forcée suivants :

    ☐ Certificate of Judgment (Form 20A) to the clerk of the
    Certificat de jugement (formule 20A), au greffier de la Cour des petites créances de
    Small Claims Court.

    (Name of court where the judgment is to be filed / *Nom du tribunal où le jugement doit être déposé*)

    ☐ Writ of Seizure and Sale of Personal Property (Form 20C) directed to the bailiff of
    Bref de saisie-exécution de biens meubles (formule 20C) adressé à l'huissier de la Cour des petites créances de
    Small Claims Court.

    (Name of court location / *Emplacement du tribunal*)

    ☐ Writ of Seizure and Sale of Land (Form 20D) directed to the sheriff of
    Bref de saisie-exécution de biens-fonds (formule 20D) adressé au shérif du/de la

    (Name of county/region in which the enforcement office is located / *Comté/région où est situé le bureau de l'exécution*)

APPENDIX 11.8 Affidavit for Enforcement Request (Form 20P) *continued*

FORM / *FORMULE* 20P	PAGE 2	SC-00-81632-00
		Claim No. / *N° de la demande*

☒ Notice of Garnishment (Form 20E)/Notice of Renewal of Garnishment (Form 20E.1).
Avis de saisie-arrêt (formule 20E)/Avis de renouvellement de la saisie-arrêt (formule 20E.1).

I believe that the garnishee   **Bank of North Ontario**
Je crois que le tiers saisi   (Name of garnishee / *Nom du tiers saisi*)

at   **77 Spirit Road North, Sault Ste. Marie, Ontario P5A 1Z2**
à/au   (Address of garnishee / *Adresse du tiers saisi*)

is indebted to the debtor or will become indebted to the debtor for the following reasons:
est ou sera redevable d'une dette au débiteur pour les motifs suivants :
                    Contents of savings account #8099.

The Notice will be served on the debtor   **Christine Michaeli**
L'avis sera signifié au débiteur,   (Name of debtor / *Nom du débiteur/de la débitrice*)

at   **55A Tranquillity Boulevard, Sault Ste. Marie, Ontario P6S 1C5**
à/au   (Address of debtor for service / *Adresse du débiteur/de la débitrice aux fins de signification*)

within five days of serving it on the garnishee.
dans les cinq jours qui suivent sa signification au tiers saisi.

☐ Notice of Examination (Form 20H).
Avis d'interrogatoire (formule 20H).

☐ Writ of Delivery (Form 20B).
Bref de délaissement (formule 20B).

☐ Other *(Set out the nature of your request):*
Autre (Indiquez la nature de votre demande) :

Complete this section if you are requesting a Writ of Delivery.
Remplissez la présente section si vous demandez un bref de délaissement.

2. An order for the delivery of the following personal property:
Une ordonnance de délaissement des biens meubles suivants :
(According to the court order, set out a description of the property to be delivered. Identify any marks or serial numbers. / Selon l'ordonnance du tribunal, donnez la description des biens qui doivent être restitués. Indiquez toute marque d'identification ou tout numéro de série y figurant.)

APPENDIX 11.8   **Affidavit for Enforcement Request (Form 20P)** *continued*

FORM / *FORMULE* 20P   PAGE 3   SC-00-81632-00

Claim No. / *N° de la demande*

was made in this action against: _____
a été rendue dans l'action contre :   (Name of person against whom the order was made / *Nom de la personne contre qui l'ordonnance a été rendue*)

on _____ , 20 ___ , in the _____
le   *à la Cour des petites*   (Name of court location where order was made / *Emplacement du tribunal où l'ordonnance a été rendue*)
                              créances de

Small Claims Court. Since the above listed personal property has not been delivered, I make this affidavit in support of a request that the clerk of the court issue a Writ of Delivery (Form 20B) to the bailiff of the
Étant donné que les biens meubles susmentionnés n'ont pas été restitués, je fais le présent affidavit à l'appui d'une demande visant à enjoindre au greffier du tribunal de délivrer un bref de délaissement (formule 20B) à l'huissier de la Cour des petites créances de

_____ Small Claims Court.

(Name of court location / *Emplacement du tribunal*)

Complete this section if you are requesting a Certificate of Judgment, Writ of Seizure and Sale of Personal Property, Writ of Seizure and Sale of Land, Notice of Garnishment, Notice of Renewal of Garnishment or Notice of Examination.
Remplissez la présente section si vous demandez un certificat de jugement, un bref de saisie-exécution de biens meubles, un bref de saisie-exécution de biens-fonds, un avis de saisie-arrêt, un avis de renouvellement de la saisie-arrêt ou un avis d'interrogatoire.

3. A judgment was made in this action against   Christine Michaeli
Un jugement a été rendu dans l'action contre   (Name of debtor(s) / *Nom du/de la/des débiteur(s)/débitrice(s)*)

on ___December 15___ , 20 _--_ in the
le   *à la Cour des petites créances de*

___Thunder Bay___   Small Claims Court
(Name of court where judgment was made / *Nom du tribunal où le jugement a été rendu*)

for the following sums:
à l'égard des sommes suivantes :

(A) **DEBT** $ _____8,000.00_____
    LA CRÉANCE $

(B) **PRE-JUDGMENT INTEREST** calculated
    LES INTÉRÊTS ANTÉRIEURS AU JUGEMENT calculés

    on the sum of $ _____8,000.00_____ at the rate of __2.5__ %
    sur la somme de $ *au taux de*   *pour cent*

    per annum from ___February 28___ , 20 _--_ to ___December 15___ , 20 _--_ ,
    par an du   *au*

    being _____290_____ days. $ _____158.90_____
    soit   *jours.* $

                            SUBTOTAL (Amount of Judgment) $ _____8,158.90_____
                            TOTAL PARTIEL (montant du jugement) $

(C) **COSTS** to date of judgment $ _____235.00_____
    LES DÉPENS à la date du jugement $

APPENDIX 11.8 Affidavit for Enforcement Request (Form 20P) *concluded*

FORM / *FORMULE* 20P   PAGE 4   SC-00-81632-00
_____
Claim No. / *N° de la demande*

(D) **TOTAL AMOUNT OF PAYMENTS RECEIVED FROM DEBTOR**
after judgment (if any)   (minus) $ _____ 0
LE MONTANT TOTAL DES PAIEMENTS REÇUS DU   *(moins)* $
DÉBITEUR après le jugement (le cas échéant)

(E) **POST-JUDGMENT INTEREST** to date calculated
LES INTÉRÊTS POSTÉRIEURS AU JUGEMENT à ce jour, calculés

on the sum of $ _____8,393.90_____ at the rate of __2.0__ %
sur la somme de $ *au taux de*   *pour cent*

per annum from __December 15__ , 20 _--_ to __July 3__ , 20 _--_ ,
par an du   *au*

being __200__ days. $ _____ 91.99
soit _____ *jours.* $

> **NOTE:** Calculation of interest is always on the amount owing from time to time as payments are received. This is true for both pre-judgment and post-judgment interest. Attach a separate sheet setting out how you calculated the total amount of any pre/post-judgment interest.
> **REMARQUE :** *Les intérêts doivent toujours être calculés sur la somme due. Le calcul doit tenir compte des paiements reçus de temps à autre. Ceci s'applique autant aux intérêts antérieurs au jugement qu'aux intérêts postérieurs au jugement. Annexez une feuille distincte indiquant comment vous avez calculé le montant total des intérêts antérieurs et postérieurs au jugement.*

(F) **SUBSEQUENT COSTS** incurred after judgment (including the cost of issuing
the requested enforcement(s)) $ _____ 154.00
LES DÉPENS SUBSÉQUENTS engagés après le jugement (y compris le $
coût de la délivrance de la ou des mesures d'exécution forcée demandées)

                                              TOTAL DUE $ 8,639.89
                                              SOLDE DÛ $

Sworn/Affirmed before me at _____ **Sault Ste. Marie**
Déclaré sous serment/Affirmé   (Municipality / *municipalité*)
solennellement devant moi à

in _____ **Ontario**
en/à/au   (Province, state or country / *province, État ou pays*)

on __July 3__ , 20 _--_ _____
le

                    Commissioner for taking affidavits
                    Commissaire aux affidavits
              (Type or print name below if signature is illegible.)
              (Dactylographiez le nom ou écrivez-le en caractères
              d'imprimerie ci-dessous si la signature est illisible.)

_____
Signature
(This form is to be signed in front of a
lawyer, justice of the peace, notary public
or commissioner for taking affidavits.)
(La présente formule doit être signée en
présence d'un avocat, d'un juge de paix, d'un
notaire ou d'un commissaire aux affidavits.)

WARNING: **IT IS AN OFFENCE UNDER THE *CRIMINAL CODE* TO KNOWINGLY SWEAR OR AFFIRM A FALSE AFFIDAVIT.**
AVERTISSEMENT : *FAIRE SCIEMMENT UN FAUX AFFIDAVIT CONSTITUE UNE INFRACTION AU CODE CRIMINEL.*

APPENDIX 11.8 Notice of Garnishment (Form 20E)

ONTARIO
Superior Court of Justice
Cour supérieure de justice

Notice of Garnishment
Avis de saisie-arrêt
Form / *Formule* 20E Ont. Reg. No. / *Règl. de l'Ont.* : 258/98

(Seal / *Sceau*)

Sault Ste. Marie

Small Claims Court / *Cour des petites créances de*
426 Queen Street East
Sault Ste. Marie, Ontario
P6A 6W2
Address / *Adresse*

705 945 8000
Phone number / *Numéro de téléphone*

SC-00-81632-00

Claim No. / *N° de la demande*

☐ Additional creditor(s) listed on the attached Form 1A.
Le ou les créanciers additionnels sont mentionnés sur la formule 1A ci-jointe.

Creditor / *Créancier*

Last name, or name of company / *Nom de famille ou nom de la compagnie* **Flood**		
First name / *Premier prénom* **Emma**	Second name / *Deuxième prénom*	Also known as / *Également connu(e) sous le nom de*
Address (street number, apt., unit) / *Adresse (numéro et rue, app., unité)* **c/o Victor Oblomov PC Attention: Victor Oblomov**		
City/Town / *Cité/ville*	Province	Phone no. / *N° de téléphone*
Postal code / *Code postal*		Fax no. / *N° de télécopieur*
Representative / *Représentant(e)* **Victor Oblomov PC Attention: Victor Oblomov**		LSUC # / *N° du BHC* ######
Address (street number, apt., unit) / *Adresse (numéro et rue, app., unité)* **648 Queen Street East**		
City/Town / *Cité/ville* **Sault Ste. Marie**	Province **Ontario**	Phone no. / *N° de téléphone* **705 945 8032**
Postal code / *Code postal* **P6A 6W4**		Fax no. / *N° de télécopieur* **705 945 8033**

Debtor / *Débiteur*

Last name, or name of company / *Nom de famille ou nom de la compagnie* **Michaeli**		
First name / *Premier prénom* **Christine**	Second name / *Deuxième prénom*	Also known as / *Également connu(e) sous le nom de*
Address (street number, apt., unit) / *Adresse (numéro et rue, app., unité)* **55A Tranquillity Boulevard**		
City/Town / *Cité/ville* **Sault Ste. Marie**	Province **Ontario**	Phone no. / *N° de téléphone* **705 945 6789**
Postal code / *Code postal* **P6S 1C5**		Fax no. / *N° de télécopieur*

Garnishee / *Tiers saisi*

Last name, or name of company / *Nom de famille ou nom de la compagnie* **Bank of North Ontario**		
First name / *Premier prénom*	Second name / *Deuxième prénom*	Also known as / *Également connu(e) sous le nom de*
Address (street number, apt., unit) / *Adresse (numéro et rue, app., unité)* **77 Spirit Road North**		
City/Town / *Cité/ville* **Sault Ste. Marie**	Province **Ontario**	Phone no. / *N° de téléphone* **705 945 5544**
Postal code / *Code postal* **P5A 1Z2**		Fax no. / *N° de télécopieur* **705 945 5545**

NOTE:	**THE CREDITOR SHALL SERVE THIS NOTICE** on the debtor with an Affidavit for Enforcement Request (Form 20P) and serve on the garnishee this notice with a blank Garnishee's Statement (Form 20F).
REMARQUE :	*LE CRÉANCIER SIGNIFIE LE PRÉSENT AVIS au débiteur conjointement avec un affidavit en vue d'une demande d'exécution (formule 20P) et signifie au tiers saisi le présent avis avec une déclaration du tiers saisi (formule 20F) en blanc.*

SCR 20.08-20E (September 1, 2010 / *1er septembre 2010*) CSD

APPENDIX 11.8 Notice of Garnishment (Form 20E) *continued*

FORM / *FORMULE* 20E PAGE 2 SC-00-81632-00

Claim No. / *N° de la demande*

TO THE GARNISHEE:
AU TIERS SAISI :

The creditor has obtained a court order against the debtor. The creditor claims that you owe or will owe the debtor a debt in the form of wages, salary, pension payments, rent, annuity or other debt that you pay out in a lump-sum, periodically or by instalments. (A debt to the debtor includes both a debt payable to the debtor alone and a joint debt payable to the debtor and one or more co-owners.)
Le créancier a obtenu une ordonnance du tribunal contre le débiteur. Le créancier prétend que vous êtes ou serez redevable au débiteur d'une dette sous forme de salaire, de prestations de retraite, de loyer, de rente ou autre que vous payez par somme forfaitaire, périodiquement ou par versements échelonnés. (Une dette envers le débiteur comprend à la fois une dette payable au débiteur seul et une dette payable conjointement au débiteur et à un ou plusieurs autres cotitulaires de la créance.)

YOU ARE REQUIRED TO PAY to the clerk of the _____ **Sault Ste. Marie** _____ Small Claims Court
VOUS ÊTES REQUIS(E) DE PAYER au greffier (Garnishment issuing court / *Tribunal qui prononce la*
de la Cour des petites créances de   *saisie-arrêt)*

   (a)   all debts now payable by you to the debtor, **within 10 days** after this notice is served on you; **and**
          d'une part, toutes les dettes dont vous êtes maintenant redevable au débiteur, dans les 10 jours qui suivent la signification du présent avis;

   (b)   all debts that become payable by you to the debtor after this notice is served on you and **within 6 years** after this notice is issued, **within 10 days** after they become payable.
          d'autre part, toutes les dettes dont vous deviendrez redevable au débiteur après la signification du présent avis et dans les 6 années qui suivent sa délivrance, dans les 10 jours qui suivent la date à laquelle elles deviennent exigibles.

The total amount of all your payments to the clerk is not to exceed $ _____ 8,639.89 .
La totalité des paiements que vous ferez au greffier ne doit pas dépasser (Amount unsatisfied / **$.**
Montant impayé)

THIS NOTICE IS LEGALLY BINDING ON YOU until it expires or is changed, renewed, terminated or satisfied. If you do not pay the total amount or such lesser amount as you are liable to pay, you must serve a Garnishee's Statement (Form 20F) on the creditor and debtor, and file it with the clerk within 10 days after this notice is served on you.
LE PRÉSENT AVIS VOUS LIE LÉGALEMENT jusqu'à ce qu'il expire ou qu'il soit modifié, renouvelé ou résilié, ou qu'il y soit satisfait. Si vous ne payez pas le montant total ou le montant moindre dont vous êtes redevable, vous devez signifier une déclaration du tiers saisi (formule 20F) au créancier et au débiteur et la déposer auprès du greffier dans les 10 jours qui suivent la signification du présent avis.

EACH PAYMENT, payable to the Minister of Finance, MUST BE SENT with a copy of the attached garnishee's payment notice to the clerk at the above court address.
CHAQUE PAIEMENT, libellé à l'ordre du ministre des Finances, DOIT ÊTRE ENVOYÉ au greffier, à l'adresse du tribunal indiquée ci-dessus, avec une copie de l'avis de paiement du tiers saisi ci-joint.

If your debt is jointly owed to the debtor and to one or more co-owners, you must pay the debtor's appropriate share of the amount now payable, or which becomes payable, or such a percentage as the court may order.
Si votre dette est payable conjointement au débiteur et à un ou plusieurs autres cotitulaires de la créance, vous devez payer la quote-part appropriée du débiteur du montant dont vous êtes maintenant redevable, ou qui devient redevable, ou le pourcentage que le tribunal ordonne.

SCR 20.08-20E (September 1, 2010 / *1er septembre 2010*) CSD   **Continued on next page /** *Suite à la page suivante*

APPENDIX 11.8 Notice of Garnishment (Form 20E) *continued*

FORM / *FORMULE* 20E   PAGE 3   SC-00-81632-00

                                                                Claim No. / *N° de la demande*

The amounts paid into court shall not exceed the portion of the debtor's wages that are subject to seizure or garnishment under Section 7 of the *Wages Act* (information available at: www.attorneygeneral.jus.gov.on.ca and www.e-laws.gov.on.ca). The portion of wages that can be garnished may be increased or decreased only by order of the court. If such a court order is attached to this notice or is served on you, you must follow the direction in that court order.

Les montants consignés au tribunal ne doivent pas dépasser la partie du salaire du débiteur qui peut faire l'objet d'une saisie ou d'une saisie-arrêt aux termes de l'article 7 de la Loi sur les salaires *(pour de plus amples renseignements, reportez-vous aux adresses : www.attorneygeneral.jus.gov.on.ca et www.lois-en-ligne.gouv.on.ca). La partie saisissable du salaire ne peut être augmentée ou réduite que sur ordonnance du tribunal. Si une telle ordonnance du tribunal est annexée au présent avis ou vous est signifiée, vous devez vous conformer à la directive qui y est énoncée.*

_____, 20 _____   _____

                                      (Signature of clerk / *Signature du greffier*)

CAUTION TO GARNISHEE:	**IF YOU FAIL TO PAY** to the clerk the amount set out in this notice and do not file a Garnishee's Statement (Form 20F) disputing garnishment, **JUDGMENT MAY BE OBTAINED AGAINST YOU BY THE CREDITOR** for payment of the amount set out above, plus costs. If you make a payment to anyone other than the clerk of the court, you may be liable to pay again [R. 20.08(17) and (18)].
AVERTISSEMENT AU TIERS SAISI :	*SI VOUS NE VERSEZ PAS au greffier le montant précisé dans le présent avis et ne déposez pas la déclaration du tiers saisi (formule 20F) contestant la saisie-arrêt, **LE CRÉANCIER PEUT OBTENIR CONTRE VOUS UN JUGEMENT** ordonnant le paiement du montant précisé ci-dessus et des dépens. Si vous effectuez un paiement à une personne qui n'est pas le greffier du tribunal, vous pouvez être tenu(e) de payer de nouveau [par. 20.08 (17) et (18)].*

NOTE:	Any party or interested person may complete and serve a Notice of Garnishment Hearing (Form 20Q) to determine any matter related to this notice. To obtain forms and self-help materials, attend the nearest Small Claims Court or access the following website: www.ontariocourtforms.on.ca.
REMARQUE :	*Toute partie ou personne intéressée peut remplir et signifier un avis d'audience sur la saisie-arrêt (formule 20Q) en vue de décider une question relative au présent avis. Vous pouvez obtenir les formules et la documentation à l'usage du client auprès de la Cour des petites créances de votre localité ou en consultant le site Web suivant : www.ontariocourtforms.on.ca.*

APPENDIX 11.8 Notice of Garnishment (Form 20E) *concluded*

FORM / *FORMULE* 20E   PAGE 4   SC-00-81632-00

Claim No. / *N° de la demande*

The top portion of the garnishee's payment notice, below, is to be completed by the creditor before the Notice of Garnishment is issued. Where it is anticipated that more than one payment will be made by the garnishee, the creditor should supply extra copies of the garnishee's payment notice. Additional copies of the garnishee's payment notice are available at court offices or online at www.ontariocourtforms.on.ca (see Form 20E or 20E.1). *Le créancier doit remplir la partie supérieure de l'avis de paiement du tiers saisi figurant ci-dessous avant la délivrance de l'avis de saisie-arrêt. S'il est prévu que le tiers saisi fera plus d'un paiement, le créancier doit fournir des exemplaires supplémentaires de l'avis de paiement du tiers saisi. Vous pouvez obtenir des exemplaires supplémentaires de l'avis de paiement du tiers saisi aux greffes des tribunaux ou en ligne à l'adresse www.ontariocourtforms.on.ca (consultez la formule 20E ou 20E.1).*

GARNISHEE'S PAYMENT NOTICE / *AVIS DE PAIEMENT DU TIERS SAISI*

Make payment by cheque or money order payable to the Minister of Finance and send it, along with this payment notice to the clerk of the court at the following address:
Effectuez le paiement par chèque ou mandat-poste à l'ordre du ministre des Finances et envoyez-le, avec une copie du présent avis de paiement, au greffier du tribunal à l'adresse suivante :

Court address: **Sault Ste. Marie**
Adresse du tribunal :

Claim No.:   **SC-00-81362-00**
N° de la demande :

Creditor: **Emma Flood**
Créancier/créancière :

Debtor: **Christine Michaeli**
Débiteur/débitrice :

Garnishee: **Bank of North Ontario**
Tiers saisi :

TO BE COMPLETED BY GARNISHEE FOR EACH PAYMENT
À *REMPLIR PAR LE TIERS SAISI LORS DE CHAQUE PAIEMENT*

Date of payment: _____ , 20 _____
Date du paiement :

Amount enclosed: $ _____
Montant inclus : $

APPENDIX 11.8 Garnishee's Statement (Form 20F)

ONTARIO
Superior Court of Justice
Cour supérieure de justice

Garnishee's Statement
Déclaration du tiers saisi
Form / Formule 20F Ont. Reg. No. / Régl. de l'Ont. : 258/98

Sault Ste. Marie
Small Claims Court / *Cour des petites créances de*
426 Queen Street East
Sault Ste.Marie, Ontario
P6A 6W2
Address / *Adresse*

705 945 8000
Phone number / *Numéro de téléphone*

SC-00-81632-00
Claim No. / *N° de la demande*

BETWEEN / *ENTRE*

Emma Flood

Creditor(s) / *Créancier(s)/créancière(s)*

and / *et*

Christine Michaeli

Debtor(s) / *Débiteur(s)/débitrice(s)*

Name of Garnishee
Nom du tiers saisi

(Full legal name of garnishee / *Nom et prénoms officiels du tiers saisi*)

A Notice of Garnishment was issued on _____, 20 -- , naming me/us as garnishee
Un avis de saisie-arrêt a été délivré le , *me/nous désignant comme tiers saisi(s)*

in relation to the debtor _____ .
en rapport avec le débiteur (Name of debtor / *Nom du/de la débiteur/débitrice*)

☐ **I/WE DO NOT OWE** and do not expect to owe to the debtor the amount set out in the Notice of Garnishment for the following reason(s):
JE NE SUIS/NOUS NE SOMMES PAS REDEVABLE(S) *et je ne m'attends/nous ne nous attendons pas à être redevable(s) au débiteur du montant énoncé dans l'avis de saisie-arrêt pour le ou les motifs suivants :*

☐ **I/WE OWE OR WILL OWE** the debtor (or the debtor and one or more co-owners), wages or periodic payments based on the terms explained below:
JE SUIS OU SERAI/NOUS SOMMES OU SERONS REDEVABLE(S) *au débiteur (ou au débiteur et à un ou plusieurs autres cotitulaires de la créance) des montants suivants exigibles à titre de salaire ou de versements périodiques et selon les modalités suivantes :*

(State the amount(s) and how often the debtor is paid. If the debtor is paid wages, state the gross amount of the debtor's wages before any deductions required by law and the net amount after those deductions, and attach a copy of a pay slip. If you owe or will owe the debtor a lump sum, state when and how much will be paid.)
(Indiquez le ou les montants et la fréquence des paiements faits au débiteur. Si le débiteur touche un salaire, indiquez son salaire brut avant les retenues que vous êtes tenu(e)(s) de déduire, selon la loi, ainsi que le montant net après les retenues, et annexez une copie d'un bordereau de paie. Si vous êtes ou serez redevable(s) d'une somme forfaitaire au débiteur, indiquez-en le montant et à quel moment le paiement sera effectué.)

SCR 20.08-20F (April 11, 2012 / *11 avril 2012*) CSD

Continued on next page / *Suite à la page suivante*

APPENDIX 11.8 Garnishee's Statement (Form 20F) *concluded*

FORM / *FORMULE* 20F   **PAGE 2**   **SC-00-81632-00**

Claim No. / *N° de la demande*

☐ **I/We are making payment of less than** the amount stated because the debt is owed to the debtor and to one or more co-owners, or for another reason explained below:
J'effectue/Nous effectuons un paiement inférieur au montant indiqué parce qu'il s'agit d'une dette envers le débiteur et envers un ou plusieurs autres cotitulaires de la créance, ou pour un autre motif indiqué ci-dessous :

(Identify the amount(s) and percentage owed to the debtor and each co-owner / Précisez le ou les montants et le pourcentage redevable au débiteur et à chaque autre cotitulaire de la créance)

Co-owner(s) of the debt:
Cotitulaire(s) de la créance :   (Full legal name(s) / *Nom et prénoms officiels*)

(Address (street & number, unit, municipality, province) / Adresse (numéro et rue, unité, municipalité, province))

☐ **I/We are not making a payment at this time or are making a payment of less than the amount stated** because I/we have been served with other notice(s) of garnishment against the debtor. (Provide details below.)
Je n'effectue/Nous n'effectuons aucun paiement présentement ou j'effectue/nous effectuons un paiement inférieur au montant indiqué parce que j'ai/nous avons reçu signification d'un ou de plusieurs autres avis de saisie-arrêt contre le débiteur. (Donnez-en les détails ci-dessous.)

Name of creditor *Nom du créancier*	Name of issuing court *Nom du tribunal délivreur*	Location of court or Sheriff's Office where payment is currently being made *Emplacement du tribunal ou bureau du shérif où le paiement est actuellement effectué*	Date Notice of Garnishment received *Date de réception de l'avis de saisie-arrêt*

☐ **I/We will dispute the garnishment** by completing and serving a Notice of Garnishment Hearing (Form 20Q) on the creditor, debtor and co-owner(s) of the debt (if any) and any other interested person, and filing it with the clerk of the court.
Je contesterai/Nous contesterons la saisie-arrêt en remplissant et en signifiant un avis d'audience sur la saisie-arrêt (formule 20Q) au créancier, au débiteur et au(x) cotitulaire(s) de la créance (le cas échéant) et à tout autre intéressé et en le déposant auprès du greffier du tribunal.

_____ , 20 _____   _____

(Signature of garnishee or representative / Signature du tiers saisi ou du/de la représentant(e))

_____

(Address, phone and fax number of garnishee or representative / Adresse, numéro de téléphone et de télécopieur du tiers saisi ou du/de la représentant(e))

NOTE TO GARNISHEE: ***REMARQUE AU TIERS SAISI :***	The garnishee must serve a copy of the Garnishee's Statement on the creditor and the debtor and file it with the court. You can get an electronic version of this form online at www.ontariocourtforms.on.ca. *Le tiers saisi doit signifier une copie de la déclaration du tiers saisi au créancier et au débiteur et la déposer auprès du tribunal. Vous pouvez obtenir une version électronique de la présente formule en ligne à l'adresse www.ontariocourtforms.on.ca.*

NOTE TO CREDITOR: ***REMARQUE AU CRÉANCIER :***	A creditor who is served with a Garnishee's Statement must send it to the co-owners of the debt, if any, together with a Notice to Co-owner of Debt (Form 20G). You can get forms at court offices or online at www.ontariocourtforms.on.ca. *Le créancier qui reçoit signification de la déclaration du tiers saisi doit la faire parvenir aux cotitulaires de la créance, le cas échéant, avec l'avis au cotitulaire d'une créance (formule 20G). Vous pouvez obtenir des formules aux greffes des tribunaux ou en ligne à l'adresse www.ontariocourtforms.on.ca.*

SCR 20.08-20F (April 11, 2012 / *11 avril 2012*) CSD

APPENDIX 11.9 Garnishee's Statement (Form 20F)

ONTARIO
Superior Court of Justice
Cour supérieure de justice

Garnishee's Statement
Déclaration du tiers saisi
Form / Formule 20F Ont. Reg. No. / Règl. de l'Ont. : 258/98

Sault Ste. Marie
Small Claims Court / *Cour des petites créances de*
426 Queen Street East
Sault Ste. Marie, Ontario
P6A 6W2
Address / *Adresse*

705 945 8000
Phone number / *Numéro de téléphone*

SC-00-81632-00
Claim No. / *N° de la demande*

BETWEEN / *ENTRE*

Emma Flood

Creditor(s) / *Créancier(s)/créancière(s)*

and / *et*

Christine Michaeli

Debtor(s) / *Débiteur(s)/débitrice(s)*

Name of Garnishee   **Bank of North Ontario**
Nom du tiers saisi   (Full legal name of garnishee / *Nom et prénoms officiels du tiers saisi*)

A Notice of Garnishment was issued on   **July 3**   , 20 **--** , naming me/us as garnishee
Un avis de saisie-arrêt a été délivré le   , *me/nous désignant comme tiers saisi(s)*

in relation to the debtor   **Christine Michaeli**   .
en rapport avec le débiteur   (Name of debtor / *Nom du/de la débiteur/débitrice*)

☐ **I/WE DO NOT OWE** and do not expect to owe to the debtor the amount set out in the Notice of Garnishment
for the following reason(s):
*JE NE SUIS/NOUS NE SOMMES PAS REDEVABLE(S) et je ne m'attends/nous ne nous attendons pas à
être redevable(s) au débiteur du montant énoncé dans l'avis de saisie-arrêt pour le ou les motifs suivants :*

☒ **I/WE OWE OR WILL OWE** the debtor (or the debtor and one or more co-owners), wages or periodic
payments based on the terms explained below:
*JE SUIS OU SERAI/NOUS SOMMES OU SERONS REDEVABLE(S) au débiteur (ou au débiteur et à un ou
plusieurs autres cotitulaires de la créance) des montants suivants exigibles à titre de salaire ou de
versements périodiques et selon les modalités suivantes :*

*(State the amount(s) and how often the debtor is paid. If the debtor is paid wages, state the gross amount of the debtor's wages before
any deductions required by law and the net amount after those deductions, and attach a copy of a pay slip. If you owe or will owe the
debtor a lump sum, state when and how much will be paid.)*
*(Indiquez le ou les montants et la fréquence des paiements faits au débiteur. Si le débiteur touche un salaire, indiquez son salaire brut
avant les retenues que vous êtes tenu(e)(s) de déduire, selon la loi, ainsi que le montant net après les retenues, et annexez une copie
d'un bordereau de paie. Si vous êtes ou serez redevable(s) d'une somme forfaitaire au débiteur, indiquez-en le montant et à quel
moment le paiement sera effectué.)*

SCR 20.08-20F (April 11, 2012 / *11 avril 2012*) CSD

Continued on next page / *Suite à la page suivante*

APPENDIX 11.9 Garnishee's Statement (Form 20F) *concluded*

FORM / *FORMULE* 20F PAGE 2 SC-00-81632-00
Claim No. / *N° de la demande*

☒ **I/We are making payment of less than** the amount stated because the debt is owed to the debtor and to one or more co-owners, or for another reason explained below:
J'effectue/Nous effectuons un paiement inférieur au montant indiqué parce qu'il s'agit d'une dette envers le débiteur et envers un ou plusieurs autres cotitulaires de la créance, ou pour un autre motif indiqué ci-dessous :

Amount owed to debtor = $843.45 (50%); amount owed to co-owner = $843.45 (50%)
(Identify the amount(s) and percentage owed to the debtor and each co-owner / *Précisez le ou les montants et le pourcentage redevable au débiteur et à chaque autre cotitulaire de la créance*)

Co-owner(s) of the debt: **Anton Zupetti**
Cotitulaire(s) de la créance : (Full legal name(s) / *Nom et prénoms officiels*)

55A Tranquillity Boulevard, Sault Ste. Marie, Ontario P6S 1C5
(Address (street & number, unit, municipality, province) / *Adresse (numéro et rue, unité, municipalité, province)*)

☐ **I/We are not making a payment at this time or are making a payment of less than the amount stated** because I/we have been served with other notice(s) of garnishment against the debtor. (Provide details below.)
Je n'effectue/Nous n'effectuons aucun paiement présentement ou j'effectue/nous effectuons un paiement inférieur au montant indiqué parce que j'ai/nous avons reçu signification d'un ou de plusieurs autres avis de saisie-arrêt contre le débiteur. (Donnez-en les détails ci-dessous.)

Name of creditor *Nom du créancier*	Name of issuing court *Nom du tribunal délivreur*	Location of court or Sheriff's Office where payment is currently being made *Emplacement du tribunal ou bureau du shérif où le paiement est actuellement effectué*	Date Notice of Garnishment received *Date de réception de l'avis de saisie-arrêt*

☐ **I/We will dispute the garnishment** by completing and serving a Notice of Garnishment Hearing (Form 20Q) on the creditor, debtor and co-owner(s) of the debt (if any) and any other interested person, and filing it with the clerk of the court.
Je contesterai/Nous contesterons la saisie-arrêt en remplissant et en signifiant un avis d'audience sur la saisie-arrêt (formule 20Q) au créancier, au débiteur et au(x) cotitulaire(s) de la créance (le cas échéant) et à tout autre intéressé et en le déposant auprès du greffier du tribunal.

July 11 , 20 --

(Signature of garnishee or representative / *Signature du tiers saisi ou du/de la représentant(e)*)
Bank of North Ontario Attention: Jacob Marley
77 Spirit Road North, Sault Ste. Marie, Ontario P5A 1Z2
TEL: 705 945 5544   FAX: 705 945 5545
(Address, phone and fax number of garnishee or representative / *Adresse, numéro de téléphone et de télécopieur du tiers saisi ou du/de la représentant(e)*)

NOTE TO GARNISHEE: The garnishee must serve a copy of the Garnishee's Statement on the creditor and the debtor and file it with the court. You can get an electronic version of this form online at www.ontariocourtforms.on.ca.
REMARQUE AU TIERS SAISI : *Le tiers saisi doit signifier une copie de la déclaration du tiers saisi au créancier et au débiteur et la déposer auprès du tribunal. Vous pouvez obtenir une version électronique de la présente formule en ligne à l'adresse www.ontariocourtforms.on.ca.*

NOTE TO CREDITOR: A creditor who is served with a Garnishee's Statement must send it to the co-owners of the debt, if any, together with a Notice to Co-owner of Debt (Form 20G). You can get forms at court offices or online at www.ontariocourtforms.on.ca.
REMARQUE AU CRÉANCIER : *Le créancier qui reçoit signification de la déclaration du tiers saisi doit la faire parvenir aux cotitulaires de la créance, le cas échéant, avec l'avis au cotitulaire d'une créance (formule 20G). Vous pouvez obtenir des formules aux greffes des tribunaux ou en ligne à l'adresse www.ontariocourtforms.on.ca.*

SCR 20.08-20F (April 11, 2012 / *11 avril 2012*) CSD

APPENDIX 11.9   Notice to Co-owner of Debt (Form 20G)

ONTARIO

Superior Court of Justice
Cour supérieure de justice

Notice to Co-owner of Debt
Avis au cotitulaire d'une créance
Form / *Formule* 20G Ont. Reg. No. / *Régl. de l'Ont.* : 258/98

Sault Ste. Marie	SC-00-81632-00
Small Claims Court / *Cour des petites créances de*	Claim No. / *N° de la demande*
426 Queen Street East	
Sault Ste. Marie, Ontario	
P6A 6W2	
Address / *Adresse*	
705 945 8000	
Phone number / *Numéro de téléphone*	

☐ Additional creditor(s) listed on the attached Form 1A.
Le ou les créanciers additionnels sont mentionnés sur la formule 1A ci-jointe.

Creditor / *Créancier*

Last name, or name of company / *Nom de famille ou nom de la compagnie*		
Flood		
First name / *Premier prénom*	Second name / *Deuxième prénom*	Also known as / *Également connu(e) sous le nom de*
Emma		
Address (street number, apt., unit) / *Adresse (numéro et rue, app., unité)*		
c/o Victor Oblomov PC Attention: Victor Oblomov		
City/Town / *Cité/ville*	Province	Phone no. / *N° de téléphone*
Postal code / *Code postal*		Fax no. / *N° de télécopieur*
Representative / *Représentant(e)*		LSUC # / *N° du BHC*
Victor Oblomov PC Attention: Victor Oblomov		######
Address (street number, apt., unit) / *Adresse (numéro et rue, app., unité)*		
648 Queen Street East		
City/Town / *Cité/ville*	Province	Phone no. / *N° de téléphone*
Sault Ste. Marie	Ontario	705 945 8032
Postal code / *Code postal*		Fax no. / *N° de télécopieur*
P6A 6W4		705 945 8033

Debtor / *Débiteur*

Last name, or name of company / *Nom de famille ou nom de la compagnie*		
Michaeli		
First name / *Premier prénom*	Second name / *Deuxième prénom*	Also known as / *Également connu(e) sous le nom de*
Christine		
Address (street number, apt., unit) / *Adresse (numéro et rue, app., unité)*		
55A Tranquillity Boulevard		
City/Town / *Cité/ville*	Province	Phone no. / *N° de téléphone*
Sault Ste. Marie	Ontario	705 945 6789
Postal code / *Code postal*		Fax no. / *N° de télécopieur*
P6S 1C5		

Garnishee / *Tiers saisi*

Last name, or name of company / *Nom de famille ou nom de la compagnie*		
Bank of North Ontario Attention: Jacob Marley		
First name / *Premier prénom*	Second name / *Deuxième prénom*	Also known as / *Également connu(e) sous le nom de*
Address (street number, apt., unit) / *Adresse (numéro et rue, app., unité)*		
77 Spirit Road North		
City/Town / *Cité/ville*	Province	Phone no. / *N° de téléphone*
Sault Ste. Marie	Ontario	705 945 5544
Postal code / *Code postal*		Fax no. / *N° de télécopieur*
P5A 1Z2		

NOTE:	**THIS NOTICE SHALL BE SERVED BY THE CREDITOR** on each co-owner of debt together with a copy of the Garnishee's Statement (Form 20F) received from the garnishee.
REMARQUE :	*LE CRÉANCIER SIGNIFIE LE PRÉSENT AVIS à chaque cotitulaire d'une créance conjointement avec une copie de la déclaration du tiers saisi (formule 20F) qu'il reçoit du tiers saisi.*

SCR 20.08-20G (September 1, 2010 / *1er septembre 2010*) CSD

APPENDIX 11.9 Notice to Co-owner of Debt (Form 20G) *concluded*

FORM / *FORMULE* 20G	PAGE 2	SC-00-81632-00

Claim No. / *N° de la demande*

TO:
DESTINATAIRE :

(Attach a separate sheet, in the same format, for additional co-owners of debt. / Annexez une autre feuille, présentée selon le même format, en cas d'autres cotitulaires de la créance.)

Name of co-owner(s) of debt / *Nom du ou des cotitulaires de la créance*
Anton Zupetti

Street and number / *Numéro et rue*
55A Tranquillity Boulevard

City, province, postal code / *Ville, province, code postal*
Sault Ste. Marie, Ontario P6S 1C5

The creditor has obtained a court order against the debtor. The creditor has served a Notice of Garnishment
Le créancier a obtenu une ordonnance du tribunal contre le débiteur. Le créancier a signifié un avis de saisie-arrêt

(Form 20E), dated _____ July 3 _____ , 20 -- , on _____ Bank of North Ontario _____ ,
(formule 20E), daté du _____ *à* _____ (Name of garnishee / *Nom du tiers saisi*)

claiming that the garnishee owes or will owe the debtor a debt in the form of wages, salary, pension payments, rent, annuity, or other debt that the garnishee pays out in a lump-sum, periodically or by instalments. (A debt to the debtor includes both a debt payable to the debtor alone and a joint debt payable to the debtor and one or more co-owners.)
dans lequel il prétend que le tiers saisi est ou sera redevable au débiteur d'une dette sous forme de salaire, de prestations de retraite, de loyer, de rente ou autre que le tiers saisi paie par somme forfaitaire, périodiquement ou par versements échelonnés. (Une dette envers le débiteur comprend à la fois une dette payable au débiteur seul et une dette payable conjointement au débiteur et à un ou plusieurs autres cotitulaires de la créance.)

The garnishee has set out in the attached Garnishee's Statement (Form 20F) that you are a co-owner of debt. Under the Notice of Garnishment, the garnishee has paid or will pay to the clerk of the Small Claims Court the appropriate share of the amount payable or such a percentage as the court may order.
Le tiers saisi a indiqué dans la déclaration du tiers saisi annexée (formule 20F) que vous êtes un cotitulaire de la créance. Aux termes de l'avis de saisie-arrêt, le tiers saisi a payé ou paiera au greffier de la Cour des petites créances la quote-part appropriée du montant redevable ou le pourcentage que le tribunal ordonne.

IF YOU HAVE A CLAIM to the money being paid to the clerk of the Small Claims Court by the garnishee, you have 30 days from service of this notice to request a garnishment hearing by completing and serving a Notice of Garnishment Hearing (Form 20Q) on the creditor, debtor and garnishee, and filing it with the clerk. If you fail to do so, you are not entitled to dispute the enforcement of the creditor's order for the payment or recovery of money and the funds may be paid out to the creditor unless the court orders otherwise.
SI VOUS PRÉTENDEZ AVOIR UN DROIT sur l'argent que le tiers saisi verse au greffier de la Cour des petites créances, vous disposez de 30 jours à compter de la signification du présent avis pour demander une audience sur la saisie-arrêt en remplissant et en signifiant un avis d'audience sur la saisie-arrêt (formule 20Q) au créancier, au débiteur et au tiers saisi, et en le déposant auprès du greffier. Si vous ne le faites pas, vous n'aurez pas le droit par la suite de contester l'exécution forcée de l'ordonnance obtenue par le créancier en vue du paiement ou du recouvrement de sommes d'argent et ces sommes pourront être remises au créancier, sauf ordonnance contraire du tribunal.

To obtain forms and self-help materials, attend the nearest Small Claims Court or access the following website: www.ontariocourtforms.on.ca.
Vous pouvez obtenir les formules et la documentation à l'usage du client auprès de la Cour des petites créances de votre localité ou en consultant le site Web suivant : www.ontariocourtforms.on.ca.

_____ July 16 _____ , 20 -- _____

(Signature of creditor or representative / *Signature du créancier/de la créancière ou du/de la représentant(e)*)

NOTE:	Within seven (7) calendar days of changing your address for service, notify the court and all other parties in writing.
REMARQUE :	*Dans les sept (7) jours civils qui suivent tout changement de votre adresse aux fins de signification, veuillez en aviser par écrit le tribunal et les autres parties.*

SCR 20.08-20G (September 1, 2010 / *1er septembre 2010*) CSD

APPENDIX 11.9 Notice of Garnishment Hearing (Form 20Q)

ONTARIO

Superior Court of Justice
Cour supérieure de justice

Notice of Garnishment Hearing
Avis d'audience sur la saisie-arrêt
Form / *Formule* 20Q Ont. Reg. No. / *Règl. de l'Ont.* : 258/98

Sault Ste. Marie

Small Claims Court / *Cour des petites créances de*
426 Queen Street East
Sault Ste. Marie, Ontario
P6A 6W2

Address / *Adresse*

705 945 8000

Phone number / *Numéro de téléphone*

SC-00-81632-00

Claim No. / *N° de la demande*

☐ Additional creditor(s) listed on the attached Form 1A.
Le ou les créanciers additionnels sont mentionnés sur la formule 1A ci-jointe.

Creditor / *Créancier*

Last name, or name of company / *Nom de famille ou nom de la compagnie*		
Flood		
First name / *Premier prénom*	Second name / *Deuxième prénom*	Also known as / *Également connu(e) sous le nom de*
Emma		
Address (street number, apt., unit) / *Adresse (numéro et rue, app., unité)*		
c/o Victor Oblomov PC Attention: Victor Oblomov		
City/Town / *Cité/ville*	Province	Phone no. / *N° de téléphone*
Postal code / *Code postal*		Fax no. / *N° de télécopieur*
Representative / *Représentant(e)*		LSUC # / *N° du BHC*
Victor Oblomov PC Attention: Victor Oblomov		
Address (street number, apt., unit) / *Adresse (numéro et rue, app., unité)*		
648 Queen Street East		
City/Town / *Cité/ville*	Province	Phone no. / *N° de téléphone*
Sault Ste. Marie	**Ontario**	**705 945 8032**
Postal code / *Code postal*		Fax no. / *N° de télécopieur*
P6A 6W4		**705 945 8033**

Debtor / *Débiteur*

Last name, or name of company / *Nom de famille ou nom de la compagnie*		
Michaeli		
First name / *Premier prénom*	Second name / *Deuxième prénom*	Also known as / *Également connu(e) sous le nom de*
Christine		
Address (street number, apt., unit) / *Adresse (numéro et rue, app., unité)*		
55A Tranquillity Boulevard		
City/Town / *Cité/ville*	Province	Phone no. / *N° de téléphone*
Sault Ste. Marie	**Ontario**	**705 945 6789**
Postal code / *Code postal*		Fax no. / *N° de télécopieur*
P6S 1C5		
Representative / *Représentant(e)*		LSUC # / *N° du BHC*
Address (street number, apt., unit) / *Adresse (numéro et rue, app., unité)*		
City/Town / *Cité/ville*	Province	Phone no. / *N° de téléphone*
Postal code / *Code postal*		Fax no. / *N° de télécopieur*

NOTE:	The Notice of Garnishment Hearing must be served by the person requesting the hearing on the creditor, debtor, garnishee, co-owner of debt, if any, and any other interested person [R. 8.01(9)].
REMARQUE :	*L'avis d'audience sur la saisie-arrêt doit être signifié par la personne qui demande l'audience au créancier, au débiteur, au tiers saisi et au cotitulaire de la créance, le cas échéant, et à tout autre intéressé [par. 8.01 (9)].*

SCR 20.08-20Q (September 1, 2010 / *1er septembre 2010*) CSD

APPENDIX 11.9 Notice of Garnishment Hearing (Form 20Q) *continued*

FORM / *FORMULE* 20Q	PAGE 2	SC-00-81632-00
		Claim No. / *N° de la demande*

Garnishee / *Tiers saisi*

Last name, or name of company / *Nom de famille ou nom de la compagnie*		
Bank of North Ontario Attention: Jacob Marley		

First name / *Premier prénom*	Second name / *Deuxième prénom*	Also known as / *Également connu(e) sous le nom de*

Address (street number, apt., unit) / *Adresse (numéro et rue, app., unité)*		
77 Spirit Road North		

City/Town / *Cité/ville*	Province	Phone no. / *N° de téléphone*
Sault Ste. Marie	Ontario	705 945 5544

Postal code / *Code postal*	Fax no. / *N° de télécopieur*
P5A 1Z2	705 945 5545

Representative / *Représentant(e)*	LSUC # / *N° du BHC*

Address (street number, apt., unit) / *Adresse (numéro et rue, app., unité)*	

City/Town / *Cité/ville*	Province	Phone no. / *N° de téléphone*

Postal code / *Code postal*	Fax no. / *N° de télécopieur*

Co-Owner of Debt (if any) /
Cotitulaire d'une créance (le cas échéant)

☐ Additional co-owner(s) listed on attached Form 1A.
Le ou les cotitulaires additionnels sont mentionnés sur la formule 1A ci-jointe.

Last name, or name of company / *Nom de famille ou nom de la compagnie*		
Zupetti		

First name / *Premier prénom*	Second name / *Deuxième prénom*	Also known as / *Également connu(e) sous le nom de*
Anton		

Address (street number, apt., unit) / *Adresse (numéro et rue, app., unité)*		
55A Tranquillity Boulevard		

City/Town / *Cité/ville*	Province	Phone no. / *N° de téléphone*
Sault Ste. Marie	Ontario	705 945 6789

Postal code / *Code postal*	Fax no. / *N° de télécopieur*
P6S 1C5	

Representative / *Représentant(e)*	LSUC # / *N° du BHC*

Address (street number, apt., unit) / *Adresse (numéro et rue, app., unité)*	

City/Town / *Cité/ville*	Province	Phone no. / *N° de téléphone*

Postal code / *Code postal*	Fax no. / *N° de télécopieur*

Other Interested Person (if any) /
Autre intéressé (le cas échéant)

☐ Additional interested person(s) listed on attached Form 1A.
Le ou les intéressés additionnels sont mentionnés sur la formule 1A ci-jointe.

Last name, or name of company / *Nom de famille ou nom de la compagnie*		

First name / *Premier prénom*	Second name / *Deuxième prénom*	Also known as / *Également connu(e) sous le nom de*

Address (street number, apt., unit) / *Adresse (numéro et rue, app., unité)*		

City/Town / *Cité/ville*	Province	Phone no. / *N° de téléphone*

Postal code / *Code postal*	Fax no. / *N° de télécopieur*

Representative / *Représentant(e)*	LSUC # / *N° du BHC*

Address (street number, apt., unit) / *Adresse (numéro et rue, app., unité)*	

City/Town / *Cité/ville*	Province	Phone no. / *N° de téléphone*

Postal code / *Code postal*	Fax no. / *N° de télécopieur*

Continued on next page / *Suite à la page suivante*

FORM / *FORMULE* 20Q   PAGE 3   SC-00-81632-00

Claim No. / *N° de la demande*

TO THE PARTIES:
AUX PARTIES :

(The person requesting this garnishment hearing or the person's representative must contact the clerk of the court to choose a time and date when the court could hold this garnishment hearing. / *La personne qui demande l'audience sur la saisie-arrêt ou son représentant doit communiquer avec le greffier du tribunal pour choisir la date et l'heure où le tribunal pourrait tenir cette audience.*)

THIS COURT WILL HOLD A GARNISHMENT HEARING on   August 15   , 20 -- , at
LE TRIBUNAL PRÉCITÉ TIENDRA UNE AUDIENCE SUR LA SAISIE-ARRÊT le   , à

, or as soon as possible after that

   9:30 a.m.   **time, at**   (Address of court location and courtroom number)
(Time / *heure*)   *, ou dès que possible par la suite, à/au*   (*Adresse du tribunal et numéro de la salle d'audience*)

26 Queen Street East
Sault Ste. Marie, Ontario P6A 6W2
Courtroom 8D

because (*Check the appropriate box.*)
parce que (*Cochez la case appropriée.*)

☐ the creditor   ☐ the debtor   ☐ the garnishee   ☒ the co-owner of debt
   le créancier   *le débiteur*   *le tiers saisi*   *le cotitulaire d'une créance*

☐ other interested person:
   une autre personne intéressée :   (Specify / *Précisez.*)

states the following: (*In numbered paragraphs, provide details of your dispute and the order(s) requested.*)
déclare ce qui suit :   (*Donnez, sous forme de paragraphes numérotés, le détail de votre contestation et l'ordonnance ou les ordonnances demandées.*)

1. I am the co-owner of savings account 8099 at the Bank of North America, Spirit Road branch, with my partner, Christine Michaeli.

2. I am a trained instructor of Bikram yoga (also known as "hot yoga"). I am currently employed by the Hot Yoga and Meditation Centre at 101 Spirit Road, Unit 8, Sault Ste. Marie, Ontario P5A 2Y3. My employment income is approximately $1,950.00 per month before deductions. I earn additional income by teaching extra classes from time to time. I have attached copies of all pay statements for the past six months to this form.

3. Christine has been employed part-time at Hot Yoga as a receptionist for the past three months. Her income is approximately $900.00 per month before deductions. Prior to that she was unemployed with no sources of income. I was her sole support.

4. By the time Christine has paid for rent and food every month, she has nothing left. I help her with her other living expenses.

5 For the past year, I have made deposits to the savings account whenever I can afford to. Christine has contributed nothing to the savings account. All of the money in the savings account is mine.

☐ **Additional pages are attached because more space was needed.**
Des feuilles supplémentaires sont annexées en raison du manque d'espace.

   July 24   , 20 --

(Signature of party or representative / *Signature de la partie ou du/de la représentant(e)*)

NOTE:	If you fail to attend this garnishment hearing, an order may be made in your absence and enforced against you.
REMARQUE :	*Si vous ne vous présentez pas à cette audience sur la saisie-arrêt, une ordonnance peut être rendue en votre absence et être exécutée contre vous.*

SCR 20.08-20Q (September 1, 2010 / *1er septembre 2010*) CSD

APPENDIX 11.10   Notice of Termination of Garnishment (Form 20R)

ONTARIO

Superior Court of Justice
Cour supérieure de justice

Notice of Termination of Garnishment
Avis de mainlevée de la saisie-arrêt
Form / *Formule* 20R Ont. Reg. No. / *Régl. de l'Ont.* : 258/98

Sault Ste. Marie

Small Claims Court / *Cour des petites créances de*
426 Queen Street East
Sault Ste. Marie, Ontario
P6A 6W2
Address / *Adresse*

705 945 8000
Phone number / *Numéro de téléphone*

SC-00-81632-00
Claim No. / *N° de la demande*

BETWEEN / *ENTRE*

Emma Flood

Creditor(s) / *Créancier(s)/créancière(s)*

and / *et*

Christine Michaeli

Debtor(s) / *Débiteur(s)/débitrice(s)*

TO
À

Hot Yoga and Meditation Centre
(Name of garnishee / *Nom du tiers saisi*)

AND TO the clerk of the
ET AU greffier de la Cour
des petites créances de

Sault Ste. Marie
(Name of court location / *Emplacement du tribunal*)

Small Claims Court:

The Notice of Garnishment/Notice of
Renewal of Garnishment dated
*L'avis de saisie-arrêt/l'avis de
renouvellement de la saisie-arrêt daté du*

July 3   , 20 **--**   , served on you with respect to the debt of
*qui vous a été signifié à l'égard de la
créance de :*

Last name of debtor, or name of company / *Nom de famille du débiteur/de la débitrice ou nom de la compagnie*		
Michaeli		
First name / *Premier prénom*	Second name / *Deuxième prénom*	Also known as / *Également connu(e) sous le nom de*
Christine		
Address / *Adresse*		
55A Tranquillity Boulevard, Sault Ste. Marie, Ontario P6S 1C5		

is terminated and you are not to make any further payments under it.
prend fin et vous n'avez pas besoin de faire d'autres paiements aux termes de celui-ci.

December 28   , 20 **--**

(Signature of creditor or representative / *Signature du créancier/de la
créancière ou du/de la représentant(e)*)

Victor Oblomov PC Attention: Victor Oblomov
648 Queen Street East
Sault Ste. Marie, Ontario P6A 6W4
TEL: 705 945 8032   FAX: 705 945 8033

(Name, address and phone number of creditor or representative / *Nom,
adresse et numéro de téléphone du créancier/de la créancière ou du/de la
représentant(e)*)

NOTE: The creditor must serve this notice on the garnishee and on the court clerk.
REMARQUE :   *Le créancier doit signifier le présent avis au tiers saisi et au greffier du tribunal.*

SCR 20.08-20R (September 1, 2010 / *1er septembre 2010*) CSD

APPENDIX 11.11   Writ of Seizure and Sale of Personal Property (Form 20C)

ONTARIO

Superior Court of Justice
Cour supérieure de justice

Writ of Seizure and Sale of Personal Property
Bref de saisie-exécution de biens meubles
Form / *Formule* 20C Ont. Reg. No. / *Régl. de l'Ont.* : 258/98

Seal / *Sceau*

Brampton
Small Claims Court / *Cour des petites créances de*
7755 Hurontario Street
Brampton, Ontario
L6W 4T6
Address / *Adresse*

905 456 4700
Phone number / *Numéro de téléphone*

SC-00-34065-00
Claim No. / *N° de la demande*

Creditor No. 1 / *Créancier n° 1*

☐ Additional party(ies) listed on attached Form 1A.
La ou les parties additionnelles sont mentionnées sur la formule 1A ci-jointe.

Last name, or name of company / *Nom de famille ou nom de la compagnie*		
Greco		
First name / *Premier prénom*	Second name / *Deuxième prénom*	Also known as / *Également connu(e) sous le nom de*
Juliette		
Address (street number, apt., unit) / *Adresse (numéro et rue, app., unité)*		
c/o Prior Mustafa LLP Attention: Joseph Mustafa		
City/Town / *Cité/ville*	Province	Phone no. / *N° de téléphone*
Postal code / *Code postal*		Fax no. / *N° de télécopieur*
Representative / *Représentant(e)*		LSUC # / *N° du BHC*
Prior Mustafa LLP Attention: Joseph Mustafa		######
Address (street number, apt., unit) / *Adresse (numéro et rue, app., unité)*		
22 County Court Boulevard		
City/Town / *Cité/ville*	Province	Phone no. / *N° de téléphone*
Brampton	**Ontario**	**905 111 2222**
Postal code / *Code postal*		Fax no. / *N° de télécopieur*
A1A 2B3		**905 111 2233**

Debtor No. 1 / *Débiteur n° 1*

☐ Additional party(ies) listed on attached Form 1A.
La ou les parties additionnelles sont mentionnées sur la formule 1A ci-jointe.

Last name, or name of company / *Nom de famille ou nom de la compagnie*		
Hardwick		
First name / *Premier prénom*	Second name / *Deuxième prénom*	Also known as / *Également connu(e) sous le nom de*
James		
Address (street number, apt., unit) / *Adresse (numéro et rue, app., unité)*		
c/o Paxton Limones PC Attention: Angela Limones		
City/Town / *Cité/ville*	Province	Phone no. / *N° de téléphone*
Postal code / *Code postal*		Fax no. / *N° de télécopieur*
Representative / *Représentant(e)*		LSUC # / *N° du BHC*
Paxton Limones PC Attention: Angela Limones		######
Address (street number, apt., unit) / *Adresse (numéro et rue, app., unité)*		
82 Main Street, Suite 11		
City/Town / *Cité/ville*	Province	Phone no. / *N° de téléphone*
Brampton	**Ontario**	**905 888 9999**
Postal code / *Code postal*		Fax no. / *N° de télécopieur*
L1N 2P3		**905 888 0000**

SCR 20.06-20C (June 1, 2009 / *1ᵉʳ juin 2009*) CSD

APPENDIX 11.11   Writ of Seizure and Sale of Personal Property (Form 20C)   *continued*

FORM / *FORMULE* 20C   PAGE 2   SC-00-34065-00

                                                                            Claim No. / *N° de la demande*

TO THE BAILIFF OF THE   Brampton   **SMALL CLAIMS COURT:**
À L'HUISSIER DE LA COUR   (Small Claims Court location / *Emplacement de la Cour des*
DES PETITES CRÉANCES DE   *petites créances*)

Under an order of this court made on _____ April 18 _____, 20 -- , in favour of
En vertu d'une ordonnance rendue par ce tribunal le _____ , *en faveur de*

                                    Juliette Greco
                    (Name of creditor(s) / *Nom du/de la/des créancier(s)/créancière(s)*)

YOU ARE DIRECTED to seize and sell the personal property of
NOUS VOUS ENJOIGNONS de saisir les biens meubles de

Last name, or name of company / *Nom de famille ou nom de la compagnie*		
Hardwick		
First name / *Premier prénom*	Second name / *Deuxième prénom*	Third name / *Troisième prénom*
James		

☐   Additional debtor(s) and also known as names listed on attached Form 1A.1.
    *Le ou les débiteurs additionnels et le ou les noms sous lesquels ils sont également connus sont mentionnés
    sur la formule 1A.1 ci-jointe.*

situated within your jurisdiction and to realize from the seizure and sale the following sums:
qui se trouvent dans votre ressort et de procéder à leur vente pour réaliser les sommes suivantes :

(A) **AMOUNT OF JUDGMENT** (debt and pre-judgment interest) $ 3,748.36
    LE MONTANT DU JUGEMENT (créance et intérêts antérieurs au jugement) $

(B) **COSTS** to date of judgment $ 1,350.00
    LES DÉPENS à la date du jugement $

(C) **TOTAL AMOUNT OF PAYMENTS RECEIVED FROM DEBTOR** after
    judgment (if any) $ 0
    LE MONTANT TOTAL DES PAIEMENTS REÇUS DU DÉBITEUR après le $
    jugement (le cas échéant)

    Post-judgment interest continues to accrue
    Les intérêts postérieurs au jugement continuent à courir

    at the rate of _____ 10 _____ % per annum from _____ April 18 _____ , 20 -- .
    au taux de   *% par an à compter du*

(D) **SUBSEQUENT COSTS** incurred after judgment (including the cost of issuing this writ) $ 35.00
    LES DÉPENS SUBSÉQUENTS engagés après le jugement (y compris le coût $
    de délivrance du présent bref)

(E) Your fees and expenses in enforcing this writ.
    Les honoraires et frais qui vous sont dus pour l'exécution forcée du présent bref.

          Continued on next page / *Suite à la page suivante*

APPENDIX 11.11 Writ of Seizure and Sale of Personal Property (Form 20C) *concluded*

FORM / *FORMULE* **20C**   **PAGE 3**   SC-00-34065-00

Claim No. / *N° de la demande*

YOU ARE DIRECTED to calculate the amount owing at the time of enforcement and to pay the proceeds over to the clerk of this court for the creditor.

ET NOUS VOUS ENJOIGNONS de calculer la somme due au moment de l'exécution forcée et de verser le produit de la vente au greffier du tribunal précité pour le compte du créancier.

_____, 20 _____   _____

(Signature of clerk / *Signature du greffier*)

Reasonable disbursements necessarily incurred to enforce this writ *Débours raisonnables qui ont dû être engagés pour exécuter le présent bref* (Bailiff (enforcement office) fees and expenses / *Honoraires et frais de l'huissier (bureau de l'exécution)*)	$ .... $ (filled in and initialled by the enforcement office / *à remplir et à parapher* *par le bureau de* *l'exécution*)

NOTE: **THIS WRIT REMAINS IN FORCE FOR SIX YEARS** after the date of its issue and for a further six years after each renewal. The writ may be renewed before it expires by filing a Request to Renew a Writ of Seizure and Sale (Form 20N) with the bailiff (enforcement office).

REMARQUE :   **LE PRÉSENT BREF RESTE EN VIGUEUR PENDANT SIX ANS** *après la date de sa délivrance ou après chaque renouvellement. Le bref peut être renouvelé avant qu'il n'expire en déposant une demande de renouvellement du bref de saisie-exécution (formule 20N) auprès de l'huissier (bureau de l'exécution).*

SCR 20.06-20C (June 1, 2009 / *1er juin 2009*) CSD

APPENDIX 11.11
Direction to Enforce Writ of Seizure and Sale of Personal Property (Form 200)

ONTARIO

Superior Court of Justice
Cour supérieure de justice

Direction to Enforce Writ of Seizure and Sale of Personal Property
Ordre d'exécution d'un bref de saisie-exécution de biens meubles

Form / *Formule* 200 Ont. Reg. No. / *Régl. de l'Ont.* : 258/98

Brampton

Small Claims Court / *Cour des petites créances de*
7755 Hurontario Street
Brampton, Ontario
L6W 4T6

Address / *Adresse*

905 456 4700

Phone number / *Numéro de téléphone*

SC-00-34065-00

Claim No. / *N° de la demande*

BETWEEN / *ENTRE*

Juliette Greco

Creditor(s) / *Créancier(s)/créancière(s)*

and / *et*

James Hardwick

Debtor(s) / *Débiteur(s)/débitrice(s)*

My name is
Je m'appelle

Joseph Mustafa

(Full name / *Nom et prénoms*)

1. In this action, I am the
   Dans la présente action, je suis le/la

   (Check one box only. / *Cochez une seule case.*)

   ☐ creditor.
   créancier/créancière.

   ☒ representative of the creditor(s).
   représentant(e) du/de la/des créancier(s)/créancière(s).

   A Writ of Seizure and Sale of Personal Property (Form 20C) directed to the bailiff of the
   Un bref de saisie-exécution de biens meubles (formule 20C) adressé à l'huissier de la Cour des petites créances de

   Brampton
   (Small Claims Court location / *emplacement de la Cour des petites créances*)

   Small Claims Court was issued on:
   a été délivré le :

   April 18, 20 -- , in favour of
   , *en faveur de*

   Juliette Greco
   (Name of creditor / *Nom du/de la créancier/créancière*)

2. I am filing this direction to enforce the Writ of Seizure and Sale of Personal Property, and direct the bailiff to seize and sell (if required) the personal property belonging to the following debtor(s):
   Je dépose le présent ordre d'exécution du bref de saisie-exécution de biens meubles et ordonne à l'huissier de saisir et de vendre (s'il y a lieu) les biens meubles appartenant au(x) débiteur(s) suivant(s) :

Last name, or name of company / *Nom de famille ou nom de la compagnie*		
Hardwick		
First name / *Premier prénom*	Second name / *Deuxième prénom*	Third given name (individual only) (if applicable) / *Troisième prénom (particulier seulement) (s'il y a lieu)*
James		

   ☐ Additional debtor(s) and also known as names are listed on attached Form 1A.1.
   Le ou les débiteurs additionnels et le ou les noms sous lesquels les débiteurs sont également connus sont mentionnés sur la formule 1A.1 ci-jointe.

   Set out a description of the property to be seized. Identify any marks or serial numbers.
   Donnez la description des biens qui doivent être saisis. Indiquez toute marque d'identification ou tout numéro de série y figurant.
   2000 Toyota RAV4, green, tinted windows, rusted hubcaps, some damage to front bumper

SCR 20.06-200 (June 1, 2009 / *1ᵉʳ juin 2009*) CSD

APPENDIX 11.11

Direction to Enforce Writ of Seizure and Sale of Personal Property (Form 200)   *concluded*

FORM / *FORMULE* 200   **PAGE 2**   SC-00-34065-00

Claim No. / *N° de la demande*

3. The above personal property is located at: 128 George Court, Brampton, Ontario L1X 2V4
Les biens meubles susmentionnés se trouvent à/au :   (Address / *Adresse*)

If the address provided does not clearly identify where the property is located, please attach a detailed map showing the nearest intersection.
Si l'adresse fournie n'indique pas clairement l'emplacement des biens, veuillez annexer un plan détaillé qui montre l'intersection la plus rapprochée.

4. From the date that the Writ of Seizure and Sale of Personal Property was issued, the following payments
have been received from the debtor and/or subsequent costs incurred by the creditor:
*Depuis la date de délivrance du bref de saisie-exécution de biens meubles, les paiements suivants ont été
reçus du débiteur ou les dépens subséquents engagés par le créancier :*

(A) PAYMENTS RECEIVED FROM DEBTOR
PAIEMENTS REÇUS DU DÉBITEUR

Date of Payment *Date du paiement*	Payment Amount *Montant du paiement*
	$ _____ $
	$ _____ $
	$ _____ $
	$ _____ $

☐ List of additional payments attached
Liste de paiements additionnels ci-jointe

(B) SUBSEQUENT COSTS incurred since issuance of Writ of Seizure and Sale of Personal Property
DÉPENS SUBSÉQUENTS engagés depuis la délivrance du bref de saisie-exécution de biens meubles

Reason cost was incurred *Raison pour laquelle les dépens ont été engagés*	Cost Amount *Montant des dépens*
	$ _____ $
	$ _____ $
	$ _____ $
	$ _____ $

☐ List of additional costs attached
Liste de dépens additionnels ci-jointe

The bailiff will calculate the amount owing based on the information provided within the Writ of Seizure and Sale
of Personal Property and the details provided above. This amount will include any reasonable disbursements
necessarily incurred to enforce this writ.
*L'huissier calculera la somme due en fonction des renseignements donnés dans le bref de saisie-exécution de
biens meubles et des précisions données ci-dessus. Cette somme inclura les débours raisonnables qui ont dû
être engagés pour exécuter ce bref.*

____April 27_____ , 20 --   _____
                                    (Signature of creditor or representative / *Signature du créancier/de la
                                    créancière ou du/de la représentant(e)*)
                                    **Prior Mustafa LLP Attention: Joseph Mustafa
                                    22 County Court Boulevard
                                    Brampton, Ontario A1A 2B3
                                    TEL: 905 111 2222   FAX: 905 111 2233**
                                    (Name, address and phone number of creditor or representative / *Nom, adresse et
                                    numéro de téléphone du créancier/de la créancière ou du/de la représentant(e)*)

SCR 20.06-20O (June 1, 2009 / *1er juin 2009*) CSD

APPENDIX 11.12 Writ of Seizure and Sale of Land (Form 20D)

ONTARIO

Superior Court of Justice
Cour supérieure de justice

Writ of Seizure and Sale of Land
Bref de saisie-exécution de biens-fonds
Form / *Formule* 20D Ont. Reg. No. / *Régl. de l'Ont.* : 258/98

Seal / *Sceau*

Brampton

Small Claims Court / *Cour des petites créances de*

7755 Hurontario Street
Brampton, Ontario L6W 4T6

Address / *Adresse*

905 456 4700

Phone number / *Numéro de téléphone*

SC-00-34065-00

Claim No. / *N° de la demande*

☐ Additional party(ies) listed on attached Form 1A.
La ou les parties additionnelles sont mentionnées sur la formule 1A ci-jointe.

Creditor No. 1 / *Créancier n° 1*

Last name, or name of company / *Nom de famille ou nom de la compagnie*		
Greco		
First name / *Premier prénom* **Juliette**	Second name / *Deuxième prénom*	Also known as / *Également connu(e) sous le nom de*
Address (street number, apt., unit) / *Adresse (numéro et rue, app., unité)* **c/o Prior Mustafa LLP Attention: Joseph Mustafa**		
City/Town / *Cité/ville*	Province	Phone no. / *N° de téléphone*
Postal code / *Code postal*		Fax no. / *N° de télécopieur*
Representative / *Représentant(e)* **Prior Mustafa LLP Attention: Joseph Mustafa**		LSUC # / *N° du BHC* **######**
Address (street number, apt., unit) / *Adresse (numéro et rue, app., unité)* **22 County Court Boulevard**		
City/Town / *Cité/ville* **Brampton**	Province **Ontario**	Phone no. / *N° de téléphone* **905 111 2222**
Postal code / *Code postal* **A1A 2B3**		Fax no. / *N° de télécopieur* **905 111 2233**

☐ Additional party(ies) listed on attached Form 1A.
La ou les parties additionnelles sont mentionnées sur la formule 1A ci-jointe.

Debtor No. 1 / *Débiteur n° 1*

Last name, or name of company / *Nom de famille ou nom de la compagnie*		
Hardwick		
First name / *Premier prénom* **James**	Second name / *Deuxième prénom*	Also known as / *Également connu(e) sous le nom de*
Address (street number, apt., unit) / *Adresse (numéro et rue, app., unité)* **c/o Paxton Limones PC Attention: Angela Limones**		
City/Town / *Cité/ville*	Province	Phone no. / *N° de téléphone*
Postal code / *Code postal*		Fax no. / *N° de télécopieur*
Representative / *Représentant(e)* **Paxton Limones PC Attention: Angela Limones**		LSUC # / *N° du BHC* **######**
Address (street number, apt., unit) / *Adresse (numéro et rue, app., unité)* **82 Main Street, Suite 11**		
City/Town / *Cité/ville* **Brampton**	Province **Ontario**	Phone no. / *N° de téléphone* **905 888 9999**
Postal code / *Code postal* **L1N 2P3**		Fax no. / *N° de télécopieur* **905 888 0000**

NOTE: **THIS WRIT REMAINS IN FORCE FOR SIX YEARS** after the date of its issue and for a further six years after each renewal. The writ may be renewed before it expires by filing a Request to Renew a Writ of Seizure and Sale (Form 20N) with the sheriff (enforcement office.)

REMARQUE : *LE PRÉSENT BREF RESTE EN VIGUEUR PENDANT SIX ANS après la date de sa délivrance ou après chaque renouvellement. Le bref peut être renouvelé avant qu'il n'expire en déposant une demande de renouvellement du bref de saisie-exécution (formule 20N) auprès du shérif (bureau de l'exécution).*

SCR 20.07-20D (June 1, 2009 / *1ᵉʳ juin 2009*) CSD

APPENDIX 11.12 Writ of Seizure and Sale of Land (Form 20D) *concluded*

FORM / *FORMULE* 20D	PAGE 2	SC-00-34065-00
		Claim No. / *N° de la demande*

TO THE SHERIFF OF _____ **Brampton** _____ :
AU SHÉRIF DE (Name of county/region in which the enforcement office is located / *Nom du comté/de la région où est situé*
le bureau de l'exécution)

Under an order of this court made on _____ **April 18** _____ , 20 **--** , in favour of
En vertu d'une ordonnance rendue par ce tribunal le , *en faveur de*

Juliettte Greco
(Name of creditor(s) / *Nom du/de la/des créancier(s)/créancière(s)*)

YOU ARE DIRECTED to seize and sell the real property of
NOUS VOUS ENJOIGNONS *de saisir les biens immeubles de*

Last name, or name of company / *Nom de famille ou nom de la compagnie*		
Hardwick		
First name / *Premier prénom*	Second name / *Deuxième prénom*	Third name / *Troisième prénom*
James		

☐ Additional debtor(s) and also known as names listed on attached Form 1A.1.
Le ou les débiteurs additionnels et le ou les noms sous lesquels ils sont également connus sont mentionnés
sur la formule 1A.1 ci-jointe.

situated within your jurisdiction and to realize from the seizure and sale the following sums:
qui se trouvent dans votre ressort et de procéder à leur vente pour réaliser les sommes suivantes :

(A) **AMOUNT OF JUDGMENT** (debt and pre-judgment interest) $ 3,748.36
    MONTANT DU JUGEMENT *(créance et intérêts antérieurs au jugement)* $

(B) **COSTS** to date of judgment $ 1,350.00
    LES DÉPENS *à la date du jugement* $

(C) **TOTAL AMOUNT OF PAYMENTS RECEIVED FROM DEBTOR** after
    judgment (if any) $ 0
    LE MONTANT TOTAL DES PAIEMENTS REÇUS DU DÉBITEUR *après le* $
    jugement (le cas échéant)

    Post-judgment interest continues to accrue
    Les intérêts postérieurs au jugement continuent à courir

    at the rate of **10** % per annum from _____ **April 18** _____ , 20 **--** .
    au taux de % *par an à compter du*

(D) **SUBSEQUENT COSTS** incurred after judgment (including the cost of issuing this writ) $ 70.00
    LES DÉPENS SUBSÉQUENTS *engagés après le jugement (y compris le coût* $
    de délivrance du présent bref)

(E) Your fees and expenses in enforcing this writ.
    Les honoraires et frais qui vous sont dus pour l'exécution forcée du présent bref.

YOU ARE DIRECTED to calculate the amount owing at the time of enforcement and pay out the proceeds
according to law and to report on the execution of this writ if required by a party who filed this writ.
ET NOUS VOUS ENJOIGNONS *de calculer la somme due au moment de l'exécution forcée et de verser le*
produit de la vente conformément à la loi et de faire un rapport sur l'exécution forcée du présent bref si la partie
qui l'a déposé l'exige.

_____ , 20 _____ _____
(Signature of clerk / *Signature du greffier*)

SCR 20.07-20D (June 1, 2009 / *1er juin 2009*) CSD

APPENDIX 11.13 Affidavit for Enforcement Request (Form 20P)

ONTARIO

Superior Court of Justice
Cour supérieure de justice

Affidavit for Enforcement Request
Affidavit relatif à une demande d'exécution forcée
Form / *Formule* 20P Ont. Reg. No. / *Règl. de l'Ont.* : 258/98

Newmarket
Small Claims Court / *Cour des petites créances de*
50 Eagle Street West
Newmarket, Ontario
L3Y 6B1
Address / *Adresse*

905 853 4809
Phone number / *Numéro de téléphone*

SC-00-31415-00
Claim No. / *N° de la demande*

BETWEEN / *ENTRE*

Merry Clayton

Plaintiff(s)/Creditor(s) / *Demandeur(s)/demanderesse(s)/Créancier(s)/créancière(s)*

and / *et*

Richard Parker

Defendant(s)/Debtor(s) / *Défendeur(s)/défenderesse(s)/Débiteur(s)/débitrice(s)*

My name is   Merry Clayton
Je m'appelle   (Full name / *Nom et prénoms*)

I live in   Newmarket, Ontario
J'habite à   (Municipality & province / *Municipalité et province*)

and I swear/affirm that the following is true:
et je déclare sous serment/j'affirme solennellement que les renseignements suivants sont véridiques :

1. **In this action, I am the**
   Dans la présente action, je suis le/la

   (Check one box only. / *Cochez une seule case.*)

   ☒ plaintiff/creditor.
   demandeur/demanderesse/créancier/créancière.

   ☐ representative of the plaintiff(s)/creditor(s).
   représentant(e) du/de la/des demandeur(s)/demanderesse(s)/créancier(s)/créancière(s).

   I make this affidavit in support of a request that the clerk of the court issue the following enforcement process(es):
   Je fais le présent affidavit à l'appui d'une demande visant à enjoindre au greffier du tribunal de délivrer l'acte ou les actes de procédure portant exécution forcée suivants :

   ☐ Certificate of Judgment (Form 20A) to the clerk of the
   Certificat de jugement (formule 20A), au greffier
   de la Cour des petites créances de   (Name of court where the judgment is to be filed / *Nom du tribunal*
                                                            où le jugement doit être déposé)
   Small Claims Court.

   ☐ Writ of Seizure and Sale of Personal Property (Form 20C) directed to the bailiff of
   Bref de saisie-exécution de biens meubles (formule 20C) adressé à l'huissier de la Cour des petites créances de

                                                            Small Claims Court.
   (Name of court location / *Emplacement du tribunal*)

   ☐ Writ of Seizure and Sale of Land (Form 20D) directed to the sheriff of
   Bref de saisie-exécution de biens-fonds (formule 20D) adressé   (Name of county/region in which the
   au shérif du/de la   enforcement office is located / *Comté/région où*
                                                                            est situé le bureau de l'exécution)

SCR 20.04-10-20P (June 1, 2009 / *1er juin 2009*) CSD

APPENDIX 11.13   **Affidavit for Enforcement Request (Form 20P)**   *continued*

FORM / *FORMULE* 20P	PAGE 2	SC-00-31415-00
		Claim No. / *N° de la demande*

☐ Notice of Garnishment (Form 20E)/Notice of Renewal of Garnishment (Form 20E.1).
   Avis de saisie-arrêt (formule 20E)/Avis de renouvellement de la saisie-arrêt (formule 20E.1).

I believe that the garnishee _____
Je crois que le tiers saisi   (Name of garnishee / *Nom du tiers saisi*)

at _____
à/au   (Address of garnishee / *Adresse du tiers saisi*)

is indebted to the debtor or will become indebted to the debtor for the following reasons:
est ou sera redevable d'une dette au débiteur pour les motifs suivants :

The Notice will be served on the debtor _____
L'avis sera signifié au débiteur,   (Name of debtor / *Nom du débiteur/de la débitrice*)

at _____
à/au   (Address of debtor for service / *Adresse du débiteur/de la débitrice aux fins de signification*)

within five days of serving it on the garnishee.
dans les cinq jours qui suivent sa signification au tiers saisi.

☐ Notice of Examination (Form 20H).
   Avis d'interrogatoire (formule 20H).

☒ Writ of Delivery (Form 20B).
   Bref de délaissement (formule 20B).

☐ Other *(Set out the nature of your request)*:
   Autre (Indiquez la nature de votre demande) :

Complete this section if you are requesting a Writ of Delivery.
Remplissez la présente section si vous demandez un bref de délaissement.

2. An order for the delivery of the following personal property:
   Une ordonnance de délaissement des biens meubles suivants :
   (According to the court order, set out a description of the property to be delivered. Identify any marks or serial numbers. / Selon l'ordonnance du
   tribunal, donnez la description des biens qui doivent être restitués. Indiquez toute marque d'identification ou tout numéro de série y figurant.)

APPENDIX 11.13 **Affidavit for Enforcement Request (Form 20P)** *continued*

FORM / *FORMULE* 20P PAGE 3 SC-00-31415-00

Claim No. / *N° de la demande*

was made in this action against: _____ **Richard Parker**
a été rendue dans l'action contre : (Name of person against whom the order was made / *Nom de la personne contre qui l'ordonnance a été rendue*)

on _____ **May 16** , 20 -- , in the _____ **Newmarket**
le *à la Cour des petites* (Name of court location where order was made / *Emplacement*
créances de *du tribunal où l'ordonnance a été rendue*)

Small Claims Court. Since the above listed personal property has not been delivered, I make this affidavit in support of a request that the clerk of the court issue a Writ of Delivery (Form 20B) to the bailiff of the
Étant donné que les biens meubles susmentionnés n'ont pas été restitués, je fais le présent affidavit à l'appui d'une demande visant à enjoindre au greffier du tribunal de délivrer un bref de délaissement (formule 20B) à l'huissier de la Cour des petites créances de

_____ **Newmarket** _____ Small Claims Court.
(Name of court location / *Emplacement du tribunal*)

Complete this section if you are requesting a Certificate of Judgment, Writ of Seizure and Sale of Personal Property, Writ of Seizure and Sale of Land, Notice of Garnishment, Notice of Renewal of Garnishment or Notice of Examination.
Remplissez la présente section si vous demandez un certificat de jugement, un bref de saisie-exécution de biens meubles, un bref de saisie-exécution de biens-fonds, un avis de saisie-arrêt, un avis de renouvellement de la saisie-arrêt ou un avis d'interrogatoire.

3. A judgment was made in this action against _____
Un jugement a été rendu dans l'action contre (Name of debtor(s) / *Nom du/de la/des débiteur(s)/débitrice(s)*)

on _____ , 20 ____ in the _____
le *à la Cour des petites créances de*

_____ Small Claims Court
(Name of court where judgment was made / *Nom du tribunal où le jugement a été rendu*)

for the following sums:
à l'égard des sommes suivantes :

(A) **DEBT** $ _____
LA CRÉANCE $

(B) **PRE-JUDGMENT INTEREST** calculated
LES INTÉRÊTS ANTÉRIEURS AU JUGEMENT *calculés*

on the sum of $ _____ at the rate of _____ %
sur la somme de $ *au taux de* *pour cent*

per annum from _____ , 20 ___ to _____ , 20 ___ ,
par an du *au*

being _____ days. $ _____
soit *jours.* $

SUBTOTAL (Amount of Judgment) $ ....
TOTAL PARTIEL *(montant du jugement)* $

(C) **COSTS** to date of judgment $ _____
LES DÉPENS *à la date du jugement* $

Continued on next page / *Suite à la page suivante*

APPENDIX 11.13 Affidavit for Enforcement Request (Form 20P) *concluded*

FORM / *FORMULE* 20P   PAGE 4   SC-00-31415-00
                                                                  Claim No. / *N° de la demande*

(D) **TOTAL AMOUNT OF PAYMENTS RECEIVED FROM DEBTOR**
after judgment (if any)   (minus) $ _____
LE MONTANT TOTAL DES PAIEMENTS REÇUS DU   *(moins)* $
DÉBITEUR après le jugement (le cas échéant)

(E) **POST-JUDGMENT INTEREST** to date calculated
LES INTÉRÊTS POSTÉRIEURS AU JUGEMENT à ce jour, calculés

on the sum of $ _____   at the rate of _____ %
sur la somme de $ *au taux de*   *pour cent*

per annum from _____ , 20 ___ to _____ , 20 ___ ,
par an du   *au*

being _____ days. $ _____
soit   *jours.* $

> **NOTE:** Calculation of interest is always on the amount owing from time to time as payments are received. This is true for both pre-judgment and post-judgment interest. Attach a separate sheet setting out how you calculated the total amount of any pre/post-judgment interest.
> *REMARQUE : Les intérêts doivent toujours être calculés sur la somme due. Le calcul doit tenir compte des paiements reçus de temps à autre. Ceci s'applique autant aux intérêts antérieurs au jugement qu'aux intérêts postérieurs au jugement. Annexez une feuille distincte indiquant comment vous avez calculé le montant total des intérêts antérieurs et postérieurs au jugement.*

(F) **SUBSEQUENT COSTS** incurred after judgment (including the cost of issuing the requested enforcement(s)) $ _____
LES DÉPENS SUBSÉQUENTS engagés après le jugement (y compris le $
coût de la délivrance de la ou des mesures d'exécution forcée demandées)

                    TOTAL DUE $ ....
                    SOLDE DÛ $

Sworn/Affirmed before me at   **Newmarket**
Déclaré sous serment/Affirmé   (Municipality / *municipalité*)
solennellement devant moi à

in   **Ontario**
en/à/au   (Province, state or country / *province, État ou pays*)

on   **May 22**   , 20 --
le   Commissioner for taking affidavits
                                  Commissaire aux affidavits
                                  (Type or print name below if signature is illegible.)
                                  (Dactylographiez le nom ou écrivez-le en caractères
                                  d'imprimerie ci-dessous si la signature est illisible.)

_____
Signature
(This form is to be signed in front of a lawyer, justice of the peace, notary public or commissioner for taking affidavits.)
(La présente formule doit être signée en présence d'un avocat, d'un juge de paix, d'un notaire ou d'un commissaire aux affidavits.)

> **WARNING:** IT IS AN OFFENCE UNDER THE *CRIMINAL CODE* TO KNOWINGLY SWEAR OR AFFIRM A FALSE AFFIDAVIT.
> *AVERTISSEMENT : FAIRE SCIEMMENT UN FAUX AFFIDAVIT CONSTITUE UNE INFRACTION AU CODE CRIMINEL.*

SCR 20.04-10-20P (June 1, 2009 / *1ᵉʳ juin 2009*) CSD

APPENDIX 11.13 Writ of Delivery (Form 20B)

ONTARIO

Superior Court of Justice
Cour supérieure de justice

Writ of Delivery
Bref de délaissement
Form / *Formule* 20B Ont. Reg. No. / *Régl. de l'Ont.* : 258/98

Seal / *Sceau*

Newmarket
Small Claims Court / *Cour des petites créances de*
50 Eagle Street West
Newmarket, Ontario
L3Y 6B1
Address / *Adresse*

905 853 4809
Phone number / *Numéro de téléphone*

SC-00-31415-00
Claim No. / *N° de la demande*

BETWEEN / *ENTRE*

Merry Clayton

Plaintiff(s) / *Demandeur(s)/demanderesse(s)*

and / *et*

Richard Parker

Defendant(s) / *Défendeur(s)/défenderesse(s)*

TO THE BAILIFF OF
À L'HUISSIER DE LA COUR
DES PETITES CRÉANCES DE

Newmarket

(Name of Small Claims Court location / *Emplacement de la Cour des petites créances*)

SMALL CLAIMS COURT:

Under an order of this court made on **May 16**, 20 --
En vertu d'une ordonnance rendue par le tribunal précité le

YOU ARE DIRECTED to seize from **Richard Parker**
NOUS VOUS ENJOIGNONS de saisir auprès de

(Name of person against whom the order was made / *Nom de la personne contre qui l'ordonnance a été rendue*)

and to deliver without delay to
et de remettre sans retard à

Name of person in whose favour the order was made / *Nom de la personne en faveur de qui l'ordonnance a été rendue*   **Merry Clayton**
Street and number / *Numéro et rue*   **255 Pelican Court**
City, province, postal code / *Ville, province, code postal*   **Newmarket, Ontario, L2M 3N4**
Phone number and fax number, if any / *Numéro de téléphone et numéro de télécopieur, le cas échéant*   **905 853 4455**

possession of the following personal property:
la possession des biens meubles suivants :

(According to the court order, set out a description of the property to be delivered. Identify any marks or serial numbers. If the order refers to items set out in the issued claim, attach a copy of the issued claim.)
(Conformément à l'ordonnance du tribunal, donnez la description des biens qui doivent être remis. Indiquez toute marque d'identification ou tout numéro de série y figurant. Si l'ordonnance vise des articles énoncés dans la demande délivrée, annexez une copie de la demande délivrée.)

Description: 1920 X 1080 52" LCD television
Model: Doinel LN52B750 LCD TV
Value: $1,499.89
Serial number: 85X23YZ00

SCR 20.05-20B (June 1, 2009 / *1er juin 2009*) CSD

APPENDIX 11.13   Writ of Delivery (Form 20B)   *concluded*

FORM / *FORMULE* 20B   **PAGE 2**   SC-00-31415-00
Claim No. / *N° de la demande*

The above personal property is located at: **45 Longtree Street, Newmarket, Ontario L3Z 7C2**
Les biens meubles susmentionnés se trouvent à/au :   (Address / *Adresse*)

If the address provided does not clearly identify where the items are located, please attach a detailed map that shows the nearest intersection.
Si l'adresse fournie n'indique pas clairement l'emplacement des articles, veuillez annexer un plan détaillé qui montre l'intersection la plus rapprochée.

(To be completed by the clerk of the court. / Section à remplir par le greffier du tribunal.)

☒ **THE COURT HAS EXPRESSLY ORDERED** that you are authorized to use reasonable force to enter a private dwelling to execute this writ of delivery, if necessary [*Execution Act*, s. 20(2)]. A copy of the court's order on the endorsement record is attached.
EN VERTU D'UNE ORDONNANCE EXPRESSE DU TRIBUNAL, *vous êtes autorisé(e) à avoir recours à la force raisonnable pour pénétrer dans un logement privé pour exécuter le présent bref de délaissement, si cela est nécessaire [Loi sur l'exécution forcée, par. 20 (2)]. Une copie de l'ordonnance du tribunal qui figure au dossier des inscriptions est annexée.*

_____ , 20 _____   _____
(Signature of clerk / *Signature du greffier*)

SCR 20.05-20B (June 1, 2009 / *1ᵉʳ juin 2009*) CSD

Courts of Justice Act

R.S.O. 1990, CHAPTER C.43

Last amendment: 2009, c. 33, Sched. 6, s. 50.

CONTENTS

. . .

Small Claims Court

. . .

SMALL CLAIMS COURT

Small Claims Court

22(1) The Small Claims Court is continued as a branch of the Superior Court of Justice under the name Small Claims Court in English and Cour des petites créances in French.

Idem

(2) The Small Claims Court consists of the Chief Justice of the Superior Court of Justice who shall be president of the court and such other judges of the Superior Court of Justice as the Chief Justice designates from time to time.

Jurisdiction of judges

(3) Every judge of the Superior Court of Justice is also a judge of the Small Claims Court.

Jurisdiction

23(1) The Small Claims Court,

(a) has jurisdiction in any action for the payment of money where the amount claimed does not exceed the prescribed amount exclusive of interest and costs; and

(b) has jurisdiction in any action for the recovery of possession of personal property where the value of the property does not exceed the prescribed amount.

Transfer from Superior Court of Justice

(2) An action in the Superior Court of Justice may be transferred to the Small Claims Court by the local registrar of the Superior Court of Justice on requisition with the consent of all parties filed before the trial commences if,

(a) the only claim is for the payment of money or the recovery of possession of personal property; and

(b) the claim is within the jurisdiction of the Small Claims Court.

Idem

(3) An action transferred to the Small Claims Court shall be titled and continued as if it had been commenced in that court.

Composition of court for hearings

24(1) A proceeding in the Small Claims Court shall be heard and determined by one judge of the Superior Court of Justice.

Provincial judge or deputy judge may preside

(2) A proceeding in the Small Claims Court may also be heard and determined by,

(a) a provincial judge who was assigned to the Provincial Court (Civil Division) immediately before the 1st day of September, 1990; or

(b) a deputy judge appointed under section 32.

Where deputy judge not to preside

(3) A deputy judge shall not hear and determine an action,

(a) for the payment of money in excess of the prescribed amount; or

(b) for the recovery of possession of personal property exceeding the prescribed amount in value.

Summary hearings

25. The Small Claims Court shall hear and determine in a summary way all questions of law and fact and may make such order as is considered just and agreeable to good conscience.

Representation

26. A party may be represented in a proceeding in the Small Claims Court by a person authorized under the *Law Society Act* to represent the party, but the court may exclude from a hearing anyone, other than a person licensed under the *Law Society Act*, appearing on behalf of the party if it finds that such person is not competent properly to represent the party, or does not understand and comply at the hearing with the duties and responsibilities of an advocate.

Evidence

27(1) Subject to subsections (3) and (4), the Small Claims Court may admit as evidence at a hearing and act upon any oral testimony and any document or other thing so long as the evidence is relevant to the subject-matter of the proceeding, but the court may exclude anything unduly repetitious.

Idem

(2) Subsection (1) applies whether or not the evidence is given or proven under oath or affirmation or admissible as evidence in any other court.

Idem

(3) Nothing is admissible in evidence at a hearing,

(a) that would be inadmissible by reason of any privilege under the law of evidence; or

(b) that is inadmissible by any Act.

Conflicts

(4) Nothing in subsection (1) overrides the provisions of any Act expressly limiting the extent to or purposes for which any oral testimony, documents or things may be admitted or used in evidence in any proceeding.

Copies

(5) A copy of a document or any other thing may be admitted as evidence at a hearing if the presiding judge is satisfied as to its authenticity.

Instalment orders

28. The Small Claims Court may order the times and the proportions in which money payable under an order of the court shall be paid.

Limit on costs

29. An award of costs in the Small Claims Court, other than disbursements, shall not exceed 15 per cent of the amount claimed or the value of the property sought to be recovered unless the court considers it necessary in the interests of justice to penalize a party or a party's representative for unreasonable behaviour in the proceeding.

Contempt hearing for failure to attend examination

30(1) The Small Claims Court may, in accordance with the rules of court, order a debtor or other person who is required to and fails to attend an examination respecting a default by the debtor under an order of the court for the payment or recovery of money, to attend before the court for a contempt hearing.

Finding of contempt

(2) The Small Claims Court may find a person to be in contempt of court at a hearing referred to in subsection (1), if the court is satisfied that,

(a) the person was required to attend the examination;

(b) the person was served, in accordance with the rules of court, with a notice to attend the examination;

(c) the person failed to attend the examination; and

(d) the failure to attend was wilful.

Power conferred

(3) For greater certainty, the power of the Small Claims Court to order, hear and determine a contempt hearing under this section is conferred on and may be exercised by the persons referred to in clauses 24(2)(a) and (b).

Limit on imprisonment in certain cases

(4) If a contempt hearing under subsection (1) is heard and determined by a person referred to in clause 24(2)(a) or (b), the court may make such orders respecting the person in contempt as are specified by the rules of court, but the court shall not make an order that the person be imprisoned for a period of more than five days.

Authority unaffected

(5) Nothing in this section affects the authority of the Small Claims Court to order, hear and determine contempt hearings where it is otherwise authorized by law.

Appeals

31. An appeal lies to the Divisional Court from a final order of the Small Claims Court in an action,

(a) for the payment of money in excess of the prescribed amount, excluding costs; or

(b) for the recovery of possession of personal property exceeding the prescribed amount in value.

Deputy judges

32(1) A regional senior judge of the Superior Court of Justice may, with the approval of the Attorney General, appoint a lawyer to act as a deputy judge of the Small Claims Court.

Term of appointment

(2) The appointment of a deputy judge is for a term of three years, subject to subsections (3) and (7).

Annual appointment if 65 or older

(3) If the deputy judge is 65 years of age or older and under 75 years of age, the appointment shall be for a term of one year, subject to subsection (8).

Renewal before age 65

(4) The appointment of a deputy judge who is under 65 years of age may be renewed by a regional senior judge of the Superior Court of Justice for a term of three years, subject to subsection (7).

Annual renewal if 65 or older

(5) The appointment of a deputy judge who is 65 years of age or older and under 75 years of age may be renewed by a regional senior judge of the Superior Court of Justice for a term of one year, subject to subsection (8).

No limit, renewals

(6) Subject to subsections (7) to (9), there is no limit to the number of times the appointment of a deputy judge can be renewed under subsection (4) or (5).

Expiry of term at age 65

(7) If the deputy judge is 63 years of age or older and under 65 years of age, an appointment under subsection (2) or a renewal under subsection (4) shall provide for a term that expires when he or she reaches 65 years of age.

Expiry of term at age 75

(8) If the deputy judge is 74 years of age, an appointment under subsection (3) or a renewal under subsection (5) shall provide for a term that expires when he or she reaches 75 years of age.

Age limit

(9) No person shall be appointed as a deputy judge, or have an appointment renewed, once he or she reaches 75 years of age.

Current appointments

(10) For greater certainty, nothing in this section shortens or otherwise affects an appointment or renewed appointment that is in effect immediately before the day subsection 20(11) of Schedule 2 to the *Good Government Act, 2009* comes into force, but any renewals of the appointment on and after that day are subject to this section.

Deputy Judges Council

33(1) A council known as the Deputy Judges Council in English and as Conseil des juges suppléants in French is established.

Composition

(2) The Deputy Judges Council is composed of,

(a) the Chief Justice of the Superior Court of Justice, or another judge of the Superior Court of Justice designated by the Chief Justice;

(b) a regional senior judge of the Superior Court of Justice, appointed by the Chief Justice;

(c) a judge of the Superior Court of Justice, appointed by the Chief Justice;

(d) a provincial judge who was assigned to the Provincial Court (Civil Division) immediately before September 1, 1990, or a deputy judge, appointed by the Chief Justice;

(e) three persons who are neither judges nor lawyers, appointed by the Lieutenant Governor in Council on the Attorney General's recommendation.

Criteria

(3) In the appointment of members under clause (2)(e), the importance of reflecting, in the composition of the Council as a whole, Ontario's linguistic duality and the diversity of its population and ensuring overall gender balance shall be recognized.

Chair

(4) The Chief Justice of the Superior Court of Justice, or his or her designate, shall chair the meetings of the Deputy Judges Council.

Same

(5) The chair is entitled to vote, and may cast a second deciding vote if there is a tie.

Functions

(6) The functions of the Deputy Judges Council are,

(a) to review and approve standards of conduct for deputy judges as established by the Chief Justice;

(b) to review and approve a plan for the continuing education of deputy judges as established by the Chief Justice; and

(c) to make recommendations on matters affecting deputy judges.

Duty of Chief Justice

(7) The Chief Justice shall ensure that any standards of conduct are made available to the public, in English and French, when they have been approved by the Deputy Judges Council.

Complaint

33.1(1) Any person may make a complaint alleging misconduct by a deputy judge, by writing to the judge of the Superior Court of Justice designated by the regional senior judge in the region where the deputy judge sits.

Dismissal

(2) The judge shall review the complaint and may dismiss it without further investigation if, in his or her opinion, it falls outside the jurisdiction of the regional senior judge, is frivolous or an abuse of process, or concerns a minor matter to which an appropriate response has already been given.

Notice of dismissal

(3) The judge shall notify the regional senior judge, the complainant and the deputy judge in writing of a dismissal under subsection (2), giving brief reasons for it.

Committee

(4) If the complaint is not dismissed, the judge shall refer it to a committee consisting of three persons chosen by the regional senior judge.

Same

(5) The three persons shall be a judge of the Superior Court of Justice, a deputy judge and a person who is neither a judge nor a lawyer, all of whom reside or work in the region where the deputy judge who is the subject of the complaint sits.

Investigation

(6) The committee shall investigate the complaint in the manner it considers appropriate, and the complainant and deputy judge shall be given an opportunity to make representations to the committee, in writing or, at the committee's option, orally.

Recommendation

(7) The committee shall make a report to the regional senior judge, recommending a disposition in accordance with subsections (8), (9) and (10).

Disposition

(8) The regional senior judge may dismiss the complaint, with or without a finding that it is unfounded, or, if he or she concludes that the deputy judge's conduct presents grounds for imposing a sanction, may,

   (a) warn the deputy judge;

   (b) reprimand the deputy judge;

   (c) order the deputy judge to apologize to the complainant or to any other person;

   (d) order that the deputy judge take specified measures, such as receiving education or treatment, as a condition of continuing to sit as a deputy judge;

   (e) suspend the deputy judge for a period of up to 30 days;

   (f) inform the deputy judge that his or her appointment will not be renewed under subsection 32(2);

   (g) direct that no judicial duties or only specified judicial duties be assigned to the deputy judge; or

   (h) remove the deputy judge from office.

Same

(9) The regional senior judge may adopt any combination of the dispositions set out in clauses (8)(a) to (g).

Disability

(10) If the regional senior judge finds that the deputy judge is unable, because of a disability, to perform the essential duties of the office, but would be able to perform them if his or her needs were accommodated, the regional senior judge shall order that the deputy judge's needs be accommodated to the extent necessary to enable him or her to perform those duties.

Application of subs. (10)

(11) Subsection (10) applies if,

   (a) the effect of the disability on the deputy judge's performance of the essential duties of the office was a factor in the complaint; and

   (b) the regional senior judge dismisses the complaint or makes a disposition under clauses (8)(a), (b), (c), (d), (e) or (g).

Undue hardship

(12) Subsection (10) does not apply if the regional senior judge is satisfied that making an order would impose undue hardship on the person responsible for accommodating the judge's needs, considering the cost, outside sources of funding, if any, and health and safety requirements, if any.

Opportunity to participate

(13) The regional senior judge shall not make an order under subsection (10) against a person without ensuring that the person has had an opportunity to participate and make submissions.

Crown bound

(14) An order made under subsection (10) binds the Crown.

Compensation

(15) The regional senior judge shall consider whether the deputy judge should be compensated for all or part of his or her costs for legal services incurred in connection with all the steps taken under this section in relation to the complaint.

Recommendation

(16) If the regional senior judge is of the opinion that the deputy judge should be compensated, he or she shall make a recommendation to the Attorney General to that effect, indicating the amount of compensation.

Same

(17) If the complaint is dismissed with a finding that it is unfounded, the regional senior judge shall recommend to the Attorney General that the deputy judge be compensated for his or her costs for legal services and shall indicate the amount of compensation.

Maximum

(18) The amount of compensation recommended under subsection (16) or (17) shall be based on a rate for legal services that does not exceed the maximum rate normally paid by the Government of Ontario for similar legal services.

Payment

(19) The Attorney General shall pay compensation to the judge in accordance with the recommendation.

Non-application of SPPA

(20) The *Statutory Powers Procedure Act* does not apply to a judge, regional senior judge or member of a committee acting under this section.

Personal liability

(21) No action or other proceeding for damages shall be instituted against a judge, regional senior judge or member of a committee for any act done in good faith in the execution or intended execution of the person's duty under this section.

. . .

Rules of the Small Claims Court

B

ONTARIO REGULATION 258/98

RULES OF THE SMALL CLAIMS COURT

Last amendment: O. Reg. 400/12.

CONTENTS

. . .

RULE 1   GENERAL

Citation

1.01 These rules may be cited as the Small Claims Court Rules.

Definitions

1.02(1) In these rules,

"court" means the Small Claims Court; ("tribunal")

"disability", where used in respect of a person or party, means that the person or party is,

    (a) a minor,

    (b) mentally incapable within the meaning of section 6 or 45 of the *Substitute Decisions Act, 1992* in respect of an issue in the proceeding, whether the person or party has a guardian or not, or

    (c) an absentee within the meaning of the *Absentees Act*;

"document" includes data and information in electronic form;

"electronic" includes created, recorded, transmitted or stored in digital form or in other intangible form by electronic, magnetic or optical means or by any other means that has capabilities for creation, recording, transmission or storage similar to those means, and "electronically" has a corresponding meaning;

"holiday" means,

    (a) any Saturday or Sunday,

    (b) New Year's Day,

    (b.1) Family Day,

    (c) Good Friday,

    (d) Easter Monday,

    (e) Victoria Day,

    (f) Canada Day,

    (g) Civic Holiday,

    (h) Labour Day,

    (i) Thanksgiving Day,

    (j) Remembrance Day,

    (k) Christmas Day,

    (l) Boxing Day, and

    (m) any special holiday proclaimed by the Governor General or the Lieutenant Governor,

and if New Year's Day, Canada Day or Remembrance Day falls on a Saturday or Sunday, the following Monday is a holiday, and if Christmas Day falls on a Saturday or Sunday, the following Monday and Tuesday are holidays, and if Christmas Day falls on a Friday, the following Monday is a holiday;

"order" includes a judgment;

"self-represented", when used in reference to a person, means that the person is not represented by a lawyer, student-at-law or agent;

"territorial division" means,

(a) a county, a district or a regional municipality, and

(b) each of the following, as they existed on December 31, 2002:

(i) The combined area of County of Brant and City of Brantford.

(ii) Municipality of Chatham-Kent.

(iii) Haldimand County.

(iv) City of Hamilton.

(v) City of Kawartha Lakes.

(vi) Norfolk County.

(vii) City of Ottawa.

(viii) County of Prince Edward.

(ix) City of Toronto. ("division territoriale")

(2) REVOKED.

General Principle

1.03(1) These rules shall be liberally construed to secure the just, most expeditious and least expensive determination of every proceeding on its merits in accordance with section 25 of the *Courts of Justice Act*.

Matters Not Covered in Rules

(2) If these rules do not cover a matter adequately, the court may give directions and make any order that is just, and the practice shall be decided by analogy to these rules, by reference to the *Courts of Justice Act* and the Act governing the action and, if the court considers it appropriate, by reference to the Rules of Civil Procedure.

Orders on Terms

1.04 When making an order under these rules, the court may impose such terms and give such directions as are just.

Standards for Documents

1.05 A document in a proceeding shall be printed, type-written, written or reproduced legibly.

Forms

1.06(1) The forms prescribed by these rules shall be used where applicable and with such variations as the circumstances require.

Table of Forms

(2) In these rules, when a form is referred to by number, the reference is to the form with that number that is described in the Table of Forms at the end of these rules and is available on the Internet through www.ontariocourtforms.on.ca.

Additional Parties

(3) If a form does not have sufficient space to list all of the parties to the action on the first page, the remaining parties shall be listed in Form 1A, which shall be appended to the form immediately following the first page.

Additional Debtors

(4) If any of the following forms do not have sufficient space to list all of the debtors in respect of which the form applies, the remaining debtors shall be listed in Form 1A.1, which shall be appended to the form:

1. Certificate of judgment (Form 20A).
2. Writ of seizure and sale of personal property (Form 20C).
3. Writ of seizure and sale of land (Form 20D).
4. Direction to enforce writ of seizure and sale of personal property (Form 20O).

Affidavit

(5) If these rules permit or require the use of an affidavit, Form 15B may be used for the purpose unless another form is specified.

Telephone and Video Conferences — Where Available

1.07(1) If facilities for a telephone or video conference are available at the court, all or part of any of the following may be heard or conducted by telephone or video conference as permitted by subrules (2) and (3):

1. A settlement conference.
2. A motion.

(1.1) If facilities for a video conference are available at the court, all or part of an examination of a debtor or other person under rule 20.10 may be conducted by video conference as permitted by subrules (2) and (3).

Request to be Made

(2) A settlement conference or motion may be heard or conducted by telephone or video conference or all or part of an examination under rule 20.10 may be conducted by video conference if a party files a request for the conference (Form 1B), indicating the reasons for the request, and the court grants the request.

Balance of Convenience

(3) In deciding whether to direct a telephone or video conference, the judge shall consider,

(a) the balance of convenience between the party that wants the telephone or video conference and any party that opposes it; and

(b) any other relevant matter.

Arrangements for Conference

(4) If an order directing a telephone or video conference is made, the court shall make the necessary arrangements for the conference and notify the parties of them.

Setting Aside or Varying Order

(5) A judge presiding at a proceeding or step in a proceeding may set aside or vary an order directing a telephone or video conference.

RULE 2   NON-COMPLIANCE WITH THE RULES

Effect of Non-Compliance

2.01 A failure to comply with these rules is an irregularity and does not render a proceeding or a step, document or order in a proceeding a nullity, and the court may grant all necessary amendments or other relief, on such terms as are just, to secure the just determination of the real matters in dispute.

Court May Dispense With Compliance

2.02 If necessary in the interest of justice, the court may dispense with compliance with any rule at any time.

RULE 3

Computation

3.01 If these rules or an order of the court prescribe a period of time for the taking of a step in a proceeding, the time shall be counted by excluding the first day and including the last day of the period; if the last day of the period of time falls on a holiday, the period ends on the next day that is not a holiday.

Powers of Court

3.02(1) The court may lengthen or shorten any time prescribed by these rules or an order, on such terms as are just.

Consent

(2) A time prescribed by these rules for serving or filing a document may be lengthened or shortened by filing the consent of the parties.

RULE 4   PARTIES UNDER DISABILITY

Plaintiff's Litigation Guardian

4.01(1) An action by a person under disability shall be commenced or continued by a litigation guardian, subject to subrule (2).

Exception

(2) A minor may sue for any sum not exceeding $500 as if he or she were of full age.

Consent

(3) A plaintiff's litigation guardian shall, at the time of filing a claim or as soon as possible afterwards, file with the clerk a consent (Form 4A) in which the litigation guardian,

(a) states the nature of the disability;

(b) in the case of a minor, states the minor's birth date;

(c) sets out his or her relationship, if any, to the person under disability;

(d) states that he or she has no interest in the proceeding contrary to that of the person under disability;

(e) acknowledges that he or she is aware of his or her liability to pay personally any costs awarded against him or her or against the person under disability; and

(f) states whether he or she is represented by a lawyer or agent and, if so, gives that person's name and confirms that the person has written authority to act in the proceeding.

Defendant's Litigation Guardian

4.02(1) An action against a person under disability shall be defended by a litigation guardian.

(2) A defendant's litigation guardian shall file with the defence a consent (Form 4A) in which the litigation guardian,

(a) states the nature of the disability;

(b) in the case of a minor, states the minor's birth date;

(c) sets out his or her relationship, if any, to the person under disability;

(d) states that he or she has no interest in the proceeding contrary to that of the person under disability; and

(e) states whether he or she is represented by a lawyer or agent and, if so, gives that person's name and confirms that the person has written authority to act in the proceeding.

(3) If it appears to the court that a defendant is a person under disability and the defendant does not have a litigation guardian the court may, after notice to the proposed litigation guardian, appoint as litigation guardian for the defendant any person who has no interest in the action contrary to that of the defendant.

Who May Be Litigation Guardian

4.03(1) Any person who is not under disability may be a plaintiff's or defendant's litigation guardian, subject to subrule (2).

(2) If the plaintiff or defendant,

(a) is a minor, in a proceeding to which subrule 4.01(2) does not apply,

(i) the parent or person with lawful custody or another suitable person shall be the litigation guardian, or

(ii) if no such person is available and able to act, the Children's Lawyer shall be the litigation guardian;

(b) is mentally incapable and has a guardian with authority to act as litigation guardian in the proceeding, the guardian shall be the litigation guardian;

(c) is mentally incapable and does not have a guardian with authority to act as litigation guardian in the proceeding, but has an attorney under a power of attorney with that authority, the attorney shall be the litigation guardian;

(d) is mentally incapable and has neither a guardian with authority to act as litigation guardian in the proceeding nor an attorney under a power of attorney with that power,

(i) a suitable person who has no interest contrary to that of the incapable person may be the litigation guardian, or

(ii) if no such person is available and able to act, the Public Guardian and Trustee shall be the litigation guardian;

(e) is an absentee,

(i) the committee of his or her estate appointed under the *Absentees Act* shall be the litigation guardian,

(ii) if there is no such committee, a suitable person who has no interest contrary to that of the absentee may be the litigation guardian, or

(iii) if no such person is available and able to act, the Public Guardian and Trustee shall be the litigation guardian;

(f) is a person in respect of whom an order was made under subsection 72(1) or (2) of the *Mental Health Act* as it read before April 3, 1995, the Public Guardian and Trustee shall be the litigation guardian.

Duties of Litigation Guardian

4.04(1) A litigation guardian shall diligently attend to the interests of the person under disability and take all steps reasonably necessary for the protection of those interests, including the commencement and conduct of a defendant's claim.

Public Guardian and Trustee, Children's Lawyer

(2) The Public Guardian and Trustee or the Children's Lawyer may act as litigation guardian without filing the consent required by subrule 4.01(3) or 4.02(2).

Power of Court

4.05 The court may remove or replace a litigation guardian at any time.

Setting Aside Judgment, etc.

4.06 If an action has been brought against a person under disability and the action has not been defended by a litigation guardian, the court may set aside the noting of default or any judgment against the person under disability on such terms as are just, and may set aside any step that has been taken to enforce the judgment.

Settlement Requires Court's Approval

4.07 No settlement of a claim made by or against a person under disability is binding on the person without the approval of the court.

Money to be Paid into Court

4.08(1) Any money payable to a person under disability under an order or a settlement shall be paid into court, unless the court orders otherwise, and shall afterwards be paid out or otherwise disposed of as ordered by the court.

(2) If money is payable to a person under disability under an order or settlement, the court may order that the money shall be paid directly to the person, and payment made under the order discharges the obligation to the extent of the amount paid.

Supporting Affidavit

(3) A motion for an order under this rule shall be supported by an affidavit in Form 4B rather than an affidavit in Form 15A.

Costs

(4) In making an order under this rule, the court may order that costs payable to the moving party be paid out of the money in court directly to the person representing that party in the proceeding.

RULE 5   PARTNERSHIPS AND SOLE PROPRIETORSHIPS

Partnerships

5.01 A proceeding by or against two or more persons as partners may be commenced using the firm name of the partnership.

Defence

5.02 If a proceeding is commenced against a partnership using the firm name, the partnership's defence shall be delivered in the firm name and no person who admits being a partner at any material time may defend the proceeding separately, except with leave of the court.

Notice to Alleged Partner

5.03(1) In a proceeding against a partnership using the firm name, a plaintiff who seeks an order that would be enforceable personally against a person as a partner may serve the person with the claim, together with a notice to alleged partner (Form 5A).

(2) A person served as provided in subrule (1) is deemed to have been a partner at the material time, unless the person defends the proceeding separately denying having been a partner at the material time.

Disclosure of Partners

5.04(1) If a proceeding is commenced by or against a partnership using the firm name, any other party may serve a notice requiring the partnership to disclose immediately in writing the names and addresses of all partners constituting the partnership at a time specified in the notice; if a partner's present address is unknown, the partnership shall disclose the last known address.

(1.1), (1.1.1) REVOKED.

Partnership's Failure to Comply

(2) If a partnership fails to comply with a notice under subrule (1), its claim may be dismissed or the proceeding stayed or its defence may be struck out.

Enforcement of Order

5.05(1) An order against a partnership using the firm name may be enforced against the partnership's property.

(2) An order against a partnership using the firm name may also be enforced, if the order or a subsequent order so provides, against any person who was served as provided in rule 5.03 and who,

(a) under that rule, is deemed to have been a partner at the material time;

(b) has admitted being a partner at that time; or

(c) has been adjudged to have been a partner at that time.

Against Person not Served as Alleged Partner

(3) If, after an order has been made against a partnership using the firm name, the party obtaining it claims to be entitled to enforce it against any person alleged to be a partner other than a person who was served as provided in rule 5.03, the party may make a motion for leave to do so; the judge may grant leave if the person's liability as a partner is not disputed or, if disputed, after the liability has been determined in such manner as the judge directs.

Sole Proprietorships

5.06(1) If a person carries on business in a business name other than his or her own name, a proceeding may be commenced by or against the person using the business name.

(2) Rules 5.01 to 5.05 apply, with necessary modifications, to a proceeding by or against a sole proprietor using a business name, as though the sole proprietor were a partner and the business name were the firm name of a partnership.

RULE 6 FORUM AND JURISDICTION

Place of Commencement and Trial

6.01(1) An action shall be commenced,

(a) in the territorial division,

(i) in which the cause of action arose, or

(ii) in which the defendant or, if there are several defendants, in which any one of them resides or carries on business; or

(b) at the court's place of sitting that is nearest to the place where the defendant or, if there are several defendants, where any one of them resides or carries on business.

(2) An action shall be tried in the place where it is commenced, but if the court is satisfied that the balance of convenience substantially favours holding the trial at another place than those described in subrule (1), the court may order that the action be tried at that other place.

(3) If, when an action is called for trial or settlement conference, the judge finds that the place where the action was commenced is not the proper place of trial, the court may order that the action be tried in any other place where it could have been commenced under this rule.

6.02 A cause of action shall not be divided into two or more actions for the purpose of bringing it within the court's jurisdiction.

6.03 REVOKED.

RULE 7 COMMENCEMENT OF PROCEEDINGS

Plaintiff's Claim

7.01(1) An action shall be commenced by filing a plaintiff's claim (Form 7A) with the clerk, together with a copy of the claim for each defendant.

Contents of Claim, Attachments

(2) The following requirements apply to the claim:

1. It shall contain the following information, in concise and non-technical language:

    i. The full names of the parties to the proceeding and, if relevant, the capacity in which they sue or are sued.

    ii. The nature of the claim, with reasonable certainty and detail, including the date, place and nature of the occurrences on which the claim is based.

    iii. The amount of the claim and the relief requested.

    iv. The name, address, telephone number, fax number if any, and Law Society of Upper Canada registration number if any, of the lawyer or agent representing the plaintiff or, if the plaintiff is self-represented, the plaintiff's address, telephone number and fax number if any.

    v. The address where the plaintiff believes the defendant may be served.

2. If the plaintiff's claim is based in whole or in part on a document, a copy of the document shall be attached to each copy of the claim, unless it is unavailable, in which case the claim shall state the reason why the document is not attached.

(3) REVOKED.

7.02 REVOKED.

Issuing Claim

7.03(1) On receiving the plaintiff's claim, the clerk shall immediately issue it by dating, signing and sealing it and assigning it a court file number.

(2) The original of the claim shall remain in the court file and the copies shall be given to the plaintiff for service on the defendant.

RULE 8 SERVICE

Service of Particular Documents Plaintiff's or Defendant's Claim

8.01(1) A plaintiff's claim or defendant's claim (Form 7A or 10A) shall be served personally as provided in rule 8.02 or by an alternative to personal service as provided in rule 8.03.

Time for Service of Claim

(2) A claim shall be served within six months after the date it is issued, but the court may extend the time for service, before or after the six months has elapsed.

Defence

(3) A defence shall be served by the clerk, by mail or by fax.

(3.1) REVOKED.

Default Judgment

(4) A default judgment (Form 11B) shall be served by the clerk, by mail or by fax, on all parties named in the claim.

(4.1), (4.1.1) REVOKED.

Assessment Order

(5) An order made on a motion in writing for an assessment of damages under subrule 11.03(2) shall be served by the clerk to the moving party if the party provides a stamped, self-addressed envelope with the notice of motion and supporting affidavit.

Settlement Conference Order

(6) An order made at a settlement conference shall be served by the clerk by mail or by fax, on all parties that did not attend the settlement conference.

Summons to Witness

(7) A summons to witness (Form 18A) shall be served personally by the party who requires the presence of the witness, or by the party's lawyer or agent, at least 10 days before the trial date; at the time of service, attendance money calculated in accordance with the regulations made under the *Administration of Justice Act* shall be paid or tendered to the witness.

Notice of Garnishment

(8) A notice of garnishment (Form 20E) shall be served by the creditor,

    (a) together with a sworn affidavit for enforcement request (Form 20P), on the debtor, by mail, by courier, personally as provided in rule 8.02 or by an alternative to personal service as provided in rule 8.03; and

    (b) together with a garnishee's statement (Form 20F), on the garnishee, by mail, by courier, personally as provided in rule 8.02 or by an alternative to personal service as provided in rule 8.03.

Notice of Garnishment Hearing

(9) A notice of garnishment hearing (Form 20Q) shall be served by the person requesting the hearing on the creditor, debtor, garnishee and co-owner of the debt, if any, and any other interested persons by mail, by courier, personally as provided in rule 8.02 or by an alternative to personal services as provided in rule 8.03.

Notice of Examination

(10) A notice of examination (Form 20H) shall be served by the creditor on the debtor or person to be examined personally as provided in rule 8.02 or by an alternative to personal service as provided in rule 8.03.

Financial Statement

(11) If the person to be examined is the debtor and the debtor is an individual, the creditor shall serve the notice of examination on the debtor together with a blank financial information form (Form 20I).

(12) The notice of examination,

    (a) shall be served, together with the financial information form if applicable, at least 30 days before the date fixed for the examination; and

    (b) shall be filed, with proof of service, at least three days before the date fixed for the examination.

Notice of Contempt Hearing

(13) A notice of a contempt hearing shall be served by the creditor on the debtor or person to be examined personally as provided in rule 8.02.

Other Documents

(14) A document not referred to in subrules (1) to (13) may be served by mail, by courier, by fax, personally as provided in rule 8.02 or by an alternative to personal service as provided in rule 8.03, unless the court orders otherwise.

Personal Service

8.02 If a document is to be served personally, service shall be made,

Individual

    (a) on an individual, other than a person under disability, by leaving a copy of the document with him or her;

Municipality

    (b) on a municipal corporation, by leaving a copy of the document with the chair, mayor, warden or reeve of the municipality, with the clerk or deputy clerk of the municipality or with a lawyer for the municipality;

Corporation

    (c) on any other corporation, by leaving a copy of the document with,

        (i) an officer, a director or an agent of the corporation, or

        (ii) a person at any place of business of the corporation who appears to be in control or management of the place of business;

Board or Commission

    (d) on a board or commission, by leaving a copy of the document with a member or officer of the board or commission;

Person Outside Ontario Carrying on Business in Ontario

    (e) on a person outside Ontario who carries on business in Ontario, by leaving a copy of the document with anyone carrying on business in Ontario for the person;

Crown in Right of Canada

(f) on Her Majesty the Queen in right of Canada, in accordance with subsection 23(2) of the *Crown Liability and Proceedings Act* (Canada);

Crown in Right of Ontario

(g) on Her Majesty the Queen in right of Ontario, in accordance with section 10 of the *Proceedings Against the Crown Act*;

Absentee

(h) on an absentee, by leaving a copy of the document with the absentee's committee, if one has been appointed or, if not, with the Public Guardian and Trustee;

Minor

(i) on a minor, by leaving a copy of the document with the minor and, if the minor resides with a parent or other person having his or her care or lawful custody, by leaving another copy of the document with the parent or other person;

Mentally Incapable Person

(j) on a mentally incapable person,

(i) if there is a guardian or an attorney acting under a validated power of attorney for personal care with authority to act in the proceeding, by leaving a copy of the document with the guardian or attorney,

(ii) if there is no guardian or attorney acting under a validated power of attorney for personal care with authority to act in the proceeding but there is an attorney under a power of attorney with authority to act in the proceeding, by leaving a copy of the document with the attorney and leaving an additional copy with the person,

(iii) if there is neither a guardian nor an attorney with authority to act in the proceeding, by leaving a copy of the document bearing the person's name and address with the Public Guardian and Trustee and leaving an additional copy with the person;

Partnership

(k) on a partnership, by leaving a copy of the document with,

(i) any one or more of the partners, or

(ii) a person at the principal place of business of the partnership who appears to be in control or management of the place of business; and

Sole Proprietorship

(l) on a sole proprietorship, by leaving a copy of the document with,

(i) the sole proprietor, or

(ii) a person at the principal place of business of the sole proprietorship who appears to be in control or management of the place of business.

Alternatives to Personal Service

8.03(1) If a document is to be served by an alternative to personal service, service shall be made in accordance with subrule (2), (3) or (5); in the case of a plaintiff's claim or defendant's claim served on an individual, service may also be made in accordance with subrule (7).

At Place of Residence

(2) If an attempt is made to effect personal service at an individual's place of residence and for any reason personal service cannot be effected, the document may be served by,

(a) leaving a copy in a sealed envelope addressed to the individual at the place of residence with anyone who appears to be an adult member of the same household; and

(b) on the same day or the following day, mailing or sending by courier another copy of the document to the individual at the place of residence.

Corporation

(3) If the head office or principal place of business of a corporation or, in the case of an extra-provincial corporation, the attorney for service in Ontario cannot be found at the last address recorded with the Ministry of Government Services, service may be made on the corporation,

(a) by mailing or sending by courier a copy of the document to the corporation or to the attorney for service in Ontario, as the case may be, at that address; and

(b) by mailing or sending by courier a copy of the document to each director of the corporation as recorded with the Ministry of Government Services, at the director's address as recorded with that Ministry.

When Effective

(4) Service made under subrule (2) or (3) is effective on the fifth day after the document is mailed or verified by courier that it was delivered.

Acceptance of Service by Lawyer

(5) Service on a party who is represented by a lawyer may be made by leaving a copy of the document with the lawyer or an employee in the lawyer's office, but service under this subrule is effective only if the lawyer or employee endorses on the document or a copy of it an acceptance of service and the date of the acceptance.

(6) By accepting service the lawyer is deemed to represent to the court that he or she has the client's authority to accept service.

Service of Claim

(7) Service of a plaintiff's claim or defendant's claim on an individual against whom the claim is made may be made by sending a copy of the claim by registered mail or by courier to the individual's place of residence, if the signature of the individual or any person who appears to be a member of the same household, verifying receipt of the copy, is obtained.

(8) Service under subrule (7) is effective on the date on which receipt of the copy of the claim is verified by signature, as shown in a delivery confirmation provided by or obtained from Canada Post or the commercial courier, as the case may be.

(9) REVOKED.

Substituted Service

8.04 If it is shown that it is impractical to effect prompt service of a claim personally or by an alternative to personal service, the court may allow substituted service.

Service Outside Ontario

8.05 If the defendant is outside Ontario, the court may award as costs of the action the costs reasonably incurred in effecting service of the claim on the defendant there.

Proof of Service

8.06 An affidavit of service (Form 8A) made by the person effecting the service constitutes proof of service of a document.

Service by Mail

8.07(1) If a document is to be served by mail under these rules, it shall be sent, by regular lettermail or registered mail, to the last address of the person or of the person's lawyer or agent that is,

(a) on file with the court, if the document is to be served by the clerk;

(b) known to the sender, if the document is to be served by any other person.

When Effective

(2) Service of a document by mail is deemed to be effective on the fifth day following the date of mailing.

Exception

(3) This rule does not apply when a claim is served by registered mail under subrule 8.03(7).

Service by Courier

8.07.1(1) If a document is to be served by courier under these rules, it shall be sent by means of a commercial courier to the last address of the person or of the person's lawyer or agent that is on file with the court or known to the sender.

When Effective

(2) Service of a document sent by courier is deemed to be effective on the fifth day following the date on which the courier verifies to the sender that the document was delivered.

Exception

(3) This rule does not apply when a claim is served by courier under subrule 8.03(7).

Service by Fax

8.08(1) Service of a document by fax is deemed to be effective,

(a) on the day of transmission, if transmission takes place before 5 p.m. on a day that is not a holiday;

(b) on the next day that is not a holiday, in any other case.

(2) A document containing 16 or more pages, including the cover page, may be served by fax only between 5 p.m. and 8 a.m. the following day, unless the party to be served consents in advance.

Notice of Change of Address

8.09(1) A party whose address for service changes shall serve notice of the change on the court and other parties within seven days after the change takes place.

(2) Service of the notice may be proved by affidavit if the court orders that proof of service is required.

Failure to Receive Document

8.10 A person who has been served or who is deemed to have been served with a document in accordance with these rules is nevertheless entitled to show, on a motion to set aside the consequences of default, on a motion for an extension of time or in support of a request for an adjournment, that the document,

(a) did not come to the person's notice; or

(b) came to the person's notice only at some time later than when it was served or is deemed to have been served.

RULE 9   DEFENCE

Defence

9.01(1) A defendant who wishes to dispute a plaintiff's claim shall file a defence (Form 9A), together with a copy for each of the other parties with the clerk within 20 days of being served with the claim.

Service of Copy by Clerk

(2) On receiving the defence, the clerk shall retain the original in the court file and shall serve a copy in accordance with subrule 8.01(3) on each of the other parties.

(3) REVOKED.

Contents of Defence, Attachments

9.02(1) The following requirements apply to the defence:

1. It shall contain the following information:
   i. The reasons why the defendant disputes the plaintiff's claim, expressed in concise non-technical language with a reasonable amount of detail.
   ii. If the defendant is self-represented, the defendant's name, address and telephone number, and fax number if any.
   iii. If the defendant is represented by a lawyer or agent, that person's name, address and telephone

number, and fax number if any, and Law Society of Upper Canada registration number if any.

2. If the defence is based in whole or in part on a document, a copy of the document shall be attached to each copy of the defence, unless it is unavailable, in which case the defence shall state the reason why the document is not attached.

(2) REVOKED.

Admission of Liability and Proposal of Terms of Payment

9.03(1) A defendant who admits liability for all or part of the plaintiff's claim but wishes to arrange terms of payment may in the defence admit liability and propose terms of payment.

Where No Dispute

(2) If the plaintiff does not dispute the proposal within the 20-day period referred to in subrule (3),

(a) the defendant shall make payment in accordance with the proposal as if it were a court order;

(b) the plaintiff may serve a notice of default of payment (Form 20L) on the defendant if the defendant fails to make payment in accordance with the proposal; and

(c) the clerk shall sign judgment for the unpaid balance of the undisputed amount on the filing of an affidavit of default of payment (Form 20M) by the plaintiff swearing,

(i) that the defendant failed to make payment in accordance with the proposal,

(ii) to the amount paid by the defendant and the unpaid balance, and

(iii) that 15 days have passed since the defendant was served with a notice of default of payment.

Dispute

(3) The plaintiff may dispute the proposal within 20 days after service of the defence by filing with the clerk and serving on the defendant a request to clerk (Form 9B) for a terms of payment hearing before a referee or other person appointed by the court.

(4) The clerk shall fix a time for the hearing, allowing for a reasonable notice period after the date the request is served, and serve a notice of hearing on the parties.

Manner of Service

(4.1) The notice of hearing shall be served by mail or fax.

Financial Information Form, Defendant an Individual

(4.2) The clerk shall serve a financial information form (Form 20I) on the defendant, together with the notice of hearing, if the defendant is an individual.

(4.3) Where a defendant receives a financial information form under subrule (4.2), he or she shall complete it and serve it on the creditor before the hearing, but shall not file it with the court.

Order

(5) On the hearing, the referee or other person may make an order as to terms of payment by the defendant.

Failure to Appear, Default Judgment

(6) If the defendant does not appear at the hearing, the clerk may sign default judgment against the defendant for the part of the claim that has been admitted and shall serve a default judgment (Form 11B) on the defendant in accordance with subrule 8.01(4).

(6.1) REVOKED.

Failure to Make Payments

(7) Unless the referee or other person specifies otherwise in the order as to terms of payment, if the defendant fails to make payment in accordance with the order, the clerk shall sign judgment for the unpaid balance on the filing of an affidavit by the plaintiff swearing to the default and stating the amount paid and the unpaid balance.

RULE 10   DEFENDANT'S CLAIM

Defendant's Claim

10.01(1) A defendant may make a claim,

(a) against the plaintiff;

(b) against any other person,

(i) arising out of the transaction or occurrence relied upon by the plaintiff, or

(ii) related to the plaintiff's claim; or

(c) against the plaintiff and against another person in accordance with clause (b).

(2) The defendant's claim shall be in Form 10A and may be issued,

(a) within 20 days after the day on which the defence is filed; or

(b) after the time described in clause (a) but before trial or default judgment, with leave of the court.

Copies

(3) The defendant shall provide a copy of the defendant's claim to the court.

Contents of Defendant's Claim, Attachments

(4) The following requirements apply to the defendant's claim:

1. It shall contain the following information:

i. The full names of the parties to the defendant's claim and, if relevant, the capacity in which they sue or are sued.

ii. The nature of the claim, expressed in concise non-technical language with a reasonable amount of detail, including the date, place and nature of the occurrences on which the claim is based.

iii. The amount of the claim and the relief requested.

iv.   If the defendant is self-represented, the defendant's name, address and telephone number, and fax number if any.

v.   If the defendant is represented by a lawyer or agent, that person's name, address and telephone number, and fax number if any, and Law Society of Upper Canada registration number if any.

vi.   The address where the defendant believes each person against whom the claim is made may be served.

vii.   The court file number assigned to the plaintiff's claim.

2.   If the defendant's claim is based in whole or in part on a document, a copy of the document shall be attached to each copy of the claim, unless it is unavailable, in which case the claim shall state the reason why the document is not attached.

(5) REVOKED.

Issuance

(6)   On receiving the defendant's claim, the clerk shall immediately issue it by dating, signing and sealing it, shall assign it the same court file number as the plaintiff's claim and shall place the original in the court file.

(7), (8) REVOKED.

Service

10.02   A defendant's claim shall be served by the defendant on every person against whom it is made, in accordance with subrules 8.01(1) and (2).

Defence

10.03(1)   A party who wishes to dispute the defendant's claim or a third party who wishes to dispute the plaintiff's claim may, within 20 days after service of the defendant's claim, file a defence (Form 9A) with the clerk, together with a copy for each of the other parties or persons against whom the defendant's or plaintiff's claim is made.

Service of Copy by Clerk

(2)   On receiving a defence under subrule (1), the clerk shall retain the original in the court file and shall serve a copy on each party in accordance with subrule 8.01(3).

Defendant's Claim to be Tried with Main Action

10.04(1)   A defendant's claim shall be tried and disposed of at the trial of the action, unless the court orders otherwise.

Exception

(2)   If it appears that a defendant's claim may unduly complicate or delay the trial of the action or cause undue prejudice to a party, the court may order separate trials or direct that the defendant's claim proceed as a separate action.

Rights of Third Party

(3)   If the defendant alleges, in a defendant's claim, that a third party is liable to the defendant for all or part of the plaintiff's claim in the action, the third party may at the trial contest the defendant's liability to the plaintiff, but only if the third party has filed a defence in accordance with subrule 10.03(1).

Application of Rules to Defendant's Claim

10.05(1)   These rules apply, with necessary modifications, to a defendant's claim as if it were a plaintiff's claim, and to a defence to a defendant's claim as if it were a defence to a plaintiff's claim.

Exception

(2)   However, when a person against whom a defendant's claim is made is noted in default, judgment against that person may be obtained only in accordance with rule 11.04.

RULE 11   DEFAULT PROCEEDINGS

Noting Defendant in Default

11.01(1)   If a defendant to a plaintiff's claim or a defendant's claim fails to file a defence to all or part of the claim with the clerk within the prescribed time, the clerk may, when proof is filed that the claim was served within the territorial division, note the defendant in default.

Leave Required for Person under Disability

(2)   A person under disability may not be noted in default under subrule (1), except with leave of the court.

Service Outside Territorial Division

(3)   If all the defendants have been served outside the court's territorial division, the clerk shall not note any defendant in default until it is proved by an affidavit for jurisdiction (Form 11A) submitted to the clerk, or by evidence presented before a judge, that the action was properly brought in that territorial division.

Default Judgment, Plaintiff's Claim, Debt or Liquidated Demand

11.02(1)   If a defendant has been noted in default, the clerk may sign default judgment (Form 11B) in respect of the claim or any part of the claim to which the default applies that is for a debt or liquidated demand in money, including interest if claimed.

(2)   The fact that default judgment has been signed under subrule (1) does not affect the plaintiff's right to proceed on the remainder of the claim or against any other defendant for all or part of the claim.

Manner of Service of Default Judgment

(3)   A default judgment (Form 11B) shall be served in accordance with subrule 8.01(4).

Default Judgment, Plaintiff's Claim, Unliquidated Demand

11.03(1) If all defendants have been noted in default, the plaintiff may obtain judgment against a defendant noted in default with respect to any part of the claim to which rule 11.02 does not apply.

(2) To obtain judgment, the plaintiff may,

(a) file a notice of motion and supporting affidavit (Form 15A) requesting a motion in writing for an assessment of damages, setting out the reasons why the motion should be granted and attaching any relevant documents; or

(b) file a request to clerk (Form 9B) requesting that an assessment hearing be arranged.

Inadequate Supporting Affidavit

(3) On a motion in writing for an assessment of damages under clause (2)(a), a judge who finds the plaintiff's affidavit inadequate or unsatisfactory may order that,

(a) a further affidavit be provided; or

(b) an assessment hearing be held.

Assessment Hearing

(4) If an assessment hearing is to be held under clause (2)(b) or (3)(b), the clerk shall fix a date for the hearing and send a notice of hearing to the plaintiff, and the assessment hearing shall proceed as a trial in accordance with rule 17.

Matters to be Proved

(5) On a motion in writing for an assessment of damages or at an assessment hearing, the plaintiff is not required to prove liability against a defendant noted in default, but is required to prove the amount of the claim.

Service of Order

(6) An order made on a motion in writing for an assessment of damages shall be served by the clerk in accordance with subrule 8.01(5).

No Assessment where Defence Filed

(7) If one or more defendants have filed a defence, a plaintiff requiring an assessment of damages against a defendant noted in default shall proceed to a settlement conference under rule 13 and, if necessary, a trial in accordance with rule 17.

Default Judgment, Defendant's Claim

11.04 If a party against whom a defendant's claim is made has been noted in default, judgment may be obtained against the party only at trial or on motion.

Consequences of Noting in Default

11.05(1) A defendant who has been noted in default shall not file a defence or take any other step in the proceeding, except making a motion under rule 11.06, without leave of the court or the plaintiff's consent.

(2) Any step in the proceeding may be taken without the consent of a defendant who has been noted in default.

(3) A defendant who has been noted in default is not entitled to notice of any step in the proceeding and need not be served with any other document, except the following:

1. Subrule 11.02(3)(service of default judgment).
2. Rule 12.01(amendment of claim or defence).
3. Subrule 15.01(6)(motion after judgment).
4. Postjudgment proceedings against a debtor under rule 20.

Setting Aside Noting of Default by Court on Motion

11.06 The court may set aside the noting in default or default judgment against a party and any step that has been taken to enforce the judgment, on such terms as are just, if the party makes a motion to set aside and the court is satisfied that,

(a) the party has a meritorious defence and a reasonable explanation for the default; and

(b) the motion is made as soon as is reasonably possible in all the circumstances.

RULE 11.1   DISMISSAL BY CLERK

Dismissal — Undefended Actions

11.1.01(1) The clerk shall make an order dismissing an action as abandoned if the following conditions are satisfied, unless the court orders otherwise:

1. More than 180 days have passed since the date the claim was issued or an order was made extending the time for service of the claim under subrule 8.01(2).
2. No defence has been filed.
3. The action has not been disposed of by order and has not been set down for trial.
4. The clerk has given 45 days notice to the plaintiff that the action will be dismissed as abandoned.

Dismissal — Defended Actions

(2) The clerk shall make an order dismissing an action as abandoned if the following conditions are satisfied, unless the court orders otherwise:

1. More than 150 days have passed since the date the first defence was filed.
2. All settlement conferences required under Rule 13 have been held.
3. The action has not been disposed of by order and has not been set down for trial.
4. The clerk has given 45 days notice to all parties to the action that the action will be dismissed as abandoned.

Transition

(3) If an action was started before July 1, 2006, the following applies:

1. The action or a step in the action shall be carried on under these rules on or after July 1, 2006.

2. Despite paragraph 1, if a step in the action is taken on or after July 1, 2006, the timetable set out in subrules (1) and (2) shall apply as if the action started on the date on which the step was taken.

Same

(4) If an action was commenced before July 1, 2006 and no step is taken in the action on or after that date, the clerk may make an order dismissing it as abandoned if,

(a) where an action is undefended, more than two years have passed since the date the claim was issued and the conditions set out in paragraphs 2, 3 and 4 of subrule (1) are satisfied; or

(b) more than two years have passed since the date the first defence was filed and the conditions set out in paragraphs 3 and 4 of subrule (2) are satisfied.

Exception Where Terms of Settlement Signed

(5) Subrules (1), (2) and (4) do not apply if terms of settlement (Form 14D) signed by all parties have been filed.

Exception Where Admission of Liability

(6) Subrule (2) and clause (4)(b) do not apply if the defence contains an admission of liability for the plaintiff's claim and a proposal of terms of payment under subrule 9.03(1).

Service of Orders

(7) The clerk shall serve a copy of an order made under subrule (1) or clause (4)(a) on the plaintiff and a copy of an order made under subrule (2) or clause (4)(b) on all parties to the action.

RULE 11.2   REQUEST FOR CLERK'S ORDER ON CONSENT

Consent Order

11.2.01(1) The clerk shall, on the filing of a request for clerk's order on consent (Form 11.2A), make an order granting the relief sought, including costs, if the following conditions are satisfied:

1. The relief sought is,
   i. amending a claim or defence less than 30 days before the originally scheduled trial date,
   ii. adding, deleting or substituting a party less than 30 days before the originally scheduled trial date,
   iii. setting aside the noting in default or default judgment against a party and any specified step to enforce the judgment that has not yet been completed,
   iv. restoring a matter that was dismissed under rule 11.1 to the list,
   v. noting that payment has been made in full satisfaction of a judgment or terms of settlement, or
   vi. dismissing an action.

2. The request is signed by all parties (including any party to be added, deleted or substituted) and states,
   i. that each party has received a copy of the request, and
   ii. that no party that would be affected by the order is under disability.

3., 4. REVOKED.

Service of order

(2) The clerk shall serve a copy of an order made under subrule (1) in accordance with subrule 8.01(14) on a party that requests it and provides a stamped, self-addressed envelope.

Same, Refusal to Make Order

(3) Where the clerk refuses to make an order, the clerk shall serve a copy of the request for clerk's order on consent (Form 11.2A), with reasons for the refusal, on all the parties.

Notice of Setting Aside of Enforcement Step

(4) Where an order is made setting aside a specified step to enforce a judgment under subparagraph 1 iii of subrule (1), a party shall file a copy of the order at each court location where the enforcement step has been requested.

RULE 11.3   DISCONTINUANCE

Discontinuance by Plaintiff in Undefended Action

11.3.01(1) A plaintiff may discontinue his or her claim against a defendant who fails to file a defence to all or part of the claim with the clerk within the prescribed time by,

(a) serving a notice of discontinued claim (Form 11.3A) on all defendants who were served with the claim; and

(b) filing the notice with proof of service.

(2) A claim may not be discontinued by or against a person under disability, except with leave of the court.

Effect of Discontinuance on Subsequent Action

11.3.02 The discontinuance of a claim is not a defence to a subsequent action on the matter, unless an order granting leave to discontinue provides otherwise.

RULE 12   AMENDMENT

Right to Amend

12.01(1) A plaintiff's or defendant's claim and a defence to a plaintiff's or defendant's claim may be amended by filing with the clerk a copy that is marked "Amended", in which any additions are underlined and any other changes are identified.

Service

(2) The amended document shall be served by the party making the amendment on all parties, including any parties in default, in accordance with subrule 8.01(14).

Time

(3) Filing and service of the amended document shall take place at least 30 days before the originally scheduled trial date, unless,

(a) the court, on motion, allows a shorter notice period; or

(b) a clerk's order permitting the amendment is obtained under subrule 11.2.01(1).

Service on Added Party

(4) A person added as a party shall be served with the claim as amended, except that if the person is added as a party at trial, the court may dispense with service of the claim.

No Amendment Required in Response

(5) A party who is served with an amended document is not required to amend the party's defence or claim.

Motion to Strike out or Amend a Document

12.02(1) The court may, on motion, strike out or amend all or part of any document that,

(a) discloses no reasonable cause of action or defence;

(b) may delay or make it difficult to have a fair trial; or

(c) is inflammatory, a waste of time, a nuisance or an abuse of the court's process.

(2) In connection with an order striking out or amending a document under subrule (1), the court may do one or more of the following:

1. In the case of a claim, order that the action be stayed or dismissed.

2. In the case of a defence, strike out the defence and grant judgment.

3. Impose such terms as are just.

RULE 13   SETTLEMENT CONFERENCES

Settlement Conference Required in Defended Action

13.01(1) A settlement conference shall be held in every defended action.

Duty of Clerk

(2) The clerk shall fix a time, date and place for the settlement conference and serve a notice of settlement conference, together with a list of proposed witnesses (Form 13A), on the parties.

Timing

(3) The settlement conference shall be held within 90 days after the first defence is filed.

Exception

(4) Subrules (1) to (3) do not apply if the defence contains an admission of liability for all of the plaintiff's claim and a proposal of terms of payment under subrule 9.03(1).

Attendance

13.02(1) A party and the party's lawyer or agent, if any, shall, unless the court orders otherwise, participate in the settlement conference,

(a) by personal attendance; or

(b) by telephone or video conference in accordance with rule 1.07.

Authority to Settle

(2) A party who requires another person's approval before agreeing to a settlement shall, before the settlement conference, arrange to have ready telephone access to the other person throughout the conference, whether it takes place during or after regular business hours.

Additional Settlement Conferences

(3) The court may order the parties to attend an additional settlement conference.

(4) The clerk shall fix a time and place for any additional settlement conference and serve a notice of settlement conference, together with a list of proposed witnesses (Form 13A) on the parties.

Failure to Attend

(5) If a party who has received a notice of settlement conference fails to attend the conference, the court may,

(a) impose appropriate sanctions, by way of costs or otherwise; and

(b) order that an additional settlement conference be held, if necessary.

(6) If a defendant fails to attend a first settlement conference, receives notice of an additional settlement conference and fails to attend the additional settlement conference, the court may,

(a) strike out the defence and dismiss the defendant's claim, if any, and allow the plaintiff to prove the plaintiff's claim; or

(b) make such other order as is just.

Inadequate Preparation, Failure to File Material

(7) The court may award costs against a person who attends a settlement conference if,

(a) in the opinion of the court, the person is so inadequately prepared as to frustrate the purposes of the conference;

(b) the person fails to file the material required by subrule 13.03(2).

Purposes of Settlement Conference

13.03(1) The purposes of a settlement conference are,

(a) to resolve or narrow the issues in the action;

(b) to expedite the disposition of the action;

(c) to encourage settlement of the action;

(d) to assist the parties in effective preparation for trial; and

(e) to provide full disclosure between the parties of the relevant facts and evidence.

Disclosure

(2) At least 14 days before the date of the settlement conference, each party shall serve on every other party and file with the court,

(a) a copy of any document to be relied on at the trial, including an expert report, not attached to the party's claim or defence; and

(b) a list of proposed witnesses (Form 13A) and of other persons with knowledge of the matters in dispute in the action.

(3) At the settlement conference, the parties or their representatives shall openly and frankly discuss the issues involved in the action.

Further Disclosure Restricted

(4) Except as otherwise provided or with the consent of the parties (Form 13B), the matters discussed at the settlement conference shall not be disclosed to others until after the action has been disposed of.

Recommendations to Parties

13.04 The court may make recommendations to the parties on any matter relating to the conduct of the action, in order to fulfil the purposes of a settlement conference, including recommendations as to,

(a) the clarification and simplification of issues in the action;

(b) the elimination of claims or defences that appear to be unsupported; and

(c) the admission of facts or documents without further proof.

Orders at Settlement Conference

13.05(1) A judge conducting a settlement conference may make any order relating to the conduct of the action that the court could make.

(2) Without limiting the generality of subrule (1), the judge may,

(a) make an order,

(i) adding or deleting parties,

(ii) consolidating actions,

(iii) staying the action,

(iv) amending or striking out a claim or defence under rule 12.02,

(v) staying or dismissing a claim,

(vi) directing production of documents,

(vii) changing the place of trial under rule 6.01,

(viii) directing an additional settlement conference under subrule 13.02(3), and

(ix) ordering costs; and

(b) at an additional settlement conference, order judgment under subrule 13.02(6).

Recommendations to Judge

(3) If the settlement conference is conducted by a referee, a judge may, on the referee's recommendation, make any order that may be made under subrules (1) and (2).

Consent to Final Judgment

(4) A judge may order final judgment at a settlement conference where the matter in dispute is for an amount under the appealable limit and a party files a consent (Form 13B) signed by all parties before the settlement conference indicating that they wish to obtain final determination of the matter at the settlement conference if a mediated settlement is not reached.

Service of Order

(5) Within 10 days after the judge signs an order made at a settlement conference, the clerk shall serve the order on the parties that were not present at the settlement conference in accordance with subrule 8.01(6).

Memorandum

13.06(1) At the end of the settlement conference, the court shall prepare a memorandum summarizing,

(a) recommendations made under rule 13.04;

(b) the issues remaining in dispute;

(c) the matters agreed on by the parties;

(d) any evidentiary matters that are considered relevant; and

(e) information relating to the scheduling of the remaining steps in the proceeding.

(2) The memorandum shall be filed with the clerk, who shall give a copy to the trial judge.

Notice of Trial

13.07 At or after the settlement conference, the clerk shall provide the parties with a notice stating that one of the parties must request a trial date if the action is not disposed of within 30 days after the settlement conference, and pay the fee required for setting the action down for trial.

Judge Not To Preside At Trial

13.08 A judge who conducts a settlement conference in an action shall not preside at the trial of the action.

Withdrawal of Claim

13.09 After a settlement conference has been held, a claim against a party who is not in default shall not be withdrawn or discontinued by the party who brought the claim without,

(a) the written consent of the party against whom the claim is brought; or

(b) leave of the court.

Costs

13.10 The costs of a settlement conference, exclusive of disbursements, shall not exceed $100 unless the court orders otherwise because there are special circumstances.

RULE 14   OFFER TO SETTLE

14.01 A party may serve on any other party an offer to settle a claim on the terms specified in the offer.

Written Documents

14.01.1(1) An offer to settle, an acceptance of an offer to settle and a notice of withdrawal of an offer to settle shall be in writing.

Use of Forms

(2) An offer to settle may be in Form 14A, an acceptance of an offer to settle may be in Form 14B and a notice of withdrawal of an offer to settle may be in Form 14C.

Terms of Settlement

(3) The terms of an accepted offer to settle may be set out in terms of settlement (Form 14D).

Time for Making Offer

14.02(1) An offer to settle may be made at any time.

Costs Consequences

(2) The costs consequences referred to in rule 14.07 apply only if the offer to settle is served on the party to whom it is made at least seven days before the trial commences.

Withdrawal

14.03(1) An offer to settle may be withdrawn at any time before it is accepted, by serving a notice of withdrawal of an offer to settle on the party to whom it was made.

Deemed Withdrawal

(2) If an offer to settle specifies a date after which it is no longer available for acceptance, and has not been accepted on or before that date, the offer shall be deemed to have been withdrawn on the day after that date.

Expiry When Court Disposes of Claim

(3) An offer may not be accepted after the court disposes of the claim in respect of which the offer is made.

No Disclosure to Trial Judge

14.04 If an offer to settle is not accepted, no communication about it or any related negotiations shall be made to the trial judge until all questions of liability and the relief to be granted, other than costs, have been determined.

Acceptance of an Offer to Settle

14.05(1) An offer to settle may be accepted by serving an acceptance of an offer to settle on the party who made it, at any time before it is withdrawn or before the court disposes of the claim in respect of which it is made.

Payment Into Court As Condition

(2) An offer by a plaintiff to settle a claim in return for the payment of money by a defendant may include a term that the defendant pay the money into court; in that case, the defendant may accept the offer only by paying the money into court and notifying the plaintiff of the payment.

(3) If a defendant offers to pay money to a plaintiff in settlement of a claim, the plaintiff may accept the offer with the condition that the defendant pay the money into court; if the offer is so accepted and the defendant fails to pay the money into court, the plaintiff may proceed as provided in rule 14.06.

Costs

(4) If an accepted offer to settle does not deal with costs, the plaintiff is entitled,

    (a) in the case of an offer made by the defendant, to the plaintiff's disbursements assessed to the date the plaintiff was served with the offer;

    (b) in the case of an offer made by the plaintiff, to the plaintiff's disbursements assessed to the date that the notice of acceptance was served.

Failure to Comply With Accepted Offer

14.06 If a party to an accepted offer to settle fails to comply with the terms of the offer, the other party may,

    (a) make a motion to the court for judgment in the terms of the accepted offer; or

    (b) continue the proceeding as if there had been no offer to settle.

Costs Consequences of Failure to Accept

14.07(1) When a plaintiff makes an offer to settle that is not accepted by the defendant, the court may award the plaintiff an amount not exceeding twice the costs of the action, if the following conditions are met:

1. The plaintiff obtains a judgment as favourable as or more favourable than the terms of the offer.

2. The offer was made at least seven days before the trial.

3. The offer was not withdrawn and did not expire before the trial.

(2) When a defendant makes an offer to settle that is not accepted by the plaintiff, the court may award the defendant an amount not exceeding twice the costs awardable to a successful party, from the date the offer was served, if the following conditions are met:

1. The plaintiff obtains a judgment as favourable as or less favourable than the terms of the offer.

2. The offer was made at least seven days before the trial.

3. The offer was not withdrawn and did not expire before the trial.

(3) If an amount is awarded under subrule (1) or (2) to a self-represented party, the court may also award the party an amount not exceeding $500 as compensation for inconvenience and expense.

RULE 15 MOTIONS

Notice of Motion and Supporting Affidavit

15.01(1) A motion shall be made by a notice of motion and supporting affidavit (Form 15A).

(2) The moving party shall obtain a hearing date from the clerk before serving the notice of motion and supporting affidavit under subrule (3).

(3) The notice of motion and supporting affidavit,

(a) shall be served on every party who has filed a claim and any defendant who has not been noted in default, at least seven days before the hearing date; and

(b) shall be filed, with proof of service, at least three days before the hearing date.

Supporting Affidavit in Response

(4) A party who prepares an affidavit (Form 15B) in response to the moving party's notice of motion and supporting affidavit shall serve it on every party who has filed a claim or defence and file it, with proof of service, at least two days before the hearing date.

Supplementary Affidavit

(5) The moving party may serve a supplementary affidavit on every party who has filed a claim or defence and file it, with proof of service, at least two days before the hearing date.

Motion After Judgment Signed

(6) A motion that is made after judgment has been signed shall be served on all parties, including those who have been noted in default.

Method of Hearing

15.02(1) A motion may be heard,

(a) in person;

(b) by telephone or video conference in accordance with paragraph 2 of subrule 1.07(1);

(c) by a judge in writing under clause 11.03(2)(a);

(d) by any other method that the judge determines is fair and reasonable.

(2) The attendance of the parties is not required if the motion is in writing under clause (1)(c).

Motion Without Notice

15.03(1) Despite rule 15.01, a motion may be made without notice if the nature or circumstances of the motion make notice unnecessary or not reasonably possible.

Service of Order

(2) A party who obtains an order on motion without notice shall serve it on every affected party, together with a copy of the notice of motion and supporting affidavit used on the motion, within five days after the order is signed.

Motion to Set Aside or Vary Motion Made Without Notice

(3) A party who is affected by an order obtained on motion without notice may make a motion to set aside or vary the order, within 30 days after being served with the order.

No Further Motions Without Leave

15.04 If the court is satisfied that a party has tried to delay the action, add to its costs or otherwise abuse the court's process by making numerous motions without merit, the court may, on motion, make an order prohibiting the party from making any further motions in the action without leave of the court.

Adjournment of Motion

15.05 A motion shall not be adjourned at a party's request before the hearing date unless the written consent of all parties is filed when the request is made, unless the court orders otherwise.

Withdrawal of Motion

15.06 A motion shall not be withdrawn without,

(a) the written consent of all the parties; or

(b) leave of the court.

Costs

15.07 The costs of a motion, exclusive of disbursements, shall not exceed $100 unless the court orders otherwise because there are special circumstances.

RULE 16 NOTICE OF TRIAL

Clerk Fixes Date and Serves Notice

16.01(1) The clerk shall fix a date for trial and serve a notice of trial on each party who has filed a claim or defence if,

(a) a settlement conference has been held; and

(b) a party has requested that the clerk fix a date for trial and has paid the required fee.

Manner of Service

(2) The notice of trial shall be served by mail or fax.

RULE 17 TRIAL

Failure to Attend

17.01(1) If an action is called for trial and all the parties fail to attend, the trial judge may strike the action off the trial list.

(2) If an action is called for trial and a party fails to attend, the trial judge may,

(a) proceed with the trial in the party's absence;

(b) if the plaintiff attends and the defendant fails to do so, strike out the defence and dismiss the defendant's claim, if any, and allow the plaintiff to prove the plaintiff's claim, subject to subrule (3);

(c) if the defendant attends and the plaintiff fails to do so, dismiss the action and allow the defendant to prove the defendant's claim, if any; or

(d) make such other order as is just.

(2.1) In the case described in clause (2)(b) or (c), the person with the claim is not required to prove liability against the party who has failed to attend but is required to prove the amount of the claim.

(3) In the case described in clause (2)(b), if an issue as to the proper place of trial under subrule 6.01(1) is raised in the defence, the trial judge shall consider it and make a finding.

Setting Aside or Variation of Judgment

(4) The court may set aside or vary, on such terms as are just, a judgment obtained against a party who failed to attend at the trial.

Conditions to Making of Order under Subrule (4)

(5) The court may make an order under subrule (4) only if,

(a) the party who failed to attend makes a motion for the order within 30 days after becoming aware of the judgment; or

(b) the party who failed to attend makes a motion for an extension of the 30-day period mentioned in clause (a) and the court is satisfied that there are special circumstances that justify the extension.

Adjournment

17.02(1) The court may postpone or adjourn a trial on such terms as are just, including the payment by one party to another of an amount as compensation for inconvenience and expense.

(2) If the trial of an action has been adjourned two or more times, any further adjournment may be made only on motion with notice to all the parties who were served with the notice of trial, unless the court orders otherwise.

Inspection

17.03 The trial judge may, in the presence of the parties or their representatives, inspect any real or personal property concerning which a question arises in the action.

Motion for New Trial

17.04(1) A party may make a motion for a new trial within 30 days after a final order is made.

Transcript

(2) In addition to serving and filing the notice of motion and supporting affidavit (Form 15A) required under rule 15.01, the moving party shall serve and file proof that a request has been made for a transcript of,

(a) the reasons for judgment; and

(b) any other portion of the proceeding that is relevant.

Service and Filing of Transcript

(3) If available, a copy of the transcript shall, at least three days before the hearing date,

(a) be served on all parties who were served with the original notice of trial; and

(b) be filed, with proof of service.

Powers of Court on Motion

(4) On the hearing of the motion, the court may,

(a) if the party demonstrates that a condition referred to in subrule (5) is satisfied,

(i) grant a new trial, or

(ii) pronounce the judgment that ought to have been given at trial and order judgment accordingly; or

(b) dismiss the motion.

Conditions

(5) The conditions referred to in clause (4)(a) are:

1. There was a purely arithmetical error in the determination of the amount of damages awarded.

2. There is relevant evidence that was not available to the party at the time of the original trial and could not reasonably have been expected to be available at that time.

RULE 18   EVIDENCE AT TRIAL

Affidavit

18.01 At the trial of an undefended action, the plaintiff's case may be proved by affidavit, unless the trial judge orders otherwise.

Written Statements, Documents and Records

18.02(1) A document or written statement or an audio or visual record that has been served, at least 30 days before the trial date, on all parties who were served with the notice of trial, shall be received in evidence, unless the trial judge orders otherwise.

(2) Subrule (1) applies to the following written statements and documents:

1. The signed written statement of any witness, including the written report of an expert, to the extent that the statement relates to facts and opinions to which the witness would be permitted to testify in person.

2. Any other document, including but not limited to a hospital record or medical report made in the course of care and treatment, a financial record, a receipt, a bill, documentary evidence of loss of income or property damage, and a repair estimate.

Details about Witness or Author

(3) A party who serves on another party a written statement or document described in subrule (2) shall append to or include in the statement or document,

(a) the name, telephone number and address for service of the witness or author; and

(b) if the witness or author is to give expert evidence, a summary of his or her qualifications.

(4) A party who has been served with a written statement or document described in subrule (2) and wishes to cross-examine the witness or author may summon him or her as a witness under subrule 18.03(1).

Where Witness or Author is Summoned

(5) A party who serves a summons to witness on a witness or author referred to in subrule (3) shall, at the time the summons is served, serve a copy of the summons on every other party.

(6) Service of a summons and the payment or tender of attendance money under this rule may be proved by affidavit (Form 8A).

Adjournment

(7) A party who is not served with a copy of the summons in accordance with subrule (5) may request an adjournment of the trial, with costs.

Summons to Witness

18.03(1) A party who requires the attendance of a person in Ontario as a witness at a trial may serve the person with a summons to witness (Form 18A) requiring him or her to attend the trial at the time and place stated in the summons.

(2) The summons may also require the witness to produce at the trial the documents or other things in his or her possession, control or power relating to the matters in question in the action that are specified in the summons.

(3) A summons to witness (Form 18A) shall be served in accordance with subrule 8.01(7).

(4) Service of a summons and the payment or tender of attendance money may be proved by affidavit (Form 8A).

(5) A summons to witness continues to have effect until the attendance of the witness is no longer required.

Interpreter

(5.1) If a party serves a summons on a witness who requires an interpreter, the party shall arrange for a qualified interpreter to attend at the trial unless the interpretation is from English to French or French to English and an interpreter is provided by the Ministry of the Attorney General.

(5.2) If a party does not comply with subrule (5.1), every other party is entitled to request an adjournment of the trial, with costs.

Failure to Attend or Remain in Attendance

(6) If a witness whose evidence is material to the conduct of an action fails to attend at the trial or to remain in attendance in accordance with the requirements of a summons to witness served on him or her, the trial judge may, by warrant (Form 18B) directed to all police officers in Ontario, cause the witness to be apprehended anywhere within Ontario and promptly brought before the court.

Identification Form

(6.1) The party who served the summons on the witness may file with the clerk an identification form (Form 20K) to assist the police in apprehending the witness.

(7) On being apprehended, the witness may be detained in custody until his or her presence is no longer required or released on such terms as are just, and may be ordered to pay the costs arising out of the failure to attend or remain in attendance.

Abuse of Power to Summon Witness

(8) If satisfied that a party has abused the power to summon a witness under this rule, the court may order that the party pay directly to the witness an amount as compensation for inconvenience and expense.

RULE 19   COSTS

Disbursements

19.01(1) A successful party is entitled to have the party's reasonable disbursements, including any costs of effecting service or preparing a plaintiff's or defendant's claim or a defence and expenses for travel, accommodation, photocopying and experts' reports, paid by the unsuccessful party, unless the court orders otherwise.

(2) The clerk shall assess the disbursements in accordance with the regulations made under the *Administration of Justice Act* and in accordance with subrules (3) and (4); the assessment is subject to review by the court.

(3) The amount of disbursements assessed for effecting service shall not exceed $60 for each person served unless the court is of the opinion that there are special circumstances that justify assessing a greater amount.

(4) The amount of disbursements assessed for preparing a plaintiff's or defendant's claim or a defence shall not exceed $100.

Limit

19.02 Any power under this rule to award costs is subject to section 29 of the *Courts of Justice Act*, which limits the amount of costs that may be awarded.

19.03 Revoked.

Representation Fee

19.04 If a successful party is represented by a lawyer, student-at-law or agent, the court may award the party a reasonable representation fee at trial or at an assessment hearing.

Compensation for Inconvenience and Expense

19.05 The court may order an unsuccessful party to pay to a successful party who is self-represented an amount not exceeding $500 as compensation for inconvenience and expense.

Penalty

19.06 If the court is satisfied that a party has unduly complicated or prolonged an action or has otherwise acted unreasonably, the court may order the party to pay an amount as compensation to another party.

RULE 20   ENFORCEMENT OF ORDERS

Definitions

20.01 In rules 20.02 to 20.12,

"creditor" means a person who is entitled to enforce an order for the payment or recovery of money;

"debtor" means a person against whom an order for the payment or recovery of money may be enforced.

Power of Court

20.02(1) The court may,

    (a) stay the enforcement of an order of the court, for such time and on such terms as are just; and

    (b) vary the times and proportions in which money payable under an order of the court shall be paid, if it is satisfied that the debtor's circumstances have changed.

Enforcement Limited While Periodic Payment Order in Force

(2) While an order for periodic payment is in force, no step to enforce the judgment may be taken or continued against the debtor by a creditor named in the order, except issuing a writ of seizure and sale of land and filing it with the sheriff.

Service of Notice of Default of Payment

(3) The creditor may serve the debtor with a notice of default of payment (Form 20L) in accordance with subrule 8.01(14) and file a copy of it, together with an affidavit of default of payment (Form 20M), if the debtor fails to make payments under an order for periodic payment.

Termination on Default

(4) An order for periodic payment terminates on the day that is 15 days after the creditor serves the debtor with the notice of default of payment, unless a consent (Form 13B) in which the creditor waives the default is filed within the 15-day period.

General

20.03 In addition to any other method of enforcement provided by law,

    (a) an order for the payment or recovery of money may be enforced by,

        (i) a writ of seizure and sale of personal property (Form 20C) under rule 20.06,

        (ii) a writ of seizure and sale of land (Form 20D) under rule 20.07, and

        (iii) garnishment under rule 20.08; and

    (b) a further order as to payment may be made under subrule 20.10(7).

Certificate of Judgment

20.04(1) If there is default under an order for the payment or recovery of money, the clerk shall, at the creditor's request, supported by an affidavit for enforcement request (Form 20P) stating the amount still owing, issue a certificate of judgment (Form 20A) to the clerk at the court location specified by the creditor.

    (2) The certificate of judgment shall state,

        (a) the date of the order and the amount awarded;

        (b) the rate of postjudgment interest payable; and

        (c) the amount owing, including postjudgment interest.

Delivery of Personal Property

20.05(1) An order for the delivery of personal property may be enforced by a writ of delivery (Form 20B) issued by the clerk to a bailiff, on the request of the person in whose favour the order was made, supported by an affidavit of that person or the person's agent stating that the property has not been delivered.

Seizure of Other Personal Property

(2) If the property referred to in a writ of delivery cannot be found or taken by the bailiff, the person in whose favour the order was made may make a motion to the court for an order directing the bailiff to seize any other personal property of the person against whom the order was made.

(3) Unless the court orders otherwise, the bailiff shall keep personal property seized under subrule (2) until the court makes a further order for its disposition.

Storage Costs

(4) The person in whose favour the order is made shall pay the bailiff's storage costs, in advance and from time to time; if the person fails to do so, the seizure shall be deemed to be abandoned.

Writ of Seizure and Sale of Personal Property

20.06(1) If there is default under an order for the payment or recovery of money, the clerk shall, at the creditor's request, supported by an affidavit for enforcement request (Form 20P) stating the amount still owing, issue to a bailiff a writ of seizure and sale of personal property (Form 20C), and the bailiff shall enforce the writ for the amount owing, postjudgment interest and the bailiff's fees and expenses.

(1.1) If more than six years have passed since the order was made, a writ of seizure and sale of personal property may be issued only with leave of the court.

(1.2) If a writ of seizure and sale of personal property is not issued within one year after the date on which an order granting leave to issue it is made,

    (a) the order granting leave ceases to have effect; and

    (b) a writ of seizure and sale of personal property may be issued only with leave of the court on a subsequent motion.

(1.3) A writ of seizure and sale of personal property shall show the creditor's name, address and telephone number and the name, address and telephone number of the creditor's lawyer or agent, if any.

Duration of Writ

(2) A writ of seizure and sale of personal property remains in force for six years after the date of its issue and for a further six years after each renewal.

Renewal of Writ

(3) A writ of seizure and sale of personal property may be renewed before its expiration by filing a request to renew a writ of seizure and sale (Form 20N) with the bailiff.

Direction to Enforce

(4) The creditor may request enforcement of a writ of seizure and sale of personal property by filing a direction to enforce writ of seizure and sale of personal property (Form 20O) with the bailiff.

Inventory of Property Seized

(5) Within a reasonable time after a request is made by the debtor or the debtor's agent, the bailiff shall deliver an inventory of personal property seized under a writ of seizure and sale of personal property.

Sale of Personal Property

(6) Personal property seized under a writ of seizure and sale of personal property shall not be sold by the bailiff unless notice of the time and place of sale has been,

(a) mailed, at least 10 days before the sale,

(i) to the creditor at the address shown on the writ, or to the creditor's lawyer or agent, and

(ii) to the debtor at the debtor's last known address; and

(b) advertised in a manner that is likely to bring it to the attention of the public.

Writ of Seizure and Sale of Land

20.07(1) If an order for the payment or recovery of money is unsatisfied, the clerk shall at the creditor's request, supported by an affidavit for enforcement request (Form 20P) stating the amount still owing, issue to the sheriff specified by the creditor a writ of seizure and sale of land (Form 20D).

(1.1) If more than six years have passed since the order was made, a writ of seizure and sale of land may be issued only with leave of the court.

(1.2) If a writ of seizure and sale of land is not issued within one year after the date on which an order granting leave to issue it is made,

(a) the order granting leave ceases to have effect; and

(b) a writ of seizure and sale of land may be issued only with leave of the court on a subsequent motion.

(2) A writ of seizure and sale of land issued under subrule (1) has the same force and effect and may be renewed or withdrawn in the same manner as a writ of seizure and sale issued under rule 60 of the Rules of Civil Procedure.

Duration of Writ

(3) A writ of seizure and sale of land remains in force for six years after the date of its issue and for a further six years after each renewal.

Renewal of Writ

(4) A writ of seizure and sale of land may be renewed before its expiration by filing a request to renew a writ of seizure and sale (Form 20N) with the sheriff.

Garnishment

20.08(1) A creditor may enforce an order for the payment or recovery of money by garnishment of debts payable to the debtor by other persons.

Joint Debts Garnishable

(2) If a debt is payable to the debtor and to one or more co-owners, one-half of the indebtedness or a greater or lesser amount specified in an order made under subrule (15) may be garnished.

Where Leave Required

(2.1) If more than six years have passed since the order was made, or if its enforcement is subject to a condition, a notice of garnishment may be issued only with leave of the court.

(2.2) If a notice of garnishment is not issued within one year after the date on which an order granting leave to issue it is made,

(a) the order granting leave ceases to have effect; and

(b) a notice of garnishment may be issued only with leave of the court on a subsequent motion.

(2.3) A notice of renewal of garnishment may be issued under subrule (5.3) without leave of the court before the original notice of garnishment or any subsequent notice of renewal of garnishment expires.

Obtaining Notice of Garnishment

(3) A creditor who seeks to enforce an order by garnishment shall file with the clerk of a court in the territorial division in which the debtor resides or carries on business,

(a) an affidavit for enforcement request (Form 20P) naming one debtor and one garnishee and stating,

(i) the date of the order and the amount awarded,

(ii) the territorial division in which the order was made,

(iii) the rate of postjudgment interest payable,

(iv) the total amount of any payments received since the order was granted,

(v) the amount owing, including postjudgment interest,

(vi) the name and address of the named garnishee to whom a notice of garnishment is to be directed,

(vii) the creditor's belief that the named garnishee is or will become indebted to the debtor, and the grounds for the belief, and

(viii) any particulars of the debts that are known to the creditor; and

(b) a certificate of judgment (Form 20A), if the order was made in another territorial division.

(4) On the filing of the documents required by subrule (3), the clerk shall issue a notice of garnishment (Form 20E) naming as garnishee the person named in the affidavit.

(5) A notice of garnishment issued under subrule (4) shall name only one debtor and only one garnishee.

Duration and Renewal

(5.1) A notice of garnishment remains in force for six years from the date of its issue and for a further six years from each renewal.

(5.2) A notice of garnishment may be renewed before its expiration by filing with the clerk of the court in which the notice of garnishment was issued a notice of renewal of garnishment (Form 20E.1), together with an affidavit for enforcement request (Form 20P).

(5.3) On the filing of the notice and affidavit required by subrule (5.2), the clerk shall issue the notice of renewal of garnishment (Form 20E.1) naming as garnishee the person named in the affidavit.

(5.4) The provisions of these rules that apply with respect to notices of garnishment also apply with respect to notices of renewal of garnishment.

Service of Notice of Garnishment

(6) The notice of garnishment (Form 20E) shall be served by the creditor in accordance with subrule 8.01(8).

(6.1) The creditor shall serve the notice of garnishment on the debtor within five days of serving it on the garnishee.

Financial Institution

(6.2) If the garnishee is a financial institution, the notice of garnishment and all further notices required to be served under this rule shall be served at the branch at which the debt is payable.

Proof of Service

(6.3) Service of the notice of garnishment may be proved by affidavit.

Garnishee Liable From Time of Service

(7) The garnishee is liable to pay to the clerk any debt of the garnishee to the debtor, up to the amount shown in the notice of garnishment, within 10 days after service of the notice on the garnishee or 10 days after the debt becomes payable, whichever is later.

(8) For the purpose of subrule (7), a debt of the garnishee to the debtor includes,

(a) a debt payable at the time the notice of garnishment is served; and

(b) a debt payable (whether absolutely or on the fulfilment of a condition) after the notice is served and within six years after it is issued.

Payment by Garnishee

(9) A garnishee who admits owing a debt to the debtor shall pay it to the clerk in the manner prescribed by the notice of garnishment, and the amounts paid into court shall not exceed the portion of the debtor's wages that are subject to seizure or garnishment under section 7 of the *Wages Act*.

Equal Distribution Among Creditors

(10) If the clerk has issued notices of garnishment in respect of a debtor at the request of more than one creditor and receives payment under any of the notices of garnishment, he or she shall distribute the payment equally among the creditors who have filed a request for garnishment and have not been paid in full.

Disputing Garnishment

(11) A garnishee referred to in subrule (12) shall, within 10 days after service of the notice of garnishment, file with the court a statement (Form 20F) setting out the particulars.

(12) Subrule (11) applies to a garnishee who,

(a) wishes to dispute the garnishment for any reason; or

(b) pays to the clerk less than the amount set out in the notice of garnishment as owing by the garnishee to the debtor, because the debt is owed to the debtor and to one or more co-owners of the debt or for any other reason.

Service on Creditor and Debtor

(13) The garnishee shall serve a copy of the garnishee's statement on the creditor and the debtor.

Notice to Co-Owner of Debt

(14) A creditor who is served with a garnishee's statement under subrule (13) shall forthwith send to any co-owners of the debt, in accordance with subrule 8.01(14), a notice to co-owner of debt (Form 20G) and a copy of the garnishee's statement.

Garnishment Hearing

(15) At the request of a creditor, debtor, garnishee, co-owner of the debt or any other interested person, the clerk shall fix a time and place for a garnishment hearing.

Service of Notice of Garnishment Hearing

(15.1) After having obtained a hearing date from the clerk, the party requesting the garnishment hearing shall serve the notice of garnishment hearing (Form 20Q) in accordance with subrule 8.01(9).

Powers of Court at Hearing

(15.2) At the garnishment hearing, the court may,

(a) if it is alleged that the garnishee's debt to the debtor has been assigned or encumbered, order the assignee or encumbrancer to appear and state the nature and particulars of the claim;

(b) determine the rights and liabilities of the garnishee, any co-owner of the debt, the debtor and any assignee or encumbrancer;

(c) vary or suspend periodic payments under a notice of garnishment; or

(d) determine any other matter in relation to a notice of garnishment.

Time to Request Hearing

(16) A person who has been served with a notice to co-owner of debt is not entitled to dispute the enforcement of the creditor's order for the payment or recovery of money or a payment made by the clerk unless the person requests a garnishment hearing within 30 days after the notice is sent.

Enforcement Against Garnishee

(17) If the garnishee does not pay to the clerk the amount set out in the notice of garnishment and does not send a garnishee's statement, the creditor is entitled to an order against the garnishee for payment of the amount set out in the notice, unless the court orders otherwise.

Payment to Person other than Clerk

(18) If, after service of a notice of garnishment, the garnishee pays a debt attached by the notice to a person other than the clerk, the garnishee remains liable to pay the debt in accordance with notice.

Effect of Payment to Clerk

(19) Payment of a debt by a garnishee in accordance with a notice of garnishment is a valid discharge of the debt as between the garnishee and the debtor and any co-owner of the debt, to the extent of the payment.

Distribution of Payments

(20) When proof is filed that the notice of garnishment was served on the debtor, the clerk shall distribute a payment received under a notice of garnishment to a creditor in accordance with subrule (20.1), unless,

(a) a hearing has been requested under subrule (15);

(b) a notice of motion and supporting affidavit (Form 15A) has been filed under rule 8.10, 11.06 or 17.04; or

(c) a request for clerk's order on consent (Form 11.2A) has been filed seeking the relief described in subparagraph 1 iii of subrule 11.2.01(1).

(20.1) The clerk shall distribute the payment,

(a) in the case of the first payment under the notice of garnishment, 30 days after the date it is received; and

(b) in the case of every subsequent payment under the notice of garnishment, as they are received.

Notice Once Order Satisfied

(20.2) Once the amount owing under an order that is enforced by garnishment is paid, the creditor shall immediately serve a notice of termination of garnishment (Form 20R) on the garnishee and on the clerk.

Payment if Debt Jointly Owned

(21) If a payment of a debt owed to the debtor and one or more co-owners has been made to the clerk, no request for a garnishment hearing is made and the time for doing so under subrule (16) has expired, the creditor may file with the clerk, within 30 days after that expiry,

(a) proof of service of the notice to co-owner; and

(b) an affidavit stating that the creditor believes that no co-owner of the debt is a person under disability, and the grounds for the belief.

(22) The affidavit required by subrule (21) may contain statements of the deponent's information and belief, if the source of the information and the fact of the belief are specified in the affidavit.

(23) If the creditor does not file the material referred to in subrule (21), the clerk shall return the money to the garnishee.

Consolidation Order

20.09(1) A debtor against whom there are two or more unsatisfied orders for the payment of money may make a motion to the court for a consolidation order.

(2) The debtor's notice of motion and supporting affidavit (Form 15A) shall set out, in the affidavit portion,

(a) the names and addresses of the creditors who have obtained an order for the payment of money against the debtor;

(b) the amount owed to each creditor;

(c) the amount of the debtor's income from all sources, identifying them; and

(d) the debtor's current financial obligations and any other relevant facts.

Notice of Motion

(3) For the purposes of clause 15.01(3)(a), the notice of motion and supporting affidavit shall be served on each of the creditors mentioned in it at least seven days before the hearing date.

Contents of Consolidation Order

(4) At the hearing of the motion, the court may make a consolidation order setting out,

(a) a list of unsatisfied orders for the payment of money against the debtor, indicating in each case the date, court and amount and the amount unpaid;

(b) the amounts to be paid into court by the debtor under the consolidation order; and

(c) the times of the payments.

(5) The total of the amounts to be paid into court by the debtor under a consolidation order shall not exceed the portion of the debtor's wages that are subject to seizure or garnishment under section 7 of the *Wages Act*.

Creditor May Make Submissions

(6) At the hearing of the motion, a creditor may make submissions as to the amount and times of payment.

Further Orders Obtained After Consolidation Order

(7) If an order for the payment of money is obtained against the debtor after the date of the consolidation order for a debt incurred before the date of the consolidation order, the creditor may file with the clerk a certified copy of the new order; the creditor shall be added to the consolidation order and shall share in the distribution under it from that time.

(8) A consolidation order terminates immediately if an order for the payment of money is obtained against the debtor for a debt incurred after the date of the consolidation order.

Enforcement Limited While Consolidation Order in Force

(9) While the consolidation order is in force, no step to enforce the judgment may be taken or continued against the debtor by a creditor named in the order, except issuing a writ of seizure and sale of land and filing it with the sheriff.

Termination on Default

(10) A consolidation order terminates immediately if the debtor is in default under it for 21 days.

Effect of Termination

(11) If a consolidation order terminates under subrule (8) or (10), the clerk shall notify the creditors named in the consolidation order, and no further consolidation order shall be made in respect of the debtor for one year after the date of termination.

Manner of Sending Notice

(11.1) The notice that the consolidation order is terminated shall be served by mail or fax.

(11.2), (11.3) Revoked.

Equal Distribution Among Creditors

(12) All payments into a consolidation account belong to the creditors named in the consolidation order, who shall share equally in the distribution of the money.

(13) The clerk shall distribute the money paid into the consolidation account at least once every six months.

Examination of Debtor or Other Person

20.10(1) If there is default under an order for the payment or recovery of money, the clerk of a court in the territorial division in which the debtor or other person to be examined resides or carries on business shall, at the creditor's request, issue a notice of examination (Form 20H) directed to the debtor or other person.

(2) The creditor's request shall be accompanied by,

(a) an affidavit for enforcement request (Form 20P) setting out,

(i) the date of the order and the amount awarded,

(ii) the territorial division in which the order was made,

(iii) the rate of postjudgment interest payable,

(iv) the total amount of any payments received since the order was granted, and

(v) the amount owing, including postjudgment interest; and

(b) a certificate of judgment (Form 20A), if the order was made in another territorial jurisdiction.

Service of Notice of Examination

(3) The notice of examination shall be served in accordance with subrules 8.01(10), (11) and (12).

(4) The debtor, any other persons to be examined and any witnesses whose evidence the court considers necessary may be examined in relation to,

(a) the reason for nonpayment;

(b) the debtor's income and property;

(c) the debts owed to and by the debtor;

(d) the disposal the debtor has made of any property either before or after the order was made;

(e) the debtor's present, past and future means to satisfy the order;

(f) whether the debtor intends to obey the order or has any reason for not doing so; and

(g) any other matter pertinent to the enforcement of the order.

Duties of Person to be Examined

(4.1) A person who is served with a notice of examination shall,

(a) inform himself or herself about the matters mentioned in subrule (4) and be prepared to answer questions about them; and

(b) in the case of an examination of a debtor who is an individual, complete a financial information form (Form 20I) and,

(i) serve it on the creditor requesting the examination, but not file it with the court, and

(ii) provide a copy of it to the judge presiding at the examination hearing.

(4.2) A debtor required under clause (4.1)(b) to complete a financial information form (Form 20I) shall bring such documents to the examination hearing as are necessary to support the information that he or she provides in the financial information form.

Who May Be Examined

(5) An officer or director of a corporate debtor, or, in the case of a debtor that is a partnership or sole proprietorship, the sole proprietor or any partner, may be examined on the debtor's behalf in relation to the matters set out in subrule (4).

Attendance

(5.1) A person required to attend an examination may attend,

(a) in person; or

(b) by video conference in accordance with rule 1.07.

Examinations Private, Under Oath and Recorded

(6) The examination shall be,

(a) held in the absence of the public, unless the court orders otherwise;

(b) conducted under oath; and

(c) recorded.

Order As To Payment

(7) After the examination or if the debtor's consent is filed, the court may make an order as to payment.

Enforcement Limited while Order as to Payment in Force

(8) While an order as to payment is in force, no step to enforce the judgment may be taken or continued against the debtor by a creditor named in the order, except issuing a writ of seizure and sale of land and filing it with the sheriff.

(9)-(15) REVOKED.

Contempt Hearing

20.11(1) If a person on whom a notice of examination has been served under rule 20.10 attends the examination but refuses to answer questions or to produce records or documents, the court may order the person to attend before it for a contempt hearing.

Same

(2) If a person on whom a notice of examination has been served under rule 20.10 fails to attend the examination, the court may order the person to attend before it for a contempt hearing under subsection 30(1) of the *Courts of Justice Act.*

Notice of Contempt Hearing

(3) If the court makes an order for a contempt hearing,

(a) the clerk shall provide the creditor with a notice of contempt hearing setting out the time, date and place of the hearing; and

(b) the creditor shall serve the notice of contempt hearing on the debtor or other person in accordance with subrule 8.01(13) and file the affidavit of service at least seven days before the hearing.

Setting Aside Order for Contempt Hearing

(4) A person who has been ordered to attend a contempt hearing under subsection 30(1) of the *Courts of Justice Act* may make a motion to set aside the order, before or after receiving the notice of contempt hearing but before the date of the hearing and, on the motion, the court may set aside the order and order that the person attend another examination under rule 20.10.

Finding of Contempt of Court

(5) At a contempt hearing held under subrule (1), the court may find the person to be in contempt of court if the person fails to show cause why the person should not be held in contempt for refusing to answer questions or produce records or documents.

Same

(6) The finding of contempt at a hearing held under subsection 30(1) of the *Courts of Justice Act* is subject to subsection 30(2) of that Act.

Other Powers of Court at Contempt Hearing

(7) At a contempt hearing, the court may order that the person,

(a) attend an examination under rule 20.10;

(b) be jailed for a period of not more than five days;

(c) attend an additional contempt hearing under subrule (1) or subsection 30(1) of the *Courts of Justice Act,* as the case may be; or

(d) comply with any other order that the judge considers necessary or just.

Warrant of Committal

(8) If a committal is ordered under clause (7)(b),

(a) the creditor may complete and file with the clerk an identification form (Form 20K) to assist the police in apprehending the person named in the warrant of committal; and

(b) the clerk shall issue a warrant of committal (Form 20J), accompanied by the identification form, if any, directed to all police officers in Ontario to apprehend the person named in the warrant anywhere in Ontario and promptly bring the person to the nearest correctional institution.

Discharge

(9) A person in custody under a warrant issued under this rule shall be discharged from custody on the order of the court or when the time prescribed in the warrant expires, whichever is earlier.

Duration and Renewal

(10) A warrant issued under this rule remains in force for 12 months after the date of issue and may be renewed by order of the court on a motion made by the creditor for 12 months at each renewal, unless the court orders otherwise.

(11) REVOKED.

Satisfaction of Order

20.12 If payment is made in full satisfaction of an order,

(a) where all parties consent, a party may file a request for clerk's order on consent (Form 11.2A) indicating that payment has been made in full satisfaction of the order or terms of settlement; or

(b) the debtor may make a motion for an order confirming that payment has been made in full satisfaction of the order or terms of settlement.

RULE 21   REFEREE

21.01(1) A person assigned the powers and duties of a referee under subsection 73(2) of the *Courts of Justice Act* may, if directed by the regional senior justice or his or her designate,

(a) hear disputes of proposals of terms of payment under rule 9.03;

(b) conduct settlement conferences under rule 13;

(c) hear motions for consolidation orders under rule 20.09; and

(d) assess receipted disbursements for fees paid to the court, a court reporter or a sheriff under the regulations made under the *Administration of Justice Act*.

(2) Except under subrule 9.03(5)(order as to terms of payment), a referee shall not make a final decision in any matter referred to him or her but shall report his or her findings and recommendations to the court.

RULE 22   PAYMENT INTO AND OUT OF COURT

Definitions

22.01 In this Rule,

"Accountant" means the Accountant of the Superior Court of Justice;

"clerk" means the clerk in the location where the proceeding was commenced.

Non-Application of Rule

22.02 This Rule does not apply to money paid or to be paid into court,

(a) under an order or proposal for payment made under rule 9.03;

(b) under an offer to settle a claim in return for the payment of money; or

(c) for the enforcement of an order for the payment or recovery of money under Rule 20, including enforcement by garnishment.

Payment into Court

22.03(1) Subject to subrule (7), a party who is required to pay money into court shall do so in accordance with subrules (2) to (6).

Filing with Clerk or Accountant

(2) The party shall file the following documents with the clerk or the Accountant:

1. If the payment into court is under a statutory provision or rule, a written request for payment into court that refers to that provision or rule.

2. If the payment into court is under an order, a written request for payment into court and a copy of the order that bears the court's seal.

Direction

(3) On receiving the documents required to be filed under subrule (2), the clerk or Accountant shall give the party a direction to receive the money, addressed to a bank listed in Schedule I or II to the *Bank Act* (Canada) and specifying the account in the Accountant's name into which the money is to be paid.

Clerk to Forward Documents

(4) If the documents are filed with the clerk, the clerk shall forward the documents to the Accountant.

Payment

(5) On receiving the direction referred to in subrule (3), the party shall pay the money into the specified bank account in accordance with the direction.

Bank's Duties

(6) On receiving the money, the bank shall give a receipt to the party paying the money and immediately send a copy of the receipt to the Accountant.

Payment to Accountant by Mail

(7) A party may pay money into court by mailing to the Accountant the applicable documents referred to in subrule (2), together with the money that is payable; the written request for payment into court referred to in that subrule shall include the party's name and mailing address.

Accountant to Provide Receipt

(8) On receiving money under subrule (7), the Accountant shall send a receipt to the party paying the money.

Proof of Payment

(9) A party who pays money into court shall, immediately after receiving a receipt from the bank under subrule (6) or from the Accountant under subrule (8), as the case may be, send to every other party a copy of the receipt and file a copy of the receipt with the court.

Payment Out of Court

22.04(1) Money may only be paid out of court under an order.

Documents to be Filed

(2) A person who seeks payment of money out of court shall file with the Accountant,

   (a) a written request for payment out and supporting affidavit, in the form provided by the Ministry; and

   (b) a copy of the order for payment out that bears the court's seal.

Payment Out, Children's Lawyer or Public Guardian and Trustee

(3) If the person seeking payment out is the Children's Lawyer or the Public Guardian and Trustee,

   (a) the written request need not be in the form provided by the Ministry and a supporting affidavit is not required; and

   (b) a single written request that deals with more than one proceeding may be filed.

Payment Out, Minor Attaining Age of Majority

(4) Despite subrule (2), money in court to which a party is entitled under an order once the party attains the age of major-ity may be paid out to the party on filing with the Accountant, in the forms provided by the Accountant,

   (a) a written request for payment out; and

   (b) an affidavit proving the identity of the party and that the party has attained the age of majority.

Accountant's Duties

(5) If the requirements of subrule (2) or (4), as the case may be, are met, the Accountant shall pay the money to the person named in the order for payment out, and the payment shall include any accrued interest, unless a court orders otherwise.

Transition

22.05 This Rule applies to the payment into and out of court of money paid into court on and after the day on which Ontario Regulation 400/12 comes into force.

23. Omitted (provides for coming into force of provisions of this Regulation).

. . .

Small Claims Court Forms

FORM NUMBER	FORM TITLE	DATE
1A	Additional Parties	June 1, 2009
1A.1	Additional Debtors	June 1, 2009
1B	Request for Telephone or Video Conference	September 1, 2010
4A	Consent to Act as Litigation Guardian	June 1, 2009
4B	Affidavit (Motion for Payment Out of Court)	November 1, 2012
5A	Notice to Alleged Partner	June 1, 2009
7A	Plaintiff's Claim	September 1, 2010
8A	Affidavit of Service	September 1, 2010
9A	Defence	September 1, 2010
9B	Request to Clerk	June 1, 2009
10A	Defendant's Claim	June 1, 2009
11A	Affidavit for Jurisdiction	June 1, 2009
11B	Default Judgment	September 1, 2010
11.2A	Request for Clerk's Order on Consent	June 1, 2009
11.3A	Notice of Discontinued Claim	September 1, 2010
13A	List of Proposed Witnesses	June 1, 2009
13B	Consent	September 1, 2010
14A	Offer to Settle	June 1, 2009
14B	Acceptance of Offer to Settle	June 1, 2009
14C	Notice of Withdrawal of Offer to Settle	June 1, 2009
14D	Terms of Settlement	June 1, 2009
15A	Notice of Motion and Supporting Affidavit	September 1, 2010
15B	Affidavit	June 1, 2009

FORM NUMBER	FORM TITLE	DATE
18A	Summons to Witness	June 1, 2009
18B	Warrant for Arrest of Defaulting Witness	June 1, 2009
20A	Certificate of Judgment	September 1, 2010
20B	Writ of Delivery	June 1, 2009
20C	Writ of Seizure and Sale of Personal Property	June 1, 2009
20D	Writ of Seizure and Sale of Land	June 1, 2009
20E	Notice of Garnishment	September 1, 2010
20E.1	Notice of Renewal of Garnishment	September 1, 2010
20F	Garnishee's Statement	April 11, 2012
20G	Notice to Co-owner of Debt	September 1, 2010
20H	Notice of Examination	April 11, 2012
20I	Financial Information Form	April 11, 2012
20J	Warrant of Committal	September 1, 2010
20K	Identification Form	June 1, 2009
20L	Notice of Default of Payment	June 1, 2009
20M	Affidavit of Default of Payment	April 11, 2012
20N	Request to Renew Writ of Seizure and Sale	June 1, 2009
20O	Direction to Enforce Writ of Seizure and Sale of Personal Property	June 1, 2009
20P	Affidavit for Enforcement Request	June 1, 2009
20Q	Notice of Garnishment Hearing	September 1, 2010
20R	Notice of Termination of Garnishment	September 1, 2010

Source: http://www.ontariocourtforms.on.ca/english/scc/scc.

Schedule of Small Claims Court Fees and Allowances

SERVICE PAID FOR	FEES/ALLOWANCES
PAID TO CLERK	
1. Filing of a claim by an infrequent claimant	$75.00
2. Filing of a claim by a frequent claimant	$145.00
3. Filing of a defendant's claim	$75.00
4. Filing a notice of motion served on another party, a notice of motion without notice or a notice of motion for a consent order (except a notice of motion under the *Wages Act*)	$40.00
5. Filing a defence	$40.00
6. Issuing a summons to a witness	$19.00
7. Receiving for enforcement a process from the Ontario Court of Justice or an order or judgment as provided by statute	$25.00
8. Issuing a certificate of judgment	$19.00
9. Issuing a writ of delivery, a writ of seizure and sale, or a notice of examination	$35.00
10. Issuing a notice of garnishment	$100.00
11. Preparing and filing a consolidation order	$75.00
12. Forwarding a court file to Divisional Court for appeal	$20.00
13. Issuing a certified copy of a judgment or other document, per page	$3.50
14. Transmitting a document other than by mail	cost of transmission
15. For the inspection of a court file, i. by a solicitor or party in the proceeding	no charge
ii. by a person who has entered into an agreement with the attorney general for the bulk inspection of court files, per file	$1.00
iii. by any other person, per file	$10.00
16. Making a photocopy of a document not requiring certification, per page	$1.00

SERVICE PAID FOR			FEES/ALLOWANCES
17. For a copy on compact disc (CD) of a digital recording of a court hearing in respect of a case, if such a recording exists and a copy is available:	i. For a single day's recording		$22.00
	ii. For each additional day's recording, if the request is made at the same time as a request under subitem i		$10.50
18. In an application under the *Repair and Storage Liens Act*,	i. on the filing of,	A. an application	$100.00
		B. a notice of objection	$35.00
		C. a waiver of further claim and a receipt	no charge
	ii. on the issuing of,	A. an initial certificate	$35.00
		B. a final certificate	$35.00
		C. a writ of seizure	$35.00
19. Fixing of a date for trial or an assessment hearing by an infrequent claimant			$100.00
20. Fixing of a date for trial or an assessment hearing by a frequent claimant			$130.00
21. Entering of a default judgment by an infrequent claimant			$35.00
22. Entering of a default judgment by a frequent claimant			$50.00
PAID TO BAILIFF			
1. Revoked			
2. For each attempt, whether successful or not, to enforce a writ of delivery			$36.00
3. For each attempt, whether successful or not, to enforce a writ of seizure and sale of personal property,	i. where no sale is necessary		$36.00
	ii. where a sale is necessary		$60.00
4. For each attempt, whether successful or not, to enforce a writ of seizure under the *Repair and Storage Liens Act*			$36.00
5. Enforcing a writ of delivery or a writ of seizure and sale of personal property, removing property seized, advertising the sale of personal property, including obtaining assistance in seizing, securing, or retaining property			Reasonable disbursements necessarily incurred, including appraisers' fees

SERVICE PAID FOR	FEES/ALLOWANCES
PAID TO WITNESS	
1. For attendance in court, unless item 2 applies, per day	$6.00
2. For attendance in court by a barrister, solicitor, physician, surgeon, engineer, or veterinary surgeon who is not a party to the action, to give evidence of a professional service rendered or to give a professional opinion, per day	$15.00
3. For travel to court	Reasonable travelling expenses actually incurred, but not exceeding the kilometre allowance set out in Regulation 11 of the Revised Regulations of Ontario, 1990

Kilometre Allowances

ADMINISTRATION OF JUSTICE ACT

R.R.O. 1990, REGULATION 11

KILOMETRE ALLOWANCES

Last amendment: O. Reg. 498/00.

1. If payment of a travel or kilometre allowance is authorized and the authorizing instrument states that the allowance shall be in accordance with or as set out in this Regulation, the allowance for each kilometre actually travelled is,

(a) in northern Ontario, 30.5 cents; and

(b) in southern Ontario, 30 cents.

2. For the purpose of section 1, northern Ontario is comprised of,

(a) all of The District Municipality of Muskoka;

(b) everything lying north of the line consisting of Healey Lake (Municipal) Road from Healey Lake easterly to its junction with Highway 612; and

(c) everything lying north of the line consisting of Highway 60 easterly to its junction with Highway 62 at Killaloe Station and Highway 62 to Pembroke.

Glossary

action: a proceeding brought in a court *(p. 2)*

action splitting: dividing an action into two or more actions in order to bring it within the Small Claims Court monetary jurisdiction *(p. 91)*

adjournment: putting a court procedure, such as a motion, settlement conference, or trial, off to a later date *(p. 291)*

admission: a voluntary acknowledgement by a party that an allegation of fact made by another party is true—in other words, that the allegation is not in dispute *(p. 228)*

affidavit: a written statement of facts that is confirmed under oath or by affirmation by the person making the affidavit *(p. 131)*

affirmative defences: a defendant's legal grounds for disputing the plaintiff's claim *(p. 231)*

aggravated damages: damages intended to compensate the plaintiff for harm or distress suffered as a result of egregious bad faith on the part of the defendant *(p. 86)*

allegation: an assertion made in a pleading by a party to an action, setting out what she hopes to prove *(p. 12)*

alternative to personal service: alternative method of delivery of a legal document to another party in a proceeding; may be used when the party being served has a lawyer with instructions to accept service of documents or when personal service has been attempted and has failed *(p. 142)*

amend: to change or correct a pleading, with the object of improving it or making it more complete *(p. 150)*

appeal as of right: an automatic right to appeal, without first seeking permission to do so from the appeal court *(p. 405)*

assessment hearing: a hearing wherein the court determines the amount of the claim *(p. 340)*

assessment of damages: a determination of the money damages owed to the plaintiff by the defaulting

defendant(s); may be done by a motion in writing or by an assessment hearing *(p. 190)*

assessment order: an assessment order is an order made by a judge on a motion in writing for an assessment of damages in an unliquidated claim where all defendants have been noted in default *(p. 293)*

assign: to transfer a legal right or entitlement (including wages owed or the money in a bank account) to another person *(p. 440)*

assignee: a person to whom something is transferred *(p. 440)*

attorney: person authorized to act pursuant to a power of attorney *(p. 123)*

authorized requester: a person who has applied to and has been approved by the ministry for that designation, and is registered as an authorized requester with the ministry *(p. 74)*

balance of convenience: a common-law test; a court applying this test will balance the prejudice to one party of denying the relief asked for, against the prejudice to the opposing party if the relief is granted *(p. 19)*

bill of costs: an itemized list of a party's representation fees and disbursements supported by documentation *(pp. 325, 381)*

binding authority: a judicial decision by a higher court that must be followed by lower courts (also known as binding precedent) *(p. 132)*

body of the affidavit: contents comprise the facts and evidence in support of the relief sought *(p. 286)*

candid: forthright and sincere, able to look at both sides of an issue without bias *(pp. 30, 72)*

casual client: a client who consults you regarding a legal issue, but then decides not to proceed, or not to hire you to act as his legal representative *(p. 31)*

causation: for damages to be awarded to the plaintiff, the evidence must establish that the harm or loss suffered by the plaintiff resulted from the defendant's actions or negligence *(p. 106)*

cause of action: the factual and legal grounds for seeking a remedy from a court *(pp. 72, 113)*

chattel mortgage: a loan that is secured against personal property; in Ontario, such security interests are registered under the *Personal Property Security Act (pp. 79, 418)*

chattel mortgagee: one who holds a loan secured against personal property or chattels *(p. 79)*

claimant: another word for plaintiff; a claimant is anyone who commences a claim *(p. 3)*

client: a person who consults with you and hires you to represent her in a matter or a number of matters *(p. 30)*

client identification: information obtained from the client regarding who the client is and what the client does *(p. 38)*

client matter number: a unique number assigned by the paralegal firm (or the file management software) to a particular client matter in order to identify that matter for filing, docketing, and billing purposes *(p. 48)*

client verification: obtaining documentary or other confirmation that the client is who he says he is *(p. 38)*

collateral: real or personal property against which a loan is pledged *(p. 418)*

committee: a person appointed by the court to manage the property of an absentee *(p. 123)*

competent paralegal: a paralegal who has and applies the relevant skills, attributes, and values appropriate to each matter undertaken on behalf of a client *(p. 28)*

compromise and settlement: when a party agrees to waive some part of what is owing or make other concessions in order to resolve a matter without the additional costs, delay, and uncertainty of a court proceeding *(p. 313)*

conflict of interest: any circumstance that may negatively affect a paralegal's ability to adequately represent the client's best interests *(p. 33)*

consideration: something that causes a party to enter into a contract; sometimes, but not always, a party's expectation of profiting from or receiving a benefit from the contract *(p. 313)*

construe: to interpret *(p. 20)*

contribution and indemnity: the transferring of responsibility for loss or damage from one party to another, and the corresponding obligation of the party to whom responsibility has been transferred to make good on any losses suffered by the transferor *(p. 242)*

co-owner of debt: a person who is entitled to part of a debt payable to a debtor, and may assert their right to co-ownership of the debt in a garnishment of that debt *(p. 439)*

corporation: a separate legal entity from its owners—the shareholders *(p. 76)*

costs: the expenses connected with a legal proceeding; costs include a party's legal fees, plus disbursements, or out-of-pocket expenses, including court filing fees *(p. 7)*

counsel slip: a form that must be filled out on a court appearance and given to the court clerk; it gives the court notice that there is someone appearing on the matter, and tells the court what your name is, the matter you are there on, and who your client is *(p. 371)*

counterclaim: a claim by a defendant back over against the plaintiff *(p. 241)*

creditor: a person to whom money is owed; a person who is entitled to enforce an order for the payment of recovery of money (Rule 20.01) *(p. 416)*

crossclaim: a claim by a defendant over against a co-defendant *(p. 241)*

cross-examination: questions used to pinpoint weaknesses or inconsistencies in the testimony of another party or another party's witness *(p. 367)*

date of default: the date the cause of action arose *(p. 113)*

debtor: a person who owes money to another person; also, a person against whom an order for the payment of money may be enforced *(p. 416)*

defendant: the party who defends a civil action *(p. 2)*

defendant's claim: a claim by a defendant against any party named in the plaintiff's claim, including the plaintiff or a co-defendant, or against a third party not named in the plaintiff's claim *(p. 186)*

denial: an assertion by a party that an allegation of fact made by another party is not true—in other words, that the allegation is disputed *(p. 228)*

deponent: the person who makes an affidavit *(pp. 131, 174, 286)*

direct examination: the questions that you ask your own witnesses when they take the stand to shape the evidence into a clear, concise narrative that can be easily understood by the court *(p. 365)*

disbursements: the out-of-pocket expenses of a legal proceeding; these include court filing fees, charges for service of documents, photocopying charges, postage, etc. *(pp. 8, 72)*

discretionary: where an action is discretionary, the court may make up its own mind about a particular matter, giving due regard to all relevant factors *(p. 92)*

dispute: an argument or disagreement between two or more sides in which the interest of one side is in direct opposition to the interest of another side *(p. 33)*

docket: a list of matters to be heard on a particular day in a particular courtroom; it will be posted outside the courtroom for the date those matters are scheduled to be heard *(p. 371)*

due diligence: exercising the prudence and vigilance that a reasonable and prudent paralegal would exercise in similar circumstances *(p. 40)*

duress: threatening someone or otherwise forcing her to agree to something she would not have agreed to without the threat or use of force *(p. 313)*

effect service: carry out or perform valid service of a document *(pp. 143, 174)*

encumber: to mortgage or place a lien or other security interest against property *(p. 440)*

encumbrance: a security interest registered against real or personal property *(p. 440)*

encumbrancer: the person holding the lien or security interest *(p. 440)*

enforcement document: a document issued by the clerk at the request of a creditor in an affidavit for enforcement request—e.g., a notice of garnishment, a writ of seizure and sale of land, and so on *(pp. 244, 424)*

enforcement of an order: a lawful attempt to obtain an amount owing pursuant to a court order *(p. 416)*

engagement letter: confirms the terms of the paralegal–client retainer, but is not signed back by the client *(p. 29)*

equitable relief: remedies other than money damages; for example, an order compelling a person to do something (specific performance) or to stop doing something (injunction) *(p. 81)*

ex parte motion: a motion made without notice to other parties *(p. 290)*

execution of an order: see the definition for "enforcement of an order"

exhibit: an original document that is material to an issue in the action; it must be identified by a witness with personal knowledge of its contents, which may be referred to in her spoken evidence; it is then marked as an exhibit by the court clerk and placed in the court file as part of the evidence *(pp. 286, 366)*

exigible assets: assets that can be seized or garnished *(p. 429)*

expert witness: a witness who, because of education and/or specialization, has knowledge about an issue or issues in the action that the trial judge or other trier of fact does not have; the expert witness's evidence must be helpful to the court and necessary to a proper determination of the issue(s) about which the expert witness gives an opinion *(p. 356)*

express consent: also known as explicit consent; written authorization from your client to disclose particular information to specified third parties *(p. 33)*

fiduciary: a person who is required to act with scrupulous good faith, honesty, and integrity for the benefit of another person *(p. 28)*

fiduciary relationship: a relationship of absolute trust and confidence between two persons, in which one person (the fiduciary) is required to act with scrupulous good faith, honesty and integrity for the benefit of another person (the beneficiary)—in the paralegal–client relationship, the paralegal is the fiduciary and the client is the beneficiary *(p. 28)*

final reporting letter: sent to the client at the conclusion of the client matter, along with the final invoice for fees and disbursements incurred since the last interim invoice—provides a summary of the client matter, steps taken, and results achieved *(p. 47)*

finding as to credibility: where there is conflicting evidence from witnesses, a decision by the trier of fact (the judge in a non-jury trial) about whose evidence to believe, in all of the circumstances; factors to be considered are the witness's demeanour on the witness stand, knowledge of the circumstances, and relationship to the matters in question, including any issues of bias *(p. 364)*

frequent claimant: anyone who files 10 or more claims in a Small Claims Court office on or after January 1 in any calendar year *(p. 3)*

frivolous and vexatious objection: an objection that has no legal merit and is made to annoy, harass, or embarrass the other side *(p. 129)*

funds: cash, currency, securities, negotiable instruments, or other financial instruments *(p. 38)*

future performance agreement: a sales contract where the purchaser takes possession of property in return for a promise to make future payments for the property to the vendor, who retains title and a right of repossession in the property until the purchase price is paid in full *(p. 419)*

garnishee: a person who owes money to a debtor *(p. 436)*

garnishor: a creditor who enforces an order for payment or recovery of money by way of a garnishment *(p. 436)*

general account: a bank account used to pay for ongoing business expenses, such as salaries, rent, client disbursements that have not been billed, etc. *(p. 45)*

general damages: damages for pain and suffering caused by injury or harm, and for future losses and expenses, such as future care costs and loss of future income; general damages cannot be quantified precisely, but they must be itemized and explained to the extent that it is possible to do so; also referred to as unliquidated damages *(pp. 86, 107)*

harass a witness: engage in conduct that is coercive or threatening toward a witness at any stage of a proceeding *(p. 361)*

hearsay rule: a witness is not allowed to repeat in court what they were told by a third party, if the reason for putting the evidence in is to prove the truth of the contents of the third-party statement *(p. 14)*

implied consent: unwritten consent to disclose confidential information because it is required by the professional relationship (e.g., disclosure to employees) or because the matter requires it (e.g., disclosure in pleadings and other documents filed with the court) *(p. 33)*

improvident sale: sale by a lender of a debtor's property for a price that does not reflect the property's market value; grounds for a debtor to challenge the sale of the property in a court *(p. 444)*

informed consent: consent based on information that is sufficient to allow the client to assess the situation and make an informed decision *(p. 35)*

infrequent claimant: anyone who files fewer than 10 Small Claims Court claims in a Small Claims Court office on or after January 1 in any calendar year *(p. 3)*

inherent jurisdiction: judicial powers that are essential for the administration of justice *(p. 93)*

installment (or partial) payments: a partial payment of a sum of money owing at regular intervals over a period of time until the amount owing is paid in full *(p. 14)*

intellectual property: intangible property with value—for example, copyright, patents, trademarks *(p. 79)*

interim invoice: a bill delivered to the client before the client matter is concluded—usually sent with an interim reporting letter *(p. 46)*

interim relief: judge's order resolving an issue in the action that cannot wait until a settlement conference or trial *(p. 284)*

interim reporting letter: a letter sent to the client before the client matter is concluded, usually with an interim invoice—reports the steps taken in the client matter to that point, the results obtained, and the likely next steps *(p. 46)*

invitation to treat: an invitation intended to do nothing more than open up negotiations; usually does not contain essential terms, such as a fixed amount of money to be paid, terms of payment, etc. *(p. 314)*

joint and several liability: form of liability where each partner is liable for any amount up to the full amount of any judgment obtained against the partnership *(p. 117)*

judgment creditor: a person who has obtained judgment against a person and is seeking to enforce the judgment *(p. 79)*

judgment debtor: any person who owes money to another person pursuant to a court order *(p. 73)*

judgment-proof: having no income or assets against which a judgment may be enforced *(p. 73)*

judicial notice: matters of common knowledge (also referred to as "notorious facts") that a judge may accept as true without hearing evidence and without inquiry—lesser known facts (for example, matters that can be checked in a standard reference work and are not easily disputed) may be judicially noticed after inquiry *(p. 135)*

jurat: conclusion of affidavit with place and date of where affidavit sworn, signature of deponent, and signature of commissioner of oaths *(p. 286)*

jurisdiction: a court's area of legal authority; in Ontario, jurisdiction is established by the *Courts of Justice Act* and by the common law *(p. 2)*

justice: a justice is the same thing as a judge; "justice," "judge," and "court" are often used interchangeably in reported decisions *(p. 11)*

lawyer: a person who has been called to the Bar of Ontario and who is licensed to practise law in Ontario *(p. 12)*

leading question: a question that implies the existence of certain facts or suggests a correct answer to a witness (or to the trier of fact); the general rule is that leading questions may be used only in cross-examination of a witness *(p. 365)*

leave of the court: permission from the court, by way of a court order, to do something; usually obtained on motion by a party *(p. 178)*

legal fees: fees charged by a lawyer or paralegal for legal representation and advice *(p. 7)*

liberal construction: means that, when applying the Rules, the court goes beyond the exact meaning of the language in order to implement the principles behind the Rules *(p. 20)*

liberally construed: interpreting the Rules without undue emphasis on strict compliance with all procedural requirements and technicalities, with a view to bringing about a resolution that is just and fair to all parties within a reasonable time *(p. 18)*

liquidated claim: claim for a debt or fixed amount of money that does not require valuation by a court *(pp. 86, 106)*

liquidated damages: a specific amount of money that may be established by unpaid invoices, NSF cheques, or other documentation proving a debt or fixed amount; also called special damages *(pp. 85, 106)*

litigant: a party to a civil action; someone engaged in civil litigation *(p. 2)*

litigation guardian: a competent person who undertakes to direct a legal proceeding on behalf of a person under disability *(p. 121)*

lump-sum payment: a one-time payment of the full amount owing or a portion thereof *(pp. 14, 420)*

mandatory: where an action is mandatory, the court must do something if certain preconditions exist; the court has no choice *(p. 92)*

material evidence: evidence that has a logical connection to an issue or issues in dispute in the action; evidence that will assist the trier of fact to make a determination about whose allegations to believe *(p. 353)*

merits of the case: the legal principles upon which a party's assertion of rights is based *(p. 130)*

misrepresentation: an inaccurate, untrue, or incomplete version of the facts; in contract law, an inaccurate or incomplete description of the terms of the agreement, with the result that the person signing does not have a real understanding of what he is signing *(p. 313)*

mixed trust account: a trust bank account into which money from many different clients will be deposited and held in trust, until such time as invoices are rendered on their files or you are directed by the client to pay out the money to whom the money belongs *(p. 45)*

monetary jurisdiction: the amount of money that the court may order one party to pay another, not including interest and costs *(p. 7)*

money retainer: money paid to you by the client on account of future legal services and/or disbursements to be incurred; it is a deposit to secure your legal services *(p. 29)*

mortgagee: a person who holds a mortgage *(p. 418)*

mortgagor: a person who is given a mortgage by a mortgagee *(p. 418)*

motion: an application to a court or a judge for the purpose of obtaining an order directing that some kind of relief be granted to the party making the motion *(p. 190)*

motioning the other party to death: using motions to delay the action, add to the costs of other parties, or otherwise abuse the process of the court *(p. 284)*

moving party: the party in a proceeding who makes a motion *(pp. 190, 284)*

negotiable instrument: an unconditional order or promise to pay an amount of money, which can be transferred—for example, cheques or banknotes (paper money) *(p. 38)*

net wages: amount of wages after all lawful deductions *(p. 426)*

non-engagement letter: a letter confirming that the paralegal has declined to accept the retainer, or that the client has declined to retain the paralegal *(p. 29)*

non-exigible assets: assets that cannot be seized or garnished *(p. 429)*

non-pecuniary damages: damages awarded for types of harm that are real and serious, but difficult to assign a money value to *(pp. 86, 107)*

notice: service of documents on other parties to make them aware of an intended procedural step or other matter *(p. 17)*

notice period: the minimum period of time for serving documents on other parties before a procedural step takes place *(p. 17)*

objection: an argument by a party that a particular piece of evidence, line of questioning, or other matter is improper or illegal and should not be allowed by the court *(p. 129)*

offer: in the context of contracts, an offer containing all essential terms; if accepted, a binding contract is the result *(p. 314)*

offeree: the party receiving an offer *(p. 313)*

offeror: the party making an offer *(p. 313)*

open-ended, or direct, question: a question that lets the witness give his own answer without prompting; a question that does not contain any language suggesting a "correct" answer to the witness *(p. 365)*

opinion evidence: in the case of an expert witness, testimony of what the expert witness thinks, believes, or infers with regard to facts in dispute *(p. 356)*

order excluding witnesses: an order that all witnesses except the parties themselves shall leave the courtroom and wait outside the courtroom until they are called to give evidence; the purpose of an order excluding witnesses is to prevent witnesses who have not yet taken the stand from hearing, and being influenced by, the evidence of the witnesses who take the stand ahead of them; required only when there are witnesses other than the parties giving evidence; if the plaintiff and the defendant are the only witnesses, an order excluding witnesses is not required *(p. 375)*

order for substituted service: a court order permitting the plaintiff to serve the claim in a manner that is not set out in the Rules *(p. 147)*

original court: the court where an order is made *(p. 428)*

originating court: the court where an order is made *(p. 428)*

originating process: the document that commences an action *(p. 428)*

paralegal: a non-lawyer who is not an articling student and who is licensed to provide legal services in permitted areas of practice to clients for a fee in the province of Ontario *(p. 12)*

paralegal–client retainer: the terms of the contractual arrangement between the paralegal and the client, including but not limited to the scope of the legal services to be provided, fees, billing practices, and the amount of the money retainer *(p. 29)*

partnership: an unincorporated business that is formed by two or more persons with the objective of making a profit *(pp. 76, 117)*

partnership agreement: a contract that allocates liability among the partners, and specifies other terms and conditions of the partnership; binding only on the parties to the agreement *(p. 117)*

party: a person who commences or defends an action or proceeding *(p. 2)*

party under disability: in Small Claims Court, a person or party who is (a) a minor, (b) mentally incapable within the meaning s. 6 or 45 of the *Substitute Decisions Act, 1992*, or (c) an absentee within the meaning of the *Absentees Act* *(p. 121)*

payment into court: money paid to the accountant of the Superior Court of Justice pursuant to a court order, to be paid out to creditors or other parties in accordance with a court order *(p. 125)*

payment out of court: when money paid into court is paid out by the accountant of the Superior Court of Justice, in accordance with a court order *(p. 125)*

pecuniary damages: damages awarded for losses that can be estimated in money terms *(pp. 86, 107)*

per diem: per day (Latin) *(pp. 185, 424)*

per diem interest: the amount of interest that accrues per day on money owed *(pp. 185, 424)*

periodic payments: fixed amounts of money that must be paid at regular intervals, usually on a stated date such as the first day of each and every month *(p. 420)*

perjury: swearing or affirming a statement (including a document) that you know is not true; perjury is a criminal offence *(p. 289)*

personal property: property that has value, and is tangible and movable *(pp. 79, 441)*

personal service: personal delivery of a copy of a document (e.g., an issued plaintiff's claim) to another party in accordance with the procedures set out in Rule 8.02; the requirements for personal service vary, depending upon who the other party is (e.g., an individual, a corporation, a municipality, etc.) *(p. 142)*

plaintiff: the party who commences a civil action *(p. 2)*

plaintiff's claim: the document that sets out the names of the parties and their addresses for service, the amount of the claim, any other relief being sought, and the allegations of fact in support of the claim *(p. 106)*

pleadings: the documents filed at the commencement of a proceeding, in which the parties plead, or state, the allegations of fact on which they rely in support of their case; in a Small Claims Court proceeding, the pleadings are the plaintiff's claim, the defence, the defendant's claim, and the defence to the defendant's claim, if any *(p. 136)*

post-judgment interest: interest that accrues on the judgment amount, including costs, or on any outstanding balances, until such time as any balance owing has been paid in full *(pp. 113, 181)*

power of attorney: a document authorizing an individual to act on another person's behalf in a legal or business matter *(p. 123)*

prayer or claim for relief: the first paragraph in a claim, setting out in separate subparagraphs particulars of the damages, interest, and other relief that the plaintiff thinks she is entitled to *(p. 140)*

preamble: in an affidavit, statement identifying the person making the affidavit, the municipality and province in which that person lives, and an affirmation that the contents of the affidavit are true *(p. 286)*

precedent document: a legal document that is used as a template or guide for drafting subsequent documents with a similar purpose *(p. 139)*

preferred creditor: an unsecured creditor who ranks ahead of ordinary unsecured creditors in a debt collection or a bankruptcy because of priority and special rights conferred by a statute *(p. 419)*

pre-judgment interest: interest that accrues on the amount determined to be owing commencing with the date of default and ending with the date of judgment *(pp. 113, 181)*

private corporation: a corporation whose shares are not publicly traded—its incorporating documents (1) restrict the right to sell shares, (2) limit the number of its shareholders (excluding employees) to 50, and (3) prohibit public trading of its shares or securities; also called a closely held corporation *(p. 39)*

pro rata distribution: the share of each creditor in the proceeds of the distribution will be determined proportionately based on what the creditor is owed *(p. 444)*

promisee: a person who receives a promise *(p. 314)*

promisor: a person who makes a promise *(p. 314)*

promissory note: a promise to pay that is signed and dated by the debtor; it should contain the following terms: the names of the payor and the debtor, the amount advanced to the debtor, and the date on which it was advanced, and the terms of the loan, including payment terms, interest rates, penalties on default, if any, etc. *(p. 107)*

prospective client: a person who consults you about a legal issue but has not yet retained you *(p. 31)*

public company: a corporation whose shares are for sale to the general public—public companies are subject to rigorous disclosure requirements under securities legislation *(p. 39)*

punitive damages: preventive, not compensatory, these damages are intended to discourage the repetition of undesirable conduct *(p. 86)*

qualified interpreter: a person who is trained to interpret in a courtroom environment; interpreters are not under oath when they interpret; they must provide an unbiased and accurate version of what the witness under oath is saying on the stand *(p. 353)*

quantifying damages: calculating damages—that is, determining all of the different kinds of damage or injury that a party has suffered because of another's wrongdoing, and assigning money values to the different kinds of damage, based on the evidence *(p. 85)*

quantum meruit: an equitable doctrine that allows the court to imply a contract in certain circumstances and order payment for services provided pursuant to the implied contract *(pp. 81, 232)*

quash: to declare something null and void, and of no legal force and effect *(p. 91)*

question of fact: a factual dispute; in jury trials, questions of fact are determined by the jury; in non-jury trials, questions of fact are determined by the trial judge *(p. 12)*

question of law: an issue that requires the application or interpretation of a law or legal principle; in both jury and non-jury trials, questions of law are determined by judges *(p. 12)*

real property: property that has value, and is tangible and immovable *(pp. 79, 445)*

realize on the security: when a secured creditor, upon default by the debtor, seizes and sells the property pledged as security for a debt, and applies the proceeds of the sale to the balance owing on the debt *(p. 418)*

re-examination: evidence intended to clarify and, if necessary, neutralize or rebut any potentially damaging evidence brought out in cross-examination; also called "reply evidence" or "rebuttal evidence" *(p. 375)*

referee: a non-judge who is authorized by the Rules to preside at terms of payment hearings *(p. 239)*

registering court: the court in which a judgment is registered *(p. 428)*

remedy: a method of enforcing a right, or preventing or compensating for a wrong *(p. 129)*

reserve judgment: the judge will take time to review the evidence and the applicable law and provide the parties with a written or spoken decision at a later time *(p. 381)*

responding party: a party who answers or responds to a motion made by another party *(pp. 190, 284)*

retainer agreement: a letter confirming services to be rendered, your fee or hourly rate, any additional charges (disbursements, etc.), and any other terms of the paralegal–client relationship; more detailed than a retainer letter, and it must be signed back to you by the client *(p. 29)*

running account: an account where a regular customer charges purchases against a standard account number on an ongoing basis; the defendant makes payments against the account from time to time (usually on a monthly basis) *(p. 91)*

secured creditor: a creditor whose loans are secured against real or personal property; if the debtor defaults in payment, the secured creditor may seize and sell the property, and pay the balance owing on the loan out of the proceeds of the sale, in accordance with the terms of the security agreement *(p. 418)*

service: delivery of a legal document to another party in a proceeding *(p. 142)*

set aside: to declare a court order or procedural step to be of no force and effect *(pp. 122, 290)*

signatory: someone who signs a document *(p. 287)*

sole proprietorship: an unincorporated business owned and run by one individual *(pp. 75, 116)*

special damages: damages that compensate the plaintiff for all losses, including out-of-pocket expenses connected with the injury or harm, up to the date of the trial; can usually be calculated fairly precisely; also referred to as liquidated damages *(pp. 85, 106)*

statement of information and belief: in a supporting affidavit, a statement of information that the deponent received from another person or source, and that the deponent believes to be true *(p. 287)*

statute-barred: to be prevented by the terms of a statute from commencing an action to assert your legal rights *(p. 83)*

stay of enforcement: stopping enforcement by creditors against a debtor for so long as the debtor complies with the terms of a court order *(p. 421)*

strict construction: means that the language of a rule is read and applied using its exact, technical meaning; also known as "narrow construction" *(p. 20)*

submissions: legal arguments made to a judge for her consideration when deciding whether the relief requested by a party should be granted *(p. 295)*

substituted service: an order permitting the plaintiff to serve the claim in a manner that is not strictly in accordance with the Rules *(p. 147)*

successful party: the party who succeeds, or wins, at trial; it may be the plaintiff or the defendant *(p. 322)*

such terms as are just: the court looks at the conduct of the parties, the legal issues, and the potential prejudice to the parties as a result of a particular court order, and imposes conditions and/or awards costs accordingly *(p. 179)*

summons to witness: a document compelling the attendance at trial of a person whose evidence is material to the conduct of an action *(p. 350)*

support and maintenance creditor: a person to whom child or spousal support is owed by a debtor *(p. 419)*

sympathetic witness: a witness who gives evidence that supports your cause *(p. 377)*

theory of the defence: the defendant's grounds for disputing the plaintiff's claim *(p. 231)*

third party: person who is not a party to an agreement or transaction, but who may have rights or obligations with respect to the agreement or transaction, or whose presence is necessary to enable the court to adjudicate effectively on the issues in the proceeding *(p. 241)*

third-party claim: a claim by a defendant against a person not named in the plaintiff's claim *(p. 241)*

trial book: book of notes, documents, submissions and so on prepared for and used by a party at trial, containing all important information needed at the trial in a secure and organized format *(p. 370)*

true copy: an accurate copy of an original document *(p. 287)*

unliquidated claim: claim for an indefinite amount that must be valued by the court based on the evidence *(p. 113)*

unliquidated damages: an amount that is not fixed and specified, which must be determined by the court based on the evidence; *see also* general damages *(pp. 86, 107)*

unsympathetic witness: a witness who gives evidence that supports an opposing party's cause *(p. 377)*

vary a court order: to change the terms of a court order *(p. 290)*

venue: the place where a trial is held *(p. 94)*

waive the default: a decision by a lender or creditor not to insist upon strict compliance by a debtor with the terms for payment of a debt or other obligation *(p. 421)*

waiving the excess: in a plaintiff's claim or defendant's claim, giving up the right to claim any money owing above $10,000.00 (exclusive of interest and costs), in order to bring the matter within Small Claims Court monetary jurisdiction *(p. 90)*

Index

Streetfood

From the Street to Your Table

WHITE STAR PUBLISHERS

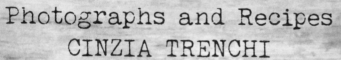

Photographs and Recipes
CINZIA TRENCHI

Project Editor
VALERIA MANFERTO DE FABIANIS

Graphic Layout
VALENTINA GIAMMARINARO

INTRODUCTION

Recipes

Introduction

Stands, food trucks, food carts, small shops: street food is starting to play an increasing role in people's everyday lives. Looking closely, one discovers that behind this new "label" there is a million different foods with the most varied of origins: foods that we eat regularly at home or in restaurants and consider a "normal" part of our diet, at times, actually have humble or far off origins. French fries, for example, are thought to have first appeared as a street food in XIX century Paris, while Ramen noodles, diffused through the streets of Japan as a quick food meant for students and laborers. In the more developed Western countries, from Europe to the United Stated, it was often the immigrants that contributed to the spread of new culinary traditions. Indians, Middle Easterners, the Chinese, Thai, and Africans transformed the "poor" cuisines of their respective countries into a profession, exporting the flavors and aromas of their places of origin and offering a low cost meal, often to laborers with just a few coins in their pockets.

This is why in today's world, made increasingly smaller by globalization, street foods can offer a unique glimpse of the traditions of far off countries and preserve that authentic and familiar flavor that large-scale restaurant industry often erases.

Throughout the world, over two billion people consume foods that can be defined as "street food" every day. Throngs of street vendors, often women, offer foods in the streets, squares, markets, transport stations and even by schools and office buildings, or in small shops with no room to sit. While in the poorer corners of the planet street food is often the only real possibility to eat a nutritious meal for little money, the reasons behind its growing popularity in the western world are certainly varied. For busy people with little time at their disposal, the informal character and the speed of a bite consumed on the street constitute the true appeal of street food. In just a few minutes, the meal – or a snack – is ready, perfect for being consumed on the go: no waiting for a table or a meal to be served at a restaurant. The cheap nature of street food on the other hand is what makes these foods perfect for those who want or have to pay more attention to their spending: decidedly cheaper than a meal at a restaurant, they are often even cheaper than cooking at home. Finally, for the curious and the experimenters, what counts is the ethnic variety of the food stands. Within a radius of a few meters, the aromas and the flavors can transport you across the world, from India to South America, Africa and China.

Almost every country has its own characteristic street foods, and in almost every corner of the world, the history of street food is all but recent. From ancient Greece to Rome, from the Aztecs to the Near East, street food has always existed. In the XVI century, Turkey, famous above all for the doner kebab, was the first to regulate the sale of food on the streets with laws. Set in a strategic location along the Silk Road, its capital Istanbul naturally developed a mix of flavors that makes its street food particularly rich and tasty: from doner kebab to mussels and simit, sesame bagels similar to American bagels but with a Polish origin.

Historically, the sale and consumption of food in the streets are typical of countries such as Turkey or the Philippines, which are characterized by a strong social life centered around outdoor spaces – the port, the market, and the square. In other cases, the development of this phenomenon is linked to the movement of populations away from rural areas and to the growth of large urban centers. Although the need to feed oneself cheaply is common and widespread, street food vendors have not always been well received by different cultures. In Japan for example, it is not considered proper to eat while walking. Foods bought from vending machines or street vendors are consumed on the spot or on a park bench, and very rarely while moving along a street.

In XIX century New York on the other hand, street vendors offered all types of foods, but above all, oysters fished from the Hudson, which could be purchased for a few cents.

When the oysters went extinct, the street vendors did not disappear with them, despite often being harassed by the authorities. At the beginning of the XX century, the "Times" asked that food carts be banned from the city, not only to facilitate the flow of traffic but also to liberate it from Italian, Greek and Chinese immigrants. In 1960 and in 1990, the mayors of New York tried first to limit the length of time a cart could be parked and then to ban them completely. Both attempts failed and today, with the exception of the most congested streets, food vendors can be found in every corner of the Big Apple, selling street food or more simple fast foods, from ice cream to falafel, hot dogs and waffles.

In Italy, there are many traditional foods that lend themselves to being eaten on the go. From pizza and focaccia to Sicilian arancini, the Roman grattachecca, Neapolitan cuoppo - a paper cone filled with deep fried cheese, vegetables and batter -, Sicilian panelle and ice cream. Now, Greek gyros and Middle Eastern doner kebabs, or even American hot dogs and the more exotic Indian and Asian foods, can be found in almost every European city. In the Western world, street food is no longer just an answer to the need for fast and cheap meals, but also an actual food trend driven by the desire to get a taste of exotic culinary traditions. This may be the real reason for the differentiation that has been growing between fast food and street food. In some cases, the most popular street food vendors become actual institutions; and in American cities, rankings of the best food trucks for the benefit of both residents and tourists are no rarity.

However, it should not be forgotten that authenticity and health don't always go hand in hand and that the savings and speed offered by street foods may be hiding low quality ingredients poor in nutrients, or even worse, unhealthy. Frying, refined flours, dips and sauces rich in fats can be a tasty once in a while meal but risk damaging your health if consumed regularly. However, there is nothing stopping us from modifying the recipes just enough to render them healthier without making them any less tasty. Cooking street foods at home also allows you to control the quality of the ingredients more carefully and to experiment by creatively adapting the recipes to your needs and tastes.

This book will introduce you to a lighter version of street food by presenting recipes that are fun and flavorful, but also - why not? - healthy. Just take more care in choosing the cooking method by baking instead of deep-frying, or replace refined flours with whole grain flours, without forgetting to use only products that are in season.

The book is divided into four sections (recipes with spices and sauces, with vegetables, with fruit and with cereals and animal proteins) and complete with splendid photographs and detailed descriptions. Page after page, this volume will propose original combinations of ingredients in a kaleidoscope of flavors. Culinary globalization revisited in a lighter and healthier key that is fun, joyful and appetizing: an inspiration for snacks and meals to brighten up pauses in the daily grind.

With Spices
and Sauces...

In this section, dedicated to street food prepared with spices and sauces, you will find some of the recipes most commonly associated with street food, including the most famous of all: hot dogs with mustard. The recipes span the American continent, Far East, Italy and Morocco, and all employ the typical spices and condiments of their countries of origin. Therefore, next to wasabi, used in Japan to accompany fish, you will find the more aromatic ingredients of meat dishes from the Arabic peninsula, India and Indonesia, which call on many spices such as chili pepper, turmeric, ginger, cumin, coriander... Chili pepper is contained in many dishes, often as a main ingredient (for example in Italian deep-fried fish). In addition to flavoring foods, the various flavorings are important to our health, due to the digestion-enhancing, antiseptic and anti-inflammatory properties that characterize them. In India, cardamom is considered helpful in cancer prevention, while curry, used in India, Africa and South America, facilitates digestion and improves intestinal health. Therefore, enjoy these tasty recipes knowing that good flavor is going hand-in-hand with health benefits.

Chicken Wings with Fresh Corn (USA)

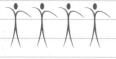

Servings

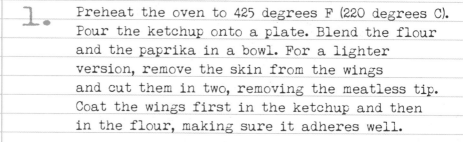

12 chicken wings - 2 fresh corncobs - 2 tbsp (34 g) ketchup - 2 tbsp (14 g) paprika - 2 tbsp (16 g) whole-wheat flour - 2 tbsp (20 g) extra virgin olive oil - salt and pepper

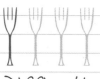

Difficulty

1. Preheat the oven to 425 degrees F (220 degrees C). Pour the ketchup onto a plate. Blend the flour and the paprika in a bowl. For a lighter version, remove the skin from the wings and cut them in two, removing the meatless tip. Coat the wings first in the ketchup and then in the flour, making sure it adheres well.

Prep Time
20 minutes

2. Line a baking sheet with parchment paper and arrange the wings on top. Bake for about 30 minutes, turning over several times.

3. In the meanwhile, wash the corncobs and cut them into four pieces each. Boil for 2 minutes, drain and season with oil.

4. Serve the chicken wings hot along with the corn, seasoning with salt and pepper to taste.

Cooking Time
30 minutes

The Origins
of Chicken Wings

Also known as "Buffalo wings", chicken wings take their name from the city of Buffalo, New York. According to one of the many stories, chicken wings were invented by Teressa Bellissimo, owner of the Anchor Bar together with her husband Frank. When their son Dominic turned up at his mother's bar unexpectedly with a group of his university friends, Teressa decided to fry some chicken wings - which were usually thrown away - and season them with Cayenne pepper sauce. New sauces were gradually introduced as the recipe spread like wildfire across the entire USA, influenced by Japanese, Chinese, Thai, or Caribbean cuisines.

Chicken wings are often served as snacks in bars or at sporting events. Around 25 billion chicken wings are eaten in the U.S every year.

Otak Otak (Indonesia)

Servings

1 lb (500 g) cod – 1 egg white – 1 1/2 tbsp (25 g) coconut milk – 5 tbsp (50 g) starch – 8 fresh spring onions – 4 fresh banana leaves – salt and pepper
For the Sambal Kacang sauce: 4 tbsp (40 g) extra virgin olive oil – 1 cup (100 g) toasted, shelled peanuts – 2 shallots – 1 fresh red chili pepper – 1 garlic clove – half a lime – 1 tbsp (15 g) coconut milk – 1 tsp (2 g) fresh minced ginger – 2 tbsp (36 g) Tamari sauce – salt

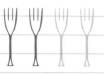

Difficulty

1. First, prepare the sauce. Finely chop the peanuts and transfer the resulting powder into a bowl. Peel the shallots. Trim the chili pepper and garlic. Finely chop everything. Transfer into a frying pan and sauté for 2 minutes. Add the peanuts, tamari sauce, ginger and lime juice. Mix, reduce and season with salt. Transfer to a bowl.

Prep Time
15 minutes

2. Trim and slice the spring onions. Remove any bones from the fish then dice and blend in a blender with the egg whites. Transfer into a bowl and add the spring onions, starch, salt, pepper and coconut milk. Blend until homogeneous. Divide the mixture between the banana leaves. Form bundles and secure with toothpicks.

Cooking Time
10 minutes

3. Grill or bake the bundles, as preferred (about 5 minutes per side are needed for a perfect result).

4. Serve the bundles hot with the peanut sauce.

An Archipelago
of Aromas

This popular Southeast Asian dish is prepared with minced freshwater or saltwater fish: it is usually made with mackerel, cod or milkfish and enriched with shrimp. The fish is finely chopped or blended and then added to a mixture of coconut milk, egg white, tapioca and spring onion: the mixture is then wrapped in banana leaves. They are usually steamed or grilled. It is custom to serve it with a spicy sauce made with peanuts, chili peppers, garlic, lime and ginger and it is truly delicious. Otak means "brain" and the Indonesian version of this specialty evokes its color and texture; Otak Otak prepared in Malaysia, on the other hand, is very bright and sunny thanks to the use of colorful spices like chili pepper, turmeric and curry. Otak Otak makes a delicious snack: often sold at bus stops, it is a typical street food, thanks to which you can immerse yourself in a magnificent archipelago of amazing flavors and aromas.

Hot Dog (USA)

Servings

4 milk buns – 4 turkey wieners – 1 head of curly lettuce – 1 purple onion – mustard to taste – ketchup to taste

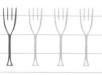

Difficulty

1. Trim the lettuce. Gently wash and dry. Peel and finely slice the onion.

2. Bring 4 1/2 cups (1 l) of water to a boil. Right before constructing the hot dogs, drop the wieners into the boiling water for about 5 minutes and drain.

3. Cut the buns, top with two well-drained lettuce leaves, the onion slices, some mustard and ketchup to taste. Set a wiener on top and add some more sauce and onion slices. Enjoy.

Prep Time
10 minutes

Cooking Time
5 minutes

There are many variations possible for a tasty hot dog: you can add cucumber, sauerkraut, tomatoes, mayonnaise; the wiener can contain pork, chicken, tofu or vegetables.

A German "Dog" Sets Off to Conquer the USA

When we think of a hot dog - succulent sausages in a soft bread roll - we think of the streets in America, which have made this cheap fast food famous. In actual fact, the hot dog was born in Germany, although the pork sausage (Frankfurter) or mixed pork and beef sausage (Wiener) were not eaten with bread. The use of the word "dog" dates back to 1800, when it was believed that sausages were also made with dog meat. It's not clear who first introduced the hot dog to the United States. Some say it was a German immigrant, Charles Feltman, on Coney Island in around 1870. Others say that the idea of the bread roll was invented by a Bavarian immigrant named Feuchtwanger, on the streets of St. Louis, Missouri. It was apparently his wife who suggested using the bread roll, so that customers could hold the sausages without burning themselves. It is estimated that annually Americans consume about 20 billion hot dogs, with an average of 70 hot dogs per person per year.

Ceviche with Lime and Chili (Peru)

Servings

1 lb (500 g) cod or grouper fillet – 8 shelled shrimp –
1 onion – 1 yellow and 1 red bell peppers – 2 lime –
1 cup (240 ml) lemon juice – 10 coriander sprigs – salt

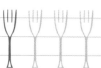

Difficulty

1. After removing any bones, place the fish on a plate with the shrimp tails. Pour the lemon juice on top and allow to sit for 30 minutes.

2. In the meanwhile, clean the chili peppers, removing the seeds, stem and white parts. If the peppers are very spicy, use only a part, choosing a dose according to personal taste. Peel and finely slice the onion.

3. After 30 minutes, drain the fish. Chop and place onto a serving tray with the shrimp tails. Season with salt, chili pepper, onion, coriander, pieces of lemon and lemon juice. Mix and serve.

Prep Time
15 minutes

Ceviche can be prepared with different types of fish as long as the meat is dense (ex. angler, perch, grouper etc.)

Turmeric Chicken (India)

Servings

14 oz. (400 g) chicken breast – 1/2 cup (30 g) whole-wheat flour – 1/4 cup (50 g) coconut milk – 1 onion – 2 tbsp (18 g) turmeric – 1 tsp (3 g) cardamom seeds – 4 tbsp (40 g) extra virgin olive oil – salt and pepper

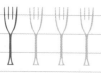

Difficulty

**Prep Time
20 minutes**

**Cooking Time
25 minutes**

1. Pour the flour and the turmeric into a bowl and mix. Dice the chicken breast and place into the breadcrumbs, making them adhere well to the meat. Crush the cardamom seeds in a mortar.

2. Peel and slice the onion. Heat the oil in a large frying pan. Add the onion and brown or 2 minutes while stirring. Add the chicken and mix. After two minutes bathe with coconut milk, add aroma with the cardamom, and season with salt and pepper to taste.

3. Cook over low heat to make sure the sauce does not reduce too quickly. Stir and check often to make sure the meat is cooked evenly. If necessary, add a few tablespoons of hot water.

4. After about 20 minutes, the chicken will be ready. You can serve it with basmati rice or soft buns.

Vegetarian Meatballs with Curry Yogurt Sauce (India)

Servings

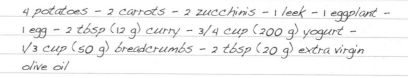

4 potatoes – 2 carrots – 2 zucchinis – 1 leek – 1 eggplant – 1 egg – 2 tbsp (12 g) curry – 3/4 cup (200 g) yogurt – 1/3 cup (50 g) breadcrumbs – 2 tbsp (20 g) extra virgin olive oil

Difficulty

1. Peel the potatoes, scrub the carrots, and trim the eggplant, zucchinis and leek. Wash the vegetables, chop into small pieces and gently cook in oil.

2. Check often, stir and add a little bit of water a spoonful at a time if necessary. Season with salt to taste. After about 20 minutes, check that the ingredients are soft. Mince.

**Prep Time
20 minutes**

3. Transfer the resulting mixture into a bowl. Add the egg and the breadcrumbs. Mix and form balls of desired size with your hands. Preheat the oven to 390 degrees F (200 degrees C). Blend the curry with the yogurt.

4. Line a baking sheet with parchment paper and set the balls on top. Bake for about 20 minutes then take out and serve with the curry yogurt sauce.

**Cooking Time
40 minutes**

Nigiri with Wasabi (Japan)

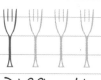

Servings

7 oz. (200 g) salmon fillet – 8 shrimp – 1 sea bream fillet – 2 1/2 cups (500 g) cooked Gohan rice – 1/4 cup (50 g) wasabi – Tamari sauce to taste

Difficulty

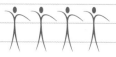

Prep Time
30 minutes

1. First, prepare the fish. Remove the shells from the shrimp, parboil for a minute and cool. Before slicing the fish, place it in the freezer for a few minutes. This will make for a more compact meat ensuring a more precise cut.

2. Use a sharp knife with a thin blade. Slice the salmon and sea bream fillet and place them in the fridge until needed. Remove the veins from the shrimp and open them. Moisten your hands, from blocks of rice onto which you will set the fish and the shrimp.

3. If you really like wasabi, place a small amount of the paste first onto the rice and then onto the fish during assembly.

4. Arrange the nigiri on a serving plate using your imagination.

5. Serve accompanied with soy sauce and wasabi.

White Rice Rolls (Japan)

Servings

1 1/2 cups (300 g) white rice – 1 tbsp (15 ml) rice vinegar – 4 sheets of nori seaweed, each cut in two – 7 oz. (200 g) salmon – 3 tbsp (50 g) lumpfish or salmon roe – 3 1/2 oz. (100 g) avocado – wasabi to taste – sesame seeds – tamari sauce to taste

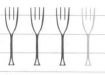

Difficulty

1. To prepare the rice for the rolls, choose rice with small, round grains and wash it until the water runs clear. Place it into a pot with double the amount of water. Cover and place a weight on top to trap the vapor formed. Cook the rice for about 8 minutes after the water begins to boil then turn off the heat. Transfer the rice into a bowl, add the vinegar and mix.

**Prep Time
20 minutes**

2. While the rice cools, prepare the ingredients for the filling: peel the avocado and cut it and the salmon lengthwise.

3. Roll out the sushi making mat, place a sheet of nori seaweed on top, cover with rice, season with wasabi to taste, and top with the salmon. Roll up the ingredients with the help of the mat. Press gently to make sure the ingredients adhere to each other then unroll. Slice using a sharp, wet knife. For a roll with rice on the outside: Form a layer of rice on a sushi rolling mat moistened with water. Top with the seaweed and the avocado. Roll up, decorate with sesame seeds, cut and top with lumpfish or salmon roe.

**Cooking Time
8 minutes**

4. Repeat until you finish all the ingredients, arranging the pieces on a serving plate as you prefer. Serve the rolls with tamari sauce and wasabi to taste.

On the Streets of Edo

Despite the sophistication it has accustomed us to, the sushi we know today actually began its life as a street food in ancient Edo - former name of Tokyo -, the capital of Japan. However, the history of sushi begins in 200 AD in Southeast Asia and China, where rice was used to preserve meat and fish. The catch was gutted, salted and wrapped in fermented rice.

A few months later, the rice was discarded and the fish (Narezushi) was eaten. This preservation method was introduced in Japan in 700 AD, but the Japanese's tastes soon turned the Narezushi into namanare, or semi-fermented fish, so that they could eat the rice and fish together. To make this dish, the raw fish was wrapped in rice and eaten fresh before the taste changed. Haya-zushi (fast food sushi), in which the ingredients could be eaten together, was invented during the Edo period (around 1800). A street food version (nigiri-zushi) was made popular by vendors who swarmed the streets of the capital, and in 1900 it spread rapidly across Japan. This is sushi as we know it: a thin slice of fish resting on an oval ball of rice.

Deep Fried Anchovies and Chili Pepper (Italy)

Servings

1 lb. (500 g) anchovies – 7 oz. (200 g) baby squid – 2/3 cup (100 g) rice flour – 1 1/3 cups (300 g) peanut oil – 8 chili peppers of desired spiciness – salt

Difficulty

1. Wash, gut and drain the fish and the baby squid. Trim and wash the chili peppers. Cut them in two and remove the seeds. Pour the flour into a bowl. Coat the fish and chili peppers.

2. Heat the oil and deep-fry a few ingredients at a time leaving the chili peppers for last (if cooked first, they will make the oil spicy altering the flavor of the fish).

Prep Time
15 minutes

3. Drain, set on paper towels and season with salt. Transfer into paper cones, small bags or plates as desired and serve hot.

Cooking Time
10 minutes

This typical Italian dish is undeniably high in calories but when the ingredients are extremely fresh and cooked in high quality oil, they are a joy to the palate.

A Fragrant History

Historical records show that the ancient Egyptians were already deep frying food in 2500 BC: the most used oils were extracted from generic seeds, while the Romans preferred olive oil. Moving on to the Middle Ages, we once again find deep-fried foods, although with the use of animal fats such as lard and butter, especially in Northern Europe. It is a simple and extremely tasty way of cooking, one that transmits regional flavors and traditions. When deep-fried, batters, donuts, vegetables, meat and fish - actually, just about any kind of food - are enriched with a wonderful crispy texture and an irresistible fragrance. Over time, the fats used to make food delicately crispy have become increasingly refined, so as to make the foods more digestible.

Many improvements have been made to improve the quality, although it is still a very high calorie dish that should only be eaten occasionally, because, despite the fact that it is delicious, it appears that it's pretty hard work for the digestive system!

Shrimp Skewers (Indonesia)

Servings

16 medium shrimp - 2 limes - 2 garlic cloves - 1 tbsp (8 g) chili pepper powder - 1 tsp (2 g) fresh, minced ginger - 1 lemon grass sprig

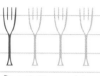

Difficulty

1. Trim the lemon grass. Wash and dice the softer portion. Wash the shrimp, remove the shells and place into a bowl. Drizzle with lime juice (save some to use during cooking). Add the lemon grass and set aside for 10 minutes.

2. In the meanwhile, peel and mince the garlic. Add the ginger and chili pepper and transfer the mixture into a plate. Drain the shrimp and coat them with the prepared mixture.

Prep Time
20 minutes

3. Wash the remaining lime. Slice and slide onto 8 skewers alternating with the shrimp. Cook the skewers on a grill, drizzling with lime juice.

4. You can serve the skewers with a fruit and vegetable salad.

Cooking Time
8 minutes

Lamb Skewers – Kefta Kebab (Morocco)

Servings

For the skewers: 14 oz. (400 g) ground lamb – 1 tsp (3 g) turmeric – 1 tbsp (5 g) fresh minced ginger – 1 tsp (3 g) cumin and 1 tsp (2 g) paprika powder – 1 tsp (6 g) minced coriander – 2 tbsp (30 g) yogurt – salt
For the sauce: 1 garlic clove – 1 onion – 2 tbsp (20 g) extra virgin olive oil – 2 small mint sprigs – 1 1/4 cups (300 g) dense yogurt – salt and black pepper

Difficulty

1. To prepare the sauce of accompaniment, trim and mince the mint and mix it with the yogurt. Peel the garlic and the onion. Finely chop. Mix all the ingredients together and season with salt and pepper to taste.

Prep Time
20 minutes

2. Preheat the oven to 425 degrees F (220 degrees C). Mix the spices and the yogurt with the meat for the kebab. Divide the mixture into 4 or 8 parts and form plump sausages around the skewer. Make sure the meat adheres well to the wood. Place on a baking sheet lined with parchment paper.

3. Coat them thoroughly with oil and place in the oven. After about 5 minutes, take them out, turn over and place back in. The cooking time can vary from 10 to 15 minutes depending on the size of the kefta kebab.

Cooking Time
15 minutes

4. Serve them hot accompanied with the yogurt sauce.

Pastel (Brazil)

For the dough: 1 1/2 cups (200 g) all-purpose flour – 2/3 cup (100 g) rice flour – 1 egg – 1 tbsp (10 g) corn oil – 1 tbsp (15 ml) Rum

For the filling: 2 tbsp (20 g) extra virgin olive oil – 1 onion – 1 garlic clove – 7 oz. (200 g) ground beef – 20 pitted olives – 1 tbsp (16 g) tomato concentrate – 1 tbsp (4 g) minced parsley – 1 minced chili pepper – salt and black pepper

Servings

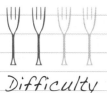

Difficulty

1. Prepare the dough by mixing the ingredients and adding a few tablespoons of water (four may suffice). Once you have a well-blended, dense and elastic dough, cover it and set aside to rest for about 20 minutes.

Prep Time
30 minutes

2. Pour the oil into a frying pan and add finely chopped onion and garlic. Next add the meat and the tomato concentrate. Mix and if necessary add a tablespoon of water but only if the filling becomes too dry. Season with salt to taste. Add black and chili peppers for some spice. Once cooked, add the parsley and olives. Mix and turn off the heat once all the cooking liquid has reduced.

Cooking Time
30 minutes

3. Roll out the dough with a rolling pin and cut it into rectangles about 4 by 6 inches (10 by 15 cm) in size. Fill with the meat. The original recipe calls for frying in oil however, for a lighter version, baking is ideal. Bake for about 15 minutes at 390 degrees F (200 degrees C) in a preheated oven, turning the bundles over halfway through.

With Vegetables...

Vegetables dominate this section, which includes street foods from four continents. Some are very healthy, such as Pupusa with marinated cabbage from the Caribbean, while others should be consumed in moderation, such as the British fish and chips. Vegetables can be an excellent substitute for meat or fish for vegetarians and vegans, or can be used to enhance and accompany meats. However, keep in mind that depending on the preparation and cooking method used, vegetable-based street foods can also be high in calories and not always healthy — especially if deep-fried! In this section, you will find common ingredients, such as onion, potato and cabbage, revisited by culinary traditions from close and far and hence new to the eye and the palate. For example, stir-fried onions and peppers can become a flavorful filling for African pockets, while an avocado and tabasco dip can enhance even simpler steamed vegetables in line with Mexican tradition.

Fried Tofu and Sautéed Eggplants, Potatoes, Celery and Bell Peppers (Indonesia)

Servings

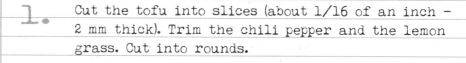

10 oz. (300 g) tofu – 1 chili pepper – 1 lemon grass sprig – 2 tbsp (36 g) tamari sauce
For the sautéed vegetables: half an eggplant – 1 celery heart – 1 potato – 1 bell pepper – salt and pepper

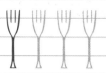

Difficulty

Prep Time
20 minutes

Cooking Time
15 minutes

1. Cut the tofu into slices (about 1/16 of an inch – 2 mm thick). Trim the chili pepper and the lemon grass. Cut into rounds.

2. Wash all the vegetables. Chop the bell pepper, celery and eggplant. Peel the potato and chop it. Transfer everything into a non-stick frying pan and cook over high heat for a few minutes. Lower the heat and add a few tablespoons of hot water if necessary. Cook until the texture is to your preference. Season with salt and pepper to taste. Take off the heat and set aside while you prepare the tofu.

3. Heat a non-stick frying pan. Toast the tofu over high heat for about 3-4 minutes. Turn it over several times and add the chili pepper, lemon grass and tamari sauce halfway through.

4. Serve the tofu with the sautéed vegetables.

Ginger Samosa (India)

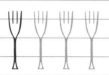

Servings

1 1/2 cups (200 g) all-purpose flour – 1/4 cup (50 g) peanut oil – 2 potatoes – 2 zucchinis – 2/3 cup (100 g) shelled peas – 1 onion – 1 medium-small bell pepper – 1 lime – 1 tbsp (8 g) Masala – 1 tsp (6 g) minced coriander – 1 tsp (2 g) fresh minced ginger – salt

Difficulty

1. Mix the flour with oil and two tablespoons of water if necessary. Prepare a firm dough then cover and set aside for an hour.

2. In the meanwhile, prepare the vegetables: Peel and dice the potatoes. Peel and finely chop the onion. Remove the seeds, white sections and stem from the bell pepper. Chop it into small pieces.

Prep Time
20 minutes

3. Place all the vegetables and the spices into a non-stick frying pan. Season with salt to taste. Drizzle with lime juice and stew for 10 minutes. Take off the heat and allow to cool.

4. Take the dough, flatten it out and cut into rectangles. Cut the rectangles into two and top the resulting triangles with the vegetables. Bake the samosas on a baking sheet lined with parchment paper. Leave in the oven for 10 minutes, turning over after 5.

Cooking Time
20 minutes

A "Half-moon" Full of Flavor

Samosas are pastry parcels with a savory filling,
a typical street food in Indian cuisine, but they
can also be found in Southeast Asia,
on the Arabian Peninsula and in North Africa.
The fillings can vary: vegetarian, cheese, meat or
legumes. The term originates from the ancient
Persian word sambusak or sanbosag, which means
"half-moon", the shape the parcels were initially.
It appears that the first samosas were made in the
X century in the Middle East, and a few centuries
later they appeared in India. Deep-fried or baked,
they are enriched with famous aromatic spices such
as "garam masala", a blend of ground spices that
makes the vegetables commonly used as a filling more
appetizing: potatoes, peas and onions. This triumph
of aromas and flavors, usually made with filo pastry
and a vegetable filling, is often served with mango
chutney, a wonderful sweet'n'sour and extremely
spicy condiment.

Fennel Salad with Oranges and Chili Pepper (Italy)

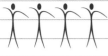

Servings

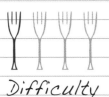

Difficulty

Prep Time
10 minutes

2 fennels – 1 thin-skinned organic orange – half an avocado –
1 fresh chili pepper of desired spiciness –
2 tbsp (30 g) lemon juice – 3 tbsp (45 g) orange juice –
2 tbsp (20 g) extra virgin olive oil – salt

1. Wash and dry the fennels. Chop finely. If you have a slicer, the result will be stunning. Cut into transparent slices, the fennel will not only be tasty but also beautiful to see.

2. Wash the orange. Peel it or if you wish to leave on the rind on, slice into thin pieces. Peel the avocado and dice.

3. Compose the salad by mixing the colorful ingredients. Flavor to taste with chili pepper. Season with an emulsion of the lemon and orange juices, oil and salt prepared beforehand.

Onion Quiche (France)

Servings

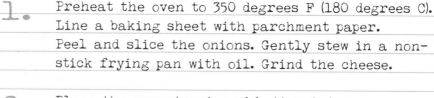

7 oz. (200 g) basic shortcrust pastry – 1 lb (500 g) white onions – 3.5 oz. (100 g) Groviera cheese – 2 eggs – 3/4 cup (2 dl) milk – 2 tbsp (20 g) cornstarch – 1 1/2 tbsp (20 g) butter – salt and pepper – 2 tbsp (20 g) extra virgin olive oil

Difficulty

1. Preheat the oven to 350 degrees F (180 degrees C). Line a baking sheet with parchment paper. Peel and slice the onions. Gently stew in a non-stick frying pan with oil. Grind the cheese.

2. Place the cornstarch and butter into a saucepan. Melt over low heat while stirring. Once the butter has absorbed the cornstarch, add the milk and bring to a boil stirring continuously. Take of the heat once the besciamella sauce has thickened.

**Prep Time
30 minutes**

3. Mix the onions with the cheese, besciamella sauce and eggs. Season with salt and pepper to taste and pour over the basic shortcrust pastry. Bake for about 25-30 minutes then check to make sure the filling is uniform and compact with a toothpick. If not, bake for an additional 5 minutes.

**Cooking Time
40 minutes**

4. Once the savory pie is ready, take it out of the oven and allow to cool. The quiche is tasty served both hot or at room temperature.

Fish and Chips (UK)

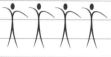
Servings

14 oz. (400 g) cod fillet – 4 potatoes – 1/3 cup (50 g) whole-wheat flour – 1 glass of ice cold beer – 1/2 glass of ice cold sparkling water – 3/4 cup (2 dl) peanut oil

Difficulty

Prep Time
20 minutes

Cooking Time
15 minutes

1. Wash and peel the potatoes. Cut them into sticks. Rinse them repeatedly in water until it runs clear. Boil for 5 minutes, drain and allow to cool.

2. In the meanwhile, pour the flour into a bowl. Incorporate the beer then drizzle in the water until the batter is homogeneous and airy using a whisk. Coat the cod with the batter.

3. Heat the oil in two non-stick frying pans and deep-fry the cod in one and the potatoes in the other. This will ensure they are ready at the same time and can be served while both are still hot. Take out the fish when the batter takes on a golden color and drain the potatoes as soon as they take on color. Before serving, season with salt.

4. A tasty dish, it should be served occasionally and can be accompanied with mayonnaise or ketchup. Remember that potatoes that have first been washed and boiled will be lighter and less oily.

"Good Companions" Wrapped Up in a Newspaper

White fish (usually cod) inside a tasty golden batter made with beer: this is the "fish"; the "chips", on the other hand, are crispy golden French fries. One of the many theories on the origin of this famous dish, is that deep-frying (already being used in countries that bordered the Mediterranean Sea) landed in the UK in the 1800s, thanks to Venetian immigrants who missed nibbling the local "scartosso de pes" while they walked. Originally fish and chips were served in a bag made from old newspapers, and sold at simple stalls where fish and potatoes fried happily in huge pots of boiling oil. Today, kiosks, street vendors and restaurants serve this dish in more hygienic containers, but the tasty recipe has kept its original characteristics, completed with a pinch of salt, a dash of malt vinegar to taste and, for those who want to go for the whole works, various condiments. The same delicious recipe that, so they say, led Winston Churchill to define the specialty as a "good companion", because it kept up the British moral during the two world wars and contributed to accelerating the industrial revolution in the UK.

Onion and Bell Pepper Pockets (Africa)

Servings

1 1/2 cup (200 g) whole-wheat flour – 2 onions – 2 bell peppers – 1 tsp (2 g) curry – 1/4 cup (50 g) dense yogurt – 5 tbsp (50 g) extra virgin olive oil – salt

Difficulty

Prep Time
20 minutes

Cooking Time
15 minutes

1. Peel and finely chop the onions. Wash the bell peppers, remove the seeds and white parts, and chop.

2. Pour 2 tablespoons of oil into a non-stick frying pan. Heat it and add the vegetables. Cook over medium heat for 4-5 minutes. The vegetables must be dry. Remove from heat while still crunchy. Add the curry and the herbs while stirring. Transfer into a bowl. Add the yogurt and salt to taste.

3. Blend the flour with 3 tablespoons of oil and a little bit of water poured in one tablespoon at a time. Knead into a firm dough. Once homogeneous and clump-free, roll it out into a sheet about 1/32 inch (1 mm) thick. Preheat the oven to 390 degrees F (200 degrees C) and line a baking sheet with parchment paper.

4. Cut the dough into rectangles. Top with the vegetables and seal by folding the rectangles onto themselves to form triangles. Press down well along the sides. Place the pockets onto a baking sheet and bake for about 10 minutes, turning them over half way through.

5. Serve the pockets warm or at room temperature.

Spring Rolls (China)

Servings

8 rice paper disks
For the filling: 3 1/2 oz. (100 g) Chinese cabbage - 3 1/2 oz. (100 g) pak choi - 1 spring onion - 8 cleaned shrimp - 1/3 cup (30 g) soy sprouts - 4 tbsp (40 g) extra virgin olive oil - tamari sauce - salt

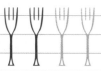

Difficulty

1. Place the rice disks into cold water one at a time then set them to dry on a cloth (they must remain soft and moist). Allow to sit for about 10 minutes.

2. Wash all the vegetables and the sprouts, setting them aside separately. Peel, trim and thinly slice all the vegetables.

Prep Time
20 minutes

3. Heat two tablespoons of oil in a non-stick frying pan or a wok. Stir-fry the vegetables to the desired crunchiness. Before turning off the heat, add the shrimp and mix them with the vegetables.

Cooking Time
10 minutes

4. Preheat the oven to 390 degrees F (200 degrees C). Line a baking sheet with parchment paper. Top the disks with the vegetables, roll them up and brush with oil. Arrange the rolls on a baking sheet. Bake until evenly cooked, turning over often. Leave in the oven for about 8-10 minutes and serve with tamari sauce.

Spicy Vegetables with Tabasco-flavored Avocado Cream (The Caribbean)

Servings

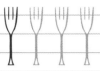

Difficulty

**Prep Time
20 minutes**

2 avocado – 2 lime – 1/2 cup (1 dl) corn oil – 2 tsp (9 g) tabasco – 4 potatoes – 2 carrots – 1 celery heart – 2/3 cup (100 g) peas – salt

1. Wash and steam the potatoes then peel and allow to cool. Trim and chop the carrots and celery. Boil the peas until soft.

2. Once the potatoes have cooled, chop and add to the other vegetables. Set aside until ready to serve.

3. Peel the avocado. Chop and place into the blender. Add lime juice, oil, salt to taste and tabasco. Blend. Once you have a smooth, homogeneous cream, transfer into a bowl.

4. Serve the vegetables with the cream, seasoning with more tabasco sauce if desired.

Cuban Mini Pizzas with Tomatoes and Onions (Cuba)

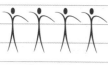

Servings

For the dough: 3/4 cup (200 g) boiled and mashed potatoes – 1 1/2 cup (200 g) whole-wheat flour – 1 tsp (2 g) extra virgin olive oil – 1 tsp (4 g) brown sugar – 1/2 tbsp (5 g) yeast

For the toppings: 2 ripe tomatoes – 1 onion – 2 tbsp (20 g) extra virgin olive oil – 1 tbsp (18 g) sweet mustard – 1 tbsp (16 g) tomato concentrate – salt

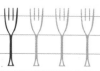

Difficulty

1. Mix the ingredients for the dough. Knead adding a little bit of water until the dough is uniform, homogeneous and malleable.

2. Preheat the oven to 390 degrees F (200 degrees C) and line a baking sheet with parchment paper.

Prep Time
30 minutes

3. Peel and finely slice the onion. Wash and chop the tomatoes. Pour the oil into a non-stick frying pan and stew the onion. After 2 minutes add the tomatoes, mustard, tomatoes and tomato concentrate. Season with salt and blend. Turn off the heat after a minute.

4. Roll out the dough. Cut out circles about 2 1/2 – 3 inches (6-8 cm) in diameter and 1/16 inch (2 mm) thick using a pastry ring. Arrange on a baking sheet placing them about 3/4 inch (2 cm) apart. Top with the onion and tomato mixture and bake for 8-10 minutes.

Cooking Time
10 minutes

5. Serve the mini pizzas hot or at room temperature.

Pupusa with Marinated Cabbage (The Caribbean)

For the cabbage: 1 lb (500 g) Savoy cabbage – 4 1/4 cups (1 l) boiling water – 1/2 cup (1 dl) white vinegar – 1 tsp (4 g) sugar – 1 tsp (6 g) salt – 1 spring onion – 1 carrot
For the tomato sauce: 4 peeled ripe tomatoes – 1 chili pepper (Jalapeño) – half an onion, finely chopped – 2 tbsp (20 g) extra virgin olive oil – salt and pepper
For the Pupusa: 1 1/2 cups (200 g) corn flour – 1/3 cup (50 g) all-purpose flour – 3 1/2 oz. (100 g) Queso or Mozzarella for pizza – 2 tbsp (20 g) extra virgin olive oil

Servings

Difficulty

Prep Time
30 minutes

Resting time
10 hours

Cooking Time
4-10 minutes

1. To prepare the cabbage, you will need at least 10-12 hours. Keep this in mind when planning to prepare this recipe. Trim, wash and dry the cabbage then chop into thin strips. Transfer it into a deep bowl. Pour boiling water over the chopped cabbage. Add freshly grated carrot, sliced spring onion, vinegar, sugar and salt. Mix and set aside in a cool spot.

2. Place the chili pepper cleaned of its seeds and stem into a blender together with the onion, tomatoes and oil. Blend until creamy. Transfer the mixture into a pot and thicken for about 20 minutes. Season with salt and pepper to taste.

3. Mix the flours with a little bit of water added one tablespoon at a time in a bowl (start with 3 tablespoons). Knead until the dough is uniform and homogeneous. Corn flour tends to break up. However, the presence of wheat flour will serve to help fuse it together. Divide the dough into eight portions. Form disks about 1/4 inch (1/2 cm) thick. Set some cheese in their centers, pressing down and partially covering with the dough. Transfer into a lightly oiled frying pan and cook for 2 minutes per side.

4. Right before serving, parboil the cabbage and place it into a bowl. Transfer the tomato cream into a bowl as well. Serve the pupusas topped with the cabbage and tomato cream.

El Salvadorian Tortillas

Pupusas, symbol of basic yet very good street food, come from Central America and, outside their place of origin, are also known as "El Salvadorian tortillas".

The base is prepared with corn flour, which can then be stuffed with beans, cheese, vegetables and even edible flowers. It is said that the specialty was already being made by the Spanish in the 1500s, but this theory doesn't tie in with the hypothesis that it was actually the Spaniards to introduce them in the first place. It appears that pupusa means "well mixed", because the base of a good pupusa must go really well with the filling.

Since 2005, thanks to a legislative decree, they celebrate "National Pupusa Day" in El Salvador on the second Sunday of November.

It is considered a national dish - the recipe has been handed down for generations - and information on the dish indicates that it is part of Pre-Columbian cuisine. This magnificent dish, which has fed people for generations, contains few ingredients while maintaining its unique characteristics, making pupusa a tasty and energy-boosting food.

Ful Mudammas (Egypt)

1 cup (200 g) dried broad beans – 2/3 cup (120 g) lentils – 3 garlic cloves – 1 spring onion – 2 lemons – 1 tsp (3 g) turmeric powder – 4 tbsp (40 g) extra virgin olive oil – salt and pepper

For the salad: 3 tomatoes – 1 cucumber – 2 spring onions – 2 tbsp (8 g) minced parsley – 2 tbsp (20 g) extra virgin olive oil – 2 tbsp (30 g) lemon juice – 3 boiled eggs cut in half – salt

Servings

Difficulty

1. Soak the broad beans for 10 hours then boil over low heat with the lentils, sliced spring onions and garlic. Keep the heat very low for 3-4 hours, adding boiling water whenever necessary.

2. By the end, the legumes should be a soft, dense puree. When ready, squeeze the lemons into the puree, and add the turmeric, oil, salt and pepper to taste. Mix energetically and transfer into a bowl.

Prep Time
10 minutes

3. Prepare the salad by chopping the vegetables and seasoning them with parsley, oil and lemon juice. Season with salt to taste, add the eggs and serve the puree with salad and toasted bread.

Resting time
10 hours

Cooking Time
3-4 hours

Crêpe with Vegetables and Yogurt (Bulgaria)

Servings

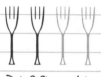

Difficulty

Prep Time
20 minutes

Cooking Time
30 minutes

4 eggs – 4 tbsp (40 g) starch – 4 tbsp (30 g) all-purpose flour – 3/4 cup (2 dl) milk – salt and pepper
For the filling: 1 leek – 1 bell pepper – 1 zucchini – 1 tsp (2 g) paprika – 1/2 cup (100 g) dense yogurt – 1/4 cup (50 g) pureed tofu – 2 tbsp (20 g) extra virgin olive oil – salt and pepper

1. Trim and slice the leek. Wash the bell pepper, remove the stem, white parts and the seeds, and chop into small pieces. Wash the zucchini and cut into rounds.

2. Pour the oil into a wok. Add the vegetables and paprika. Stew over low heat for 10 minutes, adding tablespoons of water when necessary to make the cooking process gentler. Season with salt and pepper to taste then remove from heat. Allow to cool and mix with the tofu and the yogurt.

3. Prepare the batter for the crêpes by mixing the eggs with the starch, flour and milk then seasoning with salt and pepper to taste.

4. Heat a non-stick frying pan about 9 1/2 inches in diameter. Coat it in oil using a piece of paper towel dipped in oil. Pour a ladleful of the batter into the frying pan making sure to cover the bottom completely. Allow to thicken for about 20 seconds then detach the crêpe and flip it over. Cook as long as necessary for firm crêpes (10-15 seconds) and transfer onto a plate. Continue until the batter is finished.

5. Preheat the oven to 390 degrees F (200 degrees C). Fill the crêpes with the vegetables and the yogurt, forming bundles of any shape you wish. Bake the bundles for 5 minutes and serve.

Gyros (Greece)

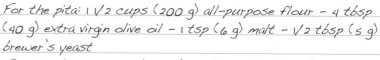

For the pita: 1 1/2 cups (200 g) all-purpose flour – 4 tbsp (40 g) extra virgin olive oil – 1 tsp (6 g) malt – 1/2 tbsp (5 g) brewer's yeast

For the Gyros: 14 oz. (400 g) pork – 1 tbsp (15 ml) vinegar – 1 tsp (2 g) paprika – 1 tsp (1 g) oregano – 1/2 tsp (1.5 g) turmeric powder

For the filling: 1 tomato – 1 cucumber – half an onion – 1/2 cup (100 g) Greek yogurt

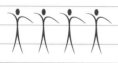

Servings

Difficulty

**Prep Time
30 minutes**

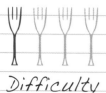

**Resting time
60 minutes**

**Cooking Time
15 minutes**

1. Preheat the oven to 480 degrees F (250 degrees C). Prepare the flatbread (pita) by mixing the flour with 3 tablespoons of oil, malt and brewer's yeast in a bowl. Drizzle in about 1/2 cup (1 dl) of water and mix until the mixture is homogeneous.

2. Set aside to rise for 30 minutes in a warm spot. Divide into 4 parts and set aside to rise for an additional 30 minutes. Flatten the balls and form sheets about 1/16 inch (2 mm) thick and 7-8 inches (18-20 cm) in diameter.

3. Place on a baking sheet lined with parchment paper. Brush with an emulsion prepared using the remaining oil and a tablespoon of water. Bake for 5 minutes at 480 degrees F (250 degrees C). Take out of the oven and store in an airtight container until needed.

4. Cut the pork into thin strips. Season them with oregano, paprika and vinegar. Bake for about 10 minutes.

5. Wash and slice the tomato and cucumber. Slice the onion.

6. Before serving, top the flatbread with the yogurt, onion, tomato and finally the meat. Close the pita and serve. In Greece, this sandwich is usually accompanied with French fries.

A Multi-faceted Kebab

This Greek specialty is reminiscent of the Turkish
doner kebabs or Arabic shawarma; the main difference
is that the meat used to stuff gyros is usually
pork, which is prohibited in Islamic countries.
The dish consists of pita bread (made with flour, oil
and yeast), which is used as a base for a tasty blend
of flavors: well-cooked lemon-marinated meat, garlic
and herbs, dressed with yogurt, tomatoes, onions
and, at times, also accompanied by French fries.
Street food par excellence, it is a complete meal
that bursts with the flavors of Greece, rich with
multi-faceted taste sensations that are more than
likely thanks to the country's geographic position,
which put Greece in contact with the countries that
border the Mediterranean Sea. Presumably the recipe
is extremely old, (excluding potatoes and tomatoes,
which were brought to Europe by Columbus),
and it is said that the culinary art of Magna Graecia
was very fashionable in the Mediterranean basin
and that having a Hellenic chef was the symbol
of a person's high status!

With Fruit...

In the recipes included in this section, fruits are transformed into quick and tasty snacks, many of which come from Italy. Among them, those most typically associated with street food are probably the French crêpes - here, presented in the wild berry variation - and the American caramel apples, which can be eaten on a stick like an ice cream. For a more exotic touch, you can push towards the Orient and practice preparing kumquat in syrup or Thai coconut cream, which can be served with any fruit you would like. According to Indonesian culinary tradition, coconut milk enhanced with a touch of cinnamon and a bit of Rum is an excellent way to flavor steamed bananas. Just like vegetable-based street foods, these fruit-based recipes can also be rich in calories. Hence, eat them in moderation. Just think of the nougat with its numerous dried fruit and nut variations, the hazelnut muffins and apple hot cakes.

Apple Frittella (Italy)

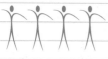

Servings

2 Reinette apples - 3/4 cup (100 g) semi whole-wheat flour - 2 eggs - 1/4 cup (0.5 dl) milk - 1/2 tsp (2 g) baking powder - 4 tbsp (30 g) confectioner's sugar - 1/2 cup (1 dl) peanut oil

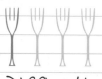

Difficulty

Prep Time
20 minutes

Cooking Time
10 minutes

1. Wash and peel the apples. Eliminate the cores containing the seeds and slice.

2. Pour the flour into a bowl. Add the eggs, mix and incorporate the yeast. Add the apples to the batter.

3. Heat the oil to 350 degrees F (180 degrees C) in a non-stick frying pan and drop in the apples. As soon as the batter sets, puffs up and becomes golden (about 2 minutes), flip the apples over. This will ensure they are evenly cooked.

4. Drain excess oil from the hot cakes by setting them on paper towels. Transfer into a serving dish, sprinkle with confectioner's sugar and serve.

Crêpes with Berries (France)

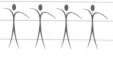

Servings

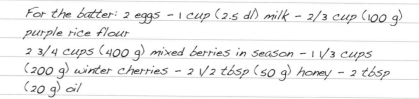

For the batter: 2 eggs – 1 cup (2.5 dl) milk – 2/3 cup (100 g) purple rice flour
2 3/4 cups (400 g) mixed berries in season – 1 1/3 cups (200 g) winter cherries – 2 1/2 tbsp (50 g) honey – 2 tbsp (20 g) oil

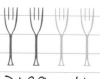

Difficulty

1. Clean all the berries and place half in a frying pan with half of the honey. Cook over high heat for 10 minutes. Remove from heat and set aside until needed.

2. Pour the flour into a bowl and slowly pour in the milk. Add the eggs while mixing with a whisk. Mix until the mixture is homogeneous and fluid. Take out a non-stick frying pan with a diameter of about 10 inches (25 cm). Pour the oil into a bowl and dip in a piece of folded paper towel. Use it to oil the frying pan (without leaving any oil behind).

Prep Time
30 minutes

3. Set the frying pan on the stove and pour in the batter covering the bottom. Tip the frying pan to make sure the batter is of the same thickness throughout. After about 30 seconds, the crêpe will begin to detach from the pan. Turn it over, let it firm up and remove from heat. Repeat until the batter is finished.

Cooking Time
20 minutes

4. Fill the crêpes with half cooked and half fresh berries. Flavor with the remaining honey and serve.

A Fashionable Crêpe

Despite not appearing so, crêpes are of medieval origin, created, as legend has it, to feed French pilgrims and wayfarers who came to Rome for religious festivals. The few ingredients, which can be found almost anywhere in the world, have meant that these thin delicacies cooked on stones, griddles or other equipment, with more or less ambitious variations, are present almost anywhere you go. However, they have only become a true passion in France, where they have transformed the extremely thin and evolved crêpe into a timeless myth. Not only are the French able to eat crêpes taken away from kiosks or super-equipped vans, but also at tables in elegant and refined restaurants which, with a sweet version drizzled with liquor and set on fire, have made this dish even more fascinating and evocative. Today there are many variations that permit the crêpe to be stuffed with both sweet and savory fillings, becoming a perfect, yummy snack, dessert, appetizer, starter... making it still a much loved choice everywhere.

Nougat (Italy)

Servings

2/3 cup (200 g) honey - 1 cup (200 g) sugar - 1 1/2 cups (200 g) toasted and blanched hazelnuts - 2 egg whites - wafer paper for coating

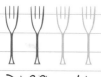

Difficulty

1. Line a rectangular baking pan with moistened parchment paper (this will allow you to shape it more easily, adhering it to the walls) and then with wafer paper.

2. Beat the egg whites until stiff. Heat the honey until it comes to a boil. Add the egg whites, blend and remove from heat.

Prep Time
40 minutes

3. Heat the sugar and, once it starts to take on color, add the hazelnuts. Mix and add the other ingredients. Pour into the pan, level the mixture, cover with more wafer paper and set aside for a few hours.

Resting time
180 minutes

Cooking Time
5 minutes

In addition to being delicious to nibble as is, the nougat makes an excellent foundation for frozen desserts and ice creams. It can also be enriched with chocolate. Very rich in calories, this sweet has many variations: with nuts, dried or candied fruits, hard or soft. In one form or another, it is present in almost all Italian regions.

The Perfect Roasted Candy

The meaning of the word nougat (from the Latin torrere) is "roast", but it could also come from the word tierra due to the candy's similarity to a block of earth. It is an extremely ancient delicacy: apparently it was already in vogue among the Romans before the birth of Christ. Widespread throughout Italy, each region prepares it with its own delicious recipes that evoke the land and its aromas: aromatic honeys, dried fruit like almonds, hazelnuts, pistachios, or candied fruit characterize this exquisite candy, which can be either soft or hard, covered with rice paper or wrapped in veils of chocolate or frosting.

Its origins, however, are not certain, as it appears that even before the Romans something similar made with mixed dried fruit bound with honey, sugar and egg white existed in the Middle East. Today's recipe is very much linked to the original, as if, from the outset, the perfection of the candy has left it unchanged over time. Its popularity in Italy unites the entire peninsula: it is sold at fair stalls and patronal festivals, and served in restaurants, transformed into irresistible desserts.

Chestnut Cream with Yogurt
(Europe)

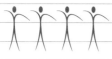

Servings

2 lb (1 kg) large chestnuts – 1/2 cup (100 g) sugar – 1/2 cup (1 dl) Rum – 1/2 cup (1 dl) hot milk – 2 1/2 cups (600 g) dense yogurt

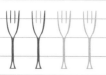

Difficulty

Prep Time
30 minutes

Cooking Time
60 minutes

1. Peel and boil the chestnuts in water for about 20 minutes. Drain and remove the skin. Place the pulp into a bowl.

2. Add the sugar and the liquor and mix. If the resulting mixture is too dense, add tablespoons of hot milk until the cream is smooth, soft and clump-free. Place the chestnut cream over very low heat and cook while mixing continuously until all the ingredients are blended and the sugar has dissolved. Take off the heat and set aside to cool.

3. You can store the cream in airtight jars sterilized for 20 minutes beforehand.

4. Right before dessert assembly, mix the yogurt to make it creamier. Alternate layers of chestnut cream and yogurt, starting with the cream, until the containers are full.

5. Serve at room temperature or after cooling it in the fridge for one hour if you prefer the dessert cold.

Whole-grain Blueberry Baci (Italy)

Servings

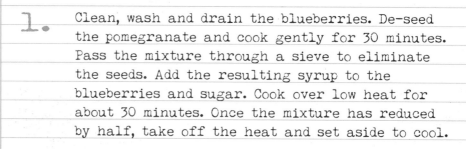

1 1/2 cups (200 g) whole-grain emmer flour – 1 egg – 1/4 cup (50 g) corn oil – 1/4 cup (50 g) brown sugar – 1/2 tsp (2 g) baking powder
For the preserves: 1 1/3 cups (200 g) blueberries – 2 pomegranate – 4 tbsp (50 g) sugar

Difficulty

1. Clean, wash and drain the blueberries. De-seed the pomegranate and cook gently for 30 minutes. Pass the mixture through a sieve to eliminate the seeds. Add the resulting syrup to the blueberries and sugar. Cook over low heat for about 30 minutes. Once the mixture has reduced by half, take off the heat and set aside to cool.

Prep Time
60 minutes

2. Preheat the oven to 350 degrees F (180 degrees C) and line a baking sheet with waxed paper.

3. Pour the flour onto a comfortable working surface. Add the egg, sugar, yeast and oil. Knead until the mixture is homogeneous.

4. Flatten out the dough and cut out disks 3 inches (8 cm) in diameter with a pastry ring. Cut into halves, creating half-circles. Set aside to rise for 30 minutes in a warm spot. Transfer onto a baking sheet.

Cooking Time
60 minutes

5. Bake the half-circles for about 20 minutes. Allow to cool and fill with the preserves.

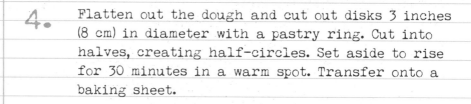

Caramel Apples (USA)

Servings

4 green apples – 3/4 cup (150 g) brown sugar – 3 1/2 oz. (100 g) dark chocolate – 1/3 cup (50 g) chopped peanuts – 1 tbsp (14 g) sugar

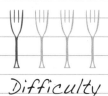

Difficulty

1. Wash and dry the apples. Dissolve the sugar in three tablespoons of water in a saucepan. As soon as it begins to caramelize, remove from heat, mix and incorporate the chocolate and chopped peanuts.

2. Insert wood skewers into the apples. Dip them into the caramel, making sure they are completely coated, and set on parchment paper. To make sure the apples detach with ease, sprinkle the paper with a tablespoon of sugar.

Prep Time
20 minutes

3. Allow the caramel to harden and serve.

Cooking Time
10 minutes

There are many varieties and decorations possible for these apples. From colored caramel to caramel with white chocolate, milk or dark chocolate, and nuts such as almonds, pistachios, walnuts, peanuts and hazelnuts.

A Brilliant Idea

Caramel apples first appeared in 1950. They were the brainchild of Dan Walker, an employee of Kraft. Walker recounts how he invented the recipe, experimenting with caramels that weren't sold at Halloween. At the beginning of the 1900s, apples were already being sweetened with sugar and cinnamon, and the caramelized version spread like wild fire thanks to the introduction of a machine that automated production. In large-scale production, a layer of caramel is applied to the apple and it is then heated so that the caramel is evenly distributed. This facilitates transport, but makes the caramel harder and therefore more difficult to eat. At home, caramel apples can be made by melting caramels or preparing the caramel with sugar, butter, vanilla and chocolate. The apple on a stick is then immersed in the mixture. The covering can be enriched with walnuts, hazelnut or chopped peanuts.

Coconut Cream (Thailand)

Servings

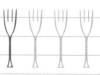

Difficulty

Prep Time
10 minutes

Cooking Time
30 minutes

1 3/4 cups (200 g) coconut flour – 1/2 cup (100 g) coconut milk – 4 tbsp (50 g) sugar – 3 eggs – 1 1/2 tbsp (20 g) butter

1. Blend the sugar with the flour and milk. Transfer into a mixing bowl and heat the cream in a water bath.

2. Beat the eggs and incorporate very slowly, passing them through a colander.

3. Cook in the water bath steering regularly. Once the spoon remains coated when you pull it out, add the butter.

4. Preheat the oven to 350 degrees F (180 degrees C). Transfer the cream into ramekins and set onto a baking pan. Add enough water to reach half way up the sides of the ramekins.

5. Bake for 30 minutes. Serve the cream with fruit of your choice.

Chocolate Muffins (USA)

Servings

1 cup (150 g) semi whole-wheat flour - 1/2 cup (50 g) hazelnut flour - 2 eggs - 3/4 cup (2 dl) milk - 1/4 cup (50 g) butter - 2 oz. (50 g) dark chocolate - 4 tbsp (56 g) sugar - 1/2 tbsp (5 g) baking powder

Difficulty

Prep Time
20 minutes

Cooking Time
35 minutes

1. Preheat the oven to 350 degrees F (180 degrees C). Place paper muffin liners into single-serving baking cups. Melt the butter in a water bath, stirring to make sure it does not get too hot. Chop the chocolate and melt in a water bath.

2. Break the eggs into a bowl. Add the milk and butter. Incorporate the flours, sieved to avoid clumps, the yeast and the sugar.

3. Mix until the mixture is smooth and soft. Incorporate the chocolate. Fill the baking cups with the batter 2/3 of the way up.

4. Bake the muffins for about 30-35 minutes. Turn off the oven, take out and set the muffins aside to cool.

5. You can leave the muffins in the baking cups until service. This will keep them from crumbling or breaking.

Coconut and Cinnamon Bananas
(Indonesia)

Servings

4 bananas - 3/4 cup (200 g) coconut milk - 1 tbsp (10 g) cornstarch - 2 tbsp (28 g) brown sugar - 1/2 tsp (1.5 g) cinnamon - 2 tbsp (30 ml) Rum - lemon leaves

Difficulty

1. Prepare the sauce by combining the cornstarch, cinnamon, Rum and brown sugar in a saucepan. Mix until the ingredients are well blended and clump free. Incorporate the coconut milk and set the saucepan over heat. The heat should be very low. Bring to a boil stirring continuously. As soon as the sauce begins to thicken, take off the heat. Cover and set aside until needed.

Prep Time
10 minutes

2. Wash the bananas, cut off the ends and cook in a bamboo steamer lined with lemon leaves.

3. Take out after 5 minutes. Peel, arrange on a serving plate and pour the sauce on top.

Cooking Time
10 minutes

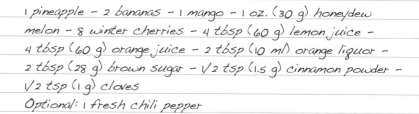

Seasoned Fruit Salad (Mexico)

Servings

1 pineapple – 2 bananas – 1 mango – 1 oz. (30 g) honeydew melon – 8 winter cherries – 4 tbsp (60 g) lemon juice – 4 tbsp (60 g) orange juice – 2 tbsp (10 ml) orange liquor – 2 tbsp (28 g) brown sugar – 1/2 tsp (1.5 g) cinnamon powder – 1/2 tsp (1 g) cloves
Optional: 1 fresh chili pepper

Difficulty

1. Trim the pineapple and chop. Peel and slice the bananas. Wash, peel and chop the mango. Peel the honeydew melon and chop. Mix all the fruits together in a bowl. Finally, add the winter cherries. For greater impact, leave the membrane surrounding the berry intact.

2. Place all the other ingredients into a saucepan and cook stirring continuously until reduced by half.

3. Add chili pepper if you wish, stir and set aside to cool.

4. Season the fruit salad with the mixture.

Prep Time
10 minutes

Cooking Time
10 minutes

With Cereals and Animal Proteins...

This section includes recipes that are immediately associated with street food, such as the Sicilian arancini, the Turkish doner kebab and the American donuts. The presence of cereals – from rice and corn to bread – makes these foods able to fill you up without requiring you to use a fork and a knife. In some cases, the cereal is at the center of the recipe, for example in Turkish sesame bread or the farinata, while in others it accompanies meat and is flavored with cooking juices. This is the case for chili tacos, doner kebab and Creole pockets. The combination of bread and meat can be found in almost all culinary traditions, from Europe to Asia because it provides a good source of carbohydrates and proteins in a single dish. The differences lie in the types of flour and meat used and in the cooking method. Lamb is characteristic of the Middle East, while in Europe (as well as in South America) pork and veal are more common.

Louisiana Cookies (USA)

Servings

2 1/3 cups (300 g) all-purpose flour, half white and half whole wheat - 1/2 cup (100 g) brown sugar - 1/2 cup (100 g) diced butter - 3 tbsp (50 g) buttermilk - 1/2 tbsp (5 g) baking powder - 1/4 cup (50 g) cream
Optional: 1 3/4 cups (200 g) whipped cream, or 1 1/2 cups (200 g) cherry preserves or chocolate cream

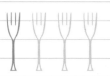

Difficulty

Prep Time
40 minutes

1. Combine the flour, sugar, yeast and butter. Mix until the mixture is homogeneous then add the buttermilk.

2. Preheat the oven to 425 degrees F (220 degrees C). Line a baking sheet with parchment paper. Roll out the dough on a comfortable working surface. Continue until you have a disk about 1/2 inch (1 cm) thick. Cut out cookies about 2 inches (5 cm) in diameter with a cookie cutter.

3. Place them on a baking sheet, brush with cream and bake for about 12-15 minutes. The cookies are ready once they have a nice golden color.

4. If you wish, fill them with whipped cream, chocolate paste or fruit preserves.

Cooking Time
15 minutes

If you want to make some buttermilk at home, you can use the following method: for 1/2 cup (120 g) of buttermilk, take 1 cup (250 g) of cream, 1/4 cup (50 g) of skim milk and 1 tablespoon (15 g) of lemon juice. Combine everything and continue mixing until the cream has separated (you will need about 20 minutes). Filter out the solid portion (butter). The remaining liquid is the buttermilk.

Pretzel with Seeds (Germany)

Servings

Difficulty

Prep Time
60 minutes

Cooking Time
25 minutes

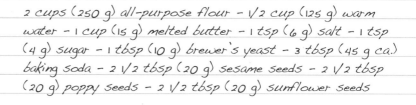

2 cups (250 g) all-purpose flour – 1/2 cup (125 g) warm water – 1 cup (15 g) melted butter – 1 tsp (6 g) salt – 1 tsp (4 g) sugar – 1 tbsp (10 g) brewer's yeast – 3 tbsp (45 g ca.) baking soda – 2 1/2 tbsp (20 g) sesame seeds – 2 1/2 tbsp (20 g) poppy seeds – 2 1/2 tbsp (20 g) sunflower seeds

1. Dissolve the baking soda in 4 1/4 cups (1 l) of cold water and set aside. Pour the flour onto a comfortable working surface. Dissolve the yeast and sugar in warm water.

2. Combine the butter with the flour. Add the warm water and knead until the dough is soft and well developed. Set aside to rise for 30 minutes in a warm spot.

3. Line a baking sheet with waxed paper and preheat the oven to 390 degrees F (200 degrees C).

4. Form strings of the dough and give them the classic pretzel shape. Set aside to rise for an additional 30 minutes. Dip into the baking soda solution for a few seconds using a skimmer.

5. Drain on some cloth and coat with seeds. Position then on the baking sheet and sprinkle with salt. Bake for about 20-25 minutes.

Monks' Bread

It seems that the bretzel or "pretzl, pretzel, laugenbrezel" was invented in French and Italian monasteries during the Middle Ages, and was made to represent the arms of a monk in prayer. It was used as a prize for young boys who diligently studied the sacred scripts. Even then, thanks to the movement of pilgrims and travelers, the bread arrived in Germany and it is said that the unusual texture was due to the fatigue of a baker, who transformed the bretzel from soft and semi-raw to hard because he forgot to take them out of the oven.

Today, there are many different varieties of bretzels in respect to the initial product, and the basic ingredients – wheat flour, malt, yeast, water and baking soda – may also include salt, butter, lard, sunflower, sesame or poppy seeds, or dark, milk or white chocolate icing and nuts for sweet versions. They love them in Germany, especially the savory ones, which are often served with sausages and spicy condiments.

Stuffed Farinata (Italy)

Servings

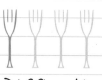

Difficulty

Prep Time
10 minutes

Resting time
10 hours

Cooking Time
10 minutes

2 cups (200 g) chickpea flour - 2 1/2 cups (6 dl) water - 3 tbsp (30 g) extra virgin olive oil - salt
For the topping: 1 tbsp (6 g) fresh minced rosemary - 1 purple onion - 2 oz. (50 g) melting cheese

1. Pour the flour into a bowl and mix with water until the batter is fluid, soft and clump free. Cover and set aside for 10 hours, skimming of the foam that will form on the surface. Season with salt, add the oil and mix.

2. Chop the cheese and thinly slice the onion.

3. Preheat the oven to 480 degrees F (250 degrees C). Oil a baking pan and fill with the batter to a height of about 1/16 inch (2 mm). Bake for 10 minutes.

4. Take out of the oven, top with the onion, the rosemary and cheese. Place back into the oven until the cheese melts and a delicious aroma permeates the kitchen.

Thanks to an Accident at Sea...

The origin of Farinata appears to have been accidental: in fact, it is quite common for great dishes to have an accidental history! It is said that in the XIII century a ship full of chickpeas took on water while making its way across the Ligurian Sea. The water that entered the ship's hold reduced the cargo of dried legumes to a sloppy puree, which was then given to the prisoners on board. Some ate it, others threw it away, but the next day, thanks to the heat and sun, the puree had thickened and turned into a kind of focaccia bread, which even if not great, was edible! The Genoese found this extremely interesting and began experimenting with cooking methods and textures, eventually transforming the polenta into a very appetizing specialty. This thin, savory pie is diffused throughout Italy, and the original ingredients are: chickpea flour, water, salt and olive oil.

It is usually cooked in wood-fired ovens for a few minutes, the time needed for it to thicken and brown.

It is also excellent stuffed with onion, cheese, rosemary and a generous amount of freshly ground black pepper.

Rice Noodles with Tofu and Peanuts (Thailand)

Servings

10 oz. (300 g) rice noodles – 3.5 oz. (100 g) tofu – 1/2 cup (50 g) peanuts – 1/3 cup (30 g) soy sprouts – 2 garlic cloves – 1 ground chili pepper – 4 tbsp (72 g) tamari sauce – 1 spring onion – 2 tbsp (20 g) peanut oil – salt

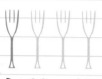
Difficulty

Prep Time
10 minutes

Cooking Time
5 minutes

1. Trim, wash and drain the sprouts. Soften the spaghetti in cold water for 10 minutes. Chop the tofu, mince the garlic and cut the spring onion into rounds. Coarsely chop the peanuts.

2. Pour the oil into a wok. Add the tofu, the tamari sauce, garlic and spring onion. Mix. Drain the pasta and add to the wok. Add the chili pepper and the peanuts. Cook for 2 minutes over lively heat.

3. Add the sprouts and stir. Season with salt (remember that tamari sauce is already salty!) and serve.

Turkish Sesame Bread (Turkey)

Servings

1 cup (100 g) oat flour – 1 cup (150 g) semi-whole wheat flour – 2/3 cup (1.5 dl) water – 1/2 tbsp (5 g) brewer's yeast – 2 1/2 tbsp (20 g) sesame seeds

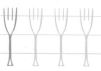

Difficulty

1. Combine all the ingredients except the sesame seeds. Once the dough is homogeneous, cover and set aside to rise in a warm spot.

2. Divide the dough into eight parts and form balls. Cover and set aside to rise for 30 more minutes.

3. Using a floured rolling pin, flatten the balls. Sprinkle with the sesame seeds and press down to make sure they adhere well.

**Prep Time
30 minutes**

4. You can cook the bread in two ways: bake at 480 degrees F (250 degrees C) for 10 minutes or cook in a hot non-stick frying pan, flipping over often, until a fantastic aroma of cooked flour permeates the room (about 5-6 minutes).

**Cooking Time
10 minutes**

5. Store the bread wrapped in dishtowels and serve hot.

Corn Cake (Brazil)

Servings

1 1/2 cups (200 g) corn flour - 3/4 cup (100 g) all-purpose flour - 2/3 cup (150 g) milk - 1/2 cup (100 g) softened butter - 1/2 cup (100 g) sugar - 2 eggs - 1 tbsp (10 g) baking powder - 1 tsp (3 g) confectioner's sugar

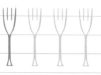

Difficulty

1. Pour the flours into a bowl and mix. Add the sugar then the butter, eggs and yeast. Blend the ingredients incorporating the milk a little at a time until the batter is soft and airy.

2. Line a baking pan about 9 1/2 inches (24 cm) in diameter with parchment paper and preheat the oven to 350 degrees F (180 degrees C). Pour the batter into the baking pan and level with a spatula.

Prep Time
20 minutes

3. Bake the cake for about 60 minutes. After 30 minutes, cover with more parchment paper to make sure the surface does not burn.

4. Once the cooking time is up, take out of the oven and set aside to cool. Sprinkle with confectioner's sugar and serve.

Cooking Time
60 minutes

Donuts (USA)

10-12 donuts

2 cups (250 g) all-purpose flour - 2 cups (250 g) manitoba flour - 1 cup (2.5 dl) warm milk - 1 tsp (4 g) sugar - 2 eggs - 1/3 cup (75 g) softened butter - 2 vanilla pods - 1 1/2 tbsp (15 g) brewer's yeast - 7 oz. (200 g) dark chocolate - 3 tbsp (18 g) almond flour - 20 whole almonds

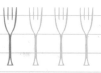

Difficulty

1. Boil the milk with the vanilla bean broken into pieces for 5 minutes. Allow to cool and filter. Dissolve the yeast in the milk along with a teaspoon of sugar. Pour the flours into a stand mixer then incorporate the milk, eggs and butter. If you do not have such an appliance, knead the ingredients together on a comfortable working surface.

Prep Time
40 minutes

2. Once the dough is smooth and soft, cover and set aside to rise for 30 minutes in a warm spot. Preheat the oven to 390 degrees F (200 degrees C).

3. Roll out the dough to a thickness of about 1/2 inch (1 cm) with a rolling pin. Cut out some donuts using two pastry rings (one 3 inches (8 cm) and the other 3/4 inch (2 cm) in diameter). Arrange on a baking sheet lined with parchment paper.

Cooking Time
30 minutes

4. Bake for 30 minutes, turning over half way through. Take out of the oven and decorate with dark chocolate, almond slices and almond flour.

The original recipe calls for deep-frying.

Rice Balls with Tofu and Vegetables (China)

Servings

1/2 cup (100 g) minced tofu – 1/2 cup (100 g) boiled white rice – 1/3 cup (50 g) Venere rice flour – 1 bell pepper – 1 onion – 1 carrot – 1 tsp (6 g) coriander – 1 lemon grass sprig – 1 chili pepper – 2 tbsp (20 g) extra virgin olive oil – 1 tbsp (7.5 g) all-purpose flour – salt

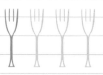

Difficulty

Prep Time
20 minutes

Cooking Time
20 minutes

1. Preheat the oven to 390 degrees F (200 degrees C). Oil a baking sheet.

2. Wash the vegetables removing the hard sections and slice finely. Mince the chili pepper and the lemon grass. Pour the rice into a bowl along with minced tofu, vegetables and minced chili pepper and lemon grass. Season with salt to taste.

3. Pour the flour into a bowl with 2 tablespoons of water and mix, obtaining a batter. Pour the Venere rice flour onto a plate.

4. Using both hands, form balls of the desired shape and size. Coat them first in the batter and then the Venere rice flour, making sure it adheres well. Arrange the balls on the baking sheet. Brush with oil on both sides.

5. Bake for 20 minutes turning over half way through to ensure they cook evenly.

Churros (Spain)

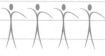

1 cup (150 g) all-purpose flour – 1/4 cup (60 g) diced butter – 2 eggs – 1 cup (2.5 dl) water – 3 tbsp (40 g) sugar – 1 tsp (3 g) cinnamon powder – 2 tbsp (16 g) confectioner's sugar

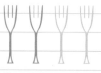

Difficulty

Prep Time
20 minutes

Cooking Time
60 minutes

1. Preheat the oven to 390 degrees F (200 degrees C) and line a baking sheet with parchment paper.

2. Pour the water into a pan. Add the sugar and mix. Add the butter and let it melt. Incorporate the flour mixing continuously. Once the dough begins to detach from the walls of the pan, transfer it into a bowl. Allow to cool and incorporate the eggs one at a time.

3. Transfer the mixture into a pastry bag and pipe out lines about 4 inches (10 cm) long directly onto the baking sheet. Bake the churros for 30 minutes then lower the temperature to 350 degrees F (180 degrees C). Continue to bake for an additional 30 minutes, checking to make sure they don't become too dark. If you see them darkening too much, cover with parchment paper. Allow to cool in the oven with the door cracked open.

4. Take the churros out and sprinkle with confectioner's sugar mixed with cinnamon before serving.

Delicacies from a Star-shaped Syringe

The name Churros derives from the distinct syringe with a star-shaped nozzle, the churrera, which is used to portion out the batter. Some say that this specialty is of Spanish origin, whereas other sources say that it originated in Portugal, although it seems that the first to actually make them were the Chinese. This demonstrates how this food loved to travel and how with each journey it was enriched with different flavors and creative imaginations.

As well as being sold on the streets, in Venezuela and South America in general, these pastries are served for breakfast in bars, accompanied by a delicious cup of hot chocolate. In Spain, where they were allegedly invented, you can find a variety of sweet, salty and spicy churros at well-equipped street stalls, which, by immersing the batter in hot oil, transform the few ingredients into a fragrant sweet pastry dusted in sugar. There are many different varieties of churros, enriched with butter, eggs and irresistible fillings, and they are sometimes baked in the oven so as to make them more digestible.

Empanada (Argentina)

Servings

For the dough: 1 1/2 cups (200 g) all-purpose flour –
1/4 cup (50 g) chopped butter
For the filling: 7 oz. (200 g) ground veal – 1 finely chopped
onion – 2 tbsp (20 g) raisins – 1 tbsp (7 g) paprika – 1/2 tsp
(1.5 g) cumin – 2 tbsp (20 g) extra virgin olive oil – 1 tsp (6 g)
minced coriander – 8 pealed quail eggs – salt and pepper

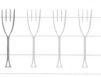

Difficulty

1. Prepare the dough by mixing the flour with the butter and some water (begin by adding 2 cups (~ 5 dl and continue a little at a time) until the dough is elastic, soft and smooth.

2. Soak the raisins in warm water and drain.

3. Pour the oil into a non-stick frying pan. As soon as it heats up, add the onion and sweat it. Add the raisins, meat, paprika, cumin and coriander. Mix, season with salt and pepper, and cook for about 15 minutes adjusting the heat so the filling does not burn. Turn off the heat and allow to cool.

**Prep Time
40 minutes**

4. Preheat the oven to 425 degrees F (220 degrees C) and line a baking sheet with parchment paper. Cut the eggs into four slices each.

5. Roll out the dough and form disks 1/32 inch (1 mm) in thickness and 4 inches (10 cm) in diameter. Fill the disks with meat and egg slices. Fold over and seal to form half-circles. Arrange on the baking sheet and bake for about 10-12 minutes. Take out of the oven and serve.

**Cooking Time
30 minutes**

Tamari Quail Eggs (Japan)

Servings

12 quail eggs – 1/4 cup (0.5 dl) tamari sauce – 1/4 cup (0.5 dl) water – 1/4 cup (0.5 dl) Mirin (sweet rice liquor) – 1 tsp (2 g) Kombu seaweed powder

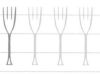

Difficulty

1. Wash the eggs and place them into cold water. Cook until hard-boiled. About 2 minutes should be sufficient. Allow to cool in water. Peel the eggs and place into a bowl.

2. Mix the water, tamari sauce, seaweed powder and the liquor together. Pour over the eggs. Marinate until the white of the egg changes color or, if time is of the essence, cook the eggs in the marinade for about one hour over very low heat.

**Prep Time
10 minutes**

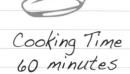

**Cooking Time
60 minutes**

Tamari eggs are a tasty savory snack that is also great paired with "udon" (typical Japanese noodles).

Doner Kebab (Turkey)

Servings

4 pitas or piadina - 7 oz. (200 g) chicken - 7 oz. (200 g) turkey - 1 lemon - 1 onion - 1 tsp garlic, cumin, coriander, chili pepper, pepper powder mix
For the filling: 1 tomato - 8 lettuce leaves - 1 purple onion - 4 tbsp (60 g) yogurt - 1 tsp (2.5 g) harissa

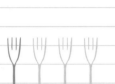

Difficulty

1. Thinly slice the onion and juice the lemon. Slice the chicken and turkey into thin strips. Place into a bowl and drizzle with the lemon juice, spice mix and onion. Allow to marinate for 20-30 minutes.

2. In the meanwhile, clean and trim the vegetables for the filling. Slice the onion and the tomato. Mix the harissa and the yogurt together. When the marinating is done, transfer the meat into a hot non-stick frying pan. Cook over high heat while bathing with the marinade for 5-7 minutes. Season with salt to taste while cooking.

Prep Time
20 minutes

3. Heat the pitas. Divide the meat into four portions and fill the pitas. Add some flavor with onions, tomatoes, lettuce and yogurt.

Resting time
30 minutes

Cooking Time
7 minutes

Meat that Travels around the World

The first thing that springs to mind when you hear the word kebab is a rotating skewer with pieces of meat marinated in yogurt and herbs exuding appetizing aromas. But where was this specialty invented?

The word kebab is of Persian origin and means "grilled" or "roasted." Initially the dish was made up of strips of golden meat cooked on hot plates and the first historical references to the kebab date back to the X century.

The most famous kebabs are: the "doner kebab", consisting of thin strips of meat in a sandwich, and the "durum kebab", which is served in a tortilla or flatbread. Eaten throughout the world, the original recipe uses meat such as lamb, beef and chicken (never pork, as it is forbidden by Islam), seasoned with aromatic herbs such as oregano, mint, cumin etc. and harissa (a spicy sauce made with chili peppers and garlic) and marinated in yogurt. Today this dish, a favorite across the world, is also made with fish and, in Australia, even with kangaroo meat.

Creole Pockets (USA)

For the dough: 1 1/2 cups (150 g) oat flour – 1/3 cup (50 g) rice flour – 1/2 cup (100 g) diced butter – 1/4 cup (50 g) milk – 1 egg
For coating the pockets: 2 tbsp (20 g) extra virgin olive oil
For the filling: 9 oz. (250 g) cod – 12 shrimp – 1 tsp (3 g) Cajun spice mix (garlic, onion, black pepper, white pepper, paprika, thyme and oregano) – 1 tbsp (5 g) fresh parsley – 1 tbsp (10 g) extra virgin olive oil – salt

Servings

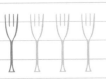

Difficulty

Prep Time
30 minutes

Resting time
30 minutes

Cooking Time
25 minutes

1. Prepare the dough by mixing all the ingredients until homogeneous and well amalgamated. Set aside for 30 minutes.

2. Remove any bones from the fish and chop. Deshell, devein and wash the shrimp. Pour the oil into a non-stick frying pan. Add the cod and cook stirring often for 5 minutes. Add the shrimp, season with the spices, parsley and salt to taste. Turn off the heat after a minute.

3. Preheat the oven to 390 degrees F (200 degrees C). Roll out the dough to a thickness of about 1/32 inches (1 mm). Cut out disks 3-4 inches (8-10 cm) in diameter with a pastry disk. Add the filling and fold the dough over forming a half-circles. Press down along the edges and arrange the pockets on a baking sheet lined with parchment paper.

4. Brush the tops with oil and bake for 20 minutes.

Cajun spices can be purchased in specialized stores or prepared at home by drying garlic, onion, thyme and oregano, and mincing them with black and white pepper, and paprika.

Arancini (Italy)

Servings

1 1/2 cups (300 g) rice – 1 saffron packet – 4 tbsp (40 g) extra virgin olive oil – 3.5 oz. (100 g) ground beef – 3.5 oz. (100 g) ground pork – 1 carrot – 1 celery stick – 1 finely chopped onion – 2 tbsp (32 g) tomato concentrate – 2/3 cup (100 g) peas – 3/4 cup (100 g) grated Ragusano or Caciocavallo cheese – salt and pepper
For the breading: 1 tbsp (8 g) flour – 1/2 cup (1 dl) water – 1 1/2 cups (200 g) breadcrumbs

Difficulty

1. Pour the rice into a pan with twice the amount of water. Add the saffron and 2 tablespoons of oil. Season with salt and pepper to taste. Cover and cook over low heat until all the liquid has been absorbed. Set aside until needed.

Prep Time
30 minutes

2. Pour 2 tablespoons of oil into a non-stick frying pan. Gently sauté chopped vegetables. Add the meat and peas after 3-4 minutes. Mix, add the tomato concentrate, and season with salt and pepper to taste. Add a glass of hot water and cook for 60 minutes: if the sauce reduces too much, add a few tablespoons of water. Turn off the heat, allow to cool and add half of the cheese. Shape into small meatballs the size of walnuts.

3. Mix the flour with a glass of water and pour into a bowl. Pour the breadcrumbs into a plate and mix with the grated cheese.

Cooking Time
100 minutes

4. Start making arancini by placing about 2 tablespoons of rice onto the palm of one hand. Top with a meatball and wrap the rice around it. Coat the resulting ball in the batter and the breadcrumbs. Preheat the oven to 390 degrees F (200 degrees C). Arrange the balls on parchment paper and bake for about 20 minutes, turning them over often.

The original recipe calls for deep-frying the arancini. If you prefer this cooking method, you will need at least 1 1/4 cups (3 dl) of peanut oil at 350 degrees F (180 degrees C).

Blini (Russia)

Servings

2/3 cup (80 g) buckwheat flour – 1/2 cup (80 g) rice flour –
3/4 cup (2 dl) milk – 2 eggs – 1 1/2 tbsp (20 g) butter –
1/2 tbsp (5 g) yeast – 3/4 cup (200 g) sour cream –
2 1/2 tbsp (10 g) minced dill – black pepper

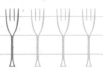

Difficulty

**Prep Time
20 minutes**

**Cooking Time
30 minutes**

1. Break the eggs and pour the whites into a bowl. Beat until stiff. Pour the flours into a bowl and mix.

2. Mix the egg yolks with the milk and yeast then blend with the melted butter and flour. Mix until the batter is smooth. Gently fold in the egg whites, making sure they don't deflate.

3. Heat up a small non-stick frying pan. Oil it using a piece of paper towel dipped in oil and cook the batter a little at a time. You can make blinis thin as crêpes or thicker like pancakes.

4. Top with sour cream mixed with minced dill, and if desired with abundant freshly ground pepper.

Ideal for a tasty appetizer, in Russia, they are served with sour cream, caviar or salmon.

Warm and Golden
Like the Sun

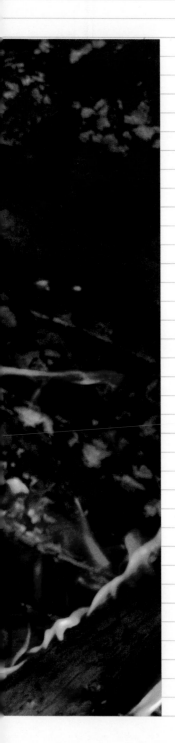

Whether made with wheat flour, buckwheat flour, or mixed flours; with buttermilk, milk or yogurt; with a sweet or savory filling, this specialty of Russian origin is truly delicious. Tradition tells how these thin pancakes were offered in religious rites and represented the sun: warm and golden. We should also add that, besides their wonderful color, blinis are fragrant, yummy and irresistible. Legend has it that they were served for anniversary celebrations, at happy events such as births and weddings, but also at funerals. Like crêpes, the skill in making blinis lies in the ability to make them consistent, soft and thin, so that they can be easily stuffed to create exciting dishes. The savory version is usually filled with red or black caviar, herring, salmon, sour cream and spices. Unlike the French crêpe, blinis need to rise so that the result is soft and delicate. When eaten fresh from the frying pan they are a real treat.

Buckwheat Soba in Hot Broth
(Japan)

Servings

7 oz. (200 g) whole-grain buckwheat noodles – 3/4 oz. (20 g) bonito or dried fish – 2 spring onions – 4 chicken egg yolks – 4 tbsp (72 g) tamari sauce – 1 tsp (2 g) minced ginger

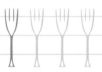

Difficulty

Prep Time
20 minutes

Cooking Time
25 minutes

1. Place the bonito into 4 1/4 cups (1 l) of water and bring to a boil. Cook for 15 minutes then filter.

2. Wash the spring onions and slice whole, including the green portions. Add to the fish broth and place back on heat for 5 minutes. At the end, add the ginger.

3. Break the eggs and separate the egg yolks from the whites.
In a second pan, boil the noodles in fresh water (if they are fresh, they will be ready in about 4–5 minutes). Drain, run under cold water and divide between four soup plates. Pour the broth on top, season with a tablespoon of tamari sauce, mix and add the egg yolk.

You can find this buckwheat pasta in ethnic stores. Soba is a thin noodle similar to the Italian tagliolini or spaghetti. They can be served cold or hot, depending on the season.

The Author

A naturopath, freelance journalist and photographer specializing in wine and food itineraries, CINZIA TRENCHI has collaborated in the writing of numerous recipe books published by Italian and foreign publishing houses. A passionate cook, she has also worked for many Italian magazines covering regional, traditional, macrobiotic and natural cuisine specialties, providing both the text and the photographs, and including dishes of her own creation. Her recipe books include original and creative meals. They propose new flavor associations and unusual pairings that result in unique preparations that keep with the spirit of flavor without forgetting the nutritional properties of foods, in order to achieve the best equilibrium during a meal and the consequent improvement in well-being. She lives in Monferrato, in the Piedmont region, in a home immersed in greenery. Using the flowers, aromatic herbs and vegetables grown in her garden, she prepares original sauces and condiments, in addition to decorations for her dishes, allowing herself to be guided by the seasons and her knowledge of the earth's fruits. In the past years, she has realized several books for White Star Publishers, with great enthusiasm and creativity.

Index of Ingredients

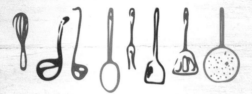

All photographs are by Cinzia Trenchi except the following:
Pages 16-17: Takamex/Shutterstock - Pages 20-21: gracethang/iStockphoto -
Pages 24-25: Cem Ozdel/Anadolu Agency/Getty Images - Pages 36-37: Paulavigeorge/iStockphoto -
Pages 40-41: ELENAPHOTOS/istockphoto - Pages 54-55: ElenaMirage/iStockphoto -
Pages 62-63: SUNG KUK KIM/123RF - Pages 74-75: Kobby Dagan/123RF - Pages 82-83: Anna Bryukhanova/
iStockphoto - Pages 90-91: Neyya/iStockphoto - Pages 94-95: Augusto Colombo-ITALIA/Alamy Stock
Photo/IPA - Pages 102-103: Svetlana Iakusheva/Shutterstock - Pages 118-119: Jane Rix/123RF -
Pages 122-123: Realy Easy Star/Toni Spagone/Alamy Stock Photo/IPA -
Pages 136-137: Anna Bryukhanova/iStockphoto - Pages 144-145: Anna Bryukhanova/iStockphoto -
Pages 152-153: Maximilian Buzun/123RF

WS White Star Publishers® is a registered trademark
property of White Star s.r.l.

© 2017 White Star s.r.l.
Piazzale Luigi Cadorna, 6 - 20123 Milan, Italy
www.whitestar.it

Translation and Editing: TperTradurre s.r.l.

ISBN 978-88-544-1093-0
1 2 3 4 5 6   21 20 19 18 17

Printed in China